Freshwater Fish
of the
British Isles

A Guide for Anglers and Naturalists

Freshwater Fish of the British Isles

A Guide for Anglers and Naturalists

Nick Giles

SWAN HILL
PRESS

DEDICATION
I wish to record my thanks to Helen, Tom and Will Giles who
patiently waited for me to write the text and to take the
photographs for this book in my spare time without any
complaints – the result is dedicated to them.

Photo credits
All the photographs are by the author unless credited
otherwise.

Copyright © 1994 by Nick Giles

First published in the UK in 1994 by
Swan Hill Press an imprint of Airlife Publishing Ltd

British Library Cataloguing in Publication Data
A catalogue record for this book
is available from the British Library

ISBN 1 85310 317 9

Printed and bound in Great Britain by
Butler & Tanner Ltd, Frome and London

Swan Hill Press
an imprint of Airlife Publishing Ltd.
101 Longden Road, Shrewsbury SY3 9EB

Contents

Preface   7

Introduction   8

Part 1: Conservation and Preservation: The Stewardship of Natural Resources   9
     Protecting the Ecology of Rivers and Lakes   13
     Fish Populations in Britain   18

Part 2: Ecology and Conservation of British Freshwater Wetlands   23
     Rivers   34
     Lakes   44

Part 3: The Cold-Water Fish Community: Mountain Rivers and Glacial Lakes   53
     British Salmonid Fish and their Relatives   55
     Arctic Charr   64
     The Coregonids   69
     Atlantic Salmon   72
     Brown Trout and Sea Trout   91
     Rainbow/Steelhead Trout   107
     Grayling   112
     Pike   115
     Perch   119

Part 4: The Warm-Water Fish Community: Lowland Rivers, Lakes and Ponds   125
     British Cyprinid Fish and their Close Relatives   127
     Carp   131
     Tench   135
     Bream   140
     Barbel   145
     Chub   151
     Roach   154
     Rudd   160
     Dace   163
     Catfish   166

Eel 168
Zander 174

Tailpiece 179

Bibliography 181

Glossary 185

Index 188

Preface

I have been fascinated by fish for as long as I can remember. My childhood in the West Country gave me the opportunity to see trawlers returning to the Barbican at Plymouth with their varied catches. Cod, whiting, bass, pollack, coalfish, mackerel, gurnards, plaice, dabs, sole, monkfish, rays, dogfish, squid, lobsters, crabs — what young child could fail to become interested in the creatures from the depths of the Channel displayed before his eyes! The Marine Biological Association on the Hoe had (and still has) a large aquarium open to the public where the lifeless creatures on the fishmonger's slab were transformed into superb, colourful, living organisms ideally adapted to their underwater environment.

When I was six years of age we moved from Plymouth to a small village near Bath in Somerset. At the bottom of the garden ran a small brook, the River Somer and in the deeper pools brown trout finned actively in the current, taking mayflies and caddisflies as they struggled to emerge at the water surface. Under the stones in the faster flowing riffles lived bullheads and stone loach, surrounded by an abundance of shrimps, caddis larvae and mayfly nymphs.

Crayfish lurked in burrows excavated in the softer clay banks. Kingfishers nested in the steep banks on river bends and I often watched them diving for bullheads and sticklebacks from branches overhanging the riffles and pools. I have a vivid memory of seeing a water shrew diving beneath the surface, covered with a silver envelope of air, turning over small stones in its search for caddis larvae and shrimps. Water voles peered myopically from the bankside reed beds, or swam quickly away across the crowfoot beds at the sound of approaching danger. Herons took their toll of the less wary voles and fish, whilst grass snakes, which were very common, stalked frogs in the wet, boggy waterside pastures. On one warm summer evening all this changed. A farmer had allowed a slurry tank to overflow into the river upstream, de-oxygenating the water and killing trout, bullheads, stone loach and many of the invertebrates. It took a long time for the kingfishers to return. This experience demonstrated for me the vulnerability of aquatic systems to sudden change and probably sowed the seed for my life-long interest in aquatic ecology and conservation.

Since my boyhood experiences by the River Somer I have been fortunate to live by the Thames at Runnymede as an undergraduate, Loch Lomond and the River Endrick as a postgraduate, the River Great Ouse in Buckinghamshire as a lecturer and research biologist and now to work at Burgate beside the Hampshire Avon; it is said that time spent at the waterside is added to your alloted span . . . I wonder?

I wish to thank the following for their help with the production of this book: my wife, Helen Giles and my mother, Marjorie Giles (grammar, punctuation, spelling, moral support), the ever-patient and helpful staff of the Buckingham Public Library (inter-library loans), Ian Watson (fisheries, fishing and comments on the text), David Jordan (fisheries, fish for photography), Len Gurd (fish for photography), Peter Gathercole (photographs, advice on taking fish pictures and the long-term loan of a flash-gun), Colin McKelvie (useful discussions about publishing and comments on the text) and the Swan Hill team for their professional input. Mistakes which remain (and I am sure that there must be some) are my responsibility.

Introduction

This book represents a personal view of the natural history of freshwater fish found in the waters of the British Isles. Where helpful, information from North America, European countries and elsewhere is included.

It is not intended to be a comprehensive review of all of the British species of freshwater fish; neither time nor space would permit such an exercise. It is, rather, a selection of topics which I hope that you will find interesting and informative. For the angler, all of the species of interest to both coarse and game fishermen are included; for the naturalist the biology of the fish is set in the context of the ecology of the lakes or rivers where it lives. Also, for the benefit of anglers and natural historians, I have tried to explain in simple terms many of the principles and areas of interest within the science of freshwater ecology.

This book has a minimum of unexplained jargon in the hope that it will prove to be readable for people without a technical background (*see* Glossary). I have not, however, shied away from the use of Latin names that are necessary for the unambiguous identification of particular plants and animals. For example brown trout/ sea trout are known under a wide variety of common names but scientifically the species is a member of the Family 'Salmonidae' within the genus *Salmo* and of the species *trutta*. No other species is called *Salmo trutta*. Many of the invertebrate animals and plants mentioned do not have well-known common names and are, therefore, given their Latin names. Non-specialist readers are likely to be bored by long lists of names of animal and plant species. I have, therefore, tried to set these aside as tables which can, I hope, be 'skipped over' without losing the thread of the argument.

The text concentrates upon the larger fish species which are of interest to anglers and many naturalists. Smaller species (sticklebacks, minnows, bullheads, loaches, gudgeon, bleak etc) are mentioned in appropriate sections of text.

Perhaps this book will stimulate thoughts on the fascinating world which exists beneath the surface of our rivers, streams and lakes and recruit more active conservationists. I have been fortunate indeed to have been able to make a career out of what has always been my favourite hobby.

PART 1

Conservation and Preservation: The Stewardship of Natural Resources

I think that it is worth making the distinction between conservation and preservation: a preservationist seeks to maintain the *status quo*, striving for an unchanging system. A conservationist seeks to manage natural resources on a long-term sustainable basis, sometimes by exploiting them in a rational manner; always ensuring that an adequate breeding stock remains to produce the next generation. In short, this is the principle of 'wise use'. The species concerned must, of course, have access to sufficient areas of suitable habitat within which to sustain its populations.

Thus habitat management combines with population management of an exploited species to produce a conservation strategy for its long-term survival. This philosophy, especially for species which yield a sporting harvest, is summed up rather well in the document *Game 2000: a manifesto for the future of Game in Britain*, published in 1989 by the Game Conservancy (Fordingbridge, Hampshire). The objectives of conservation through wise use promote the concept of the stewardship of nature:

1. That populations of game, wildfowl, deer and fish should be conserved and husbanded at densities which allow cropping on an optimal sustainable basis, in a way which is sympathetic to other users of the countryside and which benefits game, the natural environment and rural communities.

2. That game conservation should be regarded as a valid use of sustainable natural resources and valued as a prime example of conservation through wise use. The dependency of use creates a self-interest on the part of the user in sustaining the natural resource and in defending it from unwise use or destruction.

It is a central concept in fisheries biology that a reduction in fish population density (up to a point!) through exploitation will lead to an increased growth rate and higher proportion of surviving fish through reduced competition. The increased survival of fish within the stock after fishing is termed *compensatory*; if this did not occur then the fishing mortality would be *additive* (i.e. added to natural forms of mortality occurring over the same period). Animal populations are able to compensate (to varying degrees) for exploitation losses because the *proportion* of animals which die often increases as numbers within the population increase (i.e. mortality is *density-dependent*). Fisheries can, therefore, potentially stimulate the productivity of natural waters by efficiently harvesting the fish. If populations of animals (like salmon or trout) are to be exploited in the long term, great efforts must be made to understand the factors which control the numbers of fish present so that we can calculate how many can safely be harvested from the adult population each season. In this way the salmon and trout will not be over-fished, the rivers where they live will be carefully safeguarded to ensure the health of the fisheries and rural fishing-based economies will have secure futures. Putting it another way, when this ideal is achieved, 'you can have your fish and eat it' over the long term.

The Brundtland Commission (1987) used the following definition of 'sustainable development': 'meeting the needs of the present without compromising the ability of future generations to meet their own needs'. If we can do this for fisheries (and this looks very doubtful at present) we will have achieved a great deal.

This argument holds true for any species which generates an income through sporting use, be it red grouse, grey partridge, brown trout or Atlantic salmon. Many of the animals harvested by the sportsmen may well have died naturally through winter starvation, disease or social stress (territoriality, etc) which commonly occur in high density wild animal populations; a quick, clean death at the experienced hands of a hunter or fisherman could be viewed as preferable. Also, the animals are eaten and, therefore, provide valuable food. Traditional cultures like the Arctic Eskimos, North American Indians, Australian Aborigines, Amazonian Pygmies and remote African tribes still hold on to a 'hunter-gatherer' lifestyle, living wisely in balance with the natural productivity of their environment. Many regard their cultures as primitive but they know a thing or two about conservation.

In our crowded society which is largely divorced from an appreciation of wilderness and ecological principles, both game and coarse anglers do a great deal to conserve our rivers and stillwaters and their contribution to this worthwhile cause should be acknowledged and respected. Anglers are often the first people to spot a river pollution incident and to alert the appropriate authorities. Field sports often enhance countryside management, protecting the interests of game fish, birds and mammals as well as many of the other species living in these habitats.

Protecting the Ecology of Rivers and Lakes from Habitat Degradation

The year 1816 saw such a prodigious run of salmon to the Thames that the price at Billingsgate fish market fell to just threepence a pound. Twenty years later the run had been all but exterminated by gross pollution. Michael Faraday wrote to *The Times* in 1855 to complain about the raw sewage pollution of the river. The situation became so bad that in 1858 Parliament was closed for a time until the 'Great Stink' dispersed. The River Pollution Act of 1876 arose from this and became the first in a line of key legislation leading to the present day Water Act (1989), the Environmental Protection Act (1990) and the Water Resources Act (1991). Today, of course, there is a project to rehabilitate salmon to the river; some of the released fish have returned, but successful breeding remains to be confirmed.

It is sobering and salutory to realise that the pollution of so large a river as the Thames was so easily brought about by unthinking human abuse of the environment over a short period of time. Isaak Walton wrote of Thames salmon: 'There is no better salmon than in England; and that although some of our northern rivers have salmon as fat and as large as the River Thames, yet none are of so excellent a taste.'

Twenty years ago the principal pollutants of inland waters were thought to be sewage, detergents and industrial discharges; now we also realise the damage wrought by agricultural inputs (pesticides, herbicides, fertilisers, liquid slurry, silage liquor, etc) and other diffuse sources of pollution such as 'acid rain'. The pollution of groundwater aquifers, for example, in the chalk and greensand beds, is also now causing concern and, because the water abstracted may be routinely used for agricultural and domestic uses, requires further research studies to determine the scale and extent of the problems.

The Anglers' Co-operative Association (ACA) is a good example of the practical way in which fishing interests are maintained by voluntary efforts via the prosecution of individuals and companies which pollute freshwaters. The ACA has a long history of success which is now being augmented in England and Wales by the excellent environmental protection work of the National Rivers Authority (NRA, a statutory body).

The outlook for many British rivers appears to be encouraging at the time of writing (summer 1992), with salmon being restocked in the Thames and the estuaries of the Rivers Tyne and Taff now clean enough to support large runs of breeding salmon and sea trout. In the mid 1980s the first runs of salmon were returning to the middle reaches of the River Clyde following water quality improvements to the grossly polluted lower reaches. The Welsh NRA is active in combating the long history of industrial pollution in South Wales where many rivers have been rehabilitated as trout fisheries after severe degradation from coal mining effluents.

Acidification

The widespread, progressive and insidious effects of acidification are very evident in upland peat bog river catchments of Scotland, Wales and Ireland. The primary cause of acidification is the burning of fossil fuels, coal, oil and gas in power stations, factories, motor vehicles etc. This produces oxides of sulphur and nitrogen which are carried in the smoke into the atmosphere. Once in the air-stream the acidic particles can dissolve in water droplets or remain in gaseous form, to be swept along by the prevailing winds and eventually precipitated, often in upland areas. Power stations are currently responsible for more than 70 per cent of sulphur dioxide emissions. In the U.K. there has been a reduction in acidic air pollution since the early 1970s. A European Commission directive requires us to reduce further the sulphur dioxide emissions from large combustion plants by 20 per cent of the 1980 level by 1993, 40 per cent by 1998 and 60 per cent by 2003. For oxides of nitrogen the agreed reductions are 15 per cent by 1993 and 30 per cent by 1998. All new petrol-engined cars are to be fitted with catalytic converters (which greatly reduce polluting exhaust gases) by 1992.

Coniferous afforestation

Where blanket coniferous afforestation coincides with air-borne acidic pollution or salt-laden sea winds, the trees act as a 'sponge', absorbing and concentrating the acidic or saline constituents and transfering them to the ground waters. Where the soils are already lime-poor the acid remains largely un-neutralised and metals such as aluminium, lead, copper and zinc dissolve to form a toxic cocktail of pollutants. Salmonid eggs incubating in the gravel of acidified upland streams suffer ill effects, both from the increased acid and metal concentrations and siltation by peaty sediments mobilized during ditching and tree-planting forestry operations. In conifer-shaded nursery streams, surviving young salmon and trout fry and fingerlings must cope with the reduced abundance of invertebrate food organisms and with a cooler shaded habitat where the scope for growth is less than in more open natural (un-afforested) streams.

Perhaps the saddest aspect of the large scale wiping out of salmon and trout streams by acidification is that its effects are gradual and progressive; stocks of fish are likely to dwindle away over long periods, so that people do not notice the loss until most of the fish are gone. By this stage restoration of the habitat by techniques such as liming (to neutralise excess acid) is a prohibitively expensive prospect and, therefore, usually out of the question.

The Welsh NRA have, however, decided to treat the acidified reservoir Llyn Brianne with finely powdered limestone to try and restore the salmonid spawning beds of the upper River Towy immediately downstream of the reservoir. The early results are promising, with a rise in pH of the Towy water to 6.7 and the improved potential for successful incubation of eggs. This project, of course, is treating the symptoms rather than tackling the root cause (air pollution) but it is a very worthwhile exercise. The damage to fisheries from acidification in Wales alone already amounts to a massive cumulative financial loss of many millions of pounds to the riparian owners and a loss of wetland quality for us all.

Other forms of pollution

Other forms of environmental damage are also widespread, for example, the persistent pesticide Dieldrin (from sheep dips) is still affecting the trout and eels of certain West Country rivers. Herons and otters living on a diet of eels and trout from the River Taw in Devon are considered to be at long term risk from the accumulation of pesticides in their tissues. In Somerset, the River Chew is significantly polluted with Dieldrin. Agricultural damage to rivers from silage and slurry leaks in dairy farming areas and pesticide/fertiliser leaching from sheep dips and on arable land still occurs regularly, posing major problems for the conservation of fisheries and the maintenance of water quality.

Aldrin was used to control large narcissus fly on daffodil bulbs and wireworm in potatoes, and both Aldrin and Dieldrin were used on brassicas to control root fly. Cornish rivers have received these pesticides in considerable quantities in rainwater run-off. Examples include the Newlyn River where eels contained 40 times the government recommended Dieldrin levels and invertebrates were badly contaminated; trout fishing was banned for a period. The Marazion Stream, the Angarrack Stream and the Penberth River were also found to have significant pesticide loads. Sediments in the River Hayle will probably carry a significant pesticide burden for many years to come. Since pesticide use has been so widespread (sprays, sheep dips, wood preservatives etc) it is likely that contamination of freshwaters is also very widespread. Approvals for the agricultural use of Dieldrin were withdrawn during the 1970s and for all other uses in March 1989.

Heavy metals are also finding their way into freshwater fish in high concentrations. For instance, eels from the Mersey were recently found to contain four times the safe European limit of mercury, eels from the River Axe had eight times the expected cadmium levels and eels from the River Piddle had high levels of copper and zinc. Fish are excellent indicators of persistent pollutants because they are top predators in the system, are often long-lived and, especially in the case of eels, have fatty flesh which acts as a reservoir of toxic compounds. Sadly, many anglers catch and eat eels, hopefully not in the sort of quantities which will lead to serious contamination.

With regard to fertilisers, there are considerable problems of widespread eutrophication (chemical enrichment) with phosphorus and nitrate both of rivers, streams and their associated lakes and reservoirs and, increasingly, groundwaters. The following rivers have recently been shown by the NRA to have increasing trends of nitrate concentrations: Otter, Piddle, Axe, Parret, Blackwater, Dove, Derwent, Tweed, Lyne, Lune, Teme, Wye and Tywi.

Urban rivers have to carry away the sewage effluent and industrial waste products of large cities, sometimes leading to chemical barrages in estuaries which can prevent the upstream migration of adult salmon, sea trout and shad and the downstream passage of smolts. The successful management of the water environment represents a great challenge for the future.

Aquatic ecosystems naturally bio-degrade many materials, oxidising them progressively as they are broken down. Bacteria and fungi are fundamentally important in the continual cleaning up of biological waste products to produce nutrients which are then re-cycled by the ecosystem through plant and animal growth. For instance, a certain amount of sewage effluent can be coped with naturally by a given river or lake system. The problems arise when the system is overloaded and too much oxygen is used up in the breakdown of organic matter and/or the system is over-enriched (made *eutrophic*). The oxygen required for the respiration of micro-organisms engaged in breaking down organic matter can be determined precisely: it is termed the Biochemical Oxygen Demand (B.O.D.) and, together with an ammonia reading, is a useful simple measure of the organic pollution load carried by a stream. Silage liquor has an extremely high B.O.D. and can, therefore, rapidly de-oxygenate small salmon and trout nursery streams, killing the fish by asphyxiation. Raw sewage also has a high B.O.D. but that of treated sewage is very much less.

In 1958, over 2000 km of rivers and canals in England and Wales were termed 'grossly polluted'; in 1980 the figure remained at 800km. The past decade has probably seen an increase in rivers with poor water quality although, overall, a NRA survey in 1990 found that nearly 90 per cent of freshwater rivers and canals were of 'good' or 'fair' quality. In Scotland, water quality has improved over the past decade (Royal Commission on Environmental Pollution, Report 16 (1992), *Freshwater Quality*).

The former National Water Council devised a river quality classification scheme with the following categories (the quality criteria should be met 95 per cent of the time). (The NRA are currently refining a new scheme of Statutory Water Quality Objectives.)

Good
1a.   80 per cent dissolved oxygen saturation; B.O.D. not greater than 3 mg/l; ammonia not greater than 0.4 mg/l: suitable for potable supply and for game and coarse fishing.
1b.   60 per cent dissolved oxygen saturation, B.O.D. not greater than 5 mg/l, ammonia not greater than 0.9 mg/l: suitable for potable supply and for game and coarse fishing.

Fair
2.   40 per cent dissolved oxygen saturation, B.O.D. not greater than 9 mg/l, ammonia greater than 0.9 mg/l: suitable for potable supply after advanced treatment and for coarse fishing.

Poor
3.   10 per cent dissolved oxygen saturation, B.O.D. not greater than 17 mg/l, ammonia greater than 0.9 mg/l: not suitable for potable supply, few or no fish.

Bad
4.   Likely to be anaerobic (no D.O.), B.O.D. greater than 17 mg/l, ammonia greater than 0.9 mg/l: grossly polluted and likely to cause a public nuisance.

An alternative to taking water samples and analysing them chemically is to sample the aquatic invertebrate animals which live in the stream permanently. They must survive all pollution incidents, many of which are likely to be missed by occasional water sampling. John Wright and colleagues from the Institute of Freshwater Ecology based at the River Laboratory, East Stoke, Wareham, Dorset have developed this approach and produced a computer programme, 'RIVPACS', which allows the prediction of invertebrate communities for a given river type. Where expected species or groups are missing from invertebrate samples, pollution and/or other forms of habitat degradation is indicated.

We all want clean tap water and crystal-clear rivers alive with fish, but, by our very existence, we all also produce and spread polluting substances. Science (even when poorly funded) is usually expected to come up with solutions to the pollution dilemma; however, research is expensive, often long-term and is by no means guaranteed to produce the required results. It is not easy to solve all of the problems all of the time. It is refreshing, therefore, that the government White Paper on the Environment (1990) included the following section.

Where there are significant risks of damage to the environment, the Government will be prepared to take precautionary action to limit the use of potentially dangerous materials or the spread of potentially dangerous pollutants, even where scientific knowledge is not conclusive, if the balance of likely costs and benefits justifies it.

This gives scope for prudent action by a vigilant body such as the NRA. A serious river pollution is normally signalled by the death of large numbers of fish; if such a situation occurs sufficiently often, then local fish stocks become extinct. This is still happening in Britain today.

Fish Populations in Britain

There are 42 native and 12 introduced freshwater fish species in Great Britain. The habitat available to these species exceeds 80,000 standing waters (1 per cent of the land area) and 190,000 running waters of which 10,000 enter the sea; clearly we have the potential for diverse and productive fish communities which are worth looking after. It is worth remembering that an historical series of fish extinctions (many of them probably induced by human activities) has taken place in Britain, including the following (see Peter Maitland, 1990): 1830s, Arctic Charr from Loch Leven; 1840s, Allis Shad from the River Severn; 1850s, Twaite Shad from the River Thames; 1900s, Burbot from the River Foss; 1910s, Vendace from Castle Loch; 1920s, Smelt from Rostherne Mere and Burbot from the River Trent; 1950s, Arctic Charr from Loch Dungeon; 1960s, Arctic Charr from Loch Grannoch, Smelt from River Forth, Burbot from Rivers Derwent, Waveney and Cam; 1970s, Vendace from Mill Loch; 1980s, Arctic Charr from Llyn Peris.

I wonder for which species the bell will toll in the 1990s?

Selecting sites and species for fish conservation

As Peter Maitland has pointed out, the total value of fish communities to society is far greater than is usually appreciated; fish represent a healthy food source and are valuable in sporting and commercial fisheries and for aesthetic, educational and scientific purposes. Sadly, the rarer species, especially those with poor powers of dispersal are being gradually eradicated to be replaced by more robust species which are usually stocked for angling purposes. The status of some rare fish species in Britain, e.g. Allis shad, *Alosa alosa*, Twaite shad, *Alosa fallax*; Arctic charr, *Salvelinus alpinus*; the Whitefishes, *Coregonus sp*; Smelt, *Osmerus eperlanus*; Sturgeon, *Acipenser sturio* and Burbot *Lota lota*, are poorly-known and urgently need further study before they disappear for good. In the case of burbot, this may already have happened. Houting *Coregonus oxyrinchus* and sturgeon, are marine vagrants which do not breed in Britain and need conserving both in their natal countries and on an international basis.

Peter Maitland and Alex Lyle have drawn attention to the conservation needs of rare forms of commoner species, including the following examples: spineless three-spined sticklebacks in the Outer Hebrides, dwarf brook lampreys in the Inner Hebrides, freshwater feeding ('landlocked') river lampreys in Loch Lomond and the remaining locally-adapted stocks of brown trout (*Gillaroo, Sonaghen, Ferox, Dollaghan* and others) which have been unadulterated by extensive stocking.

As a practical approach to conserving freshwater fish we should be vigilant for changes in the distribution and number of discrete populations of a given species. Maitland and Campbell (*Freshwater Fish*, Collins, 1992) consider a freshwater fish species to be under threat if it has five or less discrete populations. The current criteria for the selection of Sites of Special Scientific Interest (S.S.S.I.s) with respect to freshwater fish are:

1. The presence of a diverse natural community (20 breeding species in southern waters, 15 in Wales, 10 or more in northern England and southern Scotland, 6 or more in northern Scotland).

2. The presence of one or more rare fish species, ideally in a rare (pristine) habitat with other rare species.

The fish communities present within water bodies enclosed by each of the British National Nature Reserves (N.N.R.s) are presently being investigated by Peter Maitland who has recently advocated setting up new reserves on the basis of interesting and rare fish species in their own right.

Fish introductions

It is really quite amazing how few natural diverse fish communites have remained unstocked by small boys with jam jars or bigger boys with aerated tanks on the back of lorries. Often the species chosen for stocking is exotic (eg rainbow trout, brook trout, wels, zander, grass carp) and for many years introductions were made seemingly with little regard for either other fish species, the invertebrate life or any knock-on effects to the waterfowl and other animals dependent on the aquatic habitat. These days the situation has improved, with NRA and English Nature (formerly Nature Conservancy Council) officers being careful to advise the Ministry of Agriculture, Fisheries and Food (MAFF) in their granting of consents to stock fish only where they will do little damage. The legislation in Ulster and in the Irish Republic is possibly stronger than in the rest of the British Isles; a licence is required to import any cold water fish or their eggs into Irish waters.

There are many cases of fish stocking, as in the large scale introduction of rainbow trout into chalk streams like the River Test, where we know little of the biological effects of their introduction. On the Hampshire Avon at Burgate, where I work, the river is often thronging with escapee farmed rainbows. Local anglers feel that these trout eat large numbers of coarse fish fry, harming the future sport fishing. We simply do not know whether these fears are well grounded. We also have a situation, particularly in the south of England, where more or less all formerly wild brown trout fisheries are now stocked with hatchery brown trout to sustain the angling pressure. These stock fish are likely to suppress the numbers of wild trout inhabiting a given stream.

I hope that many more anglers will adopt the voluntary catch-and-release philosophy pioneered so successfully by 'Trout Unlimited' in the United States over the past 30 years, whereby the majority of wild native trout caught are returned to live to fight another day. This does not mean that a small number of wild fish can't be taken for the pot but it does mean a reduced pressure on hard-pressed stocks of brown and sea trout. It could also herald a gradual change away from almost universal put-and-take trout fishing to a more natural low-exploitation management of fisheries. American research, for example in Yellowstone Park, Montana, has shown that when the stocking of hatchery trout is stopped, wild trout stocks increase greatly. Catch-and-release then maintains high densities of large wild fish which are challenging to catch and which spawn each winter to produce wild progeny for future seasons. Wild fish breed wild fish which are adapted to their local rivers in a way that tatty-finned inbred domesticated hatchery brown trout strains can never be. If we don't get away from the present heavy stocking of our lowland trout fisheries we may soon have very few genetically distinct, locally-adapted stocks left. If we lose them, then we no longer have future access to a valuable natural resource.

The introduction of non-native species to natural communities can also have serious long-term repercussions and both the NRA and English Nature (or its Welsh/Scottish/ Irish equivalents) *must be consulted* before fish or other animals such as crayfish, or plants are introduced.

It is worth pointing out that the stocking of lakes with high densities of common carp or bream as day ticket or syndicated coarse fisheries will often lead to a great reduction in the invertebrate populations and submerged weed growth due to the shoals of large fish rooting around as they feed on the lake bed. This, in turn, will reduce the food available to waterfowl which depend upon the weeds and invertebrates for food. In addition amphibians and large slow-moving invertebrates such as dragonfly nymphs will be depleted due to fish predation.

A good example of this happening is at the Mallory Park fishery in Leicestershire, managed by Roy Marlow. The large head of cyprinid fish led directly to a wiping out of most of the other aquatic wildlife. Here the nature conservation interests are being restored by the building of marginal wetlands around the main fishery lakes so that invertebrates, amphibians, birds and mammals can thrive in areas which are not heavily stocked as fisheries. The improved diversity of wildlife which is given a home gives increased enjoyment to the anglers and is probably self-financing in the long term as the fishery gains a reputation as a pleasant place to fish and relax. In our modern crowded countryside, due consideration should be given to the welfare of other animals and their food supplies before any fish are stocked into lakes and rivers for sporting purposes. This is particularly important when the lake or pool concerned does not naturally already contain fish or where rare fish species occur. Fish-free pools often contain populations of large invertebrates such as fairy shrimps which are sensitive to fish predation; they soon disappear when fish become established.

In a survey conducted by the Angling Foundation in 1988, it was estimated that there are almost four million anglers in Britain — more than eight per cent of the population. In recent years the number has been increasing by around 3.5 per cent per year. Ron Edwards has stressed the need for anglers to limit any negative impacts which they and their sport have on the fisheries which they exploit. These impacts include the following:

1. Habitat modification (digging out bankside platforms, beating down pathways)
2. Disturbance (especially of reedbed nesting and roosting birds and wintering wildfowl flocks)
3. Litter (take home all waste line, hooks and lead weights).

It is very important that all anglers respect and minimise stress and harm caused to the fish they catch, the other fish in the water and the rest of the animals and plants which share our precious wetland areas. When conducted responsibly, angling can be a positive force aiding conservation efforts. Thoughtlessly discarded tackle can kill birds and other wildlife.

Origins of the fish fauna of the British Isles.

It appears, from evidence collected and published by Alwynne Wheeler, that all 31 non-migratory species of British fish living in rivers were exterminated during the last major phase of the ice-age (around 12,000 years ago). Conditions are thought to have been too cold for the successful completion of their life cycles. Whilst 12,000 years sounds a long time to us with our 'three score and ten' lifetimes, it is extremely short over geological and evolutionary time scales. The coldest phase of the last (Anglian) ice incursion thrust glacier fields southwards to cover Scotland, northern and central Ireland, Wales and northern England. The freshwater fish communities which we see now are the result of subsequent immigrations from the rivers of north-western Europe (the Elbe, Weser, Rhine, Scheldt and Meuse) into systems such as the Thames and Great Ouse. These fish must have ascended the rivers which drained the retreating ice-fields to the north and which ran across the short-lived land bridge which is now submerged to form the bed of the North Sea. This land bridge was severed about 7500 years ago. The eastern rivers of Britain tended therefore to have a richer variety of species than those of the north and west. Despite subsequent natural and artificial movements of species this pattern is still evident today. All of Ireland's indigenous freshwater fish species entered from the sea. Of course, Man has subsequently introduced many others (for example, pike, carp, gudgeon, tench, roach, rudd, bream, dace, minnows, perch). The fish fauna of Scotland is dominated by salmonids and other coldwater species such as pike and perch (which were probably stocked artificially in many instances). Peter Maitland and Niall Campbell (*Freshwater Fish*, Collins, 1992) have reviewed the origins of the British freshwater fish fauna, and the following table is based on their work.

Native species		Introduced species	
Marine origin	*via Land bridge*	*European*	*USA*
Lampreys	Grayling	Common Carp	Brook Trout
Shads	Pike	Crucian Carp	Pink Salmon
Sturgeon	Barbel	Goldfish	Rainbow Trout
Atlantic Salmon	Breams	Orfe	Pumpkinseed
Brown Trout	Tench	Bitterling	Rock Bass
Arctic Charr	Rudd	Wels	Largemouth Bass
Whitefishes	Roach	Zander	
Eel	Dace		
Sticklebacks	Chub		
Mullets	Loaches		
Smelt	Perch		
Sea Bass	Ruffe		
Common Goby	Bullhead		

Clearly, both the marine and freshwater immigration routes have been very important in the post-glacial recolonisation of British freshwater habitats by fish.

Important fish communities in the British Isles

The following rivers have been noted for their unusually diverse fish communities: Severn (39 species), Thames (36 species), Hampshire Avon (33 species), Great Ouse (30 species), Tweed (16 species), Annan (14 species).

The following lakes have diverse or unusual fish communities: Loch Lomond (20 species including river lamprey and powan), Llyn Tegid (16 species including Gwyniad and grayling), Lough Corrib (14 species including charr), Lough Erne (14 species including charr and pollan), Windermere (13 species including charr and rudd), Lough Leane (9 species including goureen and charr), Loch Eck (9 species including charr and powan), Haweswater (9 species including charr and schelly) and

Lough Melvin with its three distinct wild brown trout stocks (sonaghen, gillaroo, ferox). As knowledge is gained, this list will grow. Let us hope that these and fish communities of lesser note will be conserved for future generations.

PART 2
Ecology and Conservation of Freshwater Wetland Habitats

Human impacts on British Wetlands

The history of wetland habitats in Britain (and almost everywhere else) has been one of human intervention, often leading to rapid changes, both positive and negative. On the positive side many lakes and ponds in the south of England (including dammed lakes, reservoirs, sand, gravel, clay and marl pits) are man-made anyway. The most surprising set of man-made lakes in England is, to my mind, the Norfolk Broads which are actually very extensive, flooded peat diggings excavated in the thirteenth century and before. Before their recent demise (due to increasing eutrophication and water plant-loss) the Broads were splendid examples of the way in which nature is able to colonise and exploit new habitats to form interesting and valuable new wetland communities. Many are so rich that they have been designated Sites of Special Scientific Interest (S.S.S.I.s). On the negative side, man has drained vast areas of the wetlands which developed following the last glaciation of Britain.

Oliver Rackham in his excellent *History of the Countryside* (1986) notes that much of the native British vegetation, from alders to primroses, is adapted to 'differing kinds, degrees and seasons of waterlogging'. Indeed, before the large-scale agricultural transformation of our landscape, around a quarter of the British Isles had been a wetland of one type or another. What remains today represents a tiny fraction of the former panoramic flooded woodlands, meadows, swamps, bogs and fens which once flourished, giving homes to vast wetland wildlife populations. Accurate figures on the recent rate of wetland loss in the British Isles are difficult to establish. An overview of the drastic situation 'on the other side of the pond' has, however, recently been published.

Wetland losses in the United States

Thomas Dahl has recently documented the tremendous loss of wetland habitat in the U.S.A. over the 200-year period from the 1780s to the 1980s. In a sobering report to Congress he describes how the 48 lower states have lost an estimated 53 per cent of their original wetlands, this equals one acre lost for every minute of the 200 years. Twenty-two states have lost 50 per cent or more of their original wetland, with California losing a staggering 91 per cent and Florida an equally staggering 9.3 million acres; Hawaii has lost 12 per cent, but the wilderness of Alaska retains 99 per cent of its aquatic landscapes. Most of the lost wetland was, of course, drained for agricultural use, with the nation losing approximately one third of its total wetland area over the 200 years. Quite apart from the enormous loss of habitat for wildlife, groundwater supplies, water purity, floodwater storage, sediment trapping and climatic changes are all now threatened from this major change in land use.

This loss of wetlands also has important implications for outdoor recreational facilities for the estimated 60 million American anglers who collectively fish for a billion days per year. Sport fishing is thought to generate around 30 billion dollars to the American economy annually. The U.S. Fish and Wildlife Service recently (April 1987) launched an initiative to develop a National Recreational Fisheries Policy and the policy document was duly signed by the President, Vice-President and other V.I.P.s in June 1988. The key elements of the policy statement (which are highly relevant to fisheries in all developed countries) are as follows:

1. The nation's recreational fisheries provide substantial benefits to all Americans, to the health and welfare of our society, and to the national economy.
2. These benefits derive from achieving and maintaining healthy and robust fish populations and related habitats. A concerted and diligent effort is required to maintain, restore and increase the productivity of these populations and the habitats to provide for continuing public benefits.
3. Governments are vested with stewardship responsibilities and must work in concert with recreational fisheries constituencies and the general public to conserve, restore and enhance recreational fisheries and their habitats.
4. Constituency groups, the recreational fishing industry and individual anglers have an obligation to support natural resource stewardship, practise responsible angler ethics and actively participate in individual and co-operative fishery resource conservation efforts.

The four goals of the Policy are to:
1. Effect the protection and/or increase the productivity of fishery resources.
2. Ensure and enhance the quality, quantity and diversity of recreational fishing opportunities.
3. Enhance partnerships between governments and the private sector for conserving and managing recreational fisheries.
4. Achieve and maintain a healthy recreational fisheries industry.

This document has done the important job of focusing public attention on the value of wetlands and their fisheries and has led directly to many large-scale fisheries development/improvement programmes nationwide. The NRA are instituting similar approaches in England and Wales where the aims of the fishery function are to maintain, improve and develop fisheries. Currently (1993) the specific objectives are as follows:
1. Assessing the status of fish stocks.
2. Regulating, preserving and protecting fish stocks.
3. Improving and developing fisheries — especially with regard to restoring and rehabilitating damaged fisheries.
4. A fishery service based on a sound charging policy which is sensitive to the needs of the Public.

The East Anglian Fens . . . important British wetlands

The large-scale drainage of England's extensive East Anglian Fens, such as the River Great Ouse washes, to provide fertile arable fields is a typical example of wetland loss and has occurred in three major phases. The first works, revealed by the analysis of aerial photographs, were carried out at the end of the Iron Age in Roman times. The second (Anglo-Saxon) phase, completed by the year 1250, has been revealed through archaeological studies. The third, best documented and by far the most familiar phase was organised by the famous Dutch engineer Cornelius Vermuyden and others in the mid-1600s. It was at this time that the 'Bedford Level' was drained through the digging of many ditches and the Old and New Bedford rivers, each 21 miles long, were dug, both considerable feats of engineering.

Some of the earthworks involved are truly amazing. Oliver Rackham explains how, in the early Middle Ages, the 'Roman Wall', a 60-mile-long embankment running all around the Wash and its inlets was made (or re-made). This great bank held back the sea for 500 years, protecting more than a million acres of farmland. By the fourteenth century, Fenland had the greatest concentration of agricultural prosperity in England, all created by imaginative water management and civil engineering.

Increased agricultural production was the incentive for the destruction of much of our wet habitats and still is today (it has recently been grant-aided). On the Somerset Levels farmers were, until recently, draining the small remaining fragments of the wildfowl-rich winter floodplain. In Fenland, Swallowtail butterflies and Great raft spiders still cling on in the last remnants of habitat conserved as nature reserves at Wicken and Woodwalton Fens. In the wilds of Sutherland and Caithness (Scotland's 'Flow country'), large scale coniferous afforestation (stimulated until 1990 by lucrative tax incentives) has changed the water regime of the extensive blanket bogs which are home to many rare birds (for example, breeding red and black-throated divers). We seem to want to exploit every last British wilderness in the name of profit and economic growth. The ecologist hopes and strives for *sustainable development* which encompasses the careful management of natural resources and habitats. If greater legal restrictions are not placed upon overly exploitative developments then we will soon have very little left to go and see. The evocative 'call of the Loon' (the Great Northern Diver) will no longer be heard in the wetlands of the far north.

Natural lakes

Natural lakes in the British Isles are usually the result of either faulting in the earth's crust (such as the extremely deep lochs Ness and Morar) or glacial action. Glacial waters can be huge lakes such as those of the Scottish Highlands and English Lake District, or abundant small ponds which can occur in many types of countryside both upland and lowland. Oliver Rackham has analysed the distribution and abundance of ponds in England and Wales on the first edition six-inch maps and has estimated that there was a total of around 800,000 (or 14 per square mile, on average) in the year 1880. Many of these have now gone. 'Ancient countryside' areas now average 12 ponds per square mile compared with only around 5 per square mile in our modern 'planned countryside'. Some areas are far richer in ponds than others, for example, south Norfolk, north-east Suffolk and parts of Cheshire, where there are still around 30 ponds per square mile. Many Cheshire and Shropshire meres are 'kettle holes', formed when a block of ice embedded in a glacial moraine melted. The eastern edges of the Fens and Breckland have numerous (up to 100 per square mile) 'pingos'. These round or lobe-shaped ponds are surrounded by a bank of soil and also date back to the Ice Ages. In this case it seems that a frozen lozenge of ice, formed by the freezing of a sub-terranean spring and covered with soil, gradually melted so that the soil ran down around the ensuing pond to form the characteristic surrounding soil bank.

Swallow-holes and sink-holes are other natural pond formations, both being created by underground solution-hollows in chalk or limestone into which the overlying soil has fallen. These lakes fluctuate in level in response to changes in the groundwater table and they often 'swallow' inflowing streams but have no obvious outlet. The Millstone Grit mountains of South Wales have thousands of swallow-holes where the rock has collapsed into underlying limestone caves and galleries. In western Ireland there occur 'Turloughs', which are small lakes which fluctuate greatly in level from year to year, sometimes drying out altogether and being grazed by cattle. These lakes are also connected to the water table in underlying limestone formations and can be biologically very rich and of high conservation value. The vast western Irish loughs of Corrib and Mask and the smaller Lough Carra are also limestone-based and hence hard-watered and biologically productive.

Wetland Conservation in Britain

Conservation bodies such as English Nature (formerly the Nature Conservancy Council, N.C.C.), the Wildfowl and Wetlands Trust, the Game Conservancy Trust, the Royal Society for the Protection of Birds, the Salmon and Trout Association, the Atlantic Salmon Trust, the Anglers' Co-operative Association, the Scottish and Irish river purification and fisheries boards and the newly-constituted National Rivers Authority (NRA for England and Wales) all combine to safeguard what remains of our natural wetland heritage. Wetlands are very rich in animal and plant species compared with other habitats and often contain rarities. The push over recent decades for ever greater agricultural yields from farmland throughout Britain (and elsewhere) has led both directly and indirectly to massive wetland damage and loss.

The major agents of damage have been drainage and pollution. Pollutants include industrial waste products, sewage effluent, agro-chemicals, silage liquor, cattle and pig slurry and fertiliser run-off. Pollution which increases the amount of dissolved chemical plant nutrients (especially phosphate and nitrate) in both flowing and still-waters has far-reaching ecological effects and is termed *eutrophication*. Department of the Environment (DoE) data shows that phosphate levels in many lowland British rivers are in many cases orders of magnitude above natural background levels. The principal rivers in the NRA's Anglian, Thames and Severn-Trent regions are heavily chemically enriched, as are many rivers in the North-West, Yorkshire, Southern and Wessex regions. Reservoirs fed by these eutrophic rivers rapidly become hypertrophic and subject to dense algal blooms which, if largely comprised of 'blue-green algae' (cyanobacteria), can lead to the poisoning of livestock and poor quality potable water supplies. The cost of treating drinking water from these reservoirs is considerable. Eutrophication hits the headlines when it affects well-known natural and naturalised lakes such as Windermere, Loughs Neagh and Sheelin, Loch Leven and the Norfolk Broads, but the problem is pernicious and widespread.

The Norfolk Broads: a problem of eutrophication.

The Norfolk Broads have been studied extensively by Brian Moss and co-workers from the University of East Anglia. The Broads used to be clear-watered, botanically-rich habitats with abundant water plants, dragonflies, aquatic birds and fish. This wetland complex encompasses three N.N.R.s (National Nature Reserves) and 24 S.S.S.I.s. As with all freshwater systems, the Broads are filling in gradually with silt and aquatic vegetation (reed-bed material). About two-thirds of the original water area is now dry and much of the rest is very shallow. This process, which has taken place over hundreds of years, has quickened suddenly over the past century with greatly increased rates of siltation.

The term 'broad' derives from the local dialect for a broadening of the river and most of the present-day lakes lie adjacent to the rivers Waveney, Yare, Bure, Thurne and

Ant which drain eastern Norfolk. Traditionally the Broads have provided a living for local peat-diggers, wildfowlers, fishermen (eels) and thatchers who use either the 'Norfolk reed' (*Phragmites communis*) or Great Fen-sedge (*Cladium mariscus*). Reed-cutting prevented large areas of reed bed from gradually being overtaken by alder scrub and thus helped to preserve the system. However, the reed-cutters also cut channels to link the river systems with the broads in order to move their produce more easily by barge. By this process they sowed the seeds of destruction for the delicate Broads' ecosystems. Algae and higher plants require (amongst a host of more available elements) both nitrogen and phosphorus for growth, in fact they need around seven times more nitrogen than phosphorus. If the nitrogen to phosphorus (N:P) ratio falls below about 5:1, plant growth will be limited by nitrogen; if it is higher than 12:1 it will be phosphorus-limited. The N:P ratio for *oligotrophic* (nutrient-poor) lakes is around 100:1, whilst that for *eutrophic* (nutrient-rich) lakes is around 10:1. The Broads' water chemistry was shifted across the scale by the influx of enriched waters from upstream.

As time went by the river water, which had now gained access to the lakes, brought with it increasing quantities of fertilisers washed from farmland upstream and nutrient-rich sewage effluent from the treatment works servicing the growing city of Norwich. This chemically-enriched (phosphorus and nitrogen) water led to dramatic changes in the Broads' aquatic vegetation. Strumpshaw Broad has turned from a clear-watered marl lake, rich in stonewort (*Chara*) through a phase of chara-loss and the growth of ranker weeds such as hornwort (*Ceratophyllum demersum*), milfoil (*Myriophyllum spicatum*) and fennel pondweed (*Potamogeton pectinatus*) to its present state as a weed-free, bare silt-bottomed lake. The water clarity has progressively declined because of increasingly frequent algal blooms which prevent light from reaching the lake bed in only 3–5 feet of water. Furthermore, if algal blooms suddenly die off they can cause a catastrophic depletion in the dissolved oxygen levels with the consequent death of many fish. Even the more tolerant submerged water weeds are now found in only four out of more than 40 broads. This process of eutrophication is occurring to varying extents in many rivers and lakes worldwide. It leads ultimately to the loss of water plants and then of sensitive invertebrates, fish and birds. Even in areas where lakes are naturally poor in chemical plant nutrients, like Windermere in the English Lake District, increasing sewage and agricultural inputs have had noticeable detrimental effects upon the biology of the waters. The naturally productive (alkaline) Lough Sheelin in the Republic of Ireland and Loch Leven in Scotland are two famous brown trout fisheries which have suffered badly from eutrophication in recent years. Remedial action has now improved Lough Sheelin where the mayfly hatch and attendant trout fishing is returning to its former high quality, but Loch Leven suffered very dense algal blooms and brown trout kills in the summer of 1992 and fly-fishing competitions had to move venue. Rainbow trout are to be stocked in 1993.

Wetland Amphibians and Reptiles

Stillwater and slowly-flowing wetlands can provide homes for both reptiles and amphibians, two groups of key importance to conservationists because of their dwindling numbers. With the loss of wetland habitats through drainage and pollution the populations of newts, frogs, toads and snakes which rely upon these habitats have declined too. Britain has only one common frog species (*Rana temporaria*) and one common toad (*Bufo bufo*). There are, however, other rarer species which are of considerable interest. The Edible frog, *Rana esculenta* has been introduced and gone extinct several times, whilst the Marsh frog, *Rana ridibunda*, is slowly expanding its range since its introduction in 1935, based around the River Rother and Old Military Canal in Sussex. The Natterjack toad is native to Britain but is now very rare, being restricted to a few coastal marsh habitats which are under pressure from a variety of threats from developers.

The common frog prefers to live in shallow ponds and is active during the day whilst the common toad prefers deeper water and tends to be nocturnal. The two species are seldom found together. Frogs live in bankside rush and reedbeds eating slugs, snails and flies, often falling prey themselves to herons and grass snakes. Frogs are well camouflaged, with green/yellow/black and even red smooth skins, whilst toads are dark brown and more conspicuous when in the open. Toads benefit from a warty skin which exudes a bitter-tasting liquid to deter predators. Even grass snakes are said to spit out toads (and warty newts).

Toads wander far away from water to live in woods and along canal banks, sleeping in cool damp crannies under boulders and logs during the day and becoming active at night when they forage for invertebrates. The old saying that it 'rained toads' probably refers to the marked increase in activity after rain storms when food in the form of worms, slugs and snails is abundant. Migrations are common for toads and they have an annual hibernation which starts in October/November. Frogs often remain in ponds during the winter, going into a state of suspended animation, burrowed into the mud from October to February. The widespread decline of frogs in Britain in recent decades is thought to be due largely to habitat-loss.

Britain has three newt species, the Warty or Great crested newt, *Triturus cristatus*; the Smooth newt, *T.vulgaris*; and the Palmate newt, *T.helveticus*. All are aquatic during the breeding season and as tadpoles. As its alternative name suggests, the Great crested newt (like the toad) can exude an evil-smelling/tasting fluid from its warty skin and so deter predators. It stays in water longer than the other two species and is considerably larger, males average 14cm (5.5 inches). In spring the males develop bright orange bellies with black spots and a large saw-toothed dorsal crest along the back and tail. This disappears after breeding. The species is rare and is legally protected under the Wildlife and Countryside Act; it must not be disturbed and its breeding ponds must not be damaged by industrial development, pollution, drainage, etc.

Smooth newts are the commonest species throughout lowland Britain, being replaced to some extent in upland habitats of the north and west by the Palmate. The two species overlap widely, however, and Palmate newts are often found in the ponds and canals in the Midlands and eastern England. Palmates are smaller (8cm) than Smooth newts and are distinguishable by their webbed back feet and short thread at the tip of the tail. Smooth newts remain in the water as adults for three to four months each year, beginning with spawning in April/May when females lay several hundred eggs, one at a time, on submerged plants. By August most adult Smooth newts retreat to bankside habitats where they live under stones, logs and amongst vegetation, eating small insects and molluscs. The bright orange breeding colouration of the male fades to a dull brown for the terrestrial phase of the life cycle.Most young newts leave the water in October to brave life on land.

Of Britain's three snake species (Adder, Smooth and Grass snake) only the Grass snake, *Natrix natrix* is aquatic, the other two being confined largely to dry, sandy heathland habitats. Grass snakes are widely distributed except in Scotland and Ireland and often hunt in wetlands for newts, frogs, fish, large invertebrates and small mammals and birds. Growing to a large size (1 metre or more) they make a splendid sight as they swim sinuously through weedy shallows in search of prey on a hot summer's day. Grass snakes are active by day and are very shy, retreating at the footfall of a passing person by gliding back into the undergrowth where they are well camouflaged. Whilst they have no venom, grass snakes will strike out in self defence but they keep their mouths closed and will do no harm. Grass snakes mate in the early spring after emerging from their winter rest. The females lay their eggs in compost heaps and piles of decaying grass/straw where the development is speeded by the heat generated by the fermenting vegetation. Our modern 'tidy' farmland leaves little room for grass snake breeding habitat; more's the pity, as they are beautiful, graceful creatures which do no harm and deserve to be protected as part of our diverse wetland heritage.

Wetland mammals

Clearly it is beyond the scope of this book to describe adequately the natural history of all of the British wetland fauna and flora. In particular aquatic birds are only dealt with in passing as there are so many good ornithological texts available to the keen reader. Aquatic mammals, on the other hand are not so well documented, perhaps because they are so difficult to see, let alone study scientifically. Our native primarily aquatic mammals are the Otter, *Lutra lutra*, the Water vole, *Arvicola terrestris*; and the Water shrew, *Neomys fodiens*. Until the twelfth century the European beaver, *Castor fiber* was very common in the East Anglian Fens and along Welsh river valleys. Attempts at reintroduction have been unsuccessful and the species is becoming rare over its whole range.

I suspect that otters are almost everybody's favourite aquatic mammal. Sadly they are now a rare sight on English wetlands, although they are more abundant in Wales and locally common in Scotland and Ireland. Being very shy and largely nocturnal when disturbance is common, it has never been easy to watch otters except where they are very abundant; usually the water naturalist has to be content with footprints (6cm width, mink 3cm), tracks, otterslides down clay banks and droppings ('spraints') left on prominent rocks as territory markers. In Scotland and Ireland, where coastal foraging is common, otters are often seen during the day.

Otter numbers declined steeply in the late 1950s, almost certainly due to Dieldrin and D.D.T. pesticide poisoning. Surveys in the mid-1980s indicated extensions of the species' range in the south-west of England whilst in East Anglia the range continued to contract. Dead animals were (and still are) also found to contain Polychlorinated Biphenyls (P.C.B.s) and heavy metals. Since the stricter control of organochlorine pesticides has been in force, habitat-loss is thought to be the major factor curbing a recovery in numbers. However in the West Country rivers Taw and Torridge, one in seven otters were recently (1992) found to be so polluted with P.C.B.s that they are rendered sterile. P.C.B.s are used in the manufacture of electrical components and persist in the environment for long periods, passing up and being concentrated in the foodchain. The poor old otter at the top of the chain carries the highest accumulated burden of poisons. P.C.B.s have recently been found in otters throughout Britain and the pathways of these chemicals into the natural environment must be found and blocked to prevent further pollution.

Acidified headwaters of the River Severn do not support otters whilst adjacent unaffected streams do. Acidification, which can seriously affect fish stocks, appears to have 'knock-on' effects on fish predators too. Dog otters which can cover many miles (perhaps 5–10) of river bank a night in search of food (eels, crayfish, salmon, trout, coarse fish) clearly need large areas of quiet suitable habitat to live out their lives in peace. Females tend to occupy smaller home ranges and in productive coastal sites females may only range over a few hundred metres. Female otters seem also to live fairly solitary lives in smaller territories than the males, only consorting with males during courtship. Breeding can occur throughout the year (litters usually of two to three cubs) but late autumn/winter cubs probably survive less well in harsher northern areas than those born in the summer and/or in more southerly habitats.

Water shrews are our largest shrew species and are dark-backed, white-bellied, less aggressive than common or pigmy shrews and occupy home ranges of 30-80 square metres. The species occurs throughout mainland Britain and on many of our islands, but is probably localised in northern Scotland and absent from Ireland. They dive for caddis larvae, shrimps, crayfish, small fish (bullheads) and amphibians, searching for food whilst turning over small stones on the river bed and thriving particularly in watercress beds. Being voracious feeders, water shrews eat half of their body weight each day. They either dig small (2cm) burrow systems or they use existing water vole or woodmouse burrows. Several shrews can live in the same burrow system but they are solitary animals which probably have territorial boundaries. Breeding occurs from April–September, peaking in May and June, females generally have one to two litters per year. The life span is 14–19 months with high levels of mortality during and after the breeding season. It is difficult to know how common water shrews are nowadays as they are little studied but it is thought that habitat destruction has adversely affected them in the south of England. I think that they are worth conserving for their intrinsic interest alone.

Water voles are quite large herbivorous rodents which dig burrow systems in river banks and browse reeds, rushes, grasses and herbaceous plants, eating 80 per cent of their body weight per day. The males defend territories of perhaps 100 metres length and the females live in smaller home ranges within the male territories. Breeding occurs from April–September and up to five litters, each with around six young are produced per year, this gives the populations a considerable ability to absorb heavy predation by herons, foxes, etc. The burrow systems have both underwater and bankside entrances and water voles can easily be watched as they go about their daily routine. I used to enjoy watching them from the comfort of a hammock strung up between two mature willows at the bottom of our garden on the banks of the Great Ouse in Buckingham, that is until the mink arrived. Soon after I saw mink regularly along the upper Ouse I saw water voles less and less frequently. Now I don't see them there at all. It is tempting to draw the obvious conclusion. Even with their high reproductive capacity I wonder whether the vole population was predated out of existence by mink?

The introduction of mink, *Mustela vison*, by fur farmers and their subsequent escape and proliferation in the wild throughout almost the whole of Britain is an example of the folly of exotic introductions. Whilst there is no proof, many ecologists believe that mink eat large enough numbers of water voles, aquatic birds (especially moorhens and ducklings), crayfish and fish, to have severe effects upon local populations of their main prey species. Ducks breeding on islands to avoid foxes, which hunt mostly on the mainland, are particularly vulnerable to this amphibious mustellid which can easily kill the adult bird on the nest and/or eat the eggs or the brood of ducklings.

Some of my own experiences with mink have not led me to regard them fondly. The prey are killed by a single bite at the nape of the neck. I know this to my cost, having had fifteen Tufted ducklings which were almost ready for release to the wild killed overnight by a mink. None of the birds were eaten, it was a total waste. When the mink came back for some more the following day it was met by a colleague with a shotgun. Whilst field-working on Loch Lomond in the late 1970s I had a mink steal over 30 perch which I had left in a tub over lunchtime. The last fish was being borne triumphantly away along the bank as I rowed back into my sampling bay near Rowardennan. More recently, Ros Wright and I had young pike stolen from experimental tanks by mink at the ARC Wildfowl Centre, Great Linford, Buckinghamshire. Here, the mink had taken up residence in the back-yard and were systematically raiding our fish house for their daily meals. Mink are cheeky devils.

Fur farmers also introduced two large burrowing rodents into Britain; Muskrats, *Ondatra zibethicus*, and Coypu, *Myocastor coypus*. Both of these species were subsequently eradicated by trapping campaigns; muskrats from the River Severn, Shropshire and River Earn, Perthshire and coypu from the Fenlands of East Anglia where they wrought havoc by digging away the banks of the dykes. When you consider that adult coypus weigh as much as an adult fox you can imagine the size of the burrows they make! In addition to managing feral pest species, man must address the need to manage wetland systems themselves.

Rivers

The Management of a River during its Lifetime

Rivers, lakes and streams are, by their very nature, ever-changing features in the landscape. Rivers cut their way inexorably down through their bedrock to sink ever closer to sea level. As they descend through the Earth's surface they erode clay, sand and gravel particles which are swept away downstream in the upper torrential reaches only to be deposited lower down as the current slows. Eventually the headwaters lie in a deeply-eroded river canyon and the water flows more slowly until the whole system is a meandering lowland river with oxbow lakes. Oxbows are formed when the river breaks its old bank to take the shortest course, cutting off a large loop of former river bed which is then left as a small isolated 'C'-shaped lake. The slowest of lowland reaches become silted and are rapidly colonised by abundant aquatic vegetation (rush, reed, pondweed and lily beds) more typically found in ponds. The reed beds grow ever larger year by year until they turn the lowest part of the river basin into a reedswamp. This process continues gradually to work its way backwards upstream until the river or stream is choked by vegetation and dries out to become willow and alder carr and then woodland. This process of *ecological succession* necessitates routine river dredging to reduce the risk of winter flooding — people do not take kindly to having their homes flooded. The potential for new river systems to develop occurs (in geological timescales) after periods of local uplifting of the Earth's crust (i.e. mountain-building) to form new upland areas which are drained by newly-forming rivers and streams.

Maintenance dredging — a history of ecological damage

The task of managing the ever-changing conditions in river channels falls to river engineers and ecologists. River engineers have, over past centuries, been responsible for the systematic destruction of much high quality habitat along river corridors through the practice of dredging. Their aim is to remove periodically the silt and waterplants from a section of river and thus speed up the run-off of water after rainfall. The best shape for shedding water is a gutter and this is what the engineer aims for although he uses the term 'trapezoidal section' to make the thing sound technical and therefore perhaps more acceptable. Gutters work less well when they have bends and obstructions in them so, accordingly, bends and gravel shallows are removed from rivers and streams during traditional dredging programmes.

Gravel beds and deep corner pools with undercut banks provide breeding and shelter habitat for many fish species. With the loss of steep clay banks goes the kingfisher's nest burrow. Bankside willows with their underwater root masses are ideal habitat for trout, chub, dace and barbel below the surface and for lesser spotted woodpeckers, mallard or tawny owls nesting above. If you look amongst willow root masses on the right rivers you might still be lucky enough to find the holt of an otter or a nest of water shrews, although increasingly nowadays feral mink are a more likely find. These species are evicted, however, with one sweep of the bulldozer blade.

The benefits of willow management

It is estimated that during 1985/86 the Anglian Water Authority dredged 350km of rivers, removing many of the bankside trees and often leaving steep banks, devoid of marginal aquatic plants. This habitat is very important for the survival of cyprinid fish fry. Bankside willows are often rooted out in case they split and fall into the river on a future occasion. Regular pollarding would be a much better management practice. Sallow (or goat willow, *Salix caprea*) provides a home for the caterpillars of two hawk moths (Poplar hawk and Eyed hawk), those of the Notodontid (Prominent) moths and the Puss moth. Puss moth caterpillars are remarkable in having large warning 'eye' spots ready for display and the ability to spray formic acid over potential predators like treecreepers or great tits. Old willows are home to many wood-boring beetles including longhorn species like the musk beetle which emerges as an amazing bright green 3cm long adult beetle after its larval existence. The leaves of willows are often covered with small brightly metallic chrysomellid beetles and the catkins are early sources of pollen and nectar for Small tortoiseshell butterflies and Hebrew character moths. Willows and the closely-related poplars harbour very rich insect communities along our river banks. When they are felled, this whole community goes with them.

Quite apart from the loss of wildlife through tree-felling, willow species, if correctly managed, can provide renewable crops of firewood from pollards (*Salix fragilis*), osier (*Salix viminalis*) cuttings for basketwork, or wood for cricket bats (*Salix alba coerulea*). Bankside trees also help to shade-out excessive weed growth on the river bed and so reduce the need for frequent weed cutting, a very expensive operation. The engineer's 'headache' of river bed management might even have been cured with some Aspirin made from Salicin (salicylic acid) extracted from willow bark, if he hadn't already sawn down the tree! The ecological damage which has been wrought over past decades on our river and stream banks in the name of drainage works is, in my opinion, criminal.

Effects of river dredging on fish communities

Stephen Swales has studied the effects of river dredging on the fish populations of the lowland River Soar in Leicestershire. By comparing pre- and post-drainage fish surveys Swales showed that the total fish population was reduced by about 75 per cent by the drainage work, largely through the removal of bankside trees and shrubs which provide vital shelter for fish. Brown trout, which were relatively rare before the drainage work, disappeared from the study stretch, dace numbers fell by 72 per cent and chub by 87 per cent; roach were the most resilient species, with their numbers being reduced by 30 per cent.

These effects are likely to be relatively long-lasting as it takes time for trees to re-seed and grow large enough to provide enough cover for sheltering fish shoals. Fortunately, given time, nature is resilient and many species return to recolonise worked river sections.

Modern river management

I recommend Jeremy Purseglove's *Taming the Flood* for a well-written, authoritative and up to date review and analysis of this problem. Purseglove, who was for 11 years senior landscape architect with the former Severn-Trent Water Authority helped to pioneer a new approach to the management of river channels through sympathetic engineering techniques. He cites numerous examples of damaged wildlife communities along river banks dredged using the old methods. Populations of reed and sedge warblers, coots and moorhens declined after the removal of bankside vegetation and fish were left with no cover and little food. Kingfishers and sand martins lost nesting habitat on the River Ouzel in Bedfordshire and doubtless on many other watercourses after maintenance dredging. In upland areas pied flycatchers and redstarts which nest in streamside alders have suffered similar habitat loss.

Fish (for example, trout) are also adversely affected by tree-loss from the banks of unproductive upland streams as they no longer derive the benefits of terrestrial insects (especially caterpillars) falling from the overhanging branches. Less obviously the lack of leaf litter falling into the water in these habitats reduces the potential for the production of aquatic invertebrates (shrimps, caddis larvae, mayfly and stonefly nymphs). Many of these animals feed by shredding and processing the dead leaves, eating the fungi and bacteria which grow on the particles of decaying plant material.

In Essex it is estimated that up to 70 per cent of river bank trees were cleared between the years 1879 to 1970. Even in 1986 the then South-West Water Authority was clearing the trees from the banks of beautiful Cornish rivers. One hopes that the conservation message will filter through universally before too much longer.

Thankfully the new attitude to river management (pioneered in Bavaria and Britain) is now gaining a hold at grass roots level amongst Water Company and NRA managers. Drag-line and bulldozer operators are now advised (often by an overseer on the river bank) to retain key habitat features such as gravel shoals, water plant beds, pools and riffles. The earthmoving machinery works from one bank only leaving the opposite bank untouched. Instead of cutting a clean 'trapezoidal section' the bank is often shaped to include a shoulder with a shallow water zone close to the bank. This shelf is then re-planted with clumps of aquatic plants (arrow-head, lilies, bullrush, etc); this greatly speeds up the subsequent recolonisation by invertebrates and fish fry.

In some projects it is possible to retain some meanders where the current flows slowly and water-lily beds fringe the banksides. Where winter floods are a damaging problem, relief channels can be cut to take away excess floodwaters and allow a less severe dredging of the main river bed. Bays and riverside boggy patches can be extended and key trees of importance to the landscape (and wildlife) can be left. The whole approach is less clinical and more at-one with nature.

Where drainage would ruin important adjacent wetlands the decision must sometimes be taken not to dredge at all. Engineers take advice from ecologists and *vice versa* to marry the twin objectives of land drainage and conservation. Excellent!

Fish Habitat Zones in Rivers

Where rivers have escaped the worst ravages of drainage work there exists a natural in-stream pattern of key habitat types usually referred to as Riffles, Runs, Flats and Pools. Riffles have fast broken water, often with boulders or large cobbles which slow the current along the stream bed by frictional resistance. They harbour rich populations of caddis larvae, shrimps, mayfly and stonefly nymphs which sometimes lose a foothold and drift away downstream. Fish living in riffles shelter behind rocks and dart out to take food organisms which are swept by on the current. Young salmon and trout thrive in these zones. Runs are rather slower with less turbulence and little or no broken water; the cobbles grade into gravels and weed beds occur under favourable conditions. Grayling, larger trout, dace and chub like to live in runs, especially where overhead cover is afforded by bankside vegetation or stands of water crowfoot. Flats or glides have beds of sand or fine gravel and grade into the final category of pools where slack water occurs in back-eddies and silted corners allowing the growth of lilies and pond weeds. In slacker water areas species such as roach, bream, perch, pike and eels tend to predominate.

In each of these river habitat zones, different fish species have to balance their key biological needs for *comfort* (oxygen, temperature, current speed), *safety* (cover) and *food supply*. If a fish can compete successfully for these requirements it will grow to maturity and breed to perpetuate its genetic line. The process of the differential survival of individuals as they grow, mature and finally breed is called *natural selection*.

Each species of fish has its own optimal combination of factors such as water temperature, oxygen content, current speed, food availability and proximity of cover. Individual fish position themselves in a stream to gain the best mix of these factors for their needs. Brown trout, for instance, tend to live in fast riffles when young and then gradually drop back to take up feeding lies in the slower runs and glides as they grow larger. In each zone, the trout balance the energy needed to hold station in the current against their food intake of flies and drifting shrimps etc. The fattest, fastest-growing fish defend the most profitable feeding locations; these provide shelter from the main current flow and a steady supply of food.

Brown trout prefer to *lie* in current speeds of 7–15 cm per second and *feed* in currents of 30 cm or more per second. The best fly-fishermen learn to 'read' a stream and are able to predict where the best lies, holding the biggest trout, will be. If a trout survives to be a large old fish it may finally end up defending its feeding area in the depths of a pool where it can shelter from the main force of the current and chase minnows or hunt crayfish for its food. Field studies of upland trout streams have shown that a ratio of around 50:50 pools:riffles is best for a thriving population which will provide good fishing.

Different river types and their fish communities

The gradient of a river bed and the current speed are of fundamental importance for the types of fish which can inhabit a given stretch of river. This fact was recognised by Marcel Huet who proposed a system of classifying European river zones by the dominant fish species present. The table on page 38 relates Huet's classification to current speeds and the nature of the river bed.

The Trout zone is classically fast-flowing, cold, even in summer and well-oxygenated. It occurs either in the upland headwaters of rain-fed river systems or, less commonly in strongly flowing chalk streams. The fish community is dominated by Salmonids; trout (brown and sea trout) and salmon parr (or spawning adult salmon). Minnows, bullheads and stone loach also occur commonly. The aquatic plant community is often restricted to mosses and liverworts in upland catchments.

The Grayling zone is represented either by the river sections immediately below the trout zone on rain-fed rivers or by the special conditions provided by chalk streams (fed by chalk-groundwater aquifers). The water is swiftly-flowing, generally cool and well-oxygenated throughout the summer. The fish community is mixed, dominated by grayling and trout, but also with a variety of cyprinids; barbel, chub, dace, gudgeon and

River characteristics and fish zones			
Average Current speed (cm. per second)	*River bed*	*Habitat zone*	*Fish community*
More than 120	rock	torrential	**fishless**
More than 90	heavy shingle	torrential	
			Trout zone
More than 60	light shingle	non-silted	
More than 30	gravel	lightly-silted	**Grayling zone**
More than 20	sand	moderate-silting	
			Barbel zone
More than 10	silt	silted	
Less than 10	mud	pond-like	**Bream zone**

bleak. Perch, pike and eels occur in areas sheltered from the main current. The aquatic plant community is prolific (especially in chalk streams and limestone rivers where the pH is high) and is dominated by water crowfoot (*Ranunculus*) species with other species such as starwort (*Callitriche*) water cress (*Rorippa*) and water parsnip (*Berula*).

The Barbel zone has a moderately strong current with bare gravel sections and silted areas around weed beds and on the slack current side of bends. The water temperatures and dissolved oxygen conditions can fluctuate quite widely with the seasons. The fish community is dominated by Cyprinids; barbel, chub, roach, dace, bleak with perch, pike and eels, especially in marginal reed beds. The submerged aquatic plant community tends, once more, to be dominated by water crowfoot, with bulrush (*Schoenoplectus*) beds. The river margins support a prolific growth of reedmace (*Typha*), arrow-head (*Sagittaria*), bur-reed (*Sparganium*) water plantain (*Alisma*), water mint (*Mentha*) and reed-grass (*Glyceria*).

The Bream zone is classically the slow-flowing, meandering lowland section of river catchments where the conditions can become almost pond or canal-like. Here the water temperatures and concentration of dissolved oxygen can fluctuate widely through a 24-hour period. Oxygen levels may be very low at night in warm weather on heavily weeded sections. This happens because warm water holds relatively little dissolved oxygen and dense weed beds use up much of the dissolved oxygen which is available through respiration. During daylight photosynthesis liberates oxygen and helps relieve the situation. The fish community of the bream zone is characterised by a diverse assemblage of Cyprinids, many of which also live in lowland lakes and ponds. Bream, silver bream, tench, common carp, crucian carp, roach, rudd, bleak, gudgeon, perch, pike and eels all occur commonly. Large shoals of bream dominate the fish fauna where the sediments are rich enough to support thriving populations of chironomid midge larvae (bloodworms), orb shells and oligochaete worms (e.g. *Tubifex*). Aquatic plants grow prolifically with marginal lily (*Nymphaea* and *Nuphar*) and common reed (*Phragmites*) beds, yellow flag (*Iris*), marsh marigolds or king cups (*Caltha*), mare's tail (*Hippuris*), amphibious bistort (*Polygonum*) and submerged stands of milfoil (*Myriophyllum*), Canadian pondweed (*Elodea canadensis*) and broad-leaved pondweeds (*Potamogeton*).

It is important to realise that, of course, these theoretical fish zones are artificial and tend, in the real world, to merge into each other. Species of fish usually expected in upstream reaches are sometimes to be found in slower downstream sections.

Water plant communities

The detailed nature of freshwater plant communities is strongly affected by water chemistry as well as current speed. Nigel Holmes, then working for the Nature Conservancy Council, surveyed over 1000 sites on British rivers, carefully identifying the plant species present (over 450 in total) and relating the communities to the river type. An analysis of this large set of data showed that the rivers could be split up into four broad groups on the basis of their plant communities. These groups are as follows:

A) Lowland Fen, clay-bedded, chalk-based rivers and ditches. Alkaline waters support a rich flora including Great water dock (*Rumex hydrolapathum*), Lesser water parsnip (*Berula erecta*), Horned pondweed (*Zannichelia palustris*), Brook water-crowfoot (*Ranunculus calcereous*), Great tussock sedge (*Carex paniculata*) and others.

B) Large Sandstone/Old Red Sandstone and Limestone rivers. The Sandstone rivers are rich in mosses and also have Curly pondweed (*Potamogeton crispus*), Common spike rush (*Eleocharis palustris*), River water-crowfoot (*Ranunculus fluitans*) and Canadian pondweed (*Elodea canadensis*).

C) Large, stable nutrient-rich upland or oceanic rivers. Upland rivers represent a variable group; their floras are dominated by species of mosses, Willow moss (*Fontinalis antipyretica*), liverworts, Common spike-rush (*Eleocharis palustris*), Hemlock water-dropwort (*Oenanthe crocata*), and Canadian pondweed (*Elodea canadensis*).

D) Mountain, highland acid bog and moorland rivers. Acid waters support a sparse flora which is adapted to this water type and includes many species of moss and liverwort together with Hemlock water-dropwort (*Oenanthe crocata*), Bog pondweed (*Potamogeton polygonifolius*), Intermediate Water-starwort (*Callitriche hamulata*), Round-leaved Crowfoot (*Ranunculus omiophyllus*) and Bulbous rush (*Juncus bulbosus*).

The sediments are richest in class A (bream zone) rivers and progressively poorer through to class D waters which often correspond to the fishless and upper trout zones in Huet's classification. Rich sediments on the river bed provide essential nutrients for plant growth. Chalk rivers and streams with their alkaline (high pH) waters have high concentrations of dissolved calcium and bicarbonate ions: the calcium ions aid bacterial decomposition of decaying plants and animals (detritus) and thus the rapid recycling of nutrients; the bicarbonate ions are actively taken up by the aquatic plants to provide carbon dioxide for the photosynthesis of sugars. High pH rivers and lakes, i.e. those based upon chalk and limestone catchments are, therefore, characteristically highly productive with high densities of aquatic plants and invertebrates and fast-growing fish. Good examples include the Wessex rivers Frome, Piddle, Hampshire Avon, Wylye, Ebble and Nadder.

Some of the finest river trout fisheries are based on chalk streams, for example the rivers Test and Itchen in Hampshire or Yorkshire's Driffield Beck. The highest quality stillwater brown trout fishing is found on Scottish limestone lochs (such as the Assynt lochs and lochs Borralie, Lanlish and Caladail in Sutherland), or the machair lochs of the Outer Hebrides (such as lochs Grogarry, Stilligarry and Bornish). In Ireland, land of superlative game fishing, the limestone loughs of the western region (Mask, Corrib and Carra) and the north-west (loughs Arrow and Conn) have the crystal-clear waters typical of limestone areas and are tremendous wild brown trout fisheries. The Aberdeenshire River Don, a superb wild brown trout fishery, is a relatively alkaline river, flowing over outcrops of basic (calcium-rich) rocks; its sister river, the Dee, is much more peaty and acid, and consequently supports a more sea trout and salmon-dominated fish community.

Upland acid (low pH) peaty waters are poor in *available* plant nutrients, both through the insoluble nature of the bedrock and because of rapid leaching (high rainfall) of those nutrients which are present. The build-up of peat deposits in acid bogs is primarily due to a lack of calcium ions and a subsequent very slow rate of bacterial decomposition of the dead plant material. These waters tend, therefore, to have sparse plant and invertebrate communities and to have meagre populations of slow-growing fish. The mildly acid headwaters of major river systems are, however, often vital spawning and nursery areas for Salmonid fish. The fast currents keep the spawning gravels silt-free whilst the large areas of habitat produce many young trout and salmon which spread out through the system to make the best use of the modest food supply.

Aquatic invertebrate communities

The fish zones described above, with their characteristic plant communities also tend to have groups of species of invertebrates which live in their own well-defined ecological niches. H. B. N. Hynes in his classic book, *The Ecology of Running Waters* (1970), gives a full account of this fascinating subject.

Fast-flowing reaches of river have invertebrates specifically adapted for clinging on to rock, moss and algal surfaces. The friction at the surface of the stones retards the current and creates an envelope of slower-flowing water close to the stone surfaces. Flattened mayfly nymphs like those of the March Brown (*Rithrogena haarupi*) and the August Dun (*Ecdyonurus dispar*) can thus live in the fastest-flowing riffles and yet avoid the main force of the current. These species also use tiny claws and their streamlined shape to lessen the chances of being swept away only to fall prey to the trout and salmon parr waiting downstream. During a brief survey you may find:

On the surface of rocks: freshwater limpets (*Ancylus*), mayfly nymphs (*Ecdyonurus* and *Rithrogena*), reed smut larvae (*Simulium* species), *in moss and algae:* mayfly (*Ephemerella, Caenis*) and stonefly (*Leuctra, Perla, Chloroperla, Isoperla*) nymphs, chironomid larvae (*Tanytarsini, Tanypodinae*) and riffle beetles (*Elminthidae*).

Hiding under stones: shrimps (*Gammarus*), leeches (*Erpobdella*), flatworms (*Polycelis*) or living in heavy cases (caddis larvae, like *Silo*) or within silk nets like the caseless caddis (*Hydropsyche* and *Polycentropus*). Shrimps and the various life cycle stages of mayflies, stoneflies and caddisflies provide the staple diet of the Salmonid fish community which lives in our upland streams.

As you progress downstream and the river bed becomes more silted and submerged vascular plants become established, the invertebrate community becomes much more diverse. The aquatic plants tend not to be eaten directly by aquatic invertebrates but provide a rich source of food material growing on their surfaces (*Epiphytes*) and when they die and decay. In some nutrient-poor rivers and ponds the autumnal input of dead leaves from bankside trees can be an important source of plant material to support the subsequent food-chain. When the plants are alive they provide a vast surface area which is colonised by a great variety of bacteria, fungi, algae (diatoms, filamentous green algae) and protozoan animals. This film of epiphytic lifeforms ('Aufwuchs') which coats all stable underwater surfaces is constantly grazed by a wide variety of invertebrates. In slower-flowing river sections you might find:

On the sediment surface: the water louse (*Asellus aquaticus*), many species of midge (chironomid) larvae, snails (*Ancylus*), Alder fly larvae (*Sialis fuliginosa*), many species of caddis larvae (*Sericostoma, Agapetus, Hydroptila*), leeches and flatworms.

In burrows in the silt: the nymphs of the anglers 'Mayfly' (*Ephemera danica, E. vulgata*), chironomid larvae, oligochaete worms, pea mussels (*Pisidium*) and larger bivalves, e.g. *Margaritifera* the pearl mussel and *Unio* (the painter's mussel). In clean alkaline streams native crayfish (*Austropotamobius pallipes*) may still occur but the introduced Signal crayfish is becoming increasingly common and widespread and carries a disease which wipes out stocks of our native species.

Plant surface grazers: snails (*Planorbis, Lymnaea*), some actively swimming genera of mayfly nymph (*Cloeon, Centroptilum and Baetis*).

Open-water dwellers: predators, e.g. damselfly larvae (*Ischnura elegans, Calopteryx virgo*) waterbugs, e.g. pond skaters, water boatmen (*Velia, Gerris, Notonecta*)

In slow-flowing river sections the diversity of invertebrates increases still further.

On and under the silt surface: snails (*Lymnaea peregra, Lymnaea stagnalis*), Swan and Duck mussels (*Anodonta cygnea and Anodonta anatina*), crustaceans (water fleas, shrimps, water lice), worms (Tubificids and many others), flatworms (*Polycelis, Dendrocoelum*), leeches (*Erpobdella, Glossiphonia, Piscicola*), water mites, mayflies (*Cloeon, Caenis*), caddisflies (*Leptocerus, Phryganea, Limnephilus, Mystacides, Molanna*)

On the plants and in open water: dragonfly nymphs (*Aeshna, Cordulegaster, Libellula*), damselflies (*Coenagrion, Phyrrosoma, Calopteryx*) great diving beetle (*Dytiscus*), whirlygig beetles (*Gyrinus species*), water boatmen (*Corixa, Notonecta*), water scorpions (*Nepa*), water measurers (*Ranatra*), Pond-skaters (*Gerris*), sponges, micro-crustaceans, protozoans. . . . and others! Such is the diversity of freshwater life.

Ecological food webs

Some groups of invertebrates live amongst the plants, being either predators or relying on camouflage for protection; some burrow into the silt and live within the river bed, whilst others brave life out in the open-water, gaining protection from hard shells (mussels) or strong biting mouthparts — alderfly larvae (*Sialis*) and beetle larvae (*Dytiscus*).

Green plants (including photosynthetic bacteria, algae and higher plants) provide the primary source of biological production in almost all ecosystems. Part of this primary production is then eaten by herbivorous animals and the rest by detritus-feeders and organisms of decay (fungi and bacteria). The herbivores and detritus feeders (detritivores) are, in turn, eaten by predatory invertebrates (like dragonfly nymphs, alderfly and beetle larvae) or enter the pool of dead and decaying organisms processed by the detritus-feeders.

The first-level predators are eaten by secondary predators like fish (for example trout) or birds (dippers or ducks). The fish are eaten by top predators such as the otter, kingfisher, heron or man. The total of these complex feeding inter-relations is called a *food web* and is nature's way of converting the energy provided by heat and light from the sun via green plants into the animal food chain. Freshwater biologists are only now beginning to understand the complex food webs of aquatic ecosystems.

Life in Estuaries

Whilst this book is principally concerned with the ecology of freshwaters, I cannot resist a brief mention of estuaries, where life is very demanding but where the few species adapted to meet the difficult conditions are often present in large numbers. Estuarine communities must survive organic and industrial pollutants from upstream and marine inputs on the incoming tide. Badly polluted estuaries often have severely depleted dissolved oxygen concentrations and significant pollution by heavy metals in the sediments. Rivers also bring with them a loading of decaying plant and animal matter which is added to in the estuary by rotting seaweeds, etc; this is a principal food source for estuarine animals to process. There is a thriving community of detritus-feeders and algal-browsers including invertebrates such as shrimps, ragworms, lugworms, clams, etc, and fish such as thick and thin-lipped grey mullet.

The sandy or muddy shores are washed by a constantly changing flow of water of differing salinity, ranging from pure seawater at high tide to pure freshwater at the river mouth at low tide. Saline water sinks below the incoming freshwater and between them lies a zone of mixing where rapid changes in temperature, salinity and oxygen concentration occur. The fishes which have adapted to survive in this ever-changing environment and which venture into freshwater have behaviour patterns closely linked to the tidal cycle and fall into the following groups:

1. Nursery ground species, e.g. sea bass, pollack, flounder, eel, mullets.
2. Migratory (anadromous) species breeding in freshwater, e.g. salmon, sea trout, shads, smelt, lampreys; and breeding in the sea (catadromous), e.g. bass, flounder, mullets, eels.
3. Adult residents, e.g. bass, mullets, flounder, common goby, sticklebacks.

In a large estuary, such as Christchurch harbour in Dorset, one can find the following species venturing into the lower reaches of the rivers Stour and Avon.

Occasional large adult and abundant shoals of young school bass (*Dicentrarchus labrax*), feeding on worms, crustaceans and fish. Where tide rips scour sand and gravel banks, shoals of lesser sand eel will be actively chased by bass of all ages. Bass move to deep inshore areas to spawn from February to May; there are probably several separate stocks and tagged adult fish seem to home back to the same sections of shoreline each year. Commercially very valuable, bass stocks are under heavy commercial and sport-fishing pressures. As they are on the northern edge of their distribution in Britain these warm-water loving fish grow slowly, mature relatively late and potentially live a long time. Thirty-year-old specimens have been recorded. Hot summers tend to give rise to abundant and long-lived year classes. The slow-growing stocks are vulnerable to over-fishing and are not very resilient in the face of heavy exploitation.

Large shoals of adult and young mullet of three species (thick-lipped *Chelon labrosus*, thin-lipped *Liza ramanda*, and golden *Liza aurata*), suck and graze mud banks for microscopic algae, bacteria, fungi, detritus and micro-worms and crustaceans. Mullet guts are usually full of mud and it is difficult to know which of the potential food organisms in this 'soup' provide them with their staple nutrition. Mullets move offshore in winter (and may migrate south), returning to shallow shores to feed and spawn in mid-summer.

Flounders (*Platichthys flesus*) of all ages follow the incoming tide to pick invertebrates from newly-flooded sand and mud banks. In certain Scottish estuaries they are in turn preyed upon by coastal-nesting ospreys. Flounders migrate offshore to spawn in April and May, returning inshore to feed and regain condition during the summer and autumn. Flounders will sometimes run many kilometres upriver to spend time feeding in lakes such as Loch Lomond which is 50km from the sea. Flounders in this loch eat molluscs and midge larvae which they browse from silt banks, occasionally in deep (100m) water.

Lakes

Fish Habitat Zones in Lakes

At first sight, stillwaters might appear to be rather featureless, with few well-defined habitat zones for fish. In fact this is far from the truth. Inflowing rivers and streams provide clean gravel spawning habitats for fish such as trout, charr and grayling which may spend most of their adult lives in the lake but which breed and live as juveniles in the streams. Outflowing rivers allow access for migratory species such as eels which spend their adult lives in freshwater, and sea trout or salmon which reach adulthood in the sea.

Around the marshy edges of many lakes, pike migrate into the shallows to spawn in the early spring; the marshes then act as nursery grounds for the fry. The large reedbeds which fringe some shallow bays are important nursery grounds for the fry of many species and for adult fish like rudd and perch. On shallow shores, in the *littoral* zone, light penetrates to the lake bed to promote the growth of weedbeds which in turn provide important spawning and feeding areas in lowland lakes for fish such as roach, tench, perch and crucian carp. Littoral weedbeds are rich in invertebrates which are an important food source for most freshwater fish. There is often intense competition for food in lakes, both between fish of the same and different species, leading to stunting of growth. The invertebrate-feeding fish of the littoral weedbeds are stalked by pike which ambush their prey from cover, and large solitary perch which actively chase and catch small fish in more open water.

In salmonid lakes, trout like gillaroos (a snail-eating, red-spotted sub-species of brown trout) are thought to be able to outcompete charr for invertebrate food in the littoral zone, forcing the charr to live out in the open water or *pelagic* zone of lakes. Adult salmon and sea trout rest in littoral zones on their upstream spawning migrations, occupying well-defined 'lies' ('salmon stones') in successive seasons. Loch and Lough fly-fishers cover these traditional lies and similar well-known sea trout 'drifts' on stillwater wild game fisheries in western Ireland, mainland Scotland and the Hebrides.

Just as in streams, where fish lie in slack current 'seams' to feed on a concentration of drifting invertebrate food, in the surface waters of lakes 'wind lanes' concentrate emerging insects like midges, mayflies and caddisflies for trout to rise to. Fly-fishermen, angling from a drifting boat, can exploit these subtle feeding zones, knowing that their artificial flies are much more likely to be taken when cast into wind lanes than on the relatively 'dead' water either side.

In open water there are no weed beds to support invertebrates and the resident fish community must adapt to feed upon planktonic crustaceans such as *Daphnia* and midge (chironomid) pupae which drift up from the sediments of the deep lake bed prior to emergence at the water surface. In upland lakes, the fish community of the open-water includes coregonids (whitefish), charr, perch, and sonaghen (an open water plankton-feeding sub-species of brown trout); this contrasts with numerous small fry of cyprinid species such as roach, bream and carp in richer lowland waters.

The rich silt and mud which lies on the bed of deep bays and lake basins harbours burrowing forms of invertebrates like chironomid larvae, oligochaete worms and small mussels. These comprise the food resource of the *profundal* zone of lakes and are exploited by fish which can dig down into the sediments for their food. Carp and common bream are specialists in this form of feeding; they suck up mouthfuls of sediment and then blow it back out through their gills, filtering out the invertebrates on their gill rakers. Both species are very efficient at this form of feeding and reduce the abundance of sediment-dwelling invertebrates through their feeding activity.

In shallow lakes dense shoals of carp and/or bream will stir up the lake bed so thoroughly that they make the water turbid, killing submerged weed beds and favouring the production of thick planktonic blooms of algae which further colour the water. Silver bream, tench and eels also probe the surface of sediments for food, digging much more shallowly than common bream or carp.

Lakes, then, are far from featureless habitats and, like rivers, have well-defined zones where particular fish species can eke out a living amongst the competition for food and space and threats from predators which surround animals in the wild.

The lifetime of lakes

As with rivers, the processes of ageing and ecological succession also occur in lakes and ponds so that they too gradually fill in with decomposing plant material which forms a deep layer on the lake bed. This can finally develop into a floating peat bog (a quaking bog, which you can bounce up and down on, as David Bellamy is fond of demonstrating!) as it reaches the surface of the former lake.

When the original lake is grounded on nutrient-poor, hard acidic bedrock these processes can take hundreds of thousands of years. These long-lived 'ancient lakes' have time to develop a varied and locally adapted fauna and flora, sometimes with their own unique animal species. Lake Baikal in Russia has its own endemic species of seal, *Phoca baikalensis*.

Where a lake is fed by nutrient-rich inflowing water and is shallow and productive the basin may remain water-filled for only a few hundreds or thousands of years, progressing rapidly through the natural ecological succession towards the final woodland community.

The main phases of typical freshwater wetland successions are: open water → submerged plants → emergent reed beds → build-up of decaying plant material (detritus, ie. peat) → reed swamp (which slowly lowers the lake level) → drying out of lake.

After the reed swamp has developed the subsequent succession depends upon the environmental conditions at a given site. *Sphagnum* moss *Blanket bogs* are formed under wet acid conditions; heather and cotton grass moorland develops under less wet acid conditions and birch/pine/oakwoods are based on drier acid soils. Where conditions are more alkaline, *Fens* develop in wet areas, succeeding to alder/willow/hazel scrub and then ultimately to ash/beech woods on drier soils. The final woodland is known to ecologists as the *climax community* which, if undisturbed by man, exists in a relatively stable state for long periods of time.

Managing ecological successions

Active management can be used to halt a given succession at a stage which is deemed to be most desirable, for example for the conservation of the reed-bed bird community.

Freshwater Fish of the British Isles

This habitat can support rarities like bitterns, marsh harriers and bearded tits as well as the commoner reed warblers, reed buntings, coots and moorhens. The alarming decline in Britain of large (more than 5 acres) *Phragmites* reed beds has encouraged conservationists throughout the country to manage this habitat in a sustainable way by regular cutting/burning and scrub-clearing. This prevents the natural build-up of dead reed material in the base of the reedbed which would otherwise make the system prone to invasion by willow and alder seedlings.

Lake types and their characteristic fish communities			
Shape of basin	*Lake bed*	*Physical conditions*	*Dominant fish community*
Shallow pools in blanket peat bog	Peat-bedded *Sphagnum* moss with other sparse weed growth	Water stained with peat, can be warm, low nutrients	**No-Fish** perhaps some sticklebacks
Deep, steep-sided, in mountainous region	Rock/stone, shingle shore. Few plants	Cold, clear or peaty water. High oxygen, low nutrients	**Salmonid** Trout, Charr often with sticklebacks
Deep, shelving sides with some shallow bays	Rock/stone, sand with some silt. Localised weed beds	Cool water, High oxygen, moderate nutrients	**Salmonid** Trout, Charr Whitefish, Pike, Perch
Medium depth in shallow valley. Well developed bays and shallows	Sand with silt and mud. Many submerged plants/ reed beds	Warm surface waters, cool depths. Medium nutrient levels. Oxygen level varies with seasons	**Mixed** Trout, Perch, Pike, Roach, Minnow, Eel
Shallow depth in lowland valley	Silt/mud. Dense weed growth with lilies and reed beds	Warm water down to lake bed. Low levels of oxygen at times. High nutrients – rich plankton	**Cyprinid** Bream, Carp, Tench, Roach, Rudd, Pike, Catfish, Eel, etc
Small shallow farm pond used for watering livestock	Mud with Lilies and pondweeds	Warm/Hot water with low or very low oxygen and very high nutrient levels. Thick algal blooms	**Cyprinid** Carp, Crucian Carp, possibly Tench

Classifying lakes by their fish communities

As with rivers it is possible to classify lakes by the typical fish communities which they are able to support. The table opposite summarises the major lake types and their key physical and biological features. As with Huet's river zones, this is a classification of convenience and the lake types described below are artificial categories within a continuous range of habitat types.

Over long periods of time, lakes gradually build up nutrients and can change progressively from one of the above categories into the next. The succession is far more rapid in rich lowland catchments than in nutrient-deficient glacial upland lakes. Each lake type has its own characteristic fauna and flora.

Typical members of the plant and animal bog pool community

Aquatic plant community: is dominated by *Sphagnum* mosses with bladder-wort (*Utricularia minor*) and white water lilies (*Nymphaea alba*).

Invertebrate fauna: is dominated by dragonflies (*Sympetrum danae, Aeshna juncea, Aeshna caerulea, Pyrhosoma nymphula, Lestes sponsa,* and *Libellula quadrimaculata*), water boatmen (*Sigara* and *Corixa* species) and water beetles (*Hydroporus, Agabus* and *Gyrinus* species). The alderfly larva (*Sialis lutaria*) often occurs together with caddis genera such as *Phryganea* and *Limnephilus*. Chironomid (non-biting) midge larvae are often fairly abundant, as are the larvae of the biting midges (Ceratopogonids). Biting midges can make a misery of fishing and camping trips in the uplands. Molluscs are rare except in the richer pools which may also contain sticklebacks and a few small brown trout.

On the Isle of North Uist in the Outer Hebrides, where Red and Black-throated Divers nest next to the peat bog lochans, Niall Campbell of the N.C.C. discovered that the three-spined sticklebacks living in these calcium-poor bog pools sometimes lack spines or bony plates on the sides of the body (which normally occur in the species). My own research suggests that this may be an adaptation to life in calcium-poor habitats, with the sticklebacks gradually adapting over the generations to the very soft water by 'losing' non-essential parts of their skeletons. Although these spine-deficient fish are eaten by both trout and several species of aquatic birds, the populations still survive, despite their lack of protective spines. Fully-spined fish are found in the calcium-rich machair lochs close to the coast and ten-spined sticklebacks occur in both loch types.

The steep sided oligotrophic (low nutrient) lakes of glacial or geological fault origin form the majority of natural British lakes, including those of the English Lake District, north Wales and the Scottish Highlands and Islands. The waters are cool and usually remain well oxygenated down to the lake bed. In the cold, dark depths of a few of these waters (such as Ennerdale and loughs Neagh, Erne, Derg and Ree) lives the glacial relic crustacean *Mysis relicta*, a rare shrimp which has been transplanted to various European and Canadian lakes in an effort to boost food availability for trout.

Plankton productivity is limited by the low availability of phosphate ions (which remain bound up in the oxidised sediments) and the water is, therefore, usually clear. Since the plankton productivity is low and there are few weed beds, the production of invertebrates is modest and the food supply for fish restricted. Accordingly, upland lakes tend to produce small, slow-growing trout and charr. In some waters especially in the Scottish Highlands (for example Loch Rannoch) a small proportion of genetically distinct trout (so-called 'ferox') switch their diet from invertebrates to fish (small charr or whitefish) at an age of around six years. This high-protein food source allows them to grow rapidly and reach large sizes. Ferox anglers troll spinners, spoons and plugs slowly in deep waters often spending many days in search of a single heavyweight specimen. The total fish biomass supported by oligotrophic lakes (i.e. the 'standing stock') is likely to be from 5–50 kilogrammes per hectare of lake surface area.

In a few locations (Scotland, English Lake District) there are interesting populations of whitefish (*Coregonus* species) which are relics of the last ice age and have been left land-locked in these large, deep, cold waters where they feed mostly on zooplankton. Despite the fact that the zooplankton tends to be thin on the ground these lakes do support a wide diversity of species of both copepods and water fleas. You may also find:

Aquatic plants: Milfoil (*Myriophyllum alterniflorum*) or the pondweeds (*Potamogeton gramineus*, *perfoliatus* and *natans*). In sheltered bays reed (*Phragmites*) beds are interspersed with marestail (*Equisetum*), bulrush (*Schoenoplectus*) and several species of sedges and rushes. The sandy shoreline is often vegetated by Quillwort (*Isoetes lacustris*) and shore-weed (*Littorella uniflora*) with some *Ranunculus flammula*.

Invertebrates of deep water and mud-bottom burrowers. In the depths of the lake the mud is inhabited by numerous species of midge (chironomid) larvae, small worms (oligochaetes) and pea mussels (*Sphaerium cornutum* and *Pisidium* species). The midges become available to the salmonids, whitefishes and perch when the pupae drift slowly up through the water, prior to emergence at the water surface. These midge hatches are often at their height at dawn and dusk.

In the weedy shallows and on sandy shores are found: snails tolerant of low calcium conditions, e.g. *Planorbis contortus*, *Physa fontinalis* and *Lymnaea pereger*, shrimps (*Gammarus pulex*), Mayfly nymphs (*Caenis horaria*, *Cloeon simile*, *Centroptilum luteolum*, *Leptophlebia vespertina* and *Ephemerella ignita*). Stoneflies are commonly found in these waters, including the genera *Chloroperla*, *Leuctra* and *Nemoura*. Dragonflies (*Enallagma cyathigerum*, *Phyrrosoma nymphula* and *Libellula quadri-maculata*) occur regularly. Water boatmen (*Corixa* and *Sigara* species) are sometimes abundant as are whirlygig beetles.

Caddisfly larvae include net-spinning species such as *Cyrnus flavidus* and *Polycentropus flavomaculatus*, together with many cased species, e.g. *Limnephilus* (Cinnamon sedge) species and members of the family Leptoceridae (Silverhorn sedges). The alderfly larva (*Sialis*) is also common. Any stones may be encrusted with the sponge *Ephydatia fluviatilis* and have leeches (*Erpobdella*, *Helobdella*, *Piscicola*) and flatworms (*Polycelis*, *Crenobia*) crawling underneath them.

Medium nutrient-status ('mesotrophic') lakes are intermediate between the nutrient-poor ('oligotrophic') upland waters and the nutrient-rich ('eutrophic') lowland waters. In the intermediate lakes the invertebrates which live on the lake bed have to withstand occasional de-oxygenation of the sediments. They cope with this by having the red oxygen-carrying pigment haemoglobin in their tissues. This on-board oxygen store is slowly consumed until water currents bring dissolved oxygen down to the lake bed from the water surface when the autumn storms mix up the water column. This is an important time for nutrient-cycling; phosphorus ions are released from de-oxygenated sediments and are circulated throughout the lake at turnover. This flush of nutrient gives a boost to late summer algal productivity.

Medium nutrient lakes have more prolific weedbeds and invertebrate populations than oligotrophic waters and they can harbour a wealth of amphibians and reptiles. The total fish biomass supported by mesotrophic lakes is likely to be in the range 100–250 kg per hectare of water area.

Aquatic plants include: stoneworts (*Chara, Nitella*), Canadian pondweed (*Elodea canadensis*) and the pondweeds (*Potamogeton praelongus, obtusifolius* and *alpinus*). In sheltered bays, reed beds are often prolific, merging into Fens at the lake edges. *Littorella* beds are often abundant in shallow water.

Invertebrates. The water louse (*Asellus aquaticus*) the duck mussel (*Anodonta anatina*), freshwater shrimps (*Gammarus*), and several snail species can be abundant. The weed-dwelling mayfly *Cloeon dipterum* (the pond olive) occurs here and the large *Ephemera danica* (the 'Mayfly') lives in silted areas. Caddisflies abound with weed-dwelling families (*Phryganidae* [Great red sedge], *Limnephilidae, Leptoceridae* and *Hydroptilidae*) all being abundant. The larval Chironomid populations are also very abundant with many silt-bed and weed-dwelling species occuring in profusion. The midge and caddis populations provide a multitude of hatching flies ('buzzers' and 'sedges') which make for great feeding conditions for trout and great fishing for the imitative fly-fisher.

Lake stratification

In summer these lakes heat up at the surface and a distinct layer of (lower density) warm water floating on the underlying cold water develops. If these conditions persist, the temperature and water density difference between the two water layers increases until they are effectively cut off from each other by a zone of rapid temperature (and density) difference. This process is called *stratification*, the warm surface water layer is termed the *epilimnion*, the cold lower layer the *hypolimnion* and the boundary between them the *thermocline*. The oxygen concentration in the hypolimnion can fall after a prolonged period of thermal stratification, only to be restored when the lake is mixed again at the autumn turnover. This effect is most pronounced in eutrophic waters where the oxygen demand, from decaying organic matter in the sediments, is relatively high. In the depths of winter the coldest water in a lake is at the surface where freezing may occur; water of around 4° Celsius will sit in the deeper basins because at this temperature water reaches its maximum density and sinks to the bottom. This is very important for the survival of fish under severe winter weather conditions.

Lowland nutrient-rich lakes are the domain of the Cyprinid fishes which can tolerate higher water temperatures and lower oxygen concentrations than the Salmonids. In these eutrophic waters, the total fish biomass might range from 300–500 kg per hectare. Stratification can be prolonged during periods of hot weather and when the dissolved oxygen levels in the hypolimnion are depleted the fish are forced to live in the warm layer above the thermocline until the water cools and the lake mixes again in the autumn, when the thermocline breaks down. Trout find it difficult to cope with these conditions although rainbow trout are more warm-water tolerant than browns.

Aquatic plants. The plankton is rich, with occasional algal blooms and dense swarms of water fleas (e.g. *Daphnia hyalina*). Daphnia are eaten by all young Cyprinids and adult roach, rudd, bream and perch. The dense growths of phytoplankton mean that eutrophic lakes often have a brown or green tinge and strong light penetration can be restricted to the upper three to four metres of water. Submerged weedbeds can therefore be limited by a lack of light to the zone around the lake edges. In this shallow littoral zone dense weedbeds are formed, often dominated by milfoil (*Myriophyllum*) in the summer and hornwort (*Ceratophyllum*) in the autumn together with the pondweeds,

Potamogeton pectinatus, lucens, filiformis and *berchtoldii*. Horned pondweed, *Zannichellia palustris*, Canadian pondweed (*Elodea canadensis*) and starwort *Callitriche stagnalis*.

In sheltered bays duckweed (*Lemna trisulca*) can choke the water surface; the little Fringed water lily *Nymphoides peltata* can also grow in dense patches. The battle for available light and nutrients carries on up the shoreline with a lush growth of emergent species including Common reed (*Phragmites communis*), Greater reedmace (*Typha latifolia*), Lesser reedmace (*Typha angustifolia*), Yellow flag (*Iris pseudacorus*), Bulrush (*Schoeneplectus lacustris*), Horsetail (*Hippuris vulgaris*), Bur-reed (*Sparganium erectum*), Reed grass (*Glyceria maxima*), and rushes (*Butomus umbellatus, Carex pseudocyperus, acutiformis* and *riparia*).

Invertebrates. The thick rich mud on the lake bed teems with midge larvae and oligochaete worms, and there are often tens of thousands of these animals living under every square metre of lake bed. Cyprinids such as carp and bream specialise in digging through these sediments to filter out the midge larvae, worms and pea mussels (*Sphaerium, Pisidium*). Tench pick water lice (*Asellus*) and alderfly larvae from the plants or sift the surface sediments for pea mussels and midge larvae. The Zebra mussel (*Dreissena polymorpha*) forms thick beds attached to any solid underwater surface. Mayflies are usually only represented by *Caenis horaria* nymphs which crawl over the silt surface. A diverse invertebrate community lives in the weedbeds including virtually all of the species of snail and bivalved molluscs (mussels), many species of water 'fleas' (chydorids, daphnids, etc) and larger crustaceans (shrimps, water lice), mayfly nymphs (*Ephemera danica* and the Olives, *Cloeon dipterum* and *simile* and tiny *Caenis* species, *horaria* and *moesta*), caddisflies (*Leptocerids, Limnephilids*), *Oecetis* (Longhorn sedges), *Phryganidae* and *Polycentropids* (Yellow-spotted sedge), damselflies, dragonflies, water beetles, water boatmen, water mites, leeches and flatworms. A diverse community indeed.

Farm ponds

In our final category of stillwater habitats, the farm pond, the water tends to be very eutrophic, often receiving regular dollops of manure from the watering livestock. This gives rise to an explosion of algal growth, pea-green water and extremely organically-rich bottom mud. This mud can be thick with the few species of chironomid midge larvae, oligochaete worms and insect (hover-fly, *Eristalis*) larvae which can withstand the low oxygen levels experienced on warm summer nights. At this time the algae are not producing oxygen by photosynthesis but are using it up by respiration and the high water temperatures make for low levels of dissolved oxygen anyway. Only the toughest fish can tolerate these conditions, probably by periodically respiring anaerobically (i.e. without oxygen). The Crucian carp is thought to be able to do this. Common carp and tench are able to withstand very low oxygen tensions, initially by gulping surface water and then probably by lying dormant in the mud and waiting for conditions to improve. The high productivity of these ponds means that either a few large carp or hordes of stunted common and crucian carp thrive on the rich invertebrate fauna which is characterised by large numbers of individuals of a few adaptable species. Organically polluted rivers also have invertebrate communities characterised by large numbers of individuals of a relatively few hardy species. Rich farm ponds can support very high population densities of fish with perhaps 600–1200 kg of fish per hectare (2.5 acres) surface area of water. At this upper limit of fish stock density, each square metre of lake bed is supporting, on average, 120 g (4 ounces) of fish throughout the year.

Amongst this profusion of river and lake systems, our freshwater fish have evolved to take their place in the functioning of their particular habitats. Since the retreat of the last ice sheets 10–15,000 years ago, great changes have occurred in our freshwater habitats — the fish have had to adapt or perish. The various species changed to live efficiently within the constraints imposed by the environment. As species are forced to compete with each other so they tend to avoid the head-to-head clash and to become more specialised. This process of *adaptive radiation* is seen most clearly in ancient lake systems such as the Rift Valley lakes of east Africa where hundreds of species of cichlids survive through elaborate feeding and breeding specialisations. The British freshwater fish fauna is less specialised and diverse but, nevertheless, interesting.

The following chapters attempt to give a concise account of the natural history of our most popular freshwater fish species, splitting them into two main groupings, the 'cold water' and 'warm water' communities. Salmonids predominate in cool habitats and are dealt with first, whilst Cyprinids thrive in warm waters, often only breeding successfully in unusually warm summers (for example, carp, tench, chub, bream and catfish). For the sake of convenience, I have grouped the 'cool' water dace with the 'warm' water cyprinids and the shads with the salmonids.

The table on page 52 briefly summarises the breeding seasons of the 'warm water' and 'cold water' species groups which we have in Britain; it is based on figure 15 from Margaret Varley's book *British Freshwater Fishes*, 1967, and on information from Peter Maitland's *Key to British Freshwater Fishes*, published by the Freshwater Biological Association in 1972.

Breeding seasons (x) of major fish species

Sep   Oct   Nov   Dec   Jan   Feb Mar Apr   May   Jun   Jul   Aug

Daylength: decreasing   SHORT   increasing   LONG   decreasing

Temperature;   falling   COLD   rising   HOT

COLD WATER SPECIES

Rainbow Trout / Brook 'Trout'
xxxxxxxxxxxxxxxxxxxxxxxxxxxxxx

Whitefish
xxxxxxxx

Salmon   Pike/Smelt
xxxxxxxxxxxxx   xxxxxxx

Brown Trout   Grayling/ Sea Lamprey
xxxxxxxxxxxx   xxxxxxxxxxxx

Charr   Bullhead/Perch/Eel
xxxxxx xxxxxxx   xxxxxxxxxxxxx

Burbot
xxxxxxxxxxxxxxxxxx

COOL WATER SPECIES

Dace
xxxxxxx

Stone/Spined loach/
River & Brook Lampreys
xxxxxxxxxxxxx

Allis & Twaite Shads
xxxxxx

WARM WATER SPECIES

Zander/ Ruffe/ Chub/
Gudgeon/Barbel/ Bleak
xxxxxxxxxx

Minnow/ Bream/ Roach/
Rudd/ Silver Bream
xxxxxxxxx

Crucian Carp/
Carp/Tench/Wels Catfish
xxxxxxx

PART 3

The Cold-Water Fish Community: Mountain Rivers and Glacial Lakes

British Salmonid Fishes and their Relatives

The following section relates largely to species with an adipose fin, this being an easy way to decide which families to include in the collective term 'salmonid'. The adipose is a small fleshy fin with no fin rays, positioned on the back just in front of the tail and well back from the dorsal fin. By any standards the salmonids are a beautiful, interesting and economically important group of fishes. In this section I will describe very briefly the species found in Britain and mention some other related fishes from continental Europe and North America.

Salmonids are slimly-built active predatory fish of inland freshwater and marine habitats across the Northern hemisphere. Much of the following information on North American species was gleaned from the excellent *Freshwater Fishes of Canada*, written by W. Scott and E. Crossman (Fisheries Research Board of Canada, Bulletin 184, 1973).

The genus *Salmo* includes the Atlantic salmon, *Salmo salar*, and the brown/sea trout, *Salmo trutta*. Both species have 'anadromous' populations where individuals spawn in freshwater and migrate to sea as smolts for a period of rich marine feeding (eating euphausid and decapod crustaceans, sand-eels, herring, smelt, mackerel, capelin), returning to their natal stream as mature adults after 0.5–8 years. The amazing ability to navigate from the open ocean faithfully back to the precise stretch of upland stream where they hatched involves the use of a memory for both visual landmarks and a phenomenally sensitive sense of smell. The water chemistry of each stream must be slightly different and salmonid parr become imprinted with the olfactory fingerprint of their home waters before transforming into smolts and migrating downstream to the sea. In some species wandering individuals which run up non-natal rivers are quite common. This behaviour must have been vital in the past to allow species to colonise new habitats, and recently for the recolonisation of previously polluted rivers.

Both *Salmo* species can mend after spawning, going through a 'kelt' stage, before regaining condition to spawn again the next season. Some fish biologists regard the Atlantic salmon as a large species of trout because of this basic difference in biology from the 'true' Pacific salmon of the genus *Oncorhynchus* (chinook, coho, sockeye, pink and chum), all of which die soon after spawning. Certainly the biological differences between Atlantic salmon and sea trout are few and far between (the two species occasionally hybridise in nature), perhaps the most notable being the long trans-oceanic sea migrations to feeding grounds undertaken by salmon which compare with the more usual (presumed) short journeys to inshore feeding areas by sea trout.

Pacific Salmon

Pacific salmon of the genus *Oncorhynchus* die after their first spawning season. The five Pacific salmon; the Chinook (*O. tshawytscha*), Sockeye (*O. nerka*), Coho (*O. kisutch*), Chum (*O. keta*) and Pink (*O. gorbuscha*), plus two further species, the biwa and masou which are found only in Russia or Japan, are of enormous economic and sporting importance. From the sport fishing viewpoint the Chinook salmon (alias spring, king or tyee) is the most exciting, providing angling of a quality which draws anglers from all over the world to legendary fishing centres such as Campbell River on Vancouver Island. Early spring-running Chinook of 50–70 lb are still taken here on deep-trolled or live-baited (mooched) herring whilst the rod-caught record stands at 92 lb from the Skeena River, British Columbia in 1959. I recommend Silvio Calabi's *Trout and Salmon of the World* (Wellfleet Press, 1990) for a stunning photographic review of the *Oncorhynchus* and other salmon and trout genera alive today.

Rainbow Trout

The freshwater resident rainbow trout and its migratory form, the steelhead, was formerly named *Salmo gairdneri* but has recently been moved over (with the Cut-throat trout) to join its fellow North American salmonids as an *Oncorhynchus* species (*O. mykiss*). The rainbow trout is a very widely-stocked sport fish which tolerates warmer, less clean water than the brown trout and also grows more quickly than this species, making it a favourite with both anglers and fish farmers. In Britain specimens of 20 lb or more are grown-on in stock ponds before being released into put-and-take fisheries (like Avington in Hampshire). The current rod-caught record changes regularly between put-and-take waters which vie to stock the largest grown on hatchery fish (often an old brood stock fish). In 1989 the Pennine fishery in Lancashire 'produced' a 24 lb 2 oz (10.96 kg) fish for angler John Moore*. In its home waters the rainbow trout can attain greater weights, with a 52-pounder reported from Jewel Lake (British Columbia). Unlike the other *Oncorhynchus* species, the rainbow can survive for more than one breeding season (as can the *Salmo* species). In California rainbows are thought to be able to spawn twice a year.

Cut-throat Trout

A further recent addition to the genus *Oncorhynchus* is the Cut-throat trout, (*O. clarki*), so called because of the blood-red streak below the lower jaw which is used in threat displays. Today, the Yellowstone Park region still has prolific Cut-throat populations; the species is still common in Utah, Montana and Wyoming but has declined markedly in many former strongholds of the northern Pacific continental seaboard. The Yellowstone River fishery is a good example of the success of a catch-and-release fly fishery. The stock of fish remains abundant and the average size is high, indicating that survival is good despite the high angling pressure. This system may well be the way ahead for hard pressed British wild brown trout fisheries.

Sea-run Cut-throats occur commonly in Oregon, Washington and British Columbia, with 2 lb fish being usual and large specimens weighing 4–5 lb. An exceptional fish of 17 lb is the largest on record. The migratory instinct seems to be less strong in Cut-throats than in either Brown or Rainbow trout. Whilst at sea Cut-throats are thought to feed mainly in and around the estuaries of their home rivers without venturing far out to sea. In freshwater habitats Cut-throats can reach prodigious weights; John Skimmerhorn caught a 41-pounder from Pyramid Lake, Utah in 1925, but you would be rather lucky to catch one so large today. The Lahontan basin region

---

*D. Lloyd caught a 25 lb 9 oz stocked rainbow at Maesglyn fishery, Swansea in May 1993.

of northern California still has populations of the very large local race of Cut-throats, and Pyramid Lake still produces 10-pounders after recent efforts to revitalise the damaged natural stocks.

Atlantic Salmon

Atlantic Salmon are regarded as the most prestigious fish to catch in British freshwaters; the commercial value to the rural economies of Scotland, Wales and the Republic of Ireland is enormous. *Salmo salar* which return to their native rivers to spawn after a single sea-winter are termed 'grilse' whilst multi sea-winter fish are termed 'salmon'. On many river systems 'salmon' run upstream in the early spring, the so-called 'springers' which often weigh 20 lb or more, whilst the main grilse-run occurs through the summer months, being composed usually of fish in the 4–8 lb size class. The sport fishing commercial value of salmon ensures that considerable efforts are made to preserve and even to attempt to enhance any rivers which support an appreciable run of fish. The rehabilitation of rivers which have lost their salmon runs is also attempted in many countries.

Whilst salmon are at sea they are subject to substantial commercial fishing pressures. Salmon in the north Atlantic produce an annual commercial marine catch of around 8000 tonnes, with the catch fluctuating over the past 30 years between a range of 6000-12,000 tonnes. The fish are caught mainly off the coasts of Canada, Norway, Republic of Ireland, Scotland, Greenland and the Faroes, with lesser numbers from England and Wales, the former Soviet Union, Iceland, Sweden, Northern Ireland, France, Spain and the U.S.A. In the early 1960s a rapidly-growing salmon cage-farming industry sprang up in suitable sheltered west-coast Norwegian fjords, then along west-coast Scottish and Irish sea lochs and now along the Canadian eastern sea-board.

Over the decade 1971–1981 the annual production of farmed salmon rose from virtually zero to approaching 10,000 tonnes. In 1981 the commercial catch of wild salmon was almost equalled by the production of farmed fish (which are available all year round). By 1986 the world farmed salmon production had risen to nearly 60,000 tonnes! (see Derek Mills' excellent *Ecology and Management of Atlantic Salmon*, Chapman and Hall, 1989, for further details.) One of the ironies of this new industry is that whilst farmed salmon may reduce the commercial pressures on wild stocks, the pelleted feed for the caged farm fish is produced from sand eels (amongst other species) and the sand eel fishery may be leading to declines in sea trout due to reduced food availability at sea! The effects of the industry on wild salmon populations are considered further in the later section on *Salmo salar*.

Whilst the majority of salmon populations produce smolts which descend to the sea, not all *Salmo salar* populations are anadromous. In North America 'ouananiche' (landlocked salmon) occur, reaching average adult weights of 2–4 lb. These fish can grow much larger with records of specimens of 35 lb (Lake Sebago, Maine) and 44.7 lb from Lake Ontario. The Lake Ontario population was exterminated by crass water management involving damming of the inflowing spawning streams!

Hugh and Mary Horrex (Landlocked Salmon Europe Ltd) have imported landlocked Atlantic salmon from Maine into the British Isles and have produced sterile stock fish which have been released into a small number of stillwater salmon fisheries. This project has been carefully researched, with all known disease transmission problems covered. The beauty of these fish is that they naturally feed in freshwater and so will maintain condition, or even grow in suitable cool-watered but productive lakes. The first fishery to advertise fly-fishing for these fish was 'Berwick loch Salmon' at Halliford Mere, Middlesex in 1991, and time will tell whether the enterprise is a commercial success.

Throughout their native ranges, salmon require access to clean, clear-watered streams and sufficient escapement (survival) of mature adults to ensure stock replenishment on the spawning grounds. Threats from hydro-electric schemes, water abstraction, organic pollution (paper mills, agricultural inputs, sewage effluent), acidification, afforestation, pesticide residues, over-fishing and 'genetic pollution' from inter-breeding with escaped cage-farmed fish all combine to threaten the future of these marvellous fish. Fortunately, organisations including the North Atlantic Salmon Conservation Organisation, National Rivers Authority, Atlantic Salmon Trust, Atlantic Salmon Conservation Trust, Salmon and Trout Association, and others are battling to conserve the precious resource which this species represents.

The Charrs

Fish of the genus *Salvelinus* are noteworthy for their spectacular spawning colourations; the males have bright red bellies with green or blue/grey backs, vermiculated yellow striped flanks and vivid red, white and black spots. The red pectoral, ventral and anal fins have pure white leading edges completing the striking breeding livery. Our native Arctic charr, *Salvelinus alpinus*, has only landlocked populations in Britain but is anadromous throughout Scandinavia, Iceland, Greenland and on many Arctic islands. The Arctic charr has the most northerly (circum-polar) geographical distribution of any species of freshwater fish, growing slowly and living for 20 years or more (perhaps 40 years) in these icy waters. The average weight of sea-run char is 2–10 lb but specimens of up to 27 lb have been reported from the Tree River in Canada's North-West Territories.

The brook 'trout', *Salvelinus fontinalis*, actually a charr, which is endemic and widespread in North America is sometimes stocked in the U.K. as a sport fish, especially in poor, acid waters where it grows well. It seems to be able to produce young under difficult spawning conditions where brown trout fail and has become established after initial stocking in at least eight British locations. Alan Pearson holds the present (stocked) rod-caught record for a 5 lb 13 oz (2.65kg) fish from Avington fishery in Hampshire. In nature it has both anadromous and landlocked populations. Brook trout are a short-lived species (up to eight years maximum) with a maximum recorded (rod-caught) size of 14.5 lb from the Nipigon River, Ontario in 1915.

The lake 'trout', *S.namaycush*, can be artificially crossed with (male) brook trout to produce the fertile hybrid 'splake' which have been stocked, for example in the Great Lakes, to be recaptured five or six years later at weights up to 16 lb. Lake trout grow quickly on a diet of fish and are long-lived, consequently reaching prodigious sizes, regularly in excess of 50 lb (the angling record is 63 lb 2 oz.) and on at least one occasion over 100 pounds! This fish, weighing 102 lb, was 20–25 years old and was gill-netted on Lake Athabasca, Saskatchewan in August 1961. The lake trout is the least salt-water tolerant of all the charrs but is occasionally reported from coastal waters.

The Dolly Varden charr *S.malma*, is another finely-coloured anadromous/landlocked charr and is a popular sporting species amongst the diverse North American fish fauna. This species too can reach large sizes (32 lb from Lake Pend Oreille, Idaho in 1949) and ages of up to 20 years. In Alaska a bounty (2.5 cents each) was paid for Dolly Varden charr as they were thought to be serious predators of juvenile salmon; nowadays it is recognised that they are probably no worse than many of the other resident fish species. As other species decline, the Dolly Varden is gaining in popularity with game anglers.

Taimen

The lake trout has a north Asian/ Siberian counterpart, the Taimen (*Hucho taimen*) which occurs in large rivers such as the Ob and Lena and various deep cool lakes. This is the world's largest living salmonid species, feeding on an adult diet of fish (especially nase), living for up to 15 years and reaching weights of 100 lb or more. A strange-looking salmonid, this species is long and thin, darkly-coloured with reddish anal and caudal fins and a mouth full of large teeth. Taimen are caught commercially on a local scale and are an exciting sport fish, filling the niche of top predator in rivers such as the Amur. The classic habitat is fast flowing sections of mountain rivers, adults migrate upstream in early spring to spawn in gravel-bedded streams. They must make an impressive sight in their copper-red spawning livery.

In the middle and upper reaches of the River Danube basin there lives a Taimen-like salmonid fish called the Huchen (*Hucho hucho*). It is declining rapidly in numbers in recent years but is still of considerable interest to sport fishermen. Living for around 15 years and reaching weights in excess of 100 lb this fish-eating 'trout' is usually caught at weights of 5–20 lb on spinners and spoons. Conservation measures are now being implemented to safeguard the future of this species. The latest information from a local fisheries biologist, Juraj Holcik is that hutchen have disappeared from almost 40 per cent and are rare in a further 28 per cent of their former range in the Danube system.

Grayling

Grayling are usually grouped with the salmonids but are given a family of their own by ichthyologists, namely the *Thymallidae*. The name refers to the smell of the flesh which is said to resemble the herb thyme. In Britain we have an odd attitude to our native grayling *Thymallus thymallus* in that we persecute it on chalk streams as a potential competitor with trout but revere it elsewhere, especially in northern England, as a beautiful and prized sport fish. Grayling in breeding colouration are handsome fish indeed; in the male the very large dorsal and pelvic fins develop a mottled bright blue and iridescent red sheen.

In Northern Mongolia, Western Siberia and Canada the Arctic grayling (*Thymallus arcticus*) lives in glacial lakes and rivers. As the ice melts in early spring these fish migrate from lakes and larger rivers into smaller headwaters to spawn, the eggs are not deposited in a proper redd but may be partly covered by sand and gravel. Adults live for up to 12 years and reach a rod-caught record weight of 5 lb 15 oz. from the Katseyedie River in the North-West Territories in 1967. In 1980 over 80,000 Arctic grayling were estimated to have been caught from Alaska's Tanana River system. The angling pressure is thought to cause a decline in average size and age of the adult fish and may lead to early sexual maturation.

Arctic grayling live in milky glacial meltwater streams, eating a wide range of terrestrial insects and aquatic invertebrates. Anglers will fly, at considerable expense, into remote areas of northern Canada to fly-fish for these beautiful fish. Slow growth, late maturity (6–9 years), ease of capture and a requirement for pristine water quality make Arctic grayling rather vulnerable to exploitation and pollution and thus a conservation priority.

Whitefish or Coregonids

The Whitefish (Ciscoes or Lake Herring, family *Coregonidae*) are a difficult group of fishes to identify; each so-called species tends to be rather variable, depending upon the type of lake in which a given population lives. W. B. Scott and E. J. Crossman recognise this difficulty and tentatively name 18 whitefishes within the Canadian fish fauna: one *Stenodus*, three *Prosomium* and 14 *Coregonus* species. The largest is the Inconnu (*Stenodus leucichthys*) which grows to around 80 lb at 20 years of age and has a large underslung mouth armed with small teeth. This allows the species to eat fish (smaller Coregonids) in contrast to the planktonic crustaceans (Daphnids and copepods) and benthic invertebrates (midge larvae, small mussels) which typify the diet of other whitefishes. The Inconnu occurs in Europe and North America in waters close to the Arctic ocean and north Caspian sea and supports a range of large commercial inland fisheries in Canada and Russia.

The three *Prosomium* species comprise the Mountain whitefish and two pigmy ciscoes. The Coregonids appear to have colonised and recolonised various deep cold inland lakes from the brackish waters of the post glacial Northern hemisphere. Closely related species appear to have hybridised and back-crossed to produce a myriad of similar forms which bemuse the modern taxonomist. Man has moved larger species into lakes where, previously, smaller species occurred, either to improve the coregonid fishery or to increase the forage fish availability for lake trout or taimen.

In Arctic Siberia, Finland and Sweden lives the Peled (*Coregonus peled*) which grows to 10 lb and is a commercially important species, *C. pidschian*, the Arctic whitefish, is also commercially important in Arctic Europe and the Baltic regions. The broad whitefish (*C. nasus*) grows to 20 lb over a lifespan of 10 years, living on a diet of aquatic insects and small molluscs (pea mussels) in lakes and rivers adjacent to the Arctic Ocean.

Scott and Crossman give a brief history of the demise of the Great Lakes ciscoe (=chub) fishery which operated by deep-water gill-netting a variety of coregonid species. The catch was preserved by smoking. As the stocks of one species were over-exploited, the fishery moved on to smaller species; over-fishing was exacerbated by environmental degradation and the influx of parasitic sea lampreys, *Petromyzon marinus* to the Great Lakes.

Sea lampreys in the Great Lakes of North America

The opening of the Welland Canal in 1829 allowed sea lampreys into the upper Great Lakes region from whence they spread throughout the whole system, undergoing a population explosion and decimating host fish species such as lake trout in the process. The impending catastrophe was recognised as long ago as 1946; by 1955 the average commercial lake trout catches from lakes Huron and Michigan had declined by 99 per cent of the average 1930's catches. The following methods have been tried to combat the menace of these alien parasites:

1. Spawning streams are treated with selective larval lamprey-killing chemical (TFM).

2.   Spawning adults are trapped and destroyed, spawning streams are dammed, sterile males are released.

3.   Differing lake trout strains have been developed which survive lamprey attacks better than native stocks.

In 1991 between 8–9 million dollars was spent on the Great Lakes lamprey control programme. In 1985 the regional economic output of the Great Lakes commercial and recreational fisheries was estimated at being worth between 2–4 billion (thousand million) dollars. The lampreys are threatening a major economic force! Computer models developed in the late 1980s indicated that lampreys were still killing as many lake trout each year as were caught by the human fisheries. This example should underline the potential folly of alien fish introductions to native fish communities.

Coregonids in Britain

British whitefish are a relative rarity, being of very local distribution and probably declining where they do exist. There is great confusion over the taxonomy of the various species; Andy Fergusson from Queen's University, Belfast has analysed their muscle tissue biochemically and groups them as follows.

Coregonus lavaretus (or *C.clupeoides*) which we call the schelly in the Lake District (e.g. Ullswater, Haweswater, Red Tarn) the gwyniad in Wales (Lake Bala) and the powan in Scotland (Loch Lomond, Loch Eck) has a very localised distribution (six separate stocks) but is locally common. This species also occurs in sub-arctic lakes in southern Sweden, southern Norway, the Alps, Carpathians, Finland and western Russia.

C.albula (or *C.pollan*), the pollan, freshwater herring (or Arctic ciscoe) is found in the Shannon region of Ireland in loughs Erne, Ree and Derg and in Lough Neagh. Britain now has only five remaining populations. *C.albula* is widespread all around the Baltic and central Poland, northern Russia and the Gulfs of Finland and Bothnia. A landlocked population lives in the depths of Russia's Lake Baikal where it feeds upon the crustacean *Mysis relicta* and various other invertebrates.

In the Lake District (Derwentwater, Bassenthwaite) lives the Vendace (*C.vandesius*). These are the only two remaining English populations. Eutrophication from a local sewage treatment works has recently exterminated this species from Castle Loch in Dumfriesshire, Scotland, but it may still be alive (although this is doubtful) in the nearby Mill Loch.

The Houting (*C.oxyrinchus*) is indigenous to Britain but is a very rare (possibly extinct), local, anadromous species which occurs occasionally in estuaries but has never been recorded breeding in the U.K. Some landlocked populations occur in Alpine lakes and in large Scandinavian lakes such as Sweden's Lake Valern.

Shads

Shads are related to Herring, Pilchards and Sprats and spend their lives at sea, save for migrations into freshwater to spawn in the brackish downstream reaches of large rivers. The Twaite Shad (*Alosa fallax*) is now much commoner in Britain than the Allis Shad (*Alosa alosa*) which may now only breed in one or two southern Irish rivers (e.g. the Shannon). Allis shad were formerly common, spawning in many British rivers as far north as the Tay; they run further upstream to spawn than Twaite shad and may have suffered more from polluted rivers and the construction of impassable weirs in the recent past. Prior to the pollution of the Thames, migrating Twaite shad were caught from May–July at netting sites around Putney Bridge.

Britain's best known Twaite shad population runs the River Severn each year in April and May, spawning in May and June. The adult fish are often caught in fixed salmon nets set in the estuary. There are some land-locked populations of Twaite shad, for example in the Killarney lakes in south-west Ireland and in some southern Alpine lakes. In Killarney's Lough Leane the Twaite shad are known as Goureen and grow to only around 25cm. Anadromous populations have larger fish averaging 1.5–2 lb as adults, with 3 pounders being very exceptional. In looks, shad are like large herrings, with large, easily dislodged silver scales and deeply forked tails which have runs of small scales almost reaching the tips of the forks.

Smelts

The final member of the varied group of fishes which I have grouped as 'salmonids' is the smelt *Osmerus eperlanus*. Smelts are anadromous shoaling fish which are indigenous in estuaries along the east coast of Britain. Although formerly common, smelt are now thought to breed in only around ten British river systems. A voracious feeder with a mouth full of large teeth, smelt progress from an invertebrate diet when small to small fish when adult. A single freshwater population of this species was recorded in Rostherne Mere, Cheshire but it became extinct in the 1920s. Peter Maitland notes that this local extinction may well have been caused by eutrophication of the mere.

The Lampreys

The British Isles harbour three species of the family Petromyzonidae (literally 'stone-suckers'), namely, the Brook Lamprey (*Lampetra planeri*), River Lamprey (*Lampetra fluviatilis*) and Sea Lamprey (*Lampetra marinus*). These primitive Agnathan (jawless) fishes have a toothed sucker-like mouth as adults, no paired fins and are scale-less. All three species live for several years as ammocoete larvae in freshwater streams and lakes, burrowed into silt beds where they filter-feed on algae (diatoms), microscopic animals and bacteria-covered decaying organic matter (detritus). The larvae metamorphose to adults by changing colour, developing a toothed mouth, and clearing the skin over the eyes to allow adequate vision for finding food fishes. The brook lamprey metamorphoses into a non-feeding adult (10–15cm) which matures sexually before migrating upstream to spawn in groups on stony gravel shallows before dying.

Adult river and sea lampreys migrate to sea to feed as external parasites on various fishes (flounder, herring sprats, salmon, cod, haddock) before returning to freshwater to spawn in May or June. Adult river lampreys average around 30cm length whilst sea lampreys average 50cm and can reach lengths of one metre. Loch Lomond has a very unusual land-locked population of river lampreys which parasitise the endemic powan and trout. In Sweden and Finland river lampreys are caught commercially in basket traps on their upstream spawning migration and sold grilled or smoked as a local delicacy. Commercial river lamprey fisheries used to exist on British rivers (for example the Severn), providing the basis for various pies and other dishes. King Henry I is thought to have died from eating a surfeit of lampreys . . . such gluttony is no longer possible in England!

Remarkably, brook lampreys and river lampreys have identical karyotypes (their chromosomes are the same) and the haemoglobin (red blood pigment which often differs in structure between species) is also identical. This means that the two 'species' are, in fact, one. The brook lamprey may be a non-migratory form of the river lamprey, having adapted to feed only as a larva but not as an adult.

The Burbot, *Lota lota*

Before I describe in detail the salmonid fishes which now dominate our coldwater habitats it is worth remembering that we may still have a freshwater member of the cod family living quietly in our rivers. The last reported burbot was caught near Cambridge in the Old West River, a tributary of the Great Ouse 20 years ago, but none have been recorded since. It is dangerous to assume that they are now extinct in Britain, but they certainly are not common! This is a distinct change from the situation in the sixteenth century when burbot were so abundant in certain East Anglian Fenland rivers that they were scooped out and fed to pigs as a cheap, high-protein food source.

Burbot are elongate, dark-coloured fish which look like the marine Ling in shape, with a broad head and single long sensory barbel on the lower jaw. They are nocturnal, hiding in cover during the day and foraging on small fish and large invertebrates at night. A key feature of their biology is their love of very cold water, they like temperatures below 7°C and climatic warming (combined with pollution) may be the key to their recent demise in Britain. The species still thrives across the northern hemisphere from Europe, across Siberia and the whole of North America, extending far into northern waters of Siberia, Arctic Europe, Canada and Alaska. In its widely differing habitats across a wide geographical range the burbot lives with trout and grayling in rivers or with a range of cyprinids at the northern edge of their distribution in cool lakes. Having an opposite activity cycle to the cyprinids, burbot feed voraciously in the winter and retreat to the cold depths for the summer months at which point the cyprinids leave the depths to feed over the shallow littoral zone as the water warms up in spring.

Burbot reach large sizes, up to 32kg and over a metre long at 20 years plus, and are fished for in winter through holes cut in the surface of frozen lakes. Spawning occurs in mid-winter (December/January) beneath the ice, with females laying up to 5 million eggs over stony and gravelly sections of river and lake bed. The 1mm diameter eggs hatch in 40–50 days at 2°C and the young 3mm long larval fish eat small planktonic invertebrates, gradually grading on to larger benthic prey as they grow. By the end of the summer they measure 10–15cm and are almost jet black, hiding under stones in shallow streams and around the edges of lakes. Maturity is reached after two to four years depending on conditions. The species supports commercial fisheries; in Siberia the tasty flesh is relished, the oily liver considered a delicacy, the roe sold as caviar and even the skin is tanned. Waste not, want not.

The following sections give more details of the biology of those salmonid species which are fished in U.K. waters.

Arctic Charr, *Salvelinus alpinus*

Habitat, distribution and population trends

The Arctic charr has the most northerly (circum-polar) geographical distribution of any freshwater fish, and most populations are anadromous running both rivers on Arctic islands and continental landmasses. The fish tend to be long-lived (up to 40 years) and relatively slow-growing ultimately reaching a large size (up to 88cm). Many of these populations support important local fisheries especially in Canada, Iceland and Norway where fish are usually caught during the autumnal spawning migration and then frozen for use during the long winter.

Canadian and Scandinavian charr go to sea after spending several years as juveniles in freshwater. They leave the rivers after the spring ice melt and feed in the rich inshore waters during the summer before returning to spawn in the autumn. These northern charr often over-winter in large lakes.

In Britain, our few remaining charr stocks are freshwater resident. Peter Maitland estimates that there are a little over 200 charr populations in the British Isles (200 in Scotland, 10 in England, 4 in Wales and several populations in the Republic of Ireland). Within Scotland charr are common in the Western Isles (Hebrides) but rare in Orkney and Shetland which each have a single known population. British charr populations tend to be land-locked in large (greater than 5 hectares) deep nutrient-poor, acid-neutral lakes and have been isolated post-glacially for several thousand years. Most charr lakes occur at moderate or low altitudes in areas subject to marine influence (i.e. salt spray drift). In Ireland, charr live in relatively shallow, biologically productive habitats, rather different from the 'classical' cold, deep, glacial charr lakes of the Scottish Highlands.

Sadly, there has been a gradual loss of British Arctic charr populations over the past 200 years. Examples of recent extinctions include the charr in Lough Neagh and Loch Leven, both of which may have been affected by eutrophication. The Loch Leven population disappeared soon after the lake was deliberately lowered by 1.4 metres, reducing the area by nearly 30 per cent. Charr seem to be very sensitive to changes in water quality. Winifred Frost has described how the Ullswater population, which was thought to spawn in a single inflowing beck, was wiped out after lead mine washings polluted the stream; presumably subsequently killing charr eggs and alevins, leading to a recruitment failure in the population and eventual extinction. This may be an example of the vulnerability of salmonid populations which home faithfully to small areas of spawning habitat susceptible to degradation by human activities.

Eutrophication problems for Lake Windermere charr.   Charr populations in the north basin of Lake Windermere in the English Lake District have fared well in recent years, probably because of the removal of large numbers of pike. In Windermere's south basin, however, anglers' catches of charr have declined markedly in recent years. The apparent population decrease is thought to be real and linked to eutrophication caused by treated sewage effluent and perhaps also to climatic change. Sewage and detergent-rich effluent, which was discharged via inefficient water treatment works into the south basin of the lake for many years has gradually increased the chemical fertility (especially phosphate concentration) of the water, leading to huge blooms of blue-green algae through the warm summers of the late 1970s and 1980s. When the algal blooms died off and during periods of calm warm weather, large quantities of blue-green algae sedimented down and died off, causing large-scale de-oxygenation of the lower water layers at around 30 metres depth.

The charr were driven towards the lake surface by the low dissolved oxygen concentrations where they encountered unusually warm water in the upper layers of the lake. These occurred because of a run of hot summers in the late 1980s. The summer surface temperatures of Windermere can be uncomfortably warm for the cold-water-adapted charr which grow best in cool (12–16°C) waters. Charr eggs are vulnerable to heat damage at temperatures above 8°C and the autumn spawning stock (90 per cent of the population) could be badly affected by a global warming influence on the lake. As the Americans say, the Windermere charr are 'caught between a rock and a hard place' . . . the heat of the lake surface in summer and the de-oxygenated depths.

Scientists at the Institute of Freshwater Ecology Windermere laboratory have persuaded the North-West Water plc. to install phosphate-stripping equipment to the sewage treatment plants responsible for changes in the lake's water chemistry. Phosphates in solution can be precipitated as metal salts by the addition of compounds such as iron chloride, iron sulphate, aluminium sulphate, calcium oxide or calcium hydroxide, all of which readily react to form insoluble metal phosphates. This should reduce the annual phosphate input by 80 per cent and limit further damage to the charr population of the lake's south basin. Climatic change, if it proves to be a significant influence, will be a much harder nut to crack.

Acidification. In Norway many charr populations have been lost through acidification of base-poor granitic watersheds. This form of damage has also occurred in Galloway, south-west Scotland where Loch Grannoch has suffered from both acidification and afforestation. Lochs Grannoch, Dungeon, Achray, and Venacher may all have recently lost their charr due to acidification; recent gill-netting and angling surveys have failed to produce any fish.

New charr populations. In Loch Doon acidification is advanced and the charr population may soon be lost; as a practical conservation measure Scottish Natural Heritage (formerly N.C.C. Scotland) have funded a research project in which Peter Maitland has moved adult Loch Doon charr to the nearby man-made Talla reservoir to found a new population. This appears to have been successful, with young charr being caught in the reservoir in 1990 arising from adults stocked in 1987/88. This is an excellent example of the conservation of a species which is rare in Britain, utilising a suitable man-made water where there will be no disruption of a natural fish community. Charr have deliberately been introduced to several Scottish waters in the past, for example on the Isle of Mull and in the Uaine lochs. There are two known examples of the accidental creation of charr populations in Scotland, both through engineering schemes. In the first case charr moved through a tunnel from Loch Garry, via the River Garry, into the newly-made Loch Errochty in the late 1950s to found a new population. In the second case charr must have been inadvertently pumped up through a 1400 metre tunnel over a vertical height of 365 metres into the Cruachan mountain reservoir which is part of a hydro-electric pump storage scheme utilising water from Loch Awe. The charr have settled in happily to found a new population. Perhaps charr are more adaptable than was formerly thought.

Food, growth and reproduction

In Lake Atnsjo, north-east Norway, trout and charr coexist in the upper water layers of a deep, cold unproductive lake. Charr feed almost exclusively on zooplankton day and night, selecting large individual *Daphnia* and *Bosmina* from the swarms of potential prey. Brown trout in this lake also eat zooplankton by day, but switch to midge pupae and adult flies taken from the water surface at night. The trout also occasionally eat fish. Charr appear to be more efficient plankton-feeders than trout because of their long, finely-divided gill-rakers which can be used to filter large zooplankton from the water. This may, however, be an illusion as some researchers believe that both charr and coregonids take tiny planktonic crustaceans one by one, hunting them visually in the open expanses of clear-water lochs. Trout have fewer, short gill-rakers and prefer to eat larger food items such as aquatic and terrestrial insects.

Charr are characteristically a very variable species with size, colouring, feeding and breeding biology differing between races within a single lake. Some examples will serve to illustrate these points.

Thomas Pennant, writing in the eighteenth century, suspected that differing kinds of charr lived in Lake Windermere in the English Lake District. A latter-day 45-year continuous study of this population by fisheries scientists at the Windermere laboratory, including Winifred Frost, Charlotte Kipling, David Le Cren, and Chris Mills, has told us much about the biology of this fascinating fish. Windermere is split into two basins, the north and south, with each basin containing separate autumn and spring-spawning charr stocks. Tagged adults return each year to the same spawning sites and it may be that each of the four distinct spring and nine distinct autumn-spawning grounds have their own genetically separate stocks. Spring and autumn-spawning fish are distinguishable by fine differences in the number and length of their gill-rakers. These differences are, however, minor compared with those shown by some Scottish and Scandinavian forms of charr.

Scotland's highland Loch Rannoch, home of monster brown trout, has two forms of charr. Andy Walker and his colleagues from the Pitlochry fisheries laboratory discovered these fish whilst gill-netting in different zones of the loch. A large-headed, wide-jawed race of charr which eats benthic invertebrates and fish was caught in deep water whilst in shallower and mid-water sites a slimmer-headed, plankton-feeding race occurred. The wide-headed benthic form (race) is dull-coloured with persistent parr marks along the flanks, few spots and orange pectoral fins. The narrow-headed pelagic form has dark pectoral fins (like sonaghen trout), pink spots and a dark claret-coloured body. In Loch Stack the brightly-coloured charr are plankton feeders, whilst Loch Eck fish are dull-coloured bottom-feeders.

Growth potential seems to be related to the general productivity of the water. S. E. Barbour and S. M. Einarsson studied the growth of charr in three differing Scottish lochs: Loch Builg, a cold, deep unproductive Cairngorm mountain lake, Loch Doine, a deep nutrient-poor fjord-like glacial lake with a milder climate and Loch Meallt, a relatively benign temperate Hebridean lake of medium productivity. These authors found that the age of charr (especially that of older fish) could be estimated most reliably from annual rings seen on sections of bones taken from the inner ear (otoliths), rather than from growth rings on scales. Growth checks were clearest in the large, fast-growing fish from Loch Doine and least distinct in the small, thin fish from Loch Builg which often formed 'false' growth checks, possibly due to periods of cold weather.

Loch Meallt fish tended to be intermediate in growth and ease of ageing. It is true for all long-lived fish that ageing by scales alone will often lead to under-estimates of the true age of an old specimen.

Given a good clear set of scales, a competent fish biologist can tell you the species, age, growth rate, frequency of spawning, freshwater and seawater growth phases, and whether a given fish was reared in a hatchery before stocking or was spawned naturally.*

In very productive lakes, charr can achieve sizes of, for example, 55–60cm after 8–10 years (Myvatn in Iceland and Korsvattnet in Sweden), 55cm at age 6 (Lake Geneva) and 74cm at age 12 (Lake Vattern, Sweden). In general, charr grow at least as well as trout in the first year of life; thereafter, trout tend to outgrow them. In some populations dwarf forms of charr occur, for example in Norway where adult fish of 20g (less than 1 oz) occur in lakes where the normally-growing individuals reach 700–800g (over 1½ lb). In Lake Windermere autumn-spawning male charr average 27cm length whilst the much rarer 'dwarves' average only 22cm. The larger spring-spawning males average 33cm whilst the smaller form averages only 19cm. Clearly, charr often evolve into complex communities even within a single lake; perhaps the different forms diverge (evolve) slowly, avoiding competition with one another for food and space.

Spawning. Charr congregate for spawning into large shoals, usually in autumn (October-December) over boulder-strewn lake beds or up rivers and streams. Mature males defend territories and pair singly with ripe females. The large (4–5mm) orange eggs are laid in depressions dug by the hen fish in gravel lake or stream beds where they incubate through the winter and hatch in the following spring. In Canadian waters, spawning occurs during the day at water temperatures of around 4°C. In Loch Meallt (Outer Hebrides) the young charr live in a stream for some time before dropping down to the lake below. Charr usually reach sexual maturity at 3–6 years and females can produce 200–7500 eggs depending on body size and condition.

In Thingvallavatn, a large (84 km^2) Icelandic lake, the charr can be separated into four distinct forms: a large bottom-feeding type which eats mainly snails and spawns in July-August at lake bed sites with cold inflowing springs; separate open-water plankton-feeding and fish-feeding forms which spawn in September-November away from the cold spring areas; and a small bottom-feeding form which is variable in its choice of spawning habitat and feeds on benthic invertebrates. A commercial fishery operates on the plankton-feeding form when they shoal up prior to spawning on stony shorelines in the autumn. Males of all four forms appear on the spawning grounds to set-up and defend territories before the females arrive, and leave after them.

Charr fisheries

The Windermere charr population supported a commercial net fishery for several centuries until, in 1921, netting ceased due to worries of over-fishing and the development of a popular sport fishing interest on the lake. Anglers still fish for charr today, with the total Cumbrian catch being (in 1987) around two tonnes (=two thousand kilos). Traditionally the pink/orange-boned flesh was potted in clarified butter with pepper, mace and nutmeg and sold in decorative pots as a gourmet food at Fortnum & Mason, London and other celebrated emporia. On Windermere, anglers

*The Salmon and Trout Association have recently suggested that scales from record fish could be used to classify specimens into 'cultivated' or 'wild' categories.

troll spinners above a heavy keeled lead behind rowing boats at depths of up to seventy feet. The take of a fish is signalled by the ringing of a bell fixed to the top of the stout rods which are rigged either side of the boat. In Scotland, charr are angled for on Lochs Garry, Bhrodain, Ericht, Lubnaig, Maree, Voil, Insh and Doon. On Loch Doon and on Haweswater in Cumbria, charr are said to rise freely for flies in the evening and are, at times, taken on fly-fishing tackle. As mentioned earlier, acidification may soon exterminate the Loch Doon charr stock.

Claims for the rod-caught charr record became somewhat dubious when, in 1987, a fish of 4 lb 14 oz (2.18 kg) was caught in Loch Garry, Inverness; this fish is thought to have grown un-naturally large by feeding on waste food pellets from a cage-trout farm on the loch. The most recent (at the time of writing) capture of this type was of a charr of over 6.5 lb from Loch Arkaig in 1990. As a conservation measure, rod-caught record claims for charr are no longer accepted in Britain. Very large (20-lb) wild freshwater charr do occur naturally, however, as fish-eating 'ferox' forms in Central European and Scandinavian lakes.

Peter Maitland has pointed out that charr are cage-farmed in Canada and Norway and gill-netted commercially in Norway; both activities have been proposed for British waters, posing potential threats for remaining (genetically distinct) populations.

Competition and predation effects on charr populations

Over the course of the long-term Windermere study, charr numbers in the north basin (as gauged by gill-net catches) have risen 6–8 fold, probably as a consequence of the pike-removal by winter gill-netting. Three tonnes (3000kg) of pike were caught in the first year and around one tonne in each year since. This amounts to the annual removal of around one third of the lake's adult pike population.

Pike are known to eat charr in the shallows on their autumn spawning grounds and Charlotte Kipling has proposed that more mature charr now survive to spawn successfully and have given rise to the increased stocks in recent years. Pike are known to eat charr in Loch Luichart, but in most large Scottish lochs the ferox form of trout appears to be the main natural predator of charr. In Loch Rannoch large charr are sometimes cannibalistic.

Where they co-exist, brown trout are thought to out-compete charr for the relatively rich invertebrate food supply in lake shallows, driving them out into the plankton-feeding zone of the open water where the pickings are relatively thin. Where trout are absent, charr are found feeding on invertebrates such as snails, insect larvae, nymphs and small fish in the weedy lake margins. In Lake Orne, Sweden, whitefish were introduced in 1965, apparently leading to a large decline in charr net catches. The whitefish may have out-competed the charr for food.

Even though biologists think that competition for food and space is a powerful force in the evolution of animals, the demonstration of its existence in nature has not proved to be easy. We think that animals and plants avoid strong competition for scarce resources by becoming more specialised. The collective specialist needs of a particular species are termed its *ecological niche*.

The Coregonids

The Coregonids are primarily fish of Arctic seas which live a marine adult life and return to rivers to spawn. In Britain and Ireland we have a few widely-dispersed relict freshwater populations which have become landlocked mostly in deep, cool glacial lakes. The fish have small toothless mouths and they usually feed on planktonic crustaceans (like *Daphnia* and *Bosmina*) during the summer months and spasmodically upon lake bed prey (chironomid larvae, *Asellus, Pisidium* bivalves, snails) during the winter. The food is either strained from the water and silt by long bony projections on the gill arches, gill-rakers, which form a type of filter along the sides of the throat or the prey are hunted visually and eaten singly.

Spawning takes place in mid-winter when large shoals congregate over stony and gravel-bedded areas to undertake mass-spawning, rather like marine herrings. The eggs are slightly sticky and undergo a long period of incubation (around 100 days) whilst lodged in crevices in the gravel and on weedbeds. The alevins hatch in the spring and then undergo a prolonged juvenile life in the open water where they feed on plankton and insects. Whitefish typically mature at lengths of 20–30cm and at ages of 3–4 years. Adult females produce 1000–25,000 eggs and, because of their relatively high productivity and growth rates, Whitefishes are often fished commercially in large European and North American lake systems. Overfishing and environmental degradation have limited the once prolific catches to much reduced levels.

Powan, *Coregonus lavaretus*

I was fortunate to live on Loch Lomondside at the University Field Station, Rowardennan for three years in the late 1970s while I studied for my doctorate at Glasgow University. During this period I became used to seeing gill-netted powan caught for research purposes by David Scott and his research students from the University of St Andrews. Powan are splendid, streamlined fish which live in large shoals and can give rise to large catches when the nets are set on the bottom in medium depths in the mid-basin of the loch around spawning time. Pike shoals congregate on the powan spawning grounds and predate the mature fish; they also congregate around the mouths of inflowing rivers when salmon and sea trout smolts and adults are migrating.

Powan in Loch Lomond invariably spawn during the month following the winter solstice (i.e. late December/early January), whilst powan in the nearby Loch Eck sometimes spawn a month later. The (falling) water temperature at spawning time is around 6°C. Mature male fish remain close to the gravel-bedded spawning grounds whilst females move onto the grounds as they ovulate. The pale orange eggs are around 3mm diameter and they lodge in crevices amongst the gravel and stones of the preferred spawning areas. Silted areas of lake-bed are avoided by spawning powan.

Harry Slack, based at the Rowardennan Field Station, discovered that many powan eggs fall prey to carnivorous caddis larvae (*Phryganea* species); during the past ten years this predation has been augmented by that from Ruffe (*Gymnocephalus cernua*), an introduced fish species which may pose a threat to Loch Lomond's powan stocks. Adult powan are also known to eat many of their own eggs after breeding, remaining over the spawning grounds for up to two months. Individual fish have been found to contain up to 500 ova in their guts.

In the cold winter depths of the lake, egg development is slow (perhaps 100 days) and it is a characteristic of glacial relict fishes that cool conditions are required for successful embryonic development. After hatching, the 12mm-long alevins take two to three weeks to fully absorb their yolk sacs and to start to prey on tiny crustaceans. We do not know where the Loch Lomond powan go between this size and that of 15cm or so (weight 30g.) which is reached at an age of 2 years, by which stage they start to be caught in fine-meshed research gill-nets.

Loch Lomond and its inflowing River Endrick is particularly interesting in that it has a very diverse fish fauna including populations of all three British species of lamprey (the sea lamprey, *Lampetra marinus*, the brook lamprey, *Lampetra planeri* and the river lamprey, *Lampetra fluviatilis*) together with 12 other freshwater species and an additional four brackish species. The adult river lamprey population is very unusual in that it feeds in freshwater, on the powan; it is a common sight to see healed lamprey sucker marks on the flanks of gill-netted specimens. I never saw a lamprey still attached to a powan and can only assume that they are 'wise' enough to drop off before reaching the surface.

Almost nothing is known of the early life of powan as small specimens are next to impossible to net from the Loch . . . no one knows where they live. The few specimens which have been caught have had a similar diet to the adults. The stomach contents of a single adult powan caught from Loch Lomond in early summer can contain up to 50,000 tiny crustaceans, such as *Chydorus coregoni* and *Daphnia hyalina*: the diet broadens in later months to include the larger predatory planktonic crustaceans *Bythotrephes longimanus* and *Leptodora kindti*.

Powan mature at 3–4 years and live for up to ten years. The large populations in Lochs Lomond and Eck were fished commercially during both the First and Second world wars during which periods several hundred thousand fish were taken.

There is an interesting difference in the feeding ecology of powan in Loch Lomond and Loch Eck: Loch Eck fish feed largely on the lake bed (on chironomid larvae and *Pisidium* mussels) throughout the year whilst Lomond fish feed predominantly on plankton during the summer, switching to benthic food in the winter. It appears that the plankton in Loch Eck is fairly abundant (similar to that in Loch Lomond) and it seems strange that neither the powan nor charr regularly feed on it: both species forage on the lake bed. It is possible that both powan and Arctic charr in Loch Eck are forced into feeding on the deep-water benthos because of aggressive competition for invertebrate food in the shallow littoral zone from brown trout. I wonder whether there is an undiscovered pelagic (openwater) race of charr in the loch which feeds on plankton? Recent research has turned up some plankton-feeding charr from the loch but whether they are the same race as bottom-feeding individuals remains to be seen.

Lochs Lomond and Eck, with their unusual assemblage of fishes, have a high conservation value amongst British wetlands. *Coregonus lavaretus* also occurs in Llyn Tegid in Wales, where it is known as the Gwyniad and in Ullswater, Haweswater and Red Tarn in Cumbria where it is known as the Schelly. In Haweswater, schelly feed on small crustaceans living in the weedbeds and also on some bottom-living invertebrates. In Llyn Tegid the gwyniad has a similar diet.

In 1986, S. M. Barbour caught a Schelly of 2 lb 1 oz (0.95 kg) from Haweswater on rod and line to hold the British record. Whitefishes are now protected and no further record claims will be considered (even for accidental captures).

Vendace, *Coregonus albula*

The vendace occurs across north-west Europe; in Britain, however, it now exists only in Cumbria's Bassenthwaite Lake and Derwentwater. A relatively small species, the vendace grows to around 1 lb in weight at a length of perhaps 30cm. Vendace formerly occurred in two Scottish waters at Lochmaben; Castle Loch was polluted by sewage effluent from a treatment works built adjacent to the water in the early 1900s and vendace disappeared from the water soon after. The fate of the Mill Loch population is less sure, but no fish have been reported from the site for the past decade and it seems likely that vendace are now extinct in Scotland.

The English populations are, one hopes, relatively secure but the Cumbrian lakes are now subject to a wide range of man-made influences which are causing measurable environmental deterioration. Vendace are plankton-feeders and ecological changes in their habitats which affect the plankton and hence their food supply could damage populations badly.

Given that Coregonids are fish of cold seas and cool glacial lakes, it is possible that the projected effects of global warming could potentially warm-up British waters to a level where they are no longer inhabitable by whitefishes.

Pollan, *Coregonus autumnalis*

The Pollan occurs widely through north-eastern Europe, Asia and north-west North America. It is normally an anadromous species but is landlocked in freshwater in the British Isles. The species occurs in several large Irish lakes including Loughs Neagh, Erne, Ree and Derg, the Lough Neagh population still supporting a commercial fishery. Lough Neagh pollan sometimes feed on the relict crustacean *Mysis relicta* which lives in the dark cool depths of the lake.

Houting, *Coregonus oxyrhynchus*

This Coregonid is essentially a fish of the eastern North Sea and the Baltic but is now restricted to a much reduced number of river systems due to pollution, for example of the Rhine.

The houting is a close relative of the powan but is the only British whitefish to remain anadromous in its life cycle. Adults used to ascend coastal rivers in south-east England, but these fish may not have been intending to spawn, rather, they may have been strays from mainland European rivers. Unfortunately, a combination of over-fishing and deterioration of its natal rivers seems to have combined to exclude this species from British rivers of today; none have been caught for many years. The status of the North Sea population may now be doubtful. Even in its stronghold of the Baltic, houting are much less abundant than they used to be and only a few localities support a continuing commercial fishery.

Atlantic Salmon, *Salmo salar*

Identification and Habitat

In British waters the only species of fish which is likely to be confused with an adult salmon is a large sea trout. This is not surprising since these Salmo species are capable of hybridization in the wild and are very closely related. The main features which can be used to distinguish pure bred specimens are as follows:

Salmon	Sea Trout
Tail forked at all sizes.	Tail square or convex in large fish.
Caudal peduncle (tail wrist) wide, allowing fish to be held vertically.	Caudal peduncle slim, not giving enough purchase to hold fish.
Innermost ray of anal fin longer than next ray.	Innermost ray of anal fin shorter than next ray.
With mouth closed, rear edge of maxilla (upper lip) is level with rear edge of eye.	With mouth closed, rear edge of maxilla reaches beyond rear edge of eye.
Black body spots X shaped.	Black body spots round, often with a pale halo.

In general, salmon have longer heads than sea trout of a similar size and sea trout tend to look stockier in build. Both species are splendid when fresh in from the sea, having dark backs, fully-silvered flanks sprinkled with small black spots mostly above the lateral line and a white belly. Sea lice (parasitic copepods, *Lepeophtheirus*) are often dotted around the skin between the anal fin and the tail, these drop off after the salmon has been in freshwater for a few days. After a prolonged stay in freshwater, prior to spawning, the silver colouration which provides camouflage at sea gradually fades to be replaced by brown/green mottlings interspersed with red and golden orange. In freshwater, this broken colouration is more cryptic when fish are lying deep in pools or under root masses or undercut banks. Cock salmon and sea trout tend to go very dark and may be largely grey/black on reaching the spawning grounds.

Cock salmon develop a greatly enlarged, hooked lower jaw (kype) which is armed with newly-grown long sharp teeth for fighting. When sea trout have been in freshwater for several weeks they may be indistinguishable to the naked eye from resident brown trout. Only an expert analysis of the growth rings on the scales (or the chemical content of the scales) will tell a sea trout long in freshwater from a brown trout.

Salmon and sea trout have similar habitat requirements and the two species are usually found together in pure, fast-flowing British waters. The precise habitat requirements are difficult to define since salmon thrive in rivers as different as Hampshire chalk streams (such as the Hampshire Avon, Test and Itchen) and relatively unproductive rain-fed rivers (such as the Teifi, Towy, Teign, Dart, Spey, Helmsdale, Thurso, etc.). Different stocks of salmon have different body shapes probably related to the physical nature of their natal rivers. Fast mountain stream salmon are slim 'greyhounds' with large fins, whilst lowland large river fish are broader, deeper and

72

generally stocky in build. These differences are said to be discernable to the experienced eye in parr and smolts from different streams.

Recent research indicates that there are probably separate salmon stocks (i.e. isolated breeding populations) even within some river systems, early-running (multi sea winter, MSW) springers often travel up to headwater spawning sites whilst summer-running grilse (one sea-winter, 1 SW fish) remain downstream to spawn in the middle and lower reaches. These sub-populations probably represent different stocks, at least for fisheries management considerations. It is not known whether the large MSW springers, which have declined in most (all?) British rivers in recent years after a peak of abundance in the 1950s, are a genetically distinct type. It is always difficult to establish whether genetics or environmental factors are most important in determining the life history and growth patterns of individual fish. Willie Shearer believes that the recent widespread decline of spring salmon is a biological event, possibly part of a long-term cycle, rather than a direct effect of overfishing at sea and in freshwater. It is, nevertheless, true that springers are rather vulnerable to rod-fishing in coldwater early season conditions and are sometimes exploited to a very high degree.

In Scotland, spring salmon occur almost entirely on east coast rivers whilst west coast salmon rivers are grilse-dominated. Where both MSW salmon and grilse occur in a river, the grilse can tend to be mostly male and the larger MSW fish female. Within the U.K., salmon may run a river in any month of the year; a fish entering freshwater in October may not spawn until the following October, remaining without food for more than 12 months and steadily losing body condition.

Two vital freshwater habitat characteristics are required for healthy salmon populations: 1. unpolluted and unsilted headwaters for spawning and early feeding and 2. estuaries which will allow the upstream passage of mature fish and the downstream migration of smolts. Unfortunately many British estuaries are badly polluted and suffer periods of low dissolved oxygen concentrations, especially when hot weather coincides with prolonged low flow conditions. Salmon and sea trout can be barred access to their breeding grounds by an impenetrable chemical barrier where the river meets the sea. Recent research work by John Alabaster and Peter Gough has indicated that salmon are stopped from migrating upstream by prolonged water temperatures of 24–25°C and by accompanying low levels of dissolved oxygen. These results seem to hold for fish on the rivers Axe, Frome and Thames.

A further form of habitat degradation which affects both salmon and trout stocks is that of silting spawning gravels, thereby suffocating incubating eggs and trapping alevins. Bank trampling/erosion by sheep and cattle, together with land drainage or forestry schemes, early ploughing and cultivation right up to the river edge have all contributed to increased silt inputs to salmonid nursery streams in recent times. This is a critically important area for both research and practical fishery rehabilitation work. Grant-aided set aside land on farms could be used to form valuable riparian buffer zones along river banks.

Salmonids need cool, well-oxygenated, clean gravel-bedded nursery streams where incubating eggs are bathed by pristine water. Low winter flows can lead to 'armouring' of the river bed such that the gravels are cemented together by organic and inorganic deposits and the salmon are unable to excavate their redds. Episodes of sudden acid flushes of spring meltwater can also devastate salmonid nursery areas, wiping out eggs and newly-hatched fry. Hydro-electric dams which influence flows and temperature regimes in the headwaters of salmon rivers can lead to losses of spawning habitat and unsuitable conditions for fry survival. The area and quality of nursery habitat available to young salmonids largely determines the abundance of wild salmon runs in British rivers.

Salmon fry and parr eat insects drifting in the current and thus must live in areas where aquatic invertebrates (mayflies, stoneflies, caddisflies, chironomids, Simulids) are in adequate supply. Young salmon tend to occupy faster riffle habitats with larger boulders than young trout which grade into lower current speed areas. Adult salmon may select coarser spawning gravels than trout, although large hen sea trout will dig redds 'side by side' with spawning salmon both in main river stems (channels) and in tributaries. On the River Feale in Ireland, Ken Whelan and co-workers estimated that around 60 per cent of total salmon parr production came from the main river channel despite an abundance of suitable spawning tributaries. Sea trout, in contrast, will often penetrate even the smallest spawning streams and thus make use of the maximum amount of habitat whilst salmon tend to remain in the main stems of most river systems. There are, of course, many exceptions to prove these 'rules'.

Population trends and habitat rehabilitation

The last two hundred years, which have encompassed the industrial revolution and subsequent environmental degradation of many of the developed world's salmon rivers have seen major changes in the distribution and abundance of this important fish. European rivers like the Rhine, Seine and Elbe, which once held abundant salmon stocks, lost them through gross water pollution. In New England (U.S.A.), the Connecticut, Merrimack and Penobscot rivers also lost their salmon. In Britain, many formerly productive salmon rivers such as the Thames, Trent, Clyde, Taff and Tyne have been decimated by pollution from untreated sewage, agricultural and industrial effluents, depressing or even extinguishing the resident salmon and sea trout populations. Brown trout often survived in the cleaner headwaters as they did not have to negotiate the filthy downstream sections to complete their life cycle.

Organically-polluted water consumes oxygen as bacteria digest the biological material in suspension; this microbial respiratory drain on the dissolved oxygen supply is termed the *Biochemical Oxygen Demand (B.O.D.)*. Where pollution has led to high B.O.D. levels in salmon rivers, stocks have either declined (for example in the rivers Aberdeenshire Don, Tyne, Yorkshire Ouse and Loire) or have been extinguished (for example in the rivers Clyde, Gryfe, Carron, Tees, Trent, Thames, Taff, Rhine, Meuse, Seine, Dordogne, Garrone, Jacques Cartier).

In the last 25 years there have been widespread improvements in water quality produced by better sewage treatment processes and tighter controls over industrial discharges. This has led to stock recoveries through recolonisation by stray salmon from adjacent river systems of several central Scottish rivers (Gryfe, the Firth of Forth Leven, Avon, Almond, Leith and River Esk at Musselburgh). In other systems, rehabilitation programmes have led to the presence of runs of salmon in the Thames, Tyne and Taff. It is very difficult to know to what extent our attempts at salmon rehabilitation have been successful. Often, improving water quality conditions will allow a natural recolonisation of degraded rivers. Additionally, there is usually little or no information on the numbers of wild fish running a river immediately before the start of a restoration programme; this makes it impossible to quantify the effectiveness of subsequent fish stocking.

The attempted rehabilitation of the Northumbrian River Tyne is a good case in point, as whilst considerable efforts have been made to restore the salmon run by stocking around 250,000 parr per year for the past ten years from a purpose-built hatchery, nothing has been done recently to help the sea trout stock and yet the two species have recovered in tandem. In the early 1960s the annual rod catch of both species was less than 50, whilst 20 years later 200–300 of each species were caught annually and by the late 1980s over 1000 of each species were caught each year. Maybe the salmon would have recovered just as well if they had been left to their own devices to re-populate the cleaned-up river. This dose of scepticism is healthy as stocking programmes are expensive; they do, however, appear to be important to the public perception of how much is 'being done' to aid ailing salmonid fisheries. Tony Champion, the former NRA fishery manager for the Northumbrian region suggests that hatchery salmon now represent around 10 per cent of the salmon run on the Tyne; hatchery parr are stocked in areas not used by wild salmon for spawning. A recovery rate of up to 2 per cent of batches of stocked salmon parr to the rod and net fishery has been estimated from recoveries of micro-tagged fish.

Conditions in the Tyne catchment have varied greatly over the years; the estuary was grossly polluted at the mouths of the northern and southern arms of the river whilst the upper reaches of the South Tyne were damaged by lead mine washings. To add insult to injury, the North Tyne headwaters have recently been impounded by a major new reservoir scheme: Kielder Water.

The hydro-electric dam at the head of the North Tyne holds back the 200,000,000 cubic metres of Kielder Water which flooded seven miles of salmon spawning and nursery area and barred access to many nursery tributaries. Water released from the reservoir to compensate reduced river flows below the dam tends to be cooler than the river water in summer and warmer in winter. This latter period is critical for the survival of salmon spawned in the river section below the dam since the warmer water speeds up the incubation time of the eggs such that they hatch too early in the spring. The young salmon fry then find themselves in river water too cold to initiate feeding and therefore starve to death. Subtle effects like these are difficult to foresee in the planning of a hydro-electric scheme. It appears that adult salmon which spawn at the base of the dam are largely hatchery stock and so damage to the wild stock is probably minimal. Wild fish, spawned elsewhere in the system, probably return to their natal spawning grounds.

Salmon rehabilitation programmes tend to take a long time. Derek Mills thinks it reasonable to set a minimum 10-year time scale for restoring salmon runs to a suitable river through a restocking programme. Great care must be taken to use salmon produced from stocks native to the river itself or from biologically and physically similar systems. Hopefully natural selection will act swiftly to mould the gene bank of a recovering population to produce a strain well adapted to the present-day conditions experienced by the fish in their new environment. The conservation of genetic diversity in salmon and trout populations is currently an 'in vogue' research area in fisheries management.

Research in Scotland and Ireland has started to address the problem of how to restore salmonid rivers which have been damaged by land drainage and forestry schemes. The Irish River Boyne is an example of a large catchment drained in recent decades to boost agricultural productivity. Martin O'Grady and colleagues have worked extensively on the salmon and trout populations of the lowland Irish River Boyne catchment which drains an area of 2500 square kilometres in the central/eastern region of the country, entering the sea near Dublin. This river is of interest because it was subjected to extensive drainage works which removed many pools and other features which create complex patterns of water flow, important for fish which shelter from the main current. Electro-fishing surveys showed that the highest densities of salmon parr and adult brown trout occurred in water of around 70cm depth and current speeds of 30–100cm per second with a rubble and broken bedrock substrate. The boulders and rocks create small riffle, gully, back-eddy and glide micro-habitats within the river which can hold large numbers of small salmonid fish.

Unproductive river stretches ranged from 50cm–2.5m depth but had *uniform* beds which did not break up the current flow and provide shelter for fish. Both types of habitat hold adequate supplies of invertebrate food for the salmonid fish, but only the rubble-bedded sections hold reasonable stock densities of fish.

Rivers modified by drainage schemes are designed to discharge flows as quickly as possible, like a rainwater gutter, but with little regard for the biological quality of the habitat. O'Grady and his team have been experimenting with various sizes and configurations of limestone rubble which they have placed along experimental sections of dredged river to try and re-instate a high density salmonid population. The results are encouraging, with significant increases in numbers of salmon parr and trout in the treated areas. This kind of practical rehabilitation work is very valuable for the restoration of engineered river systems.

Life in the sea and marine exploitation

The life cycle of the salmon must be one of the best known amongst freshwater fish but it is surprising how recently much of our knowledge came to light. In his benchmark book *The Salmon* (Collins, 1959) the pioneer fish biologist J. W. Jones, based at Liverpool University, noted that, at the time of writing, almost nothing was known of the sea-feeding areas used by Atlantic salmon. In 1956 the capture of a tagged Scottish salmon off the Greenland coast led to the discovery and subsequent exploitation of the Greenland and later the Faroese feeding grounds, much to the concern of conservators of wild salmon stocks. During the 1960s drifting gill-net fisheries developed off the west Greenland coast and baited-hook longline fisheries off the Faroes. These fisheries, which are now subject to catch quotas, and even buying-off of quotas, are perhaps less worrying than the uncontrolled illegal drift-net fisheries, for example those off the west coast of Ireland and off Scottish and English coasts which are known to intercept large but unknown numbers of fish returning to British rivers. The common west Greenland sea-feeding ground for salmon from far-flung natal rivers in North America and Europe may have an evolutionary basis in continental drift when the Atlantic ocean was much smaller and the continental land masses of the Northern hemisphere were much closer together. With the subsequent gradual widening of the Atlantic oceanic basin, perhaps salmon have extended their marine migration in parallel to maintain access to the prolific sub-polar feeding grounds.

Some salmon stocks remain rather less exploited at sea than others; for instance, those in the Barents sea and offshore Norwegian fish which feed near their own coast and where the commercial fishery was closed in 1984 as a conservation measure. Baltic salmon appear to restrict their migrations to the southern Baltic sea. Some Canadian stocks remain close to the continental landmass and thus 'avoid' the Greenland fishery. The extent of the annual northern movements of salmon at sea around the polar ice cap is thought to depend upon subtle annual differences in sea temperature and the distribution of forage fish and crustaceans. Grilse seem to feed in sea water regions with slightly higher (4°C-plus) surface temperatures than the larger MSW salmon. Direct relationships have recently been demonstrated between oceanic climate, sea surface temperatures and the abundance and distribution of salmon at sea. In the Faroese fishery the proportion of female salmon increases with latitude and very few potential grilse are caught in the Greenland fishery. In most years more than 90 per cent of salmon caught from these fisheries would have returned as 2SW fish. Much remains to be discovered concerning the controlling factors in salmon marine migration. This is probably fortunate for the salmon.

The annual *reported* North Atlantic salmon catch averages around 10,000 tons, i.e. 3 million salmon of 7–8 lb average weight. Angling is estimated to account for around half a million salmon annually, with the British Isles, Canada and Scandinavia sharing the bulk of the (declared) rod catch fairly evenly (see Robin Ade's *Trout and Salmon Handbook*, Christopher Helm, 1989). Clearly, the economic value of both the net and rod catch of Atlantic salmon is enormous, but the recent exponential growth in salmon cage culture has affected the market price downwards and thus, perhaps, removed some of the commercial pressures on wild stocks. Remarkably, wild salmon in Britain are now far outnumbered by farmed salmon. In Scotland alone, the projected output of farmed salmon in 1990 was estimated at 37,000 tonnes, the industry employing around 2000 people with an estimated turnover of 72 million pounds in 1988.

Salmon generate their highest economic return from game angling waters where the fishermen not only pay to fish, but also usually support ghillies, hoteliers and local shopkeepers during their holiday at the waterside. Salmon anglers visiting Scotland each year may spend as much as 50 million pounds on their sport. The average value of Scottish rod fisheries has increased by around 80-fold over the past 20 years. Anglers appear to take around 5–8 per cent of the salmon run in many Scottish rivers but rod exploitation is very variable between catchments, seasons and years. Many people believe that the development of salmon angling is the best way to ensure the economic underpinning for the conservation of stocks in the future. Most salmon fishermen want to catch a big fish and, fortunately, there are still places in the world where this is possible.

The British rod-caught record salmon was taken by Miss G. W. Ballantyne from the River Tay in 1922; it weighed 64 lb (29kg). In 1990, the Restigouche River in New Brunswick, Quebec produced a fly-caught 72 lb Atlantic salmon which was sportingly returned to continue its upstream spawning run. For the best salmon angling in the world, Scandinavia takes some beating.

Only the rivers of Norway produce 40-lb plus salmon to the rod with any regularity nowadays, with most of the large fish running in June and July. The fishing is expensive but there is no shortage of takers, for this is the cream of the world's game fishing experiences. The world rod-caught record Atlantic salmon of 79 lb 8 oz (just over 36kg) came from the Tana River which forms the border between Norwegian and Finnish Lapland. Much of the maintained excellence of Norwegian salmon fishing on rivers such as the Tana, Laerdal, Vosso and Alta, where fish can average 20 lb, may be due to the progressive restrictions on commercial netting and the phasing out of drift netting in coastal waters.

The tales of epic battles with huge Norwegian salmon must be tempered with a reminder of the damage which 'acid rain' (much of it originating in the U.K.) has done to salmonid stocks in the country. Acidification has virtually wiped out salmon populations in 25 rivers. Over 340km of river are affected with an estimated annual loss of between 92,000 and 300,000 adult salmon weighing some 345–1150 tonnes. These losses in the south of the country have been exacerbated by further problems caused (via the fish-farming industry) by the introduction of a damaging external parasite, *Gyrodactylus salaris* which kills salmon parr and smolts.

This parasite, which is endemic in Baltic salmon populations, wreaks havoc with Norwegian stocks because the fish have no inbuilt immunity to the skin fluke which builds-up in numbers rapidly to erode the skin and fins, eventually killing the fish. Around 30 rivers, including the famous River Driva, have lost their salmon stocks to this alien parasite species. It just goes to show that moving fish (or even fish eggs) around from country to country can have unforeseen and drastic consequences for native stocks. When in doubt, don't do it!

Salmon avoiding the temptation of angling baits and lures continue with their upstream migration. A famous aspect of this journey is their ability to leap waterfalls of considerable height; Derek Mills took a famous photograph (used in both of his excellent books on salmon) of a salmon leaping 12 feet to clear the falls of Orrin in Ross-shire, Scotland.

When I lived in Scotland, I used to enjoy watching both salmon and sea trout trying to leap the waterfall at the 'Pots of Gartness' on the River Endrick; often many attempts were needed before success was achieved. It was clear that, as unsuccessful fish bounced back down the jagged rocks, a great deal of physical injury was sustained, in addition to the tremendous physical effort involved. I wondered then whether the smaller grilse had a better power:weight ratio than the larger salmon, allowing them better access to spawning beds above high waterfalls. I couldn't decide, as we sometimes watched 20 lb-plus fish sail over seemingly effortlessly whilst grilse were flattening their snouts on the unyielding rock of the falls. The famous mathematician John Napier (who discovered 'natural' logarithms) must have watched the leaping fish for hours as he sat at his desk in an old cottage next to the river by the waterfall. Perhaps counting salmon helps with maths research.

The age of salmon returning to spawn

The factors which determine how long salmon stay at sea remains to be elucidated; some fish return after one sea winter as 5–7 lb grilse, whilst others stay away for two, three or more winters to return as maiden salmon weighing 10–30 lb-plus.

In J. W. Jones' studies of Welsh Dee salmon he estimated the average sea growth of (13cm) smolts which reach 50cm if returning the following summer as grilse, 60cm by their second winter at sea, 72.5cm during their third sea-summer and 80–90cm by their third sea winter. Each of these groups of fish can be distinguished by an inspection of scales taken from the 'shoulder' region of the body below the dorsal fin.

Scale reading

Just as with other fish, the scales of salmon give an indication of the life history of an individual fish; the freshwater years are marked by modest early growth increments with marked winter checks, and marine growth years have much more widely-spaced rings as rapid growth is made but, again, with clear winter growth checks. Spawning checks are caused when the scales are eroded perhaps due to a withdrawal of calcium for reproductive needs and these mark the first spawning attempt. In fish which have spawned more than once, the scales can become so eroded that previous growth rings are destroyed and accurate interpretation becomes impossible. This is also a particular problem with large sea trout which may spawn several times during their lives and thus be much older than their scales might indicate. The only way out of this is to dissect the opercular bones and inner ear bones (otoliths) out of the fish and examine those. Otoliths are particularly good for distinguishing narrowly-spaced annuli at the outer edge of the bone added during the final years of life.

There is some evidence of cycles of abundance of grilse and salmon which may be related to changes in marine temperatures and patterns of food supply. We simply do not know. In general, at present, many of our famous British salmon rivers are tending towards summer grilse fisheries, rather than large spring fish waters. This may be due to overexploitation by anglers of the coveted large 'springers' which seem to be rather vulnerable to the angler's lure, for example on the rivers Wye and Hampshire Avon. It may be that in the colder springtime water the feeding urge tends to linger longer and sometimes fatally for the spring run of fish than for the warmer water grilse run. Some fisheries biologists think that overexploitation by both rod and net fisheries has led to the demise of large spring salmon in many rivers whilst others think that climatic conditions have swung in favour of grilse in recent decades and that the cycle may return to favour springers in future. Perhaps time will tell, meanwhile moves are afoot to conserve remaining stocks. It seems that, as with sea trout, individual salmon are more vulnerable to being caught by anglers when there are relatively few in the river than when stocks are high; this could easily lead to overfishing and is a factor of which fishery managers should be aware.

There has been a recent addition to the Atlantic Salmon Trust's fine series of blue booklets, written by D. J. Solomon and E. C. E. Potter, entitled *The measurement and evaluation of the exploitation of Atlantic Salmon*, where this subject is discussed in some detail. David Solomon and Ted Potter have analysed the Dorset Frome salmon rod catches, relating them to numbers of fish in the river (measured by records from the adjacent electronic fish counter). They found that, as stock levels declined, the *proportion* of salmon caught by anglers increased. At a stock size of three to six thousand only around 10 per cent of the salmon are caught but when the stock size declines to below one thousand, the proportion of fish caught rises steeply to 50 per cent or more when the run totals only a few hundred fish. Clearly then, on the Frome, salmon stocks are vulnerable to overexploitation by rod fishing during periods of low abundance.

The return journey

On their way back to their native rivers, salmon may use magnetic fields, oceanic currents, or celestial navigation. However they do it, the majority of fish make it back faithfully to the estuary of their natal river. Back in 1880, Frank Buckland suggested that salmon use their olfactory (taste/smell) sense to find and recognise the river where they hatched. Just as he thought, subsequent research has shown that salmon use combinations of the smell and probably the topography of their home rivers to find the tributary and even perhaps the actual gravel run where they hatched to lay and fertilise their own eggs.

There are discernable genetic differences between the stocks of salmon spawning in the different headwaters of a given river. This must mean that the separate sub-populations are reproductively isolated, i.e. they very seldom interbreed.

Salmon can run their spawning rivers at any time of year but there tend to be marked seasonal peaks of spring, summer or autumn fish in different river systems. Spring fish often seem to penetrate furthest upstream whilst autumn fish tend to spawn nearer the sea. Each sub-population seems to be differently adapted to maximise the opportunities for successful reproduction in a given river system. For this reason the conservation of these different salmon genotypes may be critical for the long-term widespread survival of the species.

Breeding biology: the cycle begins in freshwater

When these magnificent silver fish return from the sea, stimulated by cool freshets or spates to move upstream from the estuaries where they wait for suitable water conditions, they stop feeding and prepare to breed. For most fish this will be a one-way journey, during which they will die; for a small proportion (which varies with the length and physical severity of the spawning river) further breeding seasons will come after dropping back downstream to the sea as thin spent 'kelts'. On the Big Salmon River, New Brunswick, Canada, hen fish have been recorded spawning up to eight times but it is usual on most salmon rivers for around 90 per cent of fish to die after their first spawning attempt. A successful downstream migration can be followed by a rapid reconditioning on the rich inshore marine feeding grounds. Mended kelts are often mistaken for fresh fish by anglers. A small proportion of salmon mature sexually but fail to spawn and are caught and taken in mistake for fresh fish. These make poor eating and are termed 'rawners' or 'baggots' by their disgruntled captors.

Sea trout make it back for a second or third spawning run more often, on average, than Atlantic salmon. Those salmon which spawn for the first time as large multi sea-winter fish and then survive to breed again are destined to become the record-breaking 50 lb-plus fish so sought after by game anglers.

With a good warm spate, both salmon and grilse will run rapidly upstream, perhaps covering 20 miles in a single day; in cold conditions movements tend to be slower. When the water is clear, fish tend to run mostly at night, whilst in coloured water they will run all day. As the spate subsides and the water 'fines down', the fish are in their most vulnerable state for being caught by anglers. Those which evade capture settle into deep pools and under overhangs where they will lie, sometimes for months, slowly metabolising their stored food reserves (fat) until they run further upstream towards the spawning grounds. As their sojourn in freshwater extends they lose their silver sea colour and darken and redden to their spawning dress. The males' teeth lengthen as does the lower jaw and they become increasingly aggressive, sparring with other males to accompany hen fish upstream. By October most salmon have collected in pools adjacent to the gravel runs where they will spawn. November and December are the peak spawning months in many rivers, the level of activity depending primarily upon the water temperature.

Certain aspects of our knowledge of salmon have been with us for a long time; Izaak Walton, writing in the seventeenth century, stated that salmon spawn 'most cunningly and cover it over with gravel and stones and then leave it to the creator's protection'. Salmon do that to this day.

During their stay in freshwater the testes in the males and ovaries in females finally mature so that in males, large quantities of white milt (sperms) are ready for shedding into the water through the urethra to fertilise eggs. In females, the ovary walls have stretched to allow the mature eggs to fill the body cavity. Female salmon produce around 700 large orange 5–7mm eggs per pound body weight, investing a considerable proportion of their body food reserves in reproductive effort. When the eggs are shed through the urinogenital papilla (at the vent) they swell up to become spherical and slightly sticky so that they adhere to gravel particles and are less likely to be swept away by the fast current. The shedding and fertilizing of the eggs is a well-studied sequence of fish behaviour. A surprising fact concerning the spawning of salmon is that the water temperature is often as low as 1°C; under these conditions most cold-blooded animals are inactive, we do not know how salmon overcome this difficulty.

J. W. Jones observed many salmon spawnings in his stream tank built on the banks of the River Alwen, a tributary of the Welsh Dee. Jones built his tank principally to observe the spawning behaviour of sexually mature male salmon parr but, as a good scientist, he also recorded carefully the reproductive behaviour of large adult males and, of course, female fish. The following notes are based largely on his writings.

Females move up onto the gravel spawning beds accompanied by a dominant adult male and often by several sexually mature male salmon parr. The adult male chases the parr away and often kills them by biting them with the sharp teeth on his kype. The hen fish turns over on her side and lashes her tail against the river bed to suck up gravel and stones which are swept downstream by the current, leaving a depression in the river bed. This continues until the pit is deep enough for the hen fish to 'crouch' in, with her anal fin extended down to reach the bed in between two large stones. When this is achieved she will 'sit' in the redd while the male, which has been in close attendance all the time, quivers against her flank. Her mouth gapes open as she releases her eggs and the male also gapes as he releases a cloud of milt which envelopes the eggs. The hen fish then moves upstream and starts to dig the next of a short series of depressions which constitute the redd as a whole. As she digs upstream, clean *silt-free* gravel is swept down on top of the newly-spawned egg batch, enclosing it safely within the stream bed. The long period of incubation then starts; it is vital that the redd does not become clogged by fine sediments during incubation as the eggs will perish by asphyxiation and fungal infections, hence the importance of a steady flow of clean water over the redds.

A 12-lb female salmon will dig a redd of perhaps 16 feet in length whilst spawning her whole load of eggs. If too many adult fish spawn on a gravel run during the course of the breeding season there is a danger that 'over-cutting' of redds will occur, with subsequent fish dislodging fertile eggs from previously farmed redds. If all is well, the eggs will hatch in around 100 days (the exact period depends upon water temperature) and the alevins will remain in the redd for several more weeks before wriggling their way up to the surface of the gravel as the spring sunlight breathes life and a new boost of productivity into the nursery stream. A 4–5 lb grilse lays her eggs about 6–8 inches deep in the gravel whilst a large salmon may leave her alevins with 12 inches of coarse gravel to negotiate before they reach the surface. While they absorb their yolk sacs the newly-hatched yolk-sac fry avoid light but, as the need to feed develops, they start to pop up to the surface in April or early May.

Feeding ecology of salmon fry and parr

Winifred Frost studied the food of young salmon and trout from the River Forss in Caithness, Scotland. This river is a peaty upland water which runs over Old Red Sandstone and is rather uniform with a coarse sand and gravel bed. The young trout and salmon appear to live together here and may compete for resources, whereas the two species segregate to a greater degree in streams where there are more distinct fast riffle and pool sequences. In the Forss the summer diet of young salmon and trout *fry* (table below) proved to be remarkably similar (figures are percentage of fish examined in July containing a given food item):

	Salmon	Trout
Mayfly nymphs	100	96
Stonefly nymphs	22	10
Caddis larvae	17	13
Beetle larvae	13	43
Midge larvae and pupae	56	63

For salmon and trout *parr* on the Forss in July, the figures are as follows:

	Salmon	Trout
Mayfly nymphs	96	95
Stonefly nymphs	22	5
Caddis larvae	56	72
Beetle larvae	48	67
Midge larvae and pupae	44	48

It is clear from the two tables that the two species exploit similar aquatic insect groups and in similar proportions.

Amongst the mayflies, *Baetis, Ephemerella*, and *Centroptilum* species were most common; of the caddisflies, *Polycentropus, Leptocerinae, Limnophilinae, Hydropsyche* and others were common. In June, larval caddisflies outnumber nymphal mayflies in the diet of young salmonids on the Forss, whilst in July the position is reversed. These differences probably reflect the availability of hatching insects to the foraging fish which intercept prey drifting in the current.

Population biology of young salmon
David Hay recently published an interesting short review of the survival of young salmon in the Girnock burn, a tributary of the River Dee in Aberdeenshire, Scotland. Scientists on staff with the Scottish Office have been electro-fishing the burn each season for juvenile salmonids for the past 20 years, allowing estimates of the long-term average survival for the early stages of the life cycle of salmon to be made. Young fish leaving the burn are caught in a downstream trap, counted and released; mature fish migrating upstream to spawn are caught in another trap, counted and then released upstream of the juvenile trap to continue their journey.

A typical Girnock burn hen fish is around 70cm long and lays around 5000 eggs in a single redd. Salmon are careful to site their redds in clean gravel which is well percolated by oxygenated water, leading to an average 94 per cent egg hatching success; 5000 eggs therefore produce (on average) around 4700 alevins. Over the next two months of May and June, in a well-stocked stream, there is (as with trout) a massive mortality of fry which are attempting to establish feeding stations in suitable areas of habitat. This mortality is density-dependent (the proportion dying varies with stock density) and thus tends to even out between-year variations in the numbers of fry surviving to the autumn of their first year of life. Of the 4700 alevins, only around 360 parr typically survive. If they make it thus far, however, their future chances of survival are much improved. Of the 360 parr, around 140 will be alive one year later, the rest succumbing to predators, starvation or disease. Of these 140 survivors, 88 will die in freshwater and the rest (52) will migrate to sea at various ages over the next two years, most as 3-year-old smolts. The 52 fish which migrated downstream to the sea represent one in a hundred of the original 5000 eggs spawned; natural selection, plus a degree of luck, has acted to ensure that these are the best-adapted individuals to try and survive life in the sea and the arduous return spawning migration.

On Scotland's River North Esk, Willie Shearer has estimated the following salmon survival statistics, e.g. for the 1978 year-class: 7521 spawners deposited around 29 million eggs; these produced 144,000 smolts (0.5 per cent survival), 21 per cent of these smolts returned as grilse and salmon to inshore home waters and 9.9 per cent made it back to the river. Of the smolts leaving the river only an estimated 7.7 per cent returned to the spawning beds. Overall, then, 99.96 per cent of North Esk salmon spawned in 1978 died before returning to breed. Survival for salmon is a chancy business!

From 1966 to the present day, biologists at the Freshwater Fisheries Laboratory near Pitlochry, Perthshire, Scotland have studied aspects of the biology of young salmon on the Shelligan burn; much of the work was carried out by Harold Egglishaw and Peter Shackley. They found that many factors affect the production of young salmon in upland nursery streams, the major ones being:

1.   *Water temperature*, which affects the rate of development of incubating eggs, the date of fry emergence from the gravel, subsequent growth rates and the length of the growing season for fry and parr. High altitude streams tend to have slower-growing salmon parr because of lower water temperatures. Forestry plantations can overgrow and shade nursery streams, reducing the growth potential of the fish.

2.   *Density of young salmonids*. Salmon parr tended to grow largest in those stream sections which had low densities of parr and to attain smaller September sizes in densely populated areas. Stocking experiments showed that fish which migrated out of the heavily stocked sections subsequently grew better than fish which stayed 'in the crowd'. There is some evidence to show that older parr compete with young parr for food and space and reduce the survival of the younger fish. In the Shelligan burn there was no clear competitive effect from the numerous young sea trout which were evenly distributed along the stream. It seems that young salmon avoid serious competition with young trout by living in shallow, fast-flowing riffles which are avoided by the trout which tend to live in deeper, slower-flowing micro-habitats.

3.   *Underlying geology*. Salmon production is higher in streams which run over soft limestone and sandstone strata than in waters which are based on hardrock such as schists and granites. The softer rocks dissolve to increase the chemical fertility of the water and its consequent algal and invertebrate productivity, giving the young fish more food.

Harold Egglishaw suggests that the recent declines in the numbers of salmon caught in various Scottish regions relate to the degree of coniferous afforestation in the regions of the spawning and nursery streams. The effects of acidification, exacerbated by conifer plantations are currently the subject of several active fisheries research programmes. Long-term population dynamics studies are vital to our understanding of fisheries biology. Sadly, the funding for research of this type is becoming increasingly difficult to secure.

Stock-recruitment curves

Ross Gardiner and colleagues, working more recently on the Shelligan burn, have estimated from a pilot study that the highest numbers of returning first and second autumn salmon were produced in years when there was a density of emergent salmon fry of around 11 per square metre on the spawning beds. Below and above this optimal fry density, fewer salmon appear to return to spawn. This type of dome-shaped stock-recruitment relationship is called a Ricker curve (see figure below) and, if confirmed by a longer run of data, is a very useful starting point for stock management. It should be possible to optimise the run of adult salmon by regulating the catch and allowing the ideal number of fish to spawn. Malcolm Elliott found that Lake District sea trout also have a Ricker-type stock-recruitment relationship with a similar optimal density of newly-emerged fry.

David Solomon has advised caution in the interpretation of these stock-recruitment relationships because young salmon and trout redistribute themselves within nursery streams as they grow, often dropping downstream and out of a study area, appearing to die, but, in reality, just going somewhere else in the system. With such mobile fish it is very difficult to get to grips with the problem of whether high densities of spawning adults give rise to 'too many' young fish for the system and disproportionately reduced survival of fry, parr and pre-smolts.

If the curve relating salmon stock (as number of eggs spawned) to numbers of recruits to the breeding population is not dome-shaped, but reaches a plateau (a 'Beverton and Holt' curve, see figure opposite) this indicates that a ceiling *carrying capacity* for the stream is reached over a wide upper range of spawning adult densities. In theory, this type of population can be fished down to the level of spawning adults approaching the

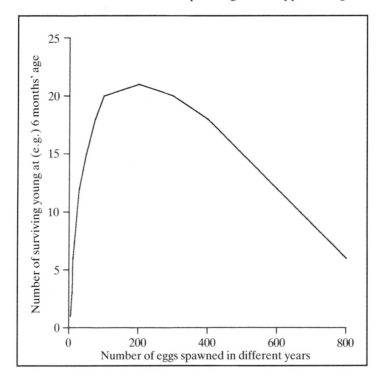

Ricker stock-recruitment curve

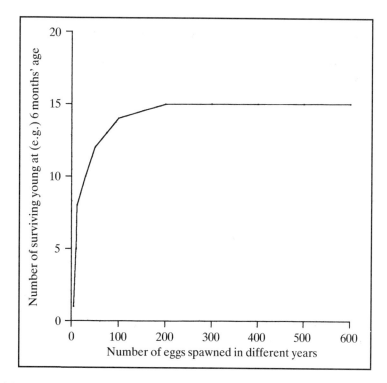

Beverton & Holt stock-recruitment curve

start of the plateau without adversely affecting future recruitment.

A clear conclusion from the research carried out on young salmonid population dynamics is that reproduction is *very efficient at low adult stock densities*, leading to a natural resilience to exploitation in salmon and trout stocks. This is a saving grace when conditions combine to reduce stock abundances. A major difficulty is to find systems where spawning stocks are very abundant so that research can be done at this end of the stock-recruitment relationship. Much more research is needed before we can understand fully and manage effectively our wild populations of salmon and sea trout.

Smolting

Young salmon feed on insect larvae, nymphs, pupae and adult flies floating downstream through the fast riffle habitats where they live. It seems that salmon fry and parr are less aggressive than trout parr and tend to form loose feeding groups where, presumably, the quickest fish off the mark get the lion's share of the available food. Most growth occurs from April to July, slowing August to October but parr will still grow slowly in winter when conditions allow. At a size of around 13–14cm the parr turn silvery and become smolts, dropping downstream, tail-first, to the sea to begin their rapid growth and maturation phase. Even before smolting some of the sexually precocious males may already have successfully fertilised eggs during the previous spawning season.

The length of time which salmon parr spend in freshwater before smolting seems to depend upon growth rate and upon reaching a critical size (around 13cm), as extreme northern (Scandinavian) river fish may not go to sea until they are 5–7 years old whilst Scottish and Welsh smolts might be 2–4 years old and southern chalk stream (for example Hampshire Avon) fish only a year old. The longer a parr remains in freshwater before smolting, the more likely the salmon is to return as a spring fish. In all rivers there is a peak smolting age with many fewer individuals going to sea either younger or older. In the Hampshire Avon salmon population 90 per cent of smolts were found by J. W. Jones to be one year old whilst in the Welsh Dee, 90 per cent were two years old. In the Grimersta River on the Isle of Lewis in the Outer Hebrides, Jock Menzies found that 60 per cent of salmon smolts were three years old.

The timing of the annual smolt run is aptly summed up by the couplet:

> The first spate in May
> takes the smolts away.

Although the 'freshwater to sea' life cycle of the salmon is familiar today, it is worth remembering that even early this century it remained to be proven that smolts return to the river of their birth. The celebrated P. D. H. Malloch did the critical experiment by tagging smolts on the River Tay in 1905 and 1906 with loops of German silver wire tied through the body below the dorsal fin. Nearly 2 per cent of these fish were recaptured over the period 1906-1909; 42 grilse (average weight 6.5 lb) in 1906, 57 salmon in 1907 (average weight 13 lb after two years at sea) and 9 fish in 1908 (average weight almost 20 lb as 3 sea-year fish). This proved not only that smolts returned as salmon but that they do so over a protracted period, to their natal river.

The imprinted memory of the 'smell' (=chemical fingerprint) of the home river which may include 'pheromones' from the salmon present in the stream, is acquired by the smolt over the final few days before downstream migration. Parr from hatcheries can, therefore, be stocked out in salmon rivers and will subsequently recognise the river using information stored between stocking and smolting. Whether this practice is likely to result in increased runs of adult fish will depend (amongst other things) upon the habitat quality of the river, the number of spawning adults and the age of stocked parr. Clearly, expert advice is needed before people rush in and stock fisheries in the blind hope of improving matters. Experience has shown that enhancement projects of this type often (but by no means always) fail dismally.

If conditions are not suitable (very low flows, hot weather), smolts may miss the 'window' for migration and remain in freshwater, losing their silver colouring before trying again the following year. This certainly seems to have happened to sea trout during the course of the Connemara stock collapse of recent years (see section on trout).

In more polluted systems, smolts have to negotiate grossly-polluted estuaries where, in summer, dissolved oxygen levels can fall close to, or even reach zero, killing any salmonids which attempt to pass through.

Where the water is clean enough to allow smolts to reach the estuary they will wait in brackish water for several hours, or perhaps days, as they gradually adjust to the full salinity of the sea. Freshwater fish tend to dry out osmotically in the sea as their blood carries a lower concentration of dissolved chemicals than the seawater flowing past their gills. Excess salts are actively excreted through the gills and by the kidneys to try to stop the fish from becoming soused in brine.

The sea is a hostile environment for fish which have spent their whole lives in freshwater; many new predators must be avoided and much food captured if a small silver smolt swimming out into the oceanic depths is to return one day as a fine adult salmon.

Predation of smolts by birds

On their downstream migration, smolts fall prey to birds such as cormorants and goosanders. Willie Shearer estimates that a total cull of sawbill ducks, Goosander and Red-breasted Merganser, if sanctioned by bird conservationists, might result in a maximum increase of 35 per cent in the returning adult salmon run on the Scottish North Esk. In reality the benefit would be less because of the difficulty in maintaining a zero sawbill population on the catchment. Also any increase in surviving parr and smolts may be reduced through increased competition for food and space amongst young salmonids in the river. On the River Bush in Northern Ireland, Gersham Kennedy has suggested that cormorant predation of salmon smolts is a major factor holding back the rehabilitation project which has been running there for several years. There is a large cormorant colony just offshore from the Bush estuary. From the conservation standpoint we have to decide how to manage the numerical balance between predators and their prey.

Predation of adult salmon by otters

In an interesting study of the foraging activity and diet of otters living on the catchment of the River Dee in Aberdeenshire, Hans Kruuk and colleagues discovered that male salmon are caught much more often than females. Throughout the breeding season, from November to January, considerable numbers of salmon, mostly males, were caught by otters in the tributaries of the Dee, probably as they travelled up and downstream over riffles between different gravel spawning runs. Males also spend longer on the breeding grounds than females and are thus more vulnerable than females which try to return to the sea soon after spawning. Otters fishing for salmon probably caught a single healthy fish (rather than a kelt) each night, eating 1–1.5kg of flesh and leaving the rest to be cleaned up by scavengers or to rot.

It seemed from this study that although a large number of salmon were killed, most were males and most died after the fishing season so that the predation probably had little adverse effect either on the rod catches or on the numbers of young salmon produced. A dominant male salmon may fertilise the eggs of several females so that the population can stand to lose more males than females, without the breeding success being lowered too much. Also, precociously-mature freshwater resident male parr can fertilise eggs from large sea-run female salmon. The traditional persecution of otters as predators of game fish probably never did much to increase stocks and is, of course, illegal nowadays.

Predation by seals . . . predator control?

The most important known marine mammalian predator of salmon is the grey seal (*Halichoerus grypus*) and the argument for and against seal control between salmon netsmen and marine mammal conservationists has been a long and acrimonious one. Seals (Grey and Common) certainly do eat large numbers of salmon, including chewing up ones conveniently hanging underwater in nets and 'skinning' fish so as to eat the flesh and leave the bones. This behaviour leads to an underestimation of salmon in the diet since prey species are identified in seal stomach contents from undigested bones.

Seals may also divert salmon shoals around netting stations by their mere presence. Whether the degree of depredation on salmon stocks warrants seal culling is a vexed and well aired question to which there is no clear answer.

As in all examples of predator control, public opinion is sharply divided depending on personal outlook and involvement. I must admit that, having done several years of research on wildfowl breeding biology, I am convinced that the great impact of crows, magpies, mink and foxes on eggs and sitting ducks can justify the *humane* control of predator populations while the birds are nesting. I also believe that pike control is beneficial to trout and salmon fisheries. The case for seal culls with respect to salmon predation remains to be proven. It is well worth pointing out that carefully managed predation control is often necessary for the production of adequate fish and game for sporting purposes. If predation pressure makes a quarry species scarce the local population will not stand further exploitation and the sporting income will be lost. If the sporting income is lost then the economic support for game conservation disappears and the habitat will be threatened by pressures from development, etc. Predator control can, therefore, safeguard habitats for a wide range of non-quarry species which might otherwise lose a home. Marshes managed for waterfowl shooting, rivers keepered for game fish, woodlands for pheasants, less intensive cereal farming for grey partridges and keepered grouse moors are all habitats safeguarded for wildlife through the interests of field sports enthusiasts. Field sports put back into conservation far more than they take away.

Salmon fisheries and their management

Derek Mills (1989) gives a full account of salmon management in his book *Ecology and Management of Atlantic Salmon*. I will only give a few pointers here to the main issues involved, leaving interested readers to refer to the specialist books should they so wish. It appears that salmon smolts migrating to sea from a given river are likely to stay together throughout their marine feeding phase. This makes a stock vulnerable to long lengths (kilometres) of drift-net which may take a high proportion of the fish from a given catchment (stock). On the high seas, catch quotas and fisheries protection vessels and aircraft attempt to police the major salmon feeding grounds and near-shore migratory routes but the manpower involved is pitiful compared to the job in hand. The system is regulated by the North Atlantic Salmon Conservation Organisation, (N.A.S.C.O.). Illegal drift-net fisheries which involve miles of cheap nylon mono-filament gill-nets strung out along key coastal salmon and sea trout migratory routes are known to account for many fish. It is difficult, for instance, for Greenland fisheries managers to accept smaller quotas for their marine salmon fisheries in order to protect 'British' salmon feeding in their waters when many of these same fish are caught illegally in British and Irish home waters where the money for adequate policing is simply not being spent. Perhaps we should introduce a tagging system (like the Canadian one) where all salmon offered for sale have a numbered tag; this would make it much more difficult for illegally-taken fish to be marketed.

At the time of writing (summer 1992) Mr Orri Vigfusson (of Iceland) has co-ordinated a buy-out for three years of the Faroese salmon quota to end the high seas fishery. Iceland, with its 80 salmon rivers, is the first country to phase out commercial fishing in favour of angling. Mr Vigfusson is said to estimate that 10–15 per cent more salmon will be available in natal rivers, and improved runs of fish in 1992 appear to be bearing out this view. The salmon anglers hope that any increased runs will be composed mainly of the large, two sea-winter spring fish which are in decline at present.*

*As this book went to press Mr Vigfusson had successfully negotiated a suspension of the West Greenland salmon net fishery. This initial agreement is set to run for 5 years.

In estuaries, salmon are often fished either by fixed net or by seine (drift) nets which are set in an arc from a boat and then pulled back onto the shore (net and coble). Commercial salmon netsmen now have to contend with a drop in price due to the huge amount of farmed salmon flooding onto the market and the threat of the buying-off of netting rights by angling interests which are attempting to increase the run of fish escaping upstream to become available to the rods. This, if successful in increasing rod catches, would of course mean a large increase in the value of the sport fishings and a high likelihood that they would be sold at great profit on a syndication or time-share basis. The Atlantic Salmon Conservation Trust points out that netting operations might begin again at some future date on rivers where appreciable increases in salmon runs occur. The loss of traditional netsmen's jobs in rural areas in the meantime is, however, a sad aspect of this approach to salmon river management.

Salmon caught on the rod, whether by fly, spinner, prawn or worm, are of much greater economic value than commercially-netted fish; an argument constantly put forward by those who seek to buy out estuarine netting consents. There is little evidence, however, that a cessation of commercial estuarine netting would either lead to greatly increased rod catches or allow populations to be adequately exploited because rod angling is such an inefficient way of catching salmon. Furthermore, salmon netting provides important employment for people in rural areas and provides a quality product for the table market. It is easy to understand the interests and points of view on both sides of this argument.

In an ideal world the salmon-spawning rivers would be kept clean and managed for optimal smolt production, leading to a well policed and scientifically managed high seas fishery which allowed an optimal escapement of fish to provide both successful netting on the estuaries and rod catches in the rivers, leaving optimal numbers of spawners to produce the next generation. There, simple! . . . and then I woke up. Lord Thurso seems to have got things about right on his splendid river, but the family do have the advantage of owning the complete catchment and are thus able to control expertly what happens to the river from 'top to bottom'. The Thurso salmon run is enhanced by stocking from an estate hatchery (using freshly-trapped Thurso brood stocks) and supports both a thriving netting station and an excellent rod fishery. Great!

Salmon farming and effects upon wild stocks

Wild Atlantic salmon alive today are thought to be outnumbered by salmon of cultured origin. Large numbers of fish-farm salmon have escaped from sea cages and are now running rivers. It is on record that over half of the adult salmon in some Norwegian rivers in the spawning season are of farmed origin. Research by John Webb, supported by the Atlantic Salmon Trust has recently shown that escapee cage-farmed salmon interbreed with wild fish under natural conditions in a northern Scottish river (the Polla). This, coupled with the knowledge that farmed salmon are becoming a common sight in anglers catches on many salmon rivers in the west of Scotland and Ireland, has led to concern over 'genetic pollution' of our wild salmon stocks. This is the same concern voiced by many over the widespread stocking of farmed brown trout into wild trout populations.

With regard to salmon, Peter Maitland has reviewed our state of knowledge of the impact of farmed fish on wild salmonid populations, and he came to the following conclusions:

1.   that isolated wild salmonid populations develop, over many generations, genetically-based stock characteristics;

2.   that hatchery stocks undergo a gradual loss of genetic diversity in captivity because of deliberate selective breeding for traits such as high growth rate, etc;

3.   that domesticated hatchery fish rarely perform as well in the wild as salmonid fish from native stocks;

4.   that releases into the wild of large numbers of non-native fish can reduce the numbers and performance of wild fish.

This last point refers to the potential of large runs of farmed salmon to swamp the gene pool of small wild populations, for example, when a cage breaks open in a storm, releasing fish close to a small river which supports a small wild population of salmon. Time may tell whether these fears are well-based or whether natural selection rapidly weeds out the poorly adapted intruders and retains a healthy salmon stock in a given river. The important study by John Webb on the interbreeding of wild and escapee farmed salmon on the Polla should help to resolve this question.

We do not know whether the wide genetic diversity displayed by our native salmonid stocks involves a high proportion of genes which are critical to the survival of fish in different rivers or whether 'any old salmon', irrespective of its genetic origin can produce offspring which will survive well enough to keep salmon populations going in the rivers of today. Some of the observed genetic diversity in wild populations may be made up of genes which have neutral survival characteristics.

This is also true for trout; will our remaining 'wild' brown/sea trout stocks be materially damaged by genetic inputs from farmed fish or are these arguments largely academic? We simply do not know at this early stage in our research. In any case it is prudent to take a precautionary approach and assume that damage will be done to native stocks and therefore that fish-farming enterprises and the haphazard stocking of angling waters should be much more carefully controlled in the future. If we wait for the scientific proof (or otherwise) of damage to native stocks it may be too late to do anything about it.

Many Scottish salmon rivers now have farmed fish running them prior to the breeding season. Final comments on possible negative effects of caged salmon farming on wild salmonids must include the strong possibility that the Connemara sea trout stock collapse which occurred in the late 1980s/early 1990s was linked to high levels of parasitic sea lice emanating from estuarine salmon sea cages. Finnock (young sea trout) returning early to the estuaries were often plastered with these parasitic crustaceans. It is not clear, however, whether the 90 per cent of the stock which appears to have died at sea was killed by sea lice or by some other factor (such as poor body condition or difficult acclimation to salt water, changed marine feeding conditions due to warm weather or perhaps to an unidentified disease).

Salmon farmers use a pesticide called Nuvan to treat sea lice infestations and this chemical may have damaging effects on commercially important crustaceans such as crabs and lobsters living in the vicinity of the cages. Finally, antibiotics are widely administered to caged fish and these may remain in the environment for fairly long periods, possibly having deleterious effects. Perhaps the recent development of offshore deepwater cages which are scoured clean by strong Atlantic currents will provide a better basis for this form of fish culture in the future.

Brown Trout and Sea Trout, *Salmo trutta*

Habitat

The trout occurs in many types of both running and still-water habitats; brown trout and sea trout combined represent the most important game fishing species over Europe as a whole. Only the rainbow trout rivals the brown in importance worldwide. The natural range of *Salmo trutta* runs from Iceland to Afghanistan; towards the southern limits (south Europe, Near East) it lives in cool mountain lakes and streams. North Africa's Atlas mountains have the most southerly natural populations. Widespread introductions have taken brown trout worldwide to North America (40 states and some Canadian provinces), South America and offshore islands (Falklands), Australia and New Zealand, Africa and India. Sea trout run most U.K. and Scandinavian rivers and some Atlantic European rivers down to Portugal. The Baltic, Caspian, Aral and Black seas also have sea trout populations. Naturalised sea trout runs, often derived from stocked browns, now provide valuable fisheries in the Maritime Provinces of Canada (Quebec, Nova Scotia, New Brunswick), southern Patagonia and the Falklands where 15–20 lb fish are commonplace, growing fat on a diet of krill. In Tasmania and New Zealand sea trout are abundant and routinely sold with chipped potatoes as take away meals; a superior form of 'fish and chips'.

North-western Europe was glaciated around 12,000 years ago, with the retreating ice sheets leaving pristine lakes and river systems, ripe for colonisation by fish, including sea trout migrating inland from the brackish coastal waters. Trout must have been very widely distributed in the immediate post-glacial period, living in cool, relatively unproductive waters throughout the south of the British Isles and following the retreating ice sheet northwards.

As the climate warmed and various water systems increased in fertility, many habitats must have become gradually less favourable for salmonids and more suitable for cyprinid species. This process continues today with eutrophication and abstraction coupled with the potential climatic change predicted from 'global warming' serving to limit further the distribution of salmonids in Britain. The habitats occupied by trout cover a wide range, from (artificially stocked) lowland reservoirs to acid bog lochans, and from mountain streams to lowland limestone rivers. In upland waters much of the trout's food comes from overhead branches (for example, alder sawfly caterpillars) or is blown on to the water from surrounding pasture and moorland (for example craneflies and beetles). The upland stream beds have sparse populations of stonefly, caddisfly and mayfly nymphs, snails and shrimps.

The population structure and growth strategies of trout stocks are very variable and poorly understood. Large nutrient-poor lakes usually harbour slow-growing, late-maturing (4–5 years) trout which may live into their teens or, in exceptional circumstances, 20 years plus. Large fish-eating individuals (*Ferox*) can be particularly long-lived. Generally it seems that the longer the period spent as a parr/fingerling in the nursery stream, the longer the lifetime of the adult fish. Upland peaty lakes often have abundant 'stunted' trout which may mature at 2–3 years and live for up to five years, achieving weights of barely one pound. Short-lived trout also occur, however, in very productive alkaline streams and lakes.

Where chalk downland produces numerous springs at ground level these aquifers can coalesce to form braided chalk streams which support some of the world's most famous brown trout fisheries such as the rivers Itchen and Test. The key features of the chalk stream environment are an alkaline ('hard') water chemistry and a steady flow of very clear water at a relatively constant temperature which cushions the ecosystem from summer highs and winter lows.

The rivers Test, Itchen and upper Hampshire Avon are all well-known chalk streams. A thriving aquatic plant community, dominated by water crowfoot (*Ranunculus*) and starwort (*Callitriche*) provides an abundance of homes for various invertebrates. In the rich organic silt trapped by the plant roots burrow mayfly (*Ephemera danica*) nymphs and alder fly (*Sialis*) larvae. On the riverbed, shrimps (*Gammarus pulex*), caddis larvae (both cased and caseless), other species of mayfly nymph, snails and midge larvae abound. On the plants live countless reed-smut larvae, mayfly nymphs, snails and many species of chironomid (midge) larvae. All of these animals provide food for the trout and grayling finning in the clear waters. The trout's chalk stream habitat is also shared by bullheads, minnows, stone loach, lampreys and eels, as well as pike, perch and various cyprinids in slower-flowing sections. The total weight (and annual production) of bullheads and other small fish can easily exceed that of the trout.

In recent years, winter droughts have combined with bore-hole abstractions to produce chronic low-flows in most chalk streams in the south of England. This damages trout habitat through the following processes:

1. Loss of insect-rich crowfoot (*Ranunculus*) beds and increased growth of blanket weed.
2. Reduced nursery areas in dried-up winterbournes.
3. Silting of spawning gravels causing egg and alevin deaths.
4. Increased pollution concentrations and water temperature, reduced dissolved oxygen concentrations.

Streams which have been particularly badly affected include the Allen, Piddle, Wallop Brook, Wey, Darent, Pang and Misbourne. All of these rivers have dwindling stocks of wild brown trout and rely increasingly on stocked hatchery brown and rainbow trout to sustain the high angling pressure.

The complex and variable life cycle of the trout

Some trout complete their life cycle in freshwater streams and lakes (brown trout), whilst others drop downstream to spend a period feeding in estuaries ('slob' trout), and a third category have a full migratory phase, becoming smolts, descending the rivers and living for a period in the sea (sea trout). All three forms can occur in the same system together and in winter on the gravel-bedded spawning grounds in the headwaters they may often inter-breed. Sea trout seem to prefer spawning and nursery areas in unproductive acid catchments where food availability for fry and parr is very limited. It has been suggested that this is why the parr (especially females), smoltify and migrate to sea where they can grow and mature on the rich marine food supply before returning to breed. Brown trout, which remain permanently in freshwater, live in both acid (for example peaty lochs) and richer alkaline waters (for example limestone rivers and chalk streams). Growth depends critically upon food supply and water temperature; sexual maturity is attained more quickly in rich and warm southern waters than colder, poor, acid upland lakes and streams. Perhaps the 'migratory genes' are present in all trout populations but are only activated when environmental conditions mean that individuals will have a better chance of growing to maturity by migrating to sea. Brown trout stocked into acid rivers in the Falkland Islands where there is rich offshore feeding (krill) have given rise to perhaps the best sea trout fisheries in the world.

In many sea trout populations the majority of migrating fish are females; they need to grow larger than males of the same age to produce large numbers of eggs. Large eggs produce large fry which probably survive better than small ones. The smaller males often remain behind in freshwater as brown trout and then try to sneak in and fertilise eggs in competition with cock sea trout on the spawning beds. A direct parallel with the salmon.

Trout have the capacity to home to their natal streams, using a combination of visual and chemical (smell) cues. This is vital in an evolutionary sense because only a relatively few rivers provide suitable salmonid spawning habitat and, therefore, it is important for the success of a breeding attempt that sea trout do not ascend the 'wrong' river very often to spawn. Local stocks tend to become adapted to their own rivers and are often of a characteristic size, shape and colour. All populations produce 'wanderers' which investigate other river systems and must occasionally found new stocks. Peter Maitland has estimated that there are somewhat less than 1000 separate sea trout stocks and several thousand brown trout stocks in the British Isles; trout therefore represent a valuable genetic resource which merits careful conservation. Very many, if not most, of our trout populations have been adulterated by stocked fish so that few now remain genetically pure.

Our native trout is a tremendously variable species, with recent genetic research showing that even within a single lake system, more than one separate breeding population (i.e. stock) can occur. In Lough Melvin, which straddles the border between the Republic of Ireland and Northern Ireland, Andrew Ferguson of Queen's University Belfast has identified three genetically distinct forms/races/species of trout. Ferguson and co-workers now regard each form as constituting a separate sub-species of *Salmo trutta* because of their reproductive isolation and distinctive looks. As he points out in his excellent scientific writings, even a small degree of inter-breeding would lead to relative genetic uniformity and this is clearly not the case. The Lough Melvin salmonid community is a rarity in Britain today, representing a relatively undisturbed ecosystem which contains a high diversity of specialised trout as well as Arctic charr and salmon. Surely it should be given a high conservation status and legal protection which forbids the wholesale stocking of either farmed brown or rainbow trout or coarse species such as pike.

The Lough Melvin trout populations include the following forms:

The Sonaghen *(Salmo trutta nigripinnis)* is an open-water form with a light/silvery background colouration, many large black spots and a few small red spots. The fins have a dark brown/ black pigmentation (hence the name *nigripinnis*) especially the elongate pectorals. Sonaghen spawn in the numerous small eastern inflowing streams and drop back down into the main lake to mature. During this phase of the life cycle they feed in open water on zooplankton (*Daphnia*) and the pupae of midges (chironomids and *Chaoborus*, the Phantom midge) as they rise up through the water column prior to emergence.

Gillaroo *(Salmo trutta stomachius)* have numerous large red spots especially below the lateral line and a background golden-yellow colouration (these fish are known locally as 'red fellows'). This may allow the fish to blend into the shallow, gravel bedded areas of the lake where they feed on benthic invertebrates including snails, caddis larvae and shrimps. The Latin name *stomachius* refers to the thickened wall of the upper gut which seems to be adapted to a diet of snails. Gillaroo spawn in the western outflowing River Drowes catchment, away from the Sonaghen spawning grounds.

Ferox (Salmo trutta ferox), which appear to be an ancient genetic strain of *Salmo trutta* can ultimately grow to much larger sizes than the other two sub-species, living on a diet of perch, Arctic charr and trout. Ferox lack spots and can be silvery or brown in colour and they share the spawning habitat of Melvin's Atlantic salmon population in the deep, shingle-bedded sections of the largest inflowing (Glenaniff) river. Ferguson has also recorded intermediate forms of trout which may have arisen from past stockings of Scottish trout from Loch Leven.

Niall Campbell, an expert on Scottish trout populations, has studied the occurence of ferox in Scotland, concluding that the following conditions are important for their presence: (a) nutrient-poor water, (b) the presence of charr, (c) a large loch (i.e. over 100 hectares). Campbell thinks it likely that ferox specialise on a diet of charr for most of the year and on salmon smolts when seasonally available. Ferox are very long-lived (up to 20 years) and appear to grow at a similar rate to 'ordinary' brown trout for the first 5–6 years of life, before switching to a fish diet and accelerating their growth over the next 10–15 years to reach large ultimate weights of 10–15 lb or more. In contrast to the ferox of Lough Melvin (silvery, few spots) Scottish ferox from lochs Rannoch, Garry, Ness, Poulary, Shin, Awe and Ericht tend to be heavily spotted against a golden-yellow background.

Trout are carnivores, feeding initially on small insect larvae and nymphs, through a range of larger invertebrates to finally grade on to a diet which includes a varying proportion of small fish and other vertebrates. Clearly the fish component of the diet of a ferox will be considerably greater than that of a small upland stream-dwelling brown trout. Even in upland catchments, however, trout will eat fish when they are available and some fishery scientists believe that they eat significant numbers of salmon fry and parr in nursery streams. This may lead to asynchronous cycles of abundance of salmon and trout which are thought to occur in some river systems where the two species co-exist.

Salmon and trout parr can be distinguished by the following features:

Salmon parr	**Trout parr**
Pectoral fins large	Pectoral fins smaller
Upper lip extends to rear edge of pupil. Eye looks large.	Upper lip extends to rear edge of eye. Eye looks smaller.
Wrist of tail narrow.	Wrist of tail broad.
Tail fin deeply forked with pointed lobes.	Tail fin shallowly forked with rounded lobes.
Adipose, pectoral and pelvic fins grey.	Adipose fin tinged red, pectoral and pelvic fins orange/yellow.
Dorsal fin 10-12 rays.	Dorsal fin 8-10 rays.
Overall shape slim. Body with sparse small spots.	Overall shape stocky. Body usually heavily spotted.

Territoriality in young trout

Most trout (save for those which are spawned on gravel-bedded lake shores) emerge from the spawning redds to start feeding in a small unproductive upland stream or a rich chalk winterbourne. At this stage in the life cycle, the fish soon become aggressively territorial, defending small feeding stations which they constantly patrol. In this way the strongest individuals exclude weaker fry from the best feeding positions in the stream and the fry spread out to occupy all available habitat. At least, this is the case where spawning adults have produced enough surviving fry. Fry emerge from the gravel and start to feed any time from March to May depending on the location of the stream (earlier in the year further south and at lower altitudes).

In Lake District streams, larger individuals occupy positions of shelter behind stones whilst smaller weaker fish are kept in shallow backwaters by aggressive chases from the larger fish. It has been shown in Canadian laboratory experiments that rainbow trout territory sizes and aggression levels are directly related to the level of food available, i.e. when food is abundant, territories are small and aggression is low. When food is scarce the young trout defend large territories very aggressively, chasing off all intruders. It seems likely that this system holds true, to a greater or lesser degree, for all species of stream-dwelling salmonids. More territories occur where there are rocks and boulders which shield adjacent fish from each other's view; and where the current is strong when the fish have to lie close to the riverbed, tending not to see each other from as far away as in gentler currents.

David Le Cren, who pioneered the study of territoriality in brown trout fry and parr in Black Brows Beck near Windermere, demonstrated neatly with field experiments that survival is *density-dependent*. This means that at higher population densities a greater proportion of fish die, so that despite stocking at a range of densities (numbers per square metre) at the beginning of his experiments, most stream sections ended up with around seven trout parr per square metre after six months.

In the highest-density areas, trout fry were found starving to death because of intense competition for feeding territories. At low population densities young trout grow more quickly, probably because of the extra food available and the reduced number of energy-demanding aggressive encounters with near neighbours. It is worth noting that larger, one- and two-year-old trout will tolerate the presence of fry and parr within their large feeding territories. This is probably because these small fish feed on different prey than the adult fish and so do not pose a direct threat to their survival.

Malcolm Elliott followed David Le Cren's work to conduct a long-term study of the Cumbrian Black Brows Beck sea trout population. This stream is firm-bedded and does not have violent spates which disrupt the integrity of the gravel. Egg survival rates are, therefore, high. Elliott found that the number of eggs deposited was related to the subsequent survival of fry, parr and adult trout by a dome-shaped ('Ricker') curve. The optimal number of eggs in the gravel, occurring at the peak of the curve, is around 40–50 per square metre, this giving rise to seven surviving fry per square metre in May/June, falling to around two per square metre by September. Drought years are characterised by higher than normal rates of mortality in young trout. Overall, the key phase of mortality in the life cycle corresponds with the period soon after hatching when the young fish try to establish feeding territories.

This is an important study since it indicates that stocking more eggs or fry than the optimal level would lead to fewer surviving parr, rather than more. Fishing clubs which stock large numbers of trout fry in nursery streams, believing that they are giving the fishery a boost may be wrong. Between 1979-85, 1.4 million hatchery-reared sea trout fry were planted out in Welsh rivers. This practice has now been curtailed until its effectiveness and consequences for the native stocks have been assessed. Experiments conducted by Welsh NRA fisheries biologists are under way on the upper Conwy system to try and answer some of these questions.

Feeding biology

Feeding trout fry dart out from their resting lies to intercept organisms (aquatic and terrestrial insects) drifting in the current. The key food of trout up to around 6cm in length are midge pupae and larvae, Ephemeropteran (*Baetis*) nymphs, caddis larvae and other dipteran and beetle larvae and shrimps. Mayfly nymphs often dominate the stomach contents. In the second year of life the diet is similar but fewer small insects are eaten and more terrestrial insects and earthworms are taken. As trout grow larger they eat much the same groups of organisms but tend to feed more on the stream or lake bed, taking larger snails, shrimps, water lice, caddis larvae, fish and crayfish.

Malcolm Elliott showed back in 1965 that the amount of invertebrate material drifting in the Walla Brook on Dartmoor varies through the day, with a peak over the three hours after sunset. Trout feed actively at dusk and into the hours of darkness taking advantage of this increased food supply. Invertebrates such as insect nymphs and shrimps may well become more active at this time, moving up onto the surface of stones on the stream bed to graze the algae growing on their surface. At this time they are vulnerable to being swept away by the current to the trout waiting downstream. These animals are added to by the nymphs and pupae of insects which are ready to hatch and often do so in the evening and under cover of darkness. All insect species such as the mayflies *Ephemera* (very large) and *Caenis* (very small) become available in large numbers seasonally; both genera have nymphs which live concealed in or on the silt for most of the year but which swim up in the water prior to emergence at which time they are taken avidly by the trout. In many habitats, trout over-winter on a diet of shrimps and other bottom-living fauna.

The challenge of fly-fishing for trout

The brown trout rod-caught record* stands at 19 lb 9 oz (8.88kg) by J. A. F. Jackson, Loch Quoish, Inverness-shire.† Fly fishermen are well aware of the selectivity of trout rising for flies and can establish the correct pattern of artificial fly to use after sampling the stomach contents of a recently-caught fish with a marrow spoon. This procedure involves scooping out the recently-consumed insects through the mouth of a dead trout with a long, narrow shallowly-curved metal spoon. The food items sit in the bowl of the spoon and can thus be identified.

On summer evenings, both on rivers and lakes, simultaneous hatches of chironomids ('buzzers') and caddisflies ('sedges') often occur. The trout usually feed selectively on midge pupae or sedge pupae sub-surface, then on hatching midges or sedges in the surface film and finally on adult flies at the water surface. On upland streams, blackflies and stoneflies are more prevalent.

*John Gardner caught the current 'cultivated' record brown of 20 lb 3 oz from Dever Springs fishery, Hampshire in 1991.

†Alistair Thorn has just beaten this fish with a ferox of 19 lb 10 oz from Loch Awe.

Coniferous afforestation planted next to an upland salmonid stream.

Loch Lomond has a diverse fish population which includes river lamprey and powan.

An example of unsympathetic river dredging.

Crack willows, providing a range of homes for wildlife.

Riffles, runs, flats (glides) and pools.

A brown trout in its lie.

A crystal-clear chalk stream with water crowfoot and starwort beds.

An acid upland river with few large aquatic plants.

A flattened (*Ecdyonurus*) mayfly nymph adapted for life in fast waters.

A stonefly nymph, a classic upland stream insect.

Alderfly (*Sialis*) larva. (*Peter Gathercole*)

The mayfly nymph (*Ephemera danica*). (*Peter Gathercole*)

A *Lymnaea snail* grazing algae.

A newly-emerged damselfly.

A duck mussel burrowing into the gravel.

The great diving beetle (*Dytiscus marginalis*).

Mayflies (*Ephemera danica*) dun below,
spinner above.

Chironomid larvae from muddy lake bed sediments.

A common bream feeding on the lake bed.

A dragonfly nymph hunts invertebrate prey.
(*Peter Gathercole*)

A fully-spined male 3-spined stickleback.

A male 10-spined stickleback.

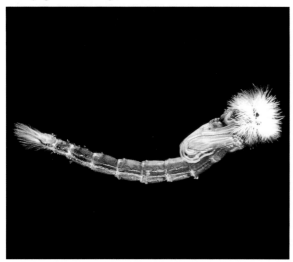

A chironomid pupa ascends towards the water surface. (*Peter Gathercole*)

A corixid (water-boatman). (*Peter Gathercole*)

An adult stonefly.

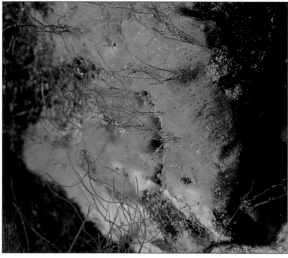

A freshwater sponge.

A cased caddisfly larva.

The water louse (*Asellus aquaticus*). (*Peter Gathercole*)

An adult chironomid midge.

Seed heads of greater reedmace.

Bur-reed.

Adult alderfly (*Sialis lutaria*).

Chum salmon with well-developed breeding livery caught on its upstream run. (*Peter Gathercole*)

Male (above) and female bullheads.

A brook trout, a species tolerant of acidic conditions. (*Peter Gathercole*)

A Twaite shad is returned to the River Severn. (*Peter Gathercole*)

A Loch Lomond powan with lamprey scar on its flank.

A cock Atlantic salmon caught on upstream migration. Note the kype developing on the lower jaw.

Vulnerable salmonid eggs and alevin lying in the gravel of a spawning stream.

A Lough Corrib grilse taken on the dapped mayfly.

A brown trout finning in the current.

The stone loach, a small species which shares the trout's habitat.

Irish lake trout (Gillaroo at top).

A marrow-spooned trout which had fed on mayflies.
(*Peter Gathercole*)

A perch shoal: food competitors and food for trout.

A brown trout from a heather moorland loch.
(*Peter Gathercole*)

Sea trout smolts.

A brace of Lake District Arctic charr (*Peter Gathercole*).

The rainbow trout, more tolerant of pollution than the brown trout.

A male grayling in spawning colours courting a female.

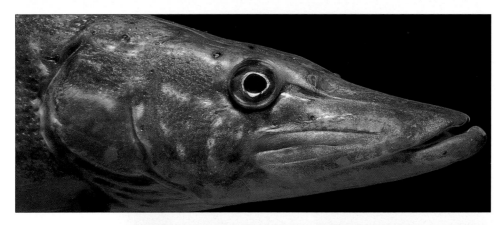

The pike: portrait of a predator.

The ruffe (or pope).

The perch, one of our most attractive fish species.

The herbivorous grass carp.

Minnows at spawning time.

A fully-scaled common carp, the ancestral form of the species.

A partially-scaled mirror carp, the fast-growing cultivated form of the species.

Koi carp, the ornamental form of the species.

The wels, a formidable predator.

Male (front) and female tench courting.

Silver bream.

A male bream, sexually mature, with spawning tubercles.

The barbel.

The gudgeon.

The freshwater shrimp, barbel food and host for parasites. (*Peter Gathercole*)

The signal crayfish.

Chub.

A shoal of roach.

An adult rudd.

Shoaling dace.

The eel.

The zander.

Each phase of feeding requires differing angling tactics if the angler is to be consistently successful. Trout are surprisingly good at distinguishing artificial from natural flies and are put off the feed by poor casting and clumsy movements. On chalk streams, you may have the added challenge of simultaneous hatches of more than one mayfly species to add to the complexity of a day's fishing. To 'match the hatch' with a well-tied artificial fly and to stalk and cast to a wily feeding fish without scaring it requires stealth, patience and skill.

When you consider that each family of flies comes in a range of sizes and colours, depending on the species living in a particular water, the challenge of imitative fly-fishing can be appreciated. Trout have very keen eyesight and can distinguish colours well, adding to the angler's difficulties. Whilst anyone can catch a trout on a worm it is a considerable 'gentleman's handicap' to fish with the fly. On most trout waters these days it is, of course, obligatory. Readers interested in angling entomology are referred to John Goddard's fine books, and that of Harris detailed in the bibliography.

In general, on lakes, surface feeding seems to be most prevalent on waters which have a limited abundance of bottom-dwelling invertebrates. This is probably because trout have a well-developed sense of caution which means that they do not venture up near the surface where they may be caught by fish-eating birds and mammals unless they are driven to through hunger or are tempted by a dense hatch of flies or a skilfully angled artificial fly.

Large trout will eat a variety of other fish including minnows, sticklebacks, roach, bream and perch fry. Perch have a very similar diet to trout and are thought to be significant food competitors in some Irish and Scottish waters; this is a complicated possibility since, whilst both perch and trout eat, for example, midge pupae and mayfly nymphs, trout also eat large numbers of perch fry and, in the end, may have a more nutritious diet where perch are present than in their absence.

Growth of Trout

The growth of trout in British waters depends largely upon the river or lake type where the fish occur and the prevailing water temperature. Water quality is directly linked to the potential for invertebrate production and hence to the trout's food supply. Alkaline waters such as limestone lakes, rivers and chalk streams which do not become too warm during the summer represent the optimal habitat for rapid growth with their abundant invertebrate populations. This point can be illustrated using data published in *The Trout* by W. E. Frost and M. E. Brown (Collins, New Naturalist 1967 appendices 3 and 4). The table on page 98 gives an estimate (back-calculated from scale readings) of the average length (in centimetres) at three years of age for brown trout from a variety of British waters. The table is split up into 'alkaline' and 'acid' water categories.

The average length of trout at three years of age from both alkaline lakes and rivers is 28–30cm, whilst that from less productive acid and rainfed systems is around 17cm. Differences in weight would, of course, be much more marked. These differences hold true for systems both in northern and southern waters although it is probably true to say that both high mountain tarns at one extreme and shallow lowland lakes at the other are sub-optimal for trout growth because of extreme temperature constraints. Water temperature is of over-riding importance for trout growth. Brown trout are known to grow slowly below 7° and above 19°C; D. R. Swift has found that brown trout grown under laboratory conditions in Lake District (Windermere) water grow fastest at

Growth of brown trout in different lakes and rivers. Average estimated length (cm.) from scale readings at three years of age.

Chalk and Limestone systems (alkaline)		*Peaty/Rainfed systems (acid)*	
Rivers			
River Test	31.2	River Dart	16.8
Hampshire Avon	28.8	River Tamar	16.5
River Lambourn	28.8	Upper Tees	12.7
River Nadder	30.0	North Esk	16.1
River Kennet	31.2	River Bela	19.7
Dorset Stour	28.8	River Forss	18.9
	average = 29.8		average = 16.7
Lakes			
Malham Tarn	27.1	Llyn Tegid	20.4
Lough Corrib	26.8	Lake Vyrnwy	16.3
Lough Rea	33.1	Windermere	20.4
Lough Derg	27.8	Ullswater	18.9
Lough Inchiquin	29.0	Haweswater	15.1
Loch Borralie	30.2	Wastwater	14.6
Loch Boisedale	22.3	Yew Tree Tarn	15.1
	average = 28.0		average = 17.25

around 12°C; Malcolm Elliott recorded figures of 13-14°C. This figure will seldom be reached in mountain tarns but will usually be exceeded during summer in lowland lakes. Trout living in differing temperature regimes probably acclimate and adapt to the local conditions and thus may have differing temperatures for optimal growth.

Water temperature controls the growth rate of brown trout rigidly; cold-blooded animals have their metabolic rate determined almost totally by the environmental temperature. A further effect on trout growth potential, as suggested by the table above, is added by the water chemistry of the lake or river which determines plant and invertebrate production levels. In nutrient-poor upland waters many fishery managers have been tempted to try and boost productivity by using plant fertilisers.

Fertilising lakes to boost trout growth potential

Alkaline waters are characteristically much more productive than acid waters and much research has been done to try and improve trout growth rates by fertilising oligotrophic waters. Acid bog lakes with peaty turbid waters are often limed (with ground limestone) to increase the pH (a measure of acidity where 7 is neutral, above 7 being alkaline and below 7 acid). When the water chemistry has been adjusted in this way, the subsequent addition of phosphorus (chemical symbol 'P') as 'superphosphate' can greatly boost algal and weed growth and so produce more invertebrates and fatter trout. In sandy-bedded lakes, which lack the large reservoir of nutrients stored in muddy sediments, it is also wise to add nitrogen (N) in a ratio of 1:2, P:N.

N. C. Morgan found that the numbers of invertebrates, particularly the chironomid larvae, on the bed of an oligotrophic Scottish loch increased by up to 25 times after limestone was applied. This increase took two years to develop, presumably via increased algal and then invertebrate growth. Trout growth improved markedly and might have been even better if forage species such as *Gammarus, Asellus* and the snail *Limnaea pereger* had been introduced after the limestone had made the lakes more suitable for their survival. It is necessary to maintain the input of limestone from year to year to sustain an improved trout growth rate.

Despite the fact that anglers will be keen to improve the growth rates of trout in their waters, it should be remembered that oligotrophic lakes and rivers are now becoming less common in Britain due to eutrophication effects from agricultural and other human inputs. The conservation value of a given low-nutrient water should be professionally assessed before any fertilisation trials are carried out. It is also possible to jump to the wrong conclusion concerning the nutrient-status of a water simply by looking at the growth rate of the trout.

Niall Campbell has pointed out that nutrient-poor lochs with a restricted amount of gravel-bedded spawning streams can support low densities of relatively large trout, whilst either limestone or acid lochs with numerous spawning streams can be overcrowded with high densities of small, slow-growing trout which are competing strongly for the available food supply. The overall growth rate of trout in such latter waters can be increased by limiting the numbers of fry produced in the feeder streams. Campbell has shown that this can be achieved by severely limiting the access of adult trout to spawning streams. Clearly, ideally, a scientific appraisal of a fishery including studies of trout growth, survival, abundance and exploitation in addition to investigating the invertebrate food supply is required before action is taken to change the fishing through management.

Spawning migrations and breeding behaviour

The evolution of the sea trout may have been a response to poor feeding conditions in freshwater habitats whereby trout parr initially dropped downstream to the estuary to feed as slob trout and subsequently developed the ability to survive fully marine conditions. Conversely salmonids may have penetrated freshwaters from the sea and thus have marine origins. We do not know.

Typically, sea trout spend two-three years as parr in the river, turning into smolts at a length of 14–20cm. Smolt age seems to increase with latitude. The seaward smolt run usually peaks in May, sea trout smolts are stockier than salmon smolts and often have brown/yellow backs and yellow fins. Where inflowing rivers enter large lakes a similar downstream migration of small brown trout occurs, paralleling the sea trout movements but within freshwater. These trout then grow on and mature within the confines of the lake.

The best of the Atlantic sea trout rivers tend to be acidic and relatively unproductive, with low numbers of aquatic invertebrates. Whilst at sea, sea trout smolts feed on planktonic crustaceans and then grade on to the abundant supply of sand eels, sprats, small herrring, shrimps, prawns, crabs and other items, growing rapidly.

Some sea trout return to their natal (or other) rivers at the end of the first summer in the sea; these fish may or may not be mature and are known as whitling or finnock. Other individuals overwinter in the sea, growing from small smolts to 2-lb fish after two years. Individuals which spend longer at sea grow to large sizes and often undergo several successful spawning migrations. In Sweden, sea trout of over 30 lb have been taken by rod fishermen from the River Em, and the famous Morrum River often produces double figure sea trout with a rod-caught record of 33 lb. Robin Ade cites the capture of a giant Caspian sea trout of 125 lb; they are occasionally caught in European commercial nets up to 60 lb but U.K. fish very rarely weigh more than 20 lb. Sea-run rainbow trout ('steelheads') grow more quickly, reaching 5–12 lb after two years of sea feeding in the Pacific Ocean.

The majority of sea trout smolts are female and this is also true of the returning mature fish . . . these then often spawn with resident male brown trout to produce a mixture of trout, some of which stay in freshwater for their whole lives whilst others migrate. It is worth noting also that female sea trout crossed with male sea trout in hatcheries can give rise to both brown trout (which do not turn into smolts) and sea trout. Adult sea trout in freshwater feed very little in spate rivers but eat rather more in productive waters such as alkaline Hebridean machair lochs. It has been pointed out by Hugh Falkus that if adult sea trout returning to spate rivers did feed avidly they would denude the natal stream of all fry, parr and flies in no time!

Marine migration and sea fisheries

Whilst salmon undergo long marine feeding migrations (for example, to Greenland) sea trout appear to be more coastal in their distribution, although east coast British fish appear to roam farther afield than west coast fish. Shoals have been located around the East Anglian coast, off the Netherlands and in the English Channel between the Isle of Wight and Land's End. Some tagged individuals are known to have travelled over 200 miles over a period of several months. Eastern river fish appear to migrate southwards down to East Anglia as smolts and then continue around the North Sea in a counter-clockwise direction to return eventually to their natal rivers. There is an important coastal fishery for salmon and sea trout in the north-east (the Northumbrian fishery) but this is to be phased out gradually in the future as a conservation measure.

The Northumbrian coastal sea trout commercial net fishery has produced, on average, nearly 30,000 fish per annum over the past 20 years with an average weight of 4–5 lb. The shores of the Orkneys and Shetland Islands and the west coasts of mainland Scotland and Ireland also hold good sea trout stocks. In Wales the rivers provide excellent sea trout fishing for specimen fish with 20,000 rod-caught fish per annum reported in the early 1980s. Over the period 1976-87, 5417 sea trout of 6 lb or over were taken by anglers. Peak rod catches occur in July, August and September. The Welsh rod-caught sea trout totals are roughly comparable with those from the whole of Ireland, 50 per cent higher than those for England and only 40 per cent less than the Scottish catch. The British record sea trout was netted at Northam on the River Tweed in 1987; it weighed 28 lb 9 oz (nearly 13kg). Samuel Burgoyne caught the rod record from Scotland's River Leven in 1989, it weighed 22 lb 8 oz (10.2kg).

Finnock (trout which have been at sea for only three to four months) usually run back up into freshwater over the summer (July-September); in some rivers larger sea trout tend to run in May or June whilst in others large runs occur as late as October. Sea trout have very variable activity patterns. Whilst sea trout can and usually do home to their natal streams or even a particular stretch in that stream in some rivers (such as the Axe in Devon) quite a few fish also go 'astray'. Finnock often spend time at least in the estuarial reaches if not further upstream in rivers other than their natal ones.

David Solomon has followed the migrations of radio-tagged sea trout in the River

Fowey, Cornwall, finding that fish will run upstream at night even under low-medium river flows but will continue to migrate through the day after freshets (small spates). Sea trout are much more willing to run under low-water conditions than salmon. Once they were in the river fish moved 4–8km upstream within 1–10 days; after this initial long run they held up in secure lies near the mouths of inflowing streams for up to 79 days. Salmon and sea trout returning from the sea have a high flesh fat content which is gradually used up over a period of several months in freshwater during their spawning activities until the spent fish are emaciated and attempt to survive the sea-ward return run as kelts.

There is growing evidence that all is not well with sea trout stocks in the British Isles. Over the last 40 years the (declared) north-west Scottish coast commercial catch has steadily dropped from around 10,000 fish per annum in 1950 to just over 4000 fish in 1988 and 1989. Over this period the (declared) rod catch has dropped from around 3000 in the 1950s to 500 or less in the late 1980s. It has to be said that the level of reporting of sea trout catches must be very low to see totals of only 500 for such a large area. In the Republic of Ireland there has been a recent collapse of the finnock-based sea trout rod fisheries along the north-west coastline, raising much concern for the future.

The Connemara and south Mayo sea trout population crash.
Whilst sea trout catches from many British rivers reached lows during the hot summers of 1989 and 1990 the Irish west coast fisheries suffered unprecedented crashes over a wide area, with many famous fisheries giving up fishing altogether and leaving the boats in the hay lofts. The economic repercussions in this rural area are serious. At the time of writing (summer 1992) there are some signs of a stock recovery, with greater numbers of sea trout running the rivers once again.

Research co-ordinated by Ken Whelan and Russel Poole at Ireland's Salmon Research Agency laboratory at Burrishoole suggests that, in freshwater, parr and smolts were stressed by drought, high temperatures and, perhaps, acidification whilst, in the marine phase of the life cycle sea trout were stressed by high temperatures, toxic algal blooms and plagues of parasitic sea lice (originating from salmon farm sea cages).

Most of these west coast fish return as yearlings and whilst normal numbers of smolts went to sea in the late eighties very few returned to spawn. Those few fish which did make it back were often thin and emaciated, indicating a possible breakdown in the marine food chain. Some people have linked this with the large commercial sand eel fishery which has operated in the north Atlantic off Shetland in recent years, but recent climatic variations may also have caused subtle changes in marine ecosystems. Poor breeding performance in north Atlantic sea bird colonies in the eighties have also indicated a breakdown in the normal food supply; many of these birds (Arctic terns, puffins, kittiwakes) are sand eel feeders.

Another popular theory to explain the sea trout decline is that the increasing numbers of sea-cage fish farms used for salmon rearing are interfering with the biology of the wild sea trout in coastal waters perhaps via increased parasite (sea lice) burdens or disease.

The latest findings (spring 1991) suggest that a variety of environmental stresses in freshwater may be leading to the production of smolts which are poorly adapted to survive the stress of changing from a freshwater existence to life in the sea. Many fish seem to de-smoltify and return to freshwater whilst others remain in the brackish estuaries to live as 'slob' trout. Those fish which do go to sea are growing very slowly and many are dying at sea during the spring and summer. Overall, the Burrishoole sea trout population has declined steadily from 1976 and collapsed in 1989 and 1990. This is thought to be due to habitat degradation, including increases in siltation of spawning gravels by soil erosion and peat extraction, removal of gravel from streams and, perhaps the most insidious factor, increased acidification.

Acidification of freshwaters

Both brown trout and sea trout have suffered population declines due to a wide range of environmental effects, perhaps the most important of which has been the recent increase in acidification of their habitats. Upland waters often run over hard igneous rock (such as granite) which is largely insoluble and releases very few base metal ions such as calcium and magnesium. These ions are released in large amounts by the soluble basic rocks marble, chalk and limestone. Where watersheds are base-poor, any acidic rain which falls upon them is not fully neutralised and eventually increases the acid inputs into the rivers. Pure rain water saturated with carbon dioxide is acid anyway (pH 5.6; neutral = 7) but industrial pollution (coal-fired power stations) and vehicle exhausts produce large quantities of nitrogenous and sulphurous gases which dissolve in rain to make it much more acidic than this. Some rain falling from polluted airstreams is as acid as vinegar and will burn holes in nylon stockings hanging on washing lines!

Rain of this nature falling onto a chalk downland or limestone escarpment is rapidly neutralised; the acidic oxides of nitrogen and sulphur reacting with the rock to form harmless calcium and magnesium nitrates and sulphates. However, where acidic rain falls on base-poor rock it is not fully neutralised and it also releases other metals such as aluminium, copper, lead and zinc. These metals in solution are very toxic to aquatic life including trout and especially trout eggs and fry living in or on the bed of upland streams. When the water is below pH 5.5 and is low in calcium and high in aluminium and heavy metals, trout (and salmon) eggs and fry are killed outright. Fry trying to hatch are unable to rupture their egg membranes, possibly because the enzyme which helps them to break through is inactivated in very acidic (less than pH 4.5) conditions. The embryos are, therefore, entombed in their eggs and quickly die. Hugh Falkus describes the devastation which 'acid rain' brought to the sea trout stocks of the Cumbrian Esk in his book *Falkus and Bullers Freshwater Fishing* (1975, 1988, Stanley Paul, London). The watersheds in southern Norway have also suffered dreadfully from this form of pollution, much of which, sadly, probably originated in Britain.

Where conifer plantations have been established in upland water catchments acidification problems are made worse by the ability of the trees to collect and concentrate both wet and dry acidic depositions and release them into the surface waters. Furthermore, maritime westerly winds carry high concentrations of sodium ions which displace hydrogen ions (i.e. 'acid') from peaty soils. This means that coniferous afforestation can acidify rivers and lakes in regions where there is no significant industrial pollution but where the prevailing winds come from the sea. The west of Ireland, especially fisheries based on the blanket peat bogs of Connemara and south Mayo, appears to be suffering severely from this form of damage. This is in contrast to the main acid-damaged regions in England, Scotland and Wales, where atmospheric pollution appears to be the main source of acidifying material.

These harmful effects are in addition to the significant negative effects on salmonid stream communities caused by siltation, changes in water flow and stream shading arising from the planting and subsequent growth of coniferous woodlands. Many fisheries scientists are convinced that the blanket coniferous afforestation of upland regions in the northern hemisphere is having profound negative effects upon salmon and trout stocks in streams, rivers and lakes. Sadly, the last bastions of British wild trout stocks survive in the very areas where conifer planting has been in tax-assisted vogue in recent years.

When acid rain falls upon snowfields it is locked up in the ice to be released as a flush of acid water during the spring thaw at the very time when salmonid eggs are present and hatching. Southern Norway and Sweden have lost hundreds of salmonid populations due to acid deposition, as have Canada and the U.S.A. The damage so far in Britain has not been quite as severe as that in Scandinavia although Galloway in Scotland, upland regions of mid- and north Wales and the English Pennines have been markedly affected, losing many trout and one or two Arctic charr populations.

Loch Grannoch in Galloway suffered a large reduction in brown trout and an extinction of Arctic charr after the afforestation of its catchment. Peter Maitland feels that the trout will disappear too when the forest canopy grows over the single remaining viable spawning stream. Care is needed, however, in blaming forestry completely since studies of acid-sensitive phytoplankton (diatom) remains in the sediments of Galloway lakes show that acidification was evident before coniferous afforestation took place. Conifer plantations exacerbate the problems by absorbing acidic mist which often clothes these upland regions. Niall Campbell has suggested that an early sign of acidification in upland loch trout populations is the frequent occurrence of tail fin deformities in adult fish. An analysis of old records has shown that Scottish lochs where trout have developed deformed tails (with in-turned fin rays) are undergoing acidification which leads to the decline and ultimate extinction of the fish population. Consequently tail deformities (such as those found by Maitland and Campbell in trout from Galloway and the Isle of Islay) may herald the demise of these populations unless remedial action is taken.

Loch Fleet in Galloway lost its brown trout in a similar fashion but the catchment has subsequently been treated with crushed limestone to reduce the elevated acidity and restocked brown trout have spawned successfully in an inflowing burn. Time will tell whether this rehabilitation has been successful in the long-term. Anglers' catch records have often been a good indicator that all is not well in acidified lakes . . . classically the catch rate per angler-day declines steadily because of the lack of young fish recruiting into the fished population and the average weight increases due to reduced food competition between the surviving fish and the lack of small year classes contributing to the bag. This happened in the Penrhyncoch lakes of mid-Wales and at Llyn Conwy.

In September 1984, 117 fresh-run salmon and sea trout were killed in the Afon Glaslyn during a spate when the water pH was 5.4–5.9 and aluminium concentrations were high. The Welsh region NRA scientists are investigating the possibility of stocking these and other affected waters with strains of acid-resistant trout taken from lakes with naturally high acidity levels. This is a good example of the value of conserving the genetic diversity of wild brown trout stocks for use in the future.

Trout breeding biology

Where habitat quality is still good enough and fortunately this is true for the vast majority of Ireland, Scotland, Wales and most of England, brown trout spawn in the headstreams of river and lake systems in November or December. In some streams (for example, the Derwent) spawning can be as late as February. The ovaries and testes develop over the summer, maturing by late autumn by which time the ovaries can represent up to 20 per cent of the female's body weight. Brown trout which live in lakes and large rivers undergo a pre-spawning migration upstream to headwaters, this often starts in August and continues through to October. Trout will often congregate around the mouth of an inflowing stream until a spate triggers them to move upstream onto the spawning beds.

Spawning usually commences when the water temperature first drops to 6–7°C. Coarse gravel beds are selected, but not those which have turbulent current flows. Female trout assess the water flow and gravel particle size such that the redds dug with sweeps of the tail fin will have a stream of cool, well-oxygenated water flowing through them, carrying away any silt which might otherwise settle on the eggs. Siltation of trout spawning beds (from forestry activity for example) represents a severe threat to the survival of eggs and alevins through fungal infections and low oxygen levels.

Sexually mature male trout develop a hooked lower jaw ('kype') and a dark colouration on the throat and belly. They fight for the attentions of the females which move onto the spawning beds when they are ready to shed their eggs. Females dig a succession of nest hollows, moving progressively upstream. They judge the depth of their excavations by lowering the anal fin into the depression. Males and females pair up and the male quivers against the female to stimulate her to release her eggs. The spawning sequence is, therefore, essentially identical to that of salmon. A large fecund trout may lay around 200 eggs in each of two or three nests to form a single large redd. This can take up to an hour and a half. The time taken for the eggs to hatch is temperature-dependent: 100 days at 5°C, 60 days at 8°, 41 days at 10°, and 27 days at 12°. Brown trout mend well after spawning and often survive to breed again for several years in succession.

Stocking . . . pros and cons

Stocking fish is an activity steeped in history. In both North America and Fennoscandia many upland lakes have been deliberately stocked either with trout or charr, sometimes several centuries ago. In Norway many high altitude lakes contain either brown trout or Arctic charr and many of these populations are due to early transplantations: a twelfth-century runestone inscription reads *Ailifr algr bar fiska i Raudsio*, which translates as 'Ailifr carried fish into lake Rausjo'. It is customary for Laplanders to carry fish (usually Arctic charr) from one lake to another to secure future food supplies during the long annual migrations from the coastal forests to the mountains. Both charr and trout preserve well by smoking and are thus valuable food sources. There are still many 'barren' lakes in Norway, Sweden and North America but there is continuous activity to fill them with fish.

The stocking of angling waters is now taken as a matter of course where angling pressure outstrips the capacity of the fishery to maintain the stock. Trout fishermen seem also to have increasing expectations of the number and size of fish which they can take home at the end of the day. Stocking may reduce the pressure on native stocks where the introduced fish are more readily caught than wild fish. However, when farmed stock fish are introduced into a native population in large numbers there is a real danger that many will survive to inter-breed with native fish and dilute the locally-adapted genetic stock. This could have serious repercussions for the long-term survival of the original locally adapted trout stock.

In a recent review of the status of wild trout in the British Isles I found that the vast majority of lowland brown trout fisheries are now dependent upon the stocking of hatchery fish for the provision of sport. You have to go a long way north and west (north Wales, Cumbria, Highlands and Islands of Scotland and the west of Ireland) to find many truly wild brown trout fisheries. It is surprising, however, how many highland lochs have been stocked at one time or another in the past. There may now be relatively few large (greater than 50 acres) lochs that have never been stocked with trout.

It is not clear at present whether damage to trout habitats or overfishing is the principal force driving fishery managers towards put-and-take systems. I strongly believe that a widely-adopted voluntary catch-and-release philosophy could make a real contribution both to brown and sea trout conservation.

Experience of catch-and-release over the past 30 years in the U.S.A. has shown that, when stocking is stopped, wild trout populations increase greatly, and abundant stocks of large wild trout are rapidly established. Anglers visiting the Madison River in Yellowstone Park, Montana can see the success of catch-and-release for themselves: wild rainbow trout populations were reduced when stock fish were released and recovered again four years after stocking was discontinued. The recovery of the wild trout stock density was over 1000 per cent (868 per cent in terms of biomass or weight) indicating the degree to which wild trout can be supressed by stocking. During the stocking period, of course, the overall density of trout in the stream was maintained by the frequent introduction of hatchery fish so that trout were always plentiful. The Game Conservancy Wild Trout research project (Fordingbridge, Hampshire) is presently researching the benefits of catch-and-release trout fishing on lowland English chalk streams.

Trout population geneticists such as Andrew Ferguson stress the folly of the widespread introduction of farmed brown trout into natural waters with little regard for the consequences. A good maxim to follow is that local parental brood stock (50 adults of each sex) should be used to produce fish to stock a given fishery. Ideally the hatchery should be adjacent to the river/lake and run on a water supply from the natural system.

Martin O'Grady of the Central Fisheries Board of Ireland is of the opinion that stocked brown trout seldom survive long in Irish loughs, probably because of their inability to compete with the large native stocks. He has found, however, that fish stocked in the spring can survive and adapt, apparently becoming like the native trout. Where large numbers are stocked, a small proportion will compete successfully for space on the spawning beds; O'Grady estimates that such fish now contribute something less than 5 per cent to the breeding stocks of Loughs Owel and Sheelin.

In Wales Richard Cresswell has calculated that 17 per cent (519km) of the fishable rivers is supported by supplemental stocking. These stretches are mainly in the industrialised areas of the Usk/Taff, Gower, Dee and Clwyd regions. Stocking of brown trout is very uncommon in Gwynedd and west Wales. On the stocked rivers of south-east Wales Cresswell states that less than 1 per cent of the stocked fish contribute to the catch in the season after stocking and most benefit is short-term in the four to five weeks after the introduction. On average, a total of only 50 per cent of stock fish are (declared) caught by anglers on rivers (effectively doubling the price of the fish). Of more than 10,000 tagged brown trout released into south Wales' rivers only one was reported caught . . . as a sea trout in a north Wales river!

On river systems where trout stock declines have occurred it seems best, where possible, to improve the production of wild fish through water quality and habitat improvements rather than topping up the populations with farmed fish. Stillwater trout fisheries can be restocked more successfully but care (and more research) is needed so as not to damage indigenous stocks where they are present.

The widespread stocking of rainbow trout requires serious scientific study to ascertain the effects of the practice on our native fish fauna. At present in Britain we release hundreds of thousands of rainbow trout each year with seemingly no regard for the brown trout or other species which could be drastically affected through food competition, predation, aggression, disease, parasitism and other unknown factors.

Pike and other fish in trout fisheries

Richard Mann, who studied the fish communities of chalk streams for many years, based at the River Laboratory in Wareham, Dorset, has pointed out how little is really known about the inter-relationships of trout and other species. It is traditional to electro-fish out and kill grayling, dace and chub from chalk stream trout fisheries because they are thought to compete with the trout for food . . . but is this necessary or even desirable? Mann describes how, over a 10-year period around 50,000 fish (mostly grayling) were removed from a 9.6-km. section of the River Wylye without any obvious change in the numbers of trout caught by anglers. Why kill so many prime fish when there is so little evidence to justify it? It may be that on some lowland English streams the invertebrate food supply is limiting the performance of the trout fishery but, to the best of my knowledge, this remains to be demonstrated.

Perch are also thought to compete for food with trout but, as mentioned before, trout can benefit from feeding on perch fry. In 1976 'perch disease' killed around 98 per cent of the Windermere perch population but despite this major stock reduction and the slow subsequent recovery of the population, Windermere trout do not appear to have made a spectacular increase in number or size. Anglers have, however, reported better trout fishing in recent years. The autumn-spawning Arctic charr population of the north basin of Lake Windermere has increased dramatically (6–8 fold) from the mid 1950s to the present day, but this is almost certainly due to the long term removal of large pike from the water. In Irish loughs such as Corrib and Mask, pike were routinely gill-netted for many years in an effort to improve the trout fishing and the policy was generally thought worthwhile; in recent years, however, not enough staff have been available to man the nets. Richard Mann concludes similarly that on chalk stream trout fisheries pike represent a significant risk to the survival of takeable trout. On one Hampshire Avon stretch the adult pike population density was reduced to about half by spring and autumn electro-fishing sessions. This resulted in fewer trout being eaten by pike and the angling club saving money on the cost of stocking the water. Mann notes that the food consumption of pike is often overestimated; to maintain condition an adult pike needs 0.815 times its body weight annually. To gain a kilo weight the pike needs to eat a further 5 kilos of fish. A 9-kg pike which grows to 11.5kg in a year therefore needs to eat 20kg of food (or about 45 stockable trout!). It seems likely, therefore, that pike control is worthwhile, both on rivers and on the put-and-take reservoir fisheries such as Grafham and Rutland water; the most cost-effective method being springtime gill- or fyke-netting when pre-spawning pike congregate around inflowing streams. Alternatively, the pike predation on trout can be tolerated and an income derived through selling pike fishing tickets. This income could offset the cost of trout lost via the pike predation, and provide fishing for a second group of anglers each season.

Rainbow/Steelhead Trout, *Oncorhynchus mykiss*
Identification, related species and habitats

The rainbow is recognisable as a trout by its salmonid adipose fin, and distinguished from the brown trout by its carmine-red lateral stripe and heavily spotted tail fin. The natural range of the species extends from the Kuskokwim River in Alaska, down through British Columbia (with the famous 'Kamloops' strain) and the eastern seaboard United States (especially the Columbia River catchment) south to Baja, California (and upland rivers of the Sierra Nevada) and the rivers of the Mexican Pacific coastal plain. Because of extensive stocking and transfer programmes (starting in California in 1874 with a transfer of fertile eggs to New York), few rivers now hold truly wild stocks of endemic fish. Possible exceptions include the famous fisheries of Henry's Fork (Snake River, Idaho), McCloud River (California), McKenzie River (Oregon), and the Kenai-Russia River system in Alaska. Rainbows have been introduced to all the world's continents, being a spectacular success in fisheries terms, in countries as far apart as Chile, Kenya, Tanzania, Pakistan, Peru and New Zealand. The fish have often grown very well and bred to produce superb sport fisheries like that of Lake Taupo in New Zealand. On the debit side, however, rainbow trout may well have eradicated rare native endemic fish species including some of those of the vast Andean lake, Titicaca, on the Peruvian/Bolivian border.

Back home in its native range, an eight-year-old boy fishing from a dinghy off Ketchikan, Alaska in 1970, hooked and landed the current rod-caught record steelhead, a fish of 42 lb 2 oz! Many die-hard west-coast American steelhead fishermen have fished for a lifetime without catching a fish half that size. Angling is a great leveller.

Rainbow trout were formerly named *Salmo gairdneri*, but have recently been moved into the genus *Oncorhynchus* to join the closely-related Pacific salmon species. Rainbow trout, like the European brown trout, have two life cycle variations; one form stays in freshwater all of its life and the other migrates to sea to grow and mature before returning to its natal stream to spawn. Historically, the migratory form ('steelhead') was called *Salmo gairdneri* and the other, coastal river form, which often stayed in freshwater, *Salmo irideus*. Within the *irideus* stock were found landlocked populations which were termed *shasta* stocks. These occur in the Kamloops lake region of British Columbia, the Crescent lake region of Washington state and in the Sierra Nevada rivers Gila, Apache and McCloud. *Irideus* stocks spawn in the spring (January-May) whilst *shasta* stocks spawn in the autumn (November/December).

This natural variation in the breeding season has been harnessed by fish farmers to extend the annual period during which fertile rainbow trout ova can be produced. The whole complex of different forms is now regarded (like *Salmo trutta* in Britain), as a single, very variable species — *Oncorhynchus mykiss*.

Rainbow trout naturally live in cool, clear-watered mountain rivers and lakes which range from unproductive oligotrophic waters where growth is slow, to rich, productive waters like Kamloops Lake where growth is spectacularly fast. Malcolm Greenhalgh describes the ecology of the Kamloops region lakes as follows: the waters are rich in dissolved salts and therefore in aquatic vegetation. This leads directly to abundant invertebrate populations and very rapid trout growth. Jewel Lake was reported to have produced a 56-lb fish in 1932! And a 25-pounder fell to the dry fly on Kootenay Lake in 1977.

These highly productive waters are, however, prone to algal blooms and periodic deoxygenation during hot summers. At these times and during prolonged periods of ice-cover in winter the whole stock of trout in a lake can suffocate. The small parr in the feeder streams would eventually repopulate the lakes naturally, although these days most trout are stocked from local hatcheries to supplement wild stocks. This is necessary because of despoilation of many spawning streams through mining wastes, erosion and siltation and through the intense pressure on the adult trout stocks from the sport fishing tourist industry.

Wild rainbow trout are a rarity in today's heavily exploited environment. Readers interested in the status of wild rainbow trout (and other trout species) are referred to Malcolm Greenhalgh and Rod Sutterby's fine book *Wild Trout* (George Phillip, London, 1989) and to Robin Ade's *Trout and Salmon Handbook*.

Steelhead, returning from their rich marine feeding grounds also show rapid growth and fine condition; they are much prized as sport fish although many populations are now supplemented by large-scale stocking programmes. Ernie Schweibert, the famous American angler/entomologist, has noted that some steelhead populations (in the rivers Columbia and Skeena for example) are noted for their very large average size of fish. He thinks that the torrential spawning beds of these mountain rivers, with their large cobbles, require big, powerful hen fish to dig the redds under the arduous conditions and large cock fish to defend the spawning territories. To gain the sizes required (10–20 lb) the steelheads stay at sea for one year longer than fish from rivers with steelheads of a smaller average size. These fish are, in some ways, a parallel of spring salmon in British rivers.

Rainbows are tolerant of poorer water quality and higher water temperatures than brown trout and are, therefore, more suited for stocking into rivers and lakes of marginal value to brown trout stocks. As rainbows also grow much faster than browns they are cheaper to farm and produce as stock fish for fly fisheries; hence their preponderance in today's stillwater put-and-take waters. Sterile, genetically manipulated 'triploid' rainbows are now available for stocking; these fish do not lose condition before the normal spawning season in the way that intact individuals do.

Rainbow trout in Britain and competition with brown trout

A technical breakthrough in the 1870s allowed live fertile trout eggs to be transported alive over long distances. This led in the early 1880s to the transfer of McCloud River rainbow trout ova from east to west in North America and then to Germany (in 1882) and subsequently to England on 14 February 1884. The famous Scottish, Howietoun trout farm (now operated by Stirling University) obtained rainbow stocks in 1887. Since then rainbows have been stocked into a wide variety of rivers, and natural and man-made lakes. In the 1930s concern was expressed that wild brown trout and grayling stocks were being ousted by rainbows in British waters and this led Barton Worthington to survey by questionnaire the status of rainbow trout in Britain. The study was published in 1940/41; he found that rainbow trout were reported as spawning successfully at the following locations: Blagdon reservoir (Somerset), a lake near Newstead Abbey, Nottingham, and the rivers Derbyshire Wye, Derwent, Gwash (Empingham, Rutland), Granta (Cambridgeshire), Gade and Garron (Hertfordshire), Chess, Mimram and Misbourne (Buckinghamshire), Wey (Surrey), Malling Bourne (Kent) and Lough Shure on Aranmore Island, Donegal, Ireland. In addition to these reports I have been told recently of spawning rainbows in the rivers Frome (Dorset), West Beck (Yorkshire), Biss (Somerset), Plym (Devon) and the Lake of Menteith (Scotland's only lake . . . all the rest are lochs). Clearly, despite widespread intensive stocking over many years, rainbow trout have not out-competed our native browns for breeding habitat.

In almost all cases of successful rainbow trout spawning, the rivers or lakes are markedly alkaline (on chalk or limestone) and are spring-fed, with equable temperature regimes. These factors seem to be important for completion of the rainbows' life cycle in British waters. The case of Donegal's Lough Shure is a peculiar one since, although it sits in the warm influence of the west coast Gulf Stream drift, it is an acid peat-bedded bog lake with no inflowing streams. Small native brown trout share the water with the introduced population of breeding rainbow trout which stem from a single stocking in 1905. As E. B. Worthington stated, this unusual acid-tolerant rainbow stock would repay further study (if it still exists) and may be a useful source of broodstock for new stocking ventures. Breeding rainbow trout have also been recorded in Ireland's Lough na Leibe (County Sligo) and White Lake (County Westmeath).

Steelheads (or at least sea-run rainbows) have been reported from the River Awe in Scotland (where a cage farm for trout has operated on Loch Awe for some years), the Newport River in County Mayo, Ireland, the Gowla River in Connemara, Ireland and from the Northumbrian sea trout drift net fishery off the coast of north-east England. It seems likely that steelheads are spawning in small numbers in British rivers.

Worthington concluded that rainbow trout were more tolerant of warm, slightly polluted waters than brown trout or grayling and that they posed few threats to native British stocks under normal conditions. However, in the Derbyshire Wye, Malling Bourne and Buckinghamshire Chess rainbows did seem to have an advantage over the brown trout stocks and were doing well. The case of the Derbyshire Wye rainbows is well documented and worthy of further comment: until 1908, angling records for the Wye show good catches of brown trout and grayling only. In 1912/13, 750 yearling rainbows were stocked into a stretch above the Haddon Hall waters at Bakewell. Between 1912 and 1935 rainbows spread downstream steadily and, despite the stocking of more than 50,000 brown trout, the native trout population dwindled to nothing whilst the rainbows thrived. The grayling catches also declined at this time.

By 1940 rainbows had spread downstream to the confluence with the River Derwent and were colonising that river too. The Wye rainbows spawn in March-May and the young fish thrive on a rich invertebrate diet of mayfly and stonefly nymphs, caddis larvae, shrimps, water lice, snails, river limpets, midge larvae and pupae and reed smuts. It would seem that rainbow trout were proved to be the cause of the demise of the native trout and grayling. However, during the period of the decline, raw sewage effluent from the town of Bakewell was increasingly discharged to the river and grayling were routinely netted and removed from the fishery to try and improve the quality of the trout fishing. It may well be that the rainbows simply withstood the decline in water quality better than the native fish and flourished as the native stocks declined. The dirty-water tolerant rainbows would also have benefited from increased midge populations in the sewage-polluted river. It is interesting to note that the River Chess rainbow population also gained a foothold (finhold?) after a bout of sewage pollution in 1937 wiped out the native browns. Under clean-water conditions perhaps the brown trout in both systems would have held sway.

Diet, growth, feeding biology and fishing methods

Where they have been studied under natural conditions, rainbow trout appear to be rather different from browns in their feeding behaviour. Whilst browns occupy a particular 'lie', moving across current to intercept food items, rainbows wander over long distances, either as individuals in streams or as small shoals moving upwind on lakes and reservoirs. Browns tend to be more bottom-living than rainbows. Rainbows also seem to be more ready to feed on any available food items (even algae) than the more selective and wary brown trout.

In productive lakes and reservoirs (like Grafham Water in Cambridgeshire or Chew and Blagdon in Somerset), rainbows will cruise between mid-water and the surface, feeding on dense swarms of *Daphnia* and other planktonic crustaceans. From early spring throughout the fishing season rainbows will immediately take advantage of hatches of midges, olives or sedges, taking the flies as nymphs/larvae, pupae and adults under and on the water surface. Chironomid pupae are often the staple diet. Much of the fun in fly-fishing lies in understanding what the trout are likely to be feeding on at a given time and then fishing with the appropriate flies and methods. Even stocked rainbows can be surprisingly difficult to catch when they are preoccupied with a particular food item. Fly fishermen spend many a happy winter hour tying new patterns of flies to imitate trout food items in anticipation of the coming season's fishing. For an excellent read on this subject, which is beyond the scope of this book, I suggest Brian Clarke's classic *The Pursuit of Stillwater Trout* (A&C Black, London, 1975).

In the autumn, reservoir-living rainbows show their adaptability once again by switching to a diet of small roach, bream and perch, which they chase actively at dawn and dusk and for short sharp feeding bouts during the day. At the back end of the season lures imitating small fish underwater or floating stunned fry at the surface account for many specimen grown-on trout.

Rainbows seem to forage more readily on stream and lake beds during the summer whilst browns tend to be seen feeding actively when hatches of fly are on the water. Browns do, however, feed extensively on bottom fauna (especially shrimps) during the winter. Perhaps because of their very active foraging behaviour, rainbows grow much more quickly than browns; in chalk streams browns take three years to reach 12–14 inches whilst rainbows can top this in only two years. For the fishery manager such differences are very important, especially when combined with the rainbow's willingness to feed during the warm 'dog days' of summer when all self-respecting brown trout are lying up. As they grow on quickly and mend the fins damaged by nipping and abrasion in cages, rainbow trout become fine-looking fish which are a great prize for the keen fly-fisherman. As this book went to press an enormous rainbow trout of 29 lb 12 oz was caught on a fly from Scotland's Loch Tay; this fish must have grown on largely in the wild and may become the first 'wild' rainbow trout rod-caught British record fish.

Breeding biology

Rainbows can mature sexually in only two years whilst browns take three to four years. Rainbows can usually spawn for two or three seasons before they die at perhaps five years of age, whilst browns can live for ten years or more (perhaps 20 years in the north) and spawn for many seasons where conditions are favourable. Californian rainbow trout may spawn twice in a year when conditions are very favourable.

Rainbow/steelhead trout show the typical salmonid pattern of territorial defence of spawning areas of clean gravel river bed where hen fish excavate redds to lay several hundred large (4-mm diameter) orange eggs. The eggs incubate in the cold, well-oxygenated water flowing through the gravel to hatch in the warming waters of early spring. Incubation is slow, taking from 100–150 days depending on water temperature. Young fry and parr defend feeding territories, fighting for the best positions in the stream until all of the available habitat is occupied.

This assumes, of course, that enough adults and clean gravel spawning sites are available to produce the next generation of wild fish. Sadly, these days, this is increasingly rare and the expense and difficulty of maintaining high quality trout streams the world over is leading to the simpler/cheaper expedient of stocking with takeable-sized fish which are rapidly caught and replaced in an artificial cycle of production and consumption. How much better it would be to improve the habitat for the benefit of self-sustaining wild trout populations. By relying on stocking, the link between fisheries management and the quality of vital trout-breeding habitat is lost.

Grayling, *Thymallus thymallus*

Identification and habitat

The *Thymallidae* or graylings comprise six species which occupy cool swiftly-flowing rivers, lakes or estuaries in North America, Europe and Asia. There is only one European species, *Thymallus thymallus*. All grayling have the characteristic large colourful dorsal fin which is more prominent in the male, and the fleshy adipose fin which groups these fish with the family Salmonidae. In Britain grayling are common in the chalkstreams of Hampshire and Dorset and the rivers Severn and Wye, several Yorkshire and Lancashire rivers, the Welsh Dee and Llyn Tegid and in the Scottish rivers Tweed, Nith, Tay, Isla and Earn. When Gouthwaite reservoir was formed by impounding Yorkshire's River Nidd, grayling were trapped in the new lake and a population appears to be adapting to this new habitat. The species is absent from Ireland.

Classic grayling habitat (Huet's 'grayling zone') is the middle reaches of clean gravel-bedded, cool, rapidly-flowing rivers; where riffles and rapids are interspersed with pools. The gradient of the river bed and flow rate both tend to be less than that found in classic 'trout zone' reaches. Clean water is important and grayling are recognised as being a good 'indicator species' of high water quality. In northern Europe grayling are less dependent on rivers and thrive in lakes and even in coastal waters off northern Sweden and Finland.

Breeding biology

In Sweden, coastal-dwelling grayling either migrate into rivers to spawn or spawn along the shores of the northern Gulf of Bothnia. The young fish leave the coastal stream after their first summer and return to spawn about four years later. In freshwater habitats grayling spawn close to their normal lies where the habitat is suitable or they undergo seasonal spawning migrations to suitable areas after the spring thaw. Grayling attain maturity at 3–4 years and spawn from March-June, depending on latitude, when the water temperature rises above 4°C. Males develop a dark body colouration which contrasts with the beautiful iridescent blue/red dorsal and pelvic fins which are held erect whilst displaying to females. Each male takes up position on a breeding territory in the late morning and displays to ripe females which shoal close to the clean gravel spawning beds.

Males leave their territories at night and return the next day. Females cut shallow (10-cm deep) redds into which the 3.5-mm diameter sticky yellow eggs are laid. Grayling tend to be prolific in suitable habitats; a 45-cm female will spawn around 10,000 eggs which hatch in 20–30 days depending on water temperature. Grayling eggs require 180 degree-days (e.g. 20 days at 9°C) to develop fully. Most spawning activity takes place in the afternoon when the water temperatures peak; cold spells of weather may delay spawning activity for several days.

Feeding behaviour and growth

Alasdair Scott studied post-hatching larval grayling in the River Frome, Dorset in 1983 and recorded the following information. The hatchlings stay in the gravel for four to five days absorbing their yolk sacs until, at a length of 15–19mm (in mid-April), they swim up to live close to the water surface near bankside vegetation. At this stage the young fish form small shoals, feeding on insects drifting downstream; 80–90 per cent of the diet being larval, pupal and adult chironomid midges. Lesser numbers of small mayfly nymphs and reed smuts (*Simulium*) are also eaten. Feeding activity peaks at dawn and dusk but stops during the night.

The abundant food supply on the Frome is more than sufficient for the young fish and during the three weeks when they live close to the surface the grayling grow very rapidly. At a length of around 25mm (one inch) they drop down to take up small territories on the streambed which they seem to defend aggressively. By occupying a habitat away from streambed-living predators and with a current speed of around 10cm per second which is too fast for small pike, grayling larvae are relatively safe in their small shoals. Also, by living within about 5cm from the surface for their early life cycle they avoid direct competition with midwater-dwelling trout fry and bottom-living salmon fry. Perhaps in this way the different species share the available chalk stream habitat.

From this stage the young grayling fry eat progressively larger invertebrates including mayfly and stonefly nymphs, caddis larvae, shrimps, snails and freshwater limpets. During the spawning period grayling often eat their own eggs. Large grayling will take small fish and even small voles when they get the chance. The relatively small, underslung mouth is, however, adapted primarily for picking invertebrates from stones on the streambed.

J. M. Hellawell studied the diet of adult grayling from Herefordshire's River Lugg; almost all of the stomach contents examined contained a wide variety of prey species. The list includes: cereal seeds, berries, filamentous algae (silkweed), caterpillars, spiders, adult flies, beetles, bugs, lacewings, stonefly nymphs (*Taeniopteryx, Nemoura*), mayfly nymphs (*Ecdyonurus, Heptagenia, Baetis, Ephemera, Cloeon, Ephemerella*), caddis larvae (*Hydropsyche, Hydroptilidae, Limnephillidae*), dipteran larvae (*Simulium, Tipulids, Chironomids* and angler's maggots), beetle larvae and adults, Corixids, molluscs (*Theodoxus, Valvata, Ancylastrum, Limnaea, Planorbis, Sphaerium*), shrimps, water lice, water mites, leeches and fish eggs – cyprinids (dace?) in April and salmonids in December. Interestingly the cyprinid eggs were taken by adult grayling whilst the salmonid eggs were eaten by young (underyearling) fish. Grayling clearly have a catholic diet.

Grayling grow rapidly, especially in the chalkstreams of southern England where at one year they average 16cm, two years 22cm, three years 34cm, four years 32cm and five years 38cm (around 600g). These fast-growing populations produce fish which live for perhaps eight to nine years but further north the slower-growing grayling can attain ages of 15 years or more. In these waters typical sizes would be around 12cm at one year, 22cm at two years, 28cm at three years and 32cm at four years. The typical adult size (at 3–4 years) for grayling is 25–35cm (250g) with the largest fish scaling perhaps 50cm (2.5kg) in Britain. On the River Lugg, J. M. Hellawell found that grayling grow fastest during the spring and summer, with the annual growth 'check' on the scales forming in November. In Llyn Tegid, north Wales the check is formed earlier, in August or September. Grayling from both populations have similar growth rates which are markedly less than those recorded for River Test fish. Whilst a 5-year-old (male or female) Test grayling would be around 41cm, on the Lugg the average length would be only 32cm – a considerable difference.

Angling for grayling

The British rod-caught record for grayling stands at 1.89kg (4lb 3oz) by Sean Lanigan from the River Frome, Dorset in 1989. Grayling continue to feed well in cold weather, providing sport for anglers well into the winter after the end of the trout season. Fly-fishermen catch them on deeply-sunk leaded nymphs (such as the 'grayling bug') or on traditional wet flies fished downstream. Grayling will rise to a dry fly but their attempts at taking it are often splashy and they appear to miss at times . . . no one knows whether this is cunning or sheer ineptitude at surface-feeding. When the water is too coloured for fly-fishing, good catches are taken on float fished worm or maggot. By whatever method you catch them, grayling are good to eat, with a firm, dry, white flesh of excellent flavour and texture.

Relationship with trout and salmon stocks

Grayling often share their habitat with trout and salmon parr and are thought by many anglers to adversely affect these species by competition for food and space. This may or may not be true; much probably depends upon the details of the habitat type and fish stocks in a given situation.

Each year many thousands of grayling are electro-fished and removed from English chalk stream trout fisheries such as the rivers Test and Kennet. This probably has little long-term impact on these prolific fish but there is little evidence to justify the activity. Some river keepers, including the famous Mick Lunn, formerly head keeper of the Houghton Club water on the Test at Stockbridge, maintain that grayling removal promotes the growth of trout in feeder streams. They should know, as they have years of practical experience upon which to base their opinions.

Scientific studies in Scandinavia, however, indicate that grayling and trout have subtly different diets and overlap little in their choice of aquatic invertebrates. Grayling have a small underslung mouth with no teeth which can probe in between pebbles on the river bed. Trout have a large terminal mouth with many large teeth which is adapted to seizing food organisms as they drift by in the open water or move over the surface of stones. Adult grayling also tend to select deeper runs and pools than trout, where the current speed is slower. I suspect that where the two species co-exist naturally they have evolved to split up the available resources and share the habitat efficiently.

Where grayling have been introduced to trout waters, however, it is a different story and this may be because the local trout have no experience of competing with the introduced alien species. In Jutland, Denmark, the trout population of a stream was decimated after a grayling introduction and similarly in Lake Anjan, Sweden, both trout and charr stocks declined markedly as an introduced grayling population flourished.

A recent general decline in trout and increase in grayling stocks in north-western Sweden is thought to be due to climatic amelioration, with grayling faring better in a run of mild years. As always in ecology there are many factors which influence animal populations, making it difficult to link directly causes and effects.

The Pikes: Family *Esocidae*

In Europe we have only one pike species, *Esox lucius*, whilst in North America there are another four; the mighty muskellunge ('musky' or 'lunge') *E.masquinongy* and the three small pickerels, the chain pickerel (*E.niger*), the redfin pickerel (*E.americanus americanus*), and the grass pickerel (*E.americanus vermiculatus*). The pickerels are essentially 'pikelets' which live in well-weeded waters over a wide range in North America; they include more invertebrates in their diets than pike but otherwise have a similar biology. Pickerels can be distinguished from small pike through their full-scaled cheek and operculum (structures which are half-scaled in pike). The River Amur catchment in Russia has a distinct pike species, *E.reicherti*, which occupies the European pike's niche in this system.

The muskellunge merits a brief paragraph because of its notable size: specimens of 100 lb have been recorded. They grow to around 10 lb in five years, 30 lb at ten years and 50 lb plus at 15 years; the lifespan can exceed 20 years. The present rod-caught record is 69 lb 15 oz from the St Lawrence River system, New York, in 1957. Muskies live in lakes and slow-flowing river meanders where they hunt over wide areas for large prey (fish, mammals, waterfowl), usually stalking them in lily or pondweed beds or large root masses/log piles. A hard-fighting sport fish, they are angled for with large spinners, spoons and plugs or bait fish. Large specimens are much prized but rare today, perhaps because of large scale nocturnal spearing of spawning fish in the last century and more recent sport angling pressure.

Pike, *Esox lucius*

Identification, habitat and feeding behaviour

Esox lucius inhabit most types of stillwater and slow-flowing rivers in temperate Europe, Asia and North America. Pike are superbly camouflaged ambush predators with the dorsal and anal fins set back near the tail to provide a powerful thrust when striking at prey. The large eyes are directed forwards to provide a degree of binocular vision which allows an accurate estimation of distance from predator to prey. The snout, which houses the huge toothed jaws, has sighting grooves along which the pike can watch its intended prey.

Like their predatory marine counterparts, the sharks, pike have an ancient lineage. The Cromer Forest fossil beds in Norfolk have yielded finely-preserved *Esox lucius* dating back half a million years. The closely-related and very similar *Esox papyraceus*, a fossil from lignite beds near Bonn in Germany dates back an estimated 30 million years, whilst in Canada, the fossil pike *Esox tiemani* was recently discovered in Eocene sediments of 60 million years age; clearly, our modern pike is a tried and tested design!

As it fins slowly through reed and weedbeds stalking small fish, the pike blends perfectly into the background; the stalk is followed by a curving of the body prior to the final 'leap' through the water at the target. This coincides with a sudden opening of the jaws which sucks the prey into the mouth. The roof of the mouth and tongue are covered with numerous small backward-pointing teeth which usually prevent the prey from escaping. Only spined fish like sticklebacks can sometimes overcome seizure by sticking in the pike's mouth or throat and being spat out, somewhat the wiser for the experience.

Whilst pike will take large prey, including ducklings and rats, they usually prefer to take fish of around 10–15 per cent of their own weight. Exceptionally this is increased to nearly 40 per cent, and large Irish lough pike will take grilse and salmon when available. Indeed large Scottish and Irish lakes have yielded many of the largest pike on record. In Loch Lomond pike congregate around the mouths of the rivers Leven, Endrick and Falloch to intercept migrating salmon and sea trout. Whether pike shoal and hunt co-operatively is unknown but it's an intriguing possibility.

Growth and lifespan

Pike seem to evoke one of two basic instincts in fisheries people; they either love them or hate them! Some game fishery managers ruthlessly cull all pike caught whilst specimen coarse fishery managers pay high prices for large (30 lb-plus) specimens which are stocked into day ticket waters. Pike do not seem to tolerate high angling pressure very well and many die after being caught and badly handled. Specimen coarse fisheries for bream, roach, perch, rudd, etc, may often rely on the presence of a healthy predatory pike population to prevent high population densities and consequent intense food competition amongst the prey species. Predators and their prey often acheive a good balance for all concerned in such circumstances. This seldom seems to be the case in game fisheries where pike find trout and salmon easy prey, and fishery managers wish to maximise the game fish populations.

To maintain condition (i.e. steady weight) adult pike need to eat around 80 per cent of their body weight per year. Active growth requires more food and pike need to eat 5kg of fish to grow 1kg; a 20-lb pike will eat about 50 newly stocked rainbow trout in a year to grow by around 5 lb. In an Irish lough, a pike population of 1170 fish was calculated to eat 51.5 tonnes of trout per year. No wonder trout fishery managers often remove pike from their waters.

Pike feed and grow most quickly from May to June. They switch from an invertebrate diet to one of fish at a length of around 3cm. At this stage larval perch and smaller pike fry are the usual prey.

Cannibalism

When introduced into waters containing muskellunge, pike seem rapidly to gain the upper hand; this may be because pike spawn before muskies and young pike fry can then eat newly hatched muskellunge, thus gaining a growth advantage. Certainly amongst sibling pike fry, early fast-growers turn around and cannibalise any smaller brethren at the first available opportunity. Once these fish have a growth advantage they will eat their way through as many brothers and sisters as they can. There is no love lost between pike.

Cannibalism in pike starts at an early age, continues through life and may well be important in the regulation of numbers; where many large pike are removed, small 'jack' pike subsequently flourish. Ros Wright and I found that cannibalism amongst pike fry stocked in experimental ponds is proportionately higher at greater population densities, i.e. that it is density-dependent. Pike spawn early, often in off-river swamps, and it may be that in such habitats smaller siblings form an important component of the diet of those few individual pike which make it through the vulnerable fry stage.

Certainly we found that the growth rate of cannibals is much higher than that of invertebrate-feeding fry. Rapid growers reach 20cm by their first autumn. Thereafter, growth is very dependent on habitat quality: slow in deep, cold, unproductive northern waters but very fast in benign shallow, rich lakes.

Fred Buller, in his classic *Pike* (Macdonald, 1971) lists a top 69 pike of 35 lb or more in weight caught in recent years. Of these, 35 are known to have been caught in large Irish loughs and three from Scottish lochs.

I would like, briefly, to recount two of Buller's excellent pike stories, one absurd, the other amazing.

The Emperor's Pike

In 1497, from a German lake near Mannheim a pike 19 feet long and weighing 350 lb was reputedly taken. A copper ring on its gill recorded that it had been stocked 267 years before, in the year 1230, by the Emperor Frederick II. The mortal remains (i.e. the skeleton), hanging on the wall of Mannheim Cathedral, enthralled a gullible public until an interested naturalist revealed the presence of hundreds of extra vertebrae inserted strategically to extend the length of the fish!

The Endrick Pike

I was fortunate to study the fish of Loch Lomond as part of my doctoral research and I have many happy memories of this magnificent lake. Despite netting for three years, however, I never saw a fish the size of the amazing 'Endrick pike'. In about 1934, on the River Endrick marshes at the south-eastern corner of Loch Lomond the receding floodwaters left stranded an enormous pike. The head was taken from the carcass, dried and preserved; over 30 years later it was examined by Fred Buller, Dick Walker and friends. Dick Walker, upon seeing the head and measuring its length from snout to gill cover at just over 12.5 inches estimated the body weight of the pike to have been around 70 lb in its prime!

We will never know the true weight of this fish and no estimate of its age has been made, but one thing is certain, pike far larger than the current rod-caught record have existed and probably still exist in waters such as the Scottish lochs Lomond and Ken and Irish loughs Corrib, Mask, Conn, Ree, Derg and Erne. Pike are known to achieve lengths of perhaps 1.5 metres, weights of up to 31kg (70-plus lb) and ages of 20-plus years. Such fish are, however, very exceptional and are always female; male pike are much smaller, seldom growing larger than 12lb.

The heaviest pike netted in the long-term Windermere study weighed 35 lb and was 14 years old. This was also the average age of the six largest Windermere pike caught (average weight 32 lb). The oldest fish netted was 18 years old, weighing 18 lb 4 oz. Irish lough pike often reach 30 lb in only 8–9 years and one fast-grower examined by Michael Kennedy weighed 41 lb at 8 years! Clearly Ireland has great potential for the pike specimen hunter.

Pike fishing

If you wish to learn about pike fishing, read Fred Buller's book (*Pike*) for there is no better text on the subject. Space permits only a brief review here. Pike are traditionally caught on small live fish but static and wobbled dead baits are also very effective and, undoubtedly, more humane. Spinning with lures is a well-tried and tested method, with jointed plugs (such as Rapalas) being especially effective. Barbless treble hooks will enable you to unhook fish very easily and safely with minimal damage both to you and to the fish.

A final note on care of pike is in order: large pike take several years to produce and are valuable members of the fish community . . . treat them carefully, unhook them gently and return them to the water quickly. Far too many fish are left to suffer on the bank whilst proud captors pause to make sure that they look their best for the photograph.

Pike thrive on a diet of trout, especially where naive stock fish are tipped into the water in front of their noses at regular intervals through the fishing season. Several noted reservoir trout fisheries are now recouping some of the financial losses of pike predation by letting pike fishing days through the winter; Ardingly and Ardleigh reservoirs are now full-time winter pike waters whilst Rutland, Grafham and Llandegfedd in Wales have short-term experimental pike fisheries underway.

This latter-noted trout water, built in the early 1960s, is situated south-east of Pontypool, Gwent, South Wales and covers around 435 acres; it is a principal water supply for the city of Cardiff. The reservoir opened for brown trout fishing in 1966 and by 1970 anglers had started to catch pike on the fly. By the mid 1970s research biologists had netted some very large pike and analyses of the stomach contents revealed that they were eating mostly coarse fish species and only a few trout.

In October 1988 pike angling trials produced about 50 pike over 20 lb including 15 over 30 lb and 4 over 40 lb — remarkable catches indeed. The present rod-caught record pike* was caught at Llandegfedd by the well-known rugby player/salmon angler Gareth Edwards who captured the fish on a Mepps spinner on his first ever day of deliberate pike fishing. The huge specimen scaled 45 lb 6 oz (20.58kg) but larger fish have come from the water. In 1988 a 48-pounder was netted from the reservoir, tagged and returned and also during that year a trout angler found a dead pike of 53 inches length in Sor Bay; this fish is likely to have weighed over 50 lb in its prime. Llandegfedd reservoir may well be the best pike fishery in England and Wales, although I am sure that in years to come Rutland Water and Grafham reservoir will also produce large specimens.

Breeding biology

Pike are spring-spawners, breeding when the first daffodils bloom (March in south to May/June in far north), migrating into shallow bays, up streams and ditches and into flooded bogs and marshes. Males reach maturity at 2–3 years and females at 3–4 years. Large females are accompanied by two or three smaller males which vie to fertilise the eggs which are laid on any available silt-free vegetation. Females can take one to two hours to lay a batch of eggs. The eggs stick to plants and twigs and are thus saved from suffocation in the soft silt below. Spawning is often triggered by a sudden rise in water temperature to 6–7°C. Large pike can produce half a million eggs (15–20,000 per kg body weight), shedding them in three to four batches at traditional sites. At 6°C pike eggs hatch in 26 days but at 10° this is reduced to 12 days. Young hatchling pike have an adhesive organ on top of the head which allows them to stick to plants and hang motionless whilst absorbing their yolk sacs.

*Roy Lewis from Teddington has subsequently caught a 46-lb Llandegfedd pike which awaits ratification as the new rod-caught record fish.

Perch, *Perca fluviatilis*

Identification, distribution and habitats

Six Perciform (spiny-finned) fishes may be encountered in British freshwaters, the perch (*Perca fluviatilis*), zander (*Stizostedion lucioperca*), ruffe (*Gymnocephalus cernua*) and, in a very few localities, Largemouth bass (*Micropterus salmoides*), Rock bass (*Ambloplites rupestris*) and Pumpkinseeds (*Lepomis gibbosus*); the first three belong to the family Percidae and the last three to the Centrarchidae or Sunfishes.

Perch have around five dark vertical bar markings on the flanks, two separate dorsal fins, the first being sharply spined with a dark spot at the base, and pelvic, anal and caudal fins which are bright red. Ruffe are like small sandy-coloured perch; the fins are not red and the two dorsal fins run into each other. Zander have much more prominent teeth than either of the former species, the second (rear) dorsal fin is separate from and larger than the first and the fins are not red.

Both ruffe and zander have a strange shining, opalescent look to their eyes because of a light-reflective layer behind the retina which allows both species to feed visually in low light levels, either at dawn and dusk or in turbid waters. Perch and ruffe probably avoid direct competition by perch feeding in open water during the day and ruffe feeding on the bottom at night (when different groups of invertebrates become active). Ruffe are now thriving in Loch Lomond where they eat large numbers of powan eggs on the lake bed, and their impact on the whitefish stocks remains to be seen*. Ruffe are also rapidly colonising the North American Great Lakes region.

Zander, an introduced species (see separate chapter), are more predatory than either of the other two, although large adult perch can become largely piscivorous and are often cannibalistic. Percids and pikes have open sensory pores on the head which allow them to detect moving prey under low-light conditions — many fish have senses which we neither have nor can readily appreciate.

Sunfish

The North American sunfishes are an interesting group, often having parental care of the eggs and fry which are spawned in a 'nest', usually a depression dug out of a sandy/gravel lake bed area and defended by the male. These are warm-water species, breeding in May and June. The largemouth bass has a single isolated British breeding population, near Wareham in Dorset. In its native North America and in eastern Canada largemouth (and the related smallmouth) bass are very important sport fish.

Largemouth bass grow to a maximum size of 6.4kg (14 lb-plus) at a length of 80cm at perhaps 15 years, but the more usual sizes are 20–40cm. The upper jaw extends back behind the eye and the lower jaw protrudes beyond the upper one to give the impression of a fish which is aggressively sticking its chin out. Freshwater bass eat crustaceans and insect larvae, grading on to larger invertebrates and fish as they grow.

The rock bass is also established as a breeding fish in a very few south-west English waters, reaching a maximum length of 34cm and weight of 1.7kg or around 4 lb at an age of 10 years. This species is similar in appearance to the largemouth but has a larger eye and a characteristic spiny anal fin with six spined rays (the anal fin on the

*It appears that as Ruffe stocks have increased so perch have declined – perhaps the two species compete strongly after all.

largemouth has only two small spined rays). The biology is typical of sunfish, with male parental care of the nest, eggs and young fry and food consisting of insect nymphs, larvae, crustaceans and small fish.

Pumpkinseeds are colourful little fish, with spiny dorsal and anal fins. The males in breeding colours are a superb golden-yellow, with red throats and vivid blue wavy stripes over the gill covers. The breeding and feeding biology is similar to that of freshwater bass, but pumpkinseeds only reach lengths of around 20cm and weights of 300 grammes (12 oz) and may live for up to 8–9 years.

This group of introduced North American fishes are hanging on by their fingertips (fintips?) and may not survive in the long-term, especially if our climate enters a cool phase instead of staying as warm as in recent summers. Conversely, if global warming becomes a reality they may become established U.K. sport fish species.

The perch has a very wide distribution in slow rivers and lakes over most of northern Europe, Asia and eastern North America, where it is termed the yellow perch (*Perca flavescens*). This species is, however, virtually identical to our own *Perca fluviatilis* with an equivalent biology. Perch prefer rivers with a moderate flow, often shoaling in marginal reed and bulrush beds. The species cannot survive in fast-flowing rivers or in very oligotrophic or very eutrophic lakes. Large cool lakes of relatively high dissolved oxygen content are ideal habitats. In Scandinavian and North American lakes that have become acidified, perch often survive the low pH conditions, feeding on the resistant *corixa*, dragonfly and aquatic beetle faunas characteristic of acid lakes.

Where large upland lakes such as Lake Constance have undergone moderate eutrophication, the perch population seems to have responded by sustaining a high yield of fast-growing fish to the commercial fishery. This is fine as long as the process of enrichment does not go too far. In Lake Balaton, Hungary, the perch population has declined to very low levels probably owing to the hypereutrophic status of parts of the lake due to sewage inputs and fertiliser/slurry run-off from adjacent farmland. As with the charr in Lake Windermere, low dissolved oxygen concentrations have probably made life difficult for perch which formerly thrived in the clear waters.

Moderate chemical enrichment of lakes can have beneficial effects for the production of some fish species but when prolonged these benefits can toll the doom of other, more sensitive species. In Lake Balaton, as the perch and zander decline, bream and carp are thriving in the stagnant, soupy-rich waters.

Regulation of Perch populations

Perch are prone to periodic plagues of 'ulcer disease', a condition where holes are eroded in the lateral body wall of the fish, leading to large-scale deaths in the populations. Scientists of the Freshwater Biological Association estimated that more than 98 per cent of the perch in Lake Windermere were killed by the disease during the warm summer of 1976. Outbreaks occur every so often in most perch populations and may be a natural regulating mechanism when population densities get too high and particularly also when there is a hot summer.

Cannibalism of fry is another potential mechanism for perch to self-regulate their abundance. It is very widespread, perhaps universal in perch stocks during breeding seasons that produce strong year-classes. Cannibalism is also the norm in pike and zander populations.

In unexploited perch populations, long-term cyclical fluctuations in abundance appear to be normal. In some populations 'ulcer' disease and/or cannibalism may generate these cycles.

Commercial perch fisheries

The long-term (45-year) perch and pike fishery on Lake Windermere, initially set up for wartime fish production studies (1941-1947) and subsequently operated for scientific purposes by the Freshwater Biological Association (now the Institute of Freshwater Ecology), has produced many important population dynamics studies over the years. John Craig has recently reviewed the main findings on perch. The following notes are based on his account (see *The Biology of Perch and Related Fish*, Croom Helm, 1987).

Perch in Windermere were reduced by the wartime fishery from 136 tonnes to around 55 tonnes, and large scale perch removal continued in the north basin until 1948 and in the south basin until 1964. It was feared that the removal of so many perch might lead to an increase in pike predation on the valuable charr stocks and, therefore, a winter gill net fishery for adult pike has been continuously operated from 1944 to the present day. Each year around 33 per cent of the pike larger than 55cm are removed from the lake.

Tagging experiments showed that the north and south basin perch populations within the lake are quite separate and thus operate as discrete stocks. The estimates of the perch stock sizes from 1941 to 1976 parallel each other for the two lake basins. From 1941 to 1950 the trap fishery decreased total perch abundance from somewhat over six million fish down to around one million. In the warm years of the late 1950s the stock recovered to peak at over 5 million by 1960. It then declined again to around one million by the late 1960s, increased to two million in the early 1970s and declined severely once more with the perch disease outbreak of 1976. Interestingly, the pike population densities follow a similar pattern of abundance.

Although perch numbers declined because of the fishery, the weight of fish present (biomass) did not decline to such a high degree because of better growth by the surviving fish. This is probably a good example of growth stimulated by fishing pressure. Also, at lower population densities the fecundity (egg production) of the female perch increased by close to 50 per cent. The number of eggs produced, however, has little effect on the subsequent year-class strength. The main factors which have been found to affect the strength of perch year classes (numbers produced each year) in Lake Windermere are 1. summer water temperatures in the year of hatch; 2. the biomass of adult perch present (i.e. degree of cannibalism) and 3. the year-class strength of pike (i.e. predation) in the same year. David Le Cren also showed that perch in several Lake District waters simultaneously produced strong year-classes in warm years, indicating that weather was the causative agent, rather than internal changes in individual lakes.

Essentially, summer water temperature (a *density-independent* factor) increased year-class strengths in warm years and cannibalism and predation (both *density-dependent* factors) decreased year-class strengths. The relative importance of the three factors varied as the years went by. This sort of long term experimental study is vital to our understanding of fish population dynamics.

Breeding Biology

Perch of an age and size tend to shoal together. Some tagging work that I did on Loch Lomond in 1977 showed that, even in this very large lake, adult perch tended to stay in the same groups and areas over extended periods. In Loch Lomond, and other large lakes, the species has a marked rhythmic annual migration, from the cool depths in winter, up onto the shallows in the spring to spawn in May, and then feeding in open water and along shorelines for the summer before returning to the depths in late autumn for the winter.

Male perch running with milt reach the spawning grounds in spring before the females. Female perch shed all of their eggs (4000–300,000, depending on body weight) at once in a large (up to 1 metre) ribbon-like, inter-connected mucus sheet on sunken branches and inshore weedbeds when spring water temperatures reach 7–8°C. A single ripe female is chased through the weeds by two or three males which compete to fertilise the eggs as they are shed. Hatching success is high, perhaps because of the protective mucus sheath and the 8mm long fry emerge in two to three weeks and form shoals which feed on small planktonic crustaceans.

Feeding and Growth

The size of prey that larval perch take is determined by the gape of the mouth and increases progressively as they grow. As with all young fish it is critical that the timing of hatching coincides with the availability of suitably sized prey. Sometimes, especially

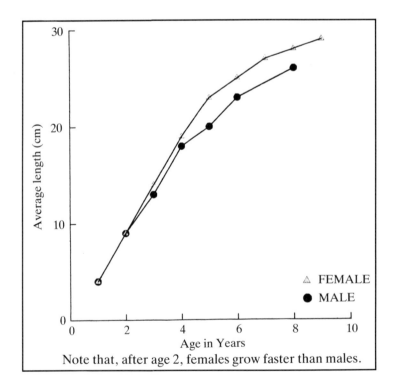

Growth of perch in Rostherne Mere

Note that, after age 2, females grow faster than males.

in marine fisheries, a 'mis-match' occurs because of unusual weather conditions and whole year-classes of a species in a given sea area can be wiped out through starvation. Less severe effects of this type are likely to occur in freshwater systems.

At 15–20mm, young perch form dense shoals close to weedbeds near the banks of rivers and lakes. At one year they measure around 4–6 cm, at two years 8–12cm and at three years 15–25cm. Young perch usually mature at 2–3 years and may live for 10 or more years. In cold climates, slow-growing perch tend to be long-lived. An illustration of the comparative growth rates of perch in two contrasting waters is given in the figures on pages 122 and 123. Rostherne Mere in Cheshire is a productive lowland lake and Ullswater in Cumbria a less productive upland glacial lake.

Note that, after age 5, females are marginally larger than males. Early growth in Ullswater is faster than in Rostherne Mere but final sizes are smaller. As in many populations, small numbers of exceptionally large (45cm max.) perch occur in Ullswater; these fish initially grow at normal rates and then in mid-life, accelerate to reach large ultimate sizes. This change in growth may reflect a dietary switch from invertebrate to fish-eating in these individuals, perhaps they are the perch equivalent of ferox trout.

As they grow, young perch are able to take larger planktonic crustaceans, such as *Daphnia, Bythotrephes, Polyphemus* and *Leptodora* and small chironomid pupae and phantom midge (*Chaoborus*) larvae. Open water feeding in summer grades into littoral feeding upon mayfly nymphs, caddis larvae, shrimps and water lice in the autumn. In my studies of gravel-pit perch diet I found that 90 per cent plus of the food of adult fish was comprised of chironomid pupae.

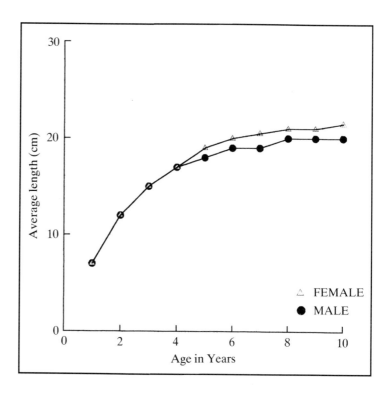

Growth of perch
in Ullswater

Perch fishing

Perch are a popular angling fish, being caught on ledgered or float-fished worms or maggots and by spinning. They are also caught commercially in nets and traps in mainland Europe and sold as table fish. Perch are very good to eat, having a firm-textured, well-flavoured white flesh. In Austria and Switzerland, Alpine lakes provide the fish for gourmet perch dishes, both for locals and visiting tourists. Most European countries conserve perch stocks by having minimum takeable sizes of 15–25cm. The largest perch recorded rarely exceed 50cm (3.5kg) although there are old European records of huge fish of up to 6.5kg (14 lb). In Britain, perch of two pounds are rare specimens, the rod-caught record came from a private water in Kent in 1985 by J. Shayler and weighed 5 lb 9 oz (2.52kg).

Perch in trout fisheries

Where perch are thought to compete for food with trout in natural waters, water bailiffs sometimes lower bunches of brushwood into suitable shallow bays in the spring and then lift them out when covered in perch spawn to limit the breeding success. Certainly, when allowed to spawn naturally, perch often 'overpopulate' their habitats to produce stunted stocks of small, late-maturing fish. In nutrient-poor Scottish lochs the competition for invertebrate food (especially midge pupae, mayfly nymphs and shrimps) may have a more marked negative effect upon trout growth than in richer southern waters where the invertebrate food supply is far greater; such relationships are not easy to prove under natural conditions.

PART 4
The Warm-Water Community: Lowland Rivers, Lakes and Ponds

British Cyprinid Fishes and their Close Relatives

Diversity

The family Cyprinidae is the largest family of fish species, comprising the carps or minnows, and it occurs in most parts of the world except South America and Australia. There are around 275 different genera in the family and, in all, around 2000 known species. In Europe there are 80 cyprinid species, with Britain having a total of 16. The British species are as follows: Common Carp, Crucian Carp, Goldfish, Barbel, Gudgeon, Tench, Silver Bream, Common Bream, Bleak, Minnow, Bitterling, Roach, Rudd, Chub, Orfe and Dace.

The European cyprinids can be split up into a number of major and minor groups as follows:

Carps: Common Carp (*Cyprinus*), Crucian Carp, Goldfish (*Carassius* species).

Barbels: (*Barbus* species) including Turkish, Macedonian, Caucasian, Greek, Albanian, Mediterranean, Bulatmai, Aral, Iberian and our own Barbel.

Roaches: (*Rutilus* species) including Danube, Adriatic, Portuguese, Pardilla, Macedonian, Pearl, Calandino and our own Roach.

Dace: (*Leuciscus* species) including Danilewskii's, Adriatic, Yugoslavian, Croatian, Ukliva, Makal, Turskyi, our own Dace, Black Sea Chub, Caucasian Chub, our own Chub, Orfe and Golden Orfe (known as Ide in continental Europe).

Breams: (*Abramis* species) Common (Bronze), White eye, and Blue Bream and the *Blicca* species the White (Silver) Bream.

Nase: (*Chondrostoma* species) nine species of dace-like fishes.

Minnows: (*Phoxinus, Paraphoxinus, Phoxinellus* species) 11 species of small minnow-like fishes.

Gudgeons: (*Gobio* species) five species of miniature barbel-like bottom-living fish. Plus the Dalmatian Barbelgudgeon which has four barbels whilst the other five species have two.

Bleaks: (*Alburnus* species) three species of small silver surface-living fish.

Rudd: (*Scardinius* species), the Greek and our own Rudd.

Tench: The single species *Tinca tinca*, the Tench.

Bitterling: *Rhodeus sericeus*, single species which, unusually, spawns in freshwater mussels.

Three other large (50-cm plus), central European cyprinids distributed in river catchments around the Baltic, Black and Caspian seas are the Asp (*Aspius aspius*), the Vimba (*Vimba vimba*) and the Chekhon (*Pelecus cultratus*), and all three form the basis of net and trap commercial fisheries. The Asp is unusual in being the only European cyprinid to regularly eat large fishes as its adult diet.

Feeding

All cyprinids are freshwater residents, with a few species able to tolerate weakly brackish conditions. Carp family species have no teeth in their jaws but they do possess one to three rows of crushing/grinding teeth in the throat (pharynx) called pharyngeal teeth. These can be useful in identifying species and distinguishing hybrids (which occur commonly) from pure-bred specimens. The pharyngeal teeth crush and grind plant and animal foods against horny pads in the throat, making gut content samples difficult to identify during dietary studies. Of our British species we can distinguish some specialisation in feeding ecology in differing habitats and under differing degrees of food competition from their own and other species.

Herbivores: Rudd, Roach, Dace, Nase, Chub, Orfe, Carp and particularly Grass Carp can all eat water plants including microscopic algae and larger species. Grass carp, a Chinese species from the River Amur, have been introduced (with permission from the NCC/NRA) for the control of unwanted aquatic plants which can clog ponds and canals. They can eat their own body weight each day when the water is warm enough to stimulate their appetites. Soft plants are selected first in preference to harder-stemmed species which are eventually eaten when the more palatable and digestible fare is exhausted. In a Dorset lake near my home, run as a put-and-take trout fishery, grass carp have completely cleared a formerly heavily-weeded water and now pull reedmace plants down into the water before chewing them up. These fish have grown to weights approaching 20 lb in only a few years. Grass carp are unlikely to breed naturally in British waters since they require very warm water to come into spawning condition.

Benthic (lake/river bed) sediment-feeders: e.g. Carp, Bream, Silver Bream, Gudgeon and Tench, all of which have protrusible mouths which can suck up silt, sand or gravel, filter out the midge larvae, small worms and mussels and then spit out the inedible fraction. Carp are the most competitive silt-filterers, reducing the numbers of midge larvae to very low levels where dense feeding shoals have been actively foraging. Common bream are also very efficient at this form of feeding. Large carp and bream dig deeper into sediments and eat larger chironomid larvae than smaller specimens. It is thought that one reason for carp and bream to feed extensively at night is that midge larvae move closer to the sediment surface at this time and are, therefore, easier for the fish to catch. Bream make characteristic conical feeding pits as they dig down into the sediments.

Picking invertebrates from the water and plant surfaces: Rudd, Orfe, Dace and Bleak all take flies from the surface of the water, whilst tench, crucian carp and roach can all specialise in picking molluscs and insect larvae from the underwater surfaces of plants. Carp in lakes and barbel in rivers will also quite audibly suck snails and snail eggs from the under surfaces of floating pond weed and lily leaves. Barbel, gudgeon and loaches are all able to probe gravel river beds and in between stones to winkle out invertebrates hiding under cover.

Zooplankton feeding: Carp, Bream, Tench and Crucian Carp are all able to feed efficiently on small planktonic crustaceans, for example *Daphnia hyalina* when these animals form dense 'blooms' in summer. The zooplankters can be eaten singly, slowly pump-filtered through the gill-raker system or 'tow-net' filtered by swimming along with the mouth open. Bleak (*Alburnus alburnus*) are known to be able to feed in this way. Bream will switch from lakebed feeding to plankton when the abundance of water fleas outweighs the profitability of finding burrowing midge larvae in the mud.

Fish-eating: The Asp (*Aspius aspius*) is the only routinely piscivorous European cyprinid, but many other species sometimes cannibalise their own fry or eat the fry of other species (e.g. bream, carp, roach, chub) and large chub and barbel can derive a considerable proportion of their nutrition from small fish.

Breeding

During the breeding season male cyprinids develop a rash of white spawning tubercles on the head, shoulders and fins. These are rubbed against the female during courtship chasing but serve no known function other than perhaps tactile and visual stimulation. Some male cyprinids develop very striking courtship colours, the minnow is one of our most attractive fish in full courtship dress.

Cyprinids can be split up into groups which spawn on differing surfaces. Some species, including roach and bream, do not fit easily into the classification as they will, in different habitats, choose to spawn on a wide variety of substrates from rock to gravel, weeds, reeds, mosses or even terrestrial vegetation overhanging the water. However, other species tend to be more specific in their choice of breeding habitat, as follows:

Lithophils: Dace, Chub, Barbel, which select stones and gravel.

Psammophils: Gudgeon, which select sandy areas for spawning.

Phytophils: Carp, Tench, Crucian Carp, Rudd, which spawn on plants.

Pelagophils: Grass Carp, Silver Carp, Big-head Carp which have buoyant eggs and which spawn in open water where the eggs drift slowly downstream as they develop.

This last group is very interesting as the mature adult fish (particularly grass carp) must migrate many miles upstream before spawning so that the egg and larval drift takes the young fish back to suitable habitats for their early development.

For other cyprinids too, the downstream displacement of small fry by the current means that pre-spawning upstream migrations are normal; dace, minnows, roach, bream, barbel, nase and chub often move upstream, sometimes by as much as a few kilometres. Roach and bream in the Black, Caspian, Aral and Asov seas migrate hundreds of kilometres up inflowing rivers to spawn. These populations would be in danger of extinction from dams and weirs which blocked their path in just the same way that salmon runs are sometimes disrupted. Our river-dwelling cyprinids can also have their spawning migrations blocked by water control structures.

Perhaps because cyprinids tend to have relatively unspecialised spawning behaviour, hybridization occurs quite commonly. The following natural cross-bred fish have been identified: Carp x Crucian Carp, Bream x Orfe, Bream x Rudd, Roach x Rudd, Roach x Bream, Roach x Bleak, Chub x Bleak, Dace x Bleak, and Dace x Rudd.

Senses

A characteristic of carp-like fish is the common occurrence of sensory whiskers or barbels which are used to taste food while it is still outside the mouth, a useful ability when there are anglers around! The sense of smell/taste can be extremely sensitive, with carp having a million times the human capacity to detect dissolved chemicals in the region of the mouth/nasal linings. This sense is likely to be vital in finding food in turbid, low-light conditions. Both common and silver bream have light-reflecting layers behind their retinas, improving vision in dimly-lit conditions; both zander and ruffe have a similar adaptation. The vibration-sensitive lateral line systems and sense of hearing are well developed, probably for defensive reasons, as cyprinids represent the principal prey group for many predatory fish and birds. Wels catfish also appear to have an acute sense of hearing/vibration detection. The hearing ability is achieved by vibrations being transmitted through the gas-filled swim bladder, via a string of small bones (the Weberian ossicles) to the labyrinth of the inner ear and thus to the brain. A heavy footstep on the bank is more than sufficient, therefore, to warn a wary carp or chub of the approach of an angler. This caution, coupled with an ability to learn to recognise fishing line as a potential danger makes large carp in particular very difficult fish to catch and a challenge for anglers. To consistently catch large carp from heavily fished waters is a difficult task; the interest generated by this pastime has given rise to the modern 'specimen-hunting' fraternity of coarse anglers who will spend long periods in pursuit of the largest carp in a lake.

Carp, *Cyprinus carpio*

Identification, original distribution and habitats

Common carp can be recognised by their long dorsal fin and two pairs of barbels (one short and one long) on the upper lip. Gudgeon have one pair of barbels and a short dorsal fin, barbel have two pairs and crucian carp (*Carassius carassius*) have no barbels at all. Hybrids between common and crucian carp usually have a single pair of small barbels and grow much larger than pure crucians generally do.

Carp live in rich weedy ponds, lakes, canals and slow-flowing rivers. They can feed in a diversity of ways and on a very wide range of food materials. Most usually, they will grub and root around in organically rich sediments for small worms, chironomid larvae (*Chironomus* species or 'bloodworms') and bivalved molluscs, Swan (*Anodonta cygnea*), Duck (*Anodonta anatina*), and Pea mussels (*Pisidium and Sphaerium* species). They can also filter zooplankton, especially large species of *Daphnia* from the water and, where feeding conditions are very poor, subsist on a diet of decaying organic matter ('detritus') and filamentous algae.

The natural range of carp is throughout eastern Europe and western Asia, but the species has been very extensively introduced to western Europe, North America, Turkey, Israel, India, Australia, South Africa, North Africa . . . almost everywhere that the climate is warm enough to support it. In the U.S.A., since their introduction in 1877, carp have multiplied to pest proportions in many states where they root out submerged aquatic plants, making formerly attractive wetlands turbid and bare-looking with reduced food supplies for waterfowl and native fish species. The Americans counter this by poisoning them with rotenone (an organic piscicide) where they are unwanted, and even hunting them in swampy areas with bows and arrows with a line attached to the arrow to haul them in with. The latter tactic would cause some raised eyebrows and heated exchanges on British carp fisheries! In Lake Mendota, Wisconsin, Peter Johnsen and Arthur Hasler radio-tracked carp, finding concentrated winter shoals which collected together in a synchronised way in the autumn before the freeze-up. This allowed commercial netsmen to locate the shoals and harvest over 46 tonnes . . . rather more effective than bows and arrows.

The Romans were probably responsible for distributing carp widely in European waters. By the reign of England's King Richard II (1377-99) carp are recorded in the royal kitchen. In Britain, carp have been distributed widely to fish ponds since at least the 1400s; the estate records of the Duke of Norfolk show that he had a number of stocked carp ponds on his East Anglian estates in the 1460s. By the reign of Henry VIII (1509–47), the carp is the most mentioned species in contemporary records, being found from the Welsh borders to London and south to the coast. Even today, carp are commonest in the south eastern counties where the climate is sometimes warm enough for them to breed successfully during hot summers.

An historical perspective on carp farming

As the archetypal cyprinid, carp have a long and complex association with man, being selectively bred for hundreds of generations to produce many varieties, all stemming from the long lean form of the 'wild' carp. Carp are traditionally a pond fish in Europe and under ideal conditions of clean water, constant 28°C and abundant high-quality food, domesticated strains can grow from an egg to a 2-kg (4.4-lb) fish in only one year. This prodigious growth rate, which has been selected for over many generations of breeding, applies to the high-backed, heavy shouldered 'king' carp. The partially-scaled 'mirror' and scaleless 'leather' varieties originated in the fish farms of Europe and Asia. In northern China and Korea, ornamental goldfish, probably originally a coloured variety of Prussian carp (*Carassius auratus*) have also been cultured for thousands of years. The relationship between Man and cyprinid fishes goes back a long way.

The breeding cycle of farmed carp can be carefully controlled by keeping the brood stock under strict temperature and light cycle regimes. The fish can be primed for spawning by injecting them with extracts of dried pituitary hormones, taken from fish killed for the table market. This allows for a carefully planned and timed production cycle. The abundant tiny eggs (a 17-lb fish can produce well over a million) are spawned onto artificial spawning 'ropes' or bunches of water plants, incubated and hatched under optimal conditions.

The tiny fry are then kept and grown-on in highly fertile warm shallow 'Dubisch' ponds where they develop quickly. These ponds are drained down annually, allowed to dry out to eradicate disease and parasitic organisms, fertilised with liberal dollops of manure and then seeded with a new generation of fish. The tiny carp larvae (3–4mm) initially eat 'infusoria' which is a soup of bacteria, algae, rotifers and minute crustaceans. As they grow, they grade on to larger zooplanktonic crustaceans and benthic invertebrates.

Modern commercial carp farming is of great importance in southern and eastern Europe, mainly in the countries of the former U.S.S.R., Poland, Yugoslavia, Czechoslovakia, Austria, Germany and France. Even back in the late 1960s the total annual production was estimated at around 200,000 tons; it must be much higher now.

Koi

In Japan, coloured varieties of 'golden' or 'koi' carp have been intensively selected to produce true-breeding metallic 'ogons'and a wide range of red, black and white variegated fish. When a high-quality genetic line of well-marked and shaped koi has been produced and the best specimens have won places in show competitions their progeny become valuable and fetch very high prices. These are the pedigree specimens of the fish world and the finest fish change hands for esoteric prices of tens of thousands of pounds.

There is a thriving local industry of small one-family koi farms in northern Japan where, through rigorous selective breeding, only the best marked and shaped individuals are allowed to survive and grow to a saleable size. To maintain such fish you need large ponds with meticulously filtered clear water, a high quality diet and freedom from the onslaught of disease, parasites and predators which fish have to endure under natural conditions.

Carp have come a long way from medieval monastic fish ponds where they were grown for the table under crowded conditions, fed on scraps and killed at a size of 1–4 lb which was usually reached in three or four years. The growth rate of carp is critically temperature-dependent; they will overwinter happily in cold water but will gradually lose condition and perhaps 5–15 per cent body weight. To produce large carp quickly you need a source of warm water. Cheap sources of heat from power stations and other industrial sites have allowed carp and eel farms to grow fish in unfavourably cool climates at the northern edge of their European distribution.

Density-dependent growth

Nature is clever in limiting the growth potential of common carp under conditions of extreme crowding. This accounts for the phenomenon of large fish not growing in small ponds. Carp appear to secrete a hormone into the water in response to low oxygen and high ammonia levels which has the effect of slowing both the growth rate and heart-beat rate of the individual fish and fellow shoal members. This may be an adaptation to cope with the stresses of high-density fish farm conditions and it is not known whether this phenomenon occurs under natural conditions.

Carp can endure prolonged bouts of very low dissolved oxygen concentration and can even live out of water in wet moss for long periods, as long as they are kept cool and the gill chambers remain moist. Apart from their need for warm water, carp are an ideal fish farm species being hardy, adaptable, non-aggressive, fast-growing and well flavoured with firm white flesh.

Natural breeding biology

Spawning takes place in warm, shallow, heavily-weeded lake margins and flooded water meadows in May or June, when the temperature reaches around 17-20°C. Carp acclimate to cool water temperatures at the northern extreme of their distribution, often spawning as early in the year as fish breeding further south. The relatively high water temperature requirement means, however, that carp only occasionally breed successfully in central and northern Europe. In England, deep, shaded lakes that warm up slowly in the spring probably never produce young carp, but they can support long-lived populations of (stocked) adult fish.

The roe can weigh up to one third of the body weight of ripe female carp, and farmed fish in good condition produce around 60–70,000 eggs per pound of body weight. Wild carp mature their eggs together but shed them in batches over an extended period on bulrush (*Schoenoplectus*), pondweeds (*Potamogeton*) and milfoil (*Myriophyllum*) beds. They require three to four months at 20°C to mature their ovaries. In southern European and Asian waters this allows two or even three reproductive cycles per year. Spawning involves much chasing and splashing amongst large shoals of fish in shallow weedy bays; at this time carp lose much of their natural caution and can be observed at close quarters. The small (1-mm diameter) sticky eggs swell up to 1.6mm in water and hatch after incubating for around 100 degree-days (e.g. five days at 20°C). The 4–5mm fry lie amongst the weed for two to three days before filling their swim-bladders with air at the surface and swimming off in search of tiny rotifers, algae, large clumps of bacteria and the smallest of crustacean larvae.

Feeding and growth

Under natural northern European conditions, carp feed very actively from around 20°C upwards and little, if at all, below 8°C; the lower threshold for active growth is around

12–15°C. Where they are fished for, carp often feed mostly at night and in all waters dawn and dusk feeding sorties are probably a normal pattern of feeding behaviour. In hot thundery weather carp lakes are often turned muddy by shoals of actively feeding fish. Like bream, carp have very protrusible mouths, allowing them to dig deep in the mud for large bloodworms and mussels. At three to four years wild carp measure 20–40cm and are long thin fully scaled golden bronze-brown fish with reddish/purple pectoral, pelvic, and anal fins and dark caudal and dorsal fins.

The cultivated 'king' carp stocks are portly by comparison. Mirror and 'king' (fully scaled) common carp, stocked into productive lakes, will grow on at a rate of at least a kilogramme per year (double this in rich waters) for many years to reach ultimate sizes of 50 lb plus. Chris Yates' rod-caught record fish from Redmire Pool, Herefordshire in 1980 was a spawn-bound female of 51 lb 8 oz (23.36kg), Richard Walker's more famous previous record fish ('Clarissa'), weighed 44 lb and was only 15 years old when caught in 1952. Clarissa went on to live until 1972 in the London Zoo aquarium, dying at an age of 35 years. The longevity record for carp is much disputed and often subject to wild quesswork, but captive fish, especially those kept on low rations in cool waters can certainly live for approaching 40 years or more. In the warm productive lakes of southern France and Spain, where insect larvae, mussels and crayfish abound, carp regularly grow to 60 lb plus and over a metre in length, with occasional specimens being much heavier still, but this fast growth probably leads to a relatively short life span.

Carp fishing

It is difficult to believe that an animal with a brain the size of your little finger nail would be hard to outwit, but it's true! This fact has spawned the craft of 'high-tech' carp specimen hunting during which grown men (and women) will sit for days on end at the side of a lake waiting for a carp to take a specially-prepared bait which has been groundbaited for weeks previously to lure the carp into a false sense of security. Successful baits are soon shunned by fish that have learnt to associate them with danger.

Large carp swim around in small loose shoals or as individuals, often patrolling a set route which they follow at particular times of day. Detailed patient observations over several days can allow a keen angler to predict where a given fish will be feeding at a given time and so greatly increase his chances of success. Carp are a wary and challenging fish to catch; they learn very quickly to avoid food items that have a length of stiff nylon monofilament line attached to them, and thus are difficult to deceive.

On a hard-fished carp water, a handful of floating bread crusts will be taken stealthily, one by one, leaving the single piece with a hook inside floating forlornly, rejected until it falls off the hook . . . then it is eaten instantly. These fish are not stupid! This animal cunning, combined with a great fighting strength and attractive and varied appearance ensure that carp fishing will remain a popular pastime for years to come. The pioneer of the craft was the clever and innovative Richard Walker whose book *Stillwater Angling* has become a classic in angling literature.

Tench, *Tinca tinca*

Tench fishing

I think it was Fred Taylor's classic book *Tench* (Macdonald, 1971) which captured for me the interest and pleasure to be derived from tench fishing. Tench are, in every way, a nice fish to see and handle. As a young teenager, before girlfriends took over from fishing, I used to have an annual pilgrimage in the early morning on 16 June to Emborough Pond in Somerset to go fishing for tench. There is something mystical and magical about being next to a lake at dawn, with a thin mist shimmering over the water and a red-tipped porcupine quill float, surrounded by clouds of needle-fine bubbles as a tench noses around the bread flake bait. The float would bob and wave around for several minutes before gently sliding away as a tench swam off with the bait. We always used barbless hooks so as to cause minimal damage to the fish and soon dispensed with keepnets so that the tench could be released immediately. And what fish they were — golden yellow, with that little red eye and large dark rubbery fins. The males could be clearly distinguished as they have larger, spoon-shaped, pelvic fins than the females.

My largest tench, a six-pounder, came from Hyde Lane lakes at Buckingham, Buckinghamshire, but this fell somewhat short of the British record — a magnificent specimen of 14 lb 3 oz (6.44kg) by P. Gooriah from Wraysbury number 1 gravel pit, Middlesex in 1987.

Identification, distribution and habitats

Tench are a solid, characterful fish, heavily built, with a thick 'wrist' to the tail. A single pair of small barbels fringe the upper lip. The scales are small and deeply embedded in the thick layer of mucus which covers the body. Folk lore would have you believe that tench slime has magical curative powers, healing skin sores and abrasions. Maybe this is so, I haven't tried, but the local name 'doctor fish' is still applied to the tench in some areas. The following quotation is attributed to Dame Juliana Berners (*A Treatyse of Fysshynge wyth an Angle*, 1496) 'A Tench is a good fyssh, and heelith all mannere of other fysshe that ben hurt yf they may come to him'.

Isaac Walton made the following statement: 'The tyrant pike will not be a wolf to his physician, but forbears to devour him though he be ever so hungry.'

I have found tench in pike stomachs and so, perhaps, modern-day pike have overcome their former reluctance to prey upon an occasional 'doctor fish'.

The golden-yellow colour of the tench that I used to catch is typical of fish from clay-bedded lakes, while in chalk pits a brassy pale form with white belly and red fins occurs, and in silty, well-weeded waters tench can be a very dark olive green. Just occasionally a golden tench turns up, this natural colour variant is selectively bred for the garden pond market and most of the golden tench caught by anglers are probably from this source.

I think that adult tench are so distinctive that they are unmistakable, but young fish might be confused with small stone loach in rivers or perhaps with spined loach in silty lakes and streams. Stone loach (*Noemacheilus barbatulus*) are a small, dark, bottom-living species, like tench, but they have three pairs of barbels, distinguishing them immediately. In still waters, such as gravel pits and in some streams, spined loach (*Cobitis taenia*) are locally common; these also have three pairs of barbels and a movable pair of small spines below each eye which distinguish them from stone loach. Spined loach are also much more laterally compressed than stone loach which are round-bodied, rather like miniature barbel.

Tench occur in rich weedy lakes and slow-moving rivers throughout most of Europe except in the far north where conditions are too cold for them to spawn. The species is very tolerant of low dissolved oxygen concentrations, only Crucian carp are tougher in this respect.

The best tench lakes have a mosaic of Canadian pondweed (*Elodea canadensis*), milfoil (*Myriophyllum*), hornwort (*Ceratophyllum*), lilies (*Nymphaea, Nuphar*), bulrush (*Schoenoplectus*) and pondweeds (*Potamogeton*). A diversity of submerged aquatic plants is important for both feeding and spawning. Tench waters are often ruined by the stocking of large numbers of adult carp and/or bream which make the water turbid and lead to the demise of most of the submerged plants. After this has happened the tench gradually die out.

Despite their great popularity as a sport species, tench remain little studied, particularly in British waters. The species is common in south-east England and Ireland but is rare in Scotland and Wales.

Food and Growth

In Britain, under natural conditions, tench grow slowly and potentially live for many years. The oldest specimen that Ros Wright and I recorded from our studies of the St Peter's gravel pit lake (Linford, Buckinghamshire) tench population was 15 years old. In Ireland, Michael Kennedy and Paddy Fitzmaurice recorded Coosan Lough tench of

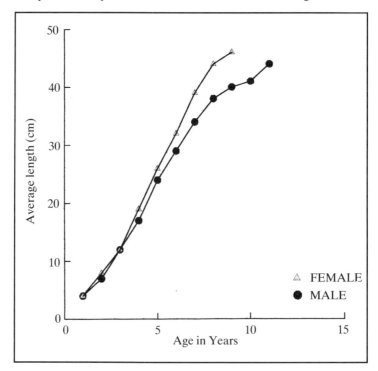

Growth of Tench in Coosan Lough

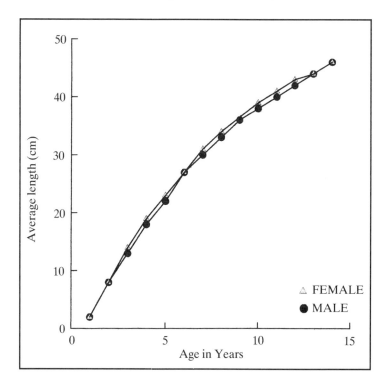

Growth of
St Peter's Lake
Tench

up to 11 years of age. The growth rates of male and female Coosan Lough tench are as in the figure opposite.

Coosan Lough is a rich water and the tench growth rates are good; females clearly grow more quickly than males after age 3. The largest fish of around 45cm in this population would weigh around 1600 grammes (4 lb plus).

In our study of St Peter's Lake tench we found the smoothed average growth rates for male and female fish as in the figure above.

The data were smoothed to even out the effects of small sample sizes for some age groups (for some reason, for example, we caught no 10-year-old females). It is clear that the growth of males and females in our gravel pit tench population is extremely similar, the females not showing the increased growth of the Irish fish. Also, our tench took much longer (five years for females) to reach the same ultimate size as the Coosan Lough fish (46cm). The St Peter's tench grow at a rate similar to that of Irish tench in 'average' waters; the Coosan Lough fish are fast growers by Irish standards.

These growth differences are probably due to differences in habitat quality. Coosan Lough is a productive, 200-acre lake with beds of Marestail (*Hippuris vulgaris*). St Peter's Lake is a well-weeded, 5-acre, firm-bedded gravel pit which has a diverse, but not very abundant invertebrate community. When we electro-fished and netted the fish out of St Peter's in October 1987, to try and improve the feeding conditions for the breeding ducks, we found that tench numbered 176 adult fish to the hectare (= 2.5 acres) or 102kg per hectare (around 100 lb to the acre). Tench accounted for about 30 per cent of the total weight of fish present, the rest being comprised of bream, roach, perch, rudd and pike. We concluded that well-weeded gravel pits represent an ideal habitat for tench and that, whilst the growth rates might be modest in some waters, these man-made lakes will provide a wealth of good fisheries in the future.

In our analysis of St Peter's tench growth, we compared age estimates using otoliths, scales and opercular bones from each of a small sample of dead fish. The estimated ages tallied well for fish up to nine years old, but thereafter scales under-estimated ages whilst opercular bones showed up clear zones between the outermost annuli which were obscured on the scales. It seems to be generally true for cyprinids (and perhaps all fish) in Britain that scale readings are fine for estimating the age of relatively young fish but, when old age sets in and growth in length slows to a trickle or stops, opercular bones and otoliths are better for distinguishing the true age of large specimens.

As can be seen from the graphs above, young tench reach only 2–4cm in their first year of growth, living quietly amongst dense weedbeds where they feed upon algae and very small crustaceans (*Bosmina, Ceriodaphnia, Cyclops,* and *Chydoridae*). After their first year, older tench start to venture further out into open water to take chironomid larvae, small shrimps, water lice (*Asellus*, which remain a favourite food throughout life), small caddis larvae and mayfly nymphs. Tench of all sizes are adept at picking small invertebrates, especially crustaceans (shrimps, water lice, chydorids) from the surfaces of plants. In this respect they are rather like Crucian carp. *Asellus* often form the bulk of tench diet through the summer when they are abundant and when the tench are feeding actively.

Tench will also probe the sediments for shallow-burrowing prey, particularly chironomid larvae, small mussels (*Sphaerium, Pisidium*) and alderfly larvae (*Sialis*) which they actively select. When they are disturbing the sediments, bubbles of marsh gas (methane) bubble up through their gills and form the patches of finely-divided 'tench bubbles' which are so familiar to anglers.

Finally, and typically for a cyprinid fish, tench can adapt their feeding behaviour to filter out dense blooms of zooplankton, such as *Daphnia hyalina*, in open water. We found that this form of feeding occurred in our Main lake at Great Linford which was almost weed-free; the benthic fauna were heavily exploited by bream, and the roach and tench (as well as the bream at times) switched their attention to the crustacean soup that surrounded them and which they only had to breath in to eat.

Breeding Biology

Tench are an unusual cyprinid fish in that the genus *Tinca* has only one species, which seems to be structurally distinct from the rest of the family. Perhaps for this reason, tench do not form natural hybrids in the way that so many other cyprinids do. Adults mature early at three to four years and at small body sizes compared with bream. Mature male tench do not develop the temporary white spawning tubercles characteristic of other cyprinids but they do develop large pelvic fins which allow the sexes to be distinguished at all times of year. This is very unusual amongst freshwater fish where external recognition of the sexes outside the breeding season is usually impossible. The large pelvic fins may serve to convey the milt (sperm) efficiently to the eggs during spawning; certainly male tench do not produce the large volumes of milt typical of, for example, male roach, bream, chub or dace.

Small groups of tench (one ripe female with two to three males) spawn during short bursts of swimming activity amongst weeds. The eggs tend to be widely dispersed compared with those of other cyprinid species where spawning often occurs amongst concentrated shoals. Tench spawn in May-June or even July in cool summers and, typically, strong year-classes are produced in hot summers. In cool years (which are not rare in England), spawning is delayed and female tench, heavy with spawn, are caught at the beginning of the coarse fishing season. This is a pity as the fish are vulnerable to bad handling at this time and certainly shouldn't be cooped up in a crowded keepnet for hours on end.

Spawning usually takes place when the water temperature reaches around 18–20°C. Females are very fecund and produce 250,000–800,000 1-mm diameter sticky eggs which are shed in successive batches in dense vegetation in shallow water. The tiny larvae hatch in three to six days and remain stuck to the weeds until they swim up to fill their swim bladders and then start to eat minute crustaceans, rotifers and clumps of bacteria and algae. Very little is known of the early life history of tench because of the difficulty of catching large enough samples of young fish in their dense weedy habitats.

Bronze or Common Bream, *Abramis brama*

Identification, distribution and habitats

Bronze bream have a deep, laterally compressed body with a thick slime layer overlaying the deep bronze skin. Young 'skimmer' bream are silver and can easily be mistaken for small Silver (or White) bream (*Blicca bjoerkna*); the latter species has 40–45 scales along the lateral line whilst the Bronze bream has 51–60. Silver bream also have relatively large eyes and scales in comparison to those of the Bronze bream. Young Bronze bream can be distinguished from roach by the much longer anal fin and the generally dark fin colouration compared to the red fins of the roach. Bream have olive/gold irises whilst those of the roach are red.

Hybrids

Roach–bream hybrids are intermediate in character and can be the devil's own job to distinguish from either parental species. The hybrids grow vigourously and can mature sexually, sometimes back-crossing with either parental species to give rise to second generation hybrids which can be very similar-looking to purebred specimens. Record claims for large rod caught roach need careful expert examination to establish the likely pedigree of the specimen concerned.

In Britain, bream spawn between mid-May and mid-June and the eggs are shed both on littoral vegetation, and on submerged weeds in water down to 10 feet in depth. Rudd spawn at the same time and in similar habitats and rudd–bream hybrids are thus very common in certain waters.

Habitats

Bronze bream are a warm-water species at the northern edge of their distribution in Britain; they are common throughout Europe and central Asia. The species thrives in rich lowland lakes and the slow flowing reaches of lowland rivers where their characteristic habitat is termed the 'Bream zone'. In Britain and Ireland, bream are an important angling species, forming the backbone of many match fishing bags and featuring largely in most angling competition results. In central Europe the species is caught commercially in nets and traps and sold for food.

Annual migrations

David Jordan and Jon Wortley found that, in the Norfolk Broads, adult bream spread out into the shallow lakes (such as Malthouse Broad) to feed and spawn during the summer months and then migrate to congregate at very high densities in wintering holes in the adjacent rivers (such as the River Bure). This type of annual cycle of movement seems to be characteristic of bream throughout their range. Ken Whelan found a similar situation on the River Suck in Ireland; here, after tracing the 4 per cent of recaptures of 2763 tagged fish, he established that most adult bream seemed to display regular spawning migrations of up to 10km. Four separate large feeding shoals coalesced to spawn and then redistributed themselves back into their former groups to resume feeding for the summer in their normal 'home' stretches of river. In the Caspian sea, bream begin their spawning migration into inflowing rivers as soon as the spring ice-melt begins in April.

Turbid bream waters: Feeding biology

Bream feed very actively at night when they will move into the extreme shallows in search of invertebrate-rich feeding areas. They thrive in silty waters where they can sift through the sediments in search of chironomid larvae, small oligochaete worms and mussels. The mouth can be extended to form a long tube which is thrust down into the mud as a mouthful of silt is sucked up. Numerous taste buds allow the invertebrates to be winnowed from the grit and mud which is then either spat out or squirted out through the gills. As the silt-laden water passes over the gill arches and rakers a subtle form of filtering takes place so that the food organisms are retained and passed to the back of the throat for grinding by the pharyngeal teeth before swallowing.

Eddy Lammens, who works on the feeding ecology of bronze and silver bream in the Netherlands, has suggested that bronze bream feed most efficiently in fine silt/sandy substrates whilst silver bream, which have a coarser gill-raker system, are better at feeding in gravel-bedded areas. Age Braband, who studied the ecology of these two bream species in Lake Oyeren, southern Norway, found that bronze bream fed on invertebrates which were deeper down in the sediments than those taken by silver bream. Perhaps the two species split up the available habitat in these ways and thus avoid strong inter-specific food competition.

It is usual for both immature and adult bream to form feeding shoals comprised of fish of a similar size and age; this may be to minimise the individual risk of predation by pike and/or it may help individual fish to find richer patches of invertebrate food. It is usual for invertebrates like chironomid larvae to be clumped in their distribution on the lake bed. If many mouths are sampling the sediments, the whole shoal can benefit from the discovery of a rich feeding area. It could be a very difficult task for individual bream to find such areas on their own. A disadvantage of feeding socially is that intense competition for the available food is likely to occur where the population density of the bream is high for the habitat type concerned.

Research that Ros Wright and I did on gravel-pit bream showed that 11–14 year old fish, produced in the hot summers of the mid-1970s, had become stunted in our lakes at a size of around 3.5 lb. We greatly reduced the bream population density by netting out most of the fish (to increase the food supply for wildfowl) and the few remaining bream which avoided the nets grew rapidly, putting on an extra pound in weight over only one year. This showed that the fish were previously very short of food and that a large reduction in the population density led directly to a spurt in growth, even amongst these old specimens. Strong competition for food in bream-dominated fish communities is probably a common occurrence.

The Tjeukemeer

The likely importance of competition for food in bream-dominated fish communities is highlighted by the interesting research of Eddy Lammens, working on Lake Tjeukemeer in the Netherlands. In this shallow productive water it seems that the following feeding relationships occur between bream, eels and smelt (*Osmerus eperlanus*). In years when young smelt are abundant they graze the *Daphnia hyalina* population down to a low level, forcing the bream to switch from *Daphnia* to chironomid larvae and molluscs and the eels to switch from chironomids to small fish. In these years the condition of both the bream and the eels declines. When the smelt year classes are weak, however, the bream feed on the abundant *Daphnia*, the eels forage for chironomid larvae and both bream and eels grow fat and sleek.

By stirring up the lake bed during the summer months as they feed, bream make waters turbid, and in addition they release mineral nutrients both from the sediments and from their own waste products which cause algal populations to flourish. As the microscopic algae bloom, so the *Daphnia* and other zooplanktonic crustaceans thrive, sometimes building up huge populations through the summer. The bream take advantage of these self-induced conditions by switching their feeding to zooplankton, especially *Daphnia hyalina*, when they have depleted the supply of midge larvae in the sediments. In these rich, turbid 'pea soup' bream lakes, submerged weedbeds have no chance to bask in the sunshine, and typically the only large plants to survive are tough ones with floating leaves such as marginal lilies and pondweeds.

When we removed the bulk of the bream (about three tonnes, plus 2.5 tonnes of roach) from the lakes of the Great Linford Wildfowl Reserve, the water cleared, algal blooms diminished and submerged weedbeds sprouted up across the whole bed of a 30-acre lake which had been weed-free whilst the fish were resident. In addition, the invertebrate food supply for the ducks increased substantially and the survival of tufted ducklings, which had previously been very poor improved markedly. Some of the new weed growth was probably due to the roach removal as I had found that roach were eating germinating plant seedlings amongst their usual diet of *Daphnia*. Bream and roach have profound effects upon the ecology of the lakes in which they live.

Michael Kennedy and Paddy Fitzmaurice studied the biology of bream in Irish waters where they found that adult fish eat large numbers of shrimps (*Gammarus*), water lice (*Asellus*) and molluscs (the mussels *Sphaerium* and *Pisidium*), in addition to the normal fare of worms and midge larvae.

A final point to make on bream diet is that the largest adults will take small fish and they are sometimes caught on large lures, fished deep on sinking lines by reservoir trout anglers. Fish-feeding by large bream has been recorded so many times that it must be regarded as a normal part of their foraging behaviour.

Growth

The average adult size of bream is 20–50cm, although much larger fish occur where the food supply is plentiful. Growth is usually rather slow with 10-cm fish being two to three years old and 10–12-year-olds reaching 45–50cm in good waters. Rarely, specimens grow to 60cm (3kg) and exceptionally to 80cm (9kg). The British rod-caught record bronze bream, caught by A. Bromley, weighed 16 lb 6 oz (7.43kg) and came from a small Staffordshire lake*. This compares with the far smaller record silver bream, a fish of 15 oz (0.43kg) caught by Dennis Flack at Grime Spring, Suffolk in 1988.

Bream usually mature at 3–5 years of age, although in Ireland maturity seems to be delayed until 7–10 years; adult fish may live for up to 20 years or more. The growth potential of bream in a lake can be related directly to the abundance of chironomid

*This fish has been surpassed by a 16 lb 9 oz specimen caught by M. McKeown.

larvae (bloodworms) in the sediments: less than 5 grammes per square metre wet weight and growth is poor, more than 20 grammes and growth is very good, with all intermediate conditions being found.

The average length (cm) of bream (sexes combined) from the moderately productive Cole Mere Lake in Cheshire, England, studied by Colin Goldspink is as follows:

Growth of
Bream in
Cole Mere Lake

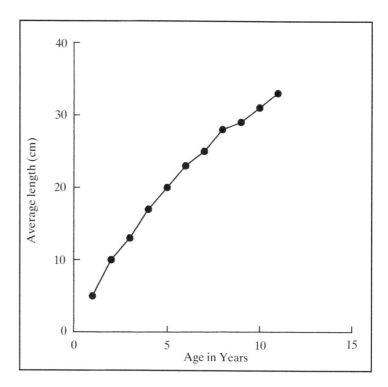

These growth rates were exceeded by bream from both Ellesmere and Tatton Meres: 10-year-old bream in these two lakes averaged 35cm plus; Tatton Mere fish grew to 46cm at an age of 16 years.

Slow growth in bream, as in other cyprinids, often leads to a long life span; fish from a northerly population in Loch Maben, Scotland have been recorded at 21 years of age. Irish bream were also found to be long-lived and slow-growing. Michael Kennedy and Paddy Fitzmaurice found that little growth occurred during the winter, whilst young bream started to increase in length in May and adult fish after July. The oldest Irish bream studied was 23 years of age. Other things being equal, Irish bream grew fastest in large alkaline ('hard water') lakes. In a rich water, Irish bream reach a length of 47cm at 10 years and weigh around 1360 grammes (3.5 lb). In slower-growth waters, 10-year-old bream averaged 30.5cm (the same as in Cole Mere) and weighed 540 grammes (1 lb 6 oz). Specimen (7-lb plus) bream, so sought after by keen coarse anglers holidaying in Ireland, are fast-growing fish from rich waters, they are usually 12–15 years old but may be as young as 9 years or as old as 23.

Breeding biology

Bream spawn from May to July depending on the warmth of the weather and the siting of the lake or river. Spawning is well synchronised throughout the shoal, often occurs at night and usually commences when the water temperature is around 12°C. Females produce 100,000–500,000 small (2-mm diameter) yellow, sticky eggs which hatch in five to ten days. Male bream develop a dark body colouration and numerous white spawning tubercles on their head and shoulders; as the spawning period approaches they become aggressive and start to defend small territories in shallow areas around lake edges. The territories occupy about one square metre in open situations and up to five square metres adjacent to reedbeds. The males defend these areas, chasing away rivals and trying to attract ripe females from shoals which patrol the lake margins. When a female enters a male's territory the male swims under her from behind and drives her into a weedy area where spawning takes place.

Newly hatched bream alevins are small (6mm) and they remain stuck to the plants on which they hatched with a special organ on the head until they have absorbed their yolk sacs and are ready to swim off in search of rotifers, tiny crustaceans and algae which form their early diet. Bream fry have grown their adult fins at 16mm length and start to form scales at 20mm. The small fry are found around the warm shallow margins of lakes and in quiet river backwaters; they often associate with young roach and rudd, sheltering from predators close to weed beds. As they grow, the young bream move on to larger zooplankton prey and then subsequently as 'skimmers' they move down to begin foraging on the lake bed for benthic invertebrates.

By comparison with bream, roach and rudd show no male territoriality, spawning in shoals where the males chase females in a mêlée of activity; there may be some subtle mate choice going on but it is not understood at present.

The importance of warm summers to bream breeding success and subsequent year class strengths is highlighted both by the work at Great Linford, where the adult bream stock was totally dominated by 1973 and 1976 fish and by Colin Goldspink's work on bream in the Cheshire Meres. In the Cheshire lakes Tatton, Ellesmere and Cole Mere, bream have variable recruitment and, at the time of Goldspink's study, the three populations were dominated by fish spawned during the relatively warm summers of 1959, 1966, 1969 and 1973. As at Great Linford, dominant year-classes were abundant but cool summers seemed to produce a total recruitment failure. There may be a threshold temperature (number of 'degree-days' through the summer) required for bream (and other cyprinids) to spawn and produce fry that survive in the medium-long term.

Barbel, *Barbus barbus*

Identification, habitat, distribution and related species.

A handsome fish with bronze-gold body colouring and pale-pink/red fins, barbel occupy the middle reaches of large rivers in central Europe and are indigenous and widespread in waters from eastern England eastward to the Black Sea. Where conditions are right, the species thrives and can dominate the fish community. The barbel appears to be native to the rivers of eastern England from Yorkshire southwards to the Thames. Alwynne Wheeler and David Jordan have published an up-to-date account of the spread of the species in Britain and the following section relies heavily upon their research.

Wheeler and Jordan suggest that barbel are truly native to the following main British Rivers; the Yorkshire Ouse, Derwent, Wharfe, Aire, Swale, Don, the Trent system, Witham, Welland, and the Great Ouse and Thames systems. Several other smaller rivers may also have provided a home for post-glacial barbel populations which subsequently either died out or survived at low densities in localised pockets of suitable habitat. Anglers have, in recent years, aided the slow natural spread through British rivers. No one knows what effects such introductions have had on the former fish communities of these rivers but it seems likely that the newly-introduced barbel will overlap for both food and space requirements with chub and, to a lesser degree, dace and roach.

Some invertebrate species may well have been subjected to predation pressures which they are ill-equiped to withstand, whilst others, like the parasitic hookworm *Pomphorhyncus laevis*, have thrived. *Pomphorhyncus* lives as an adult parasite in the upper gut of cyprinid fish including barbel, chub, roach and dace. The fish are infected when they eat shrimps (*Gammarus pulex*) that are carrying *Pomphorhynchus* larvae in their blood systems. Fish which eat a lot of shrimps can build up heavy infestations of the adult hookworms and lose body condition through the drain on their systems. The chub in the Hampshire Avon were badly affected in this way during the 1960s/70s. It seems likely that the translocation of barbel from river to river, for example from the Kennet to the Hampshire Avon and Severn, has aided the spread of this damaging parasite, infecting chub, roach dace and other species in the process.

Redistribution of barbel in Britain began in the 1890s when fish could lawfully be moved anywhere without consent: in 1896 barbel were stocked in the Dorset Stour from where they spread into the confluent Hampshire Avon. These fish are thought to have come from the Thames. Barbel from the rivers Lea and Kennet were subsequently stocked into the Avon. In 1956, 509 Kennet barbel were transferred to the Severn. This population has subsequently thrived and spread into the tributaries (Vyrnwy, Tern, Worfe, and Teme). Fish from the Swale were released into the Warwickshire Avon in 1964 and a series of stockings from the Kennet during the 1950s and 60s firmly established the species in the Bristol Avon. From here fish have been moved to Bristol Avon tributaries, the Somerset Frome and the River Chew. In Northumbria, barbel were illegally stocked into both the lower Wear and Tees. The Great Ouse, Welland and Wensum all contain small localised barbel populations which have been supplemented by stocked fish. Barbel also occur in both the Kentish Stour and the Medway system. Barbel were never native to Wales but have been stocked illegally into the Wye in mid-Wales, the Usk and possibly the Dee. Fishery scientists and anglers have also spread the species to north-west England where it now inhabits the Ribble, Dane/Weaver and Bollin.

Advances in fish culture techniques have recently made it possible to produce fish-farmed barbel and to stock out intensively-reared fry and fingerlings. This development will ensure that barbel continue to spread (both legally and illegally) to a further range of suitable rivers in the British Isles. The species is not recorded (so far!) in Ireland or Scotland.

Barbel are able to cope with the demands of a swiftly flowing current through their streamlined shape and choice of sheltered lies. The 'pay-off' in biological terms of occupying this difficult habitat is likely to be the avoidance of competition for food and space from other cyprinid species such as bream, tench and carp and, to a lesser extent, roach — all species that typify slow-flowing habitats. Predation by pike is also likely to be much reduced in good barbel habitat, since pike prefer slower river sections with marginal reedbeds.

In Britain barbel may live for perhaps as long as 20 years and reach sizes of 8–9kg; the British rod-caught record* weighed 14 lb 6 oz (6.52kg) and was caught by Aylmer Tryon from a boat on the Royalty fishery, Hampshire Avon in 1934. The young Aylmer was being instructed on the finer points of barbel fishing by his experienced father and the then Royalty fishery manager when he caught first a four pounder and then the monster fish. The family had the fish set-up by the famous taxidermists J. Cooper & Sons but didn't realise that it was a record until a little while later when it was recognised as such by the Record Fish Committee. Aylmer Tryon still fishes actively today (1993) and has a long string of fine salmon from the Dorset Frome to his name.

The largest rod-caught barbel to date weighed-in at 16 lb 1 ounce and was foul-hooked by a salmon angler on the Hampshire Avon. This fish pales into insignificance, however, when compared to the Aral barbel, one of nine other continental races or species. The Aral barbel is found in saline, brackish and freshwater regions of river deltas in the Caspian and Aral seas. Specimens caught commercially from rivers such as the Volga during the upstream spawning migration have weighed up to 22.5kg (almost 50 lb!). The other eight European species, which are localised in their distributions attain weights of around half of that of British *Barbus barbus*, but are nevertheless of local commercial and sporting importance. Turkish barbel occur in the rivers around the Black and Aegean seas, whilst the Macedonian barbel is found only in one small area of northern Greece. The Greek barbel is confined to the Aspropotamus in western Greece; the Caucasian, Bulatmai, Iberian and Albanian species also have very restricted distributions and consequently have a high conservation value. The Mediterranean barbel, conversely, is a widespread species, occurring in waters throughout south-western and central Europe. A 50-lb Aral barbel hooked on a sultry summer evening on the banks of the Volga must, surely, represent an electrifying prospect for the footloose specimen coarse angler of the 1990s.

Growth

Barbel are long-lived and grow slowly to reach sexual maturity after 4–5 years. The average adult size is 30–50cm. Maximum lengths of around 90cm, or exceptionally one metre, can be achieved after 15 or more years of life.

*The 15 lb 7 oz barbel caught by R. Morris from the River Medway in 1993 has now surpassed Aylmer Tryon's long-standing record fish.

146

The annual growth checks on scales, which fish biologists use to estimate the age of captured specimens, are formed by barbel in May when these fish stop feeding and concentrate their efforts on spawning. Annual growth checks are readily identifiable on scales taken from young (fast-growing) fish. Scales from old fish are, however, much more difficult to interpret since 'false checks' (formed during periods of stress) are often present and several true annual rings, which are difficult to separate, may be present right at the outer edge of the scale. A further difficulty lies in the fact that slow growing fish are often long lived and thus have scales with a long series of annual growth cycles occurring very close together.

In a typical year most growth in length of barbel is made during the period June-September, with a slowing through to November. Little or no growth in length then takes place from December to June. On the Severn (and probably elsewhere) female fish grow faster than males after an age of 4 years when both species have reached a length of around 30cm. By an age of 8 years males might grow to 45cm whilst females could top 60cm (and at a much greater weight than the males).

Feeding behaviour

As a species specifically adapted for life in strongly-flowing waters, the barbel has a powerfully-muscled, streamlined body which can hold station in swift currents using the large pectoral fins angled downwards along the leading edges to press the front part of the body down against the river bed. When holding station in this position, barbel can move across current to intercept small invertebrate food items drifting downstream such as shrimps (*Gammarus*), stonefly nymphs (*Perla, Nemoura*) mayfly nymphs (*Rithrogena, Baetis, Ecdyonurus*), or they can systematically browse the surface of the stone and gravel substrate for snails (*Valvata, Theodoxus*), freshwater limpets (*Ancylus fluviatilis*), cased and caseless caddis larvae (*Anabolia, Silo, Hydropsyche, Rhyacophila*) small fish (loach, bullheads, minnows), and algae covering the stream bed. The four sensory barbels on the upper lip (gudgeon have two, stone loach have six) can detect the presence of small prey that have burrowed down below the surface (small mussels, worms, midge and mayfly larvae, crayfish); these animals can then be dug out of the gravel with the thick rubbery lips and passed back to the throat where three rows of powerful crushing (pharyngeal) teeth grind up even the toughest food. A shoal of actively-feeding barbel can, therefore, 'Hoover' the stream bed for a wide variety of potential prey.

Crayfish

The demise of our native crayfish (*Austropotamobius pallipes*) in all but a few remaining strongholds may well have depleted an important source of food for both barbel and chub. The introduction of the North American signal crayfish (*Pacifastacus leniusculus*), for instance into the River Kennet where it is thriving, has undoubtedly provided an abundant replacement food source for these species. This story does, however, have a 'down-side' in that signal crays carry the fungus that has wiped out populations of our native crayfish by causing local eruptions of 'crayfish plague'. It seems that this is an example of the folly of introducing non-native species without any regard for the consequent ecological repercussions. Anyone considering stocking this or any other 'exotic' species must contact the local representative of English Nature who will advise them of their position in relation to the 1981 Wildlife and Countryside

Act. At the time of writing the stocking of signal crays is usually restricted to water bodies that are completely self-contained and where there is no danger of the introduced stock gaining access to adjacent watercourses where they might damage native species.

Barbel often shelter from the main thrust of the current in water crowfoot (*Ranunculus*) or bulrush (*Schoenoplectus lacustris*) beds where they can find abundant food amongst the silted plant roots, stems and leaves. In the silty deposits chironomid midge larvae, mayfly nymphs (*Ephemera, Caenis*), alder fly larvae (*Sialis*), snails (*Limnaea, Physa, Planorbis, Bithynia, Valvata*), orb shells (*Sphaerium*), water lice (*Asellus*), dragonfly nymphs (*Calopteryx, Gomphus*), and cased caddis larvae (*Limnephilus*) all provide potential food items for foraging fish. Water crowfoot beds also provide protective overhead cover from potential predators (herons) during the daylight hours. The eyes are positioned high up on the head, allowing the barbel a wide arc of overhead vision and thus alerting the fish to danger. Unusual bankside vibrations (like the footsteps of incautious anglers) also cause barbel to melt away back into the security of their home lies. Chub and barbel often occupy this habitat together. As the light levels fall on warm summer evenings barbel become less shy and feed high up in the water, sucking snails and insect nymphs from the floating stems and under surfaces of leaves. This foraging activity can easily be heard from the bank and often alerts anglers to the presence of feeding fish.

Groundbaiting
Through regular feeding, barbel can be readily weaned onto an artificial diet of maggots, luncheon meat, lobworms or sweetcorn introduced over extended periods by anglers pre-baiting fishing swims. Victorian footmen were famous for their slavish labours of collecting hundreds of lobworms from the lawns of riverside mansions and pre-baiting swims prior to their lords and masters fishing the weir pools. Recent research has shown that anglers' baits form a significant part of the food intake of barbel on the River Severn; indeed scales taken from these fish showed a marked check in growth when fishing was suspended for one week prior to a major national fishing match. It seems likely that the groundbait and hookbaits used by coarse anglers have a considerable effect upon the natural feeding ecology of many fish species, waterbirds and invertebrates living in our rivers, ponds and lakes.

A note on the care of barbel (and other species) by anglers
Three points concerning the care of barbel are worth making:
1. use strong line and barbless hooks; this will make playing, landing and unhooking much easier and less damaging to the fish. You will also find that you lose fewer fish whilst you are playing them. Use a knotless landing net.
2. Lay the fish on a wet plastic sheet for unhooking and for any photography. It is unwise to retain fish in keepnets, as the numerous small spines on the dorsal fin rays become firmly entangled in netting very easily. Also the fish will suffer if the net is positioned in slack water near the bank.
3. Barbel are strong fish which fight long and hard, and are usually exhausted when landed. Consequently they are best returned immediately to the water and held upright, facing upstream until they are strong enough to swim away to live to fight another day.

Quite apart from the essential requirement to respect a live animal it is worth remembering that long-lived, slow-growing fish like barbel take several years to reach specimen weights and are a valuable asset to a fishery.

Shoaling and Movements of barbel.

Barbel are most active when the water is warmest in summer and autumn when they feed avidly, especially during periods of humid thundery weather. Although they are sometimes caught by anglers during the winter, most fish are thought to lie-up in deep pools and slacks, remaining largely inactive at this time. Prolonged cold weather may induce a state of dormancy. Preferred barbel lies include gravel-bedded weir pools, deep holes, tree root masses, especially where they shelter undercut banks, rock ledges and sunken rock piles. The best-protected lies tend to be occupied by the largest fish. In the evening and throughout the night, adult barbel will venture out from their daytime retreats to feed on the shallows over gravel beds which lack the necessary cover for daytime foraging. Shoals of small barbel are often seen in these areas during the day and they may be excluded from the best lies by aggressive adult fish. Small barbel have been little studied but it is thought that they probably eat small invertebrates (insect larvae and nymphs), crustaceans (young shrimps and weed-dwelling water fleas) and molluscs (tiny snails and orb shells) whilst the adult fish tackle the larger crustaceans and small fish (loach, bullhead and minnow).

It seems that barbel are very sensitive to variations in current flow, moving their favourite holding positions on the river bed as the flow regime changes, for example after heavy rain or when sluice gates are opened and closed. Individual fish need areas within their normal 'home range' where they can hold station efficiently both at times of flood and, conversely, when the river is at a summer low. P.C. Hunt and J.W. Jones tagged more than 3000 Severn barbel in the 1970s, recapturing over 500, about half by electro-fishing and half by angling. Of the 531 recaptured fish, 287 had not moved far away from the initial site of capture since being tagged; 92 were caught downstream and 152 upstream. The vast majority of fish had moved less than one kilometre, indicating that barbel probably reside in single stretches of river for fairly long periods. Multiple recaptures of the same fish from a given spot were made on several occasions, reinforcing the view that certain fish occupy the same lie for extended periods of time. This is not always true however, since one individual moved a record 34 kilometres from its tagging site! Hunt and Jones concluded that barbel movements in a river the size of the Severn were complex and required more research before they could be understood fully. The Severn barbel population seemed to be split into two groups:
1.   Shoals of small fish which tend to stick together and which move occasionally from one stretch to another.
2.   Single (often large) fish, which seem to move often, perhaps in search of richer feeding grounds.

One clear-cut finding was that large (more than 2-kg) fish tended to be caught from deep holes or from lies where overhanging bushes with submerged root masses provided overhead cover. This is certainly the case on the upper Great Ouse where I have seen barbel occupying such spots for five consecutive years.

Breeding

An upstream migration prior to spawning occurs, with fish congregating on gravel beds below weirs to form dense shoals. This is the best time to observe barbel under natural conditions, when many of the fish abandon much of their normal caution and compete for spawning partners. To master life in fast waters, barbel have had to evolve a breeding system that enables them to spawn without their eggs being washed away by the current as soon as they are released. The solution arrived at by natural selection is the same as that adopted by both trout and salmon. Female barbel dig out redds (depressions on the river bed) with sweeps of the tail fin immediately before spawning. As the eggs are shed they are fertilised by one or more accompanying males and then covered with silt-free gravel swept over them from upstream by the female. The eggs are then securely lodged in the small spaces between the gravel particles and are bathed by a constant stream of well-oxygenated water. Gravel beds that have become silted (a common occurrence in many rivers today) are often too clogged to be permeable and any barbel or salmonid eggs spawned on them are likely to succumb either to a lack of oxygen or infection by fungus.

In a study of barbel spawning in the Driffield Beck on the Yorkshire Wolds, fish were observed from bankside hides and detailed recordings of their behaviour made. Fifty-six spawning bouts were observed. Ripe male fish were shoaled up in a deep pool below the gravel runs used for redd-cutting, awaiting the arrival of a ripe female which one or more of them would then accompany to the spawning beds. Commonly several male fish would follow a female, chasing each other away repeatedly, trying to fertilise a clutch of eggs. When more than five or six males were involved, however, a successful spawning was never observed. Two or three males seemed to be the best number for the female to be willing to shed eggs. Whilst salmonids are winter spawners, with their eggs incubating for several weeks in the cold waters of early spring, barbel spawn during periods of hot weather between May and June. Under normal summer conditions, barbel eggs take 10–15 days to hatch. The actual development period is influenced strongly by water temperature. When the yolk-sac fry hatch they are attracted strongly to light and wriggle up to the gravel surface to start the perilous journey towards adulthood. Adult female barbel produce between 3000 and 30,000 small (2-mm) yellow eggs, the number depending upon body size. The young fish (as in all species) experience such high mortality rates that very few reach maturation at 4–5 years of age.

It is a surprising thought to realise that any adult fish that you come across in your travels is literally one in many thousands out of the initial spawning when it was conceived. In order for a population to remain at a given density (assuming that all adults breed), each pair of spawning barbel (or any other species) need only give rise to two surviving offspring in their reproductive lifetimes.

Chub, *Leuciscus cephalus*

Identification and habitat requirements

On those rare occasions when family and work commitments allowed, I used to like to paddle my canoe along the upper Great Ouse, starting at the bottom of my garden in Buckingham and going upstream through the village of Radclive to Tingewick Mill where a weir blocks further progress. These journeys gave me the opportunity to watch shoals of large chub finning in the tails of pools and gliding along under the shade of bankside masses of willow roots. The fish were not afraid of the canoe (although this was less true when two small, noisy sons were on board) and could be observed closely, especially on hot days when they love to bask in the sun close to the surface, waiting for morsels of food to fall from overhanging trees.

Where recent dredging operations have cleared the banks the chub disappear and must be forced to compete for space in the diminished areas of high quality habitat left to the fish. This must lead to a higher mortality rate amongst fish which, under natural conditions, would probably occupy a favourite lie for many years.

The three features of chub that are distinctive in the wild are the broad head and shoulders, the black dorsal and tail fins and the large mouth with white lips, all of which can be seen clearly from the bank. A chub in the hand reveals the large silvery/bronze scales which are black-edged and the convex edge of the anal and dorsal fins (Dace have concave fins). Chub tend to occur in gravel-bedded clean rivers of moderate flow in the 'Barbel zone'. Whilst barbel hug the bed of the river, chub prefer to hover closer to the surface, particularly where overhanging bushes give the fish some cover and a refuge from the full force of the current. Chub frequent such places year in and year out, and are very fond of lying under floating rafts of scum and debris from which they can drift out into the current to intercept passing food items.

Young of the year-chub live in slack current areas along the edge of the banks where they hide amongst the riparian vegetation; as they grow larger they shoal up and live in faster moving glides and pool tails. Eventually, those few individuals that live to a ripe old age, live singly in deep pools and in sheltered lies where they get the pick of the passing food supply. The British rod-caught record weighed 8 lb 4 oz (3.74kg) from the Hampshire Avon at Christchurch by G. F. Smith back in 1913. Chub are versatile and can also live in gravel pits where they grow to large sizes and in natural lakes such as Lake Vyrnwy in Wales. In Britain the species is commonest in the south and east of England, rare in the West Country and upland Wales and absent from Scotland and Ireland. On the continent, chub are common throughout central and southern Europe and the species extends into brackish water in the Baltic.

Feeding and Growth

Chub fry eat tiny crustaceans (*Daphnia*), chironomid midge larvae and pupae, reed smut (*Simulium*) larvae, small mayfly nymphs and filamentous algae. As they grow slowly, young chub take larger invertebrates, especially caddisfly larvae, pupae and adults and mayfly nymphs and adults. Adult flies emerging at the water surface are a favourite food and chub can be caught readily on an artificial dry fly, much to the annoyance of anglers after specimen brown trout which often occupy similar habitats. Coarse anglers, on the other hand, seldom take advantage of this natural surface fly feeding, preferring instead to tempt the fish on floating breadcrust or a similar bait. Big chub are very shy and need to be stalked stealthily if the angler is to be successful.

Water beetles and bugs (e.g. *Corixa sp*), crayfish, small cyprinid fish, eels and even voles and mallard ducklings have all been found in the stomachs of large chub examined during scientific studies. Adult fish also take a significant amount of water plants in their normal diet including silk weed and water crowfoot (*Ranunculus*). The proportion of fish in the diet increases as the chub grows, reaching around 33 per cent in adult fish. Small roach, dace, bleak, minnows are likely prey species.

Richard Mann studied the growth of chub from the River Stour, Dorset, finding, in common with other studies, that chub are a slow-growing species in Britain and that strong year-classes with fast-growing fry occur during warm summers. This suggests that chub are on the northern limit of their European distribution in England and that the large specimens reported from mainland Europe (up to 18 lb) come from warm water rivers where fast growth can be sustained over a number of years. It is typical for British chub populations to be dominated by a few very strong year classes; fish born in 1959 dominated Richard Mann's study population. More recently fish spawned in 1976 and in the hot summers of 1989 and 1990 will provide recruits which will feature largely in anglers' catches for twenty years to come.

Chub can be very long-lived, and the oldest specimen from the Dorset Stour was a 22-year-old female. It is worth noting that scale readings will give under-estimates of the true age of specimen chub because the edges of the scales often erode and the annuli (growth rings) are so close together at the outer edge that they are indistinguishable. The only certain way to age large old specimens is to kill them and examine the opercular bones or otoliths. Since most sensible anglers would rather return a large specimen safely to the water, than kill it to get an accurate age determination, we will probably never know how many of our coarse fish live to a ripe old age. The annuli are laid down on the scales over the period mid-April to mid-June in Dorset Stour chub and scale readings are accurate on fish of up to eleven years of age. Most of the growth in length occurs during April to September when the average water temperature is above 12°C. This also seems to be true for roach and dace on the Stour.

The average length (cm) of Dorset Stour Chub at each 'birthday' taken from Richard Mann's study is given in the figure opposite.

Several interesting features arise from this study; both males and females have parallel growth until age 5 when females start to overtake males. Males more or less stop growing at age 14 whilst females carry on until death, reaching ultimate sizes of over half a metre. It seems likely that these figures will be a good guide to chub growth and longevity for most of the premier southern chalk stream fisheries. Chub are favourites with anglers since they can provide such a variety of fishing. Small shoaling chub of around a pound provide large catches for pleasure and match anglers; large solitary specimens provide a worthy challenge for specimen hunters, whilst hardy winter fishermen can still catch chub even under the coldest conditions. This is strange for a fish that feeds best during the warm summer months.

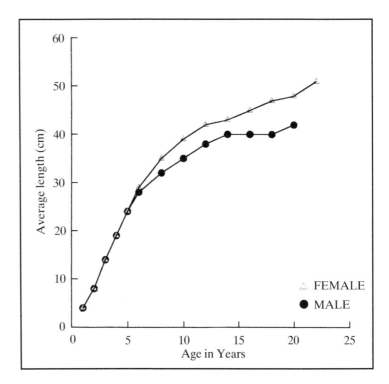

Growth of
Chub in
River Stour

Breeding

Chub spawn in steadily-flowing stretches on aquatic plants and gravel beds and then shoal up below weirs and rapids to 'clean up' after spawning. On the Stour some males mature at age 3 or 4 but mostly at age 5, whilst females mature at 5 or 6 and most by age 7 years. Chub are, therefore, slow growing, late maturing and long-lived on our chalk stream fisheries. At spawning time, male chub develop large numbers of small white tubercles over the head and shoulders. Females of 35–45cm length produce 27,000–65,000 eggs and both ovaries and testes appear to shed their gametes gradually over several days, rather than all at once (as in the Dace). In 'normal' years, spawning occurs in late May or early June and the sticky yellow eggs adhere to plants or stones, hatching quickly in around a week and giving rise to free swimming fry of 7–8mm. After spawning the ovaries and testes re-grow over the period September to May. Once maturity is reached each fish appears to spawn every year until it dies.

Roach, *Rutilus rutilus*

Identification, habitats and distribution

Roach are silver, deep-bodied fish with red fins and a distinctive red iris, they are sometimes confused with rudd. Rudd tend to be more golden-coloured and have an upturned mouth (for surface feeding) whilst roach have a downturned mouth and are more inclined to feed on river and lake beds. The origin of the dorsal fin is in line with the base of the pelvic fins in roach but is set further back in the rudd. A problem with identification of specimen fish lies in the fact that roach freely interbreed with bream and other cyprinids, to produce fast-growing hybrids that can look very like either parental species.

Roach are widely distributed and common, being found throughout mainland northern Europe and Asia. They occur in brackish river mouths in the Baltic, Caspian and Black seas; under these conditions specimens can grow to 44cm and weights in excess of 2kg (4.4 lb); such fish are, however, exceptional. Roach will tolerate a wide range of habitats and water quality, from dirty urban canals, through lowland rivers, ponds and lakes to Scottish lochs and the productive chalk streams of the south of England. It is on the chalk streams that the species really thrives and where consistent catches of large specimens occur over many years. The classic river in this respect was the Hampshire Avon, but in recent times the quality of the coarse fishing has declined on this most famous of chalk streams. It seems that the gradual loss of the water meadows, with their interconnecting ditches and feeder streams may have removed most of the habitats where cyprinid fish fry spent their first summer, prior to dropping down into the stronger currents of the main river. The Dorset Stour and Frome, with their better fry habitats, still have abundant stocks of prime roach, as do many of the rivers of southern and eastern England. Roach are scarcer in the West Country and in Wales. In Scotland they occur in the southern lowlands and north to the River Tay. They are abundant in the south basin of Loch Lomond and in the inflowing River Endrick where large shoals abound. Roach are spreading rapidly in several Irish river and lough systems after being introduced relatively recently, possibly by visiting pike anglers releasing live baits.

Man-made lakes such as gravel pits are colonised readily, often during winter floods, and many large catches of prime roach are made in these waters throughout the fishing season. When you consider that most fish species tend to occur in specific habitat zones, roach are unusual in being able to live happily in the fast-flowing grayling and trout reaches of chalk streams on the one hand and in small, polluted farm ponds on the other. They are indeed an adaptable species.

Feeding and Growth

Where food is short, stunted roach populations occur, where the largest fish struggle to reach weights of 4 oz (110g), whilst in productive chalk streams and lakes (such as the Cheshire Meres) fish of over 2 lb (nearly 1kg) occur regularly. Roach are as adaptable in their diet as they are in their habitat requirements. They will eat a wide range of foods from organic detritus and filamentous algae, through plankton (such as *Daphnia hyalina*) to insect larvae, crustaceans and molluscs. It is thought that competition for invertebrate food, for example, from perch, may force roach to eat vegetable matter in some habitats (for example lakes in Sweden). Conversely, Clive Kennedy and his students at Exeter Universty have followed some interesting changes in the fish populations of Slapton Ley in Devon where roach built up in numbers from 1967–1974 apparently almost eliminating the formerly abundant rudd and depressing the perch population. They thought that competition for planktonic crustaceans as food for the young fish may have led to these changes in the dominant fish species. A further factor in these events appeared to be the fluctuating abundance of a large parasitic larval tapeworm which lives in the body cavity of roach.

Ligulosis

The roach of Slapton Ley suffered in the mid-1970s when an outbreak of ligulosis (infection by the tapeworm *Ligula intestinalis*) caused mass mortalities. Roach with *Ligula* have distended bellies and are liable to die when handled. After this, the rudd made a short-term recovery until the roach population built up again. Whilst the roach population was sparse, growth rates amongst surviving fish improved and the fish had larger testes and ovaries. These changes underline the likely importance of a lack of strong food competition and reduced parasite burdens for the wellbeing of the roach. *Ligula* infestations appear to be cyclical in roach populations; when the parasite numbers are high the host fish are often castrated, leading to low fry production. Many heavily parasitised adult fish also die. This leads to a fall in roach population density and also subsequently a fall in parasite levels, at which point the roach start to breed efficiently and the cycle starts again. The roach population of Chew Valley Lake was also decimated by ligulosis in the 1970s and the parasite occurs almost universally in U.K. populations.

Parasitised roach that are close to death swim weakly, close to the water surface and are easily caught by gulls and herons which are the final host for the tapeworms. The tapeworms mature quickly in the gut of the birds and produce large numbers of eggs, some of which are voided into the water with the bird's droppings. The eggs then hatch into tiny larvae which are eaten by planktonic crustaceans (such as copepods) and they are then able to infect any roach that eat the crustaceans. The complex life cycle of this tapeworm therefore goes: Roach – Bird – Crustacean – Roach, etc.

Roach as adaptable feeders

In work that I did on the diet of adult gravel pit roach I found that in one lake (St Peter's at Great Linford) the fish ate filamentous algae, whilst in the adjacent Main lake they ate huge numbers of water fleas, *Daphnia hyalina*. St Peters lake was weedy and held a dense tench population and a fair head of bream leading to a shortage of invertebrate food; the plankton was also sparse. The Main lake was silty and weed-free, holding a dense population of adult bream which ate either midge larvae and pea mussels from the lake bed or plankton when *Daphnia* blooms occurred. Under these conditions the roach joined in the *Daphnia* feast and left the burrowing invertebrates for the bream to find. In the River Great Ouse which flows alongside both of these lakes the roach eat shrimps, snails and insect larvae as well as silkweed from the weir pool aprons. Thus, in three waters, all within a stone's throw of each other, roach display widely differing feeding behaviour. It is this adaptability which may account for the wide distribution and abundance of the most widely-fished-for of the European cyprinid fishes.

In the River Lugg, Herefordshire, J. M. Hellawell found that roach ate algae, submerged waterweeds, chironomid larvae, caddis larvae, shrimps, stonefly nymphs, water beetles and molluscs. Amongst the molluscs were mussels (*Sphaerium*) and snails (*Lymnaea, Valvata, Theodoxus* and *Potamopyrgus*). Richard Mann recorded that Dorset Stour roach ate midge and caddis larvae, mayfly nymphs, molluscs and algae. In Rostherne Mere, Cheshire, John Banks noted that the roach ate water weeds, algae, molluscs, *Asellus, Gammarus*, chironomid larvae, caddis larvae, alderfly larvae (*Sialis*) and copepods. The food of the species can be similar, therefore, in both rivers and lakes.

Roach are a slow-growing species with growth being dependent on habitat quality, degree of food competition and water temperature. Colin Goldspink recorded relatively rapid growth rates for roach in Tatton Mere, Cheshire, with 7-year-old males reaching 30cm and females 32cm. In Rostherne Mere, John Banks recorded 9-year-old female roach of 29cm and males of 26cm. The female River Lugg roach in J. M. Hellawell's study grew to 28cm in 11 years and the males to 25cm over the same period, the oldest fish in this study was 13 years of age. Derek Mills found that Loch Lomond roach reach 24cm at around 9 years.

These studies reflect the wide differences in growth potential for roach in different waters. David Cragg-Hine and J. W. Jones analysed the average growth of male and female roach from the Willow Brook (a tributary of the River Nene) in Northamptonshire (see figure below).

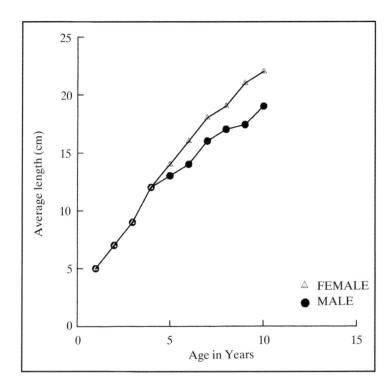

Growth of
Roach in
Willow Brook

For comparison with the Midland Willow Brook population we can now look at the growth of roach from the Dorset River Frome, a productive southern chalk stream as recorded by Richard Mann of the Institute of Freshwater Ecology.

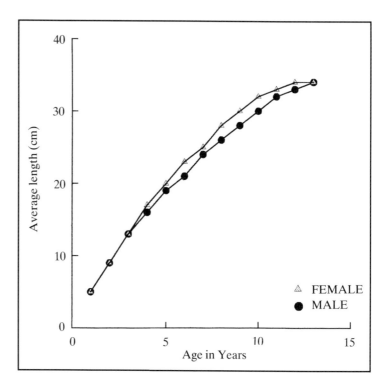

Growth of
Roach in
River Frome

Clearly, in both rivers, female roach grow faster than males after an age of 4–5 years, and in the Frome, the longevity and growth rates of both sexes are higher than for Willow Brook fish. Data like these underline the potential of chalk streams to produce specimen fish. For roach older than 9 or 10 years, opercular bones give more accurate age estimations than scales.

The Willow Brook roach population at the time of study was dominated by the 1956 year class whilst those of the Lugg and the Dorset Stour had very strong year-classes which hatched in 1959. Both of these years had notably warm summers. Perhaps in warm years, when cyprinid fry grow quickly, they are able to 'escape' rapidly from the attentions of an abundance of predatory invertebrates like corixids and backswimmers which readily eat small fish fry.

When roach scales are examined to estimate ages and growth rates of fish it is clear that warm summers give rise to wide summer growth bands and cool summers to narrow ones. The annual growth checks on the scales are formed in May/June for Stour and Frome fish and June/July on Willow Brook fish; these coincide with the switch from slow winter growth to rapid summer growth. Richard Mann estimated that roach growth in Dorset chalk streams was minimal from November to April and that rapid growth occurred (as with chub) when the average water temperatures exceeded 12°C.

Because of their abundance and widespread distribution, roach are an important part of the food webs of rivers and lakes, eating plants and invertebrate animals whilst at the same time being eaten by a host of predators including herons, grebes, kingfishers, pike, zander, wels, eels and many other species.

Breeding Biology

River Stour male roach mature at 4–5 years and females at 5–6 years. The gonads develop from September to May and spawning occurs in early May in most years. Female roach can produce 1000–100,000 eggs or even more in very large specimens. Males tend to arrive on the spawning grounds before females and have the typical cyprinid rash of small white tubercles on the head and shoulders. On the River Frome, Chris Mills found that roach spawned on moss (*Fontinalis*) clumps growing on wooden piles in fast-flowing sections of river. The eggs were concentrated near the water surface and were vulnerable to drops in river level (for example after weed-cutting). The choice of fast currents (24-36cm per second) for spawning may be due to the lack of siltation at these sites. Silt leads to poor oxygen supply and associated fungal infections on incubating fish eggs. Eels were active predators on the developing eggs, swimming through the clumps of moss in search of food.

The eggs that survived took around 11 days for a 50 per cent hatch at 13°C and the young larvae (4–6mm) lay amongst the plants for a few days, absorbing their yolk sacs before actively swimming to slack current areas to commence feeding. Young roach larvae eat rotifers and algae, gradually grading on to larger crustaceans and insects as they grow. Like larval dace, roach larvae feed most actively during the day and have little food in the gut at night. In the slower flowing rivers of the east of England, for example the Thames and Great Ouse, there is concern that increased boat traffic and changes in water quality, particularly increased phosphate and nitrate concentrations, have led to the progressive loss of submerged weedbeds and the dominance of algal plant communities. In this situation cyprinids such as roach and bream may find little suitable spawning habitat and few areas for fry to shelter from the current and from predators. These concerns, coupled with an apparent lack of young cyprinids in many East Anglian rivers led to the development of the concept of O.R.S.U.Ss. (Off-River Supplementation Units) which are shallow, man-made weedy pools linked to the river by sluiced channels. Adult roach and bream are stocked in the pools, allowed to spawn and the resulting fry develop in a warm, productive environment from which they can disperse into the main river through the linking channel when they are ready. This type of scheme, developed by Ron Linfield and colleagues in the NRA, may prove to be a valuable low-cost, long-term management technique for boosting roach and bream stocks in degraded lowland river systems.

In lakes, roach often spawn on the stems of common reed (*Phragmites communis*) where it is available; studies of lacustrine roach have shown a tendency for fish to home to spawning grounds either within the lake (as in the Tjeukemeer, Netherlands) or in inflowing streams (as in Lake Arungen, Norway). Spawning roach chase each other around, splashing at the water surface in courtship sequences which are little studied or understood; we don't know whether active mate choice takes place or whether the gametes are shed in an riotous mêlée of activity.

Roach fisheries

In Eastern Europe, roach are fished for food on a local basis; in the Black Sea region they are sold fresh, smoked or salted. The thought of a British roach angler returning home with his catch for the table would be regarded as bizarre but customs vary and European unity may lead, in the long run, to changing attitudes. The British rod-caught record roach by R. G. Jones weighed in at a spectacular 4 lb 1 oz (1.84kg) and was taken from a Nottinghamshire gravel pit in 1975.*

*This fish has recently been surpassed by a Dorset Stour roach of 4 lb 3 oz caught by Ray Clarke, another record for a Wessex river.

Rudd, *Scardinius erythrophthalmus*

Identification, distribution and habitats

Rudd are one of the more attractive cyprinid species, both because of their superb golden scales and blood-red fins and through their behaviour of swimming just below the surface on warm summer days hunting for insects. For these reasons, rudd (especially the golden variety) are popular garden pond fish and offer good sport to the coarse angler who enjoys fishing on fine summer days by an attractive lake with lightweight float tackle. As a young teenager I used to cycle many miles from our home to Priddy Pool in the Mendip Hills, Somerset, where, in the company of good friends, we used to fish for rudd and watch the dragonflies as they hawked through the reed beds where the largest and wariest rudd lived.

It was at Priddy that I saw the difference between the surface-feeding rudd and the bottom-feeding roach; you could catch either species by setting the float to fish at the correct depth. One glance at a rudd shows the upturned mouth, adapted for surface feeding and the downturned mouth of the roach which usually feeds on snails, algae and insect larvae on the lake bed. In addition to these differences, rudd have golden irises whilst those of the roach are red, and rudd have a dorsal fin which is set further back on the body than that of the roach. Overall, roach have a silver hue whilst rudd are a deep golden-yellow, especially when viewed in sunlight. Both species have red ventral, anal and caudal fins but those of the rudd tend to be a deeper red. When you consider that in some waters, roach–rudd hybrids are common you can imagine the difficulties involved in determining exactly what has taken your bait and lies resplendent in your landing net.

Rudd are closely associated with common reed (*Phragmites communis*) beds (which are distinctly uncommon these days), water lily (*Nymphaea* and *Nuphar*) clumps, bulrush (*Schoenoplectus lacustris*) beds and submerged beds of milfoil and other species. Rudd eat large quantities of aquatic plants and also spawn upon them; they suffer, therefore, in habitats where eutrophication has led to a loss of plants. Classic examples of this problem are the Norfolk Broads which were once famous for their abundant large rudd, but most of which are now devoid of submerged vegetation and are poor rudd habitats.

Rudd prefer shallow, clear-watered lakes, or slowly-flowing rivers and backwaters, rich in submerged vegetation and with a good supply of wind-blown insects landing on the surface. Despite its liking for pristine habitats, the rudd is relatively hardy and will cope with poor water quality if it must. The species is common in southern England and central Ireland but local in northern England and rare in Scotland and Wales. In continental Europe rudd are very widespread right down to the Mediterranean coastline and eastwards to Siberia, northern Turkey and the Caspian Sea. In southern Greece a separate species, the Greek rudd, *Scardinius graecus* occurs; it is slimmer than our rudd and more roach-like in appearance but otherwise has a similar biology to our own rudd.

A strange subspecies of rudd, *Scardinius erythrophthalmus racovitzai*, lives in the hot-water springs of western Romania. It is adapted to temperatures of 28–34°C and dies if kept in water below 20°C. This fish matures at 1–2 years, grows to only 9cm and dies after spawning; it is an interesting illustration of the complete adaptation of a life cycle to suit specific environmental constraints.

Breeding, Food and Growth

Male rudd usually mature at three years and females at four. An unusual aspect of rudd behaviour is their tendency to join in with the spawning activities of other cyprinids, leading to a wide variety of hybrid forms including rudd–roach, rudd–bream, rudd–silver bream and rudd–bleak. Rudd spawn in May and June over weedbeds in shallow littoral habitats. Male rudd assume a heightened colouration and develop a rash of fine white breeding tubercles on the head and shoulders. Females produce 90,000–200,000 1.5-mm diameter pale yellow eggs which stick to the plants above the silted zone on the lake bed and hatch 5–8 days later. The yolk-sac fry remain stuck to the weeds, developing a swim bladder in two days and feeding in about a week on rotifers, algae and minute crustaceans which live on the surface of the plants (i.e. on *Aufwuchs*). The adult fins are fully formed when the fry are 12–13mm long. By the end of their first summer, young rudd reach around 2–4cm length.

Rudd feed most actively in the summer and are inactive under cold winter conditions when they tend to retire to the deepest available (and warmest) water. As they grow, rudd initially eat zooplankton and then start to take aquatic insects (chironomids and caddisfly pupae and adults), terrestrial dipterans, beetles and shield bugs and small snails, water lice (*Asellus*) and shrimps (*Gammarus*), which they pick from the stems and leaves of plants. One of the best times to watch rudd in the wild is when a swarm of flying ants lands on the water — every rudd in the lake will be up to join in the feast. The tendency for surface feeding on flies is underlined by the capture of the current British rod-caught record rudd on a fly by a trout fisherman, Mr D. Webb on Pitsford Reservoir, Northamptonshire in 1986. The fish weighed 4 lb 10 oz (2.09kg) which is a huge rudd by any standards.*

Large adult rudd eat the young shoots of water milfoil (e.g. *Myriophyllum spicatum*), Canadian pondweed (*Elodea canadensis*), stoneworts (*Chara* and *Nitella* species) and pondweeds (e.g. *Potamogeton lucens*); in some waters they become predatory and chase and eat small cyprinid fry including their own. In Lough na B'Eisge in County Wexford, Ireland, rudd were found to eat adult three-spined sticklebacks. Danish rudd eat large quantities of perch spawn and this behaviour may be widespread. The surface shoaling behaviour of medium-sized rudd is replaced by a solitary lifestyle in the largest specimens.

Rudd tend to grow at similar rates to roach, with a fish of one pound being around 10 years old and two-pounders being teenage, glass-case specimens. In Ireland the fastest growing rudd occur in limestone loughs of 80 acres or more in extent. Active growth starts at the end of May or in early June in young Irish rudd and in late June or July in adult fish that have spawned. Growth ceases at about the end of October in both old and young fish. In Ireland, rudd are slow-growing and long-lived; fish older than 10 years are commonly caught and the oldest specimens examined by Michael Kennedy and Paddy Fitzmaurice were 17 years old. Female rudd appear to grow rather larger than males. Some average growth figures back-calculated from scale readings (sexes combined) for specimen Irish rudd from a high quality habitat (Coosan Lough) and for stunted fish from a poor quality habitat (Dalkey Pond) are as in the figure overleaf.

*This fish has now been deemed to be a hybrid and the official rod-caught record has reverted back to the 4 lb 8 oz fish of 1933.

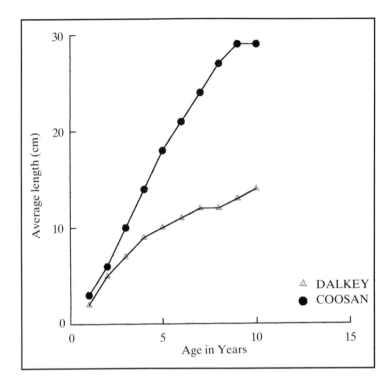

Growth of
Rudd in
Coosan Lough
and
Dalkey Pond

The difference in growth between the two groups of fish is clear, Coosan Lough rudd grow on to reach maximum lengths of 33–36cm (1000g plus) whilst Dalkey Pond fish stop at around 15cm (100g).

Small weedy ponds often hold large numbers of small, stunted rudd, which compete strongly for the limited food resources. Kennedy and Fitzmaurice describe cases of the sudden increase in growth rates of surviving rudd after rotenone treatment had killed the bulk of the fish in two loughs (Aderry and Ballybutler) prior to trout stocking. The progeny of the survivors also grew much more quickly than their parents had done. This indicates that the rudd growth had been limited by competiton prior to the rotenone treatment.

Dace, *Leuciscus leuciscus*

Distribution and habitat

Dace are found throughout most of Europe, east to the Arctic Siberian coast but not in the extreme north-west (Scotland, most of Scandinavia) or far south (Spain, Italy, Greece). Within the British Isles, dace occur throughout England north to the River Tyne but are less common in Wales, the West Country and are absent from Scotland. In Ireland only the Blackwater system seems to have an (introduced) population.

Dace thrive in cool-running waters and clear lakes, sharing habitats with trout and grayling in fast streams and with chub in slower rivers. Where dace and chub co-exist the dace prefer the fastest water, shoaling under the surface while the chub retire to the shelter of willow roots and overhanging bushes. Dace feed actively from the surface, taking a wide variety of adult aquatic and terrestrial insects; they can be caught by dry fly-fishing if your reflexes are fast enough as they eject an artificial fly with great speed. The British rod-caught record weighing 574g (1.25 lb) was taken in 1960 by J. L. Gasson from the Little Ouse at Thetford, Norfolk.

The dace is perhaps our most graceful cyprinid species, finning in quicksilver shoals in fast-flowing crystal-clear chalkstream riffles and glides. The shoals like to hover under the shade of willows or a roadbridge, intercepting flies as they drift onto the surface through the dappled shade. Large dace are distinguished from small chub by their slimmer build, concave anal and dorsal fins and small, down-pointing mouth. Dace are distinguishable from roach by their yellow iris (rather than red in the roach), their generally slimmer build and their paler fin colours; roach tend to have much redder pelvic fins.

Breeding biology

Dace are early springtime spawners, congregating on clean (unsilted) gravel shallows in early March to spawn in late March or April; because they spawn so much earlier than other cyprinids, hybrids of dace are rare. This contrasts sharply with, for example, roach–bream or roach–rudd hybrids which, because of their similar spawning seasons, are relatively common.

In the River Frome, a Dorset chalk stream, female dace mature at 2–5 (usually 3–4) years of age and then spawn each year until they die at an age of up to 10 or 11 years. All of the eggs are laid in a single batch over stony/gravel stream beds; the eggs sink quickly and stick to the stones firmly. Even in heavy floods few dace eggs (perhaps 2 per cent) are dislodged to drift downstream. Dace spawn for 2–3 weeks each April in the Frome. Under typical springtime conditions the eggs take 25–30 days to hatch. Egg survival from spawning to hatching was estimated by Chris Mills to vary between 8 and 22 per cent. Egg survival was markedly higher in silt-free gravels; a high proportion of eggs become infected by fungi in silted (low dissolved oxygen) conditions. Large bottom-living invertebrates appear to eat many moribund eggs but live eggs seem to be eaten less often, perhaps because they are in the minority.

Duncan Wilkinson and J. W. Jones studied the fecundity of dace from the Emral Brook in Clwyd, North Wales, estimating that females produce from 2000–16,000 eggs depending on body size.

Larval cyprinid habitat; bankside vegetation

Newly-hatched dace larvae are around 9.5mm long and, like all cyprinid fry, have a limited ability to hold their own against currents. This means that they rely critically on the presence of sheltering vegetation to provide essential cover from the main force of the flow, from predatory invertebrates and for the provision of abundant small crustaceans for food. Weed cutting operations which lower water levels and routine maintenance dredging, which removes vegetation to leave a smooth (fast current) bank profile can both lead to mass mortalities of cyprinid fry as they are swept downstream to their doom. In a natural stream, with fallen trees, fringing rush and reedbeds and dense submerged weed clumps there is a profusion of small food-rich shelters from the current where young fish can grow and gain strength; gradually moving out into stronger flow areas as they mature.

In modern 'managed' rivers and streams this natural habitat diversity and complexity is greatly reduced, leading to recruitment failures for many species and dwindling populations of young fish.

Warm summers mean good production of young cyprinids

Chris Mills and Richard Mann studied the River Frome dace population from 1970 to 1980, finding that the relative year class strengths varied by a factor of nearly 13-fold. In general, warm summers with low rainfall led to very strong dace year-classes, 1976 being a good example. The 1976 dace dominated samples for several subsequent years on the River Frome, accounting for 68 per cent of electro-fishing samples in 1979/80 when the fish were in their fourth year of life. In an average year, only 23 per cent of the catch would have been comprised of 4-year-old dace. The strong year-classes produced in hot summers may benefit not only from warm water and the resultant fast growth rates, but also from reduced flows and increased protection from fast currents. Abundant year classes exhibited good growth, indicating that there is little competiton for food in this highly productive chalk stream habitat. Fast-growing dace fry may soon become too large to be taken by predatory invertebrates such as dragonfly nymphs and water beetle larvae and so have better survival prospects than fish which, in cool summers, linger long as vulnerable small fry.

Feeding and Growth

Young dace fry eat rotifers, small copepod larvae and other crustaceans, grading on to midge larvae and pupae as they grow. The guts tend to contain three to four times the volume of food during the day than early in the morning, indicating that young dace are visual daytime feeders. Older dace take surface insects in summer but they also forage on the river bed for oligochaete worms, small snails, algae and water plants.

Young of the year Frome dace caught during the winter varied by up to 50 per cent length and 300 per cent weight between years, indicating the great differences in growth achieved annually. The average yearly length (cm) of dace from the Willow Brook in Northamptonshire, studied by David Cragg-Hine and J. W. Jones is as opposite.

Most growth in length occurred from May to November, with the annual growth check on the scales being formed in May at the transition between slow winter and rapid summer growth. Male dace (in contrast to roach and chub) grow more quickly than females. The Willow Brook dace growth rates are faster than those recorded for

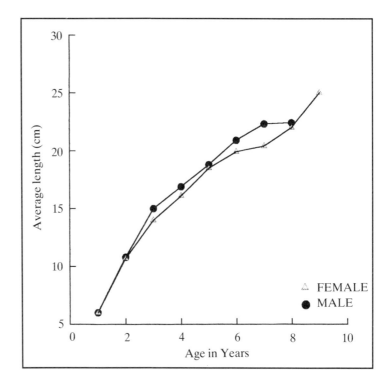

Growth of
Dace in
Willow Brook

dace from the Thames but slower than those from the River Cam, Funshion, Shepreth Brook and Hampshire Avon.

Dace fishing

Dace, because of their fast reactions and their habit of shoaling and feeding in fast water, can be difficult and exacting to catch. Favourite methods include float fishing with maggots for bait, the fish being caught at medium-long range by long-trotting the float down to the feeding shoal. Fine tackle and delicate presentation of the bait are required for consistent success with this small but very attractive and hard-fighting species.

Catfish or Wels, *Silurus glanis*

Identification, behaviour and habitats

The Siluridae is a very widespread Old World catfish family; there are many African *Siluroid* species and others in southern Europe and Asia. The Wels or Sheat fish, *Silurus glanis*, is unmistakeable, with its massive flat head, wide mouth, six flowing barbels (two on the upper lip and four on the lower) and long, tapering, slimy, scaleless body. The colour is variable but usually dark on the back, grading to an attractive marbled silver-grey on the flanks and a white belly.

In southern mainland Greece, opposite the island of Corfu, lies the Akheloos River basin with its warm, rich lakes and slow-flowing river habitats and here lives Aristotle's catfish, *Silurus aristotelis*. This species is very like the Wels, but reaches rather smaller sizes and has only four barbels as opposed to six in the Wels. These *Silurus* species have long tapering bodies with a tiny dorsal fin but very long anal fins and large pectorals, used for manoeuvring as they stealthily approach their prey under cover of darkness. Catfish are acutely sensitive to vibrations and often detect the movement of potential prey. The long barbels must be critical in the detection of food as these formidable predators patrol the shallows at night in search of their victims.

The tales of the devouring of children and small dogs must, I feel, be taken with a large pinch of salt, but when you consider that the largest Wels on record, caught in the River Dneiper, measured 5 metres (16 feet plus) and weighed 673 lb (306kg) you can see where the scope for imagination creeps in. The world rod-caught record (202 lb 6 oz) was caught by Herr Krischker and his father from the Rumanian side of the Danube delta; this gigantic fish took five hours to land!

Wels classically inhabit the lower, slowly flowing 'Bream zone' reaches of rivers and rich warm lakes in central and eastern Europe. Their popularity as sport fish has ensured that they have been widely introduced to waters outside their natural range, for example in England, France and Belgium. The ninth Duke of Bedford, who was rather keen on exotic introductions of animals stocked two lakes on the Woburn estate, Bedfordshire, with 70 wels in 1880, other specimens having been imported earlier in 1865 by the Acclimatization Society.

Rather like the zander in England, wels spread gradually to neighbouring waters, such as the Tring reservoirs and Claydon House lakes at Steeple Claydon, Buckingham-shire, but even today, more than a century after its initial introduction, it is unusual to find waters where this species is present.

Specimen-hunting coarse anglers pay handsomely for the privilege of fishing waters where wels occur and angling trips to southern European rivers in search of large specimen catfish are popular with holiday anglers. The English abroad are regarded as crazy to return their fish to the river when local fishermen are keen to convert their catches of catfish into Sunday lunch. Wels are a popular table fish on the Continent, with few bones and tasty, well-textured flesh; in Hungary they are cultured on fish farms where they are fed on white bream and other 'undesirable' species and marketed at weights of 3–4kg. They must represent an interesting alternative to the Sunday joint.

Wels are caught commercially in the Asov Sea, Caspian Sea, Lake Aral and in countries bordering the River Danube. The fish are taken in staked nets or on night lines baited with fish, frogs or offal. When ripe females are caught the eggs are often mixed with those of sturgeon or sterlets and sold as caviar. Little is wasted as the bones and swim bladder are boiled up to make fish glue.

Food and Growth

Young wels can reach 20cm at the end of their first year, eating zooplankton and then larger invertebrates, fish fry and small fish. At all stages of the life cycle growth is rapid as long as the water is warm (20°C plus) and food is abundant. A weight of 10kg (22 lb) can be reached at 10 years of age, the largest specimen ever recorded in Britain weighed 33kg (73 lb) and the rod-caught record stands at 43 lb 8 oz (19.73kg) by R. J. Bray from Wilstone reservoir, Tring, Hertfordshire, in 1970. It seems likely that wels have the capacity for sustained growth over a very long life, allowing them to become the largest European freshwater fish after the mighty Sturgeon. Most growth occurs during the summer months in northern Europe and it is usual for wels to over-winter in a state of torpid hibernation. The huge weights attained by southern European fish must be made possible by the sustained high water temperatures and good supply of small cyprinid prey fish.

Wels eat roach, bream, eels, burbot, tench, carp, crayfish, swan mussels, frogs, ducklings and even water voles. They become active at night when they swim into shallow water foraging for anything that they can catch. During the daytime they are much less active, preferring to hide under weed beds until light levels decline at dusk. Night fishing with a dead fish, piece of liver or squid ledgered on the lake bed is the usual method of catching catfish in Britain.

Breeding biology

Under normal conditions wels mature at 4–5 years, at around 50cm length and weighing about 2kg; males tend to be larger than females. Spawning takes place in water of at least 20°C and thus, in Britain, many summers are too cool for successful breeding. Like the Common carp, wels in England are at the northern extreme of their European distribution. The breeding biology is fascinating, as the male digs a nest hollow in soft mud beneath thick vegetation and then guards the fertilised egg mass until the fry hatch 2–3 days after spawning. Female wels are very fecund, with a large fish producing up to 500,000 yellow sticky 3-mm diameter eggs. The larvae hatch at around 7mm length and already have visible barbels; at a month old they can already be 30–40-mm long.

Introductions

Because of their potential for voracious predatory behaviour and unknown effects on the ecology of our native fish species, the introduction of wels must be licenced by English Nature and permission is unlikely to be given unless the water is man-made and isolated from natural watercourses. The legislation underpinning this policy is the Wildlife and Countryside Act (1981) whereby fines can be levied on individuals who stock fish illegally into waters. Despite this, some people still continue to think that they know best and the illegal stocking of exotic fish such as wels and zander and native species like barbel is still widespread.

Eel, *Anguilla anguilla*

Identification, habitats and life cycle.

Eels are found in Europe, Asia, Africa and North and South America; in all there are 16 freshwater species worldwide. The body is very elongate, the dorsal, caudal and anal fins form a continuous fringe and the pelvic fins are absent. The (paired) single, small gill openings lie just above the base of the pectoral fins.

The European eel *A.anguilla* is a similar but separate species to the American eel, *A.rostrata*: it has been suggested that no European eels survive the marine spawning migration and that stragglers from breeding American stocks drift into eastern waters, but this is now known not to be true. There also appeared to be two forms of European eel, broad and narrow-nosed, possibly having different feeding habits (broad-nosed taking more fish and larger invertebrates, such as crayfish) but recent information has established that these are extreme forms of a continuous morphological variation.

Eels are remarkably ubiquitous in their distribution, living in upland and lowland, rich and poor, running and still waters. Growth and diet vary greatly between habitats. On damp, dark nights they will travel long distances along ditches and over wet grassland, reaching landlocked pools where they may then live for many years before returning to the sea. The eyes are especially adapted to resist damage from drying out by having corneas detached from the underlying tissues. Eels are marine species which have an extended juvenile life-cycle stage in freshwater. Fish which migrate to the sea to spawn are termed *catadromous* (salmonids, which migrate to spawn in freshwater, are termed *anadromous*).

Life Cycle

Aristotle (384–322 B.C.), Alexander the Great's tutor, thought that eels generated spontaneously from mud or slime. Isaak Walton (*The Compleat Angler*) wrote the following which he believed probably to be true

> Some say they are bred by generation as other fish do; and others that they breed as some worms do, of mud, as rats and mice, and many other living creatures, by the sun's heat or out of the putrefaction of the earth, and divers other ways. And others say, that eels growing old breed other eels out of the courruption of their own age. And others say that as pearls are made of glutinous dew drops, which are condensed by the sun's heat, so eels are bred of a particular dew, falling in the months of May or June on the banks of some particular ponds or rivers — adapted by nature for that end — which in a few days are by the sun's heat turned into eels: and some of the ancients have called the eels that are thus bred, the offspring of Jove.

So there you have it! Today, we know rather more about eel reproduction, but many mysteries remain. As far as is known, all *Anguilla anguilla* and *A.rostrata* are spawned in the warm, black depths of the Sargasso Sea off central America. The origin of this distant breeding ground for European eels may lie in the history of continental drift, when the Atlantic Ocean was much smaller and Europe and North America were relatively close to each other. No breeding adult eels have actually been caught in the Sargasso (or elsewhere), however; only newly hatched, 7-mm long 'leptocephalus' larvae have been recovered at depths of 100–300 metres over submarine canyons which plummet to depths of 6 kilometres. It is worth noting in passing that marine conger eels *Conger conger* also undertake long spawning migrations and have a long planktonic life before descending to live on the sea bed. Congers and 'freshwater' eels overlap in their distributions at the lower end of estuaries. Congers can grow to well over 100 lb in weight, but they may not be the largest eels in the sea.

Are Sea Serpents Real?

In 1930 the Danish fishery research boat *Dana* went on an expedition in search of eels and whilst trawling at a depth of 70 metres in the south Atlantic between the Cape of Good Hope and St Helena a giant leptocephalus larva two metres long was captured. As Christopher Moriarty notes; if this larva bears the same size relationship to the adult as our leptocephali do to *Anguilla anguilla*, then the adults could be 70 metres long. Furthermore, adult eels tend to be shy and nocturnal in their activity patterns leading to the possibility that huge deep-sea eels may well exist, well away from the likelihood of being landed by conventional fishing gear. Perhaps the ancient mariners' tales of sea serpents were true; after all, giant squids are a reality.

Returning to our more mundane, but nevertheless fascinating, European eel; the distance of the Sargasso from European and African freshwaters where eels live, i.e. 4000–7000km, makes the adult spawning migration an amazing feat of endurance and navigation. During the return journey the transparent, leaf-shaped 'leptocephali' larvae are entrained in the surface currents of the Atlantic and of the Gulf Stream drift.

The young eel larvae eat tiny planktonic algae (diatoms) until they grow large enough to eat small planktonic crustaceans. Whilst they live passively drifting in marine currents the leaf-shaped leptocephali grow to 25mm in two months and 45mm in eight months; after approximately one year, they reach the European continental shelf and metamorphose into small elvers ('glass eels'). The elvers then migrate into estuaries and small coastal streams, reaching them in November-December in Spain and Ireland, January-March along the English west coast and March-April along North Sea coasts and the Kattegat. There then follows a period of osmotic adjustment when the elvers live in an estuary for perhaps a month, gradually acclimating to freshwater conditions. When they are physiologically prepared, at a length of 6–7cm, they can proceed upstream.

Literally billions of elvers swarm up west coast English rivers like the Severn which has a traditional spring fishery for them. In all watersheds, elvers make their way upstream, steadily spreading out to colonise all available waters and settling into a long phase of freshwater life during which they are known as yellow eels. In estuaries and the lower reaches of large rivers, eel populations are dense and are dominated by small male fish. From Irish records it seems that as you progress further upstream the eels get larger, live at lower population densities and are predominantly female, indicating that perhaps female fish have a prolonged, slow upstream migration in freshwater before finally silvering and running downstream to breed in the ocean. It is possible that the sex of individual eels is not fully determined until several years of freshwater life have elapsed. There is some evidence that environmental factors may influence the sex of eels but this is only speculative. The variation in sex ratios between upstream and downstream eel populations are just as easily explained by sexual differences in the tendency to disperse upstream as by population density effects on the sex of individuals.

Eels are found at altitudes of up to around 1000 feet above sea-level but are passive and very slow-growing in these cool, unproductive upland waters.

Feeding and Growth in freshwater

After two to six years of freshwater growth, small scales are formed in the skin, deep in the mucus layer and further scales are added in later years; for this reason eels are inaccurately aged from scales, although they often show well defined annual rings. The otoliths (inner ear bones) of eels, as in other fish species of the temperate region, are composed of concentric layers of opaque (summer) and clear (winter) growth rings. It is even possible to discern the larval marine-growth rings at the centre of eel otoliths.

When these tiny bones are burnt and snapped in half the broken surface reveals a series of concentric black (winter) and white (summer) growth rings. Interpretation of these 'annuli' has to be careful since (for example) Irish eel otoliths often contain short dark (starvation) bands within summer growth phases, such 'false rings' are also well-known on fish scales. The rhythmic seasonal pattern of growth provides a record within the skeleton of the fish of an individual's age, but considerable experience is needed before estimates can be made with a high degree of accuracy. This is very useful for analysing the age composition and growth of individuals in both marine and freshwater fish populations. An eel named 'Putte' was caught as an elver in 1863 and kept in a tank at the Museum of Salsingborg, where she lived until the autumn of 1948 . . . 85 years later.

Pliny the Elder (A.D. 23–79) wrote in his *Historia Naturalis* that eels in the River Ganges reached 300 feet in length . . . either growth rates have lessened in recent years or Pliny was somewhat off the mark! Winifred Frost, working in the 1940s at the Freshwater Biological Association on the shores of Lake Windermere, undertook a study of the growth and diet of yellow and silver eels in the Windermere catchment. She found that, in this moderately productive lake, eel growth was slow, with yellow eels reaching 10cm at 1 year, 28cm at 5 years, 50cm at 10 years and 80–100cm over 15–20 years. A half-pound eel was, on average, 10 years old and a three-pounder 15 years old.

Christopher Moriarty, who studies the fisheries biology of eels in Ireland, found that maturity at less than 15 years is unusual and that 30-year-old silver eels are not uncommon. Eels from Upper Lough Erne are relatively fast-growing and often mature at 8–9 years of age. In 1973 a large eel caught in the River Shannon was 103cm long, more than 2kg in weight and 30 years of age. This is slow growth indeed compared with most other freshwater fish. It seems likely that water temperatures play a key role in this respect; eels thrive and grow most rapidly in warm continental waters where the temperature exceeds 20°C for long periods during the summer and also where the supply of small food fish is plentiful. This is reflected in the higher weights for a given age recorded for eels from French and certain German waters. American eels, *A. americanus* from Lake Ontario grow at around twice the rate recorded for northern European eels, reaching a metre in length after only 15 years. In Britain, eels are close to the northern limit of their distribution.

The food of eels

Whilst Aristotle held that some eels subsist on pure water the truth of the matter is easier to swallow. Winifred Frost recorded eels in the River Leven and Cunsey Beck in the English Lake District eating mostly aquatic invertebrates: caddis larvae, mayfly nymphs, chironomid larvae, shrimps, water lice, snails and occasional fish. In Lake Windermere the diet was dominated by snails (*Limnaea pereger, Valvata piscinalis, Planorbis* sp.) and small mussels (*Pisidium* and *Sphaerium* sp), shrimps, *Sialis* (alderfly) larvae, caddis larvae and mayfly nymphs. Fish featured only very occasionally in the diet. It seems that eels are unable to regularly catch free-swimming pelagic (openwater) fish prey although they are regularly caught in perch traps on the lake and often eat perch within the traps.

I have retrieved gill-netted powan in Loch Lomond which have been severely chewed by eels and when scuba diving in the loch have seen the entrances of eel burrows in muddy areas of lake bed. Some of these burrow entrances were 3–4 inches across, indicating the large size of their occupants.

The long-line eel fishermen of Lough Neagh in Northern Ireland traditionally bait their hooks with either pieces of pollan (whitefish) or small live perch. These baits are sniffed out by the eels which have an exceptionally acute sense of smell. The nostrils are elongated into short 'nose tubes' which run either side of the upper lip and which must serve to conduct the scent of potential food items to the olfactory chambers in the nose.

In Lough Corrib large eels (over 50cm) often eat Arctic charr and small perch; whether they catch these fish by sneaking up to them on the lake bed or by active pursuit in open water is unknown. Fish-eating eels are able to take prey of around 10 per cent of their own body weight and seem to prefer small perch, cyprinids such as rudd or to cannibalise smaller eels.

The slow growth of eels may be due in part to their inactive lifestyle under cool conditions, lying in their burrows through the day and only foraging at night when they may not find food regularly. Many Irish eels examined for dietary analysis had empty stomachs, possibly indicating an irregular food intake. Eels from Lough Carra contained mostly *Gammarus*, chironomid larvae and snails, those from Lough Mask mostly *Asellus* and snails; whilst those from Lough Corrib ate a wide range of invertebrate prey including *Asellus, Gammarus,* chironomid larvae, ephmeropteran nymphs, caddis larvae, snails and fish.

Eels in the River Cam in south-east England are recorded eating loach, river lampreys and gudgeon, all readily accessible, bottom-living species; native crayfish (*Astropotamobius pallipes*) are also taken. German studies record eel diets including sticklebacks, burbot and fish spawn. The oft-repeated claim that eels eat a lot of salmonid eggs is unlikely to be true since, during the winter, when this potential food source is available, eels will be largely inactive in the cold water conditions.

It is claimed that yellow eels which are prevented from migrating to the sea can live for 25–50 years and reach very large sizes (2 metres long, over 5kg in weight); perhaps these are the fish that give rise to the angling record-breakers. In Scotland, where eels reach the northern edge of their distribution, growth is very slow and freshwater life prolonged; here 50-year-old-plus yellow eels have been recorded.

A specimen from a pond in the city of Cork, Ireland, measured over one metre, weighed 3.5kg and proved to be 20 years old. An analysis of the growth rings on its otoliths revealed that this fish had grown relatively rapidly up to an age of 13 years but very slowly afterwards. Perhaps it had tried to migrate at age 13 and then subsequently each year until its eventual capture.

Migration from freshwater to the sea

Upon reaching a certain length (around 40cm for males and 60cm for females), 'yellow eels' transform gradually into 'silver eels' during which time their eyes grow larger and pre-adapt to deep sea conditions. The gut shrinks with a cessation of feeding and the fat reserves represent up to a third of the body weight, compared to less than 10 per cent in typical yellow eels. The belly and flanks of both sexes change from yellow to a bright silver, presumably to aid camouflage in the hazardous marine environment. They are then ready for their long journey downstream towards the Sargasso. The ovaries and testes mature after the fish enter the sea; to reach the Sargasso in time to spawn the following spring, eels from eastern waters must travel an average 20–40 km per day! If they survive the journey at all.

Exploitation of Eels

The world commercial catch/production of eels in 1990 was between 100,000 and 110,000 tonnes of which 70-80 per cent (mostly of *Anguilla japonica* farmed in Japan and Taiwan) was eaten in Japan. In Europe, 85 per cent of the eels marketed are wild-caught and sold live, smoked or jellied. Silver eels are very nutritious and tasty, especially when skinned, cut into sections, rolled in flour and deep fried in vegetable oil. Margaret Varley has pointed out that we are wasting a valuable resource in Britain by allowing most of the eel traps that were actively fished in the last century to fall into disrepair. Lucrative silver eel fisheries still operate in both Danish (Baltic) and Dutch waters. Winifred Frost has made a study of the Toome Eel Fishery Co., based on the River Bann which drains Lough Neagh, Northern Ireland, the largest lake in the British Isles.

The Toome Eel Fishery Co. Ltd

Catch records from the Bann fishery tell us much about the biology of silver eels. Historically the catches up to the period of study (early 1940s) fluctuated considerably and concern was raised that elver access to Lough Neagh was impeded by too many obstacles. The Toome Company therefore organised the annual trap and transfer of around 20 million elvers in the early 1940s, from the headwaters of the Bann to the upper river and lough. It was estimated that between 28 and 48 million elvers entered the estuary each year. This exercise appeared to work, with increased numbers of male and longer-lived female silver eels recruiting to the fishery at the time of Frost's study.

Silver eels are caught on downstream migration in nets stretched below gaps in weirs. The nets are fished at night during an open season of 1 June to 9 January. Experience has shown that the best catches of eels occur during the 'darks' each month, just before a new moon. Eels travel most actively in the dark. An autumn flood also stimulates a run of silver eels and peak catches usually occur during the 'darks' of September and October. The runs are so well synchronised that the bulk of a season's catch can be taken over the course of just a few nights fishing.

An analysis of silver eel catches showed neatly that the average time spent as yellow eels in Lough Neagh was 7–9 years for males and 10–12 years for females. Male silver eels had an average size of around 40cm and weighed only 110g (4 oz) whilst females were around 60cm long, weighing around 550g (1 lb 4 oz). The size difference between males and females is so consistent that any silver longer than 45cm is almost certain to be female. River Bann silver eel sizes are very similar to those found for Windermere catchment fish where the largest female caught weighed 4 lb 8 oz and the average is 1 lb 3 oz for female silvers and 4 oz for males. Female Windermere fish, aged from otoliths, ranged from 9–19 years.

Angling

Eels can be caught on legered worms, small dead fish and sections of kipper or dead crayfish. Angling is most successful on warm thundery nights when tremendous battles can be waged against these powerful fish which can swim backwards and thus, rather disconcertingly, reverse out of landing nets!

Remember, large eels take a long time to reach two or three pounds, although probably not so long in the south of England as in cool lakes like Windermere. To conserve large eels in a fishery, any specimens landed should be returned as quickly as possible and kept in a dark wet sack in the meantime. The current rod-caught record is a massive (land-locked?) fish of 11 lb 2 oz (5.05kg) by S. Terry from Kingfisher Lake, Ringwood, Hampshire.

Zander or Pike perch, *Stizostedion lucioperca*

Identification and closely related species.

The zander occurs in slowly-flowing rivers, canals and productive lakes across Europe from the Netherlands, east to the Baltic Sea, extending south of the Black Sea and north far into Scandinavia. A separate species, the sea pikeperch (*Stizostedion marina*) has a restricted distribution in the Caspian and Black seas and the lower reaches of the inflowing rivers where it is commercially fished. It breeds both in fresh and saltwater in April-May. In the rivers of this region (the Volga, Danube, Ural, Don, Dneiper, Dneister for example) there also lives the Volga pikeperch (*Stizostedion volgensis*) which has a similar biology to the more widely distributed zander. The zander grows to around twice the length of these other two species. Like perch, all zanders have two dorsal fins which almost touch; the first spiny, the second soft-rayed. Perch have red ventral fins whilst the zander's are pale. Like the pike, zander have large prominent teeth, especially the large 'canines' which are characteristic of these fish. The zander's eyes are noticeably large, equipping the fish well for low light hunting. The common name 'pikeperch' describes the appearance rather well, although the zander (placed in the family 'Percidae'), is a much closer relative of the perch than the pike. A small zander could be mistaken for a Ruffe but in the zander the two dorsal fins are separate and in the Ruffe they are continuous.

In North America the walleye, *Stizostedion vitreum*, is extensively distributed from the McKenzie River in the north down to Alabama in the south. Along the Atlantic coast it occurs from Pennsylvania to North Carolina. A sub-species, the blue walleye, *S.vitreum glaucum*, used to occur in the deep clear-watered areas of Lakes Erie and Ontario but it has now disappeared, perhaps because of interbreeding with introduced walleye. The sauger, *Stizostedion canadense*, is found in Canada from Hudson's Bay southwards through the Great Lakes to West Virginia and in certain rivers in Alabama, Oklahoma, Texas, Kansas, Nebraska, Wyoming, Iowa and Montana.

A very few walleye have been released in Britain and there is a rod-caught record standing at 11 lb 12 oz (5.33kg) by F. Adams from the River Delph, Waveney, Norfolk.

Zander habitat and fisheries

The remains of both zander and perch have been recovered from archaeological excavations on the southern shores of the Baltic Sea from human habitations dating back 6000 years. Clearly, people have been catching and eating zander for a long time. The species is native to eastern Europe and western Asia and introduced to the Rhine, much of France and eastern England. Both zander in Europe and walleye in North America are most successful in relatively shallow lakes which have warm, well mixed water throughout the year and abundant populations of small prey fish. The zander's liking for warm water appears to be related to the survival of the young stages since the numbers produced each year, for example in the Dutch Lake Ijssel, is related to summer temperatures. Warm summers produce year-classes of zander that are up to 20 times more abundant than those spawned in cool summers. In Scandinavia the species is adaptable enough to survive in deeper cooler lakes where clear water and sand or gravel-bedded habitats are favoured.

Zander are tolerant of moderately acid conditions and in Finland they commonly live in peaty turbid waters with ruffe, perch, burbot and various cyprinids. Introduced into Denmark in 1879, zander are now second only to the eel as a commercially important species and are a favourite species with anglers. Most fish are stocked as two-year-olds into turbid eutrophic lakes where they eat species that are regarded by many as food competitors with the commercially valuable eels. Commercial zander fishing yields on average around 5kg per hectare of lake surface area per year. It is intended to stock many more Danish waters with zander in future years to maximise both the commercial and recreational values of the country's lakes.

The zander stocked into the German part of the Rhine in 1885 have been subsequently used to populate large numbers of Dutch fisheries where the species is an important sport fish. The recreational fishery for zander is also important in many other European countries.

In Lake Balaton in Hungary, zander have been fished by man for at least 7000 years. In 1880, 20,000 gill nets were used on the lake, zander being a major commercial species. The fishery was managed from this period and is still active today. Great changes have occurred however. In the 1950s the intensive use of fertilisers on lake-side farmland led to eutrophication of the waters and fish kills (probably due to agro-chemicals) became commonplace. In 1965 a single kill of 500 tonnes of fish including 200 tonnes of zander was recorded. In 1975 another large fish kill occurred; this time it was due to the deoxygenation of the lake after a mass die-back of an algal bloom. This is a typical problem associated with chemically-enriched waters. In recent years the changed ecology of the lake has favoured bream which now dominate the net catch; the annual zander yield from the net fishery dropped from around 175 tonnes in 1960 to around 40 tonnes by the mid-1970s. By this time, however, the recreational zander rod fishery took around 35 tonnes per year and this sport fishery (because of its high recreational and economic value) may represent a better method of exploitation of these valuable food fish in future years.

Breeding behaviour

Sexual maturity is attained by males at 2–4 years (35cm) and females at 3–5 years (40cm plus). Zander spawn from April-June at water temperatures of 8-15°C, either in slow flowing (10–20cm per second) river sections of 0.5-1 metre depth or over sandy lake bottoms at depths of up to 17 metres. The male develops a bluish belly in the spring and digs a nest in the river or lake bed sand to expose plant roots or other firm surfaces as a spawning substrate. He then courts a female by circling her for perhaps 20–25 minutes adjacent to the nest before they circle together, making the water turbid. The eggs are then laid over a 10–15 minute period. Female zander are very fecund, producing 100,000–200,000 1.3-mm diameter whitish-yellow eggs per kilo of body weight. A large female will, therefore, produce over a million eggs, all of them being laid in a single nest. The fish form a monogamous pair bond, co-operating to rear their young. The fertilised eggs are fanned by the parents with their pectoral fins to keep them clean and well aerated and hatch after around 110 degree days of incubation (e.g. 10 days at 11°C, etc). On hatching the fry are 5–6mm long and they begin to feed on tiny crustaceans after the food reserves of the yolk-sac are consumed.

Feeding and growth

Zander grow to an average of around 8cm by the autumn of their first year and to 35–55cm (1kg) by 5–6 years. Fish from the East Anglian Relief and Cut-off channels in eastern England reach around 15cm at 2 years, 30cm at 3 years, 35cm at 4 years, 45–55cm at 5–7 years and 60cm at 6–8 years. Growth is, therefore, slow compared to pike. In far northern lakes zander do not mature until they are 6–9 years old. They are, however, long-lived and can attain lengths of around 130cm and weights of 20kg after 20 years. The slower growing northern populations tend to be the longest lived. A zander might take seven years to reach 40cm at 60° north, four years at 50–60° and three years below 50°. Males generally grow more slowly than females. The British rod-caught record stands at 18 lb 8 oz (8.39kg) by R. N. Meadows from a Cambridgeshire still water in 1988*. The fastest growth rates are achieved at water temperatures of around 28°C; growth ceases around September and through the winter. It is usual for fish to lose weight through the winter and to feed voraciously, regaining condition as the water warms in the spring.

Feeding behaviour

Young zander eat small crustaceans, moving on to midge larvae and mayfly nymphs as they grow. Exactly as with pike, young invertebrate-feeding zander reach only 6–7cm in their first summer; the larger individuals switch to a diet of fish and then start to grow more rapidly reaching up to 20cm by autumn where conditions are optimal. Cannibalism occurs but is less common than in pike and perch populations. Zander catch their prey by active pursuit, swallowing roach and bream tail-first. Perch and ruffe are often swallowed head-first, perhaps to collapse the spiny dorsal fin. Feeding activity occurs at dawn and dusk and even through the night. The large eyes have a special light-reflecting layer behind the retina (the *tapetum lucidum*) which improves low-light vision by allowing light to pass through the retina twice. Walleyes are so-called because of their light-reflecting eyes. Many nocturnally hunting mammals have a similar system.

Zander eat shoaling cyprinids (roach, bream) or other species (smelt, perch, ruffe) up to around 20cm, sometimes hunting them in packs in openwater. In northern lakes young whitefish are taken. Overall, a prey size of around 10cm (or about 12 per cent of their body length) seems to be preferred by adult zander. When feeding actively in the spring and summer zander eat around 5 per cent of their body weight per day. Large zander shoals can exert a considerable predation pressure on their prey species.

Zander hunt in the depths of large clear-watered lakes, avoiding strong light, usually feeding in the late evening or at night in areas that are not too weedy. In this way they are thought to avoid direct competition with pike which prefer cooler, shallower weedy habitats where they can ambush their prey from cover during daylight. The pike's superb camouflage helps it to stalk prey under these conditions.

Do introduced zander decimate the populations of their prey species?

In 1878 the 9th Duke of Bedford introduced zander to his estate lakes at Woburn Abbey, Bedfordshire, England. The introduction was repeated by the 11th Duke in 1910. Several other English stillwaters have now been stocked including the Claydon House lakes, Old Bury Hill lake, Abberton reservoir, and Coombe Abbey lake. There are, seemingly, no problems in these waters but the introduction of zander (or any other species) into extensive river systems can have many unpredictable effects.

*This record was beaten in 1993 by R. Armstrong's 18 lb 10 oz River Severn fish.

The River Great Ouse Relief Channel
In 1963 biologists from the (then) Great Ouse River Authority in eastern England released 97 zander into the river's flood-relief channel. This is a classic case of the potential folly of introducing non-native species to new habitats. The zander population of the Great Ouse catchment subsequently exploded, rapidly colonising the rivers Ouse (1968), Wissey, Cam, Lark and Delph (1969) and countless fenland drains (1970s). Zander showed up in the Suffolk Stour in 1974, the Coventry and Oxford canal (1976) and the River Severn (1980).

Neville Fickling recorded the movements of tagged zander in the Great Ouse relief channel in the late 1970s. He found that individual fish moved up to 10km between captures but more usually distances of 3–4km were covered. One notable record was of 35.8 km (minimum) travelled by one fish in 59 days during the summer of 1979. Clearly, zander can be wide-ranging in their movements. Not all tagged fish moved; in different seasons 25–49 per cent were recaptured at the site of the initial tagging. The sudden appearance of large numbers of these mobile and hungry predatory fish caused acrimonious debate in the fishing world.

Conflicts between match and specimen anglers

The situation in the East Anglian fens is a good case in point. Whilst many people enjoy summer fishing for Fenland zander, match and casual anglers are less impressed, blaming these predatory fish for the decline of the abundant shoals of bleak, dace, rudd, silver bream, roach, common bream, ruffe and gudgeon in these waters. Ron Linfield and Barry Rickards have estimated that the rapidly-growing zander population of the Relief Channel in 1966-67 might have numbered over 20,000 fish and have eaten 16–20 tonnes of prey fish per year at that time. The circumstantial evidence points to zander predation being a principal cause of the decline in the Relief Channel's populations of small fish. Catches of large bream improved; perhaps these fish were too large for the zander to take and they benefited from an increased food supply after the demise of the huge shoals of small fish.

Scientifically the case is not proven, since other factors (for example declining habitat quality, and changes in sluice-gate opening regimes) might be responsible for the poor catches of roach and small bream subsequent to the zander's arrival. I think it likely that the zander are an important element in the overall story. As with most biological questions, comparative studies can shed light on such problems.

In 1911, zander were introduced to the large (14.5-km^2) Swedish lake Ymsen which supported a commercial fishery for perch, bream and roach. Zander were netted from 1914 and the annual catch rose to 13 tonnes by 1918. The annual catches of perch dropped, however, from around 1000 to 100 kilos; bream catches dropped from 2.4 tonnes to around 100 kilos, and roach from 300 kilos to 5 kilos. This seems like a clear-cut case of the predatory zander depleting its prey populations whilst increasing its own abundance and it may be so, but, there is a problem. Over the period of declining perch, bream and roach catches the intensity of netting for these species also decreased, leading to a difficulty of interpretation of the results. Were the population declines of the prey species real, or due simply to the reduced fishing effort? We do not know.

In most cases of zander introduction, the population seems to build up rapidly, followed by a decline in the prey species and a subsequent decline in zander stocks to a lower, relatively stable level in subsequent years. Perhaps this happened on the Great Ouse Relief Channel and in other English zander fisheries. We do not have the necessary information to form a definite opinion.

It is rather nice to end on a note of uncertainty — after all, so much remains to be discovered concerning the natural history of our freshwater fish.

Tailpiece

If you have enjoyed reading this book, and wish to make a positive contribution to the conservation of our wetland habitats and the fish and other wildlife which depend upon them for their existence, please consider joining one or more of the following organisations each of which does a good job with very modest funding:

The Game Conservancy Trust, Fordingbridge, Hampshire, SP6 1EF. Tel. 0425 652381.
    Conservation of game fish, birds, mammals and their habitats.

The Wildfowl and Wetlands Trust, Slimbridge, Gloucestershire. Tel. 0453 890333.
    Conservation of wildfowl, wetland habitats and associated wildlife.

The Anglers Co-operative Association (A.C.A.), 23 Castlegate, Grantham,
    Lincs. NG31 6SW. Tel. 0476 61008.
Prosecution of polluters of rivers and lakes and winning of compensation for restocking
    damaged fisheries.

The Atlantic Salmon Trust, Moulin, Pitlochry, Perthshire. Tel. 0796 3439.
    Active conservation of wild salmon and sea trout stocks in the U.K. and North
    Atlantic.

Institute of Fisheries Management, 22 Rushworth Avenue, West Bridgeforth,
    Nottingham, NG2 7LF.
    Scientific training and practical fisheries management advice.

The Freshwater Biological Association, The Ferry House, Ambleside Cumbria.
    Membership organisation concerned with the biology of freshwaters.
    Excellent library facilities.

Selected Bibliography

Ade, R., 1989. *The Trout and Salmon Handbook*, Croom Helm, London

Angel, H. & Wolseley, P. 1982. *The Family Water Naturalist*, Michael Joseph, London.

Angler's Mail Diary 1992 (Record fish table)

Berners, J., 1496. *A Treatyse of Fysshynge wyth an Angle*

Buller, F., 1971. *Pike*, Macdonald & Co, London.

Burgis, M. J. & Morris, P. A., 1987. *The Natural History of Lakes*, Cambridge University Press.

Campbell, R. N., 1971. The growth of brown trout in northern Scotland with special reference to the improvement of fisheries; *Journal of Fish Biology 3*, 1-28.

Campbell, R. N., 1979. Ferox trout and Charr in Scottish lochs. *Journal of Fish Biology 14*, 1-29.

Clarke, B., 1975. *The Pursuit of Stillwater Trout*, A&C Black London.

Clarke, B. & Goddard, J., 1980. *The Trout and the Fly: A New Approach*, Ernest Benn, London.

Calabi, S., 1990. *Trout and Salmon of the World*, Wellfleet Press, Secaucus, N.J.

Champion, A., 1991. Managing a recovering salmon river — the River Tyne, in *Strategies for the Rehabilitation of Salmon Rivers*, AST/IFM Conference held at Linnaean Society, November 1990.

Craig, J., 1987. *The Biology of Perch and Related Fish*, Croom Helm, London.

Dahl, T. E., 1990. *Wetland Losses in the United States 1780s to 1980s*, U.S. Dept of the Interior, Fish and Wildlife Service, Washington D.C.

Elliott, J. M., 1987. Population regulation in contrasting populations of trout *Salmo trutta* in two Lake District streams. *Journal of Animal Ecology 56*, 83-98.

Fahy, E., 1985. *Child of the Tides: A Sea Trout Handbook*, The Glendale Press, Dun Laoghaire, Dublin.

Falkus, H. & Buller, F., 1988. *Falkus and Buller's Freshwater Fishing*, Stanley Paul, London.

Ferguson, A. & Mason, F. M., 1981. Allozyme evidence for reproductively isolated sympatric populations of Brown Trout in Lough Melvin, Ireland. *Journal of Fish Biology 18*, 629-642

Fisheries in the Year 2000, Proceedings of the I.F.M. Symposium 1990 held at Royal Holloway and Bedford New College, University of London.

Friends of the Earth, 1992. *Poisonous Fish*,

Frost, W. E. & Brown, M. E., 1970. *The Trout, Fontana New Naturalist*, Collins, London.

Fryer, G., 1991. *A Natural History of the Lakes, Tarns and Streams of the English Lake District*, Freshwater Biological Association, Ambleside, Cumbria.

Gardiner, R. & McLaren, I., 1991. Decline and recovery of salmon in the Central Belt of Scotland. In *Strategies for the Rehabilitation of Salmon Rivers*, AST/IFM Conference held at Linnaean Society, November 1990.

Giles, N., Phillips, V. & Barnard, S., 1992. *Ecological Effects of Low Flows in Chalk Streams*, Royal Society for Nature Conservation Report.

Goddard, J., 1966. *Trout Fly Recognition*, A&C Black, London.

Goddard, J., 1988. *John Goddard's Waterside Guide*, Unwin Hyman, London.

Greenhalgh, M. & Sutterby, R., 1989. *The Wild Trout: The natural history of an endangered fish*, George Phillip, London.

Harris, J. R., 1956. *An Angler's Entomology*, Collins New Naturalist, London.

Haslam, S. M., 1990. *River Pollution – an Ecological Perspective*, Belhaven Press, London

Hellawell, J. M., 1972. The growth, reproduction and food of roach in the River Lugg, Herefordshire. *Journal of Fish Biology 4*, 469-486.

Howarth, W., 1987. *Freshwater Fishery Law*, Blackstone Press, London.

Hynes, H. B. N., 1970. *The Ecology of Running Waters*, University of Liverpool Press.

Kennedy, G. & Crozier, W., 1991. Strategies for the rehabilitation of salmon rivers: a post-project appraisal. In *Strategies for the Rehabilitation of Salmon Rivers*, AST/IFM Conference held at Linnaean Society, November 1990.

Kennedy, M. & Fitzmaurice, P., 1970. The biology of tench in Irish waters. *Proceedings of the Royal Irish Academy*, 69B, 31-64.

Le Cren, E. D., 1984. *The Biology of the Sea Trout*, Atlantic Salmon Trust Symposium Summary, Moulin, Pitlochry.

Lloyd, R., 1992. *Pollution and Freshwater Fish*, Fishing News Books, Oxford.

Macan, T. T. & Worthington, E. B., 1972. *Life in Lakes and Rivers*, Fontana New Naturalist, Collins, London.

Maitland, P. S., 1972. *Key to British Freshwater Fishes*, Freshwater Biological Association Publication 27.

Maitland, P. S., 1977. *The Hamlyn Guide to Freshwater Fishes of Britain and Europe*, Hamlyn, London.

Maitland, P. S., 1989. *The genetic impact of farmed Atlantic Salmon on wild populations*, NCC report.

Maitland, P. S., Lyle, A. A. & Campbell, R. N., 1987. *Acidification and fish populations in Scottish Lochs*, ITE.

Maitland, P. S. & Campbell, R. N., 1992. *Freshwater Fish*, Collins New Naturalist, London.

Maitland, P. S. & Turner, A. K., 1985. *Angling and wildlife in fresh waters*, ITE symposium No. 19.

Mann, R. H. K., 1976a. Observations on the age, food growth and reproduction of chub in the River Stour, Dorset. *Journal of Fish Biology 8*, 265-288.

Mann, R. H. K., 1976b. Observations on the age, food growth and reproduction of roach in two rivers in southern England. *Journal of Fish Biology 5*, 707-736.

Mann, R. H. K., 1985. A pike management strategy for a trout fishery. In *The Scientific Basis of Inland Fishery Management. Journal of Fish Biology*, 27A, 227-234.

Mills, C. A. & Mann, R. H. K., 1985. Environmentally induced fluctuations in year class strength and their implications for management. In *The Scientific Basis of Inland Fishery Management. Journal of Fish Biology*, 27A, 209-226.

Mills, C. A. & Hurley, M. A., 1990. Long term studies on the Windermere populations of perch, pike and Arctic charr. *Freshwater Biology* Vol. 23, No. 1, 119-136.

Mills, C. P. R., 1992. *Sea Trout in England and Wales*, NRA Fisheries Technical Report 1.

Mills, D., 1971. *Salmon and Trout. A resource, its ecology conservation and management*, Oliver & Boyd, Edinburgh.

Mills, D., 1989. *Ecology and Management of Atlantic Salmon*, Chapman and Hall, London.

Milner, N. J., 1989. Strategies to minimise the impact of forestry on fisheries. IFM study course 1989, Galway.

Moriarty, C., 1978. *Eels: a natural and unnatural history*, David and Charles, London.

Moss, B., 1988. *Ecology of Freshwaters*, 2nd Edition, Blackwell, London.

National Rivers Authority, 1992. *The Influence of Agriculture on the Quality of Natural Waters in England and Wales*.

Netboy, A., 1980. *Salmon: The World's most Harassed Fish*, Andre Deutsch, London.

O'Grady, M., King, J. & Curtin, J., 1991. The effectiveness of two physical in-stream works programmes in enhancing salmonid stocks in a drained Irish lowland river system. In *Strategies for the Rehabilitation of Salmon Rivers*, AST/IFM Conference held at Linnaean Society, November 1990.

Purseglove, J., 1988. *Taming the Flood*, Oxford University Press

Phillips, R. & Rix M., 1985. *Freshwater Fish of Britain, Ireland and Europe*, Pan Books, London.

Rackham, O., 1986. *The History of the Countryside*, Dent, London

Royal Commission on Environmental Pollution 16th Report, *Freshwater Quality*, HMSO, London.

Salmon Advisory Committee, 1992, Assessment of stocking as a salmon management strategy. MAFF/SOAFD/WOAD.

Scott, W. B. & Crossman, E. J., 1973. *Freshwater Fishes of Canada*, Fisheries Research Board of Canada Bulletin 184, Ottawa.

Shearer, W. M., 1992. *The Atlantic Salmon. Natural history, exploitation and future management*, Fishing News Books.

Solomon, D. J. & Potter, E. C. E., 1992. *The Measurement and Evaluation of the Exploitation of Atlantic Salmon*, Atlantic Salmon Trust, Moulin, Pitlochry, Perthshire.

Thorpe, J. E., 1987. *Smolting versus Residency: developmental conflict in salmonids*, Symposium of the American Fisheries Society 1, 244-252.

Varley, M. E., 1967. *British Freshwater Fishes*, Fishing News Books, London.

Walker, A., Greer, R. B. & Gardiner, A, S., 1988. Two ecologically distinct forms of Arctic Charr in Loch Rannoch, Scotland. *Biological Conservation 33*, 43-61.

Walker, R., 1975. *Stillwater Angling*, Pan Books.

Walton, I., 1653. *The Compleat Angler*, Maurice Clark, London.

Weaver, M., 1992. *The Pursuit of Wild Trout*, Merlin Unwin Books

Wheeler, A., 1969. *The fishes of the British Isles and North-west Europe*, Macmillan, London.

Winfield, I. & Nelson, J., 1991. *Cyprinid Fishes, Systematics, Biology and Exploitation*, Chapman & Hall, London.

Wootton, R. J., 1990. *Ecology of Teleost Fish*, Chapman & Hall, Fish and Fisheries Series 1, London.

Glossary

Acidification an increase in acidity (decrease in pH) usually due to atmospheric pollution

adaptive radiation the progressive evolution of a group of specialist species from a common ancestor

additive mortality deaths which the population cannot offset by better survival of remaining individuals

alevins fish fry with their yolk sacs still attached

ammocoete a freshwater-living larval lamprey

anadromous migrating into freshwater to breed (eg salmon)

back-calculated growth distances between growth checks on a scale used to estimate yearly growth of a fish based upon the population average

benthic on or in the lake bed (benthos = the animals living there)

bioaccumulation the progressive concentration of persistent pollutants in animal tissues, often increasing up the food chain

BOD Biochemical Oxygen Demand, a standardised test to measure the oxygen consumption of a water sample

carrying capacity the numbers of a species which can survive in a given area

catadromous migrating to the sea to spawn (eg eels)

Catch-and-Release returning a proportion (perhaps all) of fish caught to the water, usually to conserve wild stocks

chalk stream a braided river system originating in aquifers arising from chalk bedrock, characteristically even-temperatured and relatively even-flowing under normal climatic conditions

concretion the natural sticking together of sand and gravel particles to form a hard 'pan' on a river bed

compensatory mortality deaths which can be offset by better survival of remaining individuals

competition the struggle for limited resources, either within or between species

density-dependent mortality a factor which kills a differing proportion of a population as the numbers of animals change

density-independent mortality a factor which kills a proportion of the population irrespective of the numbers of animals present

DO a measure of Dissolved Oxygen concentration

DOE Department of the Environment

ecological succession the progressive development of one plant community into another, finally reaching the long-term stability of the 'climax community'

ecological niche the totality of environmental requirements of a given species

Freshwater Fish of the British Isles

EN English Nature (formerly Nature Conservancy Council)

ESA Environmentally Sensitive Area

endemic occuring naturally in an area

epiphytes the microscopic animal and plant community living on the surface of larger plants (macrophytes)

eutrophication progressive chemical enrichment of aquatic ecosystems

eutrophic rich in dissolved plant foods

evolution the differential survival and reproduction of genetic types within a population to gradually produce a group of well adapted individuals

food web who eats whom (or what) in a given ecosystem

genetic variability varieties of genetic types within a population, the building blocks of evolution

kilogramme two and one fifth pounds in weight

littoral the shallow sunlit lake bed

mesotrophic intermediate in dissolved plant food status

MAFF Ministry of Agriculture, Fisheries and Food

natural selection Nature's testing of individuals within a population

NRA National Rivers Authority

NNR National Nature Reserve

oligtrophic poor in dissolved plant foods

opercular bones the flat gill cover bones which can be cleaned of flesh, dried and viewed to reveal annual growth rings, especially clear in perch

otoliths tiny bones from the fish's inner ear which can be sectioned to reveal detailed (even daily!) growth rings; the best structures for ageing old, slow-growing specimens

parr a young trout or salmon with finger or 'parr' marks on its flanks

pelagic in open water

pharyngeal teeth grinding teeth in the throat of cyprinid fishes, sometimes used to identify species and hybrids

pH a logarithmic scale of acidity based upon hydrogen ion concentration where 7 is neutral, above 7 alkaline (basic) and below 7 acidic

profundal in the deep dark depths of a lake

Put-and-Take stocking-hatchery fish which are killed and taken away when caught

scale-reading the dark art of estimating the age and annual growth rates of a fish from scales taken from the 'shoulder' region (or wherever the scales are first formed in young fish of a given species)

redd gravel excavation used by salmonid fishes to protect incubating eggs

siltation the deposition of fine organic and inorganic silt on river and lake beds, often smothering fish eggs

smolt the silvery transformed salmonid parr which is ready to migrate to sea

SSSI Site of Special Scientific Interest, designated in England by EN

sustainable development growth of society within the confines of naturally renewable resources

tapetum lucidum a shiny layer of tissue behind the retina which reflects light back through the eye and permits better low-light vision

thermocline zone of rapid vertical change in water temperature (and often DO) with the epilimnion above and hypolimnion below, set up by the process of stratification

tonne one thousand kilogrammes

triploid genetically manipulated to produce a triple chromosome compliment

year class strength the numbers of a given species or proportion of a population produced in a given year; warm years often good for cyprinids, wet years for salmonids

Index

Abstraction (water) 58, 91
A.C.A. 13, 179
Acidification 13, 14, 32, 58, 65, 77, 83, 101, 102, 103
Adaptive radiation 47, 129, 133, 160
Additive mortality 11
Afforestation 14, 27, 58, 65, 102, 103
Ageing of fish 67, 170
Alkaline waters 29, 39, 40, 41, 45, 92, 97, 98, 100, 109, 143
Alevins 64, 69, 70, 82, 83, 104
American eel (*Anguilla rostrata*) 168, 170
Amphibians 20, 29, 32, 48, 88
Anadromy (migration) 42, 55, 57, 58, 62, 64, 71, 168
Angling 8, 12, 18, 19, 20, 26, 44, 48, 56, 58, 59, 63, 65, 67, 77, 78, 79, 80, 88, 89, 92, 97, 99, 104, 105, 106, 107, 108, 109, 114, 115, 116, 118, 124, 130, 134, 135, 138, 140, 143, 145, 146, 147, 148, 149, 151, 152, 158, 159, 160, 166, 173
Aquatic plants 25, 29, 34, 35, 37, 38, 39, 41, 45, 46, 47, 48, 49, 50, 65, 92, 98, 128, 129, 131, 136, 142, 153, 161, 164
Aquatic invertebrates 7, 8, 14, 15, 19, 20, 30, 31, 36, 39, 40, 41, 42, 44, 45, 47, 48, 49, 50, 59, 60, 61, 62, 63, 66, 67, 68, 70, 74, 76, 83, 92, 93, 94, 96, 97, 98, 99, 106, 107, 110, 113, 115, 117, 119, 123, 124, 128, 132, 137, 138, 141, 144, 147, '48, 154, 155, 157, 158, 164, 167, 168, 170, 171, 176
Arctic Charr 18, 21, 58, 64, 94, 103, 104, 106, 171
Atlantic Salmon Trust 28, 58, 79, 89, 90, 179
Aufwuchs 40, 161

Barbel 21, 34, 37, 38, 52, 127, 128, 129, 131, 145-150
Barbelgudgeon 127
Barbus barbus (Barbel) 127, 145-150
Bass (Sea) 7, 21, 42
　Largemouth 21, 119
　Smallmouth 119
　Rock 21, 119
Bleak 8, 38, 52, 127, 128, 129, 152, 161, 177
Bream (Common) 20, 21, 37, 38, 39, 45, 46, 50, 51, 52, 97, 110, 116, 120, 127, 128, 129, 134, 136, 137, 138, 140-144, 146, 154, 155, 158, 161, 163, 166, 167, 175, 176, 177
　Silver 38, 45, 52, 127, 128, 129, 140, 141, 161, 166, 177
　Blue 127
British rod-caught record fish 56, 58, 59, 71, 77, 96, 100, 135, 163, 166, 167, 173, 174, 176
Brown trout 7, 8, 11, 18, 19, 21, 22, 29, 35, 37, 39, 40, 44, 47, 52, 56, 58, 66, 68, 72, 74, 76, 89, 91-106, 108, 109, 110, 118, 151
　Ferox 18, 22, 48, 68, 91, 94, 123
　Gillaroo 18, 22, 44, 93
　Sonaghen 18, 22, 66, 93, 94
Brook 'trout' 19, 21, 58
Bullhead 7, 8, 21, 32, 37, 52, 92, 147, 149
Burbot 18, 52, 63, 64, 167, 171, 175

Catfish (Wels, *Silurus glanis*) 46, 51, 52, 129, 166-167
Catadromous (migration) 42, 168
Carp (*Cyprinus carpio*) 20, 21, 38, 45, 46, 50-52, 120, 127, 128, 130, 131-134, 136, 146, 167
　Crucian (*Carassius*) 21, 38, 44, 46, 50, 52, 127-131, 136
　Grass 19, 128, 129
　Silver 129
　Bighead 129
Carrying capacity 84
Chalk streams 19, 37, 38, 91, 92, 97, 106, 154, 157
Chub 21, 34, 37, 38, 51, 52, 60, 106, 127, 128, 129, 138, 145, 147, 148, 151-153, 157, 163, 165
　Black Sea 127
　Caucasian 127
Compensatory mortality 11
Conger Eel 169
Coregonids (Whitefishes) 60, 61, 66, 69-71
Coregonus albula (Vendace) 61, 71
　lavaretus (Powan) 61, 69, 70
　nasus (Broad) 60
　oxyrynchus (Houting) 18, 71
　peled (Peled) 60
　pidschian (Arctic) 60
Crayfish 7, 20, 32, 33, 41, 96, 134, 147, 152, 167, 168, 171, 173
　Signal 41, 147, 148
Cyprinidae (Carps) 20, 35, 37, 38, 46, 49, 50, 51, 63, 91, 113, 127-130, 131, 132, 138, 139, 143, 144-146, 152, 154, 157, 158, 160, 161, 163, 164, 167, 171, 175, 176

Dace 18, 21, 34, 37, 38, 51, 106, 113, 127, 128, 129, 138, 145, 151-153, 158, 163-165, 177
Density-dependent mortality 11, 82, 95, 116, 121, 133
Density-independent mortality 121

East Anglian Fens 26, 28, 31, 33, 63, 100, 158, 176, 177
Ecological niche 40, 68
Ecological succession 34, 45
Eel (European) 14, 15, 19, 21, 28, 29, 32, 37, 38, 42, 44, 45, 46, 52, 92, 133, 141, 152, 158, 166, 167, 168-173, 175
Elver 169, 170, 172
Esox americanus 115
　lucius 115-118
　masquinongy 115
　niger 115
　papyraceus 115
　tiemani 115
Eutrophication 15, 25, 28, 29, 48, 49, 50, 61, 62, 64, 91, 99, 120
Evolution 20, 68, 93, 99

Finnock (Peal, Whitling, Herling, Harvest trout) 99, 100, 101
Flounder 42, 43, 62
Forestry 14, 83, 103, 104
Freshwater Biological Association 51, 65, 120, 121, 170, 179

Frog
  Common 7, 29, 30, 31, 166, 167
  Edible 30
  Marsh 30

Game Conservancy Trust 11, 28, 179
Global warming 65, 71, 91, 120
Goldfish 21, 127, 132
Goureen 21, 62
Grass carp 19, 128, 129
Grayling 21, 37, 44, 52, 59, 63, 92, 106, 109,
  112-114, 154, 163
  Arctic 59, 60
Gudgeon 8, 37, 38, 52, 127, 128, 129, 131, 171,
  177
Grilse 72-90
  Introductions 18, 19, 20, 21, 30, 31, 32, 33, 41,
    61, 65, 69, 78, 91, 99, 104, 105, 107, 109, 119,
    120, 128, 131, 145, 147, 148, 163, 166, 174,
    176, 177, 178

Hutchen (*Hucho hucho*) 59, 60
Hydro-electricity 58, 65, 74, 75

Ice age 27, 48

Kelt 55, 80, 101
Kingfisher 7, 34, 36, 41, 158
Kype 72, 81, 104

Lake
  Alpine 62
  Anjan 114
  Arungen 158
  Atnsjo 66
  Baikal 45, 61
  Bala 61
  Balaton 120, 175
  Bassenthwaite 71
  Chew Valley 155
  Claydon House 176
  Cole Mere 143, 144
  Constance 120
  Coombe Abbey Lake 176
  Derwentwater 71
  Ellesmere 143, 144
  Emborough Pond 135
  Ennerdale 47
  Erie 174
  Geneva 67
  Great Lakes 58, 60
  Haweswater 21, 61, 98
  Hyde Lane Lakes 135
  Isjell 174
  Jewel 56, 107
  Killarney 62
  Kingfisher 173
  Kootenay 108
  Main 138, 155
  Malham tarn 98
  Malthouse Broad 140
  Mendota 131
  of Menteith 109
  Old Bury Hall 176
  Ontario 57, 170, 174
  Oyeren 141
  Penrhyncoch 103

Pyramid 57
Red Tarn 61
Rostherne Mere 123
Sebago 57
Slapton ley 155
St Peter's 136, 137, 155
Tatton Mere 143, 144
Taupo 107
Titicaca 107
Tjeukemeer 141, 158
Ullswater 61, 64, 98, 123
Vattern 67
Vyrnwy 98, 151
Wastwater 98
White 109
Windermere 21, 28, 29, 64, 66, 67, 98, 106, 120,
  170, 173
Woburn Abbey 176
Yew Tree Tarn 98
Ymsen 177
Lake District 27, 29, 47, 48, 61, 64, 66, 84, 95, 98,
  121, 170
Lake trout (Charr) 58, 59, 60, 61
Lamprey (*Lampetra & Petromyzon* species)
  Brook 18, 52, 63, 70
  River 18, 21, 62, 63, 70, 171
  Sea 52, 60, 62, 70
Land-locking 48, 62, 64, 173
Lateral line 72, 93, 129, 140
Leuciscus cephalus (Chub) 151-153
  leuciscus (Dace) 127, 163-165
Littoral zone 44, 63, 123, 140, 161
Llyn
  Brianne 14
  Conwy 103
  Peris 18
  Tegid 21, 70, 98, 112, 113
Loch
  Achrey 65
  Arkaig 68
  Assynt 39
  Awe 65, 94, 109
  Berwick 58
  Bhrodain 68
  Boisedale 98
  Bornish 39
  Borralie 39, 98
  Builg 66
  Caladail 39
  Castle 18, 61, 71
  Doon 65, 68
  Dungeon 18, 65
  Eck 21, 61, 66, 69
  Ericht 68, 94
  Errochty 65
  Fleet 103
  Garry 65, 68, 94
  Grannoch 18, 65, 103
  Grogarry 39
  Inch 68
  Ken 117
  Lanlish 39
  Leven 18, 28, 29, 64, 84
  Lomond 7, 18, 21, 33, 43, 61, 62, 69, 70, 111,
    117, 119, 122, 154, 156, 171
  Lubnaig 68
  Luichart 68

Maben 71, 143
Machair 100
Maree 68
Meallt 67
Mill 18, 61, 71
Morar 27
Ness 27, 94
Poulary 94
Quoish 94
Rannoch 66, 68, 94
Shin 94
Stack 66
Stilligary 39
Venacher 65
Voil 68
Lough
  Aderry 162
  Arrow 39
  Ballybutler 162
  Carra 28, 39, 171
  Conn 39
  Coosan 136, 137, 161
  Corrib 21, 28, 39, 98, 106, 117, 171
  Derg 47, 61, 71, 98, 117
  Erne 21, 47, 61, 71, 117, 170
  Inchiquin 98
  Leane 21, 62
  Mask 28, 39, 106, 117, 171
  Melvin 22, 93, 94
  na B'Eisge 161
  na Leibe 109
  Neagh 28, 47, 61, 64, 71, 171, 172
  Owel 95
  Ree 47, 61, 71, 98, 117
  Sheelin 28, 29, 105
  Shure 109
  Turloughs 27
Loach
  Stone 7, 8, 21, 37, 52, 92, 135, 136, 147, 149, 171
  Spined 52, 135, 136

Maintenance dredging 34, 36, 164
Mink 32, 33, 34, 88
Minnow 8, 21, 37, 46, 52, 92, 97, 127, 129, 147, 149, 152
Mullet
  Grey (thick-lipped) 42
  Grey (thin-lipped) 42
  Grey (Golden) 42
Mysis relicta (Shrimp) 47, 61, 71

National Rivers Authority (NRA) 13, 14, 15, 16, 17, 19, 20, 26, 28, 36, 75, 96, 128
NCC (EN) 128
Newt
  Great crested (Warty) 30
  Palmate 30
  Smooth 30
NNR 19
Norfolk Broads 25, 28, 140, 160

Oligotrophic 29, 47, 48, 90, 98, 99, 120
Oncorhynchus (Pacific salmon, Rainbow trout) 55, 56 107
Opercular bone 79, 138, 152, 157
Otoliths 79, 138, 152, 170, 173
Osmerus (Smelt) 18, 21, 42, 52, 55, 62, 141, 142

Parasites 132
  Hookworms (*Pomphorhynchus*) 145
  Lampreys 62
  Ligula (tapeworm) 155
  Skin flukes 78
  Sea lice 72, 101, 102
Parr 37, 40, 55, 73, 74, 75, 76, 78, 81, 82, 83, 84, 85, 86, 87, 94, 95, 96, 99, 100, 101, 108, 111, 114
Pelagic zone 44, 66, 171
Pesticides 13, 14, 15, 31, 58
Perca fluviatilis (Perch) 119-124
  flavescens (Yellow Perch) 120
Perch 21, 33, 37, 38, 44, 46, 48, 52, 92, 94, 97, 106, 110, 116, 119-124, 137, 154, 171, 174, 175, 176, 177
Pharyngeal teeth 127, 141
Phoxinus (Minnows) 127
Pike 21, 33, 37, 38, 44, 46, 52, 68, 69, 88, 92, 93, 106, 113, 115-118, 119, 121, 135, 137, 141, 146, 158
Pickerel (Chain, Redfin, Grass) 115
Pollution 12, 13, 14, 15, 16, 17, 28, 30, 32, 42, 58, 62, 63, 71, 74, 92, 102
Pumpkinseed 21, 119, 120
Put-and-Take fisheries 56, 90, 106, 108, 128
Profundal zone 44

Rainbow trout 19, 21, 50, 52, 56, 91, 92, 93, 95, 100, 106, 107- 111, 116
Redd 36, 59, 74, 81, 82, 95, 104, 108, 111, 134, 150
Reptiles 29, 49, 88
River
  Aberdeenshire Dee 40, 82, 87
  Aberdeenshire Don 40, 74
  Aire 145
  Akheloos 166
  Allen 92
  Almond 74
  Alta 77
  Alwen 81
  Amur 59, 115, 128
  Angarrack stream 15
  Annan 21
  Apache 107
  Awe 109
  Axe 15, 73, 100
  Bann 172
  Bedford (Old & New) 26
  Bela 98
  Big Salmon 80
  Biss 108
  Black Brows beck 95
  Blackwater 15, 163
  Bollin 145
  Boyne 76
  Bristol Avon 145
  Bure 29, 140
  Bush 87
  Cam 18, 165, 171, 177
  Campbell 56
  Carron 74
  Chess 108
  Chew 15
  Clyde 13, 74
  Columbia 107, 108
  Connecticut 74

Conwy 96
Cumbrian Leven 170
Cunsey beck 170
Dane 145
Danube 166, 174
Danube 59
Darent 92
Dart 72, 98
Delph 174, 177
Derbyshire Wye 108, 110
Derwent 108
Derwent 15, 18, 110
Dneiper 166, 174
Dneister 174
Don 174
Dordogne 74
Dorset Frome 39, 73, 79, 108, 112, 114, 157, 158, 163, 164
Dorset Stour 42, 98, 152, 154, 158
Dove 15
Driffield Beck 39
Driva 78
Drowes 94
Earne 112
Ebble 39
Elbe 21, 74
Em 100
Endrick 7, 70, 78, 116, 154
Erne 33
Esk 74
Falloch 116
Feale 74
Forss 81, 98
Forth 18
Forth leven 74
Foss 18
Fowey 101
Funshion 165
Gade 108
Garron 74, 108
Garry 65
Gila 107
Glennaniff 94
Gowla 109
Granta 108
Great Ouse 7, 21, 32, 63, 145, 155, 158, 177
Grimersta 86
Gryfe 74
Gwash 108
Hampshire Avon 7, 19, 21, 39, 42, 79, 85, 86, 92, 98, 151, 165
Helmsdale 72
Isla 112
Itchen 39, 92
Jaques Cartier 74
Katseydie 59
Kenai 107
Kennet 98, 114, 145, 147
Kuskokwim 107
Laerdal 77
Lambourn 98
Lark 177
Leith 74
Lena 59
Leven 100
Loire 74
Lugg 113, 155, 156

Lune 15
Lyne 15
Malling bourne 108
Marazion stream 15
McCloud 107, 108
McKenzie 107
Merrimack 74
Mersey 15
Meuse 21, 74
Mimram 108
Misbourne 92, 108
Morrum 100
Nadder 39, 98
Nene 156
Newlyn 15
Newport 109
Nidd 112
Nipigon 58
Nith 112
North Esk 83, 98
Ob 59
Old West 63
Ouzel 36
Pang 92
Penobscot 74
Piddle 15, 39, 92
Plym 108
Polla 89, 90
Restigouche 77
Rhine 21, 74
Ribble 145
Rother 30
Russia 107
Scheldt 21
Scottish Leven 116
Seine 74
Severn 18, 21, 32, 33, 62, 112, 145, 149, 169, 177
Shannon 61
Shepreth brook 165
Skeena 56, 108
Snake 107
Soar 35
Somer 7
Spey 72
St Lawrence 115
Suck 140
Swale 145
Taff 13, 74, 105
Tamar 98
Tana 77
Tanana 59
Taw 14, 31
Tay 61, 77, 86, 112, 154
Tees 74, 98
Teifi 72
Teign 72
Teme 15, 145
Tern 145
Test 19, 39, 92, 98, 105, 113, 114
Thames 7, 13, 18, 21, 73, 74, 145, 158
Thurne 29
Thurso 72
Torridge 31
Towy (Tywi) 14, 15, 72
Tree 58
Trent 18, 74, 145
Tweed 15, 21, 100, 112

Tyne 13, 74, 75, 163
Ural 174
Usk 105
Volga 174
Vosso 77
Vyrynwy 145
Wallop brook 92
Warwickshire Avon 145
Waveney 18, 29, 174
Weaver 145
Welland 145
Welsh Dee 81, 105, 112
Weser 21
West beck 108
Wey 92
Wharfe 145
Wissey 177
Witham 145
Worfe 145
Wye 15, 79, 112
Wylye 39, 106
Yare 29
Yellowstone 56
Yorkshire Don 145
Yorkshire Ouse 74, 145
River Laboratory (East Stoke, Dorset) 16, 106
Roach 21, 37, 38, 44, 46, 52, 97, 110, 116, 127,
    128, 129, 137, 138, 140, 142, 145, 152,
    154-159, 160, 163, 165, 167, 176, 177
Rutilus (Roach) 154-159

Salmon (Atlantic) 11, 13, 14, 15, 21, 32, 36, 37,
    40, 42, 44, 46, 52, 55, 57, 58, 62, 69, 72, 90,
    94, 99, 100, 101, 102, 103, 104, 108, 113, 114,
    116, 129, 146, 179
  Chinook 55, 56
  Chum 55
  Coho 55
  Pacific 55, 56, 107
  Pink 21
Sockeye 55
Salmonid 8, 14, 21, 37, 40, 44, 46, 48, 49, 51, 55,
    56, 59, 62, 63, 64, 73, 74, 75, 76, 77, 82, 85,
    87, 89, 90, 91, 93, 95, 102, 103, 107, 111, 112,
    113, 150, 168
Salmo salar (Atlantic salmon) 55, 57, 72-90
Salmo trutta (Brown/Sea Trout) 8, 55, 91-106, 107
Salvelinus fontinalis (Brook 'trout') 58
  alpinus (Arctic Charr) 18, 58, 64-68
  namaycush (Lake –trout·) 58
Sandeel 42, 55, 99, 101
Scales 62, 67, 72, 78, 79, 97, 113, 115 132, 134,
    135, 138, 140, 147, 151
Scardinius erythropthalmus (Rudd) 127, 160-162
Seas
  Aegean 146
  Aral 129, 146
Asov 129, 166
Baltic 76, 174
Barents 76
Black 127, 145, 146, 154, 159, 174
Caspian 60, 127, 141, 146, 154, 160, 166, 174
Irish 57
Sargasso 170, 172
Sea trout 8, 13, 37, 40, 42, 44, 55, 69, 72, 73, 74,
    75, 79, 80, 83, 84, 86, 90, 91-106, 109, 116
Sea-winters (salmon growth) 73, 78, 80, 86, 88
Seal
  Baikal 45
  Grey 87, 88
Sewage 13, 15, 16, 28, 58, 61, 65, 71, 74, 120
Shads (*Alosa* species)
  Allis 18, 21, 42, 51, 52, 61-62
  Twaite 18, 21, 42, 51, 52, 61-62
Silurus glanis (Wels, Catfish, Sheatfish) 166-167
Siltation 14, 28, 102, 103, 104, 108, 158
Spring salmon (Springer) 73, 79, 108
SSSI 18, 25
Steelhead 106, 107-111
Stocking 18, 19, 20, 58, 67, 75, 83, 86, 90, 93, 94,
    95, 102, 104, 105, 106, 108, 109, 111, 136,
    145, 147, 162, 167, 179
Stratification 46
Stickleback
  three-spined 8, 21, 42, 46, 47, 97, 115, 171
  ten-spined (nine-spined) 21, 46, 47
  spineless 18, 47
Sturgeon 18, 21, 167
Sunfish 119, 120
Swim bladder 130, 139, 161, 167

Tagging 86, 121, 122, 177
Tapetum lucidum 176
Tench (*Tinca tinca*) 21, 38, 44, 45, 46, 50, 52, 127,
    128, 129, 135-139, 146, 155, 167
Thermocline 49
Toad
  Common 29, 30
  Natterjack 30
Triploid 108
Tubercles 129, 144, 153, 158, 161

Ulcer disease (of perch) 120, 121

Walleye (*Stizostedion vitreum*) 174, 176
Waterfowl (wildfowl) 11, 19, 20, 27, 29, 88, 115,
    131, 142
Wildlife And Countryside Act (WACA) 147, 167

Year class strength 121, 144, 164

Zander (Pike-perch, *Stizostedion lucioperca*) 19,
    21, 52, 119, 120, 121, 129, 158, 167, 174-178

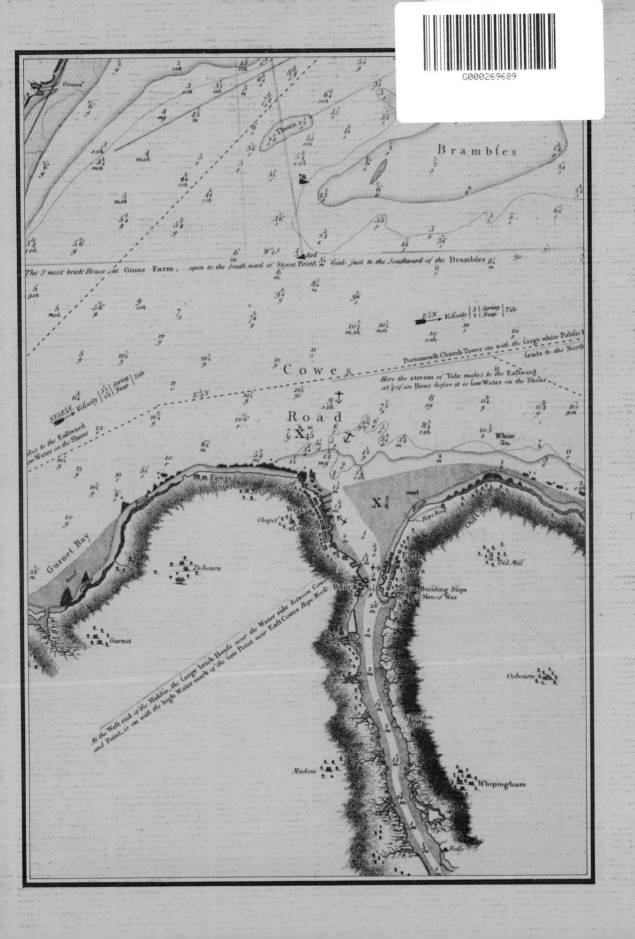

*The Royal Yacht
Squadron*

Endpapers, left The Solent was surveyed by Murdoch Mackenzie in 1783 and this chart, showing Cowes harbour, published in 1809. Soundings in fathoms. *Right* Part of the chart published in 1974 and corrected to 1978. The Squadron castle is the easternmost building, marked with a burgee. Depths in metres

The Royal Yacht Squadron

1815–1985

IAN DEAR

Foreword by H.R.H. The Duke of Edinburgh

STANLEY PAUL
London   Melbourne   Sydney   Auckland   Johannesburg

First published in 1985 by Stanley Paul & Co Ltd

An imprint of Century Hutchinson Ltd
Brookmount House, 62–65 Chandos Place, Covent Garden,
London WC2N 4NW

Century Hutchinson Publishing Group (Australia) Pty Ltd
16–22 Church Street Hawthorn, Melbourne, Victoria 3122

Century Hutchinson Group (NZ) Ltd
32–34 View Road, PO Box 40–086, Glenfield, Auckland 10

Century Hutchinson Group (SA) Pty Ltd
PO Box 337, Bergvlei 2012, South Africa

Printed and bound in Great Britain by
Butler & Tanner Ltd, Frome and London

ISBN 0 09 162590 4

Contents

Illustrations   7

Acknowledgements   12

Foreword by H.R.H. The Duke of Edinburgh   13

CHAPTER ONE   *1815–25*   15

The formation of the Club and the early years of yachting at Cowes. The first rallies, regattas, matches and overseas cruises. Crew discipline. Royal patronage

CHAPTER TWO   *1825–48*   33

Yacht racing gets under way with all the problems of rules and handicapping. Worldwide ocean voyages by members. The Royal Navy buys as warships fast yachts designed by members. The club becomes The Royal Yacht Squadron. On 'national utility'

CHAPTER THREE   *1849–81*   51

Lord Wilton's benevolent commodoreship. The visit of *America*. An Irish squabble over the White Ensign. Further race handicapping problems. A circumnavigation of the globe

CHAPTER FOUR   *1882–1919*   71

The commodoreship of the Prince of Wales and his
patronage as King Edward VII. The golden age of Cowes.
Members become power-boat champions and others help
as men of science. The club and the First World War. The
Auxiliary Yacht Patrol. The freehold of the Castle bought.
Changes in the rules for membership

CHAPTER FIVE   *1919–48*   99

The slow revival of big class yachting. The start and growth
of ocean racing. Challenges for the *America*'s Cup. Members as Olympic medallists. Worldwide cruising continues.
The Second World War. The use of members' yachts and
the Castle as of 'national utility'. The postwar start-up in
the smaller classes

CHAPTER SIX   *1948–85*   129

Small-class racing continues, and ocean racing goes from
strength to strength. The Admiral's Cup. The revival of a
challenge for the *America*'s Cup leading to worldwide
interest in the competition. The Club flourishes

Afterword by the Commodore, Sir John Nicholson Bt   157

APPENDIX 1   *Members' Yachts and Their Use in the First*
World War   159

APPENDIX 2   *Members' Yachts and Their Use in the Second*
World War   173

APPENDIX 3   *The Royal Yacht Squadron and the Town of Cowes*   189

APPENDIX 4   *Officers of The Royal Yacht Squadron*   193

Index   197

Illustrations

COLOUR PLATES

Between pages 96 and 97

A regatta off Cowes, 1776
A Trinity House regatta at Cowes, 1794
Lord Craven's *Louisa*, 1818
The Club regatta at Cowes, 1827
The Royal yacht *Royal George*, 1831
The Commodore's *Falcon*, 1831
Lord Belfast's five yachts, *Therese, Harriet, Louisa, Emily* and *Waterwitch*
Mr Joseph Weld's *Alarm*, about 1846
The cutter *Louisa*, 1832
A view of Castle Point with Squadron yachts, 1843
Lord Yarborough's brigantine *Kestrel*, 1846
The schooner *America* off Cowes, 1851
A view of Cowes, 1852
The schooner *Erminia*, about 1880
The Squadron castle with yachts, by a Japanese artist
Cowes Roads, with the Earl of Crawford's *Valhalla*, 1899
The Royal yacht *Britannia* racing in the Solent, 1921
A view from the lawn during Cowes Week, 1923
'Interior of the Yacht Club, Cowes', by Raoul Dufy, 1936
The Rt. Hon. Edward Heath's *Morning Cloud*
Redwings racing during Cowes Week, 1975
Squadron activities, 1974–80
Captain Michael Boyle's *Dauntless* on the start line

Black-and-white Photographs

Between pages 24 and 25

West Cowes, 1799
Cowes Castle, early nineteenth century
The Marquis of Anglesey's *Pearl*, 1820
A small gaff-rigged cutter off Castle Point, 1811
A Cowes skiff, 1815
Cowes esplanade, 1825
Sir William Curtis's *Emma* off Ramsgate
Starting records of cup winners
Lord Belfast's *Harriet*, 1827
The 6th Duke of Marlborough's *Wyvern*
Joseph Weld's *Alarm* off the Eddystone
Lord Belfast's *Waterwitch*, 1832
Benjamin Boyd's *Wanderer*
Lord Yarborough's *Kestrel*
A regatta at Cowes, 1844

Between pages 40 and 41

Formosa off the Fastnet
The 3rd Marquis of Ormonde's *Mirage*
Captain W. H. Roberts's *Golden Fleece*, 1882
Mosquito, 1848
The 3rd Marquis of Ailsa's *Foxhound*, 1871
Thomas Brassey's *Muriel*
The 14th Earl of Dunraven's *Valkyrie II*
The Marquis of Ailsa's *Bloodhound*, 1874
Group of members on the platform, 1870
Group of members, 1880
Group of members, 1895
Frank James's *Lancashire Witch*
Sir Allen Young's *Pandora*

Between pages 56 and 57

Thomas Brassey's *Sunbeam*
Lord Runciman's *Sunbeam II*
Lord Dunraven's *Cariad II*

Cariad II's certificate of exemption, 1903
The Duchess of Westminster, 1908
The naval review at Spithead, 1914
The 6th Marquis of Anglesey's *Semiramis*
The Duke of Bedford's *Sapphire*
The Castle from the sea, 1912
The Castle from the west
The front door of the Castle
The Castle platform
The morning room
The ladies' drawing room
Ladies on the Squadron lawn
Spectators by the Squadron landing

Between pages 72 and 73

The Prince of Wales's launch
Lord Montagu of Beaulieu's Yarrow, 1906
Sir Philip Hunloke
King Edward VII's pilot
Sir Allan Young
The 26th Earl of Crawford and Balcares
The 3rd Marquis of Ormonde
The 10th Duke of Leeds
William Jameson
Sir William Portal
The armed yacht *Ceto*
The hospital ship *Liberty*
Signor Marconi's *Elettra*
The diesel yacht *Sona*
Fantome II, now *Belem*
The 2nd Duke of Westminster's *Flying Cloud*
The three-masted schooner *Creole*
The J-class racing, 1934
Jolie Brise, the first Fastnet race winner
Lord Montagu's *Cygnet*

Between pages 120 and 121

Sir Thomas Sopwith's *Endeavour* and *Endeavour II*
Lalage, Olympic winner

Lord Moyne's *Rosaura*
Bloodhound, 1936
Peter du Cane's Motor Torpedo Boat
Sir Thomas Sopwith's *Philante* on war service
The *Cutty Sark* on war service
King George VI taking the salute, 1944
Stewart Morris, Olympic gold medallist, 1948
Captain John Illingworth's *Myth of Malham*
Sir Max Aitken's *Lumberjack*
HRH The Duke of Edinburgh's *Coweslip*
HRH The Duke of Edinburgh's *Bluebottle*
Lt. Col. Perry's *Vision*
Olympic prizegiving, Melbourne 1956

Between pages 136 and 137

Sceptre and *Evaine*
Sir Max Aitken's *Drumbeat*
The Aisher family's *Yeoman XXI*
Peter du Cane's *Brave Borderer*
Peter du Cane's *Dimarcha*
Tommy Sopwith's *Telstar*
Squadron prizegiving ceremony, 1970
Commander Peter Thorneycroft's Osprey class vessel
Commander Peter Thorneycroft's Nelson launch
Sir Max Aitken's *Gypsy Girl*
John Miller's *Maid of Honour*
Sir Peter Green's *Musketeer*
Sir Robert Crichton-Brown's *Pacha*
The Chichester trophy

Between pages 152 and 153

The Squadron platform, 1975
The library
The ladies' drawing room
The ladies' dining room
Major General Farrant's *Trifle*
Baron Edmond de Rothschild's *Gitana VI*
Cornelius van Rietschoten's *Flyer II*
John Millar's barquentine *Centurion*

ILLUSTRATIONS

Sir Maurice Laing's *Bathsheba*
The Redwing class *Redstart*
The Daring class *Deinos*
John Roome's *Flycatcher*
The Commodore, Sir John Nicholson, and *Star Ven*
Members of the Squadron, 1965
Race winners on the platform board

Acknowledgements

Spencer Herapath, Honorary Librarian and Custodian of the Pictures of the Royal Yacht Squadron, has been gathering letters, photographs and memories that make up the history of the Club for many years. He has worked on the choice of illustrations, and is responsible for the captions. He contributed Appendix 3 relating to the Squadron and to the town of Cowes.

Spencer Herapath was assisted by Maldwin Drummond, who helped organize the production of the book with Roderick Bloomfield of Century Hutchinson. They received help and advice from Sir Peter Johnson. The Commodore, Sir John Nicholson, and Lord Runciman, a predecessor in that office, read the manuscript to ensure historical accuracy.

Beken & Sons of Cowes, marine photographers by appointment to HRH The Duke of Edinburgh, provided most of the photographs, having similarly done so for the previous history published in 1939. Robert Coles MBE, of Shanklin, and Sir Geoffrey Shakerley of Photographic Records Ltd, photographed the pictures in the Squadron's collection. Pictures and photographs which do so much to contribute the visual history of the Club were provided willingly and grateful acknowledgements are made individually with the illustrations.

The charts used for the endpapers are reproduced by permission of the Hydrographer Royal.

The Club would like to express their thanks to HRH The Duke of Edinburgh, Admiral of the Royal Yacht Squadron, for his foreword which gives such an excellent introduction to the book.

Foreword

King William IV described the Royal Yacht Squadron as 'an institution of national utility' and in two world wars the members fully lived up to his expectations. The unique privilege of having permission to use the White Ensign was more than vindicated when the occasion demanded. But the Squadron has always been a club and, as this history makes clear, it has been fortunate to attract some of the most far-sighted and enthusiastic, not to say eccentric, yachtsmen of their time. They frequently led the way for others to follow. No wonder that it has come to enjoy that special prestige which the British reserve for their more venerable institutions.

For 170 years, succeeding generations of members have pursued their interest in yachting from the Castle at Cowes and this has undoubtedly had a significant influence on maintaining the Solent as a major centre for British and international yachting.

Ian Dear has put together a most interesting composite account of the Squadron and its members. I feel sure that yachting people, as well as many others, will thoroughly enjoy this book.

CHAPTER ONE

1815-25

*The formation of the Club and the earlier years of
yachting at Cowes. The first rallies, regattas, matches
and overseas cruises. Crew discipline. Royal patronage*

THE BEGINNINGS of the Royal Yacht Squadron were modest. On
1 June 1815 a group of gentlemen met at the Thatched House
Tavern in London's St James's Street and agreed to form a club for
those interested in salt-water yachting. They did not elect a Commodore – the first one, the Earl of Yarborough was not appointed until the
1820s – or any flag officers, and the possibility of a clubhouse was almost
certainly not even discussed. They merely agreed to meet twice a year –
once in London and once at Cowes – to enjoy one another's company
and to talk about their common interest.

However, from the start The Yacht Club, as it was first called, showed
itself to be a unique organization. For although sailing* clubs were by no
means unknown at that time – the Water Club of the Harbour of Cork
was in existence as early as 1720 – by gathering together under one flag
what must have been nearly all the owners of seagoing yachts which
sailed in the Solent, it created a remarkable fleet which only the Royal
Navy could equal. It cannot be proved but there is good reason to
believe that the Royal Navy did, in fact, come to regard the club as a kind
of auxiliary fleet, and there is even less doubt that the club's members
regarded themselves as such.

---

* The Yacht Club seems to have been the first sailing organization to use the word 'yacht' in its
name, though the Starcross Club, founded in 1775, may have used the word before 1815.

In 1775 the Cumberland Society, the forerunner of the present Royal Thames Yacht Club, was founded to encourage racing between small yachts on the Thames; and in the following years there sprang up, quite independently, the practice of many south-coast towns of holding sailing competitions between local fishermen, pilot boats, and even between cutters belonging to the Royal Navy. These 'regattas', as they came to be called, were especially popular at Cowes where the twenty miles of sheltered waters of the Solent made conditions ideal. It was full of the right type, too, for during the Napoleonic Wars it drew to it the complete spectrum of seafarers and those who lived by servicing their professional needs.

The first record of a sailing match at Cowes occurred well before the outbreak of war, in 1776, when what appears to be a race took place off Cowes between cutters belonging to the Royal Navy, an occasion important enough to be recorded by a noted marine artist of the time. The next known references were in 1784 when mention was made of 'a race of yachts of 24 tons with their racing flags in colour'; and in 1788 when a local paper mentioned a sailing match for a purse of 30 guineas which took place westabout around the island 'for vessels carvel built not exceeding 35 tons register'.

But the long-drawn-out war against France inhibited any sailing for pleasure away from the coast. When G. A. Fullerton, an early member of The Yacht Club, ventured beyond the Needles in his 55-ton cutter *Zephyr* in 1806 he was very nearly captured by a French privateer.* And when an original member, Sir William Curtis – an ex-Lord Mayor of London who had recently made his fortune by providing hardtack for the Royal Navy – decided to sail to Spain in 1809 to see the Peninsular War at first hand, he was only allowed to proceed provided he put his yacht under the command of a naval squadron, and this he was only too glad to do.

However, the war did not entirely stop the new pastime of yachting. The few private sailing vessels in the hands of gentlemen around the turn of the century were never apparently entered in any regatta races, but the habit gradually grew up of match racing between themselves. One of the earliest recorded was between Mr Sturt and Mr Joseph Weld – another, and very prominent, original member of The Yacht Club –

---

* *History of Lymington* by Charles Percy Jones, Chas. T. King, Lymington, 1930.

which took place off Weymouth in 1800. Local papers also record that two more took place in 1810 and another in 1812, heavy betting showing that interest in these early races were by no means confined to the participants. Horse racing was the great legitimate spectator sport of the day, but once yachting got under way it must have rivalled the Sport of Kings amongst those who had easy access to the coast.

As the years of the new century passed so interest grew amongst the gentry in visiting seaside towns along the south coast during the summer months. It became fashionable to take a house at Cowes, for instance, to enjoy the sea air and the pretty spectacle of working cutters vying with each other on the sheltered waters of the Solent. In 1813 visitors there were entertained by a parade of pilot vessels during the regatta, an addition to the usual race. According to a local reporter, both were watched by various gentlemen from the decks of their yachts before they went ashore to attend the ball at East Cowes or to dine at the Marine Hotel at West Cowes.

It was at such latter functions that the idea of a club for those interested in yachting on salt water was almost certainly put forward. Indeed, it is probable that The Yacht Club existed – in embryo form at least – before 1815. Confusion over the date of its official formation has arisen because the Club's seal, made much later, carries the date 1812.

Alongside an article about the origins of the club its first historian,* Montague Guest, pencilled a note that, 'it has always astonished me how the vessels of The Yacht Club were got together in 1815 and what caused the club to be spontaneously started at Cowes'.

Nearly a hundred years on the problem is no easier to solve, but it seems likely that some loose form of association existed, a point of view reinforced by the fact that when the first official meeting took place at least two of the original members were not present to be elected: the Earl of Uxbridge (soon to become the Marquis of Anglesey) was about to take part in the battle of Waterloo and to lose his leg there, and Sir William Curtis was aboard his yacht bound for St Petersburg.

It is not known how many were present at the Thatched House Tavern on that June day in 1815, but the club's first regulations upon which they agreed under the chairmanship of Lord Grantham have

---

* *Memorials of the Royal Yacht Squadron* by Montague Guest and William Boulton, John Murray, 1903.

been carefully preserved:

First . . . that the club be called The Yacht Club.

Second . . . that the following persons are the original members of the club [there follows a list of forty-two names, roughly half of whom belonged to the peerage, the rest being gentry].

And that hereafter, the qualification to entitle a gentleman to become a member be the ownership of a vessel not under 10 tons.

Third . . . that no vessel under 10 tons although belonging to a member shall be entitled to a number on the list.

Fourth . . . that no person be hereafter admitted as a member without being balloted for at a general meeting consisting of not less than ten members. The candidate to be proposed and seconded by two members of the club. Two black balls to exclude.

Fifth . . . that in the event of ten members not being present, the meeting may be adjourned. The day fixed to be announced in *The Courier* and *Mercury Chronicle* newspapers.

Sixth . . . that there be two general meetings in the year. One at the Thatched House on the first Saturday in May; the other at Cowes on a day in August to be fixed at the Spring meeting.

Seventh . . . that each member on his admission shall pay two guineas to the Treasurer by whom he will be furnished with two copies of signal books* and will be expected to provide himself with a set of flags according to the regulations contained therein.

Eighth . . . that each member be requested to transmit the name, tonnage, rig, and port of registry of his yacht to the Secretary; and that any change therein hereafter be duly notified in the same manner.

Ninth . . . that the distinguishing ensign of the club be – a white flag†️ with the Union in the corner.

Tenth . . . that the summer meeting of the present year be held at Cowes the 24th of August ensuing: Dinner at the Hotel East Cowes Four O'Clock. Members to give notice two days previous of their intention to dine, and of the number of friends they propose to introduce.

---

* A member would have been provided with a Royal Naval signal book as well as a club one as the two systems were different.

† The original burgee was plain white, but the 1817 signal book shows that by that date members were permitted to add their crest to it.

Eleventh . . . that John Ward Esq. of East Cowes be requested to accept the offices of Treasurer and Secretary; and that the subscriptions be paid to him at Cowes or to the House of Sir Richard Carr Glynn, Mills, Halifax & Co., London, on his account.

It can be seen from the above that the club's original purpose was to be a convivial focus for a seaborne fraternity who used Cowes as a base for their sailing during the summer months, a function well illustrated by a resolution passed in 1816 which stated that 'although many members of this club are not personally acquainted, it is hoped that no introduction to each other will be deemed necessary in any case where assistance or accommodation by boats or otherwise may be required, but that any communication by signal may be always received with that cordiality which it was the first object of the club to establish, although the parties may be personally unacquainted'.

From this statement it can be gleaned how important signalling was to members, for it was the only means of communication they had when they came across one another at sea or anchored apart in port. When the club was formed each member was given a number by which he could be identified by hoisting the necessary flags.

It took some years to perfect the club's signalling codes and much heartsearching and expense was lavished on it before a satisfactory version was published in 1831. The earliest signal book now extant is that of 1817* and contains a simple vocabulary of nearly 3000 different signals. By 1831 this had risen to over 6500 words, 2000 sentences, 900 Christian and surnames, geographical features in all five oceans and a list, updated annually, of naval ships, and this version continued with only minor changes until it was abolished in 1896 and replaced with the commercial code.

The 1831 signal book gives a fascinating insight into the social mores of the time. Sentences that could be signalled between members at sea included 'Will you dine with me?', 'Can you lend me your band?', and 'Have you any ladies on board?', while those that could be signalled to the shore included sending off for 'one hundred prawns', 'a soup tureen', or 'three hundred oysters'. It even included half a column on

---

* In the possession of the Royal Northern and Clyde Yacht Club.

what signal to fly if one member wanted to borrow from another as many as fourteen types of wine!

The signalling system baffled some members. On one memorable occasion in later years a club yacht, its bowsprit broken and its decks in considerable disarray after surviving a heavy storm, was seen limping into Torbay by a group of club yachts anchored there. This group had escaped the storm and were in immaculate condition in readiness for the local regatta. When the signal was made requesting the owner's number, he ran up his flags in the wrong order so that they read, 'Can I render you any assistance?', which caused great hilarity at dinner that night.

One of the Secretary's first acts was to write to the Admiral at Portsmouth requesting permission for club yachts to use the new Sally Port landing jetty.* This was granted provided they did not 'lag' there.

This brief exchange started a close association with the Senior Service, for at a meeting the following year it was resolved 'that officers of the Navy shall hereafter be eligible as honorary members of the club, but that the resolution respecting entrance and annual subscriptions shall not be considered as applicable to them, so long as they shall be without a yacht of their own exceeding 10 tons burthen'.

This agreed upon, Nelson's captain at Trafalgar, Admiral Sir Thomas Hardy KCB, headed a short list of distinguished naval officers granted immediate honorary membership. Later, honorary membership was not exclusively confined to naval officers. Several members of European royal houses were granted honorary membership as were two army officers and some of the club's agents abroad. Nowadays the list is a long one and divides into two, one a dozen or so names, mostly royalty, the other about twenty-five names, all of them holding ex officio appointments. Naval honorary members are now known simply as Naval Members.

The first three years of the club's existence were not marked by any outstanding event. The club's distinguishing flag and the signal book both proved unsatisfactory and were the subject of several resolutions and some considerable financial outlay, but the fact that in 1817 it was

---

* During the First World War members were granted the use of the King's Stairs in Portsmouth Dockyard, a privilege they still retain, when the landing stage at the Sally Port was opened to the public at the beginning of this century.

decided to drop the annual subscription shows that no ambitious yachting programme was planned or envisaged. New members trickled in and their 3-guinea entrance fee was thought sufficient for the club's purposes.

No sooner had this been decided upon, however, than, in 1817, the Prince Regent indicated his wish to join. Two copies of the latest signal book 'richly bound in red morocco' were dispatched to him along with a resolution by members appreciating the honour being accorded to them. Such unforseen expense as binding signal books in red morocco soon meant the reimposition of the annual subscription, but the honour bestowed upon the club, first by the Prince Regent and then by the royal Dukes of Clarence and Gloucester, who joined the following year, must also have induced its members into taking themselves more seriously. For in 1818 a club button was adopted, the qualification for membership became a yacht of 20 tons instead of 10, and the not inconsiderable sum of £70 was voted towards a prize fund for races between local boatmen during Cowes regatta – which appears to have come under the club's control soon after the latter's inauguration. Also, and significantly, club members actually took part in the regatta when thirty of them sailed in procession round the Brambles. Finally, when the Prince Regent at long last ascended the throne as King George IV in 1820, the club petitioned for him to become its patron. It also submitted that the club's name be changed to The Royal Yacht Club. Both requests were granted.

Although there was no suggestion of club members racing in the regatta, matches continued to take place at infrequent intervals between two or three of them. The year the club was founded, for example, great interest was caused at Cowes by a sailing match between Joseph Weld, in his 60-ton cutter *Charlotte*, and another original member, Thomas Assheton Smith, in his 65-ton cutter *Elizabeth*. A local paper, the *Hampshire Telegraph*, commented that the contest would 'afford as much sport as any race that was ever contested by the highest-mettled coursers at Newmarket', and it was reckoned that as much as 2000 guineas was being bet on the outcome by the large crowd that gathered to watch the two contestants.

The match consisted of three races. The first was from Cowes, round a moored vessel off Swanage, and return. The next day the course was to be from Cowes, round the light vessel at Bembridge, and return. And if a decider for the wager of £500 were needed the second course was to be repeated on the third day. It was not, for *Elizabeth* was dismasted off St Alban's Head during the first race and Assheton Smith declined to race again.

Most of the yachts belonging to the original members of the club were probably converted workboats of one kind or another. Sir William Curtis's *Rebecca Maria*, for example, was a converted Arab dhow. Smugglers' cutters were always fast and seaworthy, and the Marquis of Anglesey knew well what he was doing when in 1820 he went to Philip Sainty* of Wivenhoe, well-known builder of smugglers' boats, for the construction of his 113-ton cutter *Pearl*. In fact, cutters were the most popular type with the original members as twenty-five of them owned yachts of this rig while only three had yawls and five had schooners. There were also two brigs and one full-rigged ship (the 325-ton *Louisa*, owned by Lord Craven).

'Prior to 1820,' wrote the famous yacht designer, G. L. Watson, at the turn of the century, 'what yachts there were afloat seem to have presented but little individuality of form, and showed, in common with the faster smugglers and fishing vessels of the day, a round barrel-like bottom, full round bow and fairly clean run, the buttock lines and after riband lines being generally fair and easy. . . . the sails and equipment were of a piece with the hull, the main rigging being of hemp, and no attempt being made after flatness in the sails.'

Some idea as to the dimensions and accommodation of early yachts can also be gathered from local newspaper advertisements. For instance, when the 'elegant pleasure yacht' *Josephine and Jane* was put up for sale at Weymouth in 1812 her length was given as 40 feet and her tonnage as 29. And when the cutter *Charlotte*, which had been owned by

---

* The second volume on the county of Essex, contained in the *Victoria County History of England* (Constable, 1907), has an illuminating paragraph on Sainty and Anglesey's dealings with him. 'Philip Sainty, born in or about 1754, had been established at Wivenhoe many years and was the chief boat- and yacht-builder there at the time. Tradition at Wivenhoe speaks of him as a man of unknown origin, polygamous habits, and a confirmed smuggler, but very expert as a boat-builder. When the Marquis of Anglesey, desiring to build a yacht of unrivalled speed, had enquired for the most suitable builder and had heard of Sainty, he learned that that individual was in Springfield jail for some smuggling exploit. The marquis procured from the King a free pardon for the boat-builder; but the latter, knowing that his services were essential, refused to come out unless his brother and a brother-in-law named Pullen, both then in Maidstone jail for a similar offence, were liberated also; and the marquis had to get all three out of jail before he could get his yacht built.'

Joseph Weld until 1820, was advertised she was described with great and loving detail.

> Her beautiful proportions and first-rate sailing qualities have commanded the unqualified approval of the most eminent naval architects. She is built of the most choice materials, is coppered and copper fastened, and [is] exceedingly well found in rigging, sails, and stores, which are of the best quality.
>
> Her interior fittings are arranged on the most convenient scale, and present a main cabin 10ft by 15ft, 3 bed cabins, stewards' room, in which is a leaden cistern, store-room, and a comfortable galley for the crew. Her ballast, which comprises about five tons of lead and 25 tons of iron, is of the most expensive description, being moulded to the hold, thereby affording additional height to her cabin. The furniture is in the best style, and will be included in the purchase, together with her moorings as laid down in the Lymington river.
>
> The yacht is lying off Mr Inman's shipbuilding yard at Lymington. Any nobleman or gentleman desirous of joining The Yacht Club, and becoming the owner of a beautiful vessel in the highest style of equipment, will find the *Charlotte* in every way suited to his wishes.

From the earliest years of the club, Lymington proved a popular place for members to lay up their yachts. Joseph Weld lived there for six months of the year, at Pylewell House, and at Pylewell Hard he would supervise the construction of his yachts, for he was, by all accounts, a skilful designer.

Colonel Shedden was another original member who also lived there and it was not long before this concentration of private wealth afloat attracted talented boatbuilders to the Solent. One such was Thomas Inman who was a boatbuilder in a small way at Hastings when, in 1819, he sold up, packed his belongings and his family into his own boat, and sailed to Lymington with a view to starting in boatbuilding there.

At first Inman had to make a living as best he could, but in 1821 he impressed Joseph Weld sufficiently for him to turn over to Inman the completion of an 85-ton cutter he had under construction at Pylewell Hard. This was the famous *Arrow* and from that time Inman never looked back. He became one of the most favoured builders for club members. Today, on the same site as his yard, is located the Berthon Boat Company.

Although Cowes was the base for the club's members cruising in the Solent and round the southern coast of England, several members cruised abroad. In 1816, for instance, Lord Craven sailed to Cherbourg in *Louisa* before continuing down to Bordeaux and Cette, and eventually to Leghorn and Naples. He had a rough passage to Cette but reported that the yacht 'had not two hogsheads of water on deck'.

Cruising across to France, and vice versa, became a common enough practice once peace had made the Channel safe. But, although French yachts were allowed into British ports without paying the tonnage dues levied on all commercial craft, members of the club soon found that the French authorities were less inclined to be lenient for the avoidance of dues by commercial traffic was extremely common. The Marquis of Anglesey spent much time soliciting the help of the British Ambassador in Paris on this matter. Arrangements were made for members to enter certain French ports free of charge, but this did not work and in 1820 the Duke of Wellington was persuaded to write the following letter to the Duc de Richelieu.

My Dear Duke,

There is in England a yacht club whose members in the summer enjoy sailing between France and England in their own vessels and whose headquarters, if I may call it thus, is established on the Isle of Wight, in Cowes. These gentlemen wish to be able, from time to time, to visit the French ports; but they cannot enter them because of the enormous cost of the harbour dues, which I believe are a result of the long years of the Revolutionary wars. Accordingly, they are deprived of the pleasure and convenience of putting into the French ports, at the same time as the latter are deprived of the advantage they would gain from the visits of these gentlemen.

It appears that the late Duke de Berri had obtained permission for this club to visit the French ports and pay only the same harbour dues as French vessels, but that this was revoked, not because of abuse on the part of these gentlemen, but because others, claiming membership of this club while in fact using their vessels for trading or carrying passengers, had passed them off as yachts belonging to the club. If this is the case and the French government is prepared to grant these gentlemen the permission it had previously accorded them at the Duke de Berri's request, it seems to me possible to find ways of granting it without great danger of

A contemporary print by R. Livesay of West Cowes in 1799, showing a military
parade on the esplanade beside the Castle *(RYS collection)*

The washerwomen of Cowes outside the Castle. It was painted by Peter de Wint,
engraved by George Cooke, and published by Walker and Cockerell in the early
nineteenth century *(RYS collection)*

Top A Cowes skiff or galley with oarsmen (said to be members of the Drummond family) rowing a party of ladies and gentlemen. It is signed, and dated 1815, by Benjamin West. *(RYS collection)*

Above A coloured print of the esplanade at Cowes, after R. Cruikshank. It dates from about 1825 and is reputed to include caricatures of some members *(RYS collection)*

Top left A painting by John Schetky of the Marquis of Anglesey's cutter *Pearl* (113 tons), one of the fastest yachts of her day when she was launched in 1820. She was constructed by Philip Sainty, a builder of fast smugglers' boats. Sainty was later asked to build a 20-gun sloop on the same lines as *Pearl* for the Royal Navy which was called *HMS Pearl (RYS collection)*

Bottom left A small gaff-rigged cutter in a rough sea off Castle Point. Painted in 1811 by Nicholas Pocock *(RYS collection)*

The starting records of cup winners of the world's first handicap yacht races at Cowes *(RYS collection)*

WINNERS OF CUPS PRESENTED BY H.M. KING GEORGE IV & KING WILLIAM IV					
Year	R.Y.S	Yacht	Rig	Tons	Owner.
1827	''	Miranda.	Cut	147	James Maxse Esq.
1828	''	Lulworth.	Cut	127	Joseph Weld Esq.
1829	''	Louisa.	Cut	162	Earl of Belfast
1830	''	Alarm.	Cut	193	Joseph Weld Esq.
1831	''	Alarm.	Cut	193	Joseph Weld Esq.
1832	''	Alarm.	Cut	193	Joseph Weld Esq.
1833	''	Albatross.	Cut	74	J.L. Gower Esq.
1834	''	Harriet.	Cut	65	G.W. Heneage Esq.
1835	''	Columbine.	Cut	90	J. Smith Barry Esq.
1836	''	Breeze.	Cut	55	James Lyon Esq.
1837	''	Amulet.	Cut	51	John Meiklam Esq.

The schooner *Emma* (132 tons) off Ramsgate. Her owner, Sir William Curtis, was a supplier of hard tack to the Navy, Lord Mayor of London, and a friend of King George IV. He was an original member of the Club and was the first great cruising yachtsman. On the day the Club was founded he was on a voyage to St Petersburg in another of his yachts, *Rebecca Maria (RYS collection)*

This painting of the cutter *Harriet* (96 tons) was commissioned by her owner, Lord
Belfast, from William John Huggins in 1827. The burgee and flag were added later
to record the granting of the White Ensign in 1829 and the appointment of Lord
Belfast as Vice-Commodore in 1827 *(RYS collection)*

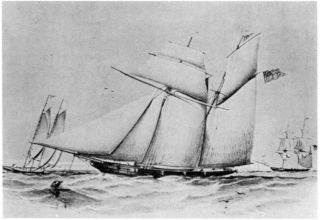

Above left: Waterwitch (331 tons) was claimed by her owner, Lord Belfast, to be the best square rigged vessel afloat. She was certainly one of the fastest, for even when armed with eighteen carronnades and two long 6-pounders, she outsailed all the ships in the Royal Navy's experimental squadron in 1832, as depicted here. After winning a match round the Eddystone, she was bought for the Royal Navy in 1834 *(RYS collection)*

Above right The schooner, *Wanderer* (141 tons), was sailed by her owner, Benjamin Boyd, to Sydney in 1842, touching at Teneriffe, Tristan da Cunha and Rio de Janeiro, probably the first yacht to have achieved such a voyage. In 1851, after sailing to the Californian gold rush, Boyd went ashore on one of the islands in the Solomon group inhabited by cannibals and was never seen again *(RYS collection)*

Top left The schooner *Wyvern* (205 tons), owned by the 6th Duke of Marlborough. In 1854 she carried his son to the Australian gold rush and averaged 194 miles a day for 36 days from the Cape to Melbourne *(RYS collection)*

Left A painting by A.W. Fowles of *Alarm* off the Eddystone. In 1852 her owner, Joseph Weld, lengthened her by 20 feet, which increased her tonnage to 248, and changed her rig from cutter to schooner, no doubt because he was influenced by the success of *America (RYS collection)*

The Commodore, Lord Yarborough, built *Kestrel* in 1837. She was changed to a
brigantine in 1845, and he died on board her at Vigo, while cruising, in 1846
(RYS collection)

This painting by N.M. Condy is of a race for yachts of 25 tons and under, all from
the Royal Thames Yacht Club, which took place in foul weather in the Cowes
regatta of 1844. Said to be one of the finest races ever seen, it was won by *Mystery*,
owned by a future RTYC Commodore, Lord Alfred Paget *(Print RYS collection)*

abuse. For example, every year on 1st March, the club could submit to the French Embassy a list and description of the vessels, together with their owners' names and the French government could grant every yacht on that list an entry permit. That arrangement would prevent repetition of the abuse that has already occurred.

These permits could last one year or another limited period and could specify that ports to which they applied, thereby excluding those it was not desired that these gentlemen should visit.

These gentlemen are ready to undertake not to sell anything or carry anyone paying his passage; and it seems to me that if someone were to abuse this privilege, it would be easy, through the above-mentioned arrangement, to deprive him of it totally. I would be grateful if you would consider this matter and be good enough to let me know if it would be possible to accede to these gentlemen's request.

I enclose the paper they sent to me.

I have the honour to be, etc.

The Duc de Richelieu consulted the Director General of the Customs in Paris whose reply to the Duke is recorded in the club minutes:

A list should be sent me, with the description, tonnage, and name of the proprietors of each yacht; I would address this list to the several directors of the Custom Houses on the Channel, not to exact the duties from any of these vessels, when the person who might make use of her for a voyage of pleasure upon our coasts, should prove that he is the proprietor of her, and that he is one of the members on the list of the Yacht Club, it being well understood that any use which might be made of her for the transportation of any kind of merchandise or any passenger would entail the obligation of paying the duties, and the privation of exemption for every future voyage, as the club itself proposes; this step which would not have the inconvenience of establishing an explicit privilege, would, nevertheless, attain the end which is proposed, since it would relieve the members of the Yacht Club from an obligation troublesome enough in effect, of applying to the Government at Paris for each of their voyages.

This should have solved the problem. But the abuse by commercial vessels masquerading as club yachts, and the crews of yachts from other clubs misbehaving themselves, prolonged it for many years, although after 1828 it was considerably eased.

In August 1819 the Prince Regent arrived at Cowes where the Royal Yacht awaited him. He 'received the compliments of most of the nobility and members of the Yacht Club at Cowes, and in the evening gave a dinner on board to the Marquis of Anglesey, General Sir E. Paget, and some other private friends'. This visit was such a success that he returned in 1821 when he was King and rented a cottage on the seafront.

This royal patronage increased interest in the club and in Cowes, and both attracted the attentions of the press. It also must have invigorated the club's participation in the annual regatta as by 1821 the annual procession round the Brambles had been supplemented by a second out to Stokes Bay. Fifteen yachts, under the commodoreship of Mr Challen, an original member, in his 44-ton yawl *Eliza*, practised the new code of signals before returning to Cowes and the admiration of the crowds that lined the shores to see them.

So successful did these processions prove to be that at the spring meeting in 1822 it was resolved 'that on the first and third Mondays of each month the yachts be assembled in Cowes Roads at 10am for the purpose of sailing together under the directions of a Commodore appointed for the day'. The first of these meetings took place on 1 July, but after the next one another resolution was passed which indicates that in the hearts and minds of some of the more active members of the club the need for organized racing was growing. It stated:

> The original proposition of assembling the vessels of the club upon certain days under the direction of a leader having been made with a far different view from that of racing and showing superiority of sailing, that inconvenience and danger arise from irregularity, and that it would tend to the comfort of all, and particularly of the ladies who may honor the meeting with their presence, if order were preserved.

It was therefore agreed at the meeting that participating yachts should keep their stations in two squadrons of equal numbers and should follow some simple directions when tacking or manoeuvring. It was also laid down that if 'any particular vessels are anxious to try rate of sailing, a signal to that effect must be made to the commodore', but there is no record of any signal being made.

Mostly the local press was full of unctuous praise for these manoeuvres but they were also watched by someone who decided that a few words of criticism would not go amiss. Writing under the name of

'Trunnion' in the October 1822 volume of a publication called *Sporting Annals*, the writer stated that:

> the naval exploits of this club appear to be represented in a way little calculated to perpetuate their celebrity, or to further some of the principal objects which ought to be connected with the institution. We have a right to assume that, where so much wealth and splendour are wasted in production of first rate specimens of naval architecture, the great object of so much competition must be to excel in that art of 'swift sailing', and yet we can gather no information whatever upon the subject from the late evolutions of the grand fleet at Spithead. . . . To make this institution really useful, and at the same time interesting, as well to the amateur ashore as to the nation at large, for everything connected with naval tactics must be interesting to Englishmen, the perfections of the structure and the rigging of the different vessels ought to be described, at the rate of sailing as compared with steam-vessels and with 'each other', the comparison between vessels of this description and the swiftest of His Majesty's fleet, and, above all, whether, as in other sciences, naval architecture, either in this country or in France, America, etc., has been lately progressing in the production of any new models for swift sailing, ought to be critically set forth and enlarged upon.

Though longwinded, the impression is gained that 'Trunnion' actually knows what he is talking about. To the modern reader one of the most interesting aspects of the article is his assumption that The Royal Yacht Club had a public duty to perform and were not fulfilling it.

On what basis 'Trunnion' made this assumption it is now impossible to say, although it does seem to underline the theory that members regarded themselves, and were so regarded by others, as a kind of auxiliary, experimental fleet. Certainly, there is no doubt that during the early years of its existence the club stimulated private yacht building to a quite remarkable degree; and that the efforts of members like Joseph Weld and Assheton Smith to improve the design and speed of their vessels was watched with interest by those responsible for the construction of naval vessels.

So for 'Trunnion' to imply that the club had not contributed to the public good is quite wrong. As proof of this, only a few months after his article had appeared, the *Weekly Register* noted that 'so unrivalled are some of the yachts on the list, in celerity of sailing and beauty of construction, that they have received considerable attention from the Government, who have lately caused to be built, on the yacht model, two very fine cutters, now employed as channel cruisers on the Portsmouth station'.

Close cooperation between the public and private sectors in this era was nothing new. Smugglers' boats and the revenue cutters built to chase them were often constructed side by side. If the former proved a flyer it would be purchased from the builder for a premium by the revenue service. So the fact that the club was in those early days a kind of school of naval architecture for small vessels is not particularly surprising. What was perhaps more unusual – at least to the modern yachtsman – is that so many of the club's yachts were armed as if they were part of the Senior Service. Sir Godfrey Webster's *Scorpion*, for example, carried four 4- and 6-pounder brass guns and a complete armoury of rifles, pistols and cutlasses, while Lord Yarborough's full-rigged ship *Falcon* was reported by a spectator as looking like a 20-gun ship-of-war when she was launched in June 1826.* In fact, so closely did club yachts often resemble their Royal Navy counterparts that Lord Anglesey's *Pearl* was used as the model for a naval sloop of the same name which was built by Sainty in 1827.†

It was common practice in those days for yachts to salute one another with guns but, as the Squadron's first historian pointed out, 18-pounders were hardly required to perform this courtesy. He could give no reason for arming a pleasure craft in so lethal a fashion but supposed it was a reflection of the insecurity felt by all those who ventured to sea after many years of being threatened with the dangers of war and privateers.

This is perhaps part of the answer. But it must be remembered that Barbary pirates‡ were still a very real danger for any yacht cruising to the Mediterranean and remained so for a good number of years; and as late as 1851 a club yacht, armed with thirteen guns, had to use her armament

---

* Not 1824, as Guest supposed.

† *One-Leg*: The Life and Letters of 1st Marquess of Anglesey, by the Marquis of Anglesey, Jonathan Cape Ltd., 1961.

‡ Pirates are still around and the crew of Robin Knox-Johnston's yacht, which included a present member, Oliver Stanley, were armed for this reason when they took part in Operation Raleigh in the Caribbean in 1984.

to defend herself, as will be seen in a later chapter. But it further emphasizes that in those early days many members must have thought of themselves as an adjunct of the Royal Navy, the division between pleasure and duty not being so clearly defined as it is nowadays.

Although 'Trunnion' was inaccurate in some of his assumptions, he had a point when criticizing the club for its lack of enthusiasm for 'swift sailing'. Cowes was the home of what even then was already acknowledged to be England's premier yacht club, yet there were still no club races for its members. If members wanted to race they had to sail down to Weymouth or Plymouth to do so. Indeed, in 1824, the club's first Commodore, Lord Yarborough, led a number of club yachts down to the West Country to do just that.

So while the club's involvement in the annual regatta amounted to no more than a series of decorous processions each summer, the racing spirit was kept alive by the few who continued to race between themselves. Yet the record of private matches during the early 1820s is sparse, although an account does survive of a particularly interesting one in 1824 between two club members, Mr James Weld, who owned the 43-ton yawl *Julia*, and Mr C. R. M. Talbot, who owned the 42-ton yawl *Giulia*. It was probably the first match between privately owned yachts to take place around the Isle of Wight. Although the two yachts were equally matched, *Giulia* was given a mile start. But *Julia* won easily, covering the distance in eight hours in a light breeze, for her opponent ran aground at the eastern end of the island.

These matches, as has been mentioned, were often for very high stakes and were taken very seriously by the participants. When the Marquis of Anglesey raced against the Weld brothers in 1825 he remarked that 'if the *Pearl* be beaten, I will burn her as soon as we get back'. From written accounts of the Marquis's character there is no doubt he would have carried out his threat, but, as it happened, *Pearl* won by a fluke and was still afloat during the last quarter of the nineteenth century.

Although only a few members raced, many cruised and it became common practice to cross the Channel to France or Spain in order to load up with wine for the summer season at Cowes and elsewhere. In September 1824, after he had rturned from the West Country and had taken part in the Cowes regatta, Lord Yarborough led nineteen club yachts across to Cherbourg in his 150-ton brig *Falcon*, which he was soon to replace with a full-rigged ship of the same name. The visit was a great success and after a stay of three days the yachts sailed for Guernsey where they anchored for a further three days before returning to England.

Individual club members were equally enterprising. Mention has already been made of the voyage of Sir William Curtis, perhaps the earliest exponent of ocean cruising, to St Petersburg in 1815. This was repeated by Lord Willoughby de Broke in 1825 aboard his 61-ton cutter *Antelope*, accompanied by Sir William. And by 1827 visits to the Mediterranean by club yachts had become so commonplace that the government ordered they receive the same courtesies as one of His Majesty's ships-of-war.

By 1820 eighteen of the original members had either died or not renewed their subscriptions, and they were only gradually replaced by new members. Two were elected in 1815, five in 1816, six in 1817 and in 1818 (excluding members of the royal family), and two in 1819. Then the numbers began to increase more rapidly, eleven joining in 1820, and the 1822 signal book lists sixty-eight names, excluding royalty, and 114 honorary members including Naval Members. An analysis of Guest's own list of members and their yachts shows that in 1824 forty-six members owned 2894 tons. This means that members must have employed around three hundred seamen, a substantial figure in those days of high unemployment. Lord Yarborough's full-rigged ship *Falcon*, for instance, employed fifty-four 'choice' hands under the command of a naval officer, and there must have been several other yachts which were crewed by almost as many.

Discipline was strict amongst the crews and in Lord Yarborough's case followed naval lines. He even got his crew to sign a paper volunteering to be flogged if the need arose. They were paid an extra shilling a week for agreeing, although, from all accounts of Lord Yarborough's character, it is extremely unlikely that such a punishment was ever enforced.

Nevertheless, sanctions were applied to any crew member who misbehaved himself. This was done by entering his name, the yacht's name, the man's misdemeanour, and the date when it occurred, in what was called the club's 'Black Book', which was kept by the Secretary.

The only one now extant covers the period between 1829 and 1866 and is described on the flyleaf as being 'An Account of Seamen discharged from yachts belonging to the Royal Yacht Squadron for disorderly Conduct, etc.' Offences ranged from drunkenness, insubordination and desertion, to 'bringing a common whore on board and sleeping with her in the owner's cabin'. In the thirty-seven years covered by the book, around 160 names were entered into it, by far the majority during the 1830s.

At the May meeting in 1872 it was resolved 'that in the future no names shall be placed in the Black Book without the authority of the Committee, who shall adjudicate upon the cases reported to them, and determine the period for which offenders shall be prohibited from vessels of the Royal Yacht Squadron'.

In 1874 certificates of conduct began to be issued to all crews and it was requested that these should always be asked for when a member was approached to engage a paid hand. This procedure was almost certainly an alternative to the 'Black Book' which, according to Guest, was condemned as libellous by the Lord Chief Justice of England, Sir Alexander Cockburn, who became a member in 1869. By the looks of it, it had in any case already fallen into disuse, for only three names were entered between the years 1860 and 1866, and none after that.

In the early days the matter of discipline was obviously taken very seriously. In 1824 J. H. Leche, who was a member between 1834 and 1844, produced detailed rules for his crew which were contained in a leather-bound book stamped with his name and crest. Called 'Rules and Regulations of the *Yida* to be observed by the men', it stated:

> First, that every man be in attendance at the undermentioned hours, namely: to breakfast at a quarter to 8, dinner at 12, supper at 6, when orders will be given for the day.
>
> Should it occur that the crew must be afloat of course they will have their meals aboard. Each man to have three pints of Ale Sunday. No grog except by my order.
>
> Secondly, that each man takes care to have himself clean and neat at his meals, likewise on a Sunday when he is expected to attend church, where seats will be procured for all.
>
> Thirdly, that the clothes will depend upon how each man conducts himself whether he has them when he leaves or not.
>
> Fourthly, should the day be bad or the boat not wanted, that the men

are employed in doing anything that may be useful according to orders given by Captain Andrews, should I not be present myself.

In the fifth place, that each man takes his turn in cleaning knives or any small matters of that kind so as to prevent confusion.

In the sixth place, that in my absence at any time, that Captain Andrews will be considered to be acting for me, by my orders. If anyone has at anytime to make any complaints, that they come through Captain Andrews, to be made known to me by him.

Although the membership figure was slow to rise at first, the club had grown sufficiently by the mid-1820s for members to feel that they should have at least a coffee room of their own at Cowes where they could meet and eat, instead of dining at the Medina Hotel or the Vine Inn at East Cowes as they had been doing up to then.

There was a rumour that the club intended to buy Brownsea Castle but eventually it was decided to purchase the lease of a house on the Parade, now the remains of the Gloster Hotel, and the club moved there in 1825. To cover the cost of the lease the annual membership was raised to £8 and the entrance fee to £10. At the same time the tonnage qualification was raised from 20 tons to 30 for new members. Obviously, the club's finances were strained so the suggestion by the honorary members that they should pay a guinea a year must have been welcomed and this was started in 1826.

It was also decided in 1826 that a gold cup, valued at £100, should be sailed for by members during that year's regatta. At long last organized racing between owners of private yachts was coming to Cowes.

CHAPTER TWO

1825-48

Yachting racing gets under way with all the problems of rules and handicapping. Worldwide ocean voyages by members. The Royal Navy buys as warships fast yachts designed by members. The Club becomes the Royal Yacht Squadron. On 'national utility'

IF THE FIRST ten years of the club passed quietly, the next twenty were full of incident. The yachtsmen who came onto the list during this time, and what, with the original members, they decided upon, became the cornerstone on which the future activities of the club were built.

In 1825 it is believed that Lord Yarborough was officially appointed the club's first Commodore, though an 1843 edition of the *Illustrated London News* states the appointment to have been made as early as July 1822, and certainly local newspapers refer to him as Commodore a good deal earlier than 1825. The club minutes do not resolve this point. But they confirm the appointment of Lord Belfast as Vice-Commodore, in 1827, and the energy with which that gentleman pursued the club's interests soon helped it into its unassailable position as the country's premier yacht club. From having a new club button designed, to being involved in negotiating with the Admiralty for a warrant to fly the White Ensign, Lord Belfast had a finger in every pie, for members were as particular about how they were dressed as they were about the code of signals with which they had wrestled for so many years.

In 1826 the *Southampton Town and County Herald* noted that the club uniform of a common blue jacket and white trousers was far from being an unbecoming dress, provided the wearer was not 'too square in the stern'. The buttons on it, however, were the subject of several resolu-

33

tions during the next few years. In 1827, when it was resolved that the band of the uniform cap should be of 'gold lace having a crown and anchor worked on it, as borne on the seal of the club', it was also decided that only members and honorary members could wear the club button. The masters of club yachts could only wear ones that bore three anchors and the letters R Y C on them.

Then in 1831 Lord Belfast presented a new button which he had had designed at his own expense. This was accepted and the naval blue, white-lined uniform coat with cloth collar, on which they were to be worn, was to have three at the cuff and at the pockets. The old button was to be retained for the use of honorary members.

Such minutiae were all part of establishing a unique identity, not only in the eyes of other yachtsmen but in the eyes of the country as a whole, the club's close association with the Royal Navy obviously influencing not only how members equipped and sailed their yachts, and disciplined their crews, but how they dressed as well.

It was not, however, the club's close links with the Royal Navy that made it apply to the Admiralty in 1829 for a warrant* to fly the White Ensign, because in those days the Royal Navy still flew the Red and Blue Ensign, as well as the White, and there was no particular privilege in flying one in preference to the other. In fact, the Red Ensign, as well as being the only legal flag for all merchant ships, was the one flown by the squadron commanded by the most senior admiral of a fleet; and it was to this that the club had changed in 1821 from the original plain White Ensign with the Jack at the canton.

It is not known why the original ensign was abandoned. In his book *British Flags*,* W. G. Perrin states that by 1821 the number of yachts, which were classed as merchant vessels, 'had so increased that the Commander-in-Chief at Portsmouth drew attention to the fact that a large number of small craft were flying an unauthorised flag. He

---

* Unfortunately, the Public Record Office no longer has either any of the correspondence regarding the granting of the White Ensign to the club, or the warrant itself, although a slip in the relevant file, ADM 3470, reveals that a copy of the warrant was sent to the Admiralty in 1889. However, there are two references elsewhere: one of which shows that the warrant was granted on 5 June 1829, and another which records that Lord Belfast applied for a warrant to fly the White Ensign on the yacht *Ondine* on 27 August 1829. According to Guest, Belfast never owned *Ondine*, though he records that one member owned her up to 1828 and another from 1830.

* *British Flags* by W. G. Perrin, Cambridge University Press, 1922.

received instructions to enforce the law, and the club had to content itself with the legal red ensign.'

This is a plausible explanation, but it would be interesting to know his source as a search in the relevant Admiralty correspondence at the Public Record Office revealed no such instructions.

It is not known, either, why the club again decided to change its ensign and burgee for a second time. But by 1829 the number of club yachts going foreign had risen considerably, and negotiations had been completed with most European governments for them to enter foreign ports without paying tonnage dues. Merchant ships, obliged to pay tonnage dues, always flew the Red Ensign. It is reasonable to suppose, therefore, that by flying the White Ensign instead of the Red club yachts could establish more easily that they were pleasure vessels not commercial ones.

At the time having a warrant to fly the White Ensign had no special distinction, and in the following decade several other yacht clubs were granted a similar warrant. This, however, caused problems and confusion and, as will be seen in the next chapter, a solution was not found until 1859. Then, the club's case to be the only one to have the right to wear the White Ensign was much strengthened by the fact that in 1833 King William IV had granted it what was a distinction unique to any yacht club in the British Isles.

Lord Belfast, who more than any other single member, except perhaps the Commodore himself, was responsible for the honour bestowed upon the club, broke the news to the club Secretary in a letter dated 4 July 1833.

> Sir,
>
> I have it in command from His Majesty to acquaint you for the information of the Commodore and the officers of the Royal Yacht Club, that as a mark of His Majesty's gracious approval of an institution of such national utility, it is his gracious wish and pleasure that it shall be henceforth known and styled 'The Royal Yacht Squadron', of which his Majesty is graciously pleased to consider himself the head.

The King also granted the Squadron its achievement, or coat of arms, bearing, uniquely, the royal motto and the royal lion and unicorn.

It has already been demonstrated how the benefits of the activities of the club during its early years had extended beyond the members

35

themselves. In the years that followed these activities took on a different dimension when a growing volume of opinion reflected the view that the design of the Royal Navy's smaller vessels was sadly lacking in both speed and seaworthiness; and it was in countering this lack that the club earned the King's praise as an institution of 'national utility'. However, before describing how it went about this task it is logical first to review the other activities of the club.

At the spring meeting in 1826 it was unanimously resolved that 'a gold cup of the value of £100 be sailed for by vessels belonging to the club, of any rig or tonnage.'

This first historic race attracted seven entries, some of them the crack boats of that year. The brand new 163-ton cutter *Menai*, owned by Assheton Smith, was one of the favourites, as was Joseph Weld's *Arrow*, which had already proved her worth in several private matches. Ranged against these two were Lord Belfast's 95-ton cutter *Harriet*, J. L. Symonds's 63-ton cutter *Emerald*, Captain P. Browne's 58-ton cutter *Dolphin*, Assheton Smith's *Elizabeth*, now owned by Daniel Magniac, and Lord Darnley's 42-ton cutter, also called *Elizabeth*.

In those days yachts started from moorings and they slipped them when the start gun fired – in this case by the Commodore who was on an anchored cutter off Cowes Castle. The wind was light and the yachts, with every sail aloft that they could muster, crept along the shore to keep out of the tide. *Menai* went too close and ran aground for a few moments. It cost her any chance of winning the race – which was from Cowes to a markboat in Thorness Bay, then back down the Solent, round the Nab Light, and back to Cowes – for although she sailed through most of the fleet to finish third she could not catch *Arrow*, the winner, or *Harriet*.

The race was voted a great success, and the local townspeople suggested a second regatta. For this they offered two cups, a 100-guinea one, for club yachts of any rig or tonnage, and a 50-guinea one for yachts not exceeding 70 tons.

The idea of a second regatta was received with enthusiasm by members and drew a large entry which included all the entries for the gold cup with the exception of *Menai*.

After winning the gold-cup race *Arrow* was the favourite and large sums of money were laid on her to win. There was a brisk breeze from the east-northeast which carried away the spars of two of the entries, and then the race developed into a tussle between *Arrow*, James Maxse's 147-ton cutter *Miranda*, which eventually won, and *Harriet*. *Harriet* took the lead but, despite a collision between her two rivals, only managed to finish in third place. The collision was described in the *Sporting Magazine* and is worth repeating here if only to show just how rugged yacht racing could be in those days.

When only a few miles from home, the distance sailed being nearly eighty miles, including the tacks made by the different vessels, the *Arrow* had the temerity to cross the *Miranda* on the larboard tack, and had not Captain Lyons taken the helm just in time she must have been run down. As it was, the two vessels became entangled, and a scene of much violence took place from the excitement of the different crews, blows being exchanged. The gallant Sir James Jordan, who was on board Mr Maxse's, had a narrow escape from a dreadful blow aimed at the back of his head by one of Mr Weld's men with a handspike as the two vessels were touching each other. He avoided the blow by ducking his head, and hitting out right and left, *à la* Spring, floored the rascal with such tremendous violence that Captain Lyons told me afterwards he thought he was done for.

No wonder some members armed their yachts!

The next day the smaller yachts raced over the same course in a strong easterly. There was another collision, showing that Joseph Weld was not alone in apparently regarding the port and starboard rule as a waste of time, and the rigging of several other entries was damaged by the high wind before Magniac's *Elizabeth* crossed the line first.

This second regatta was concluded on the third day by a match between *Arrow* and *Harriet*, which the latter won.

So successful was the racing in 1826 that the following year no less than six cups were offered. The club voted three – one of £100, and two of £50 each – while the residents of Cowes provided another Town Cup. Some ladies of rank also subscribed 250 guineas to buy a Challenge Cup, 'to be sailed for annually until won by one member in three successive matches'. The sixth one, a tankard, was donated by the King, thereby starting the tradition that the Sovereign annually donated a cup to be raced for by members during the Cowes regatta. It was this regatta that prompted the first primitive form of handicap, for the two smaller club cups were restricted to entries not exceeding 75 tons and not exceeding 45 tons. All the other races were open events.

The Challenge Cup – a novel idea in those days – and the King's Cup were raced over the same course, from Cowes to a markboat off Yarmouth, back past Cowes to the Nab Light, before returning to the finish off the Castle. All the open events attracted a good number of entries and were, not surprisingly, dominated by the large cutters. *Miranda* won the open Club Cup and the King's Cup, Lord Belfast's 121-ton cutter *Therese* won the Ladies' Challenge Cup and his *Harriet* the Town Cup.

The Cowes regatta of 1827, along with the other regattas held on the south coast, showed that the large cutters were very evenly matched. This was no doubt very popular with the spectators – the Town Cup's course had been twice round the Brambles so that the yachts were never out of sight of the townsfolk – but the difficulties of handling such large vessels and their sails, and the expense of shifting ballast during a race, created adverse comment. The *Southampton Herald*, which had that year adopted as its subtitle 'The Royal Yacht Club Gazette', came down against regatta racing altogether, but this criticism of their new sport deterred owners of the large cutters not at all. Instead, the struggle for supremacy between them showed every sign of becoming intensified. Assheton Smith had his cutter *Menai* lengthened, while Joseph Weld and Lord Belfast had new ones built.

For the 1828 regatta the club introduced more detailed regulations to govern the races. The previous year Lord Belfast had entered two of his yachts in the same race and it was now decreed that a member could enter only one yacht. No booming out was allowed, yachts were restricted to their normal sails, and the port and starboard rule was reaffirmed. The most important change was that 'no trimming with ballast or shifting of ballast be allowed, and all vessels to keep their platforms down and bulkheads standing to prevent the unnecessary expense that has heretofore taken place', and no handling of ballast was to be allowed within twenty-four hours of a race. Other rules regulated matters like moorings, running aground, the use of the hand lead, the size of dinghy to be carried during a race, and that either a member or an honorary member had to be aboard whenever a yacht raced for a prize.

Interest in 1828 centred upon the two new cutters, Lord Belfast's 162-ton *Louisa* and Joseph Weld's 127-ton *Lulworth*. The former won the open Club Cup but *Lulworth* beat her by a second in the King's Cup, and by a rather larger margin in the Ladies' Challenge Cup. *Menai*, which had been disabled in the King's Cup when she was leading, obtained her revenge on the two new cutters when she beat *Louisa* by five minutes and *Lulworth* by thirteen in the Town Cup. So keen and so close was the racing that year that Lord Belfast and Joseph Weld continued their rivalry with a private match for £1000 which Lord Belfast won. The artist, Turner, staying with John Nash at East Cowes, recorded the colourful scene for posterity.

Unfortunately, the following year this rivalry turned to open hostility. Incidents like the one already described had, until then, been isolated and infrequent, but in 1829 violence and protests and counter-protests marred practically every race. In the King's Cup, the crew of *Louisa* used hatchets to cut *Lulworth*'s mainsail from her boom when a collision occurred close to the finishing line, and protests and dissensions marred the Town Cup as well. Later, Lord Belfast was heard to remark in the club that 'in the event of any vessel on the larboard tack attempting to cross him when on the starboard tack, if he had it in his power, he would cut her in two', a volley which was obviously aimed at Joseph Weld. By way of reply both Weld and Assheton Smith announced that except for the Challenge Cup they did not propose to race against Lord Belfast again. *Louisa* came first in this race but was then disqualified on the grounds that she had 'got on board' *Menai*, and the race was awarded to *Lulworth*.

This acrimony spread to other regattas and by the end of that season Assheton Smith, for one, had had enough. He and Lord Belfast did not get on and when he suggested that the club allow steam yachts onto the list it was imputed by several members – including almost certainly Lord Belfast – that Assheton Smith had made the suggestion for self-interested motives. The matter had provoked a resolution the previous year which stated that 'as a material object of this club is to promote seamanship and the improvements of sailing vessels, to which the application of steam-engines is inimical, no vessel propelled by steam shall be admitted into the club,' a resolution which stood until 1844 when steam yachts exceeding 100 tons were allowed on the list.*

---

* This change may have influenced Queen Victoria to give up her slow sailing yacht *Royal George*, and to have built in 1844 the first *Victoria and Albert*, a steam paddle boat.

Rebuffed by his fellow members on this point and then infuriated by the behaviour of his rivals on the waters, Assheton Smith resigned and promptly ordered from Robert Napier the first of a series of steam yachts, the 400-ton *Menai*, at the cost of £20,000.

With the resignation of Assheton Smith the club lost a remarkable sportsman and a pioneer of the steam yacht. From the earliest days he had supported match racing with a fervour he only equalled on the hunting field. During his fifteen years' membership he had designed and had had built no less than five yachts. When he had lengthened *Menai* for the 1827 season he had taken the remarkable step of putting a hollow bow on her, the first vessel to be so constructed.

The principle of this shape, called the 'wave-line principle', is now commonly attributed to J. Scott Russell, but Assheton Smith, while still a schoolboy, had observed that when a flat stone was thrown into water it made a gentle curve before sinking to the bottom, and he later applied this observation to the new bows of his cutter. In fact, Robert Napier went so far as to state that the wave-line principle was Assheton Smith's invention, not Scott Russell's.*

From the evidence available it would seem to be one of those cases where a discovery is made simultaneously and quite independently. Scott Russell was the theorist, Assheton Smith the untutored practical man who put his ideas into practice first.

Though Assheton Smith retired from the action, Joseph Weld had no intention of giving up the struggle to win the Challenge Cup outright. However, he knew that *Lulworth*, some 40 tons smaller than Lord Belfast's *Louisa*, was not certain of besting her rival in all conditions. So during the winter of 1829–30 he had built the 193-ton cutter *Alarm*, the ultimate of her kind.

There is no record of Lord Belfast being present at the 1830 regatta, but in that year and the ones that followed *Alarm* showed herself to be a formidable opponent, and if Weld had not persisted in flouting the port and starboard rule she could well have swept the board. As it was, she captured many of the main prizes each year until, in 1834, most of them were put beyond her reach by new rules which limited the tonnage of yachts racing for them.

---

* From letters written by Robert Napier and Roderick Murchison in *Reminiscences of the Late Thomas Assheton Smith* by Sir John Eardly-Wilmot, John Murray, 1860.

The racing cutter *Formosa* (103 tons) painted by A.W. Fowles. She was built in 1878
for a member, Mr Sloane Stanley, who sold her to the Prince of Wales in 1880
(RYS collection)

Above left: Mosquito (49 tons) was one of the first iron yachts. She was built in 1848 and was owned by a member, Lord Londesborough, between 1851 and 1853. Designed by Tom Waterman, an original genius who also designed the *Himalaya* for P & O, she was an outstanding racing yacht, often beating vessels twice her size including, in 1852, the schooner *America* *(RYS collection)*

Above right Built in 1871, *Foxhound* (35 tons) was designed by William Fife Sr. She was owned by the 3rd Marquis of Ailsa, 'a very clever scientific man', who raced her very successfully *(Beken)*

Top left The 3rd Marquis of Ormonde's schooner *Mirage* (200 tons) in which he made many long voyages, notably one to Spitzbergen. He was Vice-Commodore 1885-1900 and Commodore 1901-1919. An outstanding seaman, he obtained a master's certificate in 1879 *(RYS collection)*

Left Depicted here is the schooner *Golden Fleece* (279 tons), owned by Captain W.H. Roberts, picking up a man overboard in mid-Channel on 21 August 1882. From running at 11½ knots, she hove-to, picked the man up, and returned on course in 31 minutes. The artist is Barlow Moore, who was marine painter to the Royal Thames Yacht Club *(RYS collection)*

The cutter *Muriel* (40 tons) was the last yacht owned by Thomas Brassey – later
Lord Brassey – before he owned his famous *Sunbeam.* Brassey was one of the most
illustrious members of the Squadron. He founded the *Naval Annual,* was Civil
Lord of the Admiralty, and was appointed Governor of Victoria in 1895
(RYS collection)

Valkyrie II, owned by the 14th Earl of Dunraven, crossing the Atlantic for the 1893
challenge for the *America's* Cup. The third, and final, race was described as 'the
greatest battle of sails that was ever fought'. This painting was commissioned by
Lord Dunraven from the Squadron marine painter Chevalier Eduardo de Martino
(RYS collection – detail)

Bloodhound (40 tons), designed by William Fife in 1874 for the Marquis of Ailsa,
was even more successful than *Foxhound*. Her tiller, presented by her owner, is on
the Squadron platform *(Beken)*

This group of members shows the Kaiser as the odd man out, wearing
a white cap. Below the battlements there is a lonely lady in white. This is
reputed to be Mrs Langtry, friend of Royalty, whose 693-ton steamer,
White Lady, lay in Cowes Roads in 1895, the year of this painting
(RYS collection)

Top left This group of members on the platform in 1870 is of historic interest,
sartorially speaking, with the presence of ladies and members wearing hats of
varying styles *(RYS collection)*

Left This group of members, photographed ten years later, in 1880, shows them in
more nautical garb but still in very varying styles. The ladies have disappeared in
the intervening decade, an event possibly linked with the abandonment of the
Club ball, and the platform remained a male preserve for several decades
(RYS collection)

Lancashire Witch (479 tons) carried her owner, Frank James, all over the world. During a hunt on the West African coast in 1890 he received a mortal wound from the tusk of a wounded elephant, certainly the only member to have died in this manner while on a cruise *(Beken)*

Pandora (426 tons) was an ex-naval five-gun sloop which Sir Allen Young bought in 1875 and fitted out for the Arctic. He sailed there twice in search of the Franklin expedition, but without success. Young, 'perhaps the best and most competent sailor who has ever flown the Squadron flag', commanded a transport in the Crimean war, a gunboat in the Taiping rebellion, and clippers on the Eastern trade routes *(Beken)*

Although *Alarm* proved almost unbeatable Lord Belfast was determined to best her somehow and during the summer of 1831 he consulted the sailmaker, G. R. Ratsey, how he was to do it. 'It is evident we can do nothing with the *Alarm* inside the island,' he remarked. 'What do you say to challenging her for £1000 round the Owers.'

'Yes, do so by all means,' Ratsey replied promptly.

Outside the sheltered waters of the Solent *Louisa* proved to be the faster boat and after he had won Lord Belfast said to Ratsey, 'I have proved to the world that I possess the fastest cutter afloat; I will now see what I can do with a square rigger.'

Being the man he was Lord Belfast did not satisfy himself with any ordinary square rigger. Instead, he decided to build a ten-gun brig which would outsail the Navy's latest design of this type.

The ten-gun brig was a much despised type both inside and outside the Navy, and for some years attempts had been made to improve its design. As with the cutter, both the Admiralty and certain club members had been working towards this end with a degree of success.

The Admiralty was, perhaps, not wholly happy in being obliged to recognize that the club's designs were often superior to its own, but by now the club's reputation in this respect stood so high that it could do little else. This reluctant acceptance was no doubt hastened when, in 1827, the Superintendent of the School of Naval Architecture at Portsmouth Dockyard, John Fincham, published a comparison of five of the club's best-known yachts – *Falcon, Pearl, Coquette, Emerald, Nautilus* and *Dolphin* – and wrote in his introduction to their detailed statistics that 'The excellency of many of the vessels belonging to the Royal Yacht Club . . . render the operations of this distinguished club highly interesting and important.'*

The following year, through his contacts at the Admiralty, Lord Vernon, a club member, secured the contract to build a ten-gun brig; and obtained the services of another member, Captain Symonds, to design it. Lord Vernon's sole purpose in doing this was to better the type's design, but it is interesting to note that at the same time both he

---

* The article was later published in a book, *The Royal Yacht Squadron. Its Yachts: and a Scientific Basis for Their Improvement* by John Fincham, G. Clayton, 1855, which also included a similar exercise Fincham carried out in the early 1850s with seven more modern Squadron yachts, *Fair Rosamund* (1846), *Novice* (1849), *Erminia* (1850), *Lotus* (1851), *Breeze* (1836), *Dream* (1840), and *Circassian* (1841).

and the Duke of Portland had similar hulls constructed for themselves, the Duke's at Troon and Lord Vernon's beside the one he was building for the Royal Navy at Fishbourne – just as the smugglers' boat and the revenue cutter were so often constructed.

Captain Symonds was a great believer in the traditional bluff bow and tapered hull of the era – the 'cod's head and mackerel tail' school of marine architecture – but the design he produced for the naval contract, *Columbine*, was certainly an improvement on earlier ten-gun brigs, while Lord Vernon's new yacht *Harlequin*, rigged as a ketch, was also a success.

The Duke of Portland's *Clown*, which was also rigged as a ketch, was a failure. He put her on the market and asked Captain Symonds to design him a larger vessel. This Symonds did and, with the benefit of three similar designs behind him, produced *Pantaloon*, which performed successfully and was eventually bought by the Admiralty which accepted her as the model for the ten-gun brig.

It was at this point that Lord Belfast entered the fray. Through whim, or perhaps a flash of genius, he came to the conclusion that *Pantaloon*, despite all the praise lavished on her, could be bettered. He therefore went to the man who had built his previous yachts, Joseph White of Cowes, and ordered a 330-ton brig to be constructed along the same lines as his yachts except that she was to have a longer and finer bow – an idea he may conceivably have filched from his arch-rival Assheton Smith.

The result was *Waterwitch*, which, when launched in 1832, was equipped and laid out in every way like a naval ten-gun brig. In the autumn of that year she joined a Royal Navy's experimental squadron off Cork and trounced every single member of it. This delighted the people of Cowes and a clamour arose in the press that she should be bought for the Royal Navy. The Admiralty, however, showed no signs of following this advice and *Waterwitch* spent the following year hanging around the Solent waiting to outsail any unfortunate man-of-war which ventured near her. Reports of these displays of speed filled the local press, but the Admiralty remained unmoved.

For the 1834 season Lord Belfast had her fitted out as a yacht, and in September of that year she sailed in a private match against C. R. M. Talbot's fore-and-aft schooner *Galatea*, which must go down in the annals of yachting as the first proper ocean race anywhere in the world.

The course was a 224-mile one, from the Nab, round the Eddystone Lighthouse, and back.

The schooner rounded the lighthouse first but on the run back she lost her jib boom and topmast, and *Waterwitch* overhauled her and won by twenty-five minutes.

It had been hoped by everyone that *Waterwitch* would meet *Alarm* in a private match, but within a week of her completing the race round the Eddystone it was announced that *Waterwitch* had been bought by the Admiralty at last. Curiously, Lord Belfast did not replace her. He stayed on the list until his death in 1881, continuing as Vice-Commodore until he became Commodore for a year in 1847–48, but it appears that he never owned another yacht.

Although the Eddystone course was used again by two members in 1843 for a private match – and there were reports that in the late 1840s a club yacht called *Sultana* raced another yacht called *Panic* around Ireland – organized ocean racing was still a good many decades away. But it was during these early years that the sailing committee which ran the regattas began to grope for a more equitable form of racing.

After the first crude attempt at handicapping had been made in 1827, a further step was taken two years later when it was decided that entrants in the Town Cup should be groped into six separate classes: from first-class yachts of over 140 tons down to a sixth class for those under 40 tons, with each class conceding a certain distance to the class below it in size. The first class gave the second half a mile over a forty-mile course and the sixth class as much as seven miles.

It is not known how well this system worked at Cowes but it was a failure at Cherbourg when a number of club yachts visited there in 1831 and raced for cups given by their hosts. The entries were divided into classes with a staggered start for each class. The smallest entry started nearly two hours before the largest which, over a course of 24 miles, was ridiculous, and not unnaturally the first boat to start won the race. These proceedings quite baffled the French, and after the race had finished several were heard to ask when it was about to begin. The system was tried again in 1837 but again proved a failure.

In 1832 a new attempt to classify by tonnage was introduced. Entries were again divided into six classes, the first consisting of yachts under 45 tons in which a difference of 5 tons was allowed. A maximum difference of 10 tons was allowed in the second class, and this gradually increased until in the sixth class, the largest, a difference of as much as 30 tons was allowed.

With this system yachts only raced against those in their own class, but certain prizes were allocated to each, either by committee decision or by ballot. This seemed to work and, although modified from time to time, continued to be used for most major races until 1843. The King gave it his early backing when two years later he intimated that he wished his cup to be raced for under this classification, thus ending the long run of wins of this prize by the large cutters.

In 1841 the first attempt was made at giving time allowances to yachts according to their tonnage. All the entries were started together, one second per mile being given for every ton of difference between them. Given that the eleven yachts varied from 31 tons to 393 tons the system worked adequately, the prize being awarded to the sixth boat home.

The success of this race no doubt encouraged the sailing committee in 1843 to introduce a more sophisticated version which gave a time allowance to a yacht calculated on her tonnage and the distance to be covered in the race. This system, known as the Ackers Graduated Scale, had been devised by a member, G. H. Ackers, who had come on the list in 1837 and was a keen racing yachtsman.

The importance of the club's efforts to improve regatta racing during these early years should not be underestimated. But it must not be thought that racing dominated this era for the majority of members were still occupied with cruising.

Under the commodoreship of Lord Yarborough cruising flourished. Where previously only the largest yachts had sailed beyond British waters, it was now common practice for much smaller ones to voyage abroad.

This increased activity was probably the result of finalizing with most European governments arrangements for entering their ports free of tonnage dues. Most of these negotiations were accomplished in 1829, sometimes with the help of the club's agents who had become established in the majority of the principal continental ports around that time. Certainly these arrangements were closely followed by an increasing number of reports of members abroad. In 1830, for instance, a letter to the club Secretary from one member, the Hon. William White, denying the rumour that his 57-ton cutter had been wrecked, shows that his cruise had taken him as far as the Greek Islands, Constantinople, the Bosphorous and the Black Sea. Two years later the newspapers recorded that Major William Lyon's 77-ton cutter *Turquoise*, Eyre Coote's 72-ton cutter *Gossamer* and Lord Anglesey's *Pearl* were all to be found at Naples, while Thomas Greg's 75-ton cutter *Iris* was refitting at Malta and J. Leveson Gower's *Albatross* was en route for Madeira.

Each succeeding year during the 1830s the lists of yachts abroad multiplied, so it can be truly said that the reign of King William IV was the time during which ocean cruising became a recognized pastime.

Other members ventured even farther. In 1830, for instance, Captain Corry sailed his 58-ton cutter *Dolphin* to Jamaica with a crew of only four, surely the first time a private yacht had accomplished a crossing of the Atlantic. And in 1839 Sir James Brooke took his 142-ton schooner *Royalist* to the far East.

Brooke's voyage seems to have been undertaken – as was typical of a member of that era – as much for the public good as for his own personal pleasure, for not only was he seeking adventure but to promote British commerce and ascendency in the area. He succeeded on both counts remarkably well for he ended up at Sarawak, helped quell a rebellion against the Sultan of Borneo, and so impressed the Governor of Sarawak that that gentleman resigned his governorship to Brooke in 1841.

As the Rajah of Sarawak Brooke abolished slavery and introduced a beneficial administration which was a model of its kind. He was helped in his policy to eradicate piracy and headhunting by one of the club's honorary members, Captain Keppel, but their actions were not appreciated by some English politicians and a commission was sent to Singapore to investigate. Brooke was entirely vindicated by the inquiry, but it is hardly surprising that when he visited England in 1847 he told Queen Victoria that he 'found it easier to govern 30,000 Malays than to manage a dozen of your Majesty's subjects'.

Not all members, of course, were as adventurous as Corry and Brooke, and most were perfectly happy to cruise for a month or two in home waters or warmer climes. Some were so enamoured with this way of life that they put their memories on paper and then published them.

The earliest book written by a member is *The Narrative of a Yacht Voyage to the Mediterranean During the Years 1840–41* by Earl Grosvenor. It is in two thick volumes, but the subject of sailing is hardly touched upon at all, a fault – to modern eyes at least – repeated by Lord John Manners when he wrote *A Cruise in Scotch Waters* in 1849, a description of a Scottish cruise in his father's yacht, the 164-ton schooner *Resolution*.

However, there does exist a book about cruising during this early period although it was not published until 1884. Called *Reminiscences of a Yachting Cruise*, it is the recollections of a cruise in company by club yachts from Cowes to Torbay in August 1843. It was written by Mrs N. W. Condy, the wife of the marine artist, who was the guest aboard J. H. W. Smyth-Pigott's 69-ton cutter *Ganymede*.

Smyth-Pigott was a keen cruising man who lived aboard his yacht. 'His vessel,' *Bell's Life* records, 'for man-of-war efficiency, order, trim, and discipline, is the *beau ideal* of the English gentleman's yacht.' This is perhaps a somewhat exaggerated description as all the yacht's linen was forgotten at the start of the cruise, the owner had shipped a bugler who confused his tunes, and a crate of live poultry kept the guests awake for most of the first night at sea.

Mrs Condy has a sharp eye for detail as she watches the activity around the yachts anchored in the Roads.

> On the decks of many of them were parties of gay ladies and gallant yachtsmen; the gigs waiting alongside with their crews in snow-white dresses, prepared to take them on shore. . . . On the deck of the *Xarifa* [Earl of Wilton], that lovely schooner which attracted me more than any of the rest, the men were standing in picturesque groups, their red caps forming a striking contrast to the white spars and blue sea and sky.

When the time came to board her host's yacht,

> we found the very perfection of a yacht's gig and crew waiting to transport us on board. No sooner had we neared the vessel than *whew - ew - ew* sounded the boatswain's whistle; the two sideboys appeared, gang-ropes in hand, and we were received in true man-o'-war style; the bugler being ordered at the same time to strike up 'Welcome, Royal Charlie!' that being the only appropriate air our kind and hospitable friend could think of at that moment.

An inspection of all the yachts going on the cruise was then made by the Commodore.

> The review commenced with the signal, 'yachts to take station according to tonnage.' Then came all the bustle and excitement of loosing sails,

slipping moorings, etc.; . . . they tacked in succession before the Commodore, then formed line, the *Brilliant* [G. Holland Ackers Esq.], taking the weather, the *Xarifa* [Earl of Wilton], the sea look-out.

Sadly, this was Lord Yarborough's last cruise. He was, by all accounts, a great character, a great seaman and a most hospitable host at his home at Appledurcombe on the Isle of Wight. In fact, his hospitality was renowned and was not confined to the times he was ashore. In 1827 he apparently somehow became involved in the battle of Navarino where *Falcon* was used as a dispatch vessel. The story goes that Lord Yarborough was so assiduous in asking the admiral for missions that the admiral, possibly deciding to relieve himself for a while of so keen a companion, gave Yarborough a message for the captain of a frigate that was sailing away from the fleet. It read: 'Give his Lordship a good meal and he'll give you a better one in return.'*

In 1835 he had been thrown across a seachest during a gale and had severely injured his legs. This, plus a severe bout of influenza, led to him selling the pride of the club's fleet, the 351-ton *Falcon*, the following year and to having built a much smaller vessel, the 156-ton cutter *Kestrel*. He then either sold her, or enlarged her and changed her rig, for in 1838 *Kestrel* is listed as a 202-ton yawl. In 1845 he converted her to a brigantine and was at Vigo in her the next summer when he quite unexpectedly died at the relatively early age of sixty-five.

The passing of the club's first Commodore brought to an end an era in which, under his steady guidance and the more volatile one of Lord Belfast, the club had grown and flourished, and become the unqestioned leader of yachting in the world. As a sign of their esteem and affection, members erected a monument to him, a conspicuous landmark on Culver Down.

During the years of Lord Yarborough's benign commodoreship the club not only grew in reputation but in numbers. In 1846 the *Sporting Magazine* reviewed the sixteen royal yacht clubs then in existence and calculated that the club had on its list 102 yachts totalling 9000 tons which were crewed by 1600 seamen. The tonnage tallies with Guest's list of yachts at that time, which shows there were 164 members (excluding royal and honorary members) in 1846, although only 102 had

---

* *Gentleman's Magazine*, 1869.

yachts on the list. It is evident from the large proportion of members not having yachts that the practice had sprung up of a candidate purchasing a yacht which he promptly sold once he had been elected, a state of affairs which became more marked by 1852 when the membership had grown to 182 without any increase in the number of yachts.

Cutters were still overwhelmingly the most popular rig – there were sixty-eight on the list in 1846 – although the majority of these were under 100 tons.* However, the increase in schooners showed the beginning of the popularity of this rig for there were twenty-eight of them, and most were over 100 tons. The rig's increasing popularity shows more clearly by 1862 when there were fifty-three schooners and twenty-eight cutters, with the number of yawls increasing from seven to thirteen.

The loss of Lord Yarborough proved hard to make good. At a special meeting on 20 January 1847 it was decided that the election of a new Commodore should take place at the annual meeting in May. When Lord Belfast, now the Marquis of Donegal, learned that the Marquis of Anglesey – a natural first choice for the post of Commodore – did not wish to be considered, he put himself forward as a candidate.

At the May meeting it was resolved before the polling took place that in order to qualify for the posts of Commodore and Vice-Commodore members had to be bona fide owners of vessels of not less than 120 tons and 80 tons respectively. Having passed this resolution, members then promptly voted the Marquis to be the new Commodore by a clear majority despite the fact he did not own a yacht!

It can only be supposed that the resolution was a tactic employed by the opponents of the appointment of the Marquis. When it failed they tried to pass another resolution which stated that he was not qualified. But this failed too, so later the same day seventeen of them wrote to the *Morning Post* complaining that he had lobbied for supporters. Lord Belfast made an indignant reply in which he pointed out that lobbying had perfectly respectable antecedents but that if the malcontents could produce a sufficiently large list of members to overturn his majority he

---

* This was at a time when other yacht clubs could only muster a handful of that size. It is interesting to note, too, the increasingly international flavour of Squadron membership, with no less than thirty members giving their residences as overseas, some as distant from Cowes as Sydney and Sarawak.

would accept that the election was void. The matter rested there until the annual dinner when it was made obvious that a rival faction existed in strength. For on the same evening as the dinner the Earl of Wilton gave a private banquet to which many members went instead of the official function.

The reasons for this sorry state of affairs are not known, but whatever the cause of the Marquis's unpopularity it created a serious rift in the club.

A similar problem had occurred after the passing of the great Reform Bill of 1832 when one of its greatest protagonists, the Earl of Durham, became active in the club. His political beliefs had not been well received in all quarters and during the next few years the Liberal and Conservative political philosophies were extended by the local papers to cover the merits and drawbacks of such matters as the holding power of *Waterwitch*'s anchors, and a visit by club yachts to Cherbourg where members dined with the citizen king, Louis Philippe.

This last occasion caused quite a furore, with the address voted by members to the King being 'cut, hashed and clipped' before becoming acceptable to those of every political persuasion. Then, when Lord Durham made a signal which involved hoisting the tricolour above the Ensign, his action was interpreted by a newspaper as displaying his own political standpoint, and Lord Durham sued for criminal libel.

In 1836 Lord Durham took up an appointment abroad but some of the political bitterness remained and it was reported in a local paper that blackballing was being conducted by a few newly elected members for party purposes. The paper bewailed the passing of tolerance in this matter and pointed out that 'in the old days' only two cases of blackballing had ever occurred. One had been when the Duke of Buckingham had not renewed his subscription and had been rejected when seeking re-election. The other had been when the owner of a yacht that looked like a river barge had failed at the ballot box, although 'more in joke than otherwise'.

The good sense of Lord Yarborough eventually prevailed on this occasion and peace returned, but in 1848 it again looked as if the old factions were coming to the fore. Then good sense prevailed again; the Marquis resigned but stayed on as a member, and the Earl of Wilton was unanimously elected in his stead.

CHAPTER THREE

1849-81

*Lord Wilton's benevolent commodoreship. The visit of
the* America. *An Irish squabble over the White Ensign.
Further race handicapping problems. A
circumnavigation of the globe*

DURING THE the final years of Lord Yarborough's commodoreship
the problem of the White Ensign occurred. It will be remembered that a general warrant to fly the White Ensign had been
granted by the Admiralty in 1829, but that this was neither an exclusive
warrant nor did it imply any privilege for at that date none existed.

Amusing proof of how little the White Ensign was regarded in those
days can be found in correspondence between the Western Yacht Club
of Ireland and the Admiralty after the club had broken away from the
Western Yacht Club in 1831. In applying for a warrant to fly an ensign of
its own choice, Maurice O'Connell wrote in January 1832 that, 'a white
ensign has been granted to the "Royal Yacht Club", a red ensign to the
"Royal Cork", a blue ensign to the "Royal Northern", and as the only
unoccupied national flag, we have assumed the green ensign'.

This rather enterprising idea was immediately quashed by their
Lordships. 'You may have as the flag for this club either a red, white, or
blue, ensign, with such device within as you may point out,' O'Connell
was advised, 'but that their Lordships cannot sanction the introduction
of a new colour to be worn by British ships.'

Reluctantly, the new club decided on the White Ensign, thinking it no
privilege, but rather the reverse.

There the matter rested for a decade. But during this time more and
more yachts from other clubs ventured abroad. Not all their owners

51

behaved themselves and the Squadron Secretary was being continually bombarded by complaints from foreign governments about those who did not. In vain did the club protest that these yachts did not belong to the Royal Yacht Squadron, but were owned by others who were also allowed to fly the White Ensign.

Eventually, in 1842, the club passed the following resolution which plainly shows that the White Ensign was still at that time of little consequence to them. 'The meeting requested the Earl of Yarborough to solicit the Admiralty to alter the present colours of The Royal Yacht Squadron, or permission to wear the blue ensign, etc., in addition, in consequence of so many yacht clubs and private yachts wearing colours similar to those at present worn by The Royal Yacht Squadron.'

Lord Yarborough, however, must have decided that instead of altering the Squadron's colours it was better to try and persuade their lordships that other clubs should wear only the Red or Blue Ensign, and he wrote to this effect on 14 July 1842. The Admiralty accepted his arguments and on 22 July 1842 sent the following circular to the Royal Thames and to the five other clubs which up to that time had flown the White Ensign as well.

> Sir,
>
> My Lord Commissioners of the Admiralty having, by their order of the 6th June 1829, granted permission to the Royal Yacht Squadron, as having been the first recognised club, and enjoying sundry privileges, to wear the white St. George's ensign and other distinctions, that their vessels might be generally known and particularly in foreign ports, and much inconvenience having arisen in consequence of other yacht clubs having been allowed by this Board to wear somewhat similar colours, my Lords have cancelled the Warrant enabling the Royal Thames Yacht Club to wear the white ensign, and having directed me to send you herewith a Warrant, authorizing the vessels belonging to the club to wear the blue ensign of Her Majesty's fleet, with the distinguishing marks of the club, as hitherto worn on the white ensign; and as it is an ensign not allowed to be worn by merchant vessels, my Lords trust that it will be equally acceptable to the members of the club.

So little did flying the White Ensign mean at the time that, with the exception of the Royal Western Yacht Club, the other clubs accepted this change without comment. The Royal Western disagreed, but then asked – and was granted – permission to fly a plain Blue Ensign with only a crown as a distinguishing mark. Later the Royal Bermuda Yacht Club asked, but was refused, permission to fly a White Ensign with a blue cross instead of a red one.

This should have ended the matter, but by an oversight the Royal Western Yacht Club of Ireland was not informed that its warrant to fly the White Ensign, along with all the other clubs, had been withdrawn. The Admiralty had overlooked the fact that in 1832 it had been told that the club was now a separate entity and no longer part of the Royal Western Yacht Club.

Two years later, in 1844, the Admiralty began issuing warrants for individual yachts belonging to yacht clubs with general warrants, although it had been issuing individual warrants to Squadron yachts ever since the club had been first granted permission to fly the White Ensign in 1829. The fact that the Admiralty was doing this must have filtered across to the Royal Western Yacht Club of Ireland at some point, but, as the Admiralty later indignantly pointed out, no requests for individual warrants for yachts belonging to the Royal Western Yacht Club of Ireland were received until 1853.

But in 1849 the Royal Western Yacht Club of Ireland asked if its privilege of flying the White Ensign had been withdrawn. Incredibly, but correctly, the club was informed that it had not been. But it still took the club another four years to submit a list of its yachts for the issuing of individual warrants. Then, and only then, did it occur to their lordships that an oversight had occurred, and the Royal Western Yacht Club of Ireland was then abruptly informed that its yachts could no longer fly the White Ensign. It was also informed that the club's yachts had been illegally flying the White Ensign since 1832 as no individual warrants had been granted to do so, an accusation totally at variance with the facts as, of course, individual warrants for yachts, other than those owned by The Royal Yacht Squadron, had only started to be granted in 1844.

It was promptly pointed out by the Royal Western Yacht Club of Ireland that its yachts had worn the White Ensign unchallenged and without interruption for twenty-one years. The Admiralty then changed its mind yet again and granted individual warrants to yachts belonging to the Irish club to fly the White Ensign. The new Commodore, Lord Wilton, and the Squadron's Vice-Commodore, C. R. M.

Talbot, protested about this decision to the Admiralty and a question was asked in the House of Commons. The spokesman for the government, however, by what might be mildly called dissimulation, managed to avoid the relevant papers being laid before the House, and the Admiralty's decision stood.

This anomaly was now seized upon by other clubs to press their claims to fly the White Ensign, for, although this was no privilege in itself, by this time it had a certain cachet because it was the ensign most closely associated with the by now prestigious Royal Yacht Squadron. As a contemporary commentator pointed out, it would not really have mattered if the Squadron had flown a 'blue, green, pink, or purple ensign, there would have been the same struggle'.

In June 1858 their lordships came to the conclusion that they either had to extend the concession made to the Royal Western Yacht Club of Ireland in 1853, or to revert to the principle established in 1842. They decided on the latter and wrote to this effect to both interested parties.

The Irish club then petitioned the Admiralty and gathered the signatures of no less than thirty-six Members of Parliament to support their case. The matter was once more taken up in the House of Commons. On this occasion, in April 1859, it was agreed to lay the relevant papers before the House. In July 1859 it was stated that this would happen within the next few days, but although the papers were printed they were never debated.

To the modern reader the tenacity with which the Royal Western Yacht Club of Ireland clung to an ensign which in itself meant very little is somewhat surprising. But some light is cast on the club's attitude by a letter published in December 1859 which stated that of the 122 yachts belonging to the club only fourteen were registered at Irish ports and that the rest were English, Welsh or Scots. The writer then revealed that the secretary of the Royal Western Yacht Club of Ireland was in the habit of 'writing to the owners of yachts belonging to other clubs, inviting them to belong to the club, and informing them that the annual subscription for non-residents in Ireland is two guineas, with two guineas entrance, and that the club flag is the white ensign of Her Majesty's fleet, and corresponding burgee with the distinguishing marks of the club'.

These distinguishing marks were a crown – identical to the one worn on the Squadron burgee – with a small wreath of very pale shamrock leaves around it. In short, any yacht owner willing to pay the required amount could fly an ensign and burgee almost indistinguishable from those flown by what was, even then, the most exclusive yacht club in the world!

After 1859 the matter was raised only rarely in the House of Commons, but there were occasions when perhaps Squadron members would have preferred not to have had the privilege of flying what, after 1863, became the ensign of the Royal Navy. The Turkish Government, for instance, regarded any vessel flying the White Ensign as a warship and they did not allow any warship through the Dardanelles without previous authority. When Lord Annersley tried to sail through in 1883 he was detained, and it was not until 1938 that the Turkish Government relented and allowed yachts flying the White Ensign through the straits. In 1912 there was a potentially even more dangerous incident when a Squadron yacht, whose owner was not on board, was challenged at night by an Italian warship in the Adriatic. The yacht's skipper panicked, and, under the glare of the warship's searchlight, hoisted the White Ensign, and was promptly fired upon.

These incidents caused some consternation at the Admiralty, and members, through the Commodore, were strongly reminded of their obligations to see that the rules governing the flying of the White Ensign were followed to the letter. Nowadays, these rules are most strictly enforced, for, whatever the origins of flying the White Ensign, it is now a very great privilege indeed and one which the Squadron is very proud to have.

*

Like Lord Yarborough, Lord Wilton was a cruising man who had a fondness for accompanying naval squadrons on manoeuvres. He had come on the list in 1832, and between 1835 and 1853 owned a whole succession of progressively larger schooners called *Xarifa*. Between 1853 and 1881 he owned three more – the 312-ton *Zara*, the 214-ton *Nyanza* and finally the 450-ton *Palatine*.

Though Lord Wilton's appointment in 1849 must have resolved the worst of the strife, a certain amount of antagonism lingered on for some years and badly affected the regatta racing.

'The good old days of the regatta have vanished,' reported *Bell's Life* in 1847, and even such important trophies as the Queen's Cup – as it had become when Queen Victoria had succeeded to the throne in 1837 – drew hardly any entries. In 1849, for instance, when the prize was alloted to yachts in the 50- to 75-ton class, it had to be made an open race because of lack of numbers.

The Prince Consort's Cup – donated by Prince Albert in 1840 – was at first raced for by the increasingly popular schooners and was considered as prestigious as the Queen's Cup. But it, too, attracted few entries and the race for it in 1848 had only three starters.

The only other race of importance in regatta week during these years was round the island for a £100 club cup. It first took place in 1850 and was open to all classes without time allowance. The first race for it produced, by the standards of the day, a large entry of eight, ranging from yachts of 60 tons up to 393 tons, and was won by the veteran *Arrow*.

The reappearance of this old favourite, after lying on a mud flat for some years, came about when Thomas Chamberlayne was elected to the list in 1847. He picked her up for a song, lengthened her and, after the visit of *America*, gave her a finer bow; and he soon proved she was as fast, if not faster, than she had ever been. She only just lost to Richard Naylor's *Sultana* in the 1848 Queen's Cup and then won it, as well as the Club Cup, in 1850 and again in 1852.

But the reappearance of *Arrow* was the one bright star in what was otherwise a dark period for club racing, and if there had not appeared upon the scene in 1851 a hitherto totally unknown yacht, the famous schooner *America*,* the ultimate result could have been the demise of the regatta, or even, as some malevolent voices hinted, the removal of the club premises to a more active locality.

America had been modelled on the lines of the American pilot boat and she possessed the long hollow bow advocated by Assheton Smith and Scott Russell, which had been developed independently by the Americans. Her arrival at Cowes was expected, for Lord Wilton had heard of her intended voyage and had written to Commodore Stevens inviting him and his afterguard to visit the club during their stay. He made no mention of racing but in his reply Stevens left no doubt that *America* expected to compete against British yachts. Consequently, at

---

* *America* was sold while she was in English waters and in 1857 she was purchased by Lord Templetown who brought her onto the list for a year under the name *Camilla*.

The auxiliary schooner *Sunbeam* (565 tons), carried her owner, Lord Brassey, and his family to many parts of the world, and in 1876-77 completed the first circumnavigation by a private yacht. During the First World War she served as a hospital ship and was finally broken up in 1929 *(Beken)*

Sunbeam was bought by Sir Walter – later Lord – Runciman, who was greatly attached to both the schooner and her late owner. So fond was he of both that when he decided to build *Sunbeam II* (659 tons), pictured here, he directed she be constructed just as if Lord Brassey had been ordering her. In many ways she was remarkably similar, though broader-beamed and much quicker in stays *(Beken)*

Below Lord Dunraven's *Cariad II* (153 tons), built in 1903, was a notable racing yacht, winning many races up to the outbreak of the First World War and in the postwar years when owned by the Rt. Hon. John Gretton MP *(Beken)*. *Right* Squadron members have always cruised widely and from the earliest days have, in common with other yachts, been exempted from certain taxes. This document certified that *Cariad* was not engaged in commerce and requested exemption. It is dated June 1903 *(RYS collection)*

SPANISH.

ESCUADRA DE REALES YACHTS.

YO, EL ABAJO FIRMADO, SECRETARIO DE LA ESCUADRA DE REALES YACHTS, CERTIFICO QUE *Ketch* NOMBRADO, *Cariad* CON EL NUMERO, *131* EN LA MATRICULA DEL PUERTO DE *Southampton* DE *87* TONELADAS, PERTENECIENTE A *Earl of Dunraven* *K^S. C.M.G.* ES EL MISMO QUE SE HALLA EN LA LISTA REMETIDA AL DIRECTOR GENERAL DE REALES ADUANAS DE ESPAÑA, Y SU DUEÑO SIENDO SOCIO DE LA ESCUADRA DE REALES YACHTS NO PUEDA EMPLEAR SU *Ketch* EN NEGOCIOS DE COMERCIO.

POR CONSIGUIENTE ESTE YACHT EN VIRTUD DELA REAL ORDEN SE HALLA EXIMIDO DEL PAGO DE GASTOS DE PUERTO, Y GOZA LOS PRIVILEGIOS CONCEDIDOS Á LOS BUQUES DE GUERRA.

FIRMADO

T.S. Pasley

TENIENTE DE LA REAL ARMADA
Y SECRETARIO.

DADO EN COWES,
1 Á Junio
DE 19 *03*

In 1908 Sheila, Duchess of Westminster, the wife of the 2nd Duke who came on the list in 1906, won an Olympic bronze medal in her 8-metre *Saskia*. She is here painted by Charles Murray Padday, who depicts her leading her class, accompanied by Philip Hunloke, acting as navigator *(Roger Hadlee collection)*

This black and grey wash drawing by Charles Dixon shows the naval review at Spithead on 10 July 1914, viewed from the deck of Sir Thomas Lipton's *Erin,* which is towing *Shamrock* through the lines *(RYS collection)*

Semiramis was a splendid 1797-ton steam yacht owned by the 6th Marquis of Anglesey who came on the list with her in 1910. She was the largest yacht ever owned by a member *(Beken)*

Sapphire (1421 tons) was built in 1912 for the Duke of Bedford, who handed her over to the Admiralty early in the First World War. She joined the Yacht Patrol and was engaged in convoy escort duties both in home waters and in the Mediterranean *(Beken)*

One of the series of photographs taken in 1912, and mounted in the Squadron photograph albums at the time. The view from the sea has changed little with the years *(RYS collection)*

The Squadron, seen from the west. A major change since this photograph was taken in 1912 has been the building of an extension comprising a ladies' balcony and a dining room *(RYS collection)*

Another photograph from 1912, this time showing the front door of the Squadron, again little different from the present day. The guns at the door were presented from the 1881 Squadron yacht *Golden Fleece (RYS collection)*

In the days of the Prince of Wales, later King Edward VII, the platform was an important reading and writing room in the Castle, and, with its fine view, was much loved by members *(RYS collection)*

The very small reading room, here photographed in 1912, where ladies were later invited as guests. They were not to be liberated into the larger rooms for another half century *(RYS collection)*

The drawing room, with its comfortable chairs, still survives today. The pictures, however, have changed with succeeding members' tastes. Shown on the left is Chevalier Martino's painting of *Valkyrie II* crossing the Atlantic *(RYS collection)*

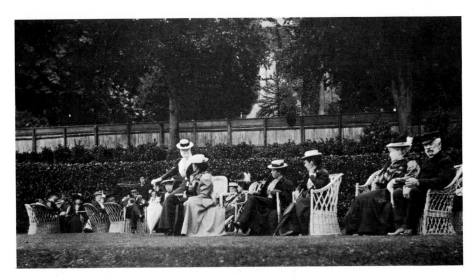

Ladies seated on the Squadron lawn in the basket chairs typical of the day, no
doubt keenly observing the assembly, and the yachting
(RYS collection)

Members of the public gaze upon the scene at the Squadron landing, while lady
members can be seen in the background on the Castle lawn *(RYS collection)*

the May meeting that year it was resolved to offer the usual £100 cup for a race round the island but that it was to be open to any yacht from any nation.

Details of this race have been well documented in other books and need not be repeated here, except to say that confusion about the correct course to take, combined with some unfortunate retirements, did not help in resolving whether one type of yacht was superior to another. Nevertheless, it was quite properly regarded at the time as a clear-cut victory for the Americans and, unlike some later races for this most coveted of yachting trophies, it was acknowledged that they had won it fairly and squarely.

The Americans were elected honorary members of the club and a dinner was held in their honour. The Queen even went aboard the schooner and is said to have been so impressed with what she saw, and those to whom she spoke, that she became, and remained throughout her long reign, a staunch and powerful ally of the new country.

There were many other visitors to *America* as well, for her victory had shaken British yachting circles to the core. One of them was the Marquis of Anglesey, then in his eightieth year. Lord Anglesey was a real 'sea dog'. He had christened his son, Lord Alfred Paget, by dipping him head first into the sea from the deck of his yacht, and when he first sighted *America* he remarked with some prescience, 'If she's right we must all be wrong.'

A rumour quickly went round Cowes that the American schooner had a propeller – though it was many years before the introduction of the auxiliary engine – a notion which it amused the Americans to foster. It must have reached the ears of the Marquis for when he went aboard the schooner he promptly clambered onto the counter. He leaned right over and peered down into the water, and was only just saved from falling in by Commodore Stevens who managed to grab him by his wooden leg.

The impact of *America*'s win in 1851 had a profound effect on British yachting. The fact that her beam was at its widest as far aft as her foremast, and that her cotton sails were laced tightly to her booms, were innovations so far as the British were concerned, and were closely copied. Yet it was the departure from the 'cod's head and mackerel's tail' style of marine architecture that caught everyone's immediate attention despite the fact that not only was it not new but had been successfully adopted by Assheton Smith and Lord Belfast amongst others.

The wave-line principle had, in fact, been only recently accommodated in the design of the 49-ton *Mosquito*, which had been built of iron in 1848 and had been brought onto the list by Lord Londesborough in 1851. But although she proved herself extremely fast her speed had been attributed to her iron build not to her bows; and it was not until *America* won her £100 cup that the success of the hollow bow was acknowledged.

In the wake of *America*'s success, therefore, came a whole vogue of building new yachts and of reconstructing old ones. Mr Ratsey, the famous Cowes sailmaker, was inundated with requests for 'Anglo–American' sails; Lord Wilton ordered a new schooner *Zara* from Joseph White; and White's archrival, Michael Ratsey, received orders for new boats from two other club members, Joseph Gee and John Naylor. Even Joseph Weld, who must have been long aware of the merits of the hollow bow, had *Alarm* lengthened to include one, and then had the famous cutter rerigged as a schooner.

The question of which type was superior was never really resolved, for, although *America* proved herself the best yacht on the day, others that came later never managed to emulate her success. In 1853, for example, a 205-ton American schooner called *Sylvie* crossed the Atlantic with the intention of beating the British just as *America* had done. Owned by Louis A. Depau, a very wealthy member of the New York Yacht Club, she was described by a local paper as being 'most magnificently fitted up. Marble, gilt work, mirrors, tapestry, pervade the whole; and we may safely assert that, for room, convenience, and elegance, she surpasses any English yacht in the Solent or out. The cabin would conveniently sit 20 persons and is seven feet high.'

This floating drawing room was regarded as being every bit as fast as her predecessor, and when the sailing committee met to vote another £100 cup for a race open to yachts of any rig and nation, they were so totally convinced she was going to win it that they also voted a second prize.

The course was from Cowes eastward to the Nab Light, thence to a station steamer twenty-four miles to the southwest, before returning to the finish at the Nab. The race drew seven entries which included a Swedish schooner, *Aurora Borealis*, and five club yachts, and was raced without time allowance. After a close tussle William Peareth's new 111-ton cutter *Julia* beat *Sylvie* by six and a half minutes.

This visit was the first of several by American yachts during the next decades, although fifteen years elapsed before the arrival of the next one. This gap was at least partly caused by the American Civil War, and the only recorded contact members had with Americans while this terrible conflict was being fought was when some were rescued by Mr John Lancaster after a fight between the Union man-of-war *Kearsage* and the Confederate commerce raider *Alabama* off Cherbourg. Lancaster was so intrigued by the battle that he sailed sufficiently close to the *Alabama* in his 190-ton steam yacht *Deerhound* to be able to rescue some of the crew, including her captain, when she was sunk by the *Kearsage*.

Once the Civil War had been resolved American yachts once more started crossing the Atlantic. The first to make the voyage was a small cutter called *Alice*, which arrived at Cowes in the summer of 1866. She was only 55 feet overall, and she rated so badly under the prevailing club handicap rules that she took no part in that year's regatta. Her urbane and witty owner, Thomas Appleton – it was he who originated the bon mot 'Good Americans, when they die, go to Paris' – looked for a private match but found no takers. So instead he cruised in the Solent, had a private unofficial race against a club yacht called *Hirondelle*, and was hospitably entertained by her owner, Lord Henry Gordon-Lennox, and by the club generally. He and his crew were invited to the annual dinner on a card 'as big as a mainsail' at which he was told to make a speech. 'Indeed,' Appleton replied. 'I have never made a speech in my life; can't conceive how it is done!' 'I will put you straight,' said the member sitting next to him, and ordered that two bottles of Château Mouton be placed next to the American. 'Stick to that,' the member advised. 'Don't mix wines, and your head will be clear as a bell.'

Only a few months after the arrival of *Alice* the first great transatlantic race took place in which three American schooners competed for a huge stake. Lord Wilton and the Commodore of the New York Yacht Club were present at the finish which J. Gordon Bennett Jr's yacht *Henrietta* crossed first. The owners were all entertained hospitably by the club as their yachts lay anchored in the Roads. So much so that on 31 December Bennett offered his yacht as a 'New Year's gift' to the Duke of Edinburgh, a club member, regarding the Queen's son as a suitable representative of the English yachtsmen who had given him such 'unbounded hospitality'. His offer had to be refused, but a firm bond now existed between yachtsmen on both sides of the Atlantic and in the following years several other American yachts arrived to race: *Sappho* in 1868, *Dauntless* in 1869 and *Enchantress* and *Faustine* in 1874, but none had the success of *America*.

In 1858 the French Emperor, Louis Napoleon, intimated his wish to join the club and came on the list with a steam yacht, *Eugenie*. The same year he presented a cup for a race for club yachts and the sailing committee decided it would be appropriate to set a course from Nab Light to a station vessel moored inside the Cherbourg breakwater.

This race was used to experiment with yet another system of handicap, this time by sail area. This had been tried in America with a degree of success and the committee sought the advice of the New York Yacht Club as to how it could best be implemented. The sail area was measured by taking the middle cloth of each sail as an average of the rest and multiplying its length in feet by the number of cloths. The allowance was threequarters of a second for each square foot of difference of sail area between vessels. To make them competitive against the yawls and cutters, schooners were allowed to deduct 10 per cent of their total area.

A Naval Member, Captain (later Admiral) Algernon de Halsey, was asked to start the thirteen competitors, which, as the following entries in his diary show, he with some reluctance agreed to do.

> Thursday, 5 August . . . The sailing committee of the club want me to start the vessels tomorrow morning under weigh off St Helens. It is a difficult and thankless task, but I suppose I must go. By the by, the *Alarm* won the schooner's cup yesterday, notwithstanding having to stop to pick up a man and losing her jib-boom. Went on board Mr Gee's vessel [his steamer] the 77-ton *Chesapeake** and got a shake down on the sofa. Found two reporters of newspapers on board for companions.
>
> Friday 6 August . . . Got under weigh at 2:45am after getting Captain Browne – the secretary – on board, and reached St Helens by 4am. I then went on board each vessel and gave them their instructions, which were to form in line astern of me according to their numbers and that I should head them out on a southerly course under their staysails only until in

---

* All restrictions on tonnage for steam yachts belonging to members had been withdrawn in 1854.

good line, when the second gun would be fired and – away. I had much difficulty in collecting them and, as they had had different instructions before, they complained a good deal at having to shorten sail to staysails. The Duke of Rutland and Lord Wilton, especially, were put out. . . . Although I could not succeed in making them follow me in good line, they got very fairly into line, and when I fired the second gun none of the 13 vessels had much advantage.

This unusual start to one of the earliest organized ocean races on record was made at 0730 in bright sunshine and a strong westerly breeze which soon had all but three of the entries reefed down. *Alarm* soon took the lead and held it all the way across the Channel. She finished at 1310, with *Zara* ten minutes behind her, followed by two more schooners, *Shark* and *Claymore*, and then the old cutter *Arrow*, which finished at 1342. However, the cup was won by the only yawl in the race, *Ursuline*, which finished at 1351, thereby saving her time by eight minutes.

Ursuline's win could be said to mark the start of the rise in popularity of the yawl rig which gathered momentum during the 1860s and 1870s – 'the most imposing in the yachting world'. *Bell's Life* called the rig during that latter decade – and led to the direct decline of the schooner. Nevertheless, it was felt after the Cherbourg race that the real honours had fallen to *Alarm*, for she had covered the course at a speed of nearly 11 knots, a rate few steamers of the day could have equalled.

The same system of handicap was used during the 1858 regatta in which *Alarm* saved her time in both the Prince Consort's Cup and the Queen's Cup. In fact, so successful was she and Joseph Weld's earlier yacht, *Arrow*, in the regattas over the next years that in 1861 *Bell's Life* expressed the hope they would both be withdrawn from racing. It was in this year that the club reverted to using a modified version of the Ackers Graduated Scale for handicapping, and followed this up by reintroducing races for mixed rigs and bringing in savage penalties for any yacht which had previously won a royal cup in a club regatta. In fact, all kinds of handicapping systems were tried to make the contests more equal between the different rigs and to keep *Alarm* and *Arrow* away from the silverware, but both kept racing and both continued to win.

Alarm eventually stopped racing in club regattas when Joseph Weld died in 1863; her place at the top of the schooner list was taken by John Mulholland's 161-ton schooner *Egeria,* which won the Queen's Cup no less than four times and in 1874 took the Prince of Wales's Challenge Cup outright.

Arrow went off the list in 1876 when her owner died and his son failed to be elected. But she went on racing under another burgee right into the 1880s, winning her last prize, the Town cup, in 1879. Although the additional penalty imposed on yachts which had previously won a royal cup severely restricted her chances after 1865, Thomas Chamberlayne continued to alter and improve her, and she remained a dangerous opponent right up to the end. Indeed, it was not until 1872 – the year the flying start was introduced – that a serious rival appeared in the shape of Count Batthyany's 105-ton cutter *Kriemhilda.*

Both *Kriemhilda,* and then Colonel Markham's 104-ton cutter *Vol-au-Vent,* launched in 1875, proved to be a match for the veteran cutter and were looked upon as the crack yachts of the day. Even so, in August 1876, as her owner lay on his deathbed, *Arrow* led *Vol-au-Vent* the whole way round the Town Cup course and won by seven minutes. She was at that time fifty-five years old, the most famous product of the early days of saltwater yacht racing.

The same year as the Cherbourg race the club moved into the Castle at West Cowes. The Castle was the surviving one of two built in 1538–39 by Henry VIII to defend the mouth of the Medina River, the other having been built at East Cowes. During the Commonwealth period it had been used as a prison. It later became a private residence, which it became possible for the Squadron to lease because of the death of its occupant, Lord Anglesey, in 1854. A stair turret had been added to the Castle in the eighteenth century at the southeast corner and after the Squadron purchased the lease, the building was further enlarged by the architect, Salvin, who also added the northwest turret. The negotiations and alterations took some time and it was not until 21 November 1857 that the servants were able to move in.

This date, plus the following ones, were jotted down in the signal-man's day book and survived an unauthorized clearout of club records at the end of the century. They were subsequently engraved on a silver plate which is now in the club's hall.

Jan 1st 1858   Lit the lamp on the battery for the first time

March 15th	Prince Albert, the Prince of Wales, and Lord Colville paid a visit to the Castle
June 4th	Stept the flagstaff on the point in front of battery
July 6th	Hoisted the flag of the RYS at the Castle
July 10th	General Meeting of members

The move to the Castle from the modest residence on the Parade was appropriately timed, for the club had, under the patronage of the Queen and her Consort, grown in both numbers and status. The racing might still not be as popular as it had once been, but socially the club's affairs were about to reach a new zenith.

The Prince of Wales's first connection with the club was in 1863, when he became its patron in the place of Prince Albert, who had died the previous year, and donated his first cup. Then, in 1865, at a meeting to mark the club's jubilee, the Commodore announced that the Prince of Wales intended to take a more active part in the club's affairs by becoming a member, and he was brought onto the list by acclamation on 8 July that year.

The Prince's first yacht was a 37-ton cutter, *Dagmar*, which he kept for three years before purchasing, in succession, two steamers, the 40-ton *Princess*, and the 38-ton *Zenobia*. Then in 1876 he brought onto the list the 205-ton schooner *Hildegarde*, and that year entered his first regatta race, the Town Cup, which he won by forty-six seconds in heavy weather. The following year he had a more notable win when he beat both *Vol-au-Vent* and *Kriemhilda* in a mixed race for the Queen's Cup. The violent squalls made it schooner weather and the finish was very exciting – the Prince winning by three and a half minutes from *Vol-au-Vent*.

'His Royal Highness's victory is held to reflect the greatest credit on his judgement in the selection not less of his craft than of John Nicholls to sail it,' commented one paper. 'Although there was half a gale of wind blowing, the Prince took passage on his own craft, and the ovation he received when he came ashore will be one of the brightest dreams of his life.'

The remaining regattas of the 1870s were dominated by yachts like *Egeria* and *Vol-au-Vent*, and by Sloane Stanley's new 103-ton cutter *Formosa*. In 1880 *Formosa* was bought by the Prince of Wales, who in that year won his second Queen's Cup aboard her.

The entry of the Prince of Wales* into regatta racing naturally increased public interest in it as well as inspiring a more competitive spirit. But it was on the social side that the Prince's continuing interest in the club was most strongly felt, and in 1881 one newspaper was led to remark that Cowes 'is no longer a half-civilised resort of the sailorman. It is now a court.'

So numerous had become the private entertainments by the 1870s, due to the presence of the Prince of Wales, that both the ball, which had become a private affair after 1848, and the annual dinner fell out of favour with members and were discontinued.

Although the racing now had royal patronage, some members felt it was breeding an attitude inimical to the club's traditional function. Their feelings were expressed in a short book which was issued anonymously in 1872 by a member, Sir Edward Sullivan, for private circulation within the club. Sullivan wrote:

> The RYS has never been a racing club, and I am of the opinion that the greatest misfortune that could befall it is that it should become so. It stands in a position that enables it to steer a course entirely independent of other yacht clubs on this subject, and to adopt rules and a system that promise to foster good fellowship in the Club, and to add to the numbers of competing vessels, and to promote seamanship and the improvement of sailing vessels.
>
> In theory racing does promote the latter objects, but practically it does not. In its present exaggerated form it has given birth to prodigies of lead and canvas, that are not sea-going craft at all.

The author then went on to back the proposal that in all club races yachts should compete in cruising trim, and a resolution was in fact passed to this effect the same year as Sullivan's book was published. Although this resolution, along with the idea of mixed races, was overturned in 1877, 'when yachting opinion,' according to Guest, 'drove them from the Solent as elsewhere,' it does show that the majority of members thought of themselves still as a seagoing society

---

* The first crowned head of Europe to join the club had been Czar Nicholas in 1847. In 1854 Joseph White built the large schooner *The Queen Victoria* for him which he adorned with a bust of the Queen. Her Majesty was reported to have giggled and to have been amused when she inspected it!

involved in the improvement of seamanship and yacht design, and not just a club for organizing yacht races. In this the Lords Brassey, Crawford and Kelvin were, as will be seen, outstanding in their individual fields.

When the Royal Navy eventually turned to steam not even the most affluent and knowledgeable member would have considered trying to improve the early designs of a destroyer or motor torpedo boat by building one to his own satisfaction. Nevertheless, the steam yachts belonging to some members were considered models of their kind and one or two found their way into naval service before the end of the century. The 1508-ton twin screw steamer *Giralda*, for instance, owned by Harry McCalmont MP, was bought by the Spanish Government at the time of the Spanish–American War and was used as an armed cruiser before becoming the Spanish royal yacht.

Although the influence the club had on naval architecture died out during the commodoreship of Lord Wilton, the enthusiasm its members had for cruising did not. And given the sense of duty imbued into them by tradition and a close connection with the Royal Navy it is not surprising to learn that some of the voyages undertaken were not solely for pleasure. For example, at the end of 1854, Lord Wilton suggested it might be appropriate to try to alleviate the suffering of British troops in the Crimea, and a subscription was opened to fill a yacht with suitable provisions. A few months later several club yachts arrived at Balaclava to unload the gifts they had aboard.

Already at Balaclava was another club yacht, the schooner *Enchantress*, which was being used by her owner, the Earl of Cardigan, as a luxurious home while at the same time his officers and men lived in squalor ashore.

Lord Cardigan does not seem to have been much liked and had been blackballed the first time he had been put up as a candidate. He eventually came on the list in 1849, a prime example perhaps of someone who had joined in order to enjoy the club's social benefits, not for his love of sailing. He was certainly no yachtsman. When asked on one occasion by his skipper if he would like to take the helm, he replied, 'No, thank you. I never take anything between meals.'

Another voyage started for at least partly altruistic reasons was that undertaken by Ben Boyd in 1851, and it was one which ended in tragedy. Boyd came onto the list in 1840 with the 141-ton schooner

Wanderer, which had been part of his share of a series of business enterprises he had set up in the Antipodes when he had gone to Sydney in 1839. He was seen at Cowes during the summer of 1841 before leaving in December of that year from Plymouth in *Wanderer*, bound for Australia by way of Teneriffe, Tristan da Cunha, and Rio, perhaps the first private yacht to have undertaken such a voyage.

In 1850 he was attracted back across the Pacific to take part in the Californian gold rush, but the following year he decided to sail once more across the Pacific as he wished to establish a Papuan Republic and to lay the foundations there for some sort of political and social organization. He sailed from San Francisco Harbour on 3 June 1851 accompanied by a smaller schooner which was to act as *Wanderer*'s tender. This tender was commanded by a John Webster who later wrote a book about this fateful last voyage. In it he describes *Wanderer* as a very handsome and fast-sailing topsail schooner. 'She had a flush deck; her cabins were fitted up with every possible attention to convenience.' She was also very well armed and carried 'four brass deck guns – two six-pounders and two four-pounders – mounted on carriages, resembling dolphins; four two-pounders, rail guns – two on each side; and one brass twelve-pounder traversing gun ["long tom"] which had done service at Waterloo'.

After stopping at Hawaii and the Gilbert Islands *Wanderer* arrived at the Solomon group. On 15 October Boyd landed on one of the islands with a native boy. Shortly afterwards the schooner was attacked by scores of natives in canoes and the crew was forced to open fire. Eventually the attackers were driven off, but neither Boyd nor the native boy was ever seen again. At the time of his death Boyd owned 381,000 acres in Australia, which must have made him one of the biggest settlers of the period. But he was not the first member to have become an Australian settler, as, in 1836, Colonel William Light, who came on the list in 1828, went to South Australia as Surveyor-General and was subsequently partly responsible for the founding of its capital city Adelaide.

Another adventurous member of this early era was Lord Dufferin, who, in 1856, took his 85-ton schooner *Foam* to within 630 miles of the Pole when he cruised to Iceland, Jan Mayen and Spitzbergen, which at the time was within a hundred miles as far north as any ship had ever succeeding in sailing. The following year he wrote a highly successful book about this voyage which became something of a best seller.*

An outstanding seaman-explorer of the later period reviewed in this chapter was Sir Allen Young, who came on the list in 1861. He was an immensely capable character who, at sixteen, had joined the Merchant Navy and had subsequently commanded a transport taking troops to the Black Sea during the Crimean War. After serving as sailing master in Sir Leopold McClintock's 1857 expedition to discover the fate of Sir John Franklin, he commanded the *Quantung* of the Chinese European navy during the Taiping Rebellion. While with the McClintock expedition he explored 400 miles of new land, including part of Prince of Wales Land in the Franklin Strait.

Young was haunted by the feeling that not everything had been discovered about the fate of the Franklin expedition and he became determined to return to the Northwest passage and, if possible, to navigate it. In 1875 he bought a naval five-gun sloop called *Pandora* and had her fitted out for the Arctic. He did not succeed in either finding out any more about the Franklin expedition or in navigating the Northwest Passage. He tried again the following year, but again had no success. Both voyages, which were carried out under the Squadron burgee, are vividly described in his book, *The Two Voyages of Pandora*, which was published in 1879.

But Sir Allen's adventures were not confined to large yachts and distant places, for in 1879 her made a wager he could run his 21-foot steam launch, also called *Pandora*, from Cowes to Torquay and back. The general opinion was that such a small vessel would soon be swamped in open water. But Sir Allen recruited an able hand in eighteen-year-old Harry Guy, one of the few young yacht hands in Cowes who knew how to handle these newfangled launches. The young Guy, by his own account, had a pretty miserable time of it, but Sir Allen won his bet, although on the return voyage they had to run for the shelter of Exmouth in a sinking condition.†

Guy's father had an engineering firm at Cowes and it was the elder man's boast that Lord Dufferin could never pass his gate without popping in for a chat – even if he was on his way to dine with the Queen

---

* *Letters from High Latitudes* by Lord Dufferin, John Murray, 1857.

† *Memories of a Cowes Born Lad* by Harry Guy, The County Press, Newport, I.O.W., 1932.

at Osborne. This is probably true, for Lord Dufferin in his later years became a keen small-boat sailor. During his time as ambassador in Constantinople he developed a taste for sailing alone in a small yacht of his own design. When he returned to England he devoted himself to perfecting, with the elder Guy's help, gadgets that enabled someone to sail single-handed. His small yawl, *Lady Hermione*, was so well equipped for this task that it was said that he could even cat his anchor from the cockpit. Another member who enjoyed sailing single-handed was General Sterling, who came on the list in 1872. Apparently, the extent of his cruises was governed by the amount of corned beef he could carry aboard his 18-ton cutter *Chough*. He always started and finished at the Squadron, and the object was to return to base before the corned beef ran out. He was affectionately nicknamed Sinbad the Sailor.

Another most unusual member was J. J. Curling. When he came on the list in 1868 with his 72-ton yawl *Lavrock* he was an officer in the Royal Engineers. He possessed a strong sense of adventure, first displayed when he took a canoe one afternoon while stationed at Dover and paddled it over to Calais, returning with it as luggage on the night ferry. He would think nothing of dining with friends in Folkestone before walking home the eight miles to Dover in his evening clothes.

In 1871, on hearing that the Newfoundland Church Ship, which attended to the spiritual needs of the local fishermen, had been lost off that coast, Curling immediately offered his yacht as a replacement. His offer was accepted and before he sailed her across the Atlantic he had her equipped with an altar and the necessary vestments, perhaps the only occasion in which a Squadron yacht has become a floating church.

After delivering the yacht Curling returned to England, but in 1873 he resigned his commission and returned to Newfoundland to work with the mission there. His jobs included being the master of his old yawl and acting as lay assistant to the bishop. Shortly afterwards he was ordained and went to live at an outlying mission which he could only get to by ship. He chartered a schooner to do this and, as the charter ended only when the ship had returned to St John's, Curling ordered the captain to return as swiftly as possible. Instead the captain anchored out of sight and waited for the approaching ice to freeze him in. When he heard about this Curling found a boat and sailed out to where the schooner was anchored as he had no intention of allowing the mission to pay for the schooner while she was in the ice for three or four months.

The captain pointed to the encroaching ice and said he could go no farther. 'Oh, nonsense,' said Curling cheerfully, 'I'll sail her out for you, if you're afraid', which is just what he did, right through the ice which was closing in fast. He sailed the schooner a hundred miles along the coast, then got the captain to drop him ashore, and walked back the fifty miles to the mission!

In 1879 he refused a colonial bishopric but the following year accepted the onerous task of being rural dean over a huge tract of coastline. In order to cover this territory he designed himself a 54-ton schooner *Sapper*, had her constructed by his own workmen at the mission, and then spent the summer in her performing his pastoral duties. Three years later he designed another, smaller yacht of 9 tons, called *Dove*, which he could sail with only one hand to the settlements close to the mission. He also wrote a book called *Coastal Navigation,* in which, by this time, he must have been an expert indeed.

In 1886 this remarkable man returned to take a degree at Oxford. He returned twice to Newfoundland during the long vacation and on the second occasion he packed his belongings into *Sapper* and sailed her across the Atlantic. 'This voyage,' his biographer noted, 'took 20 days and the arrival of the strange little craft at Portsmouth, flying the Royal Yacht Squadron burgee, was a puzzle to many an old sailor and coastguardsman.'*

The Victorian era abounded with extraordinary characters. One of the most prominent cruising members of the period over which Lord Wilton presided as Commodore was George Bentinck MP, a distant relation of the more famous politician of the same name. In many ways he epitomized the pleasures and aspirations of many members during the middle decades of the last century. He had come on the list in 1834 with a 55-ton cutter called *Zephyr*, owned another, larger cutter for a single year in 1839 and from then until his death sailed a whole succession of yachts called *Dream* which varied from a cutter of 100 tons to a topsail schooner of 238 tons.

Like the Duke of Leeds, who lived summer and winter aboard his schooner, Bentinck made his yacht his home the whole year round. He had the greatest contempt for those who did not live aboard their yachts permanently, and despised equally those who employed skippers and

---

* *Life of J. J. Curling: Soldier and Priest* by Colonel R. H. Jelf RE, printed privately, 1909.

those who confined their sailing to the Solent. He ran his yacht with great discipline but was well liked by his crew. He enjoyed taking friends with him on his cruises, but strongly resented being asked where he was going or for how long, and indeed refused to say.

'Long voyages and the difficulties of bad weather were Mr Bentinck's delight,' wrote Guest, 'and his favourite stories were of a trip, which consumed 42 days, between Cowes and Gibraltar, or of some outrageous storm in the Baltic, where the *Dream* shipped 20 tons of green water.'

He was a confirmed bachelor who resented the increasing prominence of the ladies at Cowes during his later years. He was, too, an MP with an independent view of life that delighted his political colleagues, for he loathed both Disraeli and Gladstone. On one occasion, after haranguing the front benches on both sides of the House, he shook his fist at them and said, 'You know you have all ratted; the only difference between you is that some of you have ratted twice.'

With the death of this splendid character in 1886, and that of Lord Wilton in 1882, there finally passed an era in which yachting had grown and had at last come of age.

CHAPTER FOUR

1882 - 1919

*The commodoreship of the Prince of Wales and his
patronage. The golden age of Cowes. Members become
powerboat champions and others help as men of
science. The Club and the First World War.
The Auxiliary Yacht Patrol. The freehold of the Castle
bought. Changes in the rules for membership*

AT THE May 1882 general meeting the Marquis of Londonderry,
who had become Vice-Commodore on the death of the Marquis
of Conyngham in 1875, proposed the Prince of Wales as
Commodore. The motion was seconded by the oldest member present,
Mr Milner Gibson, who had come onto the list as far back as 1828, and
was carried by acclamation.

The first result of the Prince's election was to reconcile the club with
the newly formed Yacht Racing Association, of which he was the
President. The Yacht Racing Association (YRA) had been founded in
1875 to provide nationwide regulations for all regatta racing. It was felt
by some clubs that these rules were biased in favour of the 'racing
machine' and that they disregarded the interests of the cruising yacht, a
vessel, as has been seen, particularly close to hearts of most Squadron
members. Worse, it was felt that the new rules were so stringent that
only a handful of yachts stood any chance of winning and that the prizes
would all go to the select few.

The new order of things was also particularly galling to the Squadron
which, over the last half century, had not only thought of itself as the
natural ruling body for the sport but had been closely involved in

71

ing rules that would not result in the supremacy of any one type of yacht.

The YRA, however, held out against the clubs which disagreed with it, and by 1881 the matter had reached such an impasse that yachtsmen who supported the new organization refused to race in any regatta organized by the dissenting clubs. As a result of this boycott the 1881 Cowes regatta was a miserable affair, with the prizes being divided amongst the few old schooners and even fewer cutters which still entered the various events.

The regattas of the other dissenting clubs proved to be equally uninspiring and at the end of that year the Royal Thames announced that it had had a change of heart. The Squadron, too, felt something had to be done and at the end of 1881 the sailing committee resigned 'in order that the subject of the YRA might be brought before the next meeting of the club to be held in May 1882'.

However, at the very meeting where this critical matter was to be discussed the Prince of Wales was elected Commodore, and it was immediately assumed that the Prince would not tolerate any further dissension, and this indeed proved to be the case. Within a very short time the Squadron was working closely with the Association and contributing new ideas. The Marquis of Ailsa was one of the first committee (later council) members, and within a few years other members keen on racing, like John Mulholland, Prince Batthyany-Strattman, Lord Brassey, the Earl of Dunraven, Captain J. Orr-Ewing and Lord Iveagh, were active YRA members.

It looked at first as if the critics of the new YRA rules were going to be proved wrong, for the 1882 regatta was extremely successful, with each race having a good list of entries. But in the following years the number of entries dropped right away and it was not until 1886, when the YRA adopted a new measurement rule, that the prizes began to be spread more evenly, which resulted in more yachts appearing at the starting line.

Under this rule the waterline length of a vessel and the square footage of its sails were multiplied together and the result divided by a fixed denominator, 6000. The answer gave the vessel's rating, and from then on a yacht was termed a 20-, 40-, or 60-rater, according to her size. This rule remained in force until 1895 and ended the supremacy of the narrow 'plank on edge' type of racer which had been encouraged by the earlier rule where a yacht's rating had been expressed in tonnage.

Although this rule proved to be a great improvement on the earlier

Above A rare photograph of the Prince of Wales' launch, taken when he was Commodore and before he ascended to the throne in 1901 *(RYS collection)*

Right Lord Montagu of Beaulieu, pioneer in the use of combustion engines, had successes on the water too and won championships in the Solent and in the South of France. Here is his *Yarrow* in 1906. Other contemporary members who raced power boats were Lionel de Rothschild and the Duke of Westminster *(RYS collection)*

Portraits by Lord Albemarle *Above left* Sir Philip Hunloke, born Philip Perceval Jr.,
who inherited both name and estates. He became one of the finest helmsman the
Squadron has ever had. For many years he raced *Britannia* for King George V and
was Commodore 1943-47 *Right* The pilot at the helm of King Edward VII's
Britannia, a noted character, named Giles

Above left Sir Allen Young, 'Alleeno' to his friends. He was the first member to
have a female cook aboard his yacht. *Right* The 26th Earl of Crawford and
Balcarres, owner of the 1490-ton *Valhalla*, 'sailor, astronomer, collector, bibliophile
and traveller', he voyaged to Mauritius for a transit of Venus, and became
President of the Royal Astronomical Society

Above left The 3rd Marquis of Ormonde, who succeeded the Prince of Wales as Commodore. *Right* The 10th Duke of Leeds, Commodore 1920-26, 'a lovable man, courteous and charming'. Although 53 years old at the outbreak of the First World War, he commanded his yacht *Aries* for a year in the North Sea before being given another posting. *Aries* was sunk by a mine shortly afterwards

Above left William ('Willy') Jameson was a very experienced helmsman and a friend of the Prince of Wales. He managed *Britannia* for her first five racing seasons with great success. *Right* Sir William ('Willie') Portal, who treated the Castle as a beloved second home. He was no yachtsman, but his yawl *Valdora* won the Kings Cup twice

Right: Ceto was a 185-ton steam yacht built in 1888 owned by Viscount Iveagh. At the start of the First World War she was armed and joined the Yacht Patrol, serving first of all in the Dover Patrol and then as part of the Downs Boarding Flotilla *(Imperial War Museum)*

Below At the start of the First World War, Lord Tredegar's 1571-ton *Liberty* was the largest yacht on the Squadron's list. Under the command of her owner, who held a master's certificate, she served mostly as a hospital ship but was for a time used as an armed yacht *(Imperial War Museum)*

The 693-ton steam yacht, *Elettra* came on the Squadron's list in 1922 on the election of Signor Marconi as a foreign member. He was the inventor of wireless telegraphy and King George V created him a GCVO *(Beken)*

The 555-ton *Sona*, built in 1922 for Lord Dunraven, was the first semi-diesel yacht ever constructed. Later, she came into the ownership of Lord Camrose, Vice-Commodore 1948-54 and served in the Second World War, first as an anti-submarine patrol vessel and then as an accommodation ship. She was sunk by a bomb in Poole harbour in June 1942 *(Beken)*

The Duke of Westminster had the four-masted schooner *Flying Cloud* built for him at Leghorn in 1923. At 1195 tons, and with a crew of 40, she was one of the largest private yachts afloat at that time. Her name was changed to *Fantome* when she was sold to the Hon. Ernest Guinness in 1938 *(Beken)*

Fantome II started life as a commercial trader called *Belem,* but was then bought by the 2nd Duke of Westminster, who converted her into a private yacht. Later, she was owned by the Hon. Ernest Guinness who cruised in her widely. Now renamed *Belem* again, she is in French ownership and moored alongside the French maritime museum on the river Seine *(Beken)*

Creole (699 tons) was built in 1927 by Camper & Nicholson to Charles E. Nicholson's design. In 1929 she entered the Squadron's list in the ownership of Major Maurice Pope and subsequently that of Sir Connop Gúthrie *(Beken)*

The photographer catches the beauty of sail in this 1934 portrait of the 'Big Class', the J-class: *Velsheda, Candida, Shamrock, Astra,* and *Britannia (Beken)*

Left: Jolie Brise, a French pilot cutter built at Le Havre in 1913, won the first Fastnet race in the ownership of Commander E.G. Martin who became a member in 1932. In the ownership of another member, Bobby Somerset, she won again in 1929 and 1930 *(Beken)*

Below: Cygnet, the 17-ton motor launch belonging to Lord Montagu, which he used to bring alongside the RYS landing stage 'with never a jerk, bump or scratch', to the admiration of onlookers *(Beken)*

one it had its limitations and in 1896 it was replaced by what was known as the Linear Rating Rule where length, girth and half the sail area in square feet were multiplied together and divided by 2. From this time a yacht's rating was expressed in feet, until the first International Rule was established in 1907, when yachts designed to it were known as 6-metres, 8-metres, etc.

One of the most successful club racers – and about the smallest – under the earliest rule was the cutter *Sleuthhound*, which measured as a 40-tonner. Built by William Fife of Fairlie for the Marquis of Ailsa, she started her remarkable racing career in 1882 by winning the Queen's Cup, a feat she repeated in 1883 and 1886. But her most famous win was undoubtedly that of the King of the Netherland's Cup in 1883, an event vividly described by her owner many years later.

The day of the race dawned grey and with gale-force winds from the south which later veered northwest. The Marquis came down to breakfast and was greeted by the club Steward, William, who warned him not to think of racing that day. When the Marquis asked to take away some cold pie from the dining room, William reminded him that this infringed club rules, but added, 'Of course you shall have it, and I hope you will live to eat it.'

But the Marquis was determined to race as he was intent on proving to his fellow members that his yacht was more than a mere 'sailing machine', which was their general opinion of it.

The course was round the Warner Lightship, thence to the Calshot Lightship, then to Lymington Spit buoy, and then back to Cowes. By the time the second mark was being approached, amidst a heavy squall which cut the visibility to almost nil, the Marquis judged he was already out of the race for the much larger schooners were well ahead. So he retired below for lunch. However, by the time he had finished the light had improved and to his amazement he found that *Sleuthhound* was no longer trailing the fleet but was close behind the two leading schooners and well ahead of the rest of the fleet. The Marquis wrote later:

> What had happened was this. The north-westerly squall which brought us along in a fog of its own, had, for some unaccountable reason, never reached any of our opponents, who had continued to work short tacks down the Solent against a westerly wind, whilst we had fetched a straight course down, with the wind about north-west.

Owing to the fog, they never saw us coming, and it was only when it cleared off that they discovered us, to their intense surprise.

The reefs were promptly shaken out and the large spinnaker hoisted, although all agreed it would probably take the mast out of her. After twenty minutes the sheet pulled the cleat out of the deck. Luckily, the turns stayed on the cleat which became jammed against a block, so the crew were able to haul the sheet back in, although it took sixteen of them to do it! Then, near the finish, the after guy of the spinnaker parted with a frightful crack and they crossed the line with the sail wrapped round the topmast. They saved their time by four minutes, after which the general comment in the club was that *Sleuthhound* 'was the finest all-round little boat that ever lay in Cowes Roads'.

An even more remarkable success for the Marquis came a quarter of a century later when, in 1907, he saved *Sleuthhound*'s predecessor, *Bloodhound*, from being broken up. Originally, *Bloodhound* had done remarkably, for in the six seasons between 1874 and 1880 (she did not race in 1878) she won no less than seventy-one prizes, before the new rule apparently made her obsolete.

The Marquis now speculated how, with some alteration, his old boat would compete with her modern counterparts. As an experiment he bought her and lavished a considerable amount of money on her. He gave her a new bow, the latest sails and hollow spars, and in 1908 began racing her in the handicap class.

The result of this experiment – the yachting journalist Brooke Heck-stall-Smith called it 'one of the most peculiar and interesting circumstances in yachting history' – was little short of astounding: between 1909 and 1914 *Bloodhound* won no less than 142 prizes, sixty-four of which were firsts. Out of thirty starts in 1914 she won nineteen firsts. A memento of this great yacht can still be seen at the Castle as in that year Lord Ailsa gave her mast to the Squadron where it is still used as the flagstaff, and her tiller adorns the platform.

In 1884 Sir Richard Sutton, whose grandfather and father had both been members, brought onto the list the 84-ton cutter *Genesta*, the kind of narrow, deep-drafted yacht that the 1881 rule encouraged. She proved herself a success from the start of her career and in thirty-four races during the 1884 season she won seven first and ten second prizes. At the end of that summer Sir Richard sailed *Genesta* across the Atlantic to challenge for the *America*'s Cup. He was no more successful than earlier challengers, but he made himself extremely popular with Americans by refusing to accept a walkover when the American defender fouled him. And although he was unsuccessful in bringing back the main prize he won both the Brenton Reef Cup and the Cape May Challenge Cup, and brought them back to England with him.

Genesta also won the first Round Britain Race which was held in 1887 to celebrate Queen Victoria's Jubilee. She covered the 1590-mile course in 12 days, 16 hours, 59 minutes, and appears to have led all the way.

Later the same year the club held its own long-distance race to celebrate the Jubilee. It was open to any yacht, British or foreign, above 30 tons, with £500 going to the winner on time allowance. The course was from Cowes to the Nab, across the Channel to the Cherbourg breakwater, then round the Eddystone Light, and then back to Cowes, a distance of 330 miles.

The race attracted thirty entries, nine of which were club yachts, but was won clearly by the famous cutter *Irex*, which crossed the finishing line nearly eight hours ahead of the next yacht.

It might be thought that having two organized long-distance races in one year would enthuse yachtsmen and those following the sport to agitate for ocean racing to begin on a regular basis. In fact, the reverse occurred, with *The Field* magazine stating bluntly that 'nothing came out of the long race from Cowes round Cherbourg and the Eddystone and back to recommend a repetition at any future time, and it is to be hoped that, with the Jubilee year, the fashion of long, dreary racing tramps will go out,' which indeed it did for another ten years.

Although ocean racing did not appeal in the late 1880s, regatta racing at Cowes and elsewhere saw a renaissance in the following decade when the German Emperor, William II, began to take an interest in the sport. He came onto the list in 1889 and two years later bought the 1887 *America*'s Cup challenger *Thistle* and renamed her *Meteor*. Then in 1892 he raced her at Cowes with an all-English crew as there were at the time no professional German hands capable of sailing her. She did not do particularly well as she had a very large handicap, but it can be said that the era of the large racing cutter starts from that date, for it was almost certainly the appearance of his nephew at Cowes in 1892 that prompted the Prince of Wales to build one of the famous yachts of all time, *Britannia*.

For some years the boatbuilders and designers on the Clyde had displaced those in the south from the forefront of the industry. An exception to this was the firm of Camper and Nicholson of Gosport. Camper and Nicholson had been founded in 1792, but there is no record of it constructing any yachts before 1836 when the cutter *Breeze* had been built for a member, Captain James Lyon. By the mid-1850s, however, it had established a sufficient reputation for John Fincham to choose six of William Camper's yachts as the subject for an analysis similar to the one he had carried out in 1827.

In 1842 Camper had apprenticed Ben Nicholson, who later designed many yachts for members, as did his son, Charles E. Nicholson, one of the great yacht designers of all time. The connection with the club remains, for Ben Nicholson's great-grandson, Peter Nicholson, is a present member.

With *Britannia*, however, the Prince of Wales followed the fashion of the day by employing the Scotsman, G. L. Watson, to design her and Henderson's on the Clyde to build her. She was of composite construction – wooden planks on a steel frame – even then a new method for building yachts, as most were still entirely constructed of wood.

The news that the Prince of Wales was building a first-class cutter enthused others to do the same, and in the same year as *Britannia* was launched there also appeared *Valkyrie II*, owned by a member, the Earl of Dunraven, *Satanita* and *Calluna*, and for the 1893 season these four were joined by a new American yacht, *Navahoe*, which crossed the Atlantic to try and retrieve the Brenton Reef and Cape May cups.

The sight of these five great yachts competing against one another on the regatta circuit caused enormous interest and started a revival in yacht racing which was to last some years. *Britannia* showed her clear superiority by winning twenty races out of the thirty-eight in which she took part, and although she lost the Brenton Reef Cup to *Navahoe* on a protest she retained the Cape May Challenge Cup.*

That same year, 1893, Lord Dunraven challenged for the *America's*

---

* When the American schooner *Ingomar* crossed the Atlantic in 1904 expressly to race for the Cape May Challenge Cup, the cup could not be found. An extensive search was carried out for it at the club and at Windsor Castle before it was eventually discovered amongst the silver at Sandringham. By then it was too late for a race to be arranged so the cup was returned to the New York Yacht Club and was raced for by American yachts without international competition later that year.

Cup, but lost three races in a row to the American defender *Vigilant*, which in 1894 arrived in English waters to race in the regatta circuit. The season started disastrously when *Satanita* sank *Valkyrie II* during the Clyde regatta. This left the royal cutter as the American's main rival. The two met seventeen times, and *Britannia* won twelve times.

In 1895 Lord Dunraven brought out *Valkyrie III*, and another first-class cutter, *Ailsa*, also appeared. But neither could dent *Britannia*'s superiority.

No first-class American yacht crossed the Atlantic in 1895. However, a Herreshoff-designed 20-rater, *Niagara*, arrived to challenge the English yachts of her class, but only *Audrey*, designed and owned by Lord Dunraven, could match her in speed.

Later the same year Lord Dunraven challenged again for the *America*'s Cup in *Valkyrie III*, a series of races that ended in bitterness and recrimination.* This challenge has been extensively written about and the details of it need not be repeated here. It is sufficient to say that history does not come down on the side of Lord Dunraven over the affair, whose temper has been described as being of the 'hair-trigger' variety.

Whatever his faults, Lord Dunraven was a distinguished politician and an able journalist, as well as being one of the outstanding yachtsmen of his day. In 1894 he passed his master's certificate and three years later his extra-master's, which, as will be seen, came in great use to him during the First World War. But he was more than being a practical seaman for he also wrote a book, *The Practice and Theory of Navigation*, and studied the art of yacht design under Dixon Kemp, one of the premier marine architects of the day. In *Audrey* he produced a plate-and-bulb keeler of extraordinary speed before practically anyone else in the country had thought of this kind of design for such a large yacht. He eschewed the normal method of drafting her out on paper and instead cut out the sections in millboard and then modelled her in clay.

Although he never attempted to challenge for the *America*'s Cup again Lord Dunraven continued to race for many years. In 1895 he had built a ketch, *Cariad*. She was intended mainly for cruising, but in 1898

---

* Relations between the New York Yacht Club and The Royal Yacht Squadron remained strained for many years. Then in 1912, quite by chance, the carved eagle that had adorned the stern of *America* was found in a junk shop. It was sent to the NYYC as a gift and the rift was finally healed.

he took her to Portugal for the Vasco da Gama tercentenary celebrations as the representative of the Royal Geographical Society and won the Vasco da Gama Cup with her. Later, he built *Cariad II* in which he won the King's Cup in 1905 and 1912, and again in 1921.

Though no more American yachts were to appear in British waters for a number of years the void in international racing was filled to some extent by the appearance in 1896 of the German Emperor's new *Meteor*. Except for *Satanita*, she was the largest cutter ever built, being 89 feet on the waterline compared with *Britannia*'s 88 feet. She was built to the new Linear Rating Rule and could therefore carry 2000 square feet more canvas than the royal cutter. Even so, the racing was very even that year, with *Meteor* and *Ailsa* winning thirteen races each, *Britannia* eleven and *Satanita* five.

1896 was the year that one-design racing really began in the Solent, with a number of 8-ton yachts, called the Solent One-Design Class, being launched. In their fifty-five races during this first season one member won no less than fifty prizes, including twenty-eight firsts. This was Philip Perceval, who later, as Philip Hunloke, sailed *Britannia* for many years as the King's sailing master. He came on the list in 1890 at the age of twenty-one years and two months, which made him easily the youngest member, a fact other members commemorated by presenting him with a small rush-seated chair, suitable for a three-year-old. This delighted 'Young Phil' – so called to differentiate him from his father, 'Old Phil', who was also a member – and he kept it until he was able to hand it on to his son.

The story is told that Young Phil passed the ballot box without one black ball against his name – a most unusual occurrence in those days. However, years later Hunloke corrected this story by saying that there had been one black ball in the box. Old Phil, thinking his son might get bumptious at being elected too easily, had put it there himself!*

Young Phil, probably at the behest of the Prince of Wales, was elected onto the sailing committee after only being a member for four years. This committee was chaired at the time by the Marquis of Ormonde, who had become Vice-Commodore on the death of the Marquis of Londonderry in 1884.

---

* *The King's Sailing Master* by Douglas Dixon, George G. Harrap Ltd., 1948.

Lord Ormonde apparently had the greatest difficulty in understanding the difference between a motion and its amendment. He also had the rather disconcerting habit of saying, 'Certainly not! Certainly not!' to any new suggestion before it had even been fully explained. This latter foible – although not, perhaps, the first – was quite accepted by his committee who were as amused by it as was the Marquis himself.

On one occasion the club's most junior member had to obtain a ruling on a certain racing signal. 'Shall there be two guns or one?' he asked. 'Certainly not! Certainly not!' the Marquis cried. Young Phil must have taken a deep breath before he tried again. 'Do you, sir,' he inquired, 'want the Squadron races to be run properly?' 'Certainly not! Certainly not!' the Marquis repeated to the delight of everyone present, and then joined in the general laughter.*

Although the 1896 season was successful the new Linear Rating Rule failed to please in the long run and the following year marked the start of a long decline in first-class racing. *Britannia* only appeared twenty times in 1897 compared with fifty-eight times in 1896, and at the end of the season was withdrawn from racing and sold. It has been said that the reason for this was as much the fault of the German Emperor as the handicapping of the Big Class. Certainly, the Emperor's pettiness and jealousy annoyed his uncle enormously. 'The regatta,' the Prince of Wales is said to have remarked to Baron von Eckhardstein about Cowes Week, 'used to be a pleasant relaxation for me; since the Kaiser takes command it is a vexation.'

The history of *Britannia* after the Prince of Wales ceased racing is rather a strange one. She was sold in December 1897 and changed hands several times, but continued to lie on the mud in the Medina River until the spring of 1899. She then returned to the ownership of the Prince of Wales, who used her mainly as a trial horse for Lipton's *Shamrock I*, which later that year challenged for the *America*'s Cup. Then in 1900 she was sold to a member, Sir Richard Williams-Bulkeley, who was to become the club's Vice-Commodore between 1920 and 1926 and

---

* *The King's Sailing Master* by Douglas Dixon, George G. Harrap Ltd, 1948. The Marquis might not have been much of a committee man, but he was an outstanding yachtsman. He gained his master's certificate in 1879 and voyaged far and wide in his 200-ton schooner *Mirage*, including one long cruise to Spitzbergen.

its Commodore from 1927 to 1942, and he reduced her sail area as he intended to use her mainly for cruising.

However, the following year Sir Richard decided to enter *Britannia* for what was, for the first time since the late 1830s, the King's Cup. But at the end of July he was summoned to Marlborough House and asked by the King to lend him *Britannia* for the regatta. Sir Richard, albeit without much enthusiasm, naturally agreed. 'You look disappointed,' the King said jokingly. 'Sir,' replied Sir Richard, 'I had so much wished to race for your Majesty's first cup in your Majesty's old yacht.' 'I quite understand,' said the King immediately. 'You shall have the ship back for the race, and I hope you will win.'

Sir Richard very nearly did win, for it was *Britannia* weather with the wind near gale force. She finished first, but just failed to save her time against the 98-ton yawl *Leander*, owned by the Hon. Rupert Guinness. 'Will you ever forgive me?' Rupert Guinness later asked Lady Williams-Bulkeley. 'No, never,' she replied firmly.

At the end of the 1902 season the King bought *Britannia* back from Sir Richard and used her as a cruising yacht until his death in 1910 when she passed to his son, King George V.

The withdrawal of *Britannia* from racing and increasing disillusionment with the rating rule wrought an interesting change in the Big Class. For years the big racing schooners had been in the doldrums and the yawl rig had also fallen from favour. Then both were resurrected, with one member, Captain Charles Orr-Ewing MP, commissioning G. L. Watson to design the 316-ton schooner *Rainbow*, and another, Sir Maurice FitzGerald, buying *Satanita* and rigging her as a yawl. The owner of *Ailsa* followed Sir Maurice's example, as did the German Emperor the following year.

Rainbow turned out to be one of the fastest yachts ever built – she is said to have touched 16 knots on one occasion – and in 1898 she established a new course record for the Queen's Cup by covering the fifty miles in 3 hours, 52 minutes, 26 seconds. She was, incidentally, the first sailing yacht to be constructed with a companion deckhouse, an innovation that was regarded by some at the time as being unseamanlike if not downright dangerous!

With the Big Class languishing, those members interested in racing turned to the smaller classes. In 1900, for example, Captain Orr-Ewing won fifty-one firsts in fifty-six starts with his 5-rater, and by 1905 it had become common practice for an owner of even quite large yachts to steer himself – quite a revolutionary event! In that year, for instance, members like Lord Brassey, Lord Albermarle, John Gretton and Richard Charteris raced their own yachts in the 24-ton South Coast One-Design Class.

Another kind of competition that members could participate in when the Big Class regatta racing declined was ocean racing. This started in 1897 on a regular basis when the Kaiser donated a Jubilee Cup to be raced for from Dover to Heligoland, a distance of about 310 miles. Two club yachts entered this first race: Lord Iveagh's 203-ton schooner *Cetonia* and the 160-ton ketch *Corisande*, owned by the Duke of Leeds. *Cetonia* finished first, having covered the course in 42 hours, 29 minutes, but she was later disqualified, while *Corisande* lost all chance of winning when she inadvertently passed the Terschellinger Bank Lightship on the wrong side.

This first Dover–Heligoland fixture proved to be a great success and was turned into an annual fixture to coincide with the Kiel regatta. Over the years it attracted many Squadron entries, but not always the fastest. When one member entered in his elderly and extremely slow yacht his son said to him, 'I'm sorry to see you going, we always had such good Christmases together.' But in both 1902 and 1903 it was won by a member, the Marquis Camden, in his yawl *Fiona*, and, with the exception of 1901, the year of Queen Victoria's death, it took place every year until 1908 when interest in it ceased.

One of the more unusual events organized by the club during this period was also an ocean race. In 1902 a member, Lord Crawford, gave a cup to celebrate the coronation of Edward VII. He stipulated that it was to be raced for by 'auxiliary steam vessels' of 340 tons Thames Measurement (TM) or above, but engines were only to be used to get to the start line and propellers were to be feathered thirty minutes before the gun. All competitors had to be in seagoing trim, with all boats carried, and with only the normal crew on board.

This singular fixture attracted five starters which included three club yachts: Lord Crawford's full-rigged ship *Valhalla*; Lord Brassey's 532-ton schooner *Sunbeam*; and the 564-ton schooner *Czarina*, owned by Lord Brassey's brother Albert. Another starter was the 560-ton American schooner *Utowana* belonging to the New York Yacht Club; being the only fore-and-aft rigged yacht in the race, she won easily over a course which took the entries from the Nab to Cherbourg, round the Eddystone Light, and back to Cowes.

Utowana, *Sunbeam* and *Valhalla* also took part in what was undoubtedly the major ocean racing event of the period, the 1905 Transatlantic Race.

The race was the idea of Robert E. Tod, Commodore of the Atlantic Yacht Club, but when the German Emperor heard of it he took over the idea as if it were his own and donated a large and seemingly valuable gold cup* for the winner. The race attracted eleven entries and was won by Wilson Marshall's famous *Atlantic*, which crossed in the remarkable time of 12 days, 4 hours, 1 minute, a record which remained unbroken for decades. *Valhalla* came third, crossing in 14 days, 2 hours, 53 minutes, and *Sunbeam* sixth, in 14 days, 6 hours, 25 minutes. *Utowana* finished ninth.

Another new maritime sport some members took to with enthusiasm was that of racing the early petrol-driven speedboats. Lord Howard de Walden was probably the first member to own and race a speedboat, but the most successful member was the Hon. John Montagu, who came on the list in 1906, the same year as he succeeded to his father's title, Lord Montagu of Beaulieu. Montagu joined forces with another great patron of the early motorcar, Lionel de Rothschild, who became a member in 1919, and in 1905 they bought *Napier II*, the winner of the first Harmsworth Trophy, which had been started in 1903. They won the trophy in her that year and then built *Yarrow-Napier* in which they again won the trophy in 1906 at an average speed of 21·4 m.p.h., beating, on both occasions, Lord Howard de Walden's entries into second place.

In 1908, *Ursula*, which belonged to another member, Bendor, Second Duke of Westminster, won the Championship of the Sea at Monaco at nearly 35 knots. *Ursula*'s considerable speed was put to good use on behalf of her country when, the following year, she was employed on a spying mission in Kiel Harbour. Captain Hall, later Admiral Sir Reginald Hall, was on an official visit to German ports in HMS *Cornwall*, but unofficially he had been charged with the task of photographing some secret German installations including some naval building slips. German security was strict and any ordinary incursion would have been

---

* The cup was broken up during the First World War as the owner's donation towards the war effort, but was found to be made of pewter under a thin layer of gold plate.

turned back before getting anywhere near the target. So Hall persuaded the Duke of Westminster to lend him *Ursula* and with two other officers armed with cameras he steered at top speed into the forbidden area. *Ursula* then very conveniently 'broke down', the photographs were taken, and they made their escape before the Germans could get anywhere near them, making it perhaps the first time – though not the last – when a vessel owned by a member has been used as a spy ship.*

Although *Ursula* was a very fast boat, the development of these petrol-driven craft was so rapid that in 1909 her top speed was easily eclipsed by the Duke of Westminster's *Pioneer*, which was one of the first hydroplanes to be constructed and showed her superiority by exceeding 39 knots. She was at the time the fastest hydroplane in the world, but developed engine trouble when she went to the United States to try to retrieve the Harmsworth Trophy – by then named the British International Trophy – which had been won by *Dixie* in 1907. The trophy was eventually won back in 1912 by *Maple Leaf IV*, a hydroplane driven by a future member, T. O. M. Sopwith, and he successfully defended it in Osborne Bay the following year against French and American challengers.

Although the names of Lord Crawford and Lord Brassey have been mentioned in connection with ocean racing their real contributions lay in other fields. They were both remarkable men and outstanding seamen. Lord Brassey had come onto the list in 1859 when, as Thomas Brassey MP, he owned the 110-ton schooner *Albatross*. In 1874 he built the three-masted topsail auxiliary schooner *Sunbeam* and in 1876–77, prior to a period in government as Civil Lord of the Admiralty (1880–84), went round round the world in her, the first privately owned yacht to achieve this distinction. His wife Anne wrote a book, *A Voyage in the Sunbeam*, about their experiences during this cruise which sold millions of copies and was widely translated; it has recently been reissued in paperback. By the time he lent *Sunbeam* to the Indian Navy as a hospital ship in 1916 Lord Brassey had logged half a million miles in her in voyages to every part of the globe. When he was appointed Governor of Victoria in 1895 he sailed there and received a warm welcome when he arrived. He helped develop the city and port of Melbourne, and took a major part in the federation of the states into a commonwealth in 1900.

---

* *The Riddle* by Maldwin Drummond, Conway Maritime Press, 1985.

Lord Brassey was not only the first member but the first yachtsman to obtain a master's certificate, and was as happy in a small boat as he was in a big one. When in London he exercised almost daily by rowing on the Serpentine and when at sea he was always involved in the working of his ship, of which he was not only the captain but the navigator as well.

On one occasion just after *Sunbeam* had been fitted with some studding-sail booms one of the crew began grumbling about the awkwardness of handling them aloft. 'I wish the old —— was up 'ere 'isself,' he shouted to a mate. 'The old —— is up here,' a voice shouted back, and the startled hand turned to see the owner coming out along the yard's footropes.

Another accomplishment of this versatile seaman was the publication of his *Naval Annual* in 1876, which, in its day, was the most authoritative survey of naval affairs in the world. On his death in 1919 an obituarist wrote that 'to his conscientious and persistent advocacy the Royal Navy, the Naval Reserves, and the Maritime Marine are greatly indebted'.

The Earl of Crawford came on the list as Lord Lindsay in 1874 with the 390-ton schooner *Venus*, and at the turn of the century owned two of the largest yachts on the list, the 708-ton steamship *Consuelo* and *Valhalla*, one of the two largest fully rigged yachts ever constructed, which had been built for another member, T. F. Laycock, in 1893.

Besides being a very competent seaman, Lord Crawford was a Fellow of the Royal Society.* Between 1902 and 1905 he made three voyages during which some important ornithological discoveries were made. On the last of these a collection of five hundred bird skins was made which included eight new species. Three of these, a white tern from south Trinidad (*Gygis crawfordi*), a paradise flycatcher from the Comoro Islands (*Terpsiphone lindsayi*) and a heron from Assumption Island

---

* Another member who was a distinguished scientist of the period was Lord Kelvin, who came on to the list in 1872 as Sir William Thomson with the 126-ton schooner *Lalla Rookh*. Like Lord Crawford, he was a Fellow of the Royal Society. He had a brilliant and widely educated mind and was the originator of the sounding machine and of the first really effective mariner's compass and a president of the Royal Astronomical Society. By 1871 his accomplishments as an inventor had been accepted and he was appointed a member of the Admiralty committee on designs for ships-of-war which resulted in 1904 in the Dreadnought type of battleship. He died in 1907.

(*Butorides crawfordi*) were named after Lord Crawford or members of his family.*

Lord Crawford's other passion was astronomy. He erected an observatory near Aberdeen and made several expeditions in his yacht for astronomical purposes. One of the most successful of these was a voyage to Mauritius to observe the transit of Venus, and much was achieved towards determining longitudes and establishing the solar parallax. He once displayed his enthusiasm for astronomy in the club where he was dining one clear starlit night with some other members. During the meal he pointed to the sky and remarked, 'Some day that star may run into the earth.'

'If it does,' replied one of his fellow diners, Hercules Langrishe, 'I hope to God we shall be on the starboard tack!'

Hercules Langrishe, later Sir Hercules, was an Irishman with a ready wit who was equally at home behind the wheel of a large cutter as he was at the helm of a small-keel boat. As a young man he had acted as the Squadron's representative aboard the American defender during Lord Dunraven's 1893 challenge in *Valkyrie II*. He won the Queen's Cup in 1890 in his 94-ton cutter *Samoena* and later sailed Lord Dunraven's *Cariad II* to her victories in the King's Cup.

After his victory in 1890 he sold his yacht and started racing 5-raters. His first was *Iernia*, which had been designed by Fife and built by Camper and Nicholson. She was not a success, so in 1892 he asked Charles E. Nicholson, then a young man of twenty-five, to design and build him another 5-rater, which he called *Dacia*. While *Dacia* was on the stocks, George L. Watson, at that time the most distinguished yacht designer in the country, came to visit the Camper and Nicholson yard. Tentatively, the young Nicholson suggested the master look at his new creation. Watson agreed and Nicholson took him into the shed. Watson studied the boat's lines in total silence while Nicholson held his breath. At last he turned and said, 'That'll be a verra fast boat, Charlie.'

In this Watson proved to be absolutely right, for although Nicholson knew he had designed a fast reaching boat he had no idea of her windward performance until he started racing her with Langrishe at the helm. When he did he knew he had built a champion yacht, for in six weeks her owner won fourteen firsts out of fourteen starts.

---

* *Three Voyages of a Naturlist*, by M. J. Nicoll, Witherby and Co., 1908.

Lord Dudley, who also crewed for Langrishe, was so amazed by her performance that he begged Langrishe to sell her to him. Langrishe agreed, and parted with her for twice what he had paid for her, £600. However, Dudley never did any good with her, which underlined Nicholson's adage that the secret of a successful boat is to get the right man to steer her.

Langrishe's wartime activities between 1914 and 1918 were as colourful as his yachting career, for he acted as a British agent in a neutral country. He wrote later about his adventures:

The schooner *Vergemere*, 496 tons, became my property in August 1915. She was given to me in Portsmouth Harbour. I borrowed a naval tug and towed her to Hythe and moored her there. Camper and Nicholson fitted her out in first-class style. The crew was the difficulty; I found it hard to get men to go to sea with an amateur, especially in war time. At last a skipper and crew were found and we proceeded to Corunna. My orders were to cruise about the north coast of Spain and do propaganda work. That was badly needed, for German influences were active and strong. I was supposed to be a rich Irish baronet. I liked the part and only hoped for the means to sustain it.

At Corunna I was kept for some time by invitations, which I reciprocated with interest. I was very much the white-headed boy. One day a Spanish naval officer came on board, very smart and speaking first-class English. He told me that I must take down my wireless, and he proceeded to seal up my little temporary wireless-officer's cabin on deck. Of course we cut a hole in the roof and used the set as before. All went well for a week, when another Spanish naval officer came on board to inspect. This knocked me sideways. Evidently he smelt a rat, for he asked me if I would give my word of honour not to use my wireless in territorial waters. Of course I did. . . .

A 14,000 ton German liner, the *Cap Ancona*, lay in the roads all the time. The German captain had done a lot of propaganda before I got there, and had been lavish. It was plainly my job to knock him out. This was becoming easy in a way, as the poor chap was getting a bit short of the ready. I found that to augment his purse he used to send three-quarters of his crew to work on shore. I noticed a dozen of them laying a tram line on the sea front. Some of them got very drunk and riotous, and were locked up in the state prison.

The German captain sent a valuable Bechstein piano to a musical firm at Corunna to be sold for him. I told the shopkeeper that I wanted a piano and gave him a good big tip to keep it for me. I would bet anything that the German skipper never got a penny for it. I saw it in the shop window a month later.

I had an account at a bank in Corunna. The manager was a friend of mine. I was longing to find out about the German's finances, but did not think it wise to ask a banker. I got my chance, however, in this way. I was entertaining the bank manager to luncheon on board the *Vergemere*. He did himself well, and having put away the best part of a bottle of wine, he asked if he could do any business for me. So I called a few days later and presented a cheque drawn to self for £100. He handed me the money with hardly a glance at the cheque. A few days afterwards he was with me in my launch cruising about near the German liner. We spotted the captain on board, and I laughingly asked the manager if he would cash a cheque on the captain's note of hand. He simply jeered at me and asked, 'What do you take me for?'

I am certain the German had me sized up all right. He tried many ways to trap me, but I was well guarded. The excitement was lovely. I laid a trap for him in the open country, but he did not fire a shot. Nor did I. I often think we were both cowards.

The last anecdote about Langrishe perhaps hides more than it reveals, but it does show what a great character he must have been. By the 1930s, Charles E. Nicholson's son John was working with his father. One day Langrishe turned up unannounced to look at his new Red-wing. John Nicholson recorded in a letter to a friend:

The great old rascal had a good look at his boat and chose her colour. He was going to use the gear from his old boat, and I escorted him back to his ropey old Ford V8 car. The stern-sheets were stuffed with gear including golf clubs and on the front passenger seat were a bottle of Scotch and a route guide scribbled on a large piece of Bristol board. That day, at well over 80, he had driven from Fishguard and, on saying good-bye he told me he was going on up to Claridges for the Squadron meeting next day. Some Man! I could tell you much more of this really wonderful old rascal!*

---

* Private letter to a Mr Henderson, dated 11 October 1967.

The club during this period was rich in explorers as well as in scientists and characters like Langrishe. Two of the most famous were Captain Scott and Ernest Shackleton. Scott came onto the list just before he left on his fateful expedition to the South Pole, and the White Ensign that flew on his ship was a present from the club.

Ernest Shackleton, later Sir Ernest, served under Scott before he began to command his own expeditions. His second was about to leave for the Antarctic in August 1914 when war broke out. He offered his ship and his men to the government, but was allowed to proceed. He lost his ship in the ice, made Elephant Island by sledge, and from there made a heroic 800-mile voyage in a 22-foot boat in search of a vessel that could rescue his companions. He died in 1922 at the early age of forty-eight.

Another member with a taste for exploring was Frank James, who came on to the list in 1888 with the 479-ton auxiliary schooner *Lancashire Witch*. With his two brothers, William – who also became a member, in 1891 – and Arthur, he roamed the world in her, but met a tragic end in 1890 while out hunting. With a party of friends he had taken his yacht out to the West Coast of Africa where he eventually anchored in the Gulf of Guinea. On 21 April he went ashore with four of his guests to celebrate his birthday with an elephant hunt. They shot and wounded a large bull, but on tracking it down the animal turned on them and charged. Frank was mortally wounded by one of its tusks and died later that day. His two brothers built a refuge for yacht hands at Cowes as a memorial to him. It later became a cottage hospital and continues to serve the local community.

Cruising during the late Victorian and Edwardian eras was, in fact, still closely allied to such pursuits as shooting or sightseeing, and was often incidental to them. But by the end of the century other pastimes began to encroach on the interest of members as a book by one of them, *With the Yacht, Camera, and Cycle in the Mediterranean* by the Earl of Cavan, illustrates well. However, the author was not, as might be supposed, a mere dilettante but had an early grasp of the advantages of photographs for coastal navigation.

'Admirable in every respect, as are the Admiralty charts,' he wrote in his preface, 'many of which contain sketches of lighthouses and head-lands, they cannot convey, distinctly to the navigator's mind, the exact appearance of the port he is about to visit. A photograph or picture of the place, as it appears in the offing, will supply the want.' The book, not surprisingly, sold several editions and the Earl wrote a sequel about eastern Mediterranean ports, but this time excluded his bicycle. He can be said to be a true precursor of a present member, Captain Denham, who is famous for his various Mediterranean pilot guides.

In 1907 the first International Rule came into effect and Sir James Pender, who had won the King's Cup in his 153-ton yawl *Brynhild* in 1902 and 1904, launched a 23-metre, *Brynhild II*. Despite winning the King's Cup in 1908 she was not as successful as the other 23-metre built the same year, *White Heather II*, which came on to the list in 1909 with her owner Myles Kennedy. The career of *Brynhild II* was cut short when, at the beginning of the 1909 season, her mast came out of its step during a race at Harwich. It went through her bottom and she sank immediately, luckily without loss of life.

As mentioned earlier, the Big Class never amounted to much once *Britannia* had stopped racing, and even when King George V started entering her in regattas from 1911 onwards matters did not improve much. But besides those already mentioned Cecil Whitaker was another member who helped at least to keep the Big Class in existence. He had contributed to the revival of the racing schooners earlier in the century by building *Cecily* and then *Waterwitch*, but when he could not make the latter yacht go any faster he ordered, in 1913, the schooner *Margherita* from Charles E. Nicholson. She proved to be one of Nicholson's most successful designs and when she was taken to the Kiel regatta that year, under the command of another member, Colonel Barklie McCalmont, she won every race but one.

Although the 23-Metre Class was never successful prior to the Second World War, some of the smaller metre classes had several seasons of competitive racing. Only two members competed in these classes. Almeric Paget, later Lord Queenborough, who came on the list in 1910, built a 15-metre, *Ma'oona*, and raced against the King of Spain's 15-metre *Hispania*, which, during the inter-war period was owned by a present member, Patrick Egan. Then the following year he built a 19-metre, *Corona*.

George Coats, who came on the list in 1909, built a 12-metre, and was the first member to own one, and in 1912 he built a 15-metre, *The Lady Ann*, but the flowering of the international class did not really occur until the 1920s.

It has not been necessary to dwell on the social side of the club in this chapter. With the Prince of Wales as its Commodore, and then its Admiral, it reached a zenith in exclusivity which, perhaps thankfully, it has never surpassed. Membersip rose steadily year by year until in 1914 it numbered 246. How it stood in the eyes of other yachtsmen is neatly summed up by the Comte Camille de Renesse, who visited Cowes in the yacht *Intrepid* in 1899.

'*Le Club de Cowes,*' he wrote a friend, '*ou plus régulièrement le Royal-Yacht-Squadron, est le club le plus select, le plus aristocratique, le plus ferme, le plus intransigeant, non seulement d'Angleterre, mais du monde entier.*'

But it can fairly be said that the Squadron was not alone in being cocooned in the security of the Edwardian era; and when, like other rather ossified corners of society, it was blown apart by the confrontation with Germany, it rose to the challenge and responded by contributing to the war effort in a quite outstanding way.

*

On Thursday, 30 July 1914, the Home Fleet left Portland under sealed orders and the following day the club's Commodore, Lord Ormonde, received a telegram from the King regretting that he would not be able to be present for the regatta, due to start on the following Monday.

Outwardly, however, everything appeared normal, for that night, Friday, Admiral von Eisendecher and the Kaiser's brother, Prince Henry, both honorary members, arrived to stay with the Commodore. It was not until the Saturday, when members began to assemble for the regatta, that it became apparent that war could be imminent. A letter was dispatched to ascertain whether the King thought the regatta should be postponed and the reply advised that he thought it should be. By then both von Eisendecher and Prince Henry had left Cowes.

By Sunday afternoon the decision had been taken to cancel the regatta. By this time it was known that Active and Reserve officers of the Armed Forces were being recalled. Two hundred men from the crews of the yachts had already received their orders and crossed to Portsmouth that afternoon.

When war was declared on the Tuesday, the Kaiser's *Meteor* and Frau von Krupp's *Germania* were still at sea, having left Germany to take part in the regatta the previous week. *Meteor* was being towed by a German destroyer and she managed to escape, but *Germania* was captured and taken to Southampton.

It was immediately realized that some form of patrol service was needed around the coast of the British Isles. Lord Ormonde and the club's Vice-Commodore, the Duke of Leeds, were therefore summoned to the Admiralty and asked about the capabilities of some of the club's larger steam yachts to carry guns.

As a consequence of this meeting several members began to sit on various Admiralty committees and some of them were later commissioned to command yachts. A number of club yachts were also chartered by the Admiralty, armed, and became the nucleus of what was known initially as the Yacht Patrol. The idea of the patrol came from one of the club's Naval Members, Vice-Admiral Sir Arthur Farquhar, and it was initially put under the command of Captain E. C. Carver RN.

There were a number of club volunteers for the Yacht Patrol and a few were given temporary commissions as RNR officers. However, this practice was soon discontinued when it was pointed out to the Admiralty that there would be no defence in law if an accident occurred to an HM ship commanded by an unqualified master.

Early volunteers included the Duke of Leeds, the Duke of Sutherland, A. W. Fulcher and A. Reynell-Pack. Although then aged fifty-three, the Duke of Leeds was commissioned into the RNR and commanded his own yacht *Aries* for a year in the North Sea before being transferred to other service. The Duke of Sutherland became a commander RNR in command of his yacht, while A. W. Fulcher was given command of the 44-ton steam yacht *Hersilia*, owned by another member, Sir Walpole Greenwell. He was sent on patrol in the Stornoway area, but after a winter in Scottish waters his health broke down and he had to give up his command. A. Reynell-Pack was given command of the 172-ton steam yacht *Oriana*, and as he was a master mariner he was allowed to continue in his appointment. He was given the rank of temporary lieutenant-commander and commanded his small vessel off the west coast of Scotland for the rest of the war.

Harold Swithinbank, who had come onto the list in 1912, also held a master's certificate. This enabled him to retain command of his own yacht, the 568-ton steam yacht *Venetia*, which served first in the Orkney Islands area and then in the Falmouth area, where she saw quite a bit of action.

Another member who was active in the Auxiliary Patrol was Captain Alwyn Foster, who was elected in 1918 and who joined the Yacht Patrol in command of his 265-ton steam yacht *Calista* the month after war broke out. *Calista* struck a mine in the Irish Sea in December 1917 and went down with the loss of all hands, but by then Captain Foster had relinquished his command of her.

In October 1914 the Yacht Patrol, still an embryo organization, was put under the command of Captain H. S. Lecky, CB, AM, RN, who was told to expand it as quickly as he could. When he asked what kind of ships he was to take into the Patrol, he was told to 'take up anything seaworthy that has not got a hole in its bottom'. And when he inquired as to where he was to find crews for his vessels, the answer was to pick them up from 'under the lampposts' if necessary.

The normal sources for trained crews were unhelpful and Lecky had to find his officers and men where he could. 'We were looking for men with a disciplined mind but with a piratical outlook,' Lecky commented after the war. Often suitable members of the original crews stayed on, especially the yachts' engineers, but if there were not enough of these, competent men from fishing boats, small coasters and other yachts were found. Officers also came from the yachts' original masters and mates, and where there was a shortfall properly certified Merchant Navy officers were acquired.

The Admiralty had the power to requisition yachts, but mostly they were handed over voluntarily. Not all members, however, agreed with the Admiralty's idea of arming a yacht, as a letter from Mr Alfred Farquhar, the owner of the 627-ton steam yacht *Medusa*, makes abundantly clear.

'Dear Pasley,' he wrote to the Secretary of the Squadron committee on 3 September 1914, 'I have a letter from the Admiralty (marked "secret", but of course you know all about it) which I suppose requires an answer about this arming question. What is any other yacht [owner] doing about it? As you know, arming a yacht of the size of *Medusa* which steams only 11 knots or so, seems to me the most lunatic idea I have ever heard of in my life.'

Further letters from Farquhar during the next few months show that he would be only too delighted if *Medusa* were used as a hospital ship 'for which she is well equipped', and that although he had reservations about the Admiralty charter terms he had no intention of making a profit out of the emergency. What he did object to, as did several owners, was the arming of yachts which appeared quite unsuitable for use as warships, to say nothing of the damage to them that might ensue.

Most owners acquiesced but at the beginning of 1915, according to Pasley, both the Duke of Bedford's *Sapphire* and Lord Leith's *Miranda* were requisitioned. By that time *Medusa* had been taken into service as some kind of hospital auxiliary, but the Admiralty kept pressing for her to join the Yacht Patrol. At the beginning of February 1915 Farquhar was still arguing with them about this. It was an argument which he lost for, as will be seen, *Medusa* served very successfully with the Auxiliary Patrol in several areas and survived the war in one piece. She even went on to serve in the Second World War.

At first the Admiralty charter rates for yachts joining the Auxiliary Patrol were fixed very much in the favour of the owners. Yachts were chartered for only 1 shilling a month for the first three months, but then the rate shot up to £1 per Thames Measurement ton per month. Lecky regarded this as uneconomic from the government's point of view. Charter contracts were renegotiated so that owners were paid 10 per cent of the agreed value of the yacht in rental and were relieved of all overheads. The agreed value of the yacht was paid if she was lost and the Admiralty paid for the cost of a refit at the end of her service if she was not.

Once an owner had been approached and had agreed to chartering to the Admiralty for the duration of the war, his yacht was taken to a naval dockyard – in nearly every case this was Portsmouth – and was fitted out for service. All valuable fittings were stripped out and replaced by naval ones, guns were mounted, decks strengthened, magazines created, wirelesses fitted and the hulls painted grey. Captain Lecky wrote later:

> As soon as the yachts were completed, they were despatched to their various bases and began duty at once. . . . There is very little that is delicate about the best yachts, except their appearance. Most of them are beautifully constructed to Lloyds class, have good sea-keeping speed, are fine sea boats and are excellent examples of naval architecture. . . . They carried their guns well above the water, were comfortable to live in, and afforded moral as well as material support, not only to the small types

with which they worked, but to the more nervous-minded of the populace in their neighbourhood.*

Each area had a number of units, each of which was headed by a yacht with perhaps six trawlers or drifters and a couple of motor launches under it. The motor launches were later dispensed with as they were insufficiently seaworthy. But the yachts and the fishing boats, which were used for minesweeping or for netlaying to enmesh enemy U-boats, were extremely effective in harassing German submarines which came within their range. On one occasion the Commander-in-Chief of the Grand Fleet stated that without the Auxiliary Patrol the Grand Fleet could not have gone to sea, and at the end of the war an Admiralty memorandum stated that 'This new Navy of small craft, created by the special needs of the War, has proved the vitality of the British instinct for the sea.'

Details of the thirty-seven club yachts which served in the Auxiliary Patrol, and the actions in which they took part, are in Appendix 1, but mention should be made of several other club vessels which served in other capacities. The 116-ton auxiliary schooner *Lisette*, for instance, was used as a 'Q' ship, a decoy for enemy submarines. She was owned by Eric Chaplin and was commanded later in the war by a future member, Commander F. F. Tower. *Czarina*, belonging to Albert Brassey, had a less glamorous role for she became a commercial vessel but was unfortunately torpedoed in the Bay of Biscay and sank.

Cecilia was another club yacht which never joined the Auxiliary Patrol. Owned by Sir Charles Wyndham Murray, she was a 188-ton steam yacht, built in 1890. According to the club's second historian, J. B. Atkins, she was for a time on patrol in connexion with the transportation of the Expeditionary Force, and her owner later in the war used her for taking out parties of convalescent soldiers from Netley.

Four other yachts belonging to members also served the wounded as hospital ships. Three of them continued to be commanded by their owners as they all held a master's certificate. The fourth, the 679-ton steam yacht *Sheelah*, was owned by Rear-Admiral David Beatty, who had bigger and more important ships to command.

---

* From a lecture by Captain Lecky reproduced in the February 1933 issue of *The Royal United Service Institute Journal*.

Lord Tredegar's 1571-ton *Liberty*, which had been built in 1908, was the largest yacht in the club at that time; she was mostly used as a hospital ship, although in 1916 she was turned into an armed yacht and used as the headquarters of Lord Rawlinson and his staff. Lord Rawlinson was planning an amphibious landing on the Belgian coast behind German lines, but the plan never materialized.

Lord Dunraven was another who was able to retain command of his own yacht. He was willingly drawn into war service when Lady Dudley telephoned him in August 1914, told him she had organized an Australian Voluntary Hospital, but that she had no transport. Lord Dunraven had his cruising yacht *Cariad*, but she was both unsuitable and too small. So he promptly chartered a steam yacht called *Greta*.

Greta, however, did not prove wholly suitable, so Lord Dunraven bought the 439-ton steam yacht *Grianaig* from the Duchess of Westminster and had her fitted out at his own expense. In October 1914 she was appropriated by the Admiralty as a hospital transport carrier, no. E2806, the smallest in the service. Lord Dunraven was made a commander RNVR and was directed to wear the Blue Ensign as a naval transport ship while he plied between Southampton or Dover and Le Havre, Boulogne and Dunkirk, bringing back the wounded. In May 1915 he was ordered to Malta with hospital supplies and later helped to evacuate the wounded from Gallipoli.

Grianaig stayed in the Mediterranean until 1916, when she returned home and was used for taking convalescent officers on Solent cruises. Although useful, Lord Dunraven found the work dull and in July 1918 he contrived to have *Grianaig* armed and attached as a hospital ambulance to the Harwich force. His work was much appreciated there, although he states in his autobiography that he was disappointed not to see more active service. At that time he was seventy-six years of age!*

Another famous member who also retained command of his yacht when she became a hospital ship was Lord Brassey. *Sunbeam* was first used to take out hospital supplies to Rouen and returned with wounded men. Then, in the summer of 1915, she was properly fitted out as a hospital ship and J. R. Carter, the one-time professional skipper of the King's *Britannia*, became her master. However, Lord Brassey remained on board and despite describing his 'rating' as 'idler' no doubt helped

---

* *Past Times and Pastimes* by the Earl of Dunraven, 2 vols, Hodder and Stoughton Ltd., 1922.

Carter in his duties when *Sunbeam* was sent to the Mediterranean. She was employed in the Mediterranean for a year before being sailed to India where Lord Brassey lent her to the Royal Indian Navy for use as a hospital ship.

*

The war brought the functions of the club to a virtual halt. Within three weeks of the start of hostilities the Castle was put at the disposal of convalescent naval officers and four bedrooms were put aside for their use.

In May 1915 a rule was introduced that 'Members or honorary members whose nationality is of a country with which Great Britain is at war shall, *ipso facto*, cease to be members or honorary members of the club.' This meant that the names of the Kaiser, his brother, Prince Henry, Prince Ibrahim Pasha, Baron von Eckhardstein, Admiral von Eisendecker and Vice-Admiral E. Gulich were erased from the list.

At a YRA meeting after the war it was agreed, under the chairmanship of Sir Philip Hunloke, that no British yachtsman should race against German or Austrian nationals for ten years. This ban, however, was lifted after a series of treaties had been signed at Locarno in 1925.

An event which was to have a much more lasting affect on Squadron members was the negotiation of the purchase of the Castle from the Crown. In 1914 the club's thirty-one year lease was nearing its end. A new one was fixed, and this was accepted at the May meeting when suggestions for improving and enlarging the Castle were also discussed. These plans were shelved when the war started, but towards the end of 1916 Major Oswald Magniac found that it might be possible to purchase the Castle and its grounds. At a general meeting in December of that year it was decided to try to negotiate a sale with the Crown. An offer of £6000 was eventually made and accepted.

An appeal to members was now made for this sum and so enthusiastic was the response that £8036 5s was soon raised, and by August 1917 the deal had been completed. It was then agreed that the excess should be held in reserve for the rebuilding programme decided upon in 1914, although this could not be started until the war ended.

Another matter of equal importance to the club's future was also raised during the war, although not settled finally until many years later. At the general meeting in May 1917 it was pointed out that the

96

A regatta off Cowes with naval cutters. It was painted in 1776 by Dominic Serres
RA. Serres was a founder member of the Royal Academy and marine painter to
King George III (*RYS collection*)

A Trinity House regatta at Cowes in 1794 by Joseph Farington RA. The painting is framed in oak from the Royal yacht *Royal George* (*RYS collection*)

Lord Craven's *Louisa* (325 tons) in company with *HMS Wasp* off Saint Honorat, 3 May 1818, by Antoine Roux of Marseille. Lord Craven was the first member, in 1816, to cruise to the Mediterranean (*RYS collection*)

The Club regatta at Cowes painted by J.W.M. Turner when staying in
August 1827 with John Nash (*Tate Gallery*)

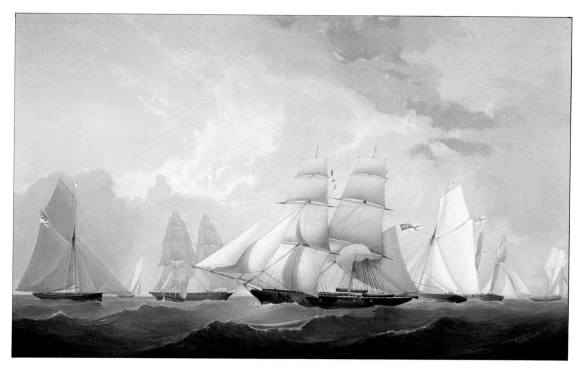

Above The five yachts owned by Lord Belfast, between 1825 and 1834: *Therese* (121 tons), *Harriet* (96 tons), *Louisa* (139 tons), *Emily* (33 tons) and *Waterwitch* (331 tons). It was painted by William John Huggins (*RYS collection*)

Left, above The Royal yacht, *Royal George* (330 tons), visiting Cowes in 1831 with King William IV aboard. The painting was executed by the King's marine painter, William John Huggins, and presented by Huggins to the Club's Vice-Commodore, Lord Belfast (*RYS collection*)

Left, below The Commodore's *Falcon* (351 tons), with Lord Yarborough aboard, at the assembly of Club yachts near the Warner Buoy off Spithead on their rally to Cherbourg in September 1831. Painted by William John Huggins (*RYS collection*)

Mr Joseph Weld's *Alarm* (193 tons), having taken on board a pilot at Plymouth. Mr
William Forster is the young man.
Painted by Nicholas Condy about 1846
(*National Maritime Museum*)

The cutter *Louisa* (132 tons) flying the flag of Lord Belfast as she finishes a race in
1832. Painted by William John Huggins (*RYS collection*)

A view off Castle Point with Squadron yachts, including *Brilliant* (393 tons), *Fairy* (143 tons), and *Flirt* (132 tons). Painted by John Lynn, 1843 (*RYS collection*)

The brigantine *Kestrel* (202 tons), with flags at half-mast, leaving Vigo with the body of her owner, Lord Yarborough, first Commodore of the Squadron. Painted by T.S. Robins, 1846 (*Captain Hammick's collection*)

The schooner *America* (170 tons) off Cowes, 1851, with numerous other yachts.
The innovative design of her sails was one reason for her success. Painted by T.S.
Robins (*RYS collection*)

A view of Cowes in 1852, with yachts in a calm sea and light airs off Castle Point,
the yacht *America* in the background. Painted by John Christian Schetky, marine
painter to King George IV, King William IV, and Queen Victoria – and to the
Squadron (*RYS collection*)

The schooner *Erminia* (276 tons) running past the Castle. Painted about 1880 by
Charles Gregory, the artist father of marine artist George Gregory
(*RYS collection*)

A view of the Squadron castle with yachts, signed by a Japanese artist yet to be
identified (*RYS collection*)

A watercolour by Charles Dixon of the splendid scene in Cowes Roads, 1899, with
the Earl of Crawford's *Valhalla* (1490 tons). It was the golden age of yachting
(*RYS collection*)

Above The French impressionist painter Raoul Dufy visited Cowes in 1936, made sketches, and later painted from them and from memory in his studio in Paris. This is 'Interior of the Yacht Club, Cowes' (*H.N. Abrams, New York, collection*)

Above left This painting of the Royal yacht *Britannia* racing in the Solent in 1921 was executed by Norman Wilkinson. It was bought by yachtsmen and presented to King George V during Cowes Week, 1923. *Britannia* competed in 569 races between 1893 and 1935, and was one of the most successful racing yachts ever built (*On loan from HM the Queen to the RYS*)

Left A view from the lawn during Cowes Week, 1923, by Paul Maze, the French artist who served with distinction in the British army during the First World War (*Lord Camrose's collection*)

The Rt. Hon. Edward Heath rose quickly to fame as an ocean racing yachtsman with his yachts named *Morning Cloud.* He won the Sydney-Hobart race in 1969 with the first one, and captained the British team which regained the Admiral's Cup in the second one, painted here by Deryck Foster (*Edward Heath collection*)

A view of Redwings racing during Cowes Week, by Richard Eurich RA,
noted for his wartime paintings of marine scenes (*Sebastian de Ferranti collection*)

A painting commissioned from David Cobb representing Squadron activities
during the commodoreship of Lord Cathcart, 1974-80. A club rally; ocean racers;
keelboats; a Seawanhaka Cup race; and the Naval Review, 1977
(*RYS collection*)

The Squadron start line has been used for well over a century and has become internationally renowned. Peter Leath painted this picture, which is of Captain Michael Boyle's Daring Class *Dauntless,* whose part owners were Peter Vanneck and Peter Nutting (*Captain Boyle collection*)

membership numbered only 198, some fifty less than in 1911. To counter this fall Sir Richard Williams-Bulkeley proposed a temporary suspension of Rule 1, which stated that the qualification for membership was the ownership of a British yacht of 30 tons or more. His proposal was firmly rejected, but, after a year's reflection, it was equally firmly accepted, although in a slightly different form.

Rule 1A was formulated whereby after scrutiny by a committee of selection a candidate without a yacht of 30 tons could be proposed for membership. Seventeen members were elected under this new rule, but then, in 1919, a motion to rescind it was carried by a majority of five. There the matter stood until a special meeting in 1922 at which Sir Richard Williams-Bulkeley, now the Vice-Commodore, reiterated that unless the continuing fall in membership was reversed the club would soon be in financial trouble. He therefore proposed that Rule 1A should be reinstated. After some discussion this was agreed with the proviso that the rule stay in force 'until the membership of the club reached the number of 250'.

Admiral Bridgeman then pointed out that Rule 1A did not encompass those who did not own a yacht nor had shown an active interest in yachting, but wanted to join the club in order to take up the sport. The Duke of Leeds, who was now the Commodore, disagreed. 'I think what the members of the Squadron want to see is young men taking to yachting for the love of yachting,' he said, 'and then they will be welcomed to the Squadron with open arms. It seems to me to be reversing the position to elect them members of the club first, and then to get them to take to yachting afterwards,' a statement which very much reflects the feeling of the Squadron today.

It was also decided to lower the size of yacht owned by a candidate seeking election under Rule 1 from 30 tons to 15, but it was not until 1923 that the White Ensign could be flown on vessels of this tonnage.*

In May 1926 Rule 1A was again rescinded, before being finally restored in May 1932 with the amendment that it stay in force until the membership had reached 275. Although it did not reach this figure until 1960, the decline in membership was finally reversed so that by 1938 there were 253 members who owned between them 24,187 tons.

---

* Nowadays the White Ensign may only be flown on yachts of 7 tons or more, or which exceed 30 feet overall.

CHAPTER FIVE

1919-48

The slow revival of big class yachting. The start and growth of ocean racing. Challenges for the America's Cup. Members as Olympic medallists. Worldwide cruising continues. The Second World War. The use of members' yachts and the Castle as of 'national utility'. The postwar start-up in the smaller classes

I F THE MATTER of membership took time to resolve, the problem of the ladies' annexe was almost as protracted and its eventual solution must go down as the most bizarre incident in the club's domestic history.

As has been mentioned, it had been decided, just prior to the outbreak of war, that the Castle should be improved and enlarged, and these proposed alterations included a 'ladies' cloakroom'. Women, of course, had been engaged in yachting for as long as men. Some of them were brilliant helmsmen, and there was nothing unusual, even before the turn of the century, in seeing a woman at the helm of a keel boat in the Solent. In the 1908 Olympics, the wife of a member, the Duchess of Westminster, won a bronze medal in the 8-Metre Class; while in recent times Sir Max Aitken's wife and daughter, both lady members, have taken part with great success in a number of powerboat races, something unique in the Squadron's history.

The Squadron, however, had been founded by men for men and until quite late in the day women were not allowed inside the Castle. There were, it seems, restrictions too on them being allowed on the Platform. They were, however, always given access to the lawn, although a member's remark in 1907 that 'these damned women have no respect for the Squadron', on hearing that the Countess of Cardigan had collapsed and died on the lawn, indicates that this privilege was perhaps not universally popular.

In prewar days there had, of course, been unwritten rules about the standard of dress. But the war had brought about an emancipation in such matters just as it had in other spheres and by the early 1920s it was noted with distress by some members that lady guests were beginning to appear on the lawn unsuitably attired. So, in 1924, ladies were banned from wearing shorts or trousers on the lawn, and when Lady Hinchingbrooke appeared there in 1937 in bright blue slacks there was an immediate uproar and she was asked to leave.

A major influence in keeping such rigorous rules was King George V. He was a stickler for correct dress as a letter from the Commodore to King George VI's private secretary reveals when inquiring in 1938 whether the King would object if the dress rule be relaxed. 'Some four or five years ago King George V, on landing at the Squadron, took me aside and pointed out some pictures in one of the daily papers of certain ladies wearing trousers, and he told me then that he hoped they would not be allowed into the garden in that rig, and that if they did come in, he would not come to the club.'*

The King readily assented that the rule should be relaxed to allow ladies to wear trousers on the lawn except during regatta week, and from 1939 onwards ladies were also allowed to lunch or dine in the club, except during regatta week. From 1953 the wife of a member was allowed to stay at the Castle with her husband; and in 1964 the Castle was extended to provide every amenity for women guests, which included changing rooms and a ladies' dining room. Finally, in 1969, the club introduced a Lady Associate Membership with two of its members being soon coopted on to the House Committee.

But in the 1920s if a member's wife had been sailing with her husband there was nowhere for her to change. This must have posed a problem even before the war, and the emancipation which was one of its consequences made a solution even more urgent.

Despite the increasing need for somewhere for ladies to change the

---

* From a letter in the Royal Archives, Windsor (RA GVI PS 1928), dated 13 August 1938. Reprinted by the gracious permission of Her Majesty the Queen.

necessary alterations had still not been carried out in 1924 when the committee heard that Castle Rock, a substantial house situated directly behind the Castle, was for sale. This must have seemed an ideal solution to the problem: a ladies' annexe close to but not actually in the Castle.

In July the club was given a fortnight's option to buy at £5000. The club made an offer which was then increased, and which was then accepted. Then, to the committee's chagrin, it heard that a higher offer had been made. A counter-bid was made but on 13 September 1926 the committee was told that, in modern parlance, it had been 'gazumped' by an unknown buyer.

It was soon revealed that the purchaser of Castle Rock was none other than Rosa Lewis, friend of King Edward VII, owner of the raffish Cavendish Hotel, and the model for Lottie Crump in Evelyn Waugh's novel, *Vile Bodies*.

Quite why Rosa chose to pay above the odds for Castle Rock will never be known, but, as the committee was soon to find out, she was an unpredictable lady who was inclined to act on the spur of the moment. She was certainly pleased with her new property – 'my little place at Cowes', she used to call it – and would fill the place with as diverse a gregarious bunch of guests as were attracted to the Cavendish Hotel.

Some of these guests were Squadron members who had known Rosa in her youth – she had been a great beauty – and who liked the jollity, the numerous pretty girls, and the chance of a quiet game of roulette in a back room.

But other members, and in particular the committee who had to deal with her eccentric business methods, found her impossible. Rosa knew the reason why the Squadron needed Castle Rock so badly and let it be known that she would be willing to rent, or sell, to the club a small and somewhat dilapidated ballroom at the bottom of her garden for use as a ladies' annexe. 'While they won't 'ave me on their old lawn,' she complained later when her relationship with the committee had soured, 'I 'ave to let their lady friends into my garden to piddle.'

But at first Rosa appeared perfectly amenable, although previously unpublished correspondence reveals that as early as July 1925 the club's lawyer was finding the negotiations heavy going. 'Mrs Lewis is evidently an extraordinary person,' he wrote the Secretary, Mr Pasley, on the 6th, '. . . I am afraid her views are impossible. On Friday and Saturday when I was away she was telephoning wildly both here and at my house and I think perhaps the best way is to leave her alone.'

The committee, however, insisted that he did not, and while the tortuous negotiations were proceeding quotes were being obtained for carrying out the improvements to the Castle first mooted before the war. To the committee's consternation it was found that inflation had struck and the money that had been earmarked for the ladies' annexe in the Castle was hopelessly inadequate to cover the costs. What had seemed a less desirable, but still possible, alternative to continuing to negotiate with Rosa now became no alternative at all.

With the pressure now really on, the Vice-Commodore wrote to the club's solicitor and told him to make an offer of £3000 for the ballroom, only £500 less than Rosa's figure. Rosa agreed with alacrity but later changed her mind, suggesting instead that the club pay a rental for the ballroom equivalent to the interest that would have accrued on the amount they were offering. Her tone was amiable – 'Everything possible shall be done to make you secure, but I do not think there is any necessity for having heavy lawyer's expenses and that kind of thing. I think a little amiable talking would be sufficient.'

Amiable talking no doubt took place. But again negotiations were protracted and it was not until 13 February 1926 that Mr Pasley, who seemed to get on with Rosa very well, was able to get her to sign her agreement to a letter he had sent her which included what they had verbally agreed: a rent of £250 a year and an option to buy at £3000.

The following year negotiations began all over again after Sir William Portal, a strong advocate for buying the ballroom, had managed to raise, through special subscription amongst members, most of the necessary money.

In September 1927 the club's solicitor reported that he had just seen Rosa and had found her 'in a very agreeable mood'. So much so that 'she expressed the wish and intention of giving the property to the Squadron by her will', and added, rather primly, that 'this would not of course meet the case'. He felt certain the Squadron would succeed in its purchase of the ballroom but advised the committee not to rush the matter, an opinion the committee doubtless received with some irritation as it had by now been trying to get its hands on the place for over three years.

The committee must have been doubly irritated when it eventually became obvious that Rosa did not want to sell – at least, not then. In January 1928 she wrote to the club's solicitor that, 'The members of the

Squadron or most of them are my friends, and have been my friends, and I have worked for most of them, but my lawyers know that I have had good offers and could have sold the ballroom for any price or let it at a very good rental just after I bought it, but I want it to belong to the Squadron and that is why I said they should always have the first option of renting it if I never sold it to them.'

This was followed shortly afterwards by a letter from Rosa's solicitors which stated that Rosa did not want to sell, but that she would rent the ballroom for £200 per annum on a seven- or fourteen-year lease provided no alteration were made to the ballroom that would affect the view from Castle Rock.

But still there was no final arrangement and at the May meeting the patience of members ran out and the club's solicitor was instructed to enforce purchase.

Rosa now dug in her heels and insisted she would not sell unless there was a restriction on the Squadron increasing the height of the ballroom. Naturally, the club's solicitor advised that the purchase must go through without any restrictions. She also started haggling about the furniture and demanded to remove the mantelpiece over the fire! Then on 17 July 1928 she finally signed.

This more or less ended the matter except that when it became necessary to rebuild the ballroom in 1934 Rosa complained that its height had been increased and blocked her view, which was not true, as can be still seen today.

But even when roused, Rosa's letters were always conciliatory and there was no sign at any time that she was carrying out a kind of vendetta against the club, as some writers have suggested. She had a large heart and a generous spirit, and her presence at Cowes, although it may have embarrassed a few, greatly added to the gaiety of Cowes in the inter-war years. When she finally sold Castle Rock* after the Second World War she said to a friend 'The fun's all over, m'dear. We won't none of us see no more of that sort of thing. The war's put paid to that little lark.'

If the Second World War put an end to the kind of life Rosa enjoyed, the first very nearly put an end to racing in the Big Class and, perhaps, to yachting altogether, for Cowes during that first summer of peace was a mere shadow of its former self. One witness wrote:

---

* It became a clubhouse for the Royal Corinthian Yacht Club.

There was no Royal yacht or guard ship and not a steam yacht to be seen. But the White Ensign flew once more at the Squadron flagstaff and the basket chairs stood in rows on the lawn under the shade of the elm trees, although there were no kings, princes or ambassadors to occupy them, only a handful of elderly gentlemen and their ladies whispering together shaking their heads and regretting the past. There were no holiday crowds on the esplanade or the green – just a few old people making the most of the August sunshine and staring rather sadly at the empty roadstead. That summer – 1919 – the pessimists gloomily declared that the sport of yacht racing was as dead as a Dodo.*

Although there was no regatta that summer some races were held. These included one for yachts between 25 and 50 tons, one for yachts between 10 and 25 tons, one for Solent One-Designs, and one for the Redwing keel boats from Bembridge which had long been a favourite with members.

But the re-establishment of regatta racing in Britain really came about because King George V decided early in 1920 that he would fit out *Britannia* for the coming season. Immediately it was known that he was going to do so others followed suit. Without his encouragement, it is extremely doubtful whether the Big Class would ever have sailed again.

The same year the International Yacht Racing Union, formed in 1907 to manage the first International Rule, was also resurrected; and as the first Rule had lapsed a new one was formulated which, it was agreed, would run for six years, from 1 January 1920.

The Big Class took some years to reach its zenith, and it was regatta racing amongst the smaller International classes, encouraged by the new Rule, that held the most interest in the years immediately following the Armistice and exemplified the increasing popularity of the smaller keel boats.

The British–American Cup, for instance, was started in 1921 and the following year the Seawanhaka Cup was revived. The Seawanhaka Cup was match racing between single boats, at first in 6 metres; while the British–American Cup was competed for by British and American teams each consisting of four 6-metres.

In the first series for the British–American Cup racing took place

---

* *Sacred Cowes* by Anthony Heckstall-Smith, Anthony Blond Ltd., 1965.

every year, alternating between Britain and the United States, the first team to win twice in succession to win the cup. This was achieved by the British team, which won at Cowes in 1923 and Long Island Sound in 1924. A second series was started in 1928 but took place every two years. Britain won on the Clyde in 1928 but the Americans won the second trophy with wins in 1930 and 1932.

The third series started in 1934, the rules providing that the team gaining 'four victories not necessarily consecutive shall gain absolute possession of the Cup'. The Americans won in 1934, 1936 and 1938, and when the series resumed after the war, they won the cup outright when they raced against the British in the Solent in 1949.

A fourth series, this time for a perpetual trophy, was then started in 1951 under the same conditions as the previous one. The Americans won in 1951, 1953 and 1955, but there was then a long gap and the fourth match was not raced until 1974. This was raced in Solings on the Clyde and was won by the Scottish team who then proceeded to draw the next two meetings, in 1976 and 1978, before finally losing to the Americans in 1980. A new match, in which The Royal Yacht Squadron will participate, is likely to take place in 1986.

When the British–American Cup was introduced in 1921 the Americans had never built any 6-metres, and the British had never built any to the new Rule. The idea behind the races was to try to bring racing on both sides of the Atlantic under one rule and the series was not only significant for the fact that it introduced team racing into the sport of yachting but that it induced the Americans to build to the International Rule which they eventually came to embrace.

The first races in 1921 took place during Cowes regatta week with Sir John Ward's *Jean* representing the Squadron. But the most outstanding exponent of this type of racing was Sir Ralph Gore who had come onto the list in 1913. He was a member of the British team no less than four times, and when the races were held for the first time on the Clyde in 1928 he won three firsts and one second out of four races in his 6-metre *Naushabah*, a record which was never equalled in the history of the series.

Another top-flight 6-metre helmsman was a present member, Sir Kenneth Preston, the son of Sir Walter Preston. In 1923 the young Preston was given the black-hulled 19-metre *Paula III* as a wedding present and spent, with the professional Edward Sycamore as his skipper, two seasons racing her on the regatta circuit. Sycamore, he says, taught him the finer points of racing. On one memorable occasion, when the wind was very light and the Big Class and the Second Class had been combined into one race, he beat *Britannia*, not just on handicap, but boat for boat, and won £100, 'a hell of a lot of money in those days'.

After the race Hunloke, who had proposed Preston for the club, came over to see him. 'You little black thief,' was his first comment, and from then on *Paula III* was known as the 'little black thief'. Sadly, in 1925 she broke her back in a storm off Ramsgate when Sycamore was bringing her round from Harwich to Cowes, and it was then that Preston turned to racing 6-metres. He bought his first, *Echo*, from Sir Ralph Gore and raced her for two seasons before going to William Fife to design him a new boat which he called *Prudence*. She was so successful that she was chosen to race in the British team for the British–American Cup in 1930 which was being raced for that year in Long Island Sound.

After *Prudence* had beaten the Baron Philippe de Rothschild's 6-metre in every Solent race in 1931, Preston sold her to him and started to share one of the increasingly popular 8-Metre Class, *Saskia*, with another Squadron member, Robert Steele. He was equally successful with her and, at short notice, was chosen to represent Britain in the 1936 Olympics* 8-Metre Class, and managed, despite having a scratch crew, to finish sixth. He continued to race her right up to the war, and after it sold her to the Australian Olympic helmsman, Bill Northam.

Postwar Preston took to racing 6-metres again. In 1949, at the helm of *Thistle*, he raced in the revived British–American Cup series and was captain of the British team. Then he built his own 6-metre, *Titia*, and took part with her in the 1953 British–American Cup series.†

Another enthusiastic racing man in the smaller keel boats was Colonel Moore-Brabazon, later Lord Brabazon of Tara. He did not rate himself very highly as a helmsman, ranking himself as the equivalent of a golfer with a handicap of eight, fair but not first rate. However, what

---

* It was at these Olympics that a future member, Christopher Boardman, won a gold medal in the 6-Metre Class in *Lalage*.

† Other members who raced 6-metres in the British–American Cup postwar were Lieutenant-Colonel J. E. Harrison, who represented Britain in the series in 1951, 1953 and 1955, Sir Charles Taylor, Air Commodore Quinnell, and a present member, Michael Crean, who raced in a Royal Thames Yacht Club 6-metre.

he lacked in skill on the water he certainly made up for in inventiveness. He owned a Redwing which he sailed at Bembridge and Cowes. These had standard hulls, but any rig was allowed provided it did not exceed 200 square feet. As one of the foremost aeronautical experts of his age, this presented something of a challenge to Moore-Brabazon, for he approached the problem of improving his boat's speed purely from an aeronautical point of view, having always believed that ordinary rigs had long since been outdated.

He first of all tried a streamlined mast with one sail before trying two masts with one sail between them. He then devised a rig with a gaff which he could control from the helm and later tried the Lungstrom rig, and finally a Flettner rotating cylinder 'mast' As someone remarked rather testily, he was always bringing down some new mechanical toy which invariably failed. But his most remarkable experiment was yet to come.

He had long cherished the idea of fitting an autogyro to his Redwing as this seemed on the face of it the most efficient way of making use of the wind. He approached an engineer who helped him with the design of a suitable mechanism which used only 35 square feet of surface against the 200 allowed under the class rules. It was, he thought, the only boat ever to be sailed without either sheets or shrouds of any kind – and although he later added a sheet to control the boom he stated it was not really necessary.

The experiment worked well at first, though great care had to be taken that the crewman's head was not chopped off by the blades. King George V saw her sailing one day and later remarked to Moore-Brabazon that he had never seen a boat point so high. In winds of around 20 knots Moore-Brabazon reported that the most astonishing speeds were achieved, although a whole new technique for sailing the boat had to be developed. The greatest point of danger was when reaching as there was a risk in a short sea that during a roll the rotor would hit the water.

Despite its limitations under certain conditions Moore-Brabazon was determined to sail his boat during Cowes Week. Unfortunately, while moored amongst a lot of other small keel boats at Cowes, one of his crew accidentally let the rotor go. A good breeze was blowing and there was nothing Moore-Brabazon could do to stop his Redwing descending on one of the neighbouring boats which the rotor promptly chewed into matchwood before it disintegrated. 'A very sad ending to an expensive but amusing experiment,' said Moore-Brabazon.*

Another outstanding aviation expert of that, or indeed any, era was T. O. M. Sopwith, who joined the club in 1930, having already established himself as a top-flight 12-metre helmsman. His first yacht was an Itchen fishing cutter which he bought in 1907, and he later owned two others. But in those early prewar days, as has been mentioned, he concentrated on racing powerboats which he did with great success, a role that his son, Tommy, took on with distinction in the 1960s, as will be seen in the last chapter.

After the war Sopwith at first turned to owning a series of diesel and motor yachts which culminated in the beautiful 1620-ton *Philante*, which, after serving in the Royal Navy during the Second World War, became, and still is, the Norwegian royal yacht.

In 1926 he bought his first 12-metre, *Doris*, and sailed her for three seasons before having the Nicholson designed *Mouette*, built in 1929. She was an outstanding success and for three successive seasons – 1929, 1930 and 1931 – he came top of the 12-Metre Class. When the Big Class ceased to exist he reverted to 12-metres again. First, in 1938, he bought *Blue Marlin*, but she was not a success, and for the following season he had *Tomahawk* built to race against his old rival, Harold Vanderbilt, who came over with his 12-metre *Vim*.

Another member, Hugh Goodson, also raced in the 12-Metre Class during the 1930s, first in *Flica*, bought from Sir Richard Fairey, and then in his new Laurent Giles-designed *Flica II*, which he had built for the 1939 season. He remembers that Vanderbilt and his crew, Olin and Rod Stephens, were much too good for either Sopwith or himself.

'The organisation behind his bringing *Vim* to England was as thorough as the subsequent American preparations for the Second Front,' he wrote ruefully in later years.† 'She won because she took the trouble to win. She left absolutely nothing to chance.'

Sopwith was a great 12-metre helmsman but his outstanding contribution to yachting was, of course, his two challenges for the *America*'s Cup, with *Endeavour* in 1934 and *Endeavour II* in 1937.

---

* *The Brabazon Story* by Lord Brabazon, Wm. Heinemann Ltd., 1956, and 'The Autogyro Rotor as a Sail' from the *Royal Aeronautical Journal* (vol. xxxviii, 1934).

† *All That and the Beauty of It* by Hugh Goodson, privately printed by the Blackmore Press, Gillingham, Dorset, undated.

After Lord Dunraven's unfortunate challenge in 1895, Sir Thomas Lipton, through the Royal Ulster Yacht Club, took over the British effort to try to retrieve 'the auld mug'. He tried unsuccessfully in 1899, 1901, 1903 and in 1920. Then in 1930 he made his last attempt, building the 'J' Class *Shamrock V* designed by Charles E. Nicholson.

The 'J' Class was governed by the American Universal Rule, a quite different concept to the International Rule, although the end products were not dissimilar. *Shamrock V* was beaten easily by Vanderbilt's *Enterprise*, and the following year Lipton was elected to the Squadron by acclaim. He vowed he would try again, with *Shamrock VI*, but he died in October 1931 before a challenge could be made.

When Lipton died Sopwith bought *Shamrock V*. He renamed her *Shamrock*, and raced her very successfully in the Big Class for two seasons before building *Endeavour* in order to challenge, through The Royal Yacht Squadron, for the *America*'s Cup in 1934.

As with the earlier challenges, much has been written about what happened in 1934, and nothing much can usefully be added here to what has already been said. It was, as the Duke of Wellington commented in another context, 'the nearest run thing you ever saw in your life', with the British yacht winning the first two races convincingly before going down 4–2 after a controversial fourth race.

Although *Endeavour* was an outstanding yacht, by far the best-known member of the Big Class during that inter-war period was the King's *Britannia*.

As already mentioned, it was the King's decision to refit *Britannia* in 1920 that saved the Big Class and revived the sport of yachting. Her record is quite astonishing and is certainly unrivalled in the annals of the sport. Under her various rigs – she had seven all told – she did amazingly well against much more modern opponents, and in a blow was virtually unbeatable. In 1927 she headed the Big Class and as late as 1932 gained twenty-three flags out of thirty-two starts, a better record than even the 'J' Class *Shamrock* could achieve that year. Only in her last season, 1935, did it become apparent that she was outclassed, and at the end of Cowes Week that year she sailed in her last race. A few days later Sir Philip Hunloke resigned from the vice-presidency of the YRA, 'because my racing days are over'. Between 1893 and 1935 *Britannia* took part in 569 races and won no less than 355 flags. Of these 231 were first prizes, and Hunloke was at the helm for 213 of them.

Early the following year the King died. Soon afterwards, as requested by him, *Britannia* was sunk in deep water south of St Catherine's Point. Her wheel and truck were saved and, along with her owner's Squadron Admiral's flag and his racing flag, were presented to the club by Queen Mary; these mementoes are on display at the Castle. Her gaff was also saved and is now on display at Sir Max Aitken's Prospect Museum at Cowes.

Thanks to the King and *Britannia*, regatta racing flourished during the inter-war period, but it was also a time when ocean racing in its modern form became established in Britain. It came about through the enthusiasm of a small group of yachtsmen who were determined to run a fixture similar to the American Bermuda Race, which had first taken place in 1906 and which had been revived by members of the Cruising Club of America in 1923. A small committee was started early in 1925 and after some argument it was decided that the course for the proposed race should be from Ryde, round the Fastnet rock off the south-west coast of Ireland, and back to Plymouth, a distance of about 630 miles.

The race was won by Commander E. G. Martin in *Jolie Brise*. At the end of the race, Martin, who became a member in 1932, and his fellow competitors' formed the Ocean Racing Club.* Sir Philip Hunloke was voted its first president while Sir Ralph Gore served on the committee. The success of the race and the persuasive influence of Hunloke and Gore no doubt influenced the Squadron to take an interest in this new sport, for the following year the race was started from the club's line, and has been ever since.

Although none of the yachts in that first race belonged to members – Michael Tennant, who entered his cutter *North Star*, became a member in 1926 – Robert Somerset, a member, was navigator aboard the winning yacht, and others soon took part and helped build up enthusiasm for this new branch of yachting. Colonel Baxendale, for example, who had become a member in 1924, entered his new 51-ton Bermudan-rigged cutter *Hallowe'en* in the 1926 race and established a course record of 3 days, 19 hours, 5 minutes, which was not beaten until 1939. On corrected time, however, she dropped to third place, for although she was a new boat Fife had designed her without regard to

---

* In 1931 it became the Royal Ocean Racing Club.

the ORC Rule governing the race. Indeed, from the amount she was penalized under the Rule some felt he had never even heard of it.

It was, in fact, some years before designers built specifically to what became the RORC Rule, and for her time *Hallowe'en* was as close to being what would now be understood to be an ocean racer as anyone was likely to get. Nearly all the entries in the Fastnet during the 1920s, and indeed even in the early 1930s, were cruising boats. A good example of such a yacht was the 12-ton cutter *Penboch*, owned by Robert Somerset, who became a member in 1925. *Penboch* took part in several Fastnets but was always outclassed. In 1928, however, she won the first Channel Race, before Somerset sold her and bought *Jolie Brise*. With this famous cutter he did much better in the Fastnet Race and won it in both 1929 and 1930.

The first member to win the Fastnet, though, was Lord Stalbridge who entered his cutter *Tally Ho!* in the 1927 fixture.

The Fastnet is notorious for bad weather and in 1927 it blew a series of ferocious gales. There were fourteen entries that year, including two Americans, but only two of them finished.

Before *Tally Ho!* even passed the Lizard, yachts were turning for home. 'Now was our chance,' Lord Stalbridge wrote afterwards when *Jolie Brise* was seen to retire, 'as, knowing from experiences in a gale in the Bay of Biscay what a wonderful sea-boat the *Tally Ho!* was, and also confident in our sails and gear, we thought by reefing her down and making things ship-shape we might be able to weather the Lizard, and if so would catch the tide and be a tide ahead of any of our competitors who failed to do so.'

They did manage to weather the Lizard but off the Longships were forced to turn back and shelter in Newlyn Roadsteads for the night, while the only American survivor, the schooner *La Goleta*, hove to under the lee of the Lizard.

The next morning both yachts plunged back into the gale and from the Longships they raced neck and neck, often in sight of one another, until they reached the Fastnet Rock which *Tally Ho!* rounded just fifteen minutes ahead of her rival.

By now they were the only two entries left in the race and both yachts clung on to their canvas for as long as they could. 'We had to drive her along for all we were worth,' said Lord Stalbridge, 'not only to beat *La Goleta* but to get sea room. And drive her we did, more under the water than over I fear, but by 4am it had got too bad and we had to heave to and reef again.'

The Americans, with a five-hour handicap to erase, kept racing and at one point *La Goleta* logged fourteen miles in an hour and twenty minutes. Then one of the crew members was washed overboard. Weston Martyr, a founder member of the ORC, was on board *La Goleta* and later, with tongue in cheek, described what happened:

> At the time the schooner was logging ten knots, and I expect Mr Tallman understood perfectly that the race could not be stopped at that stage for any man overboard, even if he did come from Pittsburgh. In any case he must have got a mighty good grip of something for it took six strong men and a watch tackle to get him back again. He came back smiling, too, with his cigar still between his teeth.

Despite all their efforts the Americans crossed the line only forty-two minutes ahead of *Tally Ho!* and the British yacht was awarded the race. 'In the whole history of yachting in British waters,' commented one magazine afterwards, 'there has never been so hard a fight between two yachts over so long a course and under such weather conditions.'

After 1931 the Fastnet was held during odd-numbered years only so that it did not clash with the Bermuda Race, and in 1932 Robert Somerset took *Jolie Brise* across the Atlantic to take part in this American classic. On the first night out in heavy weather distress flares were sighted. *Jolie Brise* went to investigate and it was found that another competitor, *Adriana*, was on fire. With great daring Somerset brought *Jolie Brise* alongside the burning yacht and managed to rescue the entire crew except one who lost his foothold, fell into the water and could not be found in the dark. For his bravery Somerset was presented with an inscribed watch and chain by the President of the United States, and with the CCA's highest award, the Blue Water Medal.

By the early 1930s ocean racing had become established, with other courses apart from the Fastnet being raced over every year. In 1929, for instance, the first Santander Race was run – Lord Stalbridge in his three-masted schooner *Cetonia* won the large class, and Robert Somerset in *Jolie Brise* won the small class – and during the 1930s there were a number of regular races in and across the North Sea as well as ones to France. Several members took part in these races with Gerald Potter winning the 1934 race to Belle Isle in *Carmela*, and Michael Mason winning the Benodet Race in 1936 and the Dinard and Ile de Brehat races in 1938 in his ketch *Latifa*, which he also raced in the 1937 and 1939 Fastnets and in the 1938 Bermuda Race. Another keen ocean-racing member was Major Rose-Richards who took part in both the 1931 and 1933 Fastnets and the 1932 Bermuda Race in his 40-ton cutter *Lexia*.

But perhaps the most successful ocean-racing Squadron member during the latter part of the inter-war period was an American, Isaac Bell, who became a foreign member in 1936. For it was he who commissioned Charles E. Nicholson to design the famous *Foxhound* and then, in 1936, the even more famous *Bloodhound*, which won the 1939 Fastnet, and which after the war, under the ownership of Sir Myles Wyatt and then the Duke of Edinburgh, became one of the best-known ocean racers in the world.

While the 1920s and 1930s saw a tremendous upsurge in racing of all kinds it should not be forgotten that the majority of members still cruised. In keeping with the prewar years were the long voyages undertaken by such members as Sir Walter (later Lord) Runciman, Lord Moyne, the Hon. Ernest Guinness and Urban Broughton.

Sir Walter Runciman was a great admirer of the late Lord Brassey and owned *Sunbeam* for some years during the 1920s. He was an old seadog who had learned to love the sea through many adventures on it as a professional seaman. As a young officer he had had to fight against a mutineer with his fists, but had survived to become one of the biggest shipowners in the country. By 1929 he realized that *Sunbeam* was worn out, and he had her broken up. But so great was his attachment to her, and to her original owner, that he directed that *Sunbeam II* be constructed just as if Lord Brassey had been ordering her, and in many ways she was remarkably similar though broader-beamed and much quicker in stays. He did not travel as far as Lord Brassey, for he was already in his eighties when he had *Sunbeam II* built, but his knowledge and love of the sea comes through on nearly every page of the logs of his cruises between 1930 and 1934 which he had privately printed.

Lord Moyne, on the other hand, appears to have voyaged to every far corner of the earth. He followed very much in the footsteps of the Earl of Crawford in using his yacht not just for pleasure cruises but for scientific purposes. He came on the list in 1906 as the Hon. Walter Edward Guinness, and, after owning a variety of vessels, converted two Newhaven–Dieppe ferries into luxury yachts which, because of their spaciousness, were ideally suited for extended cruises. The first of these was the 1489-ton *Roussalka* (ex-*Brighton)* which he bought in 1930 and converted, but lost in 1933 when she ran onto a rock off the Galway coast in thick fog. Then, in 1934, he converted the *Dieppe* and called her *Rosaura*. Her refit cost £70,000 and she was given eight staterooms, each with its own bathroom, and a swimming pool on the weather deck.

Once she had been converted, the 1538-ton *Rosaura* was well equipped for the ethnological and natural-history expeditions that were so close to Lord Moyne's heart. He was an explorer by nature and wrote in 1936 that he had spent every holiday during the last twenty-five years travelling to remote places. After the First World War he voyaged by yacht to the Pacific no less than six times. In 1929 he visited New Guinea, became intrigued with the place, and returned there in 1935 to gather flora and fauna unrepresented in the British Museum collection. The voyage in *Rosaura* covered over 30,000 miles on that occasion and he returned not only with a unique collection of photographs of native tribesmen, but with various species of fauna which proved to be quite new to the London Zoo. Judging from the long list of live animals he managed to bring back, his yacht must have closely resembled Noah's Ark on her return!

The following year Lord Moyne took *Rosaura* on another unusual voyage, his ambition this time being to circumnavigate the Atlantic ocean, sailing from the Arctic down to Brazil and back via the West Coast of Africa. Again, his real interest centred on the primitive peoples of the lands he visited, but he also returned with some rare deep-water species previously unrepresented in the British Museum.

This eighteen-month, 18,000-mile voyage was nearly cut short at the start when *Rosaura* was all but cut off from the open sea by ice while anchored at Angmagssalik. The first attempt to break out failed and when she tried a second time all her boats were swung out on their davits in case she was nipped and crushed by the ice.

Rosaura escaped being wrecked, but the Duke of Sutherland in his 830-ton diesel yacht *Sans Peur III* was not so lucky. He was cruising off a deserted part of the west coast of Mexico shortly before the Second World War when he ran aground on an uncharted rock. The damage was serious and the yacht had to be immediately beached on a nearby island. Despite this emergency action the three forward holds were flooded, which ruined all their food, and oil leaked into the water supply. Luckily, what could have developed into a very unpleasant incident turned out to be no more than an inconvenience as a fellow member soon came to their rescue.

For two years running Sopwith, a keen amateur naturalist, had visited the Galapagos Islands and its teeming wildlife in *Philante* and he was just 400 miles to the south when he picked up *Sans Peur*'s distress signal. He hurried to their rescue and, after twenty-four hours of being marooned on a totally barren island which did not even have any water, the Duke and Duchess and their crew were taken aboard *Philante*. The next day Vincent Astor arrived in his yacht and took over the salvaging of *Sans Peur III* with the help of a diver who had been brought out from the mainland. Repairs were made and *Sans Peur III* was able to make the Californian coast under her own steam where she was repaired. But she never returned to Europe, for the outbreak of war found her in Canada and she was offered to the government as a patrol ship.

The Hon. Ernest Guinness, who came on the list in 1903 with his 303-ton auxiliary screw ketch *Fantome*, was another inveterate cruising man who went all over the world during the inter-war period. He was so fond of his yacht that when he decided the time had come to have a larger vessel he ordered Camper and Nicholson to lengthen her by 33 feet rather than sell her. For this to be done she virtually had to be cut in half, and when Charles E. Nicholson found that parts of her were very rotten he advised Guinness not to proceed. But Guinness was adamant that Nicholson should finish the job and when he had done so Guinness confided to him that he had spent his honeymoon in *Fantome* and would not part with her for anything.

Fantome's engines exhausted in a rather unusual manner – up the mizzen mast. However, when it was found that this covered the guests with smuts, her owner had an exhaust pipe of flexible metal fitted and this was trailed overboard when the engine was running. Apparently it looked not unlike a sea serpent and, when not in use, it was coiled down on deck.

In 1921 Guinness bought the 611-ton auxiliary barque *Belem* from the Duke of Westminster and renamed her *Fantome II*, but he still kept the original *Fantome* until 1938 when he replaced her with the duke's 1195-ton auxiliary schooner *Flying Cloud*, and renamed her *Fantome*.

Guinness was also a keen speedboat man and after the First World War bought a triple-engined ex-naval high-speed motorboat called

Oma. It was not fast enough for him, so he ordered Camper and Nicholson to fit a fourth engine. Camper found that this could not be done, but suggested that it might be possible to fit it on deck driving an aerial propeller. This appealed to Guinness and a 450 h.p. Napier Lion engine was purchased from Air Ministry disposal stocks and installed. It only increased *Oma*'s speed by about 3 knots, but she caused quite a stir when she appeared at the Cowes regatta later that year.*

Urban Broughton also enjoyed cruising to distant places in his 1421-ton *Sapphire* with which he had come onto the list in 1924, and to do so entirely for pleasure. Rather like a much earlier member, George Bentinck, Broughton did not like to be tied down too much. He thought guests should be told the main objective of the cruise and its approximate duration, but that there was no fixed itinerary or schedule. To emphasize this he had inscribed on *Sapphire*'s mailbox, 'Do not ask when the post goes, you know as much about it as we do.'

The Duke of Westminster, the amazing Bendor, was another who liked cruising without any particular plan. Even if an itinerary had been arranged he would often tell his captain to change course in the middle of the night. When his guests appeared on deck in the morning they would peer about them with consternation and ask why the scenery looked so different. Sir Sacheverell Sitwell, a frequent guest of the Duke's, claimed that the crew were always instructed to say, 'Looks like Spain to me, sir,' when asked where they were.

The Duke's first postwar purchase was the 611-ton barque *Belem*, which he had converted into a luxury auxiliary motor yacht at a cost of £100,000. Then in 1923 he had the four-masted schooner *Flying Cloud* built for him at Leghorn. Over 200 feet long, she was one of the largest private yachts in the world and he used the architect Detmar Blow to turn her into a floating palace. Blow had designed many of the buildings on the Grosvenor estate in what might be called a neo-Queen Anne style, and he proceeded to decorate *Flying Cloud* in the same manner. She was, said Loelia, Duchess of Westminster, 'almost too odd to be believed in. The upper cabins were reached through an ornamental doorway with a big concave shell above it, which the architect had designed to resemble the front door of an old Cotswold house.'

---

* *Great Years in Yachting*, by John Nicholson, Nautical Publishing Co. Ltd., 1970.

116

The Duke was a restless soul and his yachts were rarely stationary. On the spur of the moment he would sail to Norway to fish, or to the Mediterranean to gamble in the casinos at Cannes and Monte Carlo. His yachts were so well known on the Riviera that they were immortalized by Noel Coward in his play *Private Lives*. 'What yacht is that?' Amanda asks in the first act. 'The Duke of Westminster's, I expect,' Elyot replies. 'It always is.'

But perhaps the most unusual of the Duke's yachts was the *Cutty Sark*, which had started life as the hull and engines of an 'S' Class destroyer, but had been converted for use as a private yacht. Two of her four boilers had been removed and the engines installed on the port side so that her passengers could walk the length of the ship below deck. She was immensely fast, but rolled abominably. Normally, the Duke revelled in rough weather, but he was once caught in a nasty swell off Toulon which made even him seasick. He told the captain to take her back in, but the captain said that it was not possible. The swell got worse and so did the Duke, and when he again demanded to return to harbour, and again the captain said it was not possible, the Duke snapped, 'Well, beach the bitch.'*

But although many members cruised great distances in their large motor yachts there were others who took part in the type of voyaging in small craft with which we are familiar today. General Jack Seely – who later became Lord Mottistone – was a keen cruising man who enjoyed handling his own small sailing yacht. He had learned his seamanship the hard way by becoming a supernumerary officer in a small cargo boat in the 1890s, an adventure which nearly cost him his life when the ship was almost wrecked on the Ushant rocks. In 1923 he shipped his 14-ton cutter *Isme II* to Hamburg so that he could take part in the Copenhagen and Helsingør regattas in her and then sail her back to Cowes. He described her as being very like the King's *Britannia* viewed through the wrong end of a telescope, for she had a very high-aspect-ratio rig which was regarded by many of his friends as being totally unseaworthy.

By misfortune he arrived by steamer at Hamburg on the very day the German mark finally collapsed. He went ashore to have dinner and ordered lunch in a famous restaurant which, like the city, was almost

---

* *Bendor: The Golden Duke of Westminster* by Leslie Field, Weidenfeld & Nicolson, 1983.

totally deserted. He ordered a bottle of hock which was priced at 100,000 marks, the equivalent of about 10 shillings. At the end of the meal, which took about an hour and a half, the manager approached General Seely and explained that he had just come from the Bourse and that the bottle of hock the general was just finishing should now be priced at 250,000 marks if he was not to make a loss on it. The General said that while he thought the wine was excellent he thought a rise in price of 150 per cent in one and a half hours was somewhat unreasonable, and a compromise figure was agreed upon. During that day the mark fell from 100,000 marks to the pound to 500,000 marks.

After taking part in the Copenhagen regatta the general sailed for home. He found two very competent pilots to take him to Kiel and then through the canal. But at Brunsbuttel no one seemed interested in taking them on the next leg of the voyage into the Zuider Zee. Eventually, a man who claimed he was a pilot said he would take them for £10. Before long the 'pilot' had nearly put them aground and later confessed that he was a gardener, that he had never been in a yacht in his life, but that his family were starving and he needed the money. He then started to be thoroughly seasick and the General had to put him below before eventually paying him off at a nearby port.

A new pilot was taken aboard who took them through the canals to Flushing and then on to Dover. Off Nieuport they ran into a storm and were advised by the pilot to run for the harbour. When the General pointed that it was nearly low water and that they would never get over the bar, the pilot said it was their best chance of surviving. 'The seas will lift her over the bar, and even if she breaks up, we shall be able to swim ashore in the calm waters inside.'

The general ignored this rather gloomy advice and managed to claw off the lee shore and eventually made his way to Dover. When he at last reached Cowes he was met by his old friends Sir Philip Hunloke and Sir William Portal who had strongly advised him that with a rig like *Isme*'s he should not sail outside the Solent. Where have you been, they asked, Portsmouth? No, the General proudly replied, the Baltic. It was, he said later, the most interesting voyage he had ever had in a yacht!*

*

---

* *Fear, and Be Slain* by General J. E. B. Seely, Hodder & Stoughton, 1931.

118

Like other yachtsmen club members kept cruising and racing right up to
the outbreak of the Second World War. But as soon as it was declared,
the warrant to fly the White Ensign was returned to the Admiralty – as it
had been at the start of the First World War – and members at once
offered their yachts for naval service. During the war fifty-eight club
yachts were acquired for use by the Admiralty, and although the
situation was quite different to the First World War – members' yachts
had become a good deal smaller while warships had become a good deal
larger and more sophisticated – the record of these vessels which served
their country are well worth preserving and have therefore been listed
in Appendix 2.

Again, as in the First World War, the Castle was immediately thrown
open for convalescent naval officers, with a number of bedrooms being
reserved for their use. In addition, any member was allowed to propose
one officer who was serving on the Isle of Wight as a temporary
honorary member. These members enjoyed all the privileges of the
club, but were not allowed to fly the club burgee or to wear the club
uniform or badge.

A present member and past Vice-Commodore, Lord Malmesbury,
was ordered on the outbreak of war to take a small force of 200 men from
his battalion of the Hampshire Regiment to guard vital installations on
the Isle of Wight. He made his headquarters at Cowes and was therefore
able to visit the Castle during the first months of the war. He found that
the Vice-Commodore, Lord Camden, had installed himself there as he
felt that someone had to look after the place and that it was his
responsibility.

In 1940 the question arose as to whether the Castle should stay open
at all. One member in particular, Lord Dorchester, felt strongly that it
should not and he proposed that it should be closed immediately and
remain closed until the war ended. This did not receive much support,
so Lord Dorchester then suggested that if no one agreed that it should
be closed then it should be thrown open to every commissioned
member of HM Forces who was serving on the Isle of Wight and that the
lawn should be dug up and used as a vegetable plot.

During the summer of 1940 correspondence flew back and forth
between Lord Dorchester, the Secretary and certain members of the
committee, with Lord Dorchester demanding to know if anyone was
using the club at all and repeating his grievance at having to pay his full

subscription when he could not use the club, for, as a serving army officer, he certainly felt he was too busy to use it. However, the figures showed that the club was still being used – rather more than it had been in 1939, in fact.

At the August meeting Lord Mottistone, who lived on the Isle of Wight, pointed out that rules governing those allowed to visit the island had recently been relaxed, and that there was no reason why members should not use it if they wished to. He also said he had consulted with the local agricultural committee from which he had ascertained that the lawn was not suitable for cultivation and was not, in any case, required for such a purpose.

The Commodore, Sir Richard Williams-Bulkeley, was not well enough to attend the meeting, but wrote a letter listing his objections to Lord Dorchester's proposals, and the Vice-Commodore said that the committee 'believe the members will unite in endeavouring to ensure that this club – the Premier Yacht Club in the world – shall weather the war and will be prepared to retain their membership to do so'.

It was then proposed by Colonel the Rt Hon. John Gretton that 'this meeting has the fullest confidence in the Flag Officers and the Committee, and, in the present crisis, is content to leave the management of the club under their control as provided by Rule 18, with full power to take any action which they may consider to be in the interest of the members', a proposal which was unanimously carried.

However, it must have been felt that Lord Dorchester had a point about subscriptions. Members serving overseas in HM Forces only had to pay £1 anyway, but it was agreed that for the following year the ordinary subscription should be reduced from £16 to £8. This amount was retained for 1942, but when the club was taken over by the Admiralty towards the end of that year the subscription was reduced to a £1 for all members and stayed at that amount until 1946 when the full subscription of £16 was reinstated.

It is difficult from the surviving correspondence to untangle exactly how it came about that the Admiralty made its decision to use the Castle. On 25 May 1942, the Vice-Commodore wrote the following letter to the Secretary Captain Walshe:

> Mottistone telephoned me Sunday to go to London on an *urgent & confidential* matter.

Left: Endeavour and *Endeavour II*, the two J-class cutters which challenged for the
America's Cup during the 1930s were both designed by Charles E. Nicholson for
their owner T.O.M. (later Sir Thomas) Sopwith, who became a member in 1930
(Beken).

Right: The 6-metre *Lalage,* which won a gold medal at the 1936 Olympics with
Christopher Boardman, one of her co-owners and a future member, at the helm.
At the same Olympics, Peter (later Sir Peter) Scott, who joined the Squadron in
1943, won the bronze medal in the Olympic Monotype class *(Beken)*

Right Designed by Charles E. Nicholson in 1936, *Bloodhound* was built to the 12-metre rule for an American Isaac Bell who became a foreign member in that year. A Bermudan yawl of 34 tons and 45 feet on the waterline, she won the 1939 Fastnet race and in the postwar years Sir Myles Wyatt raced her with equal success. Later, HRH The Duke of Edinburgh bought her for family cruising *(Beken)*

Below Lord Moyne's 1538-ton yacht *Rosaura,* an ex-cross channel ferry built in 1905 which he bought in 1934 and converted into a luxury yacht with eight staterooms, each with its own bathroom, and a swimming pool. He was an avid collector of zoological and archaeological specimens and to this end circled the Atlantic in 1936-37 visiting the Arctic, South America and the West Coast of Africa *(Beken)*

This prototype Motor Torpedo Boat bought by the Admiralty was designed by Peter du Cane, a noted designer of many different types of powered vessels. He designed *Bluebird II* for Sir Donald Campbell and the winner of the first Cowes-Torquay powerboat race, *Tramontana (collection Peter du Cane)*

T.O.M. Sopwith's magnificent *Philante* (1620 tons) was designed by Charles E. Nicholson in 1937. At the start of the Second World War she was requisitioned by the Admiralty and served as an escort vessel. She's seen here entering Lough Eriboll, escorting two U-boats which had surrendered. She is now the Norwegian royal yacht *Norge (Imperial War Museum)*

The 1920 Yarrow-built destroyer *Cutty Sark* (828 tons) was converted into a luxury
yacht and owned by the Duke of Westminster. She was requisitioned during the
Second World War and used as a submarine chaser and escort ship
(Imperial War Museum)

From 1942 onwards, the Castle was used as Headquarters for 'J' Force. Here King
George VI is taking the salute from the Squadron battery in May 1944 as landing
craft from 'J' Force for the D-Day landings pass by in review order
(Imperial War Museum)

Yachting World

Power and Sail

XIV OLYMPIAD

Stewart Morris, helmsman, and David Bond, crew, (Great Britain), winners of the Gold Medal in the Swallow Class

In This Issue

- XIV Olympiad
- Cowes Week
- Pavillon d'Or

2/-

SEPTEMBER 1948

Stewart Morris is a member with an outstanding racing record in dinghies and small keel boats. This cover of *Yachting World* features Morris, who won an Olympic gold medal in his Swallow-class *Swift* at Torbay in 1948 *(Yachting World)*

Right: Myth of Malham was one of the most radical yachts ever when she was designed by Laurent Giles in 1947 for Captain John Illingworth. She won the Fastnet race twice and came top of her class five times. Illingworth, an outstanding ocean racing yachtsman, was one of the donors of the Admiral's Cup *(Beken)*

Below The 54-ton *Lumberjack*, the first of Sir Max Aitken's many notable ocean racers. He was a great patron of yachting, who, among other things, started the Cowes-Torquay powerboat race and the Boat Show at Earls Court. He was also a joint 'Yachtsman of the Year' in 1963 *(Beken)*

Left The Flying Fifteen *Coweslip,* owned by HRH The Duke of Edinburgh, was frequently raced by him, often with his friend Uffa Fox, who designed her, as his crew *(Beken)*

Right The International Dragon class *Bluebottle.* She was given by the Island Sailing Club to HM the Queen and HRH The Duke of Edinburgh on their marriage. Helmed by a present Rear Commodore, Graham Mann, she won an Olympic bronze medal at Melbourne in 1956, with another present member Jonathan Janson as crew *(Beken)*

Inset right Lt-Col Perry receives his silver medal at the Melbourne Olympics *(RYS collection)*

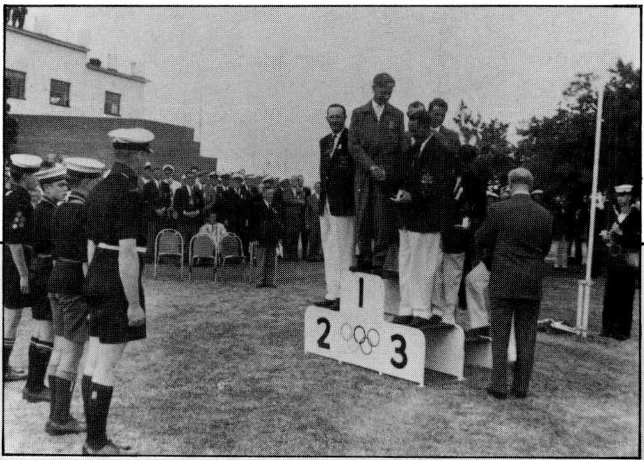

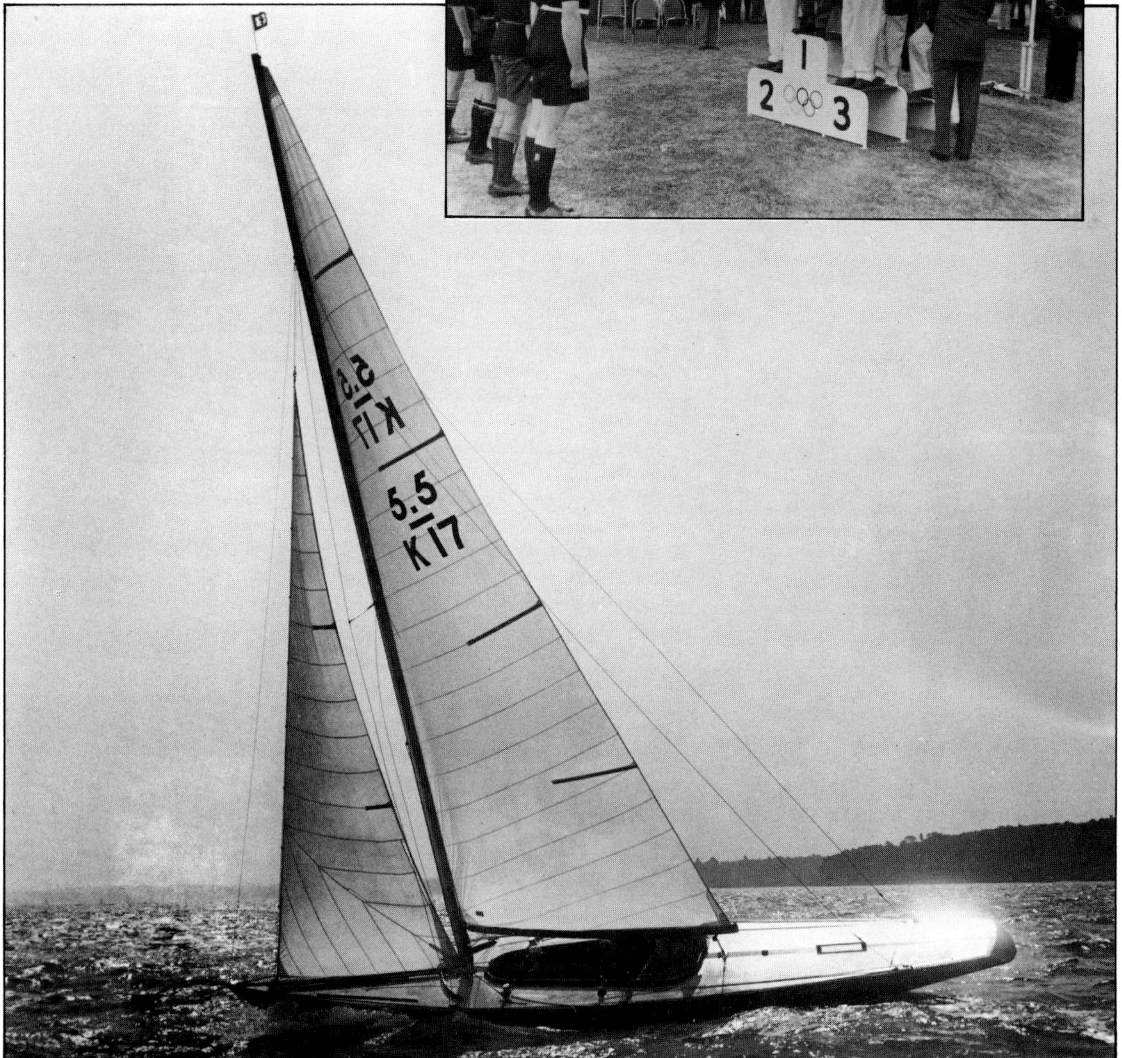

Lt-Col 'Stug' Perry was another Squadron member who won Olympic honours. He competed in the 5.5 metre class at Helsinki in 1952, and then in 1956 won a silver medal at Melbourne with *Vision*, pictured here *(Beken)*

I have been up to see him.

The Admiralty and Vice-Admiral Lord Louis Mountbatten, Command-ing Combined Operations, want the Castle as HQ for the above and I expect some other big thing and I believe the Island may be closed to the public. They want everything to go on as at present, so that *nothing* should get known, until a certain time when they would take over, with an Admiral in charge.

They would be responsible for everything and take on our present staff. I do not know if they would allow you to keep your office. They may put a Naval officer in charge, but the Admiral will be there.

The whole thing is so urgent and secret that I was told not to tell anyone, but I said I must tell the Commodore and you as you were responsible to the Committee.

I have written the Commodore and also to Mountbatten. I have told *no one* else and I had to take the responsibility, as I could not telephone the Commodore on such a secret matter.

Simultaneously, and maybe coincidentally, the C.-in-C. Portsmouth requested that the club accommodate some senior naval officers as accommodation on the island was hard to find. This was probably agreed, for the Castle first appears in the Admiralty's 'Red List' as a depot ship on 14 June 1942.

On 22 June 1942 the committee met and passed the following resolution: 'That in view of the close relationship which has always existed between the Royal Navy and the Royal Yacht Squadron, the Admiralty be informed that the Committee desires to place the Club premises, with the Annexe, at their disposal as at present furnished for the duration of the war.'

The committee then put forward some suggestions as to the terms of such an agreement and fixed the rent at 1 shilling per annum. These terms – and the rent – were accepted by the Admiralty, and HMS *Vectis* was officially commissioned on 12 August 1942, and in May 1943 became an operational training base for what was known as 'J' Force.

After the raid on Dieppe in August 1942 the landing craft and ships which had taken part in it were kept together as one force, so that they could be used as a nucleus for bigger operations, but also as a standby group for smaller ones.

This force was formally constituted on 12 October 1942. It was codenamed 'J' Force and, as part of Combined Operations, came under the overall command of Vice-Admiral Lord Louis Mountbatten. The Castle, however, was not personally used by Mountbatten but as the residence and planning HQ for the Officer Commanding 'J' Force.

The first commanding officer for 'J' Force was Captain J. Hughes-Hallett, but he was later succeeded by Rear-Admiral Sir Philip Vian. When Vian became Naval Commander Eastern Task Force (British) prior to D-Day he was succeeded by Commodore G. N. Oliver. Oliver and his staff planned the operation in which 'J' Force safely delivered the British and Canadian divisions onto Juno beach, one of the two designated British beaches during the Normandy landings.

Mountbatten, incidentally, was elected to the Squadron in 1943, but not in the usual way. It was proposed by the committee that 'having regard to the distinguished service of Vice-Admiral the Lord Louis Mountbatten GCVO, DSO, the usual procedure be suspended in his case, and that he be, and is hereby, elected a member of the Royal Yacht Squadron.'

Commander Sir Archibald Southby, Bt, MP, thought that the election of a member in this manner might be misunderstood and suggested that it might be better to have the usual ballot – the result of which, he added, was not in doubt. The meeting – chaired by the Marquis Camden, who had become Commodore on the death of Sir Richard Williams-Bulkeley the previous year – disagreed and Sir Archibald did not press the matter. The motion was put and carried unanimously and with acclamation.

This method of electing Mountbatten is perhaps explained by the fact that he had already been blackballed twice, as Philip Ziegler in his biography* of him records.

> The gossip was damaging to Mountbatten's career as well as to his pride. 'A Royal Spanking for Gay Lady Mountbatten', proclaimed the *San Francisco Chronicle* in banner headlines above a full-page story. Queen Mary was said to be displeased at her behaviour, in particular at the fact that she had danced a Charleston with Fred Astaire. In punishment the Queen had 'caused this vivacious lady's husband to be blackballed from the Royal Yacht Squadron, the very stronghold of British aristocracy'. In

---

* *Mountbatten*, by Philip Ziegler, Collins, 1985.

fact, the King thought strongly that Mountbatten *should* be a member of the Squadron and was incensed at his rejection, particularly when it happened a second time. It was a humiliating rebuff for Mountbatten, but his wife's adventures were only partly to blame; more important was the tactlessness of his proposer, Lord Beatty, and the feeling of certain members that the candidate was a rackety young man with a weakness for showing off in fast motor-boats.

Mountbatten apparently bore a grudge against the Squadron for many years after his election and Ziegler records that it was not until he became Governor of the Isle of Wight that he relented slightly and agreed to wear the club's buttons and badge. However, according to a present member, Stewart Morris, who was elected at the same time as Mountbatten, he seemed to think it all rather a joke. When they sat next to one another at dinner Morris complained that while he, Morris, had had to go through the usual ballot Mountbatten had been elected by acclamation. 'Ah,' replied Mountbatten with a laugh, 'but you weren't blackballed twice beforehand.'

Luckily, the Castle survived the war virtually unscathed, although in May 1942 furniture and effects stored at Marvin's yard was destroyed by enemy action and half the Platform glass was blown out. More serious was the damage done when a 2000-lb high-explosive bomb fell close to the club on the night of 15–16 May 1944. It blew a large crater in part of the lawn and the promenade at the western end of the Squadron grounds, causing considerable external and internal damage, but none of a permanent nature.

Not many people are still alive who knew the Castle during those war years, but through the foresight of Lord Malmesbury there exists one excellent account by someone who served there. At the request of Lord Malmesbury, Anthony Taylor, who had served as a signals officer at HMS *Vectis*, wrote down all he could remember. He was at Cowes when the Castle was bombed and wrote about the raid that nearly destroyed it.

> As far as I can recollect it started at about midnight with the dropping of flares attached to parachutes. As a result the whole of Cowes Roads were illuminated followed by a heavy though short bombing attack. Fortunately, many of the bombs dropped in the sea, some fell in the area behind the hill at the back of the Gloster and one high-explosive bomb fell

and exploded on the lawn of the Castle. All the glass in the Platform was shattered, the evergreen oak tree was destroyed. Much stonework and masonry was precipitated into the air and fell onto the roof and precincts of the Castle. I believe it was the upper rooms which were most damaged but many of the paintings and marine prints in corridors and main rooms fell to the ground and glass was broken. Generally, the scene next morning was one of chaos.

The Chief of Staff who was occupying the tower room fortunately left his bed and stood in the doorway. This action saved his life, for a minute later the whole roof and ceiling fell in with masses of stone and debris. The cupboard containing his clothes and uniforms was demolished as was the bed and other furnishings.

The Commodore [of 'J' Force] was in London but those of his staff who were occupying the Castle were a sorry sight the next morning. They came to breakfast at the Gloster, as the Castle kitchens were out of action, dressed only in their pyjamas and other night wear as many had lost their uniforms in the debris and rubble. I believe that no one was killed or seriously injured.

The old retainer caretaker,* who had remained at the Castle during its occupancy by Commodore, Force 'J', was in tears when we went next morning to view the state of affairs. He was truly heartbroken to see the chaos which had resulted. However, he was reassured that immediate and effective steps would be taken by the Admiralty to restore the Castle to its former dignity. Steps were in fact taken and all the damage was repaired so that within a few weeks all was back to normal again.

*

At the August meeting in 1942 the Marquis Camden was elected Commodore for the duration of the war, but the election of a Vice-Commodore was deferred *sine die*. However, Lord Camden died eight months later and at a meeting held in October 1944 the senior member present, Sir Walter Preston, took the chair. Sir Philip Hunloke was elected Commodore and Sir Ralph Gore Vice-Commodore, but again, both appointments were only for the duration of the war in Europe. So at the meeting the following year Sir Walter Preston, who was again in

---

* This must have been the Steward Frederick.

the chair, reminded members that the club had been without flag officers for some months and that the time had come to elect some. Both Hunloke and Gore were then unanimously elected back to their posts. Although HMS *Vectis* had been paid off on 20 May 1945, the Commodore announced that the Castle was in need of general refurbishment and would not reopen until 1 April 1946.

It is always difficult to interpret the feelings of any meeting just from its written minutes, but a change in attitude is discernible in the minutes of those immediate postwar meetings. There was much talk of attracting the young to become members, and of setting aside bedrooms for the use of those who wished to take their wives to the Castle for weekends. The Commodore even aired the possibility of converting the ladies' annexe into a dining room where members could entertain lady guests – and that such a conversion would include a cocktail bar and a central floor space for dancing.

It was generally agreed that the Castle should be enlarged, an impossibility at that time. It was also agreed that a house called Thornhill, situated directly behind the Castle, should be purchased from Lord Northampton, who had generously offered to sell it to the club for the same amount as he had paid for it. Originally, it was intended that Thornhill should be a new ladies' annexe, but eventually the decision was taken to convert it to flats for members. When the new extension to the Castle was completed in 1964, Thornhill was sold and the ladies' annexe at the bottom of the Castle Rock made into three flats for members.

As a reminder that inflation is not a modern phenomenon, in 1946 it was found that £8000 per annum was needed to run the club, while in 1939 only £5000 had been needed. The subscription was therefore raised to 20 guineas and a life membership fee of £1000 was introduced.

If the First World War had killed off yachting in the Grand Style, the Second put an end to the very large yachts, whether sail, steam or diesel, in which members had raced and cruised during the inter-war years. Instead, a new era began, one in which dinghies and the small-keel-boat classes proliferated and ocean racers, the cruiser–racers of the 1940s and 1950s, became functional objects in which efficiency and value for money mattered more than looks.

The Squadron has always prided itself in taking an interest in every aspect of enjoyment afloat, while avoiding becoming too committed to any one branch. The regatta had never included dinghy races and, although during the inter-war years, many members had started their sailing careers in this way, no specialist in this sport had joined. The war changed all that and in 1943 two outstanding dinghy sailors, Stewart Morris and Peter Scott, were elected.

It is appropriate at this juncture to cover the sailing careers of these two outstanding yachtsmen. For they, as much as anyone, are representative of those who helped alter, along with the war and the economic changes it wrought, yachting from being a pursuit of the elite few to being the most popular international pastime in the world.

In 1927, the Prince of Wales, at that time an honorary Naval member presented a cup for the, then, National 14-foot sailing dinghy. The first race for the Prince of Wales Cup took place the same year and was started from the Squadron line. The first member to take part in this annual competition was Sir Edward Stracey Bt, who came third in the 1929 race which was held at Plymouth.

The Prince of Wales Cup soon established itself as the country's most prestigious prize in the dinghy-racing world, and by the time Stewart Morris became a member he had already won it three times and had come third three times. Such an outstanding sailing record made him a natural choice to represent his country and in 1934 and 1936 he captained a team of four which beat the Canadians and Americans, and then the Americans, to win and then retain the International Trophy. Stewart's crew during the 1934 series was another future member, Roger de Quincy, who had already achieved fame in the sailing world by winning the 1933 American National Canoe Sailing Championships which he was to defend successfully in 1936.

In 1937 Morris turned to racing 6-metres and lost the championship at the Coronation regatta at Torquay by a mere 0·64 of a point to the Crown Prince of Norway. Then, the following year, he was a member of the British team which won the European 22-Square-Metre Championships from the five other competing countries.

After the war, in which he served as one of the first carrier-born fighter direction pilots, Morris went back to racing dinghies and small keel boats, and again achieved an unbeaten run of racing successes. He won the Prince of Wales Cup in 1947, 1948 and 1949, and came in second in 1950 before changing to racing Swallows, a class in which he won a gold medal at the 1948 Olympics. He went on to win the National

Swallow Championship no less than thirteen times. In 1953 he started racing again in the Prince of Wales Cup and won it in 1957, 1960, 1961, 1962 and 1965, a grand total of twelve times, a record which has never been surpassed.

Morris started dinghy racing on the Norfolk Broads, but in 1934 he moved to Chichester Harbour and has raced there ever since. He won his first race there, in an X-boat, because he made his crew sit out, 'which was quite unknown in those days, not done at all!'

His other notable successes were winning the Itchenor Gallon ten times, the Firefly Championship twice, and the Single-Handed Firefly Championship twice. He has recently handed over the presidency of the Royal Yachting Association to one of the Squadron's present Rear-Commodores, Sir Maurice Laing, and, aged seventy-five, still races regularly.

Peter Scott's dinghy racing record is second only to what Morris achieved. In his first year as an international helmsman, 1934, he joined Morris's team for Toronto with his 14-footer *Eastlight*, so called because it was the name of the lighthouse in which he painted his famous pictures of wildfowl. Besides helping his team to victory in 1934, Scott won the Wilton Morse Trophy, which made him the Canadian dinghy champion of that year.

In 1936 he was chosen to represent Britain at the Olympics and, with Morris as his reserve, he went to Kiel and won a bronze medal in the German Olympic Monotype Class. Then the following year, at the fourth try, he won the Prince of Wales Cup before crewing for Morris in the 6-metre *Coima* at the Coronation regatta.

In 1938 Scott teamed up with an old friend and rival, John Winter. Both had thought for some time that it would be better for the crewman to dictate the tactics of a race, not the helmsman. They therefore commissioned a dinghy from Uffa Fox, with the idea that they would share the helm during a race. In that year's Prince of Wales Cup they introduced two pieces of equipment which were unknown in the dinghy-racing world at that time: a wooden centreboard, with which Scott had been experimenting for two seasons, and a harness so that the crewman could get the whole of his body to windward more effectively.

Scott made a bad start in the race, but his competitors were so amazed at seeing his crewman hanging out on a trapeze that he soon caught up and went on to win by four minutes. As he had let everyone know the evening before that he intended using a trapeze no one felt they could protest its use. Nevertheless, it was decided to ban it and, on the principle, as Scott put it, of putting a thief to catch a thief, he was asked to draft an appropriate rule which did so; it was not used again until the advent of the Flying Dutchman Class seventeen years later.

After the war, in which he served in Coastal Forces, Scott won the 1946 Prince of Wales Cup, but thereafter became more involved in the organizational side of the sport, although he was chosen to steer *Sovereign,* the British *America*'s Cup challenger in 1964. In 1948 he was the IYRU's Olympic representative and chairman of the RYA Olympic Committee which organized the regatta at Torquay, and in 1955 was appointed IYRU chairman. In this latter capacity he was active for some years in getting all yachting nations to accept the same 'right of way' rules, which was eventually achieved in 1960.

In 1950, while a guest at Sandringham, Scott suggested to King George VI that as the *America*'s Cup seemed defunct it might be a good idea for the King to present another trophy which could be raced for by larger yachts, and that, like the *America*'s Cup, it should be named after a yacht. Perhaps, he suggested, it might be called the *Britannia*'s Cup, in memory of the King's father's famous cutter.*

King George liked the idea but not the name – he was not a racing man and perhaps remembered some uncomfortable days aboard his father's yacht – and when he came to present the trophy, to the RYA, it was simply called the *Britannia* Cup, which from 1951 became one of the premier races during regatta week.

The presentation of the *Britannia* Cup was certainly a boost for the bigger yachts racing at Cowes, but without doubt the biggest boost to British yachting came in 1948. At the May meeting that year the Commodore opened the meeting by announcing that the club had 'the great honour and good fortune to be able to elect Her Royal Highness the Princess Elizabeth, Duchess of Edinburgh, as an Honorary Member† and also to elect His Royal Highness the Duke of Edinburgh KG, a sailor and a keen yachtsman, as a Member.'

---

* *The Eye of the Wind* by Peter Scott, Hodder & Stoughton, 1961.

† Correspondence in the Royal Archives (RA GVI PS 1928) reveals that it was first of all suggested that HRH Princess Elizabeth be made Vice-Admiral of The Royal Yacht Squadron, but the King felt that honorary membership would be more appropriate.

CHAPTER SIX

1948-85

*Small-class racing continues, and ocean racing goes
from strength to strength. The Admiral's Cup. The
revival of a challenge for the* America's Cup leading
to worldwide interest in the competition. The Club
flourishes

IN APRIL 1948 the Island Sailing Club hit upon the inspired idea of
giving the Duke and Duchess of Edinburgh a Dragon Class yacht as a
wedding present. It was built at Camper and Nicholson and named
Bluebottle. A Royal Navy officer was appointed as *Bluebottle*'s sailing
master and he and his successors, and the Duke of Edinburgh, raced her
with great success for many years. In her first race, organized by the
Squadron on 10 July 1948, she came third; and the Duke of Edinburgh
raced her for the first time on 5 September 1948 at the Lee-on-Solent
regatta. That particular race was won by a present member, Jack
Raymond, who that season picked up sixteen firsts out of forty-four
starts. The Duke of Edinburgh finished sixth on that occasion but in
later years won several races in her as he did in his other keel boat, a
Flying Fifteen called *Coweslip*.

Interest in the Dragon Class naturally increased enormously and the
following year the Duke of Edinburgh donated the Edinburgh Cup, a
challenge cup open to Dragons belonging to any nation. It was to be
competed for annually in the main areas where Dragons were sailed in
Britain and immediately established itself in Britain as the premier race
for the class. The popularity of Dragons soon also increased in Canada
and Australia, and in 1953 and 1954 respectively these countries were
also presented with similar challenge trophies by the Duke of
Edinburgh.

129

Two present members, Lieutenant-Commander R. L. Hewitt RN and Lieutenant-Commander Graham Mann RN, became *Bluebottle*'s sailing masters, Hewitt in 1953 and 1954 and Mann in 1955 and 1956. In 1952 *Bluebottle* took part in the Olympic trials, but the choice that year to represent Britain in the Dragon Class fell to another member, Lieutenant-Colonel T. V. Somers, who raced his Dragon called *Sabre*. In the 1956 Olympic trials, however, *Bluebottle* fared better, and with Graham Mann at the helm won the right to represent Britain at Melbourne and won a bronze medal.

In the immediate postwar era several members raced Dragons with great success. Jack Raymond, who was later to part-own several keel yachts with Sir Kenneth Preston, has already been mentioned, and others included Michael Crean, Philip Colville, Jonathan Janson and Max Aitken, all of whom, except Colville, had been elected after the war.

The postwar increase in popularity of dinghies and the smaller keel boats like the Dragon, was marked, but this did not mean that the larger classes were entirely neglected. The 8-Metre Class was never resurrected, and the 12-metres, as will be seen, returned only briefly, but the 6-metres, and their successors after 1952 as an Olympic class, the 5·5-metres, continued to be raced throughout the late 1940s and the 1950s before lack of interest and the high costs of racing them killed both off.

As has already been mentioned, in the front rank of helmsmen of this period was Sir Kenneth Preston. He had the 6-metre *Juno* built for the 1948 Olympic trials, but was not selected. But in 1952, with *Titia*, he was selected to represent Britain in the 6-Metre Class but was unplaced. He then built a 5·5-metre, but it was not a success, so he turned, as did so many of his contemporaries, to Dragons, and with Jack Raymond won the Edinburgh Cup in 1955 in *Tania*.

Air Commodore Paddy Quinnell was another very skilled and popular helmsman. Immediately after the war he raced *Jade*, a West Solent Restricted Class yacht which he had owned and raced successfully in the 1930s. In 1946 he won twenty firsts, two seconds and five thirds in her out of thirty-eight starts. He then had a 6-metre, *Kyria*, built for him, in which he challenged, unsuccessfuly, for the Seawanhaka Cup, and later part-owned a 5·5-metre called *Yolaine*. When he died in 1982, aged ninety-one, a racing buoy off his old home west of Calshot was named 'Quinnell' after him.

Another member with a distinguished career in the International metre classes was Colonel R. S. G. 'Stug' Perry who, in 1952, won an Olympic silver medal at Helsinki in his 6-metre *Unique*, and was chosen again for the 1956 Olympics when he sailed at Melbourne in his 5·5-metre *Vision*.

Other members who took part in these immediate postwar Olympics were Hunter of Hunterston, Jonathan Janson and Major Desmond Dillon, while Colonel Blewitt acted as team manager for the 1948 British Olympic sailing team.

But although regatta racing in keel boats held its own, postwar yachting really polarized during the 1950s: towards dinghies at one end of the scale and towards ocean racing at the other. The Squadron's contribution to dinghies has already been mentioned, but after the war it became increasingly – though by no means exclusively – involved in ocean racing.

The decade following the end of the war has been aptly called by one member the 'age of austerity and reverse sheer'. Austerity was the inevitable result of fighting a world war for over five years and brought in its wake an urgent need for cheaper, roomier yachts. Both these necessities were part of a trend that had already been started before the war by Captain John Illingworth, who became a Naval Member in 1951, and it was one which he continued in 1947 when he built a straight-sheered, light-displacement cutter called *Myth of Malham*. Light displacement meant a cheaper boat as less materials were needed and a straight or reverse sheer gave more room below. *Myth* was not a pretty boat, but she was one of the most revolutionary yachts ever built, and in her Illingworth won both the 1947 and 1949 Fastnets and forced a change in the RORC Rule.

Another highly successful postwar design in which Illingworth was involved were the RNSA 24-footers, a small racer–cruiser type that rated extraordinarily well. One of the first of these, *Blue Disa*, was owned by a present member, Colonel Dick Scholfield, who shipped her to Buenos Aires to take part in the second Buenos Aires–Rio Race in January 1950. Although she only finished ninth in her class a contemporary writer recked her performance to be 'one of the greatest achievements of the modern, tiny, moderate displacement yacht. Though maintained as a cruiser she was able to race over one-and-a-third thousand miles of ocean.'* After *Blue Disa*, Scholfield owned an

---

* *British Ocean Racing* by Douglas Phillips-Birt, Adlard Coles Ltd., 1960.

even more radical design, *Fandango*, which he raced very successfully for a number of years.

Another highly successful ocean-racing member at this time was Michael Mason, whose adventures were every bit as colourful as those of his predecessors in the Squadron during the Victorian era. After leaving Sandhurst, where he became the Army heavyweight boxing champion, Mason went to Canada for three years and lived as a tracker, prospector, lumberjack and bootlegger. He then embarked on a whole series of explorations which took him to places as far apart as the Sahara Desert and Cape Horn, and gave him the material for a number of well-reviewed books. In one, *Where Tempests Blow*, he described how he and his wife explored and charted the still-unknown waters around the islands of Tierra del Fuego.

Mason came on the list in 1933, built the Fife-designed *Latifa* in 1936, and, as already mentioned, raced her successfully until the outbreak of war when his 'combination of seamanship, linguistic ability, physical and mental stamina, and accuracy with his revolver', as his obituary in *The Times* put it, 'brought him to the attention of the Naval Intelligence authorities'.

Actually, Mason had been involved in secret work before war broke out, for after the 1937 Round Gotland race which, rather to the consternation of the Germans, he won, he and his crew carefully noted all the fortifications in the area and duly reported what they had seen. It was possibly this action that made him the ideal choice when the Admiralty, in the summer of 1939, needed someone to survey the south-west coast of Ireland to look for remote places where a U-boat could hide and be provisioned by a mother ship disguised as a neutral merchantman.

Mason performed this difficult task in *Latifa*, possibly the only time a Squadron sailing yacht has ever been used as a spyship. He took three months to cruise the coast, the inhabitants of which had rarely if ever seen a private sailing yacht before. Mason reported that they were so bemused by the appearance of *Latifa* that they thought her White Ensign was the Guinness house flag, a mistake Mason was delighted to leave uncorrected.

This mission gave him invaluable information about that part of the Irish coast and only hours after war broke out he went back there, this time as the skipper of a requisitioned trawler. He and his crew, which included a naval signalman and another Squadron member, Alfred Rosling, who acted as his second-in-command, were all disguised as fishermen. They never caught a submarine tender disguised as a merchantman, nor did they ever sight a U-boat; but from reports Mason received from local lighthouse keepers he was able to radio back the positions of several, so they could be attacked.

After a second sally into neutral Irish territory, during which he was arrested but then released, Mason went to work for Naval Intelligence which by then had recruited people like Augustine Courtauld, also a Squadron member, and Ian Fleming. When Fleming's novels became famous, it was said that he partly modelled his character 'M' on Mason, but Mason always said that he thought Fleming took the character entirely from his own imagination.

It is not part of this history to cover the wartime careers of Squadron members, so it is sufficient to say that during 1940 Mason, working under the assumed name of David Field, acted as an undercover agent in Rumania. He then returned to Britain and spent the rest of the war training Royal Marine instructors in unarmed combat and later in commanding various landing-craft flotillas. He survived the war and went back to racing *Latifa*, which he did even more successfully than he had in the 1930s.

In 1952 Mason took to cruising, had a 46-foot gaff-rigged Loch Fyne fishing ketch built for him, for which he designed the sail plan and the deckhouse, and his wife the interior, and sailed her for many years on the west coast of Scotland. He wrote in 1971:

> For the last ten years I have never gone south of Mull, and have stuck entirely to the Minches and the Inner Sounds. . . . One thing I am perhaps eccentric over; I detest all these modern aids to navigation. I carry a sextant but never need it. I have no radio-telephone, no echo sounder, no Decca direction-finder, and no Aldis signal lamp. If anyone wants to talk to me these 'aids to navigation' turn a little ship into a parrot house. I go afloat to get peace. For three months every year I never sleep ashore and I never hear a telephone bell.

Mason, incidentally, also wrote two novels under the name of Cameron Blake. The Squadron has only had one other novelist as a member. This is Ralph Hammond Innes, known to his readers as simply Hammond Innes, who raced and cruised his yacht *Mary Deare* for sixteen years to every part of Europe, and calculates that he spent three years of that time actually at sea.

Another member who turned from racing to cruising was Major Harold Hall. During the 1930s he had shared an 8-metre, *Severn II*, with Sir Fisher Wentworth Dilke and raced her extensively. After the war, however, he decided to abandon racing in favour of putting himself and a suitable vessel at the disposal of the British Museum whose Natural History Department warmly welcomed Hall's suggestion that he help in its marine biological work. In 1946, therefore, he purchased *Dorade II*, a twin-screw diesel-engined trawler of about 200 tons, and renamed her *Manahine*. She had to be extensively refitted, but was ready by the following spring. One of Hall's problems was providing sufficient towels and teacloths for the number of people he was taking aboard, and the Board of Trade had to be lobbied by the Museum for the necessary additional clothing coupons!

The first marine biological investigations were carried out in the summer of 1947 in the English Channel, and these continued during the summer months for several years. In 1948, for instance, there were seven separate voyages of short duration in which a number of 'stations' were worked in the Hurd Deep and elsewhere.

Between these summer excursions, Hall undertook two major expeditions, one of the Gulf of Aqaba, in 1948–49, and the other to the Red Sea, in 1950–51. On both occasions he was accompanied by the marine biologist, N. B. Marshall and much new marine biological data was obtained. Several new species were discovered and one, *Oxymonacanthus halli*, was named after him.*

Both expeditions were carried out without any major problems, although, as the owner noted in his log of the first voyage, he had one moment of anxiety.

Feb. 22nd. Weighed anchor 9am for Port Said. The Pilot a little Cretan gave us no confidence. He had only one method. Full speed ahead or full astern. Met the southbound convoy [after] about two hours. He went past

---

* In 1961, Hall, who was an Australian, also funded an expedition by the British Museum's Natural History Department to Australia to obtain a comprehensive collection of native birds. The expedition was a success and several new species were discovered. One, a new species of babbler, *Pomatostomus halli*, was named after him (*Emu, Journal of the Royal Australasian Ornithologists Union*, October 1964).

the first ship, a huge tanker, at full speed. *Manahine* was steering badly for some reason. The skipper and I were terrified. He did slow down for the succeeding ships but put years on us both. Did arrive at Port Said in one piece without ramming another ship or taking a bit out of the sides of the Canal. On arrival we went full astern both, into his berth, which ended in a stone wall. A horrid little bastard and we were delighted to see the last of him. He seemed to speak no known language.

In 1947 Sir Philip Hunloke died and Sir Ralph Gore became Commodore and Viscount Camrose Vice-Commodore.

Sir Ralph was, of course, one of the Squadron's most distinguished members. An outstanding helmsman, he was also in other ways the ideal representative of the very best in English yachting. But by the 1950s he was an elder statesman who belonged to, and supported, an era that had passed. In 1955, aged seventy-eight, he resigned both his chairmanship of the RYA and the IYRU, and from about that date Viscount Camden, who had succeeded Viscount Camrose as Vice-Commodore in 1954, ran the club virtually single-handed. Lord Camden – 'Brecky' to his friends – was keener on racing cars than he was of any form of yachting, but he helped the Squadron through a difficult time with unswerving loyalty.

In retrospect, many senior members feel that the Squadron should have adjusted itelf more than it did to the postwar mood of the country. Gore, however, was against change, and the urge for innovation detected in the minutes of meetings held directly after the war slowly evaporated.

Although not strictly accurate, a letter, sent from Augustine Courtauld to a friend who had just been elected, catches the mood during the mid-1950s very well.

> Many congratulations on your election to that archaic edifice – the Squadron. I was pushed into it a few years ago, and on my only visit there in *Duet* committed every known atrocity. I thought I had done pretty well in coming ashore in a blue reefer and white flannels but everybody else, of course, had grey. And I committed the appalling outrage of wearing a beret with a Squadron badge. I was removed to the room of my proposer, dear old Sir Carne Rasch, who insisted on lending me his yachting cap which is about three sizes too small. Then when I was telephoning I told Mollie to produce herself on the sacred platform. When I returned I found

the stewards white to the gills and I found she was the first woman who had ever got on to it. We ended up by having all our four boys turned off the lawn by order of the Commodore. I got back on them in the end by making them change their rules, which only allowed midshipmen under the age of 18, to include children of members.

When the children of another member appeared on the lawn in jerseys embroidered with the name of their father's very distinguished ocean racer they were also asked to leave. In those days only paid hands wore jerseys embroidered with a yacht's name! Correct dress, in fact, was most important and woe betide anyone found wearing red socks – or, worse, none at all.

Those who felt things were fine as they were lost a strong supporter in 1950 when Frederick Draper died aged seventy-three. Draper, known to everyone simply as Frederick, had served generations of members since 1905, first as waiter and then, from 1932, as Steward. He was, as one newspaper clipping put it, 'a Victorian by birth and by inclination' and had come to rule the domestic side of the club with a severity that younger members found endearing but also, at times, rather overbearing. When asked by one member in the immediate postwar period what he thought of the recent election of a rather flamboyant but popular yachtsman, Frederick said darkly: 'If the election had been held in the pantry, sir, the result would have been very different.'*

Although socially the club, for a time, lived in the past, on the water its members lived very much in the present and for the future. One of the most forward-looking members was John Millar who came on the list in 1954. It was he who in 1958 brought the first hydrofoil to Britain, when the chief engineer of the Grumman Aeroplane Engineering Company, who was designing surface-piercing hydrofoils, sold him a 18-foot Grumman runabout with retractable hydrofoils. Powered by a 35-h.p. outboard engine, the boat could travel at 35 knots and Millar proceeded to demonstrate its speed and versatility on the Thames opposite the Houses of Parliament and then to take it across the Solent to the Squadron. As the hovercraft was then at an advanced stage of development no government money was available for further develop-

---

* The height of Frederick's career had come in 1930 when King George V made him a Member of the Victorian Order and the Squadron gave him a reception and drank his health.

Races for the *America's* Cup were revived in 1958, after a 21-year lapse, when a
syndicate of Squadron members challenged with the 12-metre *Sceptre*. Here she is
seen tuning up in the Solent with her trial horse *Evaine,* then owned by a present
member Sir Owen Aisher. *Sceptre* failed to win back the Cup, but her challenge
encouraged others which culminated in the Australian victory in 1983 *(Beken)*

Left: Drumbeat was an auxiliary centreboard sloop designed by Raymond Hunt and built in Cowes. She was the third of Sir Max Aitken's ocean racers and competed from 1960 to 1962 *(Beken)*

Right: The Aisher family are famous in the ocean racing world for their succession of yachts called *Yeoman.* The first was built in 1936. *Yeoman III* won the 1951 Fastnet race in heavy weather. *Yeoman XXI,* shown here, was designed by Doug Peterson and built in 1978, and has been chartered by HRH The Duke of Edinburgh for racing in Cowes Week. *(Beken)*

Dimarcha was designed by Peter du Cane as a pleasure yacht for his own use. A 60-ton craft, 60 feet in length, she was a great success and her owner enjoyed extensive voyages at a comfortable 15 knots *(Beken)*

At the end of the Second World War Peter du Cane was asked by the Royal Navy to design a fast patrol boat capable of a speed of 50 knots. The result was *Brave Borderer*, pictured here, while on loan as the starting boat for the Cowes-Torquay powerboat race. Subsequently, the *Brave* class, of which this boat was the first, has been sold to many countries, including the navies of Germany, Denmark and Malaysia *(Daily Express)*

Tommy Sopwith, son of Sir Thomas Sopwith, has inherited many of his father's skills. In the new sport of powerboat racing, he won the 1968 Cowes-Torquay-Cowes race in *Telstar*, pictured here *(Beken)*

In 1970 Tommy Sopwith won the powerboat race again in John Goulandris's *Miss Enfield II*. He is seen here on the left at the Squadron prizegiving ceremony. Next to him is HRH Princess Alexandra, with Sir Max Aitken, Vincenzo Balestrieri (world champion) and Sopwith's co-driver, Charles de Selincourt, who is also a member *(Daily Express)*

Commander Peter Thornycroft is another Squadron member who is an
outstanding designer of many different types of craft. It is he who proposed a
revolutionary wide-bodied hull for the Type 23 destroyer and is currently working
on a similar design for an offshore protection vessel. Pictured here is an Osprey
class, wide-bodied fishery protection vessel *(TT Designs)*

Commander Peter Thornycroft's series of Nelson launches have become
best sellers throughout the world as pilot tenders, port commercial boats,
a royal barge for *Britannia*, launches for the Royal Navy, and as pleasure craft.
Here is Spencer Herapath's *Joyeuse II*, built in 1966, alongside the first-ever
vessel built of glass-reinforced plastic for the Royal Navy
(Owner's collection)

Sir Max Aitken's *Gypsy Girl* was a 40-foot powerboat with two turbo-charged
Cummins diesel engines. She first competed in the 1968 Cowes-Torquay-Cowes
race, and, with Captain John Coote as co-driver, won an award in 1970, one of
many Aitken and Coote received as a team over the years *(Daily Express)*

Until 1955, *Maid of Honour*, pictured here, was a steam-driven launch used by the
Royal Navy at Malta. In that year she was bought by John Millar and converted to
diesel. In 1958 she acted as a tender for the squadron's *America's* Cup challenge
(John Millar)

Inset Designed by Stuart Devlin and based on lines suggested by the donor, the 5th Duke of Westminster, the Chichester Trophy is awarded for outstanding achievements in single-handed voyages. The first winner, after whom the trophy was named, was Squadron member Sir Francis Chichester in 1967. The second winner was Sir Alec Rose. The latest winner, in 1983, was Jonathan Saunders of the Royal Perth Club of Western Australia. He circumnavigated the world twice without either stopping or leaving his boat *(RYS collection)*

Left: Pacha was also designed and built by Camper and Nicholson, in 1969, for Sir Robert Crichton-Brown, a member of the Squadron and a Commodore of the Cruising Yacht Club of Australia. In 1970 *Pacha* won her class in the Sydney-Hobart race and crossed the Pacific and the Atlantic to race at Cowes Week *(Crichton Brown)*

Right: Musketeer was designed and built by Camper and Nicholson for Sir Peter Green in 1963, with a 30-foot RORC rating. Her owner is one of the donors of the Admiral's Cup and a past Commodore of the Royal Ocean Racing Club. In 1966 he described ocean racing as 'tearing up £5 notes under a cold shower' *(Beken)*

This painting of members of the Squadron, with HRH The Duke of Edinburgh at their centre, was commissioned from A.R. Thomson RA in 1965, to commemorate the 150th anniversary of the founding of the Squadron. *Bloodhound* can be seen in the background. It is interesting to compare this picture with that of members similarly depicted in 1895, which is reproduced on the jacket of this book
(RYS collection)

ment, so Millar carried out some experimentation himself and later bought a second boat which was delivered in 1959. This he drove on Lake Geneva and on the River Seine, 'to the astonishment and great interest of the French'. Millar wrote in 1984:

> Very much later, hydrofoil boats were bought for daily service from Southampton to Cowes. These are very early 1930 design, by Von Schertel, the German, made by the Aliscarfo Company in Sicily. These are not surface-piercing foils at all. . . . Boats with surface-piercing foils must have some form of sensor, like a small ski mounted under the bow of the boat, to sense the wave over which the boat is passing, because, of course, if the foils break through the waves into the trough, they immediately lose their lift and this results in a dangerous stop on that side of the boat, which could be very dangerous in rough weather. . . . In a way it is sad that there had not been more development work done with surface-piercing foils, as the speeds that are obtainable – better than 60 knots – with great economy of power, put them in a class well above the Von Schertel designs, which are only able to travel at very moderate speeds, say 30–35 knots.

Another member interested in the development of high-speed craft was Commander Peter du Cane who came on the list in 1946. After a stint in the Royal Navy, where he was trained as an engineer, du Cane joined the Auxiliary Air Force before setting up in civilian life as a consulting engineer. He then joined Vospers and in 1931 became its managing director, a job he retained for thirty-two years, eventually becoming its major shareholder.

Before the Second World War Vospers began developing the motor torpedo boat. When Lord Louis Mountbatten heard that the prototype, MTB 102, was to be tested by the Admiralty he asked du Cane if he would be willing to fit her with a 20-mm Oerlikon gun, as for some time Mountbatten had been trying to interest the Admiralty in this admirable Swiss weapon, but without success. The MTB was still Vospers' property, so that if the Oerlikon were installed the Admiralty would be obliged to test it along with the rest of the MTB's equipment.

Du Cane readily agreed and successful trials – including the firing of the Oerlikon – were carried out. The Admiralty bought the MTB – but promptly removed the Oerlikon! Thankfully, once the war had started it was soon shown to be far superior to the equivalent British weapon and was then bought for the Royal Navy.

Once the Admiralty had accepted the prototype MTB Vospers began to specialize in this type of high-speed vessel. During the war they developed MTB's, MGBs and airsea rescue craft, and after it continued development in this type which culminated in them cooperating in the design of the Brave Class of fast patrol boat.

Du Cane was also involved in the development of civilian high-speed craft. In 1938 he designed *Bluebird II* for Sir Malcolm Campbell, which unofficially broke the world speed water record, and in 1949 he began experiments with jet-propelled models mounted on skis, which led to the design of the 31-foot speedboat *Crusader* for John Cobb.

But du Cane's interests were not just confined to high-speed craft. He was a keen yachtsman and took part in several early offshore races during the 1930s, and after the war converted an MTB for his own use as a motor yacht. He converted another, called *Sea Huntress*, for another member who was a friend of his, Group Captain Loel Guinness. Soon after, Guinness asked du Cane to find him a larger vessel, and after some searching du Cane found a 150-foot ex-Canadian minesweeper which was suitable for conversion into a yacht.

When crossing the Channel on a British Rail ferry, Guinness had been impressed by how well the ship's stabilizers had worked during rough weather. He therefore suggested to du Cane that if a similar device could be developed on du Cane's own yacht, *Sea Victory*, he would be interested in having it fitted to his new yacht which he called *Calisto*. Du Cane agreed and after some experimentation with a non-retractable type, which he called 'roll-damping fins', he had them fitted to *Calisto*. The device was a great success and was later installed in many yachts, including Onassis's *Christina*, and eventually led to some being fitted to the Leander Class frigates.

Another venture in which du Cane was involved, also with a Squadron member, was the building of an offshore powerboat for the *Daily Express* Powerboat Race which was started in 1961. Sir Thomas Sopwith's son, Tommy, won this first race, from Cowes to Torquay, and a Squadron friend of his, Dick Wilkins, swore it was not a feat Sopwith would repeat if he, Wilkins, could help it. He therefore approached du Cane at the 1962 Boat Show and asked him to build a boat for him which would beat Sopwith.

With Vospers' long experience in designing high-speed craft, du Cane had little trouble in coming up with a very fast boat indeed, *Tramontana*, which duly won the race that year, although, as it happened, Sopwith was unable to compete. After the 1962 race the authorities restricted the size of engines. This rule prevented *Tramontana* from competing, so Wilkins then asked du Cane to design and build another, *Tramontana II*. She again was a very fast boat but minor mechanical trouble in the 1963 race robbed her of victory and she finished in third place.

Over the years several members have been involved in powerboat racing – Rear-Admiral Morgan Giles, Sir Robert Hobart, Charles de Selincourt and Nigel Tunnicliffe were all early competitors – while Lord Beaverbrook and the Earl of Normanton are among the current enthusiasts.

Another keen powerboat man in the early days of the *Daily Express* Powerboat Race was Peter Thornycroft. He entered nine times, nearly each time with a new boat. A designer by profession, he took part, he says, more to learn about how boats behaved at high speed than with any thought of winning.

Thornycroft underlines the theme of this history – one of continuity with change. A century and a half after the Admiralty was obliged to take heed of the club's designs, Thornycroft is attempting to revolutionize warship design with the introduction of the wide-bodied hull.

Thornycroft conceives that the warship of the future will be shorter and fatter than the present pencil-thin frigates. This shape, he says, makes a warship more seaworthy and more economical to run. It is cheaper to build and has a more flexible armament capacity. His first wide-bodied hulls, fishery protection vessels for the Mexican Navy called the Aztec Class, were designed in 1974, and there are now about seventy-five in service. He has also designed a fishery protection vessel, the Osprey Class, for the Burmese and the Danes, and a hull of one of these is currently being fitted out as a yacht for Australian yachtsman Alan Bond.

When, in 1981, the Admiralty suggested Thornycroft submit a design for the new Type 23 frigate, he produced the S90 which is 300 feet long and 62 feet wide. The Admiralty design for the same displacement type was 400 feet long and only 42 feet wide.

Thornycroft's design was not accepted, but he is currently in the process of submitting a similar wide-hulled design for a Mark 3 offshore protection vessel and is confident that it will not only be favourably received by the Admiralty but accepted by it.

In 1968 the Powerboat Race was extended to finish back at Cowes, and Sopwith, with de Selincourt as his navigator, won it in his Shead-designed *Telstar* at an average speed of 33 knots in rough weather. He then started to race for John Goulandris and, in 1970, the year he came second in the World Championship, he won the race again.

The instigator of the Powerboat Race was Sir Max Aitken, who came on the list in 1947, and he took part in the race every year between 1962 and 1972. The son of Lord Beaverbrook and for many years the chairman of *Express* newspapers, Aitken was both an outstanding yachtsman and a great patron of the sport. It was he who also started the Boat Show at Earl's Court, which first opened in 1954, and throughout the 1960s and early 1970s his yachts were major contenders on the international ocean-racing circuit.

Unconventionality was one of the hallmarks of Aitken as a young man – he would, for instance, wear a baseball cap with a Squadron badge on it, to the fury, one cannot doubt, of Sir Ralph Gore. But where it mattered – the correct etiquette for flying the White Ensign is a prime example – he was extremely meticulous.

Aitken's favourite story about the Squadron was the remark made by one elderly member to another when he was proposed for membership.

'Who's this fellow Aitken, then?'

'Don't you know? He was a Battle of Britain fighter ace. He's a pilot.'
Pause.

'Good God!'
Pause.

'A pilot?'
Pause.

'We'll be letting in dirt-track riders next.'

After racing for some years in his Dragons, *Mohoopany* and *Joel*, and a 6-metre called *Thistle*, Aitken turned to ocean racing with a 54-ton schooner called *Lumberjack*. The RORC allowed her to be measured as a two-master cutter, so she was able to set an enormous masthead spinnaker on her mainmast which came to be called 'The Great Maxwell'. Aitken was also an early supporter of the South Coast One-Designs which appeared in the early 1950s, and he owned one of the first, *Papoose*. Then, in 1957, the Hunt-designed *Drumbeat* appeared. As a launching present Sir Malcolm Sargent gave Aitken a piano stool which he would always sit on when steering her. She was not a conspicuous success and in 1962 she was superseded by the Illingworth-designed *Outlaw*. This commission came about for Illingworth because he happened to be dining with Francis Chichester who had also asked Aitken to join them. Aitken explained that although he had one yacht, *Drumbeat*, he had sufficient spars and equipment for two, so he suggested Illingworth design a second hull to utilize what was spare. It did not work out like that, but *Outlaw* was highly successful and in 1963 won the RORC Class 1 Championship and represented Britain in its successful Admiral's Cup team.

After a time gap *Outlaw* was followed by a radically designed one-tonner called *Roundabout*, possibly his most successful yacht of all. She won numerous races, including the Round-the-Island Race three times, and in 1966 received the Honeywell Performance Award for the best overall performance by any yacht during Cowes Week.

Successful though *Roundabout* was, Aitken's best-known yacht was the 62-foot *Crusade*, launched in 1969. In her he missed winning the Fastnet by 69 seconds – some say he did win it but the time-keepers erred – but headed Class 1 and was the first holder of the Figaro Trophy which had been donated by American yachtsman Bill Snaith for the second boat to finish on corrected time. Then, at the end of that year, as a member of the only British team ever to have won the Southern Cross Cup, he took line honours in the Sydney–Hobart race, the Australian classic which Illingworth had started in 1945.

A two-tonner, *Knockout*, followed *Crusade* and was almost as success-ful, but his last yacht, *Perseverance*, was a disappointment. Up to the time of his death in 1985, he still owned *Crusade* as well as a motor cruiser *Blue Max*.

'There are several things British yachting ought to be grateful to Max for,' said Captain John Coote, who for many years was a member of Aitken's afterguard. 'He started the Boat Show and sustained it against the open hostility of his father. He started the Offshore Powerboat Race as he didn't like the plywood boxes that were being passed off as cabin cruisers, so he set up the race to break a few up, which he did with enormous success. But most of all he was a marvellous ambassador with the Americans.'

There were not many areas of yachting that Aitken did not know about and was not keen to become involved in. When a syndicate of members decided in 1957 to challenge for the *America*'s Cup he wanted to join them, but was not able to do so. This syndicate, headed by Hugh Goodson, consisted of Lord Runciman, Herman Andreae, Bertram Currie, Group Captain Loel Guinness, Major Harold Hall, Sir Peter Hoare, Major Reginald Macdonald-Buchanan, Charles Wainman, Lord Camrose (the present Lord Camrose's father), Lieutenant-Colonel A. W. Acland and Sir John Wardlaw-Milne.

For some years negotiations had been going on for the resurrection of the *America*'s Cup in one form or another, but it was not until 1956 that the New York Club indicated that it was willing to alter the deed of gift to enable the cup to be raced for by 12-metres.

At that time the only 12-metre which had not been converted to a cruising yacht was *Evaine*, which Sir Richard Fairey had laid up just in case the class was ever resuscitated. Gore had sold *Tomahawk*, probably the fastest 12-metre in the country, to an Italian only two years previously; *Little Astra* and *Blue Marlin* were also in the Mediterranean; *Trivia* was in Norway; *Jenetta* in Canada; and *Westra* and *Ornsay* had been destroyed during a raid on the Camper and Nicholson Gosport yard. *Flica*, *Flica II*, *Vanity*, *Vanity V* and *Kaylena* (ex-*Morwenna**) were still all in Britain, but not in racing trim.

With the prospect of a challenge in the offing a few of the surviving 12s managed some class racing in 1957. *Evaine* was bought by a present member, Sir Owen Aisher, and became the challenger's trial horse. The only Squadron member to be picked as a crewman was Charles de Selincourt who acted as mastheadsman, but amongst the helmsmen

---

* Before the war *Morwenna* had been owned by one of the Squadron's great characters, Major R. J. B. Bolitho, known to his many friends as 'Pull-Through' as he had once been as long and as thin as the cord used by soldiers to clean their rifles. Bolitho's wife came from the Channel Islands and he knew the area blindfold. It is said that he is the only man who has sailed a 12-metre backwards. He performed this remarkable feat amongst the Ecrehous, a group of tiny islands which are just one mile closer to Jersey than they are to France. The tides there rip through at an enormous speed. Bolitho, knowing he would have more control if he went through this dangerous area slower than the current would carry him, allowed himself to be carried stern first in the direction he wanted to go while sailing on a broad reach. Apparently, he had an agreement with the lockkeeper at St Malo who, when the tide was right, would open both the lock gates so that Bolitho could sail *Morwenna* straight into the inner basin. After the war he was instrumental in helping Britain win her case in the international courts when France sued for the ownership of the Plateau des Minquiers near Jersey.

were Lieutenant-Colonel Perry, Lieutenant-Commander Mann, Lieutenant-Colonel Towers-Clark and Hugh Goodson, all of whom were members or, in the case of Mann, were about to join.

Mann was the eventual choice for the job, but *Sceptre* went down 4–0 to the American defender *Columbia*.

The most interesting aspect of the challenge now is that it revived the *America*'s Cup, and much of the credit for its resurrection is due to Hugh Goodson and his syndicate. The 1958 challenge was also instrumental in resurrecting the 12-Metre Class in the Solent between 1959 and 1964. Patrick Egan became the honorary secretary of the newly founded 12-Metre Association, and racing flourished for a number of years with as many as seven 12s competing. One season they even raced in the old regatta circuit, appearing in Scotland, Ireland and the West Country, but by the mid-60s rising costs had killed off the class.

Only two members owned 12-metres during this period: Major Reginald Macdonald-Buchanan, who owned *Kaylena*, and a present member, Captain Michael Boyle. Boyle first owned *Vanity*, which had belonged to his father, also a member, and then in 1960 bought *Vanity V*, and became the only man in the country to own two 12-metres simultaneously. This amused his Squadron friends immensely and in an era when only Sir Bernard and Lady Docker seemed willing, or perhaps able, to display their wealth both on and off the water, Boyle was promptly christened 'Docker', a nickname that has stuck with him ever since. Perhaps it originated from the occasion when Boyle was having breakfast in the Castle. The Steward approached and told him that his captain was outside and would like to know which of the 12s he wanted to race that day. Boyle lowered his paper momentarily. 'Both,' he said.

It was during this brief renaissance that a present member, Eric Maxwell, bought *Sceptre* from the Squadron syndicate and in 1967, prior to a possible challenge by him, he took her across the Atlantic to race with the American 12s during the New York Yacht Club cruise, and while there acted as trial horse for *American Eagle*.

After the 1958 challenge the Australians became interested in challenging as well. Eventually, in 1962, a separate challenge was made but at one time it looked as if two great supporters of Australian yachting, Frank and John Livingston, who both came on the list in 1963, might make a challenge through the Squadron.

Well known in Australia as ocean-racing enthusiasts, the Livingstons' cutter *Kurrewa IV* took line honours in the Sydney–Hobart race in 1954, 1956, 1957 and 1960, but in the early 1960s they turned their attention to 12-metres. They started a series of secret tank tests in Australia and submitted the results to the Squadron, and when Tony Boyden challenged with *Sovereign* in 1964 they built their own 12-metre, *Kurrewa V*, on the understanding that the management of the yacht, and a proportion of the expenses, would be borne by someone else. Owen Aisher, who over the years has done so much for British yachting, stepped forward and, helped by a team which included three other present members, Perry, Major-General Ralph Farrant and Simon Tait, sailed *Kurrewa V* in the first *America*'s Cup elimination trials ever to be held between two countries. Unfortunately, time had precluded building a different design for the Australian yacht and her hull was identical to that of *Sovereign*, although rigging and deck layout was different. *Sovereign*, with Peter Scott at the helm, won the trials and became the challenger, but she fared no better than had *Sceptre*.

By the 1960s, the 6-metres had ceased to race as a class, and when the 12-metres stopped too only the ocean racers were left of the larger yachts that used to compete in the Solent. It was this type of yacht that flourished during this period and the growth of ocean racing in the 1960s was quite astonishing. What made it additionally attractive was its international flavour, with yachts from many nations sailing against one another.

The international aspect of ocean racing was, without any doubt, encouraged by the introduction of the Admiral's Cup in 1957. This first international team racing series between ocean racers was the idea of a small group of English yachtsmen who wanted to encourage American yachtsmen to race in British waters.

During the 1950s Illingworth teamed up with a present member, Sir Peter Green, and together they owned *Myth of Malham* and then *Mouse of Malham. Mouse of Malham* – irreverently called *Bat of Balham* by some – was a minimum-waterline Class III yawl of extremely light displacement, a logical continuation of Illingworth's efforts to design smaller, cheaper yachts that took the maximum advantage of the existing Rule. It is arguable that *Mouse of Malham*, with her tiny mainsail and outsize mizzen staysail, was even more radical than *Myth of Malham*, and when Green came on the list in 1957 as her part owner, she must have been one of the most revolutionary designs to have flown the White Ensign since *Mosquito* over a century before.

In 1961 *Mouse of Malham* was sold to an Australian yachtsman and Green then bought *Myth of Malham* outright from Illingworth and raced her for a couple of seasons before building his own boat, *Musketeer*.

The season after *Mouse* had been launched, 1955, Green and another top-flight ocean-racing man, Myles Wyatt, who became a member in 1959, began discussing how best to encourage the Americans to race in British waters. Then later that year Green crewed in *White Mist* in the Bermuda Race. She belonged to an ex-CCA Commodore, Blunt White, and when Green put forward the idea of a team of five American yachts coming to the Solent to race against a similar number of British yachts, White and his friends responded enthusiastically.

The CCA also agreed to cooperate, provided the new series fitted in with their plans to run a transatlantic race which could act as a feeder race. They had planned such an event for 1957, but were not proposing to run one in 1959, so when the first series had been successfully run – and won by the British by the narrow margin of two points – Wyatt, the real instigator of the series, and Green hit upon the idea that all nations should be allowed to compete.

The search now began for a suitable team and a suitable trophy. Five yachts were eventually chosen which included Wyatt's *Bloodhound* and *Myth of Malham*; but then the Americans said they could only field three yachts, so Wyatt and another stepped down, Wyatt volunteering to do so as *Bloodhound* was rather larger than the other yachts which were competing. This left *Myth* and two other, non-Squadron, yachts, *Jocasta* and *Uomie*. An early nineteenth-century racehorse cup was then found and bought for £300 by Wyatt and the owners of the three British competing yachts, and suitably engraved.

The first series consisted of the *Britannia* Cup, the New York Yacht Club Challenge Cup, the Channel Race, which counted double points, and the Fastnet Race, which counted treble points. A third inshore race was added in 1975 and in 1979 it was decided that all the inshore races should be raced separately. Nowadays, two are raced in the week before Cowes Week, and one during it in Christchurch Bay.

It is a great pity that *Bloodhound* did not race in that first Admiral's Cup series for it would have been a fitting swansong for a top-grade ocean racer. Her history is as interesting as that of another royal yacht,

Britannia, and is worth recording briefly. After the 1939 Plymouth–La Rochelle Race, in which she was sailed by Olin and Rod Stephens, she was bought from Bell by a Scots architect called John Joass for £2000. Joass then wrote to Patrick Egan, who had crewed for Joass in various ocean races, and said he was forming a syndicate of four to sail her and would Egan like to join. Both Egan and another yachtsman put up £500 each, but then war broke out and *Bloodhound* was laid up. During the war Joass wrote to Egan again and said he was going to sell her and would return Egan's stake once he had done so. Instead, Egan bought Joass out so that he then owned 75 per cent of her. When the war finished Egan and the remaining owner sailed her very successfully for two seasons before Egan decided he could not afford to continue and sold her to Wyatt for £7000. At the time of writing she is again for sale – for £60,000.

Although during the years immediately before and after the war *Bloodhound* was very well known in the sailing world, she became the most famous yacht since *Britannia* when, in 1962, she became the property of Her Majesty the Queen and the Duke of Edinburgh, with the Duke of Edinburgh both racing and cruising her successfully for many years.

*

In the first months of 1961 Sir Ralph Gore died, aged eighty-four, and the Duke of Edinburgh was approached to succeed him as Commodore. He agreed, provided the appointment became one of a six-year duration instead of for life, as he felt strongly that it was wrong for anyone to stay on as Commodore indefinitely. He also said that, although he would not always be able to chair club meetings, he did not propose to be a figurehead. Nor was he, and a fresh wind blew through the Castle, perhaps disturbing the equanimity of some of the more senior members but delighting the younger generation.

The Duke of Edinburgh also suggested that the two Rear-Commodores were appointed so that more attention could be given to the administration of yachting generally. This was agreed and in 1962 Lord Cathcart, who became Commodore between 1974 and 1980, and Lord Runciman, who became Commodore between 1968 and 1974, were appointed the first Rear-Commodores the club had ever had. To mark this occasion a small gold cup was donated anonymously by a member.

On one side was engraved the Squadron's coat of arms and the other bore the coats of arms of the two Rear-Commodores. It was given to the Secretary with a small typewritten note which said that it was hoped that the happy juxtaposition of the mottoes of the two flag officers would not be missed. Lord Cathcart's is 'I hope to speed' while Lord Runciman's is 'By sea'. Nowadays, one Rear-Commodore is in charge of all yachting matters and the other deals with the financial affairs of the club. The Commodore and Vice-Commodore serve for six years, the two Rear-Commodores for four.

The appointment of these two flag officers also marked a rapid modernization of the whole of the organization of Cowes Week.

In those days each club holding its own regatta issued its own set of sailing instructions and the races were run from a number of different start lines. When the Duke of Edinburgh was racing in the 1963 regatta he came ashore one day and said that he was totally confused by all the different instructions and start lines, 'and if I'm confused what must foreign yachtsmen be feeling'.

As it happened, those yacht clubs with premises at Cowes had already come together, under the chairmanship of Lord Runciman, to try to persuade the local authorities to improve the amenities for yachts; and Runciman was asked to look into the possibility of combining all these clubs' different sailing instructions. However, it was soon found that no amalgamation was possible unless all the races started from the same line. The best line for this was the Squadron's. The club agreed, and one set of sailing instructions was written which covered all the races for the entire regatta, with the responsibility for the new organization being placed in the hands of Lord Runciman and his committee, which he now called the Cowes Combined Clubs. Starting from 1964, the Cowes Combined Clubs has run the regatta ever since, so far always under the chairmanship of a Squadron member.

Cowes Week used to take place over seven days, but when Sunday racing was allowed it was extended to nine days. Since 1972, a present member, Major Peter Snowden, has been Secretary of the Combined Cowes Clubs and it is upon his shoulders that the smooth running of the regatta lies. It is a very complicated organization indeed and, although a computer is now used, a large team of race officers is required to run the racing each day, and these are provided by the clubs taking part in the regatta.

In 1985 there were twenty-four classes, with over 700 yachts* to start and it all had to be achieved with split-second timing. The starting line is divided in half, with the bigger classes, called the Black group, being started on the outer half and the smaller classes, the White group, on the inner half. A class belonging to the Black group starts first and its five-minute gun is the ten-minute gun for the first class in the White group. The starting gun for the first class in the Black group is the five-minute gun for the first class in the White group and the ten-minute gun for the second class in the Black group, and so on. The first class starts at 1030 and from then on a class is started every five minutes.

To avoid confusion between the two groups, the faster classes belonging to the Black group are started with the slower ones belonging to the White group, and the course setters make sure that the two classes starting closest to one another are on diverging courses.

Setting courses is a very complicated business as they not only have to be the right length for the class racing over them but they have to be set depending on the direction of the wind and the tide. And it is, of course, essential to make sure that different classes do not all converge on the same buoy at the same time – especially if they happen to be sailing in opposite directions! Up to now the courses have been set on an ingenious board which has different-coloured pieces of string. Several courses can be set at once by stretching the strings round the buoys marking the courses. The different colours clearly show whether any of the courses converge on one another and the strings are marked so that it can instantly be calculated that the course is the right length. From 1985 the problems of the course setters were considerably eased as the computer, when fed with the relevant information, produced on a screen the best selection of courses for any particular class.

Nowadays, there are two finishing lines: the Squadron line for the Black group and one in Cowes Roads on the Shrape for the White group, which is run from a committee boat. When a class finishes it is watched by two races officers as well as by the officer in charge of the line. It is the line officer's job to call out the yacht's sail number and for the others to note this down and the finishing time. These are then written on a slip of paper and passed to a computer operator who feeds

---

* In 1938 just over 200 took part.

them into a terminal linked to the computer at the office of the Cowes Combined Clubs. Within seconds the computer calculates the yacht's corrected time from information already fed into it and displays the result on a visual display unit on the Squadron Platform and elsewhere.

The calling out of so many numbers by the line officer sometimes confuses the public who are watching the racing on the battlements below the Castle. Recently, one woman glanced up at the Platform and in all innocence asked, 'Is that a bingo hall up there?'

During the 1960s racing in keel boats continued to flourish. Dragons still remained the most popular class amongst members,* and in the 1960 Olympics, at which Preston acted as the captain of the British sailing team and Snowden as team manager, Jonathan Janson, with Graham Mann as his crew, represented Britain in his Dragon *Salamander*. Another successful Dragon sailor was Simon Tait, who came on the list in 1962. In 1965 he won both the Edinburgh Cup and the European Dragon Championship and went on to represent Britain in the 1971 Olympics at Kiel in his Dragon *Royalist*.

But it must not be thought that members' interests centred on the highly competitive world of ocean racing and Olympic sailing any more than it had done in the past. Most sailed in a far more leisurely way and even if they ocean-raced they did so for the fun of it and often in other people's boats. No better example of this type of yachting can be given than to mention the Household Brigade Yacht Club cutter *Gladeye*, which a number of present members remember with great affection. She was an ex-100-square-metre which performed credibly in a number of ocean races during the 1950s and early 1960s. In 1955, for example, she was entered for the Fastnet for the first time and won the *Jolie Brise* Cup for the first yacht home in 'A' Division and the Hong Kong Cup for winning 'A' Division, Class 1. On that occasion she was skippered by a member, the Hon. Robert Boscawen, who had with him two others, Sir Peter Thorne and Lieutenant-Colonel Ferris St George, and one future member, Maldwin Drummond.

After the race an article appeared in the Household Brigade magazine about the race. This made it clear that it was liquid sustenance that kept

---

* By the 1970s, however, the most popular class with members had become the smaller, but intensively competitive Darings.

the crew going, as it has so many other crews during an ocean race, for the skipper's order were faithfully recorded as follows:

'Three inches in on the mainsheet.'

'Get the light genoa hanked on.'

'Stop up the heavy genoa.'

'Stop up the gin bottle.'

And when at last the great moment arrived and the Fastnet was rounded a bottle of champagne was opened. Drummond happened to be off watch and in his bunk while this was happening. He was shaken and told to take a first look at the famous rock. He put his head up through the hatch and said, 'I think it's the wrong one', and returned to his bunk.

Cruising to France in *Gladeye* was also very popular with members and a present member, the Hon. Hugh Lawson, who was one of her crew in those days, recalled that not all of them were able to speak French in a manner likely to be understood by any Frenchman. On one occasion *Gladeye* was nosing her way carefully into an unfamiliar French harbour where anchoring was known to be tricky. A French yacht was lying ahead, but in the dusk no one could see for sure in which direction her anchor was lying, so one of *Gladeye*'s crew shouted out, '*Où est votre anchre, m'sieur?*' to a rather ancient Frenchman sitting in the cockpit. The Frenchman cupped his ear. '*Quoi?*' '*Où est votre anchre?*' The old man shrugged, went below and then reappeared with an even older Frenchman. '*Voici, mon oncle,*' he shouted, '*mais pourquoi?*'

Cruising farther afield than the Channel nowadays is perhaps the prerogative of the lucky few who can snatch the necessary time, and most now can only take part in the club rallies which were so popular in the time of Lord Yarborough and which were resurrected, with great success, in 1978. But Hugh Lawson managed the unusual feat of cruising from Helsinki to Leningrad in 1968, one of the only two private yachts to visit that Russian port since the war; while Lord Camrose, the son of the late Vice-Commodore, is one of those who carries on the old tradition of cruising in the Mediterranean, first with *Idalia* and now with his 119-ton *Tartar II*. He has a knowledge of that sunlit sea only equalled by Captain Denham, who has already been mentioned as the author of the long-established Mediterranean pilot guides.

Lord Camrose also maintains the long tradition of members cruising to the West Indies, while others who regularly cross the Atlantic include

John Millar, John Foote, Aylete Moore and John Power. Lord Runciman, too, has cruised extensively during the postwar years and his
ports of call have included countries as far apart as Turkey and Sweden,
while John Roome has also followed in the footsteps of previous
members by sailing up to the North Cape.

Maldwin Drummond is another keen cruising man and one who
believes that cruising should have a purpose if the time involved is to be
justified. Few yachtsmen can have explored remote islands off the
Chilean coast. Yet Drummond and his brother, Bendor, also a member,
have been there twice, sailing amongst them with the Squadron's only
South American member, Doonie Edwards, in his 50-foot cutter *Trauco*;
and on the second occasion he combined exploration with plant hunting. He has also cruised to many European countries in his own boats.
In 1968, for example, he sailed to the Baltic in search of the graves of
some British sailors killed in a battle between the British and Russian
fleets during the Crimean War. He found them, too, on the tiny island
of Fjallskar, part of the Aland Islands. Then in 1975 he went to the west
coast of Norway to look for Viking crosses as he wanted to plot their
positions to try to find a connection between them and the high crosses
in Scotland and Ireland. He is also a keen amateur marine biologist and
during the 1970s his yacht, *Gang Warily II*, was equipped with a small
marine laboratory with which he could examine specimens he trawled
up when cruising off the Norwegian coast.

But the most unusual contribution from a present member in the field
of cruising has undoubtedly come from Lieutenant-Colonel Ewen
Southby-Tailyour of the Royal Marines,* whose knowledge and
experience, like that of Lord Belfast and others over 150 years ago,
became 'of national utility' when the Falkland Islands were invaded in
1982.

Southby-Tailyour was the youngest ever Naval Member when he was
elected in 1970 and although in those days he was more involved in
ocean racing – he has taken part in six Fastnets and several single- and
double-handed races – he renewed an interest in chart making and
watercolour painting while at sea when he was sent on a tour of duty to

---

* Although the Royal Marines are part of the Royal Navy they have never been eligible to become
Naval Members. This anomaly was corrected in 1951 when Major-General R. N. Thomas was
elected the first Royal Marine to be a Naval Member.

the Falkland Islands in 1978. His idea, now come to fruition,* was to write a book to encourage others to cruise in the area, but the facts he gathered about some of the 15,000 miles of coastline were of invaluable help to planners when British Forces had to land to clear the islands of Argentine troops.

Cruising, whether for a purpose or none at all, is by its nature a leisurely pastime, the antithesis of speed, but it is speed, in all its forms, that has as much fascination for the present generation as it had with earlier ones. The involvement of members in high-speed power craft has already been noted, but it would be quite wrong to imagine that sheer speed for its own sake has not also attracted those who enjoy sailing.

Major-General Ralph Farrant, for example, became involved in the late 1960s with the design of a fast multihull. Dermot de Trafford was the first owner of a multihull to fly the White Ensign, but when Farrant, in cooperation with Derek Kelsall, designed the 40-foot trimaran *Trifle* he produced what at the time was one of the fastest multihulls in the world. He raced her successfully for a number of years. In 1970 he won the Crystal Trophy, the premier multihull prize in Britain, and took the Snowgoose Cup no less than five times for being the fastest yacht over the course. So fast was she that he entered for the first Speed Week at Portland in 1972, but this was won by another present member, Tim Colman, in his first *Crossbow*.

If Sir Peter Green came onto the list with a radical yacht, Tim Colman, when he became a member in 1982, certainly came on with the most unusual one, *Crossbow II*, designed purely and simply for speed. Colman has won every Portland Speed Week since its inception, and in 1980 achieved a world sailing-speed record of 36 knots in *Crossbow II*. He is currently trying to break the 40-knot barrier.

Another member deeply committed to speed on water, and to breaking records, was of course Sir Francis Chichester, who came on the list in 1962 with *Gipsy Moth III*. Chichester's many achievements have been well documented and there is no need to repeat them here, but it is sometimes forgotten that by turning away in 1960 from the increasingly regulated world of what might be called traditional offshore racing, in

---

* *Falkland Islands Shores* by Ewen Southby-Tailyour, Conway Maritime Press, 1985.

A series of photographs of the interior of the Castle were taken in 1975. Here is the platform, used constantly during the season for starting races, for the Cowes Week ball, and occasionally for dinners. It continues to provide members with the perfect view of the Solent scene *(RYS collection)*

The library houses the records of the Squadron and its activities since 1815, as well as a large collection of nautical books. In the background to the right can be seen the bronze head of HRH The Duke of Edinburgh, by Vincent Opap. The Honorary Librarian is seated at the desk *(RYS collection)*

Above left Maj-General Ralph Farrant is another accomplished helmsman of international standing. He was a pioneer of multi-hull design and his *Trifle*, pictured here, was in part designed by him and was a prizewinner from 1967 onwards *(Beken)*

Above right Baron Edmond de Rothschild's *Gitana VI* is a fine example of a yacht owned by a foreign member of the Squadron and raced in the Solent. Built in Holland in 1975, she is 65-feet overall and designed by Sparkman and Stephens *(Beken)*

Top left The ladies' drawing room. On the far wall can be seen the 1965 painting of members grouped on the landing stage and battlements *(RYS collection)*

Left The much valued ladies' dining room, part of the extension of the Club completed in 1964. On the wall is the 1895 painting of members of the Squadron *(RYS collection)*

Above left This is John Millar's magnificent barquentine *Centurion* (93 tons) seen against a background of powerboat racing *(Beken)*

Above right Bathsheba, a Class III ocean racer, the most recent in the long line of successful ocean racers owned by one of the Squadron's Rear Commodores, Sir Maurice Laing *(Beken)*

Left Cornelius van Rietschoten's 24-ton sloop *Flyer II* which won both line honours and the handicap prize in the 1981 Whitbread Round-the-World race. Van Rietschoten also won in 1977. He was elected a foreign member in 1979 *(Van Rietschoten)*

Above left Fourteen original Redwings were built in 1896, and another ten were added in 1901. These were replaced in 1938 by a larger boat, built at Camper and Nicholson under the supervision of John Nicholson, the son of Charles E. Nicholson. This class has been much favoured by Squadron members, and *Redstart*, pictured here, has been a consistent winner for over a decade in the hands of the Janson family. Jonathan Janson is an Olympic medallist and Vice-President of the IYRU *(Beken)*

Above right The Daring class has raced at Cowes since 1961. They are fibreglass boats designed by Arthur Robb to a near 5.5 metre design. They are very popular with Squadron members. *Deinos*, shown here, is part-owned by the captain of the class, John Green, who also shares the responsibility of the chairmanship of the Cowes Combined Clubs committee which runs Cowes Week *(Beken)*

Right John Roome, a past Rear Commodore, has been racing *Flycatcher*, pictured here, very successfully for some ten years *(Beken)*

Top right The Commodore, Sir John Nicholson, is here photographed by a member of his crew having just rounded the Fastnet in his Contessa 32 *Star Ven*. He brings a lifetime's experience of seagoing to his duties as Commodore, while continuing to enjoy cruising, and racing during Cowes Week *(Sir John Nicholson)*

R.Y.S.
NEW YORK YACHT CLUB CHALLENGE CUP

1951	LATIFA	M.H.Mason.
1952	CARIBEE	Carleton Mitchell(U.S.A)
1953	GESTURE	A.Howard Fuller.(U.S.A)
1954	KAYLENA	Maj.R.N.Macdonald Buchanan.
1955	CARINA II.	R.S.Nye. (U.S.A.)
1956	EVENLODE	T.C.Ratsey.
1957	FIGARO III.	W.T.Snaith. (U.S.A)
1958	DRUMBEAT	Hon.Max Aitken.
1959	MISTY DREAM	T.G.Clarke.
1960	WYVERN.	Britannia R.N.College.
1961	FEDALAH.	N.E.Wates.
1962	QUIVER.III.	S.H.R.Clarke.
1963	CLARION of Wight	D.J.Boyer.
1964	ROCQUETTE	P.C.Nicholson.
1965	CAPRICE of Huon	G.W.Ingate.(Australia)
1966	QUIVER.IV.	S.H.R.Clarke.
1967	RABBIT.	R.E.Carter.(U.S.A)
1968	PHANTOM of Mersea	G.P.Pattinson.
1969	RED ROOSTER	R.E.Carter.(U.S.A.)
1970	RED ROOSTER	C.A.F.Dunning.
1971	QUAILO.III	T.D.Parr.
1972	MAVERICK of Wight	R.W.Thirlby.
1973	RECLUTA.III.	Carlos A.Corna.(Argentina)
1974	MORNING CLOUD	Rt.Hon.E.Heath.
1975	MAVERICK of Wight	R.W.Thirlby.
1976	LOUJAINE.	Sir Maurice Laing.
1977	MORNING CLOUD.	Rt.Hon.E.Heath.
1978	FORMIDABLE.	R.W.Vroon.(Holland.)
1979	MARLOO.	Dr.N.S.Girdis.(Australia)
1980	BLIZZARD.	E.G.Juer.
1981	RACE	ABANDONED
1982	MARIONETTE	C.A.F.Dunning.
1983	ALMAGORES.	G.Borromeo.
1984	CONSTANCE of Lymington.	C.M.Martin.

R.Y.S.
THE BRITANNIA CUP

1951	TAISEER IV.	Group Capt.R.J.F.Barton.
1952	ZORAIDA.	Captain F. Ratsey.
1953	CARINA.	R.S.Nye (U.S.A)
1954	ST BARBARA	Royal Artillery Y.C.
1955	CARINA II.	R.S.Nye (U.S.A.)
1956	TAISEER V.	Group Capt.R.J.F.Barton.
1957	UOMIE.	S.B.SLATER.
1958	GRIFFIN II.	R.O.R.C.(S.Bishop)
1959	ZWERVER.	Capt.W.N.H.van der Vorm(Holland)
1960	FEDALAH.	N.E.Wates.
1961	FEDALAH.	N.E.Wates.
1962	QUIVER.III.	S.H.R.Clarke.
1963	STAIKA III.	S.Roden.(Sweden)
1964	ROCQUETTE	P.C.Nicholson.
1965	CAPRICE of HUON	G.W.Ingate (Australia)
1966	QUIVER IV.	S.H.R.Clarke.
1967	MERCEDES III	H.T.Kaufman.(Australia)
1968	PHANTOM of Mersea	G.P.Pattinson.
1969	PROSPECT of Whitby	A.Slater.
1970	EVAINE.	G.Godfray.
1971	PROSPECT of Whitby	A.Slater.
1972	MAVERICK of Wight	R.W.Thirlby.
1973	PROSPECT of Whitby	A.Slater.
1974	BATTLECRY III	J.O.Prentice.
1975	BUMBLEBEE 3	J.D.Kahlbetzer.(Australia)
1976	LOUJAINE	Sir Maurice Laing.
1977	YENA.	Sergio Doni.(Italy)
1978	FORMIDABLE	P.W.Vroon (Holland)
1979	TENACIOUS	R.E.Turner.(U.S.A.)
1980	WHIRLWIND VI	N.A.V.Lister.
1981	MARIONETTE VII	C.A.F.Dunning.
1982	FORMIDABLE	P.W.Vroon (Holland)
1983	JADE.	L.Woodell.
1984	HURRYCANE.	K.Bruneflod.

R.O.R.C.
FASTNET RACE

1925	JOLIE BRISE	Lt.Cdr.E.C.Martin.
STARTS FROM R.Y.S.		
1926	ILEX.	Royal Engineer Yacht Club
1927	TALLY HO.	Lord Stalbridge.
1928	NINA.	P.Hammond (U.S.A.)
1929	JOLIE BRISE.	R.Somerset.
1930	JOLIE BRISE.	R.Somerset.
1931	DORADE.	R.Stephens.(U.S.A.)
1933	DORADE.	R.&O.J.Stephens.(U.S.A.)
1935	STORMY WEATHER	P.Le Boutillier (U.S.A.)
1937	ZEEAREND	C.Bruynzeel.(Holland.)
1939	BLOODHOUND.	I.Bell.
1947	MYTH of MALHAM	Capt.J.H.Illingworth.
1949	MYTH of MALHAM	Capt.J.H.Illingworth.
1951	YEOMAN.	O.A.Aisher.
1953	FAVONA.	Sir Michael Newton.
1955	CARINA.II.	R.S.Nye.(U.S.A.)
1957	CARINA.II.	R.S.Nye.(U.S.A.)
1959	ANITRA.	S.Hansen.(Sweden.)
1961	ZWEVER.	W.N.H.Van der Vorm.(Holland)
1963	CLARION of Wight	D.Boyer & D.Miller.
1965	RABBIT.	R.E.Carter.(U.S.A.)
1967	PEN-DUICK.III.	E.Tabarly.(France.)
1969	RED ROOSTER	R.E.Carter.(U.S.A.)
1971	RAGAMUFFIN.	S.Fischer.(Australia)
1973	SAGA.	E.Lorentzen.(Brazil.)
1975	GOLDEN DELICIOUS.	P.Nicholson.
1977	IMP.	D.Allen.(U.S.A.)
1979	TENACIOUS.	R.E.Turner.(U.S.A.)
1981	NORDICUS.	E.Taylor & Volters.
1983	CONDOR.	R.A.Bell.

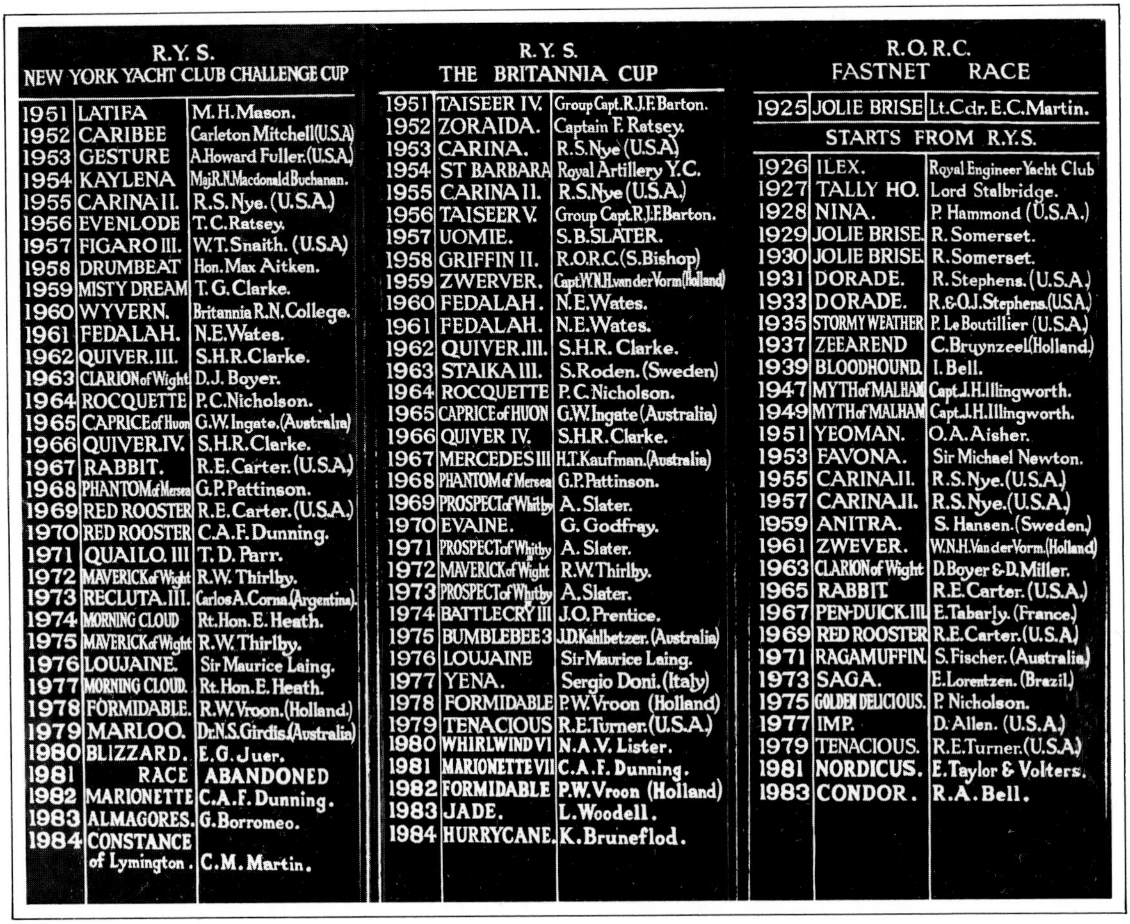

The platform of the Royal Yacht Squadron is truly a yachting hall of fame for on its walls are the names of race winners since 1827. Shown here are the winners of the Fastnet race and other principal events starting from Cowes. Another board shows winning Admiral's Cup teams *(Robert Coles)*

which he had participated for some years, Chichester became the instigator of not just one, but two new branches of the sport. In 1960 he helped organize the first Single-Handed Transatlantic Race, and then won it, which started OSTAR and numerous other single- and double-handed events that have sprung up all over the world.

Then his solo circumnavigation in 1966–67 inspired what might loosely be called inter-ocean racing, and it is interesting to record that in those early days of sponsorship Chichester was helped by Whitbread which at the time had two members, Colonel William Whitbread and the club's present Vice-Commodore, Charles Tidbury, on the board.

Sponsorship is a controversial subject, but it must be said that, between them, Chichester, whose achievements inspired it, and Whitbread, which organized it, started a new branch of the sport when the first Whitbread Round-the-World Race was inaugurated in 1973.*

When Chichester returned from his circumnavigation he was made a life member and his burgee is now on display at the Castle. In honour of Chichester's circumnavigation, another member, the Duke of Westminster, presented a trophy to the club which was to be awarded by it to any yachtsman performing an outstanding feat of single-handed sailing. Chichester, naturally, was the first recipient, and the next year it was awarded to Sir Alec Rose, who was also made a life member of the Squadron on his return in 1968.

Chichester's lead in long-distance solo racing has been followed by several other members, notably in his son Giles, the Hon. Christopher Sharples, and by Desmond Hampton, who took part in the last 'Around Alone' Race.

Although it can be seen that members take part in just about every conceivable branch of yachting, it is in the field of ocean racing as it is run today that they have most made their contribution to the sport.†
Mike Vernon's series of *Assegais*, Sir Owen Aisher's series of *Yeomans*, Sir Peter Johnson's *Innovation*, Sir Maurice Laing's two *Loujaines*, John Roome's *Flycatcher*, Peter Nicholson's *Rocquette*, Chris Dunning's series

---

* Two distinguished foreign members have taken part in this event, André Viant from France and Cornelis Van Rietschoten from Holland. Van Rietschoten has won it twice, in 1977 and 1981.

† In 1981 a Squadron team won the inter-club championship, the first time it had achieved this distinction since it won the first competition in 1935.

of *Marionettes*, David Edwards's *Hylas* and Donald Parr's two *Quailos* are all notable yachts, many of which have represented Britain in the Admiral's Cup and other international series.

But these members, and others like them, have not just supported yachting by competing, for they have all served as either flag officers of the Royal Ocean Racing Club, on the council or as chairmen of the Royal Yachting Association and the International Yacht Racing Union, on the Offshore Racing Council, or as selectors of the British Admiral's Cup team; while younger members like Commander Peter Bruce and Oliver Stanley have also contributed, Bruce by managing the 1985 British Admiral's Cup team, Stanley by being a member of the 1983 British *America*'s Cup team and by helping paraplegics to sail as part of Operation Raleigh.

One of the greatest contributors to the sport in recent years has been the Rt Hon. Edward Heath with his five *Morning Clouds*. His presence alone created better publicity for ocean racing than anything else has ever done, but his contribution is much more concrete than that for his racing record is second to none. His first big success was in the first *Morning Cloud* when he won the Sydney–Hobart in 1969. In 1971 he built the second *Morning Cloud*, which was selected for the British Admiral's Cup team. Heath captained the team which won back the cup from the Americans, but could not take part in 1973 although his third *Morning Cloud* was a member of the team. She was wrecked in 1974 and his fourth was not selected, but his fifth was, in 1979, and again Heath captained the team as he did for the Sardinia Cup in 1980.

He raced seriously for eleven seasons and in that time made fifty-four starts in RORC events and won his class in them no less than sixteen times. He was RORC points champion in his class four times and won the Roman Golden Bowl for the Round-the-Island Race four times too. On one occasion during Burnham Week he won Class 1 on each of the eight days of the regatta.

This is an outstanding record by any standard and the fact that he gained his most memorable wins whilst either Leader of the Opposition or as Prime Minister is remarkable. But the achievement of which he can be most proud is that he really did break the mould of ocean racing as it was in the early 1970s when he built his second *Morning Cloud*. Up to that time it was still customary to build an ocean racer in which it was possible to go cruising when the racing was over. Heath changed all that, for *Morning Cloud* was designed for maximum speed with the minimum of weight below, and the 'stripped out' boat is now the conventional one.

The Squadron, incidentally, has had another Prime Minister as a member. When Sir Winston Churchill became First Lord of the Admiralty he was automatically given honorary membership, a privilege he chose to retain for the rest of his life. He was never known to go to the club but while Prime Minister would often wear the club uniform with the Squadron badge in his cap.

*

In summing up it must be mentioned that many members are involved in maritime organizations like the Sail Training Association, the Royal National Lifeboat Institution, Trinity House, the Maritime Trust, the National Maritime Museum and the *Mary Rose* Trust, and are therefore helping to preserve our maritime heritage and to make the sea a safer place to sail on.

Nor must Lord Amory, with *Rona*, or the Courtauld family, with *Duet*, be forgotten, for both established charitable trusts to provide sailing instruction for the young.

No history of the Squadron would be complete either without further mention of Australia and New Zealand.

Australia, by its long – and at last successful – campaign to win the *America*'s Cup, has surely established itself as the world's top yachting nation; for not only is it at the pinnacle in 12-metre match racing but must rank very highly in ocean racing too. The Sydney–Hobart ranks only with the Fastnet and the Bermuda races and, besides John Illingworth and Edward Heath, another member who has carried off top honours in it is the well-known Australian yachtsman, Sir Robert Crichton-Brown, who came on the list in 1968.

In New Zealand, Auckland provides one of the finest yacht harbours in the world, first-class racing and a base for cruising locally and across the South Pacific. Now a top-ranking ocean-racing nation, New Zealand first emerged on the international scene when the Royal New Zealand Yacht Squadron challenged for the One Ton Cup in German waters in 1968, a trophy which it won the following year.

The return challenge in 1971 was at Auckland and was won by that redoubtable yachtsman, Syd Fischer, from Sydney. There was some consolation for the New Zealanders, however, for when the Chief of Naval Staff presented the prizes he announced that, 'As you know the Royal New Zealand Yacht Squadron has gone from strength to strength over the past hundred years. As a token of the affection in which the Yacht Squadron is held by all who have served in Her Majesty's Royal New Zealand Navy, Her Majesty the Queen has graciously authorized the Squadron Flag Officers to wear on board their vessels the White Ensign of our New Zealand fleet.'

*

Membership of the Squadron is now around 400. It includes a growing proportion of younger men, many of them descended from past and present members, which helps to preserve the club's character.

Honorary membership has grown, too. It has always been granted, not only to Naval Members, but to distinguished foreign yachtsmen as well. If a member is born in Britain he can fly the White Ensign – several Commonwealth members fly it for this reason – but foreign members may only fly the Squadron burgee. The first American to be elected was Commodore Charles Ridgeley of the American Navy, in 1839, while the first Australian, Charles Gibson Millar of Melbourne, the owner of the first steam yacht in Australia, was proposed by the Prince of Wales in 1890 and was elected by acclamation. There are several members who live in both those countries as well as in Canada, Bermuda, South Africa and in Europe. When invited to join, a candidate must still, above all else, show that he is, as the club's first rule puts it, 'actively interested in yachting or yacht racing'.

Many years ago the club's second historian, J. B. Atkins, wrote his memoirs* in which he described how, when asked by Lord Arran to become a candidate for membership, replied that he thought he could not afford it. 'His look of righteous indignation showed me that I had blundered. "It is inevitable in a club of that sort," he said, "that there should be rich men and large yachts, but if you think that candidates are welcome because they are rich, or that things are in any way difficult for the poor man, you are making the biggest possible mistake." '

Sixty years after that remark was made it still holds true today.

---

* *Incidents and Reflections* by J. B. Atkins, Christophers Ltd., 1947.

Afterword

by the Commodore, Sir John Nicholson Bt

AT THE HEART of the Club stands the Castle with its lovely marine paintings and agreeable country-house atmosphere. Behind lie the lawns, the setting for so many cheerful gatherings of yachtsmen from every part of the globe: in front is the Platform, the scene of much splendid entertainment, and beyond are the battlements created by that ardent sailor, King Henry VIII, which still form the base of the world's most famous starting line.

Against this familiar background any member from an earlier generation would find himself instantly at home in today's society of friends linked by a true zest for seafaring.

APPENDIX 1

Members' Yachts and Their Use in the First World War

There is no detailed information on club yachts which took part in the First World War by serving in the Auxiliary Patrol. The Admiralty's Naval Historical Branch has extracts from the logs of some yachts, and it also has what are known as 'Red Lists' which record in which Auxiliary Patrol area each yacht was operating at any particular time. It is from these sources that the following list is compiled as well as from information in the club's second history, *Further Memorials of the Royal Yacht Squadron*, written by J. B. Atkins.

Agatha
Owned by Sir E. Walter Greene, *Agatha* was a 450-ton steam yacht built in 1905. She was taken into service in September 1914 and served until March 1919. She was armed with one 12-pounder and one 6-pounder, and was based in the Cromarty area between 1914 and 1915 and in the Granton area between 1916 and 1918.

Amethyst
Owned by Sir Edward Coates MP, *Amethyst* was a 330-ton steam yacht built in 1877. She was taken into service in March 1915, had her name changed to *Amethyst III*, and was armed with two 6-pounders. She served until February 1917, and was based at Holyhead.

Aries
Owned by the Vice-Commodore, the Duke of Leeds, *Aries* was a 268-ton steam yacht built in 1880. She was taken into service in September 1914

and was one of the first yachts to join the improvised Yacht Patrol. Her owner, although fifty-three at the time, served with her for a year in the North Sea until he was transferred to another appointment. She served in the Tyne area in 1914 and in the Dover and Downs area in 1915. She was armed with two 3-pounders. In October 1915 she was sunk by a mine while on patrol in the vicinity of the South Goodwin Lightship with the loss of five officers and seventeen men.

Aster

Owned by Austin Mackenzie, *Aster* was a 249-ton steam yacht built in 1883. She was taken into service in September 1914 and armed with two 3-pounders. In June 1915 she had her name changed to *Aster II* and was based in the Valentia area on patrol and examination duty until May 1916 when she was paid off.

Atalanta

Owned by Lieutenant-Colonel Lord Decies, who came onto the list in 1915, *Atalanta* was a 1398-ton steam yacht built in 1903 which was taken into service in June 1915, and from November 1915 served with the Auxiliary Patrol based at Gibraltar where she had the opportunity to attack enemy submarines on three separate occasions, but without success.

Beryl

Owned by Lord Inverclyde, *Beryl* was a 1393-ton steam yacht built in 1898. She was taken into service in January 1915 and armed with one 3-inch and one 12-pounder. Until October 1915 she was on loan to the Director of the Naval Intelligence Division. Later, she was based at Queenstown with the Auxiliary Patrol and stayed there until early 1918. She was then based at Portsmouth and Kirkwall, and was based at Dundee when the war ended.

Boadicea

Owned by Lieutenant-Colonel A. Hickman Morgan, *Boadicea* was a 447-ton steam yacht built in 1882. She was taken into service in May 1915 and had her name changed to *Boadicea II*. She was armed with one 12-pounder and one 6-pounder. She was based on the Kingstown area throughout her time in the Auxiliary Patrol and served until March 1919.

Branwen

Owned by Lord Howard de Walden, *Branwen* was a 151-ton steam yacht built in 1905. She was taken into service in January 1915 and armed with two 6-pounders. She was based at Oban until December 1916, when she was paid off, and she was then bought by another member, Arthur Salvin Bowlby.

Calista

Owned by Captain Alwyn Foster, *Calista* was a 265-ton steam yacht built in 1902. She was taken into service in September 1914 and served until December 1917. She was armed with three 3-pounders and served first in the Rosyth area before being moved to the Granton area in 1915. She was then moved to the Orkneys and Shetlands where she served throughout 1916 and 1917. In December 1917 she struck a mine in the Irish Sea and was lost with all hands.

Catania

Owned by the Duke of Sutherland, *Catania* was a 668-ton steam yacht built in 1895. She was taken into service in September 1914 and was armed with two 6-pounders. She first of all served with the yacht patrol in the Cromarty area under the command of her owner, but in 1915 he was sent to serve with the British Military Mission to the Belgian Army. Later in the war, however, he returned to command her in the Mediterranean where she was serving as the flagship of a fleet of armed motor launches. These launches operated in the Suez Canal and the Straits of Otranto against Turkish mine-laying vessels and German submarines. She served until February 1919.

Ceto

Although never recorded in the club's list of yachts, *Ceto*, a 185-ton steam yacht, built in 1888, was owned by Viscount Iveagh. She served at Dover in 1914 and the following year she became part of the Downs Boarding Flotilla and served in this capacity until the end of the war.

Clementina

Owned by Frederick Harrison, *Clementina* was a 625-ton steam yacht built in 1887. She was taken into service in September 1914 and was armed with two 6-pounders. She served with the Auxiliary Patrol in the Orkney Islands area in 1914 and in the Larne area in 1915. On 8 August 1915 she was in collision off Tor Cor Point. She was beached, but the attempt to salvage her was abandoned.

Corycia

Owned by James Miller, *Corycia* was a 250-ton steam yacht built in 1896. She was taken into service in September 1914 and armed with two 6-pounders. She was used by the Auxiliary Patrol in Peterhead in 1914, the Orkney Islands area in 1915, the Portsmouth area in 1916, and the Harwich area in 1917. In November 1917 she was purchased by the Ministry of Shipping for use as a salvage vessel.

Diane

Owned by Cecil Slade, *Diane* was a 259-ton steam yacht built in 1902. She was taken into service in September 1914 and served until November 1917 with the famous Dover Patrol. On 24 April 1916 she was with the 11th Drifter Division in the vicinity of the Dunkirk Roads guarding an anti-submarine net barrage which had been laid ten miles off the Belgian coast. A U-boat – which from German records was later found to be UB13 – became fouled in the nets of one of the drifters and *Diane* dropped two lance bombs and then a depthcharge. The latter was dropped by the mate, a man named Dunstan, who after the war became skipper of Captain Slade's schooner *Diane*. Although it shattered part of the yacht's stern, the depthcharge also found its target.

'A heavy explosion took place, followed by a large eruption of bubbles and oil,' wrote Sir Reginald Bacon in the second volume of his history of the Dover Patrol.* 'The air bubbles became much reduced later on, but oil continued to come to the surface, and when the yacht *Diane* returned through this position at 5.25pm she passed through pools of oil. The vessels concerned received the usual award.'

Diane continued to serve with the Dover Patrol and sank several German mines by gunfire. In June 1917 she captured a German seaplane off Gravelines. She took two prisoners and tried to tow the seaplane into Dover, but it began to disintegrate and was cut adrift.

Hersilia

Owned by Sir Walpole Greenwell, *Hersilia* was a 454-ton steam yacht

---

* *The Dover Patrol*, in two volumes, by Admiral Sir Reginald Bacon, Hutchinson Ltd, 1920.

built in 1895. She was taken into service in September 1914, armed with one 12-pounder and became part of the Auxiliary Patrol in the Storno-way area in 1914 and 1915. In January 1916 she was caught in a bad storm while hunting a U-boat and was wrecked on North Rona.

Jason

Owned by Frank Bibby, *Jason* was a 702-ton steam yacht built in 1913. She was taken into service in February 1915 and had her name changed to *Jason II*. She served in the Orkney Islands area throughout 1915 before moving to the Humber area in 1916, and becme part of the Hydrophone Flotilla there. She was armed with two 12-pounders and one 3-pounder. She served until February 1919.

Lorna

Owned by Lord Hollenden, and then by Walter Preston, on the list with her in 1916, *Lorna* was a 484-ton steam yacht built in 1904. She was taken into service in September 1916 and armed with one 12-pounder and one 6-pounder. She was based in the Stornoway area in 1914 and 1915, and then in the Portland area between 1916 and 1918.

Lorna is the only club yacht credited with destroying an enemy submarine unaided. This remarkable incident, which happened on 26 May 1918, is most vividly described in a report of it made by Lieutenant C. L. Tottenham RNR, who was in command of the yacht.

At 8.50 the followig SOS signal was intercepted from the SS *Julian*: 'SOS. Two miles SW of Portland Bill SS *Julian* torpedoed'.

I immediately proceeded at full speed to look for and render assistance to her if required. At 9.14 I intercepted W/T message 'Proceeded to port – torpedo missed fire'. I then altered my course towards SS *War Cross*, who had by this time turned and was steering to the westward. As she had also received the SOS signal, I spoke to her and advised her captain to lay the land and endeavour to round the Bill, as I deemed this the safest course for her to take. I also informed him that I would escort him, but her captain decided to wait for darkness and get round then.

Observing another steamer approaching from the southward, I headed towards her. After steaming for about $3\frac{1}{2}$ miles I observed HM Drifter *Evening Primrose* closing the steamer. I then altered course W. by N. towards another steamer approaching the Bill from the westward. At 9.55 the ship had hardly been steadied on this course when I observed the periscope of a submarine steering west. The periscope was approximately 150 feet distant, slightly on my port bow. Considering the course the submarine was steering and his position with reference to the approaching steamer, I presumed the enemy was manoeuvring into position to attack her. I immediately starboarded my helm, and when I was close on top of the periscope (say 10 feet away) the enemy dipped, and as my vessel passed over the spot a distant jar was felt, caused presumably by our keel passing over the conning tower. I then dropped a D depth-charge set at 50 feet (time 9.57pm). I then starboarded a little more and dropped a second D charge about 50 feet from the first one.

Whilst circling to pass again over the spot I observed four objects in the water among the disturbance caused by the depth-charges. I proceeded direct to this spot, assuming objects to be wreckage, etc., from the submarine. On reaching the spot I discovered the objects to be four survivors shouting 'Kamarad' and 'Help'. Right in the middle of them I saw a disturbance in the water, caused by the rush of escaping air, etc., from the sunken submarine. I dropped another charge in the centre of this disturbance and a can buoy at the same time. This charge killed three of the survivors in the vicinity – two were blown completely out of the water (position being 4¾ miles N.65W. (m.) from Portland Bill). I eased down to pick up the remaining survivor who was still crying, 'Help, Kamarad', etc. Close up to the survivor a German naval blue jacket's cap was picked up, the ribbon marked 'Unterseeboots – Abteilung'.

Survivor was covered with oil, as by now the surface of the water over a very large area was thick with it. When survivor was received on board everything possible was done to alleviate his pain. The man was evidently seriously injured internally, and after living for about three hours he died. I remained cruising in the vicinity till relieved at 2.40pm by HMTB 81, when I proceeded to harbour.

The following information was gleaned from the prisoner: His name was Lit Wilhelm Ventland [Wendland] of Cologne. Commander's name: Uber Lt. Schtiendorff [Steindorff]. Submarine's serial number was U.74 [UB74]. Stated they were one week out from [Zeebrugge?] and had torpedoed three ships. Whether this was in one day or the whole week could not be ascertained. Number of crew 31 all told.

The Admiralty paid £1000 to the officers and crew of *Lorna* and Lieutenant Tottenham was awarded the DSO.

Medusa

Owned by Alfred Farquhar, *Medusa* was a 627-ton steam yacht built in 1906. She was taken into service in January 1915, had her name changed to *Medusa II*, and served until March 1919. She was armed with one 12-pounder and one 6-pounder, and was part of the Auxiliary Patrol in the Tyne area in 1915 and then in the Orkney Islands between 1916 and 1918.

Mera

Owned by Harold Swithinbank, *Mera* was a 293-ton steam yacht built in 1886. She was taken into service in December 1914, armed with one 12-pounder and one 6-pounder, and served until March 1919.

Minona

Owned by George Coats, *Minona* was a 249-ton steam yacht built in 1906. She was taken into service in October 1914 but does not appear in any of the 'Red lists' until 1918 when she was based in the Granton area. She was paid off the same year.

Miranda

Owned by Lord Leith, *Miranda* was a 942-ton steam yacht built in 1910. She was taken into service in January 1915, had her name changed to *Miranda II*, and was armed with two 12-pounders and one 3-pounder. She served until February 1919 and spent the war with the Auxiliary Patrol in the Tyne area. Although she first tried to engage a U-boat in 1915 it was not until August 1918 that she was able to come to grips with the enemy. On 13th of that month a convoy being escorted by *Miranda II* was attacked by UB30. The U-boat was rammed by another of the escorts and then depthcharged by *Miranda II*. It then dived, but two hours later was forced to surface and was shelled by the escort force and forced to submerge once more. It was then again attacked with depthcharges and destroyed; divers later found the wreck.

During the inter-war years *Miranda II* served as one of Trinity House's best-known yachts under the name of *Patricia*.

Narcissus

Owned by E. Miller Mundy, *Narcissus* was a 816-ton steam yacht built in 1905. She was taken into service in January 1915, had her name changed to *Narcissus II*, and was armed with two 12-pounders. She served until February 1919 with the Auxiliary Patrol, and was based at Gibraltar until the end of the war. *Narcissus II* had several engagements with the enemy. On 25 August 1916, the extract from her log records the following: 'Observed enemy submarine (1505). Heard gunfire five minutes later and at 1520 opened fire herself at extreme range. The U-boat submerged. Arrived on scene at 1540 to find a French steamer, SS *Socoa*, sinking. Searched area for submarine without success.'

Another submarine was spotted on 24 April 1917, but escaped, as did a third which was seen on 19 May 1917, when *Narcissus II* went to investigate the sinking of SS *Mardinian* after hearing gunfire.

On 7 September 1917 she had another encounter with the enemy, this time with some success as related by her captain, Captain J. P. Rolleston RNR.

> At 11.40pm being in latitude 35.36N., 6.54W., steering east at 10 knots, a submarine was seen about a mile ahead crossing the streak of light thrown by the lately risen moon. Her conning tower was showing and a small portion of the hull could be seen as she rose on the sea, she was in fact in diving trim heading about south-east, moving slowly. The ship's company were assembled at quarters and the speed increased to the utmost. I held fire for three or four minutes, as the range was decreasing, and eventually opened fire with the bow gun with common shell at 800 yards at about 11.43pm. The first shot was an undoubted hit at the very base of the conning tower, and the second was very close but short. Only two shots were fired, as the submarine submerged immediately fire was opened on her. I continued on my course and speed until a little past the spot where she disappeared, which was still obvious owing to the disturbance of the water, then dropped a type D depth-charge which unfortunately failed to explode. The evidence of an officer and a petty officer shows that the charge was correctly set to fire at 40 feet depth.

It transpired later that this was UB49. She was so badly damaged in the clash with *Narcissus II* that she was forced to make for neutral Cadiz and was interned there. However, the captain broke his parole and, much to the fury of the Spaniards, took his boat back to sea.

Although the Senior Naval Officer at Gibraltar was convinced that it was *Narcissus II* which had caused the damage to UB49, and claimed for the usual money award on her behalf, the Admiralty was equally convinced that the damage to the U-boat had been caused by ramming and not by gunshot. The award was never paid.

This was not the end of the yacht's active service for she was involved in three more U-boat sightings. On 15 September 1917 she heard heavy gunfire and, on going to investigate, found a sinking steamer with a U-boat on the surface. The enemy submerged before *Narcissus II* could approach closer but she was able to rescue the steamer's crew who had taken to their boats. Then, on 29 April 1918, she was escorting a convoy from Genoa when it was attacked by a submarine. *Narcissus II* attacked by dropping her depthcharges, but without any apparent effect. Finally, on 23 September 1918, while escorting a convoy from Gibraltar to Genoa she again attacked a U-boat with depthcharges after it had sunk a steamer, but without any result.

Ombra

Owned by Baron W. von Schroder, *Ombra* was a 275-ton steam yacht built in 1902. She was taken into service in September 1914 and after patrolling in the northern Irish Sea she became part of the Dover Patrol in June 1916. Almost immediately she had her first contact with the enemy as the following extract from her log relates. 'Struck submerged object. Turned ship round, fired depth charges, and buoyed position. Later heard explosion NW and leader 16th Division reported sub in nets.'

Later, *Ombra* was bombed while at Ramsgate. Part of her stern was blown off and one crew member was killed. She served until March 1919.

Portia

Owned by Herbert Foster, *Portia* was a 527-ton steam yacht built in 1906. She was taken into service in October 1914, had her name changed to *Portia II*, and was armed with one 12-pounder and one 6-pounder. She served until April 1919 and was based in the Orkney Islands area.

Rhiannon

Owned by Lord Howard de Walden, *Rhiannon* was a 138-ton auxiliary ketch built in 1914. She was taken into service in September 1914 and used in the Auxiliary Patrol in the Harwich area. On 20 July 1915 she was sunk by a mine off Longsands.

Rosabelle

Owned by Theodore Pim, *Rosabelle* was a 614-ton steam yacht built in 1901. She was taken into service in March 1915 and was armed with one 3-inch and two 6-pounders. She served until March 1919 and spent until August 1916 with the Auxiliary Patrol in the Falmouth area and the rest of the war in the Orkney Islands area. In both places she engaged the enemy and was unlucky not to be able to claim the destruction of at least one U-boat.

Her first sighting of the enemy was in March 1915. Soon after she had departed from Portsmouth, she spotted a U-boat and tried to ram it, but the submarine escaped by crash-diving.

On 10 April 1916 she 'sighted merchant ship on starboard quarter which suddenly gave out large volumes of smoke and steam, then took a heavy list, and disappeared under water, head foremost, torpedoed by enemy submarine'. She steamed at top speed towards the scene and managed to pick up two of the crew before making for Penzance.

In January 1917, while on patrol from Kirkwall, she saw an enemy submarine and opened fire with her aft gun, but the U-boat submerged, apparently undamaged.

In May 1917 she saw another enemy submarine which was attacking two steamers with its gun. *Rosabelle* immediately opened fire with her 3-inch gun, but the U-boat crash-dived. However, shortly afterwards its periscope was sighted and *Rosabelle* again opened fire with both her fore and aft guns. Despite this the submarine pressed home its attack on the two steamers and an hour later it torpedoed both while only about 500 yards from *Rosabelle*. The yacht dropped her depthcharges, but without any visible effect.

Finally, on 24 July 1917, *Rosabelle* saw yet another U-boat on the surface, this time off Stromness. She gave chase but the submarine dived before she could reach it.

St George

Owned by E. J. Wythes, *St George* was a 871-ton three-masted auxiliary schooner built in 1890. She was taken into service in March 1915 and renamed *Oriflamme*. She was then lent to the Director of the Naval Intelligence Division and based on the Humber, but nothing is known of her activities. She ceased her active service in June 1918 and after being renamed *Wallington* was used as a base ship on the Humber.

Sapphire

Owned by the Duke of Bedford, *Sapphire* was a 1421-ton steam yacht built in 1912. She was taken into service in September 1915, had her name changed to *Sapphire II*, and was armed with one 4-inch and one 12-pounder. She served until February 1919, first of all in the Irish Sea as a patrol and escort ship before performing the same role when based on Gibraltar. She initially patrolled between Gibraltar and Algiers, and then spent 1916 escorting convoys between Gibraltar and Malta. She had contact with the enemy three times while based in the Mediterranean. The first time, in July 1917, she sighted a U-boat but it submerged before she could attack. The second time was in January 1918 when a steamer in one of the convoys she was escorting was torpedoed. She attacked the U-boat with depthcharges, but without any positive result. The last time was in May 1918 while escorting a convoy from Genoa to Gibraltar. The wake of a submarine was spotted, but before any action could be taken two steamers were attacked and sunk. While depthcharging the enemy *Sapphire II* was in collision with another of the escorts. Despite a bad leak which had left the forepeak full of water *Sapphire II* picked up the survivors of both steamers and the escort. She then sank the crippled escort with gunfire and managed to make Toulon with the survivors.

Scadaun

Scadaun was a 157-ton steam yacht. Although she never appeared in *Lloyds Register of Yachts* or in the club's list of members and their yachts, she appears in the Admiralty 'Red Lists' as being owned by the Earl of Dunraven, although the present Earl cannot find any proof that this was so. The 'Red Lists' show that she served in Galway Bay in 1914 as part of the Auxiliary Patrol before being moved to the Nore in 1915 where she spent the rest of the war acting as escort to drifters and as a minesweeper. She was armed with one 6-pounder after being taken into service on 7 October 1914 and was based at Queenstown. On 12 May 1915 she was sent to look for survivors from the *Lusitania*. She searched for forty-eight hours but found only bodies and one liferaft. She very nearly revenged this appalling attack when, the following month, she sighted a U-boat some twenty-five miles south of Brow Head and immediately opened fire. 'First shot,' her log noted, 'appeared to take effect when s/m disappeared. Arriving on scene discovered a large quantity of oil on surface – approx 400 yards by 100 yards. Also found part of cigar and bubbles amongst oil.' However, after the war, when German U-boat records were made available, no U-boat was reported missing on the date or at the place *Scadaun* made her attack.

Shemara

Owned by Earl Fitzwilliam, *Shemara* was a 588-ton steam yacht built in 1899. She was taken into service in September 1914 and armed with one 12-pounder and one 6-pounder. She served until March 1919, first of all in the Shetland Islands area between 1914 and 1915, and for the rest of the war in the Granton area.

Vanadis

Owned by Edward Whitwell, *Vanadis* was a 333-ton steam yacht built in 1880. She was based in the Portland area until she was paid off in January 1918, but by then she had been sold by Whitwell.

Vanessa

Owned by A. Salvin Bowlby, *Vanessa* was a 445-ton steam yacht built in 1899. She was taken into service in October 1914 and armed with two 6-pounders. She served until March 1919, first of all in the Stornoway area, between 1914 and 1915, and then in the Holyhead area.

Venetia

Owned by Harold Swithinbank, *Venetia* was a 568-ton steam yacht built in 1905. She was taken into service in August 1914 and armed with one 12-pounder and one 6-pounder. She served until February 1919, first in the Orkney Islands area, between 1914 and August 1916, and then in the Falmouth area. In 1917 her name was changed to *Venetia II*.

Like *Rosabelle*, she too was unlucky not to be able to claim at least one U-boat victim. From the records she was the only club yacht to be engaged in a surface fight with a submarine.

In July 1916 she sighted the enemy for the first time when a U-boat was spotted dead ahead. She increased speed and opened fire, but the shells fell short and the submarine crash-dived.

Her next sighting was in May 1917 when she dropped depthcharges in an area where a submarine had been seen, but without any visible effect. In July 1917 she received an SOS from a steamer that was being attacked, and on arriving at the scene she opened fire on the U-boat at a range of 7000 yards. The submarine promptly dived and although depthcharges were dropped it escaped.

In September 1917 she was picking up survivors from a torpedoed steamer when a submarine surfaced. She opened fire with both her guns, but instead of diving the submarine returned the fire. The shots fell short but the engagement continued for half an hour before the U-boat decided to submerge. *Venetia II* then depthcharged the area, but the submarine escaped.

Her next sighting of an enemy submarine was in April 1918 when she spotted its periscope. She attacked with her depthcharges, but without any visible effect.

In September 1918 *Venetia II* intercepted an SOS from a steamer while on escort duty to Brest. When she arrived on the scene the submarine was still in sight and she opened fire at short range. The second shot looked like a hit. The submarine then dived while heading in a north-northeasterly direction. *Venetia II* steamed over the spot and dropped her depthcharges, and a large quantity of oil was seen on the water. However, there is no record of her being credited with a 'kill', nor was any German submarine subsequently reported sunk on that date.

Verona
Owned by Hugh Andrews, *Verona* was a 437-ton steam yacht built in 1890. She was taken into service in November 1914 and served in the Peterhead area in 1914 and 1915, before moving to the Cromarty area. On February 1917 she was sunk by a mine off Portmahomack with the loss of four officers and nineteen men.

Yarta
Owned by the Rt Hon Arnold Morley, *Yarta* was a 357-ton steam yacht built in 1898. She was taken into service in July 1915 and armed with two 3-pounders. She served until April 1919, at Portsmouth in 1915, the Stornoway area in 1916 and 1917, and in the Yarmouth area in 1918.

Zaida
Owned by the Earl of Roseberry, *Zaida* was a 350-ton steam yacht built in 1900. She was taken into service in May 1916 and served as tender to

HMS *Hannibal* in the East Indies and Egypt stations. She was sunk by gunfire from U.38 in the Gulf of Alexandretta on 17 August 1916 with the loss of three officers and eighteen men, the remainder of the crew being taken prisoners-of-war.

Zaza

Owned by Sir William Beardmore, *Zaza* was a 455-ton steam yacht built in 1905. She was taken into service in September 1914 and armed with one 12-pounder and two 6-pounders. She served until March 1919, being based in the Orkney Islands area in 1914 and 1915, and then in the Granton area.

APPENDIX 2

Members' Yachts and Their Use in the Second World War

The following details are taken from the 'Special Secret Branch Acquaint' and 'Special Military Branch Acquaint' files, and from the 'Pink Lists', retained by the Admiralty's Naval Historical Branch, as well as from the Admiralty's official War Diary and from various special reports compiled by the Naval Historical Branch on certain individual vessels. The records of some yachts are fairly comprehensive but in other cases they are patchy and, occasionally, nonexistent, beyond the fact that a certain vessel was acquired for war service.

Although most club vessels were first of all chartered and then bought by the Ministry of War Transport, the word 'requisitioned' has been used for the sake of simplicity for all vessels taken over by the Admiralty.

Taken alphabetically the yachts acquired were as follows:

Alastor
Owned by Sir John Shelley-Rolls Bt, *Alastor* was a 340-ton diesel yacht built in 1926. She was requisitioned in March 1940 for the Fleet Air Arm and was commissioned the following month as a tender. In May 1941 she went to the Ayrshire Dockyard at Irvine where she was converted to anti-submarine duties. She was equipped with depthcharge chutes and a 6-pounder gun and in October 1941 was allocated to the 35th Anti-submarine Group at Larne where she remained for the rest of the war.

Alice Hawthorne
Owned by the Earl of Albermarle, *Alice Hawthorne* was a 18-ton con-

173

verted Admiralty pinnace built in 1934. She was requisitioned in June 1940 and was used initially as an Auxiliary Patrol boat before being converted for use as a balloon barrage boat.

Angela

Owned by Captain Alwyn Foster, *Angela* was a 17-ton converted Admiralty picket boat built in 1912, and was requisitioned in October 1941 and employed as a boom defence vessel, first by South Atlantic Command and then by West African Command. She was lost, not by enemy action, in March 1944 at Freetown.

Annabella

Owned by John Musker, *Annabella* was a 49-ton diesel yacht built in 1934. She was requisitioned in January 1941 and used as a Fire Service boat for some months before being reallocated as a fire float at Preston for the remainder of the war.

Atlantis

Owned by Loel Guinness MP, *Atlantis* was a 216-ton diesel yacht built in 1926. She was requisitioned in October 1939 for danlaying* and was renamed *Sargasso*. She later became a minelaying yacht and operated with the 9th Minesweeper Flotilla in the English Channel. In June 1943 she hit a mine while off St Alban's Head and was lost.

Beryl

Owned by Lord Inverclyde, *Beryl* was an 83-ton motorboat built in 1926. She was requisitioned in August 1940 and had her name changed to *Drusilla*. She was employed initially by the Port Minesweeping Officer at Ardrossan, but was later used by the RAF and then for miscellaneous purposes by the Royal Navy. She was resold to her owner at the end of the war.

Black Arrow

Owned by Colonel F. J. B. Wingfield Digby, *Black Arrow* was a 50-ton diesel yacht built in 1934. She was requisitioned in November 1939 and

---

* Dan buoys were laid to mark a minefield or an area which had been cleared of mines.

employed initially as a Harbour Defence Patrol vessel. In February 1940 she was commissioned as a tender to HMS *Defiance* and was used for harbour defence at Plymouth.

Blue Bird

Owned by Captain W. H. Schroder, *Blue Bird* was an 80-ton motor yacht built in 1911. The Naval Historical Branch have no records of her but *Ships of the Royal Navy: Book Two* by J. J. Colledge lists her as being requisitioned in September 1939 for danlaying, and that between 1941 and 1944 she worked as a harbour boat.

Cat II

Owned by Lord Iveagh, *Cat II* was an 86-ton motor yacht built in 1917. She was requisitioned in October 1939 for danlaying. In July 1942 it was decided to make her a salvage tender but she failed to pass the survey. It is not known what happened to her subsequently.

Ceto

Owned by the Earl Fitzwilliam, *Ceto* was a 130-ton diesel yacht built in 1935. She was requisitioned in September 1939 and was employed as a danlaying vessel. In December 1939 she was transferred to the Signal School at Portsmouth where she was used as a calibration ship. Some years later, in February 1943, she was similarly employed in the Western Approaches.

Cutty Sark

Owned by the Duke of Westminster, *Cutty Sark* was an ex-'S' Class destroyer of 828 tons built in 1920. After being converted to a private yacht, she was requisitioned in September 1939 and spent the war as a submarine chaser and escort ship.

In June 1940 she took part in Operation XD, which entailed the destruction of certain French harbour facilities. She took a party of Royal Engineers to Saint Nazaire for this purpose but was damaged in the Raz de Sein by bombs and had to be towed back to Plymouth. In March 1944 she developed boiler trouble and became an accommodation ship at King's Lynn. In February 1946 she was sold to the Jewish Marine League.

Elizabeth

Owned by Captain Alwyn Foster, *Elizabeth* was a 51-ton motorboat built in 1920. She was requisitioned in June 1940 but was returned to her owner in April 1941. It is not known how she was employed, if at all.

Esmeralda

Owned by J. R. Parsons, *Esmeralda* was a 78-ton motor boat built in 1936. She was requisitioned in January 1940 and was employed as a mine recovery vessel.

Firefly

Owned by Lieutenant-Colonel R. Vaughan Wynn, *Firefly* was a 44-ton diesel yacht built in 1900. She was requisitioned in December 1939 as a harbour defence patrol boat and was renamed *Wagtail*. Later, she was renamed *Ferret*, and then reverted to the name of *Wagtail*. No details of her war service are available.

Foinaven

Owned by Viscount Chaplin, *Foinaven* was a 670-ton steam yacht built in 1919. She was requisitioned in October 1939 and was employed as an examination vessel in the Mediterranean.

Freelance

Owned by Sir Spencer Portal, *Freelance* was a 106-ton motor yacht built in 1908. It is not known when exactly she was requisitioned but from September 1940 she was based at Newhaven as an examination vessel. In November 1940 she was reallocated as an accommodation ship at Ipswich and her name was changed to *Bunting*. Then in March 1944 she became an accommodation ship at Yarmouth and again had her name changed, this time to *Freewill*.

Golden Hind

Owned by Captain J. B. Kitson, *Golden Hind* was a 144-ton motor yacht built in 1931. She was requisitioned in September 1940 and was employed as a balloon barrage boat at Rosyth until November 1944 when she became an accommodation ship at Grangemouth.

Hiniesta

Owned by Sir Frederick Preston, *Hiniesta* was a 361-ton steam yacht built in 1902. She became an Anti-submarine Patrol vessel and on 13 July 1940 narrowly missed being sunk when she was bombed twelve miles south of Anvil Point while on escort duty. She was in the Irish Sea Escort Force until May 1942 when she was converted to D/F calibrating duties.

Kalan

Owned by Lord Strathcona, *Kalan* was a 44-ton motorboat built in 1938. She was requisitioned in September 1939 and employed as an anti-submarine vessel. In April 1940 she was sent to the Ayrshire Dockyard at Irvine for conversion to an anti-submarine instructional craft which included the fitting of the type 134 Asdic set. She served in this capacity for the rest of the war. In July 1944 she was allocated to Training Captain, Western Approaches, for training duties at Larne.

Kiloran

Owned by Lord Strathcona, *Kiloran* was a 277-ton diesel yacht built in 1930. She was requisitioned in November 1939 and employed as an examination vessel. In March 1940 the Admiralty War Diary noted that she was used as a patrol vessel off the Lizard with orders to escort all neutral vessels into a British port.

On 5 August 1940 the War Diary noted the following: 'Coastguard Teignmouth reports at 0900 watcher at Labrador Cove sighted sub which surfaced and showed periscope and part of conning tower one mile from shore and immediately submerged again. *Kiloran* is proceeding to investigate.' However, as there is no further note in the War Diary, it must be assumed that *Kiloran* did not find the submarine. In February 1942 she was allocated 'for special service' and given a civilian crew and in December 1944 was employed by the US Navy at Dartmouth. At the end of the war she was sold back to her owner.

Lahloo

Owned by Robert Steele, *Lahloo* was a 55-ton diesel yacht built in 1937. She was requisitioned in October 1939 as a patrol boat, but nothing more is known of her war service.

Lorna

Owned by Sir Walter Preston, *Lorna*, as has been noted, rendered distinguished service during the First World War. In 1939 she was again requisitioned by the Admiralty and first appears in the 'Pink List' on 12 November 1939 as an armed boarding vessel of the Contraband Control Service with a Chatham crew. At the end of the year she was based at Gibraltar with the same duties, though later she was used for miscellaneous duties, which apparently included being an officers' mess. The 'Pink List' does not list her after April 1944.

Majesta

Owned by the Earl of Arran, *Majesta* was a 170-ton steam yacht built in 1899. She was requisitioned in March 1940 and was converted for use as a Harbour Defence Patrol boat in the Nore Command with an armament of 12-pounders. In July 1941 she was reallocated for use as a Mobile Mark VI Balloon Base at Aultbea, but in March 1943 was converted for use as an accommodation ship for rescue-tug personnel at Campbeltown.

Maid Honor

Owned by Major William Bell, *Maid Honor* was a 67-ton auxiliary ketch built in 1924. She was requisitioned in March 1941 for special service, and spent, it seems, the rest of her service at Lagos under the Naval Intelligence Director there. In July 1944 she was purchased by the Sierre Leone Government from the Ministry of War Transport.

Mary Jane

Owned by Lieutenant-Colonel H. S. C. Richardson, *Mary Jane* was a 27-ton motor boat built in 1936. She was requisitioned in June 1940 as an Auxiliary Patrol boat, but was paid off in August 1942. In September 1945 she was returned to her owner.

Medusa

Owned by the Rt Hon. John Gretton MP, *Medusa* also saw service in the First World War when she had been owned by Alfred Farquhar. She was requisitioned in September 1939 and renamed *Mollusc*. She was used as an anti-submarine escort vessel off the northeast coast. On 17

March 1940 she was bombed off Blyth. Two near misses sank her, but there were no casualties.

Morning Star

Owned by Major M. N. Wright, *Morning Star* was a 49-ton motorboat built in 1923. She was requisitioned in August 1940 and renamed *Festival*. She was manned by a civilian crew and was employed on pilotage duties at Milford Haven. She was later reallocated to Freetown.

Muraena

Owned by the Rt Hon. Robert Hudson PC, MP, *Muraena* was a 330-ton steam yacht built in 1907. She was requisitioned in August 1940 and used as an accommodation vessel for the mine-sweeping and anti-submarine flotilla officers based at Portsmouth, and later at Poole. At the end of the war she was sold to the War Office.

Muriel Stephens

Owned by A. E. W. Mason, *Muriel Stephens* was a 97-ton auxiliary ketch built in 1925. She was requisitioned in April 1940 and used as a barrage balloon ship at Plymouth.

Narcissus

Owned by Captain C. O. Liddell, *Narcissus* had also served in the First World War when she had been owned by E. Miller Munday. She was requisitioned in September 1939 and renamed *Grive*. Initially, she served as a training vessel for the Fleet Air Arm and was later used for evacuating British troops from Dunkirk. Under the command of Captain the Hon. L. J. O. Lambart, DSO, RN, she helped rescue hundreds of troops before being destroyed by a mine with the loss of six officers and nineteen-ratings. Lambert, who was one of those killed, was awarded a posthumous Mention in Dispatches, and one of his officers, Sub-Lieutenant J. K. B. Miles RNVR, was awarded the DSC. The official report on the heroic actions of the crew of *Grive* gives the following details:

30 May 1400 Left Dover for Dunkirk.

1900 Arrived Malo beach and embarked troops with the ship's 2 whalers and 2 M/Bs.

2130 proceeded with just under 300 troops on board.

31 May am Arrived Dover. Disembarked 325 troops.

1400 Sailed from Dover.

1830 Entered Dunkirk Harbour, and secured outside the drifter *Whitehall* which was alongside the drifter *Winchelsea*. Embarked about 400 troops from the jetty. Aircraft being sighted *Grive* left the habour, on orders from the *Whitehall*. *Grive* and *Whitehall* collided outside the harbour but both able to proceed.

2030 When clear of harbour, an aircraft was believed to have been shot down by *Grive*'s 12-pounder.

1 June 0100 Arrived Dover. Disembarked 374 troops.

0300 Sailed from Dover [with only 5 rounds of ammunition per gun].

0800 Approaching Dunkirk, at first proceeded to assistance of the drifter *Ivanhoe*; then went alongside the jetty. During heavy bombing, embarked troops and proceeded.

By now the *Ivanhoe* was in tow of the tug *Persia*, and the drifter *Havant* (with *Ivanhoe*'s troops and survivors on board), hit by a bomb, was listing heavily and on fire (she later sank). The *Grive* went alongside the *Havant* (which was taken in tow by the M/S *Saltash*), transferred her troops and survivors and proceeded to Dover with about 700 on board.

1300 Arrived Dover. Disembarked 785 troops. Captain Lambert now insisted on Lt. West going ashore for a rest; he himself remained on board.

1800 Sailed from Dover.

2230 About 1 mile outside Dunkirk the *Grive* was blown to pieces by a mine and sank immediately. The drifter *Gula*, which was about 100 yards distant, lowered a boat and picked up 11 survivors who were clinging to the wreckage. The drifter *Renascent* picked up 4, and 4 others were picked up by a M/B. A later source says that *Grive* was not mined but bombed.

Nigella

Owned by Lionel de Rothschild, *Nigella* was a 25-ton motorboat built in 1929. She was requisitioned in June 1940 for use by the RAF, but was later reallocated to the Flag Officer-in-Charge at Milford Haven.

Noressian

Owned by Captain James Buller RN, *Noressian* was a motorboat, but there are no details of her in *Lloyds Register of Yachts*. She was requisitioned in July 1941 and renamed *Trelawney*, and was used as a depot ship at Loch Alsh. She was returned to her owner in January 1945.

Ocean Rover

Owned by James Napier, *Ocean Rover* was a 300-ton steam yacht built in 1919. She was requisitioned in November 1939 and was converted at Lamont's, Port Glasgow, for use as a torpedo recovery vessel with the Fleet Air Arm. She was later requisitioned as a calibration vessel, and was employed in this capacity on the Clyde and later at Portsmouth.

Ombra

Owned by Sir FitzRoy H. Anstruther-Gough-Calthorpe, *Ombra* had also been employed during the First World War when she had been owned by Baron W. von Schroder. She was requisitioned in October 1939 for use as a danlayer, but apart from the fact that in November 1941 she was reduced to the status of a harbour vessel nothing more is known of her war record.

Panope

Owned by Brigadier G. J. W. Clark, *Panope* was a 122-ton auxiliary schooner built in 1928. She was requisitioned in September 1940. Between that date and the end of the war she was employed as a barrage balloon boat at Belfast, Methil and Rosyth. She was lost in August 1945.

Pendragon

Owned by Colonel Edward Treffrey, *Pendragon* was a 7-ton motorboat built in 1926. She was requisitioned in June 1941 and in November of that year was allocated to the Royal Navy, Scillies, and manned by a civilian crew.

Philante

Owned by T. O. M. Sopwith, the 1620-ton *Philante* was one of the few club yachts that saw a lot of active service. She was requisitioned in September 1939 for use with the Fleet Air Arm as a training vessel. But after refitting at Southampton in the summer of 1940 she was transfered to Western Approaches Command and was based at Londonderry. As an anti-submarine escort vessel she escorted a large number of convoys to various destinations. In this role she made a number of transatlantic crossings and also sailed to the West African ports of Bathurst and Freetown.

In the winter of 1941–42 she was converted to a sloop and then joined the 44th Escort Group at Londonderry and resumed her duties as a convoy escort. In October 1942 she escorted convoy KMS1, the first of the convoys for the build-up to Operation Torch, the invasion of North Africa. At the end of 1942 she became the Escort Group training ship and stayed in that role until the end of the war. She was paid off in September 1945 and in June 1946 was sold back to her original owner. However, soon afterwards she was purchased by the Norwegian people and presented to King Haakon, and she is still the Norwegian royal yacht.

When *Philante* first joined the Royal Navy she brought her peacetime crew with her. They were mainly Shetland Islanders, and her fo'c'sle boasted eight McLeods and five Macdonalds.

Donald McKillop, who had been T. O. M. Sopwith's professional skipper before the war, was commissioned as a lieutenant RNVR and became *Philante*'s first lieutenant, and the ship's chief engineer stayed with her as well. It was her commanding officer, Captain M. J. Evans CBE, DSC, RN, Training Captain to C.-in-C. Western Approaches, who personally accepted the surrender of the first two German U-boats to give themselves up off the northern coast of Scotland when Germany capitulated.

Princess

Owned by Lord Kemsley, *Princess* was a 751-ton diesel yacht built in 1924. She was requisitioned in September 1939 and allocated to the Western Approaches Command, based at Swansea. She was fitted with depthcharge equipment at Camper and Nicholson, Southampton, and then commissioned as an anti-submarine escort ship on 2 October 1939. She had early contact with the enemy when she sighted a submarine off Bull Point in the Bristol Channel. She attacked with depthcharges, but without result. Her war service was short, for on 11 January 1940 she was in collision with SS *Blairmore* near Elwell Bay in the Bristol Channel and sank soon afterwards, without any loss of life.

Radiant

Owned by Lord Iliffe, *Radiant* was a 550-ton diesel yacht built in 1927. She was requisitioned in September 1939 and after being used for kite development duties she was converted by Thornycroft's at Southampton into an anti-submarine escort vessel and was armed with a 4-inch gun. She was then employed in escort duties around the east and south coasts, and in May 1942 took *Hiniesta*'s place in the Irish Sea Escort Force when the latter was converted for D/F calibrating duties. In November 1942 she was reallocated as a training vessel to the Anti-Submarine Training Flotilla at Campbeltown.

Reindeer

Owned by Lord Glentanar, *Reindeer* was a 26-ton motorboat built in 1933. She was requisitioned in March 1940 for use of the Flag Officer at Greenock and was later used for convoy servicing with a civilian crew.

Revive

Owned by Norman Field, *Revive* was a 95-ton auxiliary ketch built in 1922. She was requisitioned in July 1940 and was employed at Plymouth as a barrage balloon boat. In March 1945 she became an accommodation ship at Fowey.

Rhodora

Owned by Lionel de Rothschild, *Rhodora* was a 709-ton motor yacht built in 1929. She was requisitioned in September 1939 for employment in an anti-submarine role, and in March 1940 took part in an unsuccessful attack on a U-boat which was sighted nine miles off Bull Point. In September 1940 she was sunk in a collision with another vessel off Cardiff. However, the motor launch was salvaged and was used by the base maintenance staff at Swansea.

Rosaura

Owned by Lord Moyne, *Rosaura* was a 1538-ton converted Cross-Channel ferry built in 1905. She was requisitioned in November 1939 and was used as an escort vessel in Home Command. She later sailed for the Mediterranean and became an armed boarding vessel. In February 1941 she was involved in the evacuation of the Cyprus garrison. On 18

August 1941 she was sunk by a mine when leaving Mersa Tobruk. Eleven of her crew were killed and thirteen wounded.

St Modwen

Owned by the Rt Hon. John Gretton MP, *St Modwen* was 1023-ton steam yacht built in 1911. She was requisitioned in September 1939 and was converted by the Thorneycroft shipyard at Northam for employment as an anti-submarine vessel. After her conversion, in November 1939, she joined A/S Group 89 based at Portland. This group served as seagoing tenders to the Anti-submarine School and *St Modwen* was employed training Asdic operators and depthcharge-release crews. In May 1941 she was reallocated to the 84th A/S Group based at Campbeltown where she was employed for the rest of the war on local escort duties and on anti U-boat patrols at the entrance to the Clyde.

Sanspareil

Owned by John Prior, *Sanspareil* was a 62-ton auxiliary ketch built in 1912. She was requisitioned in July 1940 as a barrage balloon boat, but nothing more is known about her war service.

Sans Peur III

Owned by the Duke of Sutherland, *Sans Peur III* was an 821-ton diesel yacht built in 1933. She was requisitioned in October 1939 for Canadian service as an anti-submarine vessel and she served in this capacity throughout the war. Her name was given to *Trenora*, a 28-foot motor-boat owned by The Royal Yacht Squadron, when this latter vessel was requisitioned in February 1942 and allocated to Freetown as a patrol boat.

Sapphire

Owned by Lord Fairhaven, *Sapphire* had served in the First World War. She was requisitioned in November 1939 and was renamed *Breda*. She was initially part of the 7th Submarine Flotilla based at Rothesay and was used as a submarine tender. She then became a convoy leader and was the first vessel to be so used. She came under several air attacks while escorting convoys from Kirkwall and on 27 April 1940 attacked a U-boat she had sighted with depthcharges, but without success. She escorted various convoys across the North Sea to and from Norway, but was not wholly suited to the task. While escorting her first convoy, ON.22, she had to heave to in heavy weather although the rest of the convoy was able to proceed. In March 1941, therefore, she was reallocated to Portland to be used as a submarine escort ship, and spent the rest of the war on escort duties in the Irish Sea. In June 1941 she escaped an attack by enemy aircraft off Land's End without damage, but in February 1944 she was accidentally beached in Campbeltown Loch and later sank.

Scotia II

Owned by James Bryce Allan, *Scotia II* was a 43-ton steam pinnacle built in 1909. There are no records of her in the Naval Historical Branch, but *Ships of the Royal Navy: Book Two* by J. J. Colledge lists her as having been requisitioned as a boom tender in November 1939.

Silver Cloud

Owned by Captain Arnold Wills, *Silver Cloud* was an 88-ton motor yacht built in 1930. She was requisitioned in August 1940 as an auxiliary patrol boat. After conversion to this role by Scott and Sons, Bowling, and fitted with depthcharge chutes, a 6-pounder gun and a Hotchkiss gun, she became a defence patrol craft at Tobermory. In December 1941 she was reallocated to Aultbea, and in January 1945 reallocated again for use by C.-in-C. Western Approaches as a local patrol craft.

Sona

Owned by Lord Camrose, *Sona* was a 555-ton motor yacht built in 1922. She was requisitioned in September 1939 as an anti-submarine patrol vessel but in August 1940 became an accommodation ship in Poole Harbour. On 4 June 1942 she was attacked by an enemy aircraft and hit by a bomb which later detonated and broke her back.

Sou'wester

Owned by Major Charles Prestcott-Westcar, *Sou'wester* was a 95-ton motor yacht built in 1891. She was requisitioned in June 1943, renamed *Epping*, and employed as an accommodation ship for the Captain, Minesweepers, Harwich.

Star of India

Owned by Lord Portal, *Star of India* was a 735-ton steam yacht built in 1888. She was requisitioned just before the war broke out as an examination vessel. However, she initially acted as an escort vessel, mostly in the English Channel, but in July 1942 was allocated for service at Kilindini where she was converted for examination service. In March 1943 she was found unsuitable for service abroad and reallocated to Ardrishaig as an accommodation ship for HMS *Seahawk*.

Tamahine

Owned by Major Harold Hall, *Tamahine* was a 43-ton motor yacht built in 1934. She was requisitioned in October 1939 and after serving for a short time as a patrol boat she became a boom defence boat in Portsmouth Harbour. She served in this capacity until May 1944 when she was damaged by fire.

Thendara

Owned by Arthur Young, *Thendara* was a 147-ton auxiliary ketch built in 1937. She was requisitioned in September 1940 as a barrage balloon boat, but nothing more is known about her war service.

Thoma II

Owned by Sir Thomas Thompson, *Thoma II* was a 134-ton auxiliary ketch built in 1909. She was requisitioned in July 1942 and was employed as an accommodation ship by the Port of London Authority in this capacity during salvage operations.

Three-Three-Three

Owned by James Allan, *Three-Three-Three* was a 69-ton motor yacht built in 1936. She was requisitioned in November 1939 as a Harbour Defence Patrol boat. She served in this capacity on the Clyde until the end of the war. In November 1941 her name was changed to *Trefoil*.

Virginia

Owned by S. L. Courtauld, *Virginia* was a 712-ton diesel yacht built in 1930. She was requisitioned in September 1939 and converted for use as an Anti-Submarine Patrol vessel. In May 1940 she attacked a U-boat while on patrol, but without success. In March 1941 she joined the Irish

Sea Escort Force based at Belfast and the following month was employed as an additional AA escort in the Irish Sea because of the increased air threat to convoys. In 1943 she escorted convoys to South Africa and remained at Kilindini for a few months for escort duties. At the end of 1943 she sailed for the Seychelles, India and Ceylon. In January 1946 she arrived back in Britain and was then returned to her owner.

Yarta

Owned by the Marquis Camden, *Yarta* had served during the First World War. She was requisitioned in November 1939 and was then commissioned as a danlaying vessel. In September 1942 she was converted for use as an Anti-submarine Patrol boat by Harland and Wolff and served in this capacity for the remainder of the war.

APPENDIX 3

The Royal Yacht Squadron and the Town of Cowes

By Spencer Herapath, Hon. Librarian and Custodian of Pictures, Royal Yacht Squadron

Members of the Squadron brought prosperity to Cowes by spending money in greater and greater amounts in the yards and in the shops. A further high in the golden age of the reign of King Edward VII was the introduction of 'the big spenders' of the world in their huge yachts. Then, unfortunately, both the First and Second World Wars reduced the wealth of members because of the huge taxation needed to pay for them. Still the members have contributed to the town as benefactors with permanent attributes to their generosity:

Prince's Green
The freehold of the stretch of land to the West of the Squadron was a gift from George Stephenson in 1863 on the occasion of the marriage of the Prince of Wales. This land exists now as a promenade and a beach and it is a star amenity for the people of Cowes and for tourists. The donor was a keen yachtsman member who challenged *America* to a race in 1851 in his schooner *Titania*, but he was a greater lover of Cowes and made other benefactions. George Stephenson was one of the first industrialist members of the Squadron, being the son of the locomotive engineer and in his own right one of the greatest bridge builders of his era, including the viaduct bridge over the Tweed, the Menai tubular bridge and the Victoria Bridge over the St Lawrence.

The Hospital
The Frank James Hospital in East Cowes was the gift of the James family and thirty-four members of the Squadron in 1883 – in memory of Frank

James who was killed by an elephant. Originally a home for seafarers, in 1903 it became a fullyfledged cottage hospital with a further five-figure endowment from the James family. Now extended to provide full operating facilities, it is a key hospital serving the whole island community. The hospital has continued to have a popular image, with its initial reputation for caring being maintained.

The Church

Holy Trinity Church was consecrated on Midsummer's Day, 1832, as a church for sailors and seafarers and has received continuing support from the members. The interior has been beautifully enhanced by thirty fine memorial tablets, twenty-seven in memory of members, one of a club Secretary and two of honorary chaplains. The peal of eight bells was given by a member in 1907. The church has been called the only yachtsman's church in the world.

Museums

At the Prospect in the High Street a former sailing loft has been converted into a first-class maritime museum through the monies of a charitable trust founded by Sir Max Aitken. Not only are there some fine classical marine paintings but also amusing and interesting memorabilia of yachting and yacht owners, including items once in royal possession.

Yelf Brothers

The longest-standing connection with the Squadron or the Royal Yacht Club as it then was, is with the printing firm Yelf Brothers. In fact, their works are in Newport. They started printing yacht-race programmes in 1828 with the racing flags coloured by hand. This continued until the end of the century. Yelf Brothers are still printing for the Squadron and are doing the list of members and their yachts this year, 1985.

Benzies

Mr Benzie in the High Street in the 1860s became the club's silver smith and he had his own hallmark. His finest work in the club's possession is a large solid silver model of *Britannia*. The firm continues to supply the needs of members for their yachting jewellery.

The Beken Family
They were chemists who turned their talents to photography, in which they excelled. Their photographic works of art are well known world-wide while their archive of photographs of old and new yachts is unsurpassed.

APPENDIX 4

Officers of
The Royal Yacht Squadron

Sovereign's name at head of members' list
Royal Yacht Squadron

1837	His Majesty King William IV
1838 – 1840	Her Majesty Queen Victoria
1841 – 1857	Her Majesty Queen Victoria and His Royal Highness Prince Albert
1858 – 1861	Her Majesty Queen Victoria and His Royal Highness The Prince Consort
1862	Her Majesty Queen Victoria
1863 – 1881	Her Majesty Queen Victoria and His Royal Highness The Prince of Wales K.G.
1882 – 1900	Her Majesty The Queen and His Royal Highness The Prince of Wales (Commodore)
1901 – 1952	Admirals: Their Majesties King Edward VII, George V, Edward VIII and George VI
1953 –	Patron: Her Majesty Queen Elizabeth II Admiral: H.R.H. The Duke of Edinburgh

Commodores

1825 – 1846	The Earl of Yarborough
1847 – 1848	The Marquis of Donegall
1849 – 1881	The Earl of Wilton
1882 – 1900	H.R.H. The Prince of Wales
1901 – 1919	The Marquis of Ormonde
1920 – 1926	The Duke of Leeds
1927 – 1942	Sir R. Williams-Bulkeley

1942 – 1943	The Marquis Camden
1943 – 1947	Sir Philip Hunloke
1947 – 1961	Sir Ralph Gore
1962 – 1968	H.R.H. The Duke of Edinburgh
1968 – 1974	The Viscount Runciman of Doxford
1974 – 1980	Major General The Earl Cathcart
1980 – 1986	Sir John Nicholson

Vice-Commodores

1827 – 1844	The Earl of Belfast
1845 – 1847	The Marques of Donegall
1848 – 1850	Sir Bellingham Graham
1851 – 1861	C. R. M. Tallbot Esq.
1862 – 1875	The Marquis of Conyngham
1876 – 1884	The Marquis of Londonderry
1885 – 1900	The Marquis of Ormonde
1901 – 1919	The Duke of Leeds
1920 – 1926	Sir R. Williams-Bulkeley
1927 – 1943	The Marquis Camden
1945 – 1947	Sir Ralph Gore
1948 – 1954	The Viscount Camrose
1954 – 1965	The Marquis Camden
1965 – 1971	Sir Kenneth Preston
1971 – 1977	The Earl of Malmesbury
1977 – 1983	Major General Sir Robert Pigot Bt.
1983 – 1989	C. H. Tidbury Esq.

Rear Commodores

1962 – 1964	Colonel The Earl Cathcart
1962 – 1966	The Viscount Runciman of Doxford
1964 – 1968	Lt Colonel A. W. Acland
1966 – 1970	John D. Russell Esq.
1968 – 1972	Stewart H. Morris Esq.
1970 – 1974	Roger Leigh-Wood Esq.
1972 – 1976	Major P. R. Colville
1974 – 1978	Brigadier Sir Richard Anstruther-Gough-Calthorpe

1976 – 1980 J. M. F. Crean Esq.
1978 – 1982 Sir Eric Drake
1980 – 1984 J. W. Roome Esq.
1982 – 1986 Sir Maurice Laing
1984 – 1988 Commander G. H. Mann, RN

Secretaries

1824 – 1827 J. Ward Esq.
1828 – 1833 Richard Stephens Esq.
1834 – 1851 John Bates RN
1852 – 1866 W. C. Browne, RN (as from 1858 he addressed himself as
W. C. Browne, Esq., Captain RN)
1867 – 1897 Richard Grand Esq.
1898 – 1926 T. H. S. Pasley Esq., MVO, RN
1927 – 1946 Pay Captain F. W. Walshe, MVO, OBE, RN
1947 – 1951 L. A. Drover Esq.
1951 – 1955 Commander H. H. Rogers RN
1955 – 1968 Captain M. H. Evelegh, MVO, RN
1968 – 1980 Major J. D. Dillon, DSC, RM
1981 – Major R. P. Rising, RM

Honorary Appointments as Marine Painters

1828 – 1858 John Christian Schetky
1875 – 1894 Sir Oswald Brierly, RWS
1895 – 1912 The Chevalier Eduardo de Martino, MVO
1913 – 1917 Charles Napier Hemy, RA, RI, ROI, RWS
1917 – 1946 Norman Wilkinson, CBE, PRWS, RI
1934 – 1946 Lt. Col. Harold Wyllie, OBE, RSMS, AINA

Index

Ackers, G. H., 44, 47

Ackers Graduated Scale, 44, 61

Acland, Lieut. Colonel A. W., 142

Admiral's Cup, 141, 144, 154

Admiralty, grants RYS the White Ensign, 34–5, 51, 52, 53; and RYS's yacht designs, 41–2; World War I, 91–4; 95; World War II, 119, 120, 137–9

Adriana, 112

Agatha, 159

Ailsa, 77, 78, 80

Ailsa, Marquis of, 72, 73–4

Aisher, Sir Owen, 142, 144, 153

Aitken, Sir Max, 99, 130, 139, 140–2, 190

Alabama, 59

Alarm, 40–1, 43, 58, 60, 61

Alastor, 173

Albatross, 45, 83

Albermarle, Earl of, 81, 173

Albert, Prince, 56, 63

Alfred Ernest Albert, Duke of Edinburgh, 59–60

Alice, 59

Alice Hawthorne, 173–4

Aliscarfo Company, 137

Allan, James Bryce, 185, 186

America, 56–8

America's Cup, 75, 76–7, 79, 108–9, 128, 142–3, 144, 154, 155

American Eagle, 143

American National Canoe Sailing Championships, 126

American Universal Rule, 109

Amethyst, 159

Amory, Lord, 155

Andreae, Herman, 142

Andrews, Hugh, 171

Angela, 174

Anglesey, Sir Henry Paget, Marquis of, 17, 18, 22 and n., 24, 26, 28, 29, 45, 57, 62

Annabella, 174

Annersley, Lord, 55

Anstruther-Gough-Calthorpe, Sir FitzRoy H., 181

Antelope, 30

Appledurcombe, 47

Appleton, Thomas, 59

Aries, 91, 159–60

Arran, Earl of, 178

Arrow, 23, 36–7, 56, 61–2

Assegais, 153

Assheton Smith, Thomas, 21, 22, 27, 36, 38, 39–40, 42, 56, 58

Astaire, Fred, 122

Aster, 160

Astor, Vincent, 115

Atkins, J. B., 94, 156, 159

Atlanta, 160

Atlantic, 82

Atlantic Yacht Club, 82

Atlantis, 174

Audrey, 77
Aurora Borealis, 58
autogyros, 107–8
Auxiliary Patrol, 92–4
Aztec Class, 139

Balaclava, 65
Batthyany, Count, 62
Batthyany-Strattman, Prince, 72
Baxendale, Colonel, 110
Beardmore, Sir William, 172
Beatty, Rear-Admiral David, 94, 123
Bedford, Duke of, 93, 169
Beken family, 191
Belem, 115, 16
Belfast, Lord, *see* Donegal, Marquis of
Bell, Isaac, 113, 146
Bell, Major William, 178
Bennett, J. Gordon Jr, 59
Benodet Race, 113
Bentinck, George, 69–70
Benzie, Mr, 190
Bermuda Race, 110, 112, 113, 145
Berri, Duke de, 24
Berthon Boat Company, 23
Beryl, 160, 174
Bibby, Frank, 163
Big Class, 80–1, 89, 104, 109
biological exploration, 84–5, 114–15, 134, 151
Black Arrow, 174–5
'Black Book', 30–1
Blake, Cameron, 133
Blewitt, Major, 131
Bloe, Detmar, 116
Bloodhound, 74, 113, 145–6
Blue Bird, 175
Blue Disa, 131
Blue Ensign, 51–3
Blue Marlin, 108, 142
Blue Max, 141
Bluebird II, 138
Bluebottle, 129–30
Boadicea, 160
Boardman, Charles, 106n.
Boat Show, 140, 141
Bolitho, Major R. J. B., 142
Bond, Alan, 139
Boscawen, Robert, 149
Boulton, William, 17n.
Bowlby, Arthur Salvin, 161, 170

Boyd, Ben, 65–6
Boyden, Tony, 144
Boyle, Captain Michael, 143
Brabazon of Tara, Lord, 106–8
Branwen, 161
Brassey, Albert, 81, 94
Brassey, Lady Anne, 83
Brassey, Lord, 65, 72, 81, 83–4, 95–6, 113
Breeze, 41n., 76
Brenton Reef Cup, 75, 76
Bridgeman, Admiral, 97
Brighton, 114
Brilliant, 47
Britannia, 75–7, 78, 79–80, 89, 104, 106, 109–10, 146
Britannia Cup, 128, 145
British–American Cup, 104–5, 106
British International Trophy, 83
Brook, Sir James, 45
Broughton, Urban, 113, 116
Browne, Captain P., 36, 60
Bruce, Commander Peter, 154
Brynhild, 89
Brynhild II, 89
Buckingham, Duke of, 49
Buenos Aires–Rio Race, 131
Bulkeley-Williams, Sir Richard, 97
Buller, Captain James, 180
Bunting, 176
Burnham Week, 154

Calista, 92, 138, 161
Calluna, 76
Camden, Marquis of, 81, 119, 122, 124, 187
Camilla, 56n.
Campbell, Sir Malcolm, 138
Camper, William, 76
Camper and Nicholson, 76, 85, 86, 115, 116, 129, 142
Camrose, 1st Viscount, 135, 142, 185
Camrose, 2nd Viscount, 150
Cap Ancona, 86–7
Cape May Challenge Cup, 75, 76 and n.
Cardigan, Countess of, 99–100
Cardigan, Earl of, 65
Cariad, 77–8, 95
Cariad II, 78, 85
Carmela, 112
Carr Glynn, Sir Richard, 19
Carter, J. R., 95–6

Carver, Captain E. C., 91
Castle, 157; bombed, 122–3; during World War II, 119–23; Ladies' Annexe, 125; post-war refurbishment, 125; RYS leases, 62–3; RYS purchases, 96
Castle Rock, 100–3
Cat II, 175
Catania, 161
Cathcart, Lord, 146–7
Cavan, Earl of, 88–9
Cecelia, 94
Cecily, 89
Ceto, 161, 175
Cetonia, 81, 112
Challen, Mr, 26
Chamberlayne, Thomas, 56, 62
Championship of the Sea, 82
Channel Race, 111, 145
Chaplin, Eric, 94
Chaplin, Viscount, 176
Charlotte, 21, 22–3
Charteris, Richard, 81
Cherbourg, 24, 43, 49
Chesapeake, 60
Chichester, Sir Francis, 141, 152–3
Chichester, Giles, 153
Chough, 68
Christina, 138
Churchill, Sir Winston, 155
Circassian, 41n.
Clark, Brigadier G. J. W., 181
Claymore, 61
Clementina, 161–2
Clown, 42
Club Cup, 38, 39, 56
Coates, Sir Edward, 159
Coats, George, 89, 165
Cobb, John, 138
Cockburn, Sir Alexander, 31
Coima, 127·
Colman, Tim, 152
Columbine, 42
Colville, Lord, 63
Colville, Philip, 130
conduct, 30–2
Condy, Mrs N. W., 46
Consuelo, 84
Conyngham, Marquis of, 71
Coote, Captain John, 141

Coote, Eyre, 45
Coquette, 41
Corisande, 81
Cornwall, HMS, 82
Corona, 89
Corry, Captain, 45
Corycia, 162
Courtauld, Augustine, 133, 135–6
Courtauld, S. L., 186
Courtauld family, 155
Coward, Noel, 117
Cowes, early sailing matches, 16; and the formation of the RYS, 17; Frank James Hospital, 189–90; Holy Trinity Church, 190; Prince's Green, 189; Prospect Museum, 190; RYS and, 189–91; *et passim*
Cowes Combined Clubs, 147–9
Cowes Week, 147–9
Coweslip, 129
Craven, Lord, 24
Crawford, Lord, 65, 81, 83, 84–5, 113
Crean, Michael, 106, 130
crews, discipline, 30–2
Crichton-Brown, Sir Robert, 155
Crimean War, 65
Crossbow, 152
Crossbow II, 152
cruising, 65, 88, 113, 150–1
  early, 24, 30, 44–5
Cruising Club of America, 110
Crusade, 141
Crusader, 138
Crystal Trophy, 152
Culver Down, 47
Cumberland Society, 16
Curling, J. J., 68–9
Curtis, Sir William, 16, 17, 22, 30
cutters, 48
Cutty Sark, 117, 175
Czarina, 81, 94

Davia, 85
Dagmar, 63
Daily Express Powerboat Race, 138–9, 140
Dardenelles, 55
Darnley, Lord, 36
Dauntless, 60
De Broke, Lord Willoughby, 30
De Halsey, Admiral Algernon, 60–1

De Quincy, Roger, 126
De Selincourt, Charles, 139, 140, 142
De Trafford, Dermot, 152
De Walden, Lord Howard, 82, 161, 167
Decies, Lord, 160
Deerhound, 59
Denham, Captain, 89, 150
Depau, Louis A., 58
Diane, 162
Dieppe, 114
Dilke, Sir Fisher Wentworth, 134
Dillon, Major Desmond, 131
Dinard Race, 113
dinghy sailing, 126–7, 131
discipline, 30–2
Dixie, 83
Docker, Lady, 143
Docker, Sir Bernard, 143
Dolphin, 41, 45
Donegal, Marquis of (Lord Belfast), 33–4, 35,
    38–41, 42–3, 48–9
Dorade II, 134
Dorchester, Lord, 119–20
Doris, 108
Dove, 69
Dover–Heliogoland Race, 81
Dragon Class, 129–30, 149
Draper, Frederick, 124n., 136 and n.
Dream, 41n., 69, 70
Drumbeat, 140, 141
Drummond, Bendor, 151
Drummond, Maldwin, 149, 151
Du Cane, Commander Peter, 137–9
Dudley, Lady, 95
Dudley, Lord, 86
Duet, 135, 155
Dufferin, Lord, 66–8
Dunning, Chris, 153–4
Dunraven, Earl of, 72, 76–8, 85, 95, 169
Durham, Earl of, 49

Eardley-Wilmot, Sir John, 40n.
Eastlight, 127
Echo, 106
Eckhardstein, Baron von, 79, 96
Edinburgh Cup, 129, 130, 149
Edward VII, King, (Prince of Wales), 63–4,
    71, 75–6, 78, 79–80, 81
Edward VIII, King (Prince of Wales), 126
Edwards, David, 154

Edwards, Doonie, 151
Egan, Patrick, 89, 143, 146
Egeria, 62, 63
8-Metre Class, 130
Eisendecker, Admiral von, 90, 96
Eliza, 26
Elizabeth (Assheton Smith/Magniac), 21, 22,
    36, 37
Elizabeth (Darnley), 36
Elizabeth (Foster), 176
Elizabeth II, Queen, 128 and n., 129, 146
Emerald, 36, 41
Enchantress, 60, 65
Endeavour, 108, 109
Endeavour II, 108
Enterprise, 109
Epping, 185
Ermina, 41n.
Esmeralda, 176
Eugenie, 60
Evaine, 142

Fair Rosamund, 41n.
Fairey, Sir Richard, 108, 142
Fairhaven, Lord, 184
Falcon, 28, 29–30, 41, 47
Fandango, 132
Fantome, 115–16
Fantome II, 115
Farquhar, Alfred, 165
Farquhar, Vice-Admiral Sir Arthur, 91, 92
Farrant, Major-General Ralph, 144, 152
Fastnet Race, 110–12, 113, 131, 141, 145, 149–
    50, 151
Faustine, 60
Field, Norman, 183
Fife, William, 73, 106
Figaro Trophy, 141
Fincham, John, 41 and n., 76
Fiona, 81
Firefly, 176
Firefly Championship, 127
Fischer, Syd, 155
Fishbourne, 42
FitzGerald, Sir Maurice, 80
Fitzwilliam, Earl, 170, 175
5.5-Metre Class, 130
Fleming, Ian, 133
Flica, 108, 142
Flica II, 108, 142

Flycatcher, 153
Flying Cloud, 116
Flying Dutchman Class, 128
Foam, 66
Foinaven, 176
Foote, John, 151
Formosa, 63
Foster, Captain Alwyn, 92, 161, 174, 176
Foster, Herbert, 167
Fox, Uffa, 127
Foxhound, 113
France, early cruising to, 24–5
Franklin, Sir John, 67
Freelance, 176
Freewill, 176
frigates, 139
Fulcher, A. W., 91
Fullerton, G. A., 16

Galatea, 42
Gang Warily II, 151
Ganymede, 46
Gee, Joseph, 58, 60
Genesta, 74–5
George IV, King, 21, 26
George V, King, 80, 89, 90, 100, 104, 107, 110, 136n.
George VI, King, 128
Germania, 90–1
Gibson, Milner, 71
Giles, Rear-Admiral Morgan, 139
Gipsy Moth III, 152
Giralda, 65
Giulia, 29
Gladeye, 149–50
Glentanar, Lord, 183
Golden Hind, 176
Goodson, Hugh, 108, 142, 143
Gordon Lennox, Lord Henry, 59
Gore, Sir Ralph, 105, 106, 110, 124–5, 135, 140, 142, 146
Gosport, 76
Gossamer, 45
Goulandris, John, 140
Gower, J. Leveson, 45
Grantham, 18
Green, Sir Peter, 144–5, 152
Greene, Sir E. Walter, 159
Greenwell, Sir Walpole, 91, 162
Greg, Thomas, 45

Greta, 95
Gretton, John, 81, 120, 178, 184
Grianaig, 95
Grive, 179–80
Grosvenor, Earl, 45
Grumman Aeroplane Engineering Company, 136
Guest, Montague, 17n.
Guinness, Ernest, 113, 115–16
Guinness, Group Captain Loel, 138, 174
Guinness, Rupert, 80
Gulich, Vice-Admiral E., 96
guns, 28–9
Guy, Harry, 67–8

Hall, Major Harold, 134–5, 186
Hall, Admiral Sir Reginald, 82–3
Hallowe'en, 110–11
Hampton, Desmond, 153
handicapping, 43–4, 60, 61
Hannibal, HMS, 172
Hardy, Admiral Sir Thomas, 20
Harlequin, 42
Harmsworth Trophy, 82, 83
Harriet, 36, 37
Harrison, Frederick, 161
Harrison, J. E., 106n.
Hastings, 23
Heath, Edward, 154–5
Heckstall-Smith, Brooke, 74
Hendersons, 76
Henrietta, 59
Henry, Prince, 90, 96
Henry VIII, King, 62, 157
Herreshoff, 77
Hersilia, 91, 162–3
Hewitt, Lieut. Commander R. L., 130
Hildegarde, 63
Hinchingbrooke, Lady, 100
Hiniesta, 177
Hirondelle, 59
Hispania, 89
Hoare, Sir Peter, 142
Hobart, Sir Robert, 139
hollow bows, 40, 56, 58
Honeywell Performance Award, 141
hospital ships, 94–5
Household Brigade Yacht Club, 149–50
Hudson, Robert, 179
Hughes-Hallett, Captain J., 122

Hunloke, Sir Philip (Philip Perceval), 78–9, 96, 106, 109, 110, 118, 124–5, 135
Hunter of Hunterston, 131
hydrofoils, 136–7
hydroplanes, 83
Hylas, 154

Ibrahim Pasha, Prince, 96
Idalia, 150
Iernia, 85
Ile de Brehat Race, 113
Iliffe, Lord, 183
Illingworth, Captain John, 131, 141, 144, 155
Ingomar, 76n.
Inman, Thomas, 23
Innes, Ralph Hammond, 133–4
Innovation, 153
International Rule, 89
International Yacht Racing Union, 104, 154
Intrepid, 90
Inverclyde, Lord, 160, 174
Irex, 75
Iris, 45
Island Sailing Club, 129
Isme II, 117
Itchenor Gallon, 127
Iveagh, Lord, 72, 81, 161, 175

'J' Class, 109
'J' Force, 121–2
Jade, 130
James, Arthur, 88
James, Frank, 88, 189–90
James, William, 88
Janson, Jonathan, 130, 131, 149
Jason, 163
Jean, 105
Jenetta, 142
Joass, John, 146
Jocasta, 145
Joel, 140
Johnson, Sir Peter, 153
Jolie Brise, 110, 111, 112
Jolie Brise Cup, 149
Jordan, Sir James, 37
Josephine and Jane, 22
Jubilee Cup, 81
Julia, 29, 59
Juno, 130

Kalan, 177
Kaylena, 142, 143
Kearsage, 59
Kelmsley, Lord, 182
Kelsall, Derek, 152
Kelvin, Lord, 65, 84
Kemp, Dixon, 77
Kennedy, Miles, 89
Keppel, Captain, 45
Kestrel, 47
Kiloran, 177
King of the Netherland's Cup, 73
King's Cup, 37–8, 39, 44, 78, 85, 89
Kitson, Captain, J. B., 176
Knockout, 141
Kriemhilda, 62, 63
Krupp, Frau von, 90
Kurrewa IV, 144
Kurrewa, V, 144
Kyria, 130

La Goleta, 111–12
Ladies Challenge Cup, 37–8, 39
Lady Ann, 89
Lady Hermione, 68
Lahloo, 177
Laing, Sir Maurice, 127, 153
Lambart, L. J. O., 179
Lancashire Witch, 88
Langrishe, Sir Hercules, 85–7
Latifa, 113, 132, 133
Lavrock, 68
Lawson, Hugh, 150
Laycock, T. F., 84
Leander, 80
Leche, J. H., 31
Lecky, Captain H. S., 92, 93
Leeds, Duke of, 69, 81, 91, 97, 159
Leith, Lord, 93, 165
Lewis, Rosa, 101–3
Lexia, 113
Liberty, 95
Liddell, Captain C. O., 179
Light, Colonel William, 66
Linear Rating Rule, 73, 78, 79
Lipton, Sir Thomas, 79, 109
Lisette, 94
Little Astra, 142
Livingston, Frank, 143–4

Livingston, John, 143–4
Londonderry, Marquis of, 71, 78
Lorna, 163–4, 178
Lotus, 41n.
Louis Napoleon, Emperor of France, 60
Louis Philippe, King of France, 49
Louisa, 24, 38–9, 40
Loujaines, 153
Lulworth, 38–9, 40
Lumberjack, 140
Lymington, 23
Lyon, Captain James, 76
Lyon, Major William, 45
Lyons, Captain, 37

McCalmont, Colonel Barklie, 89
McCalmont, Harry, 65
McClintock, Sir Leopold, 67
Macdonald-Buchanan, Major, 142, 143
Mackenzie, Austin, 160
Magniac, Daniel, 36
Magniac, Major Oswald, 96
Maid Honor, 178
Majesta, 178
Malmesbury, Lord, 119, 123
Manahine, 134–5
Mann, Lieut. Commander Graham, 130, 143, 149
Manners, Lord John, 45–6
Ma'oona, 89
Maple Leaf IV, 83
Margherita, 89
Marionette, 154
Markham, Colonel, 62
Marshall, N. B., 134
Marshall, Wilson, 82
Martin, Commander, E. G., 110
Martyr, Weston, 112
Mary, Queen, 110, 122
Mary Deare, 133–4
Mary Jane, 178
Mason, A. E. W., 179
Mason, Michael, 113, 132
Maxse, James, 37
Maxwell, Eric, 143
Medusa, 92, 93, 165, 178–9
Menai, 36, 38, 39, 40
Menai (steam yacht), 40
Mera, 165

Meteor, 75, 78, 90–1
Miles, J. K. B., 179
Millar, Charles Gibson, 156
Millar, John, 136–7, 151
Miller, James, 162
Minona, 165
Mirage, 79
Miranda, 37, 38, 93, 165
Mohoopany, 140
Montagu, John, 82
Moore, Aylette, 151
Morgan, Lieut. Colonel A. Hickman, 160
Morley, Arnold, 171
Morning Cloud, 154–5
Morning Star, 179
Morris, Stewart, 123, 126–8
Morwenna, 142 and n.
motor torpedo boats (MTBs), 137–8
Mottistone, Jack Seely, Lord, 117–18, 120
Mouette, 108
Mountbatten, Lady, 122
Mountbatten, Lord Louis, 121, 122–3, 137
Mouse of Malham, 144–5
Moyne, Lord, 113–14, 183
Mulholland, John, 62, 72
multihulls, 152
Mundy, E. Miller, 165–6
Muraena, 179
Murchison, Roderick, 40n.
Muriel Stephens, 179
Murray, Sir Charles Wyndham, 94
Musker, John, 174
Musketeer, 145
Myth of Malham, 131, 144–5

Napier, James, 181
Napier, Robert, 40
Napier II, 82
Narcissus, 165–7, 179–80
Nash, John, 39
Naushabah, 105
Nautilus, 41
Navahoe, 76
Navarino, battle of, 47
Naylor, John, 58
Naylor, Richard, 56
New York Yacht Club, 58, 60, 76n., 77n., 81, 142, 143
New York Yacht Club Challenge Cup, 145
Niagara, 77

Nicholls, John, 63
Nicholson, Ben, 76
Nicholson, Charles E., 76, 85–6, 89, 109, 113, 115
Nicholson, John, 87
Nicholson, Peter, 76, 153
Nigella, 180
Noressian, 180–1
Normanton, Earl of, 139
North Star, 110
Northam, Bill, 106
novelists, 133–4
Novice, 41n.
Nyanza, 55

ocean racing, 61, 75, 81, 110–13, 153–5
Ocean Rover, 181
O'Connell, Maurice, 51
Offshore Powerboat Race, 141
Offshore Racing Council, 154
Oliver, Commodore G. N., 122
Olympic Games, 99, 106 and n., 126, 127, 128, 130–1, 149
Oma, 116
Ombra, 167, 181
Onassis, Aristotle, 138
One Ton Cup, 155
Operation Raleigh, 154
Oriana, 91
Ormonde, Marquis of, 78–9, 90, 91
Ornsay, 142
Orr-Ewing, Captain Charles, 80
Orr-Ewing, Captain J., 72
Osprey Class, 139
Outlaw, 141

Paget, Lord Alfred, 57
Paget, Sir Edward, 26
Paget, Sir Henry *see* Anglesey, Marquis of
Palatine, 55
Pandora, 67
Panic, 43
Panope, 181
Pantaloon, 42
Papoose, 140
Parr, Donald, 154
Parsons, J. R., 176
Pasley, 92, 93, 101, 102
Patricia, 165
Paula III, 105–6

Peareth, William, 59
Pearl, 22, 29, 41, 45
Pearl, Lord, 28
Penboch, 111
Pender, Sir James, 89
Pendragon, 181
Perceval, Philip, *see* Hunloke, Philip
Perrin, W. G., 34–5
Perry, Colonel R. S. G. 'Stug', 131, 143, 144
Perseverence, 141
Philante, 108, 115, 181–2
Philip, Prince, Duke of Edinburgh, 113, 128, 129, 146–7
Pim, Theodore, 168
Pioneer, 83
piracy, 28 and n., 45
Plymouth–La Rochelle Race, 146
Portal, Lord, 186
Portal, Sir Spencer, 176
Portal, Sir William, 102, 118
Portia, 167
Portland, 4th Duke of, 42
Portsmouth, 93; King's Stairs, 20n.; Sally Port, 20
Potter, Gerald, 112
Power, John, 151
powerboats, 108, 138–9
Prestcott-Westcar, Major Charles, 185
Preston, Sir Frederick, 177
Preston, Sir Kenneth, 105–6, 130, 149
Preston, Sir Walter, 124–5, 163, 178
Prince Consort's Cup, 56, 61
Prince of Wales' Challenge Cup, 62
Prince of Wales Cup, 126, 127, 128
Princess, 63, 182
Prior, John, 184
Prospect Museum, 190
Prudence, 106
Pylewell Hard, Lymington, 23
Pylewell House, Lymington, 23

Quailos, 154
Quantung, 67
Queen's Cup, 55–6, 61, 62, 63, 73, 80, 85
Queensborough, Almeric Paget, Lord, 89
Quinnell, Air Commodore Paddy, 106, 130

racing, Ackers Graduated Scale, 44, 61;
    Americans first enter, 56–9; classes, 43–4;
    Cowes Week, 147–9; early, 16–17, 29–32,

racing, cont.
36–8; handicapping, 43–4, 60, 61; Linear
Rating Rule, 73, 78, 79; ocean, 61, 75, 81,
110–13, 153–5; one-design racing, 78; rat-
ings, 72–3; rules, 38, 71–3; transatlantic,
59–60; YRA rules, 71–3; *see also individual
races*
Radiant, 183
Rainbow, 80
Rasch, Sir Carne, 135
ratings, 72–3, 78, 79
Ratsey, G. R., 41
Ratsey, Michael, 58
Rawlinson, Lord, 95
Raymond, Jack, 129, 130
Rebecca Maria, 22
Red Ensign, 33–5, 51–3
Redwing keel boats, 104
Reindeer, 183
Renesse, Comte Camille de, 90
Revive, 183
Reynell-Pack, A., 91
Rhiannon, 167
Rhodora, 183
Richardson, Lieut. Colonel H. S. C., 178
Richelieu, Duc de, 24–5
Ridgeley, Commodore Charles, 156
Rocquette, 153
roll-damping fins, 138
Rolleston, Captain J. P., 166
Roman Golden Bowl, 154
Rona, 155
Roome, John, 151, 153
Rosabelle, 168
Rosaura, 114, 183–4
Rose, Sir Alec, 153
Rose-Richards, Major, 113
Rosebery, Earl of, 171
Rosling, Alfred, 133
Rothschild, Lionel de, 82, 180, 193
Rothschild, Baron Philippe de, 106
Round Britain Race, 75
Round Gotland Race, 132
Round-the-Island Race, 141, 154
Roundabout, 141
Roussalka, 114
Royal Bermuda Yacht club, 53
Royal Corinthian Yacht Club, 103n.
Royal George, 39n.

Royal Marines, 151 and n.
Royal Navy, association with RYS, 20, 34,
65; ensign, 55; goes over to steam, 65; and
the RYS as an auxiliary fleet, 15, 29; sailing
matches, 16; *see also* Admiralty
Royal New Zealand Yacht Squadron, 155–6
Royal Ocean Racing Club, 110 and n., 154
Royal Thames Yacht Club, 16, 52, 72
Royal Ulster Yacht Club, 109
Royal Western Yacht Club, 52
Royal Western Yacht Club of Ireland, 53–4
Royal Yacht Squadron, as an institution of
'national utility', 36, 65; association with
Royal Navy, 20, 34, 65; as auxiliary fleet to
Royal Navy, 15, 29; becomes 'Royal', 21,
35; burgee, 35, 54–5, 156; buttons, 33–4;
buys Thornhill, 125; coat of arms, 35;
Commodores, 33, 48, 71, 93–4, 97, 122,
124, 135, 146; early races, 29, 32, 36–8;
ensign, 18 and n., 34–5, 51–5; first regulations, 17–19; formation, 15–32; granted the
White Ensign, 34–5, 51–5, 156; influence
on naval architecture, 65; ladies' annexe,
99–103; membership, 20, 30, 32, 47–8, 90,
96, 97, 100, 156; moves into the Castle, 62–
3; officers, 193–5; purchases the Castle, 96;
Rear-Commodores, 146–7, 194–5; reform,
125, 135–6; relations with New York Yacht
Club, 77n.; royal patronage, 64; rules, 97,
100; Secretaries, 195; signal books, 18 and
n., 19–20, 21; subscriptions, 20, 21, 32,
120, 125; tonnage qualification, 21, 32;
uniform, 33–4; Vice-Commodores, 147,
194; and women, 99–100; World War I, 90–
6, 159–72; World War II, 119–25, 132–3,
173–87
Royal Yachting Association, 127, 154
Royalist, 45, 149
rules, Linear Rating Rule, 73
Runciman, Sir Walter, Lord, 113, 142, 146–7,
151
Rutland, Duke of, 61

St George, 168
St George, Lieut. Colonel Ferris, 149
St Modwen, 184
St Petersburg, 17, 30
Sainty, Philip, 22 and n.
Salamander, 149

Salvin, Anthony, 62
Samoena, 85
Sanpareil, 184
Sans Peur III, 114–15, 184
Santander Race, 112
Sapper, 69
Sapphire, 93, 116, 169, 184–5
Sappho, 60
Sardinia Cup, 154
Sargent, Sir Malcolm, 141
Saskia, 106
Satanita, 76, 77, 78, 80
Scaudaun, 169–70
Sceptre, 143
Scholfield, Colonel Dick, 131–2
schooners, 48
Schroder, Captain W. H., 175
Schroeder, Baron von, 167
Scorpion, 28
Scotia II, 185
Scott, Captain, 88
Scott, Peter, 126, 127–8, 144
Scott Russell, J., 40, 56
Sea Huntress, 138
Sea Victory, 138
Seawanhaka Cup, 104, 130
Severn II, 134
Shackleton, Sir Ernest, 88
Shamrock, 109
Shamrock, I, 79
Shamrock V, 109
Shamrock VI, 109
Shark, 61
Sharples, Christopher, 153
Shedden, Colonel, 23
Sheelah, 94
Shelley-Rolls, Sir John, 173
Shemara, 170
Silver Cloud, 185
single-handed sailing, 68, 153
Single-Handed Transatlantic Race, 153
Sitwell, Sir Sacheverell, 116
6-Metre Class, 130, 144
Slade, Cecil, 162
Sleuthhound, 73–4
smugglers' boats, 22, 28
Smyth-Pigott, J. H. W., 46
Snaith, Bill, 141
Snowden, Major Peter, 147, 149

Snowgoose Cup, 152
Solent One-Design Class, 78
Somers, Lieut. Colonel T. V., 130
Somerset, Robert, 110, 111–12
Sona, 185
Sopwith, Sir Thomas, 83, 108, 109, 115, 138, 181
Sopwith, Tommy, 108, 138–9, 140
South Coast One-Design, 140
Southby, Commander Sir Archibald, 122
Southby-Tailyour, Lieut. Colonel Ewen, 151–2
Southern Cross Cup, 141
Sou'wester, 185
Sovereign, 128, 144
Speed Week, 152
speedboats, 82
sponsorship, 153
spy ships, 83, 86–7, 132
stabilizers, 138
Stalbridge, Lord, 111, 112
Stanley, Oliver, 154
Stanley, Sloane, 63
Star of India, 186
Starcross Club, 15n.
steam yachts, 39, 65
Steele, Robert, 106, 177
Stephens, Olin, 108, 146
Stephens, Rod, 108, 146
Stephenson, George, 189
Sterling, General, 68
Stevens, Commodore, 56, 57
Stracey, Sir Edward, 126
Strathcona, Lord, 177
Sturt, Mr, 16
Sullivan, Sir Edward, 64
Sultana, 43, 56
Sunbeam, 81–2, 83, 95–6, 113
Sunbeam II, 113
Sutherland, Duke of, 91, 114–15, 161, 184
Sutton, Sir Richard, 74–5
Swallow Championship, 127
Swallows, 126–7
Swithinbank, Harold, 91, 165, 170
Sycamore, Edward, 105–6
Sydney–Hobart Race, 144, 154, 155
Sylvie, 58–9
Symonds, Captain, 41–2
Symonds, J. L., 36

Tait, Simon, 144, 149
Talbot, C. R. M., 29, 42, 53–4
Tally Ho!, 111–12
Tamahine, 186
Tartar II, 150
Taylor, Anthony, 123–4
Taylor, Sir Charles, 106
Telstar, 140
Templetown, Lord, 56n.
ten-gun brigs, 41–2
Tennant, Michael, 110
Thatched House Tavern, 15, 17
Thendara, 186
Therese, 38
Thistle, 75, 106, 140
Thoma II, 186
Thomas, Major-General R. N., 151n.
Thompson, Sir Thomas, 186
Thorne, Sir Peter, 149
Thornhill, 125
Thornycroft, Peter, 139–40
Three-Three-Three, 186
Tidbury, Charles, 153
Titia, 106, 130
Tod, Robert E., 82
Tomahawk, 108, 142
Torbay, 20
Tottenham, C. L., 163–4
Tower, Commander F. F., 94
Towers-Clark, Lieut. Colonel, 143
Town Cup, 37, 38, 39, 43, 62, 63
Tramontana, 139
Tramontana II, 139
Trauco, 151
Tredegar, Lord, 95
Treffrey, Colonel Edward, 181
Trifle, 152
Trivia, 142
Troon, 42
'Trunnion', 27
Tunnicliffe, Nigel, 139
Turner, J. M. W., 39
Turquoise, 45
12-Metre Association, 143
12-Metre Class, 130, 142–4
23-Metre Class, 89

Unique, 131
Uomie, 145

Ursula, 82–3
Ursuline, 61
Utowana, 81–2

Valhalla, 81–2, 84
Valkyrie II, 76, 77, 85
Valkyrie III, 77
Vanadis, 170
Vanderbilt, Harold, 108, 109
Vanessa, 170
Vanity, 142, 143
Vanity V, 142, 143
Vasco da Gama Cup, 78
Vectis, HMS, 121, 123, 125
Venetia, 91, 170–1
Venus, 84
Vergemere, 86
Vernon, Lord, 41–2
Vernon, Mike, 153
Verona, 171
Vian, Rear-Admiral Sir Philip, 122
Victoria, Queen, 39, 45, 57
Victoria and Albert, 39n.
Vigilant, 77
Vim, 108
Virginia, 186–7
Vision, 131
Vol-au-Vent, 62, 63
Von Schertel, 137
Vospers, 137–8, 139

Wagtail, 176
Wainman, Charles, 142
Wallington, 168
Walshe, Captain, 120–1
Wanderer, 66
Ward, Sir John, 105
Ward, Joseph, 19
Wardlaw-Milne, Sir John, 142
Water Club of the Harbour of Cork, 15
Waterwitch, 42–3, 49, 89
Watson, George L., 22, 76, 80, 85
Webster, Sir Godfrey, 28
Webster, John, 66
Weld, James, 29
Weld, Joseph, 16, 21, 23, 27, 36, 37–40, 58, 61
Wellington, Duke of, 24–5
Western Yacht Club, 51
Western Yacht Club of Ireland, 51

Westminster, Bendor, 2nd Duke of, 82–3, 115, 116–17, 175
Westminster, Loelia, Duchess of, 95, 99, 116
Westminster, Robert, 5th Duke of, 153,
Westra, 142
Whitbread, Colonel William, 153
Whitbread Round-the-World Race, 153
White, Blunt, 145
White, Joseph, 42
White, William, 44
White Ensign, 34–5, 51–5, 156
White Mist, 145
White Heather II, 89
Whittaker, Cecil, 89
Whitwell, Edward, 170
Wilkins, Dick, 138–9
William, II, Emperor of Germany, 75, 78, 79, 81, 82, 96
William IV, King, 35, 37, 44
Williams-Bulkeley, Lady, 80
Williams-Bulkeley, Sir Richard, 79–80, 120, 122
Wills, Captain Arnold, 185
Wilton, Earl of 46, 47, 49, 53, 55, 56, 58, 59, 61, 65, 70
Wilton Morse Trophy, 127
Wingfield Digby, Colonel F. J. B., 174
Winter, John, 127
World War I, 90–6, 159–72
World War II, 119–25, 132–3, 173–87
Wright, Major M. N., 179

Wyatt, Sir Myles, 113, 145, 146
Wynn, Lieut. Colonel R. Vaughan, 176
Wythes, E. J., 168

Xarifa, 46, 47, 55

Yacht Patrol, 91–4
Yacht Racing Association (YRA),71–2, 96
yachts, cutters, 48; early members', 22, 27–8; hollow bows, 40, 56; Redwing keel boats, 104; schooners, 48; steam, 39, 65; wave-line principle, 40, 58; yawl rig, 61; *see also individual classes*
Yarborough, Lord, 15, 28, 29–30, 33, 44, 46–7, 49, 51, 52
Yarrow-Napier, 82
Yarta, 171, 187
yawl rig, 61
Yelf Brothers, 190
Yeoman, 153
Yida, 31
Yolaine, 130
Young, Sir Allen, 67
Young, Arthur, 186

Zaida, 171–2
Zara, 55, 61
Zaza, 172
Zenobia, 63
Zephyr, 16, 69
Ziegler, Philip, 122–3

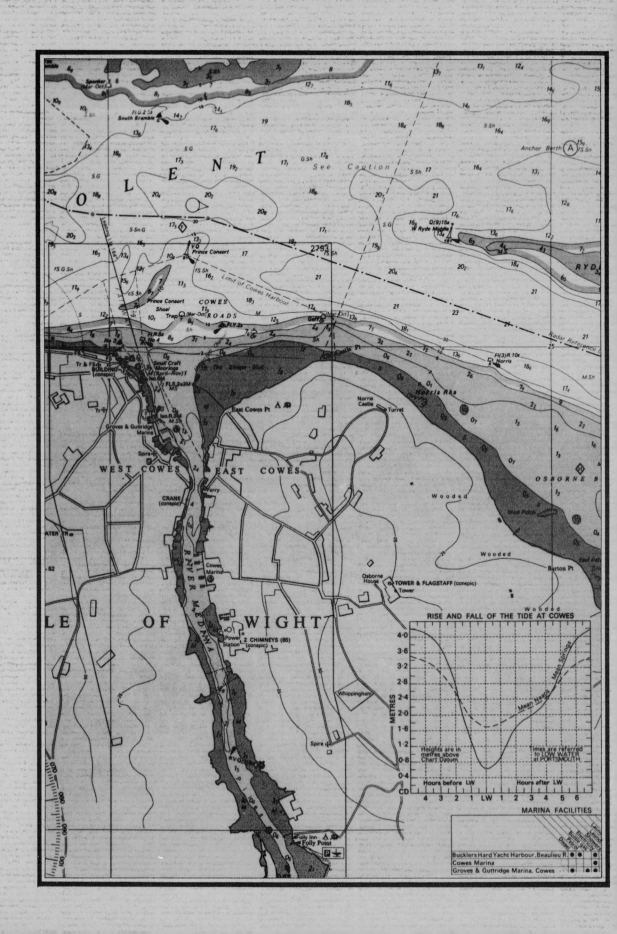